Principles of Transgender Medicine and Surgery

D1431081

A practical guide to state-of-the-art treatments and health care knowledge about gender-diverse persons, this second edition of *Principles of Transgender Medicine and Surgery* presents the foremost international specialists offering their knowledge on the wide spectrum of issues encountered by gender-diverse individuals. In this handy text, professionals of all types can get important information about various aspects of transgender health care for a full spectrum of clients, from childhood to advanced age. Key topics addressed include medical and surgical issues, mental health issues, fertility, the coming-out process, and preventive care. This essential text is extensively referenced and illustrated, and instructs both novice and experienced practitioners on gender-affirming care.

Randi Ettner, PhD, is a clinical and forensic psychologist, a staff psychologist at the Chicago Gender Center, and president of New Health Foundation Worldwide.

Stan Monstrey, MD, PhD, is professor and chairman of the Department of Plastic Surgery at the Ghent University Hospital, Belgium.

Eli Coleman, PhD, is director of the Program in Human Sexuality and Chair in Sexual Health at the University of Minnesota. He is one of the founding editors of the *International Journal of Transgenderism*, founding editor of the *International Journal of Sexual Health*, and past president of the World Professional Association for Transgender Health, Society for the Scientific Study of Sexuality, International Academy of Sex Research, and Society for Sex Therapy and Research.

"Finally, science and compassion have replaced prejudice and politics! This marvelous book is essential reading for every person who provides care, or cares about, people who don't conform to society's 'rules' about gender. How I wish this wisdom and information had been available when I was a young pediatrician working with children and families struggling with these seemingly insurmountable issues."

— **M. Joycelyn Elders, MD**, professor emeritus, University of Arkansas for Medical Sciences, 15th Surgeon General of the United States

"All new and established transgender care professionals will treasure this book because it provides extensive up-to-date information to help caregivers become informed, reflective, and involved, and will assist them to develop into the professionals they aspire to be."

—**Guy T'Sjoen, MD, PhD**, interim president of EPATH, full professor and head of the Department of Endocrinology, Ghent University Hospital, Belgium

"This second edition of *Principles of Transgender Medicine and Surgery* presents the current state of the art in all aspects of treatment and management of transgender health care. It is an absolute 'must-have and must-read' for anyone working in the field of transgender health care. I highly recommend this standard text to both trainees and experienced clinicians in the field as it represents a most valuable and much needed contribution to the field of transgender health care."

—**Walter Pierre Bouman, MD, MA, MSc, FRCPsych, UKCPreg**, consultant psychiatrist-sexologist/head of service, Nottingham National Centre for Gender Dysphoria, United Kingdom

"Written by leaders in the field, this book is a 'must-read' for health care professionals working in trans health."

—**Gail Knudson MD, MPE, FRCPC**, clinical associate professor, University of British Columbia, Vancouver, Canada

"A terrifically researched guidepost for clinicians hoping to negotiate the complexities of gender transition. This text arranges itself to provide transitional care through and beyond medicine and surgery, to include discussions of function, sexuality, reproduction, and aging among its transgender clientele. Destined to be a must-have reference for any provider serving the transgender patient."

—**Marci Bowers, MD**, gynecologic and reconstructive surgeon, Mills-Peninsula Hospital, Burlingame, CA; Mt. Sinai-Beth Israel Medical Center, New York, NY

Principles of Transgender Medicine and Surgery

Second Edition

Edited by Randi Ettner, Stan Monstrey, and Eli Coleman

Routledge
Taylor & Francis Group

NEW YORK AND LONDON

Second edition published 2016
by Routledge
711 Third Avenue, New York, NY 10017

and by Routledge
2 Park Square, Milton Park, Abingdon, Oxon, OX14 4RN

Routledge is an imprint of the Taylor & Francis Group, an informa business

First edition published by Routledge 2007

Library of Congress Cataloging in Publication Data
A catalog record has been requested for this title.

ISBN: 978-1-138-85701-8 (hbk)
ISBN: 978-1-138-85700-1 (pbk)
ISBN: 978-1-315-71897-2 (ebk)

Typeset in Minion Pro
by Out of House Publishing

Contents

List of Contributors

Walter Bockting, PhD, Columbia University Medical Center, New York, United States

Katrien Bonte, MD, Ghent University Hospital, Belgium

Jack Byrne, Human rights researcher and trans activist, Aotearoa, New Zealand

Mauro Cabral, Director of Advocacy and Programs, Global Action for Trans* Equality Argentina

Sophie Carlson, University of Sheffield, Western Bank, Sheffield, United Kingdom

Peggy T. Cohen-Kettenis, PhD, Department of Medical Psychology and Medical Social Work, VU University Medical Center, Amsterdam, Netherlands

Britt Colebunders, MD, Department of Plastic Surgery, Ghent University Hospital, Belgium

Eli Coleman, PhD, Program in Human Sexuality, University of Minnesota, Minneapolis, MN, United States

Lindsay Collin, MPH, Emory University Rollins School of Public Health, Atlanta, GA, United States

Aden M. Cook, BA Doctoral student, Medaille College, Buffalo, NY, United States

Griet De Cuypere, MD, PhD, Center of Sexology and Gender, University Hospital, Ghent, Belgium

Salvatore D'Arpa MD, PhD, Department of Plastic and Reconstructive Surgery, Ghent University Hospital, Belgium

Petra De Sutter, MD, PhD, Head of Department of Reproductive Medicine, University Hospital Ghent, Senator and MP Council of Europe University Hospital, Ghent, Belgium

Annelou L. C. de Vries, MD, PhD, Department of Child and Adolescent Psychiatry, VU University Medical Center, Amsterdam, Netherlands

Frederic M. Ettner, MD, private practice, Chicago, IL, United States

Randi Ettner, PhD, Chicago Gender Center, Chicago, IL, United States

A. Evan Eyler, MD, MPH, University of Vermont Medical Center, Burlington, VT, United States

Jamie Feldman, MD, PhD, Program in Human Sexuality, Department of Family Medicine and Community Health, University of Minnesota, Minneapolis, MN, United States

Lin Fraser, EdD, private practice, San Francisco, CA, United States

Melissa Gardner, MA, University of Michigan, Ann Arbor, MI, United States

Michael Goodman, MD, MPH, Emory University Rollins School of Public Health, Atlanta, GA, United States

Louis J. Gooren, MD, PhD, Emeritus professor of endocrinology and transgender medicine at VU University Medical Center, Amsterdam, Netherlands

Antonio Guillamon, MD, PhD, Professor Emeritus of Psychobiology, Universidad Nacional de Educacion a Distancia, Madrid, Spain

Piet Hoebeke, MD, PhD, Head of Department of Urology, Ghent University Hospital, Belgium

Eszter Kismodi, JD, International Human Rights Lawyer on Sexuality, Gender, and Reproductive Health, Geneva, Switzerland

Nicolaas Lumen, MD, PhD, Department of Urology, Ghent University Hospital, Belgium

Tom Mazur, PsyD, University of Buffalo, NY, United States

Stan Monstrey, MD, PhD, Department of Plastic Surgery, Ghent University Hospital, Belgium

Stephen M. Rosenthal, MD, University of California, San Francisco, CA, United States

David E. Sandberg, PhD, University of Michigan, Ann Arbor, MI, United States

Vin Tangpricha, MD, PhD, Emory University and Atlanta VA Medical Center, Atlanta, GA, United States

Wim Verhaeghe, MD, Department of Maxillo-Facial Surgery, Ghent University Hospital, Belgium

Steven Weijers, MD, PhD, Department of Obstetrics and Gynecology, Ghent University Hospital, Belgium

Tarynn M. Witten, PhD, LCSW, Center for the Study of Biological Complexity, Virginia Commonwealth University, Richmond, VA, United States

James Woodcock, University of Sheffield, Western Bank, Sheffield, United Kingdom

Edward Wootton, University of Sheffield, Western Bank, Sheffield, United Kingdom

Kevan Wylie, MD, University of Sheffield, Western Bank, Sheffield, United Kingdom

Foreword

More than 40 years ago, role models, such as Mortimer Lipsett, Wayne Bardin, Raymond VandeWiele, and Seymour Lieberman, taught me the challenges and joys of research and clinical practice that focused upon disorders of androgens and estrogens. Known as an andrologist, the scope of my interest was to supplant or to suppress sex steroid hormones that altered the quality of lives of people as men or women—labels of their natal sex. That is, until 1993, when a friend, unable to find a willing endocrinologist in Philadelphia, hesitantly asked "if I would mind" seeing a transsexual woman unable to find someone to treat her with estrogens. Arrogance and ignorance (the latter easy to overcome, I thought) initiated more than two decades of adventure during which a focus upon gender has taught me how complex and difficult living as one's true self can be. In addition, the privilege of helping others achieve this goal has introduced me to a village of committed caregivers—such as those in this volume.

Hormone replacement treatment remains one of the lifelong commitments of transgender persons. However, even this simplest of medical tasks requires complex decisions of timing, psychological insight and readiness, discussions of reproduction, varying use of irreversible surgery, choices of education and profession, unique views of puberty, sexual preference and conjugal life, as well as absent guidelines for developing a life plan. The curriculum for transgender care remains obscure. This volume brings together a world view of many of the complex contexts faced by parents and their children, adolescents, adults, both developing and aging, and the caregivers transgender persons must rely upon to integrate medicine, surgery, psychology, sociology, the legal system, and strategies for change.

A volume such as this not only teaches based on extensive experience, it opens opportunities for those new to the field and stimulates the imagination to develop future strategies to improve the lives of special persons whose needs are complex. Most importantly, the book serves as a self-educating resource for each of us who is privileged to provide guidance to transgender persons. Gratitude is extended to each author for valuable contributions that guide the future of transgender care. Congratulations to all.

Wylie Hembree, MD

Preface

In 1992, I saw my first transgender patient, and quickly learned about the health disparities, stigmatization, and minority stress that were pervasive in the transgender population. Not unlike society in general, the health care system was largely indifferent to the needs of people with unique gender identities and presentations.

Fifteen years later, *Principles of Transgender Medicine and Surgery*, the premier medical text on transgender health care, was published. A practical and extremely informative resource, it provided valuable guidance for medical professionals charged with caring for the health of these individuals. One hoped that in the medical field, *Principles of Transgender Medicine and Surgery* would initiate greater acceptance of, and more appropriate health care for, transgender people.

Remarkably, even in the short time since the 2007 release of that landmark volume, society at large has come a long way. Thanks to increased media attention and online social networking, general awareness of transgender issues has increased exponentially. In some ways, however, the medical field has lagged. Ironically, the public is now more informed and accepting of gender incongruity than are many health care providers.

Even medical schools have been outpaced. My medical students clamor for more information about transgender health care. But the educational institutions have not yet developed the necessary curricula.

For all medical professionals now desiring to educate themselves about appropriate, compassionate care for these individuals, the second edition of *Principles of Transgender Medicine and Surgery* fills the gap. It is a wonderfully edited text written by international experts who strive, successfully, to support wholeness and authenticity in every medical encounter with transgender individuals. This book is an invaluable resource for those requiring the most up-to-date, cutting-edge information in this rapidly evolving field.

With knowledge and gender-affirming models of care, the old, pathologizing paradigms can be dismantled, and health care systems can become more responsive to the emotional, social, and medical needs of people with unique gender identities. The second edition of *Principles of Transgender Medicine and Surgery* leads the way. It is an authoritative text that belongs not only on the shelf in every medical library, but also in the hands of every medical professional devoted to providing compassionate, appropriate health care to members of the transgender population.

Frederic M. Ettner, MD

Introduction

There has been a tectonic change in the field of transgender health care since the 2007 publication of the first edition of *Principles of Transgender Medicine and Surgery*. What was once a seemingly rare phenomenon has shown itself to be far more prevalent than previously thought.

Science, research, and the narratives of people who experience gender incongruity have informed new models of care. The old paradigm of gate-keeping has been replaced by more evolved models that affirm gender. Evidence-based, best-practice care—a culturally sensitive approach that amalgamates the disciplines of mental health, medicine, and surgery—is now the ideal.

The media has helped to shine a light on this once-obscure area of human behavior. Young people are transitioning at earlier ages, and many people are finding a home outside of the binary. The lexicon of gender non-conformity is rapidly expanding, yet the care these authors describe with deep knowledge and insight will, hopefully, empower providers to follow in their footsteps and end health disparities.

The needs and lived experiences of gender-diverse people have often out-paced knowledge and practice. The second edition of *Principles of Transgender Medicine and Surgery* was the inevitable expansion into territories, previously unmapped, that now comprise the infrastructure of the social terrain. Issues of sexual health, human rights, and the medical treatment of young people have swelled, demanding attention and responsive action. While language will continue to evolve, and the standards of care will be modified from time to time to reflect new realities, some clinical principles remain unchanged: We must first do no harm.

The authors of this second edition are true visionaries. Long before it was in vogue to care for gender-diverse people, they exhibited a deep sensitivity and great respect for all who sought care. Their willingness to witness and listen gave birth to a movement—a bold effort to defy convention—and created a new sub-specialty in health care. We are extremely fortunate that they have generously contributed their knowledge to this volume. We feel privileged to gather, in one place, this collective wisdom, which is now supported by scientific evidence.

Above all, we feel forever indebted to all the people who have shared their lives and their journeys with us in our work.

Randi Ettner
Stan Monstrey
Eli Coleman

1 Theories of the Etiology of Transgender Identity

Randi Ettner and Antonio Guillamon

Introduction

Ever since the beginning of time, human beings have sought to understand the physical world and one another. Ancient people told tales, or "myths," passed down orally, which were humanity's earliest answers to the mysteries of the unknown.

In these cosmogonic myths, supernatural beings possessing human motives created the world and other natural phenomena. They also served to explain the genesis of sickness and cure. Often, solemn recitation of the creation myth was enough to cure an illness, as symbolic return to the origins allowed for the "rebirth" of the patient. Mythmakers of all religions and cultures recognized that unseen forces needed to be heralded to make a sterile womb fertile or to cure a body or mind (Eliot, 1976).

The scientific revolution that occurred in 16th- and 17th-century Europe heralded the dawn of modern science and a revolution in physics. Theories replaced beliefs, and printing facilitated the dissemination of knowledge. The medical profession made great strides in understanding the human body and the pathophysiology of disease. But human beings and their behavior do not easily capitulate to taxonomy, and in the absence of observable disease or organ deficiency, one must settle for theory—the modern equivalent of myth—to explain enigmatic phenomena. Such is the case with gender incongruity, the most misunderstood area of human behavior.

Historical Background

Historical accounts of people engaging in cross-gender behavior date back to Biblical times. The Old Testament expostulated against such displays (Deuteronomy 22:5) and Ovid, a first-century BC poet, referred in verse to the "stuff from a mare in heat," a reference to conjugated estrogen, which is derived from pregnant mares (Taylor, 1996). But prior to the middle of the 20th century, the phenomenon of gender transition was unknown in the Western world.

In 1910, Magnus Hirschfield, a German sexologist, published *Die Transvestism*, a monograph describing cross-gender behavior, but as early as 1877,

Krafft-Ebing referenced case histories in the medical literature (Pauly, 1992). In 1921, Harry Benjamin, a German physician living in New York, and Eugen Steinach observed that vasoligation (ligation of the vas deferens) had a restorative effect in elderly men, an observation that presaged the use of hormone replacement in the aged. Benjamin was keenly interested in Steinach's experiments, in which he "changed the sex" of animals, via castration and implantation of the opposite-sex glands (Schaefer & Wheeler, 1987b). Benjamin spent the next decade of his life providing endocrine therapy to geriatric patients. In 1948, an incident occurred that shifted the focus of Benjamin's career, earning him a place in history and changing the lives of countless people.

It was the referral from famed sex researcher Alfred Kinsey of a 23-year-old man, Van, who presented a unique situation: Van claimed he wanted to change his sex. Van and his mother pleaded with Benjamin for help. The mother related that, at age 3, Van spontaneously began dressing in girl's clothing. He continued this throughout grade school, and special toilet arrangements were made. Psychiatrists assured the parents that this highly intelligent child would outgrow this behavior, but he didn't. When the high school refused to make accommodations, Van left, remained at home, and performed housework. He insisted that he be treated as a female, and became extremely agitated when he wasn't. Van refused to accept that change was impossible, and he was institutionalized by the courts a year prior to meeting with Harry Benjamin.

Benjamin urged Van to go to Germany, where recorded accounts of sex reassignment surgeries appeared in the literature as early as 1930. Van made three trips to Europe, which culminated in the surgical construction of a neovagina from skin of the thigh. Van changed his name to Susan, moved to Canada, and was never heard from again (Schaefer & Wheeler, 1987b).

But it wasn't until 1952, when U.S. citizen Christine Jorgensen underwent surgery in Denmark, that media reports of "sex-change surgery" captured the public's attention. She became Benjamin's seventh patient, and lifelong friend (Schaefer & Wheeler, 1987a). Christine Jorgensen deconstructed prevailing beliefs about gender immutability, as Harry Benjamin reconstructed a taboo area of behavior into a medical specialty.

Psychoanalytic Theories

Ms. Jorgensen's fame rose rapidly, as did opposition to the surgery. The "Christine operation" generated legal, religious, and moral controversy. But the psychiatric community struck the most damaging blow by challenging the very legitimacy of the condition (Ettner, 1999).

A 1978 article in the *Journal of the American Medical Association* stated "most gender clinics report that many applicants for surgery are actually sociopaths seeking notoriety, masochistic homosexuals, or borderline psychotics" (Belli, 1978). The reigning psychoanalytic model regarded transsexualism as a psychiatric disorder. Those desiring surgery were proclaimed to be delusional, obsessive, or otherwise severely disturbed. The cause of the "disorder" was attributed to serious object relations disturbances: an inability of mother and child to separate, leading to dysregulation of intrapsychic boundaries and an attempt, on the part of the patient, to incorporate an alternate persona (Gilpin et al., 1979; Lothstein, 1979; Macvicar, 1978; Moberly, 1986; Ovesey & Person, 1976). Some theorized that this was a psychotic process (Socarides, 1978), while others conceptualized it as a type of borderline syndrome. Lothstein (1984) described the severely dysphoric patient as being unconsciously motivated to "discard bad and aggressive features" and incorporate "a new idealized perfection."

Tragically, this conflation of gender dysphoria, homosexuality, and psychopathology often resulted in the institutionalization of people who required medical and surgical treatment. Many were subjected to electroshock or other aversion therapies when psychoanalysis failed to "cure" them (Shtasel, 1979).

Early Biological Theories

Some researchers, intent on replacing "emotional controversy by rational assessment of facts," rejected the psychoanalytic theories, and probed for a biological basis of the condition (Vogel, 1981). Roentgenological examination of skulls (Lundberg, Sjovall, & Walinder, 1975), screening for anomalous hormonal milieus (Gooren, 1986; Kula, Dulko, Pawlikowski, et al., 1986), cytotoxicity assay inspection of h-y antigen status (Eicher et al., 1980, 1981; Engel, Pfafflin, & Wiedeking, 1980; Spoljar, Eicher, Eiermann, & Cleve, 1981), and quantitative electroencephalograph analysis were among the once-promising attempts at identifying an organic marker. Despite the failure of these investigations, some researchers remained convinced that a yet-unknown change in hormonal-dependent brain structure was implicated (Gooren, 1990).

Oddly enough, psychologists provided indirect support for this position. Through the use of reliable, objective psychometric testing, they documented that transgender individuals lacked the rampant psychopathology supposedly fundamental to the condition. In fact, several studies concluded that surgical applicants demonstrated a "notable absence of psychopathology" (Cole, O'Boyle, Emory, & Meyer, 1997; Greenberg & Laurence, 1981; Leavitt, Berger, Hoeppner, & Northrop, 1980; Tsushima & Wedding, 1979). With the advent of the internet, databases became accessible for meta-analyses. Large-scale studies designed to provide quantitative epidemiological data found no evidence that child-rearing practices accounted for the development of the phenomenon (Buhrich & McConaghy, 1978).

Rapid advances in technology led to increasingly sophisticated theories and investigation into the etiology of the condition. By the 1990s, a theory emerged known as "gender transposition." Evidence of a link between steroid hormones, brain structure, and animal sexual behavior (Dorner, Poppe, Stahl, et al., 1991) was extrapolated to suggest a switch of hormone-induced cephalic differentiation at a critical gestational stage might likewise occur in humans (Elias & Valenta, 1992; Giordano & Giusti, 1995) The theory proved to be reductionistic, and was ultimately abandoned (Coleman, Gooren, & Ross, 1989).

Environmental Theories

As psychoanalytic theory lost its foothold, two movements, both reactions to Freudian doctrine, arose in concert. The first was the theory of radical behaviorism. Psychologist B. F. Skinner asserted that free will was an illusion, and that behavior—even complex human behaviors—was the consequence of environmental reinforcement histories. The infant was a tabula rasa—a blank slate. Simultaneously, the French philosopher Michel Foucault was espousing what would become known as the theory of social constructionism. Foucault, like Skinner, insisted that there is no fixed human nature. He proposed that sex and gender are social constructs imputed on to bodies. Heavily influenced by Foucault, and empowered by the view that constricted societal roles could be surmounted, the social construction of gender—the belief that people learn to become men or women—germinated. Gender was regarded as performance; i.e., people *do* gender: "In social interaction, throughout their lives individuals learn what is expected, act and react in expected ways, and they simultaneously construct and maintain gender order" (Butler, 1990). By the 1970s, a majority of scientists, most notably John Money, regarded socialization as the sine qua non of gender identity formation.

Anatomical Post-Mortem Studies

In 1995, Zhou, Hofman, Gooren, et al. reported that autopsied brains of male-to-female transsexual individuals differed in comparison to heterosexual and homosexual non-transgender men's brains. This groundbreaking study identified an area of the hypothalamus, the bed nucleus of the stria terminalis (BSTc), wherein the volume of the central sulci was comparable to that of control females, and unlike the greater volume found in control male brains. The findings were widely publicized, and *The New York Times* reported the study was "casting new light on perplexing issues of sexual identity" (Angier, 1995).

Clearly, exploring the landscape of the brain offered tantalizing clues to consciousness and identity. But the study raised additional questions. What if the volume differences found in the BSTc were the result of hormone use? A subsequent study was designed to address that issue. Kruijver et al. (2000) quantified the number of somatostatin neurons in the BSTc, rather than using volume as a metric. Neuron numbers of heterosexual males, homosexual males, lesbian women, transsexual women, males and females with sex steroid disorders, a transsexual man, and a transsexual individual who had not received hormones were compared. Consistent with earlier findings, regardless of sexual orientation or hormone usage, there was a significant difference in the somatostatin neuron number in the BSTc. Not only did the transsexual women's post-mortem brain tissue resemble that of control females, but the opposite pattern was displayed in the brain of the one transsexual man.

The verification of the ontogeny of the BSTc bolstered the theory that gender identity evolves as a result of the interaction of the developing brain and sex hormones. In 2002, Chung, De Vries, and Swaab et al. made the surprising discovery that BSTc volume was not apparent until adulthood. How could the late occurrence of sexual dimorphism be explained? The researchers hypothesized that, before a difference in BSTc appeared, changes in fetal hormone levels, neuronal activity, or differentiation were pre-paving the way for the structural change, which would occur at a later stage of life.

In 2008, another nucleus of the brain was identified that likewise appeared to be related to gender identity: the interstitial nucleus of the anterior hypothalamus number 3 (Garcia-Falgueras & Swaab, 2008). Post-mortem brain tissue revealed that the gene encoding neurokinin B (NKB) in the infundibular nucleus is sexually dimorphic. In children, both sexes have equivalent levels of NKB immunoreactivity, but adulthood ushers in dimorphism. As with the BSTc, there was a reversal in the tissue of transwomen studied post-mortem, indicating that gonadotropin-releasing hormone secretion is regulated via estrogen feedback, and a mutation in NKB creates gonadotropin deficiencies. This laid the foundation to implicate hormones, genes, and cephalic structure in a neurodevelopmental theory of gender identity formation (Taziaux, Swaab, & Bakker, 2012).

Prenatal Hormonal Influences

The notion that early hormonal influences on the fetus were the precursors to later structural brain change gained traction. Dessens, Cohen-Kettenis, and Mellenbergh et al. (1999) reported an elevated incidence of gender incongruity in the offspring of women exposed to phenobarbital and diphenylhydantoin. Phenobarbital was widely used in many countries as a prophylactic treatment for neonatal hyperbilirubinemia, owing to its ability to enhance liver function. But it also raised postnatal testosterone levels, demonstrating that certain substances could alter steroid hormone levels (Swaab, 2004).

Synchronistic evidence for the weight of prenatal influences came from a source far from the laboratory. Environmental scientists noted an alarming escalation of birth defects, sexual abnormalities, and reproductive failures in wildlife. They traced this endocrine disruption to environmental assaults—synthetic chemicals that mimic natural hormones—and derail normal reproduction and development. Biologists and animal researchers demonstrated the extreme sensitivity of developing mammals to the slightest shift in hormone levels in the womb: "hormones permanently organize or program cells, organs, the brain, and behavior before birth, in many ways setting the individual's course for an entire lifetime" (Colborn, Dumanoski, & Myers, 1996). They argued that humans were similarly vulnerable to endocrine disruption, and that could explain the escalating incidence of disorders of sexual development, infertility, hypospadias, cryptorchidism, double uterus, and blind vagina in the population.

Dietheylstilbestrol (DES), the most widely studied endocrine disruptor, has been implicated in numerous health problems in female offspring of exposed women (Langston, 2010). Few studies, however, have examined its impact on male offspring. DES Sons International, an online forum, reported that in a survey of 500 member respondents, 90 identified as "transsexual"; 48 described themselves as "transgender"; 17 identified as "gender-dysphoric"; and three as "intersex" (Kerlin, 2004).

It is well documented that the ratio of the second to fourth finger (2D:4D) is smaller in human males than in females. This sexually dimorphic trait is presumably established prenatally, due to hormones (Garn, Burdi, Babler, et al., 1975; Manning, Fink, Neave, et al., 1998; Phelps, 1952). Galis, Ten Broek, Van Dongen, et al. (2010) analyzed the digit ratio in deceased fetuses and determined that, at 14 weeks of gestation, there was a small but significant difference in the 2D:4D ratio among male and female fetuses, and that the ratio increases during childhood. This led to the conclusion that prenatal sex hormones have a lasting impact, affecting sexual dimorphism both pre- and post-natally. Schneider, Pickel, and Stalla (2006) compared the digit ratio between transgender individuals and cisgender controls. The transgender women had a digit ratio comparable to control females. No such difference was found in transgender men or control females. The researchers concluded that decreased prenatal androgen exposure is implicated in the development of gender incongruity in transgender women.

Genetic Influences

In 2000, Green reported on familial concordance of gender dysphoria in ten sibling or parent–child dyads. He forecast that advances in technology would make the exploration of genetic variants a viable area of exploration in the quest to discover the origins of atypical gender identity.

Other researchers also found a co-occurrence of gender dysphoria in families. Gomez-Gil, Esteva, Almaraz, et al. (2010) looked at a sample of 995 transgender people, and found 12 pairs of non-twin siblings. The researchers concluded that the probability of a sibling of a transgender individual also being transgender was 4.48 times higher for siblings of transgender women than transgender men probands, and 3.88 times higher for the brothers than for the sisters of transgender probands. The study suggests that a sibling of a transgender person was more likely to be transgender than someone in the general population.

Diamond (2013) reported on a study of gender incongruity amongst 112 sets of twins, illuminating the relative contribution of genetics and social factors. He found a 33.3% concordance among monozygotic male twins, and a 22.8% concordance among monozygotic female twins. Interestingly, among the twin probands, there were three sets of twins who were reared apart but concordant for gender transition (Heylens et al., 2012).

Several landmark studies undertook to directly assess the role of specific genes of the androgen (ARs) and estrogen receptors (ERs). First, Henningsson, Westberg, Nilsson, et al. (2005) found that transwomen differed from controls with respect to the mean length of the ERβ repeat polymorphism, suggesting lesser effective function of ER. Bentz et al. (Bentz, Hefler, Kaufman, et al., 2008) found transgender men to differ from non-transgender controls in a specific allele distribution pattern and to have an allele distribution akin to male controls. The identified gene, *CYP17*, is associated with gender incongruity, as is the loss of the female-specific genotype distribution. Hare, Bernard, Sanchez, et al. (2009) looked at polymorphisms in genes involved in steroid genesis. Specifically, they examined repeat length variants in the AR, the ERβ, and aromatase (*CYP19*) genes. They found a significant association between gender incongruity in birth-assigned males and the AR gene. Fernandez et al. (2014a) looked at a Spanish sample of 442 transgender women and found no significant association with AR, ER, or *CYP19*. However, in a subsequent study the same group found an association of the ERβ gene and transmasculinity (Fernandez et al., 2014b). To date, these are the two largest genetic studies conducted.

Neurodevelopmental Cortical Hypothesis

The advent of sophisticated brain imagery techniques enabled researchers to study large numbers of brains in vivo, overcoming the limitation of small sample size in post-mortem studies. Studies before and after hormone treatment have shown that transgender women, transgender men, non-transgender women, and non-transgender men present clear and distinct phenotypes, with respect to the gray and white matter of the brain. The studies of gray matter focus on the thickness of the cortex and volume of the subcortical structures, while the white matter has been approached by analyzing the microstructure of the main bundles of the brain.

The cortex, central to behavior and connected to subcortical structures, is the seat of the most consistently documented differences between transgender and non-transgender people. Additionally, the cortex contains both ARs and ERs, making it the principal focus of study. The human cortex is sexually dimorphic. Females have a thicker cortex than males (Luders et al., 2006), and the cortex thins throughout the first three decades of life (Shaw et al., 2008). Transgender men and transgender women with early-onset gender incongruity likewise have a thicker cortex than males, but there are regions of the cortex in which they do not differ from non-transgender males (Zubiaurre-Elorza et al., 2013). No cortical feminization was found in transgender women with late-onset gender incongruity (Savic & Arver, 2011).

There are also sex differences in the microstructure of brain bundles that connect cortical regions. These bundles are related to emotional and cognitive functions. Transgender people differ from non-transgender people in the microstructure of some of these bundles. Transwomen show demasculinization

(Rametti et al., 2011a), while transmen show a masculinization of these bundles (Rametti et al., 2011b).

If one considers both white and gray matter, it appears that transwomen, transmen, non-transgender women and men each display a unique phenotype. It is likely that ARs are implicated, perinatally, in the architecture of these unique developmental trajectories. The timing of the thinning of the cortex in the parietal, visuoperceptive regions and the insula follows a different pattern eventuating in the establishment of these visible distinctions. Additionally, the morphological differences in transgender individuals primarily involve the right hemisphere of the brain (Table 1.1).

The significance of the right hemisphere is salient, in that one's perceptual experience of the body and body phenomenology emanates from parietal and insular networks, located within the right hemisphere. Longo, Azanon, and Haggard (2010) anchor the right hemisphere to higher somatosensory cognitive processes. One such perceptual process is "somatorepresentation." This refers to the abstract cognitive construction of

> semantic knowledge and attitudes about the body, including: lexical-semantic knowledge about bodies generally, and one's own body specifically, configural knowledge about the structure of bodies, emotions and attitudes directed toward one's own body, and the link between the physical body and the psychological self (Longo et al., 2010).

Perhaps this is the seedbed of gender identity and consciousness of anatomical alignment or misalignment.

Hormones diminish gender dysphoria and alter secondary sex characteristics. But few studies have examined the effects of hormonal treatment on the brain. Those that have systematically investigated pre- and post-treatment in a given individual, via neuroimaging techniques, consistently report a decrease in brain volume in transwomen post-treatment. Hulshoff Pol, Cohen-Kettenis, Van Haren, et al. (2006) first reported a decrease in the total volume of the brain and the hypothalamus after short-term cross-sex hormone treatment in transwomen. More recently, Zubiaurre-Elorza, Junque, Gomez-Gil, and Guillamon (2014) measured cortical thickness after a minimum of 6 months of treatment, and found a decrease in volume of the brain and cortical and subcortical structures as well as thinning of the cortex. In addition to this generalized decrease in cortical thickness, there is an increase in the ventricular system.

After testosterone treatment, transmen show an increase in total brain volume (Hulshoff Pol et al., 2006) and cortical thickness and subcortical structures (Zubiaurre-Elorza et al., 2014), but there is no effect on the ventricular system. It appears that hormone treatment affects both the gross structure and the microstructure of the brain (Rametti et al., 2012), presumably via ARs and ERs and glucocorticoid receptors (Zubiaurre-Elorza et al., 2014).

Do these brain changes that exogenous hormones eventuate have clinical significance? In a comprehensive review of the extant literature, Guillamon,

Table 1.1

	Phenotype	Hemisphere
Transmen[1]		
Cerebral compartments		
Gray matter	Feminine	
White matter	Feminine	
Intracranial volume	Feminine	
Cerebrospinal fluid	Feminine	
Cortical thickness		
Global	Feminine	Right
Parieto-temporal	Feminine	Right and left
Parietal	Feminine	Right
Subcortical structures		
Putamen	Masculine	Right
White-matter microstructure	Masculine	Right and left
Longitudinal superior	Masculine	Right
Forceps minor	Masculine	Right
Corticospinal tract	Defeminized	
Transwomen[2]		
Cerebral compartments		
Gray matter	Masculine	
White matter	Masculine	
Intracranial volume	Masculine	
Cerebrospinal fluid	Masculine	
Cortical thickness		
Global	Feminine	Right
Orbitofrontal	Feminine	Right
Insular	Feminine	Right
Cuneus	Feminine	Right
White-matter microstructure		
Longitudinal superior	Demasculinized	Right
Fronto-occipital inferior	Masculine	Right
Forceps minor	Demasculinized	Right
Cingulum	Demasculinized	Right
Corticospinal tract	Demasculinized	

[1] Data transformed from Rametti et al. (2011a); Zubiaurre-Elorza et al. (2013).
[2] Data transformed from Rametti et al. (2011b); Zubiaurre-Elorza et al. (2013).

Junque, and Gomez-Gil (2016) conclude that, to date, this has not been systematically studied. Neuropsychological studies have focused solely on sexually dimorphic cognitive behaviors, e.g., mental rotation, after initiation of hormonal therapy. Sensitive neuropsychological instruments designed to detect subtle brain changes or to assess function in the domain of areas known to be impacted have yet to be employed.

As greater numbers of individuals access care, there is a heightened need to understand the effects of hormones on the brain, particularly long-term. Guillamon et al. (2015) have demonstrated that individuals with a history of early-onset gender incongruity evidence a specific brain phenotype that differs from those with later onset (Savic & Arver, 2011). Additional research and longitudinal studies can advance our understanding of unique identities and hopefully inform treatment across the lifespan.

References

Angier, N. (1995). Size of region of brain may hold crucial clue to transsexuality, a study finds. *The New York Times*, November 2.

Belli, M. (1978). Transsexual surgery: A new tort? *JAMA* 239(20): 2143–2148.

Bentz, E. K., Hefler, L. A., Kaufman, U., et al. (2008). A polymorphism of the CYP17 gene related to sex steroid metabolism is associated with female-to-male but not male-to-female transsexualism. *Fertil Steril* 90(1): 56–59.

Buhrich, N., & McConaghy, N. (1978). Parental relationships during childhood in homosexuality, transvestism, and transsexualism. *Aust N Z J Psychiatry* 12(2): 103–108.

Butler, J. (1990). *Gender Trouble: Feminism and the Subversion of Identity*. New York: Routledge.

Chung, W., De Vries, G., & Swaab, D. (2002). Sexual differentiation of the bed nucleus of the stria terminalis in humans may extend into adulthood. *J Neurosci* 22(3):1027–1033.

Colborn, T., Dumanoski, D., & Myers, J. P. (1996). *Our Stolen Future*. New York: Penguin Books.

Cole, C. M., O'Boyle, M., Emory, L. E., & Meyer, W. J. (1997). Comorbidity of gender dysphoria and other major psychiatric diagnoses. *Arch Sex Beh* 26(1): 13–26.

Coleman, E., Gooren, L., & Ross, M. (1989). Theories of gender transpositions: A critique and suggestions for further research. *J Sex Res* 26(4): 525–538.

Dessens, A. B., Cohen-Kettenis, P. T., Mellenbergh, G. J., et al. (1999). Prenatal exposure to anticonvulsants and psychosexual development. *Arch Sex Beh* 28:31–44.

Diamond, M. (2013). Transsexuality among twins: identity concordance, transition, rearing, and orientation. *Int J Trans* 14: 24–28.

Dorner, G., Poppe, I., Stahl, F., et al. (1991). Gene and environment-dependent neuroendocrine etiogenesis of homosexuality and transsexualism. *Exp Clin Endocrinol* 98(2): 141–150.

Eicher, W., Spoljar, M., Murken, J. D., Richter, K., Cleve, H., Stengel-Rutkowski, S., & Steindel, E. (1980). Transsexuality and X-Y antigen. *Geburtshilfe Frauenheilkunde* 40(6): 529–540.

Eicher, W., Spoljar, M., Murken, J. D., Richter, K., Cleve, H., & Stengel-Rutkowski, S. (1981). Transsexualism and the X-Y antigen. *Fortschr Med* 99(1–2): 9–12.

Elias, A. N., & Valenta, L. J. (1992). Are all males equal? Anatomic and functional basis for sexual orientation in males. *Med Hypotheses* 39(1): 39–45.

Eliot, A. (1976). *Myths.* England: McGraw Hill.

Engel, W., Pfafflin, F., & Wiedeking, C. (1980). H-Y antigen in transsexuality, and how to explain testis differentiation in H-Y antigen positive males and ovary differentiation in H-Y antigen positive females. *Hum Genet* 55(30): 315–319.

Ettner, R. (1999). *Gender Loving Care.* New York: WW Norton.

Fernandez, R., Esteva, I., Gomez-Gil, E., Rumbo, T., Almaraz, M. C., Roda, E., Haro-Mora, J. J., Guillamon, A., & Pasaro, E. (2014a). Association study of *ERb, AR,* and *CYP19A1* genes and MtF transsexualism. *J Sex Med* 11:2986–2994.

Fernandez, R., Esteva, I., Gomez-Gil, E., Rumbo, T., Almaraz, M. C., Roda, E., Haro-Mora, J. J., Guillamon, A., & Pasaro, E. (2014b). The (CA) in polymorphism of *ERb* gene is associated with FtM transsexualism. *J Sex Med* 11: 720–728.

Galis, F., Ten Broek, C., Van Dongen, S., et al. (2010). Sexual dimorphism in the prenatal digit ratio (2D:4D). *Arch Sex Beh* 39(1): 57–62.

Garcia-Falgueras, A., & Swaab, D. F. (2008). A sex difference in the hypothalamic uncinate nucleus: Relationship to gender identity. *Brain* 131: 3132–3146.

Garn, S. M., Burdi, A. R., Babler, W. J., et al. (1975). Early prenatal attainment of adult metacarpal-phalangeal rankings and proportions. *Am J Phys Anthro* 43:327–332.

Gilpin, D. C., Raza, S., & Gilpin, D. (1979). Transsexual symptoms in a male child treated by a female therapist. *Am J Psychother* 3(3): 453–463.

Giordano, G., & Giusti, M. (1995). Hormones and psychosocial differentiation. *Minerva Endocrinol* 20(3): 165–193.

Gomez-Gil, E., Esteva, I., Almaraz, M. C., et al. (2010). Familiality of gender identity disorder in non-twin siblings. *Arch Sex Beh* 39(2): 265–269.

Gooren, L. (1986). The neuroendocrine response of luteinizing hormone to estrogen administration in heterosexual, homosexual, and transsexual subjects. *J Clin Endocr Metab* 63(3): 583–588.

Gooren, L. (1990). The endocrinology of transsexualism: A review and commentary. *Psychoneuroendocrino* 15(1): 3–14.

Green, R. (2000). Family co-occurrence of "gender dysphoria": Ten siblings or parent–child pairs. *Arch Sex Beh* 29(5): 499–507.

Greenberg, R. P. & Laurence, L. (1981). A comparison of the MMPI results for psychiatric patients and male applicants for transsexual surgery. *J Nerv Ment Dis* 169(5): 320–323.

Guillamon, A., Junque, C., & Gomez-Gil, E. (2015). A review on the status of brain structure research in transsexualism (submitted).

Hare, L., Bernard, P., Sanchez, F. J., et al. (2009). Androgen receptor length polymorphism associated with male-to-female transsexualism. *Biol Psychiatry* 65(1): 93–96.

Henningsson, S., Westberg, L., Nilsson, S., et al. (2005). Sex steroid-related genes and male-to-female transsexualism. *Psychoneuroendocrino* 30(7): 657–664.

Heylens, G., De Cuypere, G., Zucker, K. J., Schelfaut, C., Elaut, E., Vanden Bossche, H., & T'Sjoen, G. (2012). Gender identity disorder in twins: a review of the case report literature. *J Sex Med* 9: 751–757.

Hulshoff Pol, H. E., Cohen-Kettenis, P., Van Haren, N., et al. (2006). Changing your sex changes your brain: Influences of testosterone and estrogen on adult human brain structure. *Eur J Endocrinol* 155: S107–S111.

Kerlin, S. P. (2004). The presence of gender dysphoria, transsexualism, and disorders of sex differentiation in males prenatally exposed to diethylstilbestrol: initial evidence from a 5-year study. DES Sons International network. TransAdvocate.org.

Kruijver, F. P. M., Zhou, J., Pool, C. W., et al. (2000). Male-to-female transsexuals have female neuron numbers in a limbic nucleus. *J Clin Endocr Met* 85: 2034–2041.

Kula, K., Dulko, S., Pawlikowski, M., et al. (1986). A nonspecific disturbance of the gonadostat in women with transsexualism and isolated hypergonadotropism in the male-to-female disturbance of gender identity. *Exp Clin Endocrinol* 87(1): 8–14.

Langston, N. (2010). *Toxic Bodies: Hormone Disruptors and the Legacy of DES*. London: Yale Unviersity Press.

Leavitt, F., Berger, J. C., Hoeppner, J. A., & Northrop, G. (1980). Presurgical adjustment in male transsexuals with and without hormonal treatment. *J Nerv Ment Dis* 168(11): 693–697.

Longo, M. R., Azanon, E., & Haggard, P. (2010). More than skin deep: Body representation beyond primary somatosensory cortex. *Neuropsychologia* 48: 655–668.

Lothstein, L. M. (1979). Psychodynamics and sociodynamics of gender-dysphoric states. *Am J Psychother* 33(2): 214–238.

Lothstein, L. M. (1984). Psychological testing with transsexuals: A 30-year review. *J Pers Assess* 48(5): 500–507.

Luders, E., Narr, K. L., Thompson, P. M., Rex, D. E., Woods, R. P., Deluca, H., & Toga, A. W. (2006). Gender effects on cortical thickness and the influence of scaling. *Hum Beh Mapping* 27: 314–324.

Lundberg, P. O., Sjovall, A., & Walinder, J. (1975). Sella turcica in male-to-female transsexuals. *Arch Sex Beh* 4(6): 657–662.

Macvicar, K. (1978). The transsexual wish in a psychotic character. *Int J Psychoanal Psy* 7:354–365.

Manning, J. T., Fink, B., Neave, N., et al. (1998). The ratio of 2nd to 4th digit length, a predictor of sperm numbers and concentrations of testosterone, luteinizing hormone and oestrogen. *Hum Reprod* 13: 3000–3004.

Moberly, E. R. (1986). Attachment and separation: The implications for gender identity and for the structuralization of the self: A theoretical model for transsexualism and homosexuality. *Psych J Univ Ottaw* 11(4): 205–209.

Ovesey, L., & Person, E. (1976). Transvestism: A disorder of the sense of self. *Int J Psychoanal Psy* 5: 219–236.

Pauly, I. B. (1992). Terminology and classification of gender identity disorders. In W. O. Bockting & E. Coleman (Eds.) *Gender Dysphoria: Interdisciplinary Approaches in Clinical Management*. New York: Haworth, pp. 1–11.

Phelps, V. R. (1952). Relative index finger length as a sex-influenced trait in man. *Am J Hum Gen* 4: 72–89.

Rametti, G., Carrillo, B., Gomez-Gil, E., Junque, C., Segovia, S., Gomez, A., & Guillamon, A. (2011a). White matter microstructure in female to male transsexuals before cross-sex hormonal treatment: A diffusion tensor imaging study. *J Psychiatric Res* 45: 199–204.

Rametti, G., Carrillo, B., Gomez-Gil, E., Junque, C., Zubiarre-Elorza, L., Segovia, S., & Guillamon, A. (2011b). The microstructure of white matter in male to female transsexuals before cross-sex hormonal treatment: A DTI study. *J Psychiatric Res* 45: 949–954.

Rametti, G., Carrillo, B., Gomez-Gil, E., Junque, C., Zubiarre-Elorza, L., Segovia, S., & Guillamon, A. (2012). Effects of androgenization on the white matter microstructure of female-to-male transsexuals: A diffusion tensor imaging study. *Psychoneuroendocrinology* 37:1261–1269.

Savic, I., & Arver, S. (2011). Sex dimorphism of the brain in male-to-female transsexuals. *Cereb Cortex* 23: 2855–2862.

Schaefer, L., & Wheeler, C. C. (1987a). Tribute to Harry Benjamin, 1885–1986. Paper presented at the Tenth International Symposium on Gender Dysphoria. Harry Benjamin International Gender Dysphoria Association, Amsterdam.

Schaefer, L., & Wheeler, C. C. (1987b). Harry Benjamin's early cases, 1938–1953. Historical influences, part 1. Paper presented at the Eighth World Congress for Sexology, Heidelberg, Germany.

Schneider, H. J., Pickel, J., & Stalla, G. K. (2006). Typical female 2nd–4th finger length (2D:4D) ratios in male-to-female transsexuals – Possible implications for prenatal androgen exposure. *Psychoneuroendocrinol* 31(2): 265–269.

Shaw, P., Kabani, N. J., Lerch, J. P.,Eckstrand, K., Lenroot, R., Gogtay, N., Greenstein, D., Clasen, L., Evans, A., Rapoport, J. L., Giedd, J. N., & Wise, S. P. (2008). Neurodevelopmental trajectories of the human cerebral cortex. *J Neurosci* 28: 3586–3594.

Shtasel, T. F. (1979). Behavioral treatment of transsexualism: A case report. *J Sex Marital Ther* 5(4): 362–367.

Socarides, C. W. (1978). Transsexualism and psychosis. *Int J Psychoanal Psy* 7: 373–384.

Spoljar, M., Eicher, W., Eiermann, W., & Cleve, H. (1981). H-Y antigen expression in different tissues from transsexuals. *Hum Genet* 57(1): 52–57.

Swaab, D. F. (2004). Sexual differentiation of the human brain: relevance for gender identity, transsexualism and sexual orientation. *Gynecol Endocrinol* 19: 301–312.

Taylor, T. (1996). *The Prehistory of Sex: Four Million Years of Human Sexual Culture.* New York: Bantam.

Taziaux, M., Swaab, D. F., & Bakker, J. (2012). Sex differences in the neurokin B system in the human infundibular nucleus. *J Clin Endocrin Metab* 97(12): E2010–E2020.

Tsushima, W. T., & Wedding, D. (1979). MMPI results of male candidates for transsexual surgery. *J Pers Assess* 43(4): 385–387.

Vogel, F. (1981). Neurobiological approaches in human behavior genetics. *Behav Genet* 11(2): 87–102.

Zhou, J. N., Hofman, M. A., Gooren, L. J., et al. (1995). A sex difference in the human brain and its relation to transsexuality. *Nature* 378(6552): 68–70.

Zubiaurre-Elorza, L., Junque, C., Gomez-Gil, E., Segovia, S., Carrillo, B., Rametti, G., & Guillamon, A. (2013). Cortical thickness in untreated transsexuals. *Cerebr Cortex* 23: 2855–2862.

Zubiaurre-Elorza, L., Junque, C., Gomez-Gil, E., & Guillamon, A. (2014). Effects of cross-sex hormone treatment on cortical thickness in transsexual individuals. *J Sex Med* 11: 1248–1261.

2 Worldwide Prevalence of Transgender and Gender Non-Conformity

Lindsay Collin, Michael Goodman, and Vin Tangpricha

Background

In 2011, the Institute of Medicine released a report on the health of lesbian, gay, bisexual, and transgender (LGBT) people (Institute of Medicine, 2011). The report emphasized the importance of transgender health research to better understand the needs of this population. The Healthy People 2020 initiative underscored the importance of the commitment of eliminating health disparities among the LGBT populations by providing accessible and quality care (Cahill & Makadon, 2014). The transgender community has been identified as a population with specific health issues that need to be identified, better understood, and better addressed.

A growing recognition that transgender health constitutes a significant gap in current knowledge has led to a notable increase in research activities and resulting publications. As of January 2015, a PubMed search using keywords "transgender health" yielded 1,039 publications, most of which appeared in press in the last 4 years. As shown in Figure 2.1, the number of articles published in the late 1990s never exceeded five per year. This number began to increase after 2000, reaching approximately 50 publications in 2010. Since the publication of the Institute of Medicine report (2011) and the Healthy People 2020 initiative, the literature assessing various aspects of transgender health has been increasing exponentially, with 299 publications appearing in 2014.

Despite increased research focus on transgender health, some of the very basic issues in this area remain largely unresolved. For example, little is known about the prevalence of gender dysphoria (GD) or the proportion of the population that should be considered transgender. The reported estimates are greatly affected by differences in methodology and variable definitions of who should be considered transgender (Coleman et al., 2012). Some studies have attempted to ascertain the prevalence of transgender by focusing on individuals who have undergone surgical gender confirmation or attended specialty hospitals and clinics (Zucker & Lawrence, 2009). This approach undoubtedly underestimates the true size of the transgender population (Coleman et al., 2012).

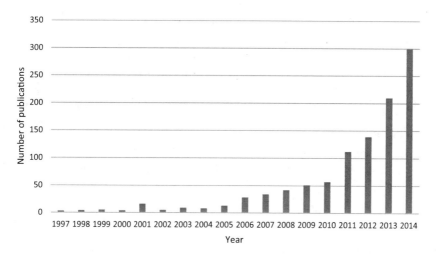

Figure 2.1 Publications on transgender health from 1997 to 2014.

A number of previous reviews sought to synthesize the available information regarding the demographic characteristics of the transgender population (Meier & Labuski, 2013; Zucker & Lawrence, 2009). However, in view of rapidly expanding literature, a re-evaluation of the data available to date is warranted. Moreover, most previous reviews of this issue focused on a summary of reported findings, but did not systematically assess the impact of methodology and definitions on prevalence estimates. With these data gaps in mind, the objectives of the present review were to: (1) evaluate the state of the science on epidemiology of transgender; (2) examine the effect of various definitions and methodological characteristics on study results; (3) compare findings reported in different countries; and (4) examine the differences between estimates reported in the peer-reviewed publications and those that appeared in the so-called "gray" literature, which includes non-peer-reviewed publications.

We followed the Preferred Reporting Items for Systematic Reviews and Meta-Analyses (PRISMA) guidelines and searched electronic literature databases MEDLINE, Embase, and PubMed for relevant journal articles published through January 2015, using multiple combinations of the search terms "prevalence," "gender identity disorder," "gender dysphoria," "transgender," and "transsexual" (Moher et al., 2015). We hand-searched the *Archives of Sex Behavior* and the *International Journal of Transgenderism* as well as reference lists from studies and relevant reviews. We also included gray literature identified through Google Scholar and general internet searches.

We aimed to find all publications reporting population prevalence estimates of transgender. We did not restrict eligibility based on language, study type, or publication status. Two reviewers, Collin and Goodman, independently reviewed each citation. Each report was assessed according to the following a priori eligibility criteria: (1) reported results with prevalence estimates in an adult population; (2) reported numerator for prevalence estimates; and (3) identification of denominator or a description of how prevalence estimates were calculated. Publications that did not report prevalence estimates or numerator that was used to calculate the prevalence were excluded from the analysis. The main outcome measure of interest in this review was population prevalence estimate of transgender. Secondary outcomes of interest included specific prevalence estimates for male-to-female (MTF) or female-to-male (FTM) transgender people.

Overview of the Literature

Thirty publications estimating the prevalence of transgender met the inclusion criteria. Sixteen of the studies were conducted in Europe, eight were based in the United States, and two were from Japan. Iran, Australia, New Zealand, and Singapore each contributed a single study. The years of publication ranged from 1968 to 2015. The design features of these studies and their main findings are presented below. We begin by discussing studies that defined transgender people as those who underwent surgical or hormonal gender confirmation therapy. We then review studies assessing prevalence of transgender-related diagnoses such as "transsexualism," GD, or gender identity disorder (GID). We conclude the review with a summary of studies that defined endpoints of interest for gender non-conformity and gender incongruence, or evaluate occurrence of legal or administrative name or gender changes.

Prevalence of Gender Confirmation Therapy

As shown in Table 2.1, eight publications have estimated the prevalence of transgender by considering only those individuals who sought or received gender confirmation surgery (GCS). Three of these publications were from the United States, four from Europe, and one from Singapore. The publication dates ranged from 1968 to 2014.

In the United States, the earliest estimate of the proportion of "transsexuals" in the general population was reported in 1968 (Pauly, 1968). Based on the data from various specialized centers (most notably the Gender Identity Clinic at the Johns Hopkins Hospital), Pauly identified 2,000 MTF and 500 FTM persons who had requested GCS since 1953. Using the total U.S. population in 1968, the resulting prevalence was estimated at 1/100,000 for MTF and 0.25/100,000 for FTM. Unlike other similar studies, which calculated the prevalence of MTF and FTM among natal men and women, respectively, Pauly divided each numerator by the total population. This produced a roughly twofold underestimate of the gender-specific results.

More recently, Conway (2002) attempted to calculate an approximate prevalence of transsexualism through estimation of annual GCS performed in the United States between 1960 and 2002. Although the source of the information is not clear, Conway estimates that there have been 32,000 transwomen in the United States who have undergone GCS. Based on the assumption that there are approximately 80,000,000 males aged 18–60 years old, the MTF prevalence in the United States was calculated to be 40/100,000.

In a similar report, Horton (2008) estimated the number of GCS performed annually based on information obtained from clinics and surgeons who were members of the Harry Benjamin International Gender Dysphoria Association (now known as the World Professional Association for Transgender Health). Based on the responses and unspecified missing data imputation, the author determined that 1,166 GCS procedures must have been performed during 2001 alone. The author further extrapolated overall prevalence by multiplying the number of surgeries by years of eligibility, or average life expectancy of males and females, and determined the prevalence estimates to be 39.5/100,000 MTF and 24/100,000 FTM. The rationale for the missing data imputation and extrapolation to average life expectancy was not clear.

Several recent prevalence estimates for the receipt of or referral for GCS are available from Europe. Reports were published in Spain, Belgium, Italy, and Sweden. In 2011, Esteva et al. sent out questionnaires to regions of Spain that have established Gender Identity Units (Esteva et al., 2012). The questionnaires inquired about both the number of applicants for GCS and the services offered at the clinic. Each clinic that received a questionnaire responded and the authors determined that there were 3,303 individuals who solicited surgical treatment. Using the total Spanish population between ages 15 and 65 years as the denominator, the prevalence estimate was reported as 10/100,000, which, according to the authors, was comparable to other European studies.

A study in Belgium estimated the proportion of the population that had undergone GCS between 1985 and 2003 through retrospective collection of data on procedures performed by plastic surgeons and gender teams (De Cuypere et al., 2007). Gender teams and plastic surgeons were sent questionnaires regarding procedures performed and 24% of the questionnaires were returned. Based on the responses, the study identified 412 Belgian-born transsexuals (292 MTF and 120 FTM), corresponding to prevalence estimates of 7.74/100,000 and 2.96/100,000. The reported figures may have underestimated the true population prevalence because of the incomplete participation of the plastic surgeons and gender teams; however, the authors indicated that, in a relatively small country such as Belgium, the number of uncounted patients would be minimal.

Based on information available from Italian clinics performing GCS procedures, Caldarera and Pfäfflin (2011) identified 424 MTF and 125 FTM surgeries performed between 1992 and 2008. Using data from the National Institute

Table 2.1 Prevalence of receipt or requests to receive surgical and hormonal gender confirmation therapy

Reference	Location, time period	Case definition	Source of numerator
Caldarera and Pfäfflin, 2011	Italy, 1992–2008	GCS receipt	Surgical clinics
Conway, 2002	USA, 1960–2002	GCS receipt	Estimate (source not clear)
De Cuypere et al., 2007	Belgium, 1985–2003	GCS receipt	Questionnaires sent to "gender teams" and plastic surgeons
Dhejne et al., 2014	Sweden, 1960–2010	Request (and receipt of) GCS	National Board of Health and Welfare Statistics
Esteva et al., 2012	Spain, 1999–2011	Request for GCS	Questionnaires sent to Gender Identity Units
Horton, 2008	USA, 2001	GCS receipt	Survey of clinics and individual members of the Harry Benjamin Society. Results multiplied by average lifespan (rationale not clear)
Pauly, 1968	USA, dates not specified	Request for GCS	Author's communication with specialized centers
Tsoi, 1988	Singapore, until 1986	Request for GCS	Documented diagnosis of transsexualism as part of pre-GCS evaluation
Bakker et al., 1993	Netherlands, 1976–1990	Receipt of HT	Free University of Amsterdam (AZVU) clinic records
Eklund et al., 1988	Netherlands, 1976–1986	Receipt of HT	Free University of Amsterdam (AZVU) clinic records

MTF, male-to-female; FTM, female-to-male; GCS, gender confirmation surgery; HT, hormonal therapy.

[1] Denominator calculated from the numerator from the reported prevalence.
[2] Prevalence calculated using total population as the denominator.

Numerator			Source and size of denominator	Prevalence (per 100,000)			Ratio MTF:FTM
Total	MTF	FTM		Overall	MTF	FTM	
549	424	125	National Institute of Statistics 2009: total 59,619,290 (28,949,747 males and 30,669,543 females)	0.9	1.5	0.4	3.39:1
	32,000		Estimate: 80,000,000 males 18–60 years of age		40		
412	292	120	January 2003 population: 3,758,969 males and 4,048,095 females		7.7	3.0	2.43:1
767 (681)	478 (429)	289 (252)	December 2010 population: 3,704,685 males and 3,791,791 females	10.2 (9.1)	12.9 (11.6)	7.5 (6.6)	1.7:1
3303			Spanish population 15–64 years old, 33,030,000[1]	10.0			1.9:1
89,782	54,464	34,400	U.S. residents 2000: 281,421,906	31.9	39.5	24	
	2,000	500	200,000 total U.S. population used for both MTF and FTM calculations[2]		1.0	0.25	4:1
458	343	115	Population June 1986: 979,300 males and 954,900 females		35.0	12.0	3:1
713	507	206	Center of Statistics: 6,019,546 males and 6,252,566 females		8.4	3.3	2.5:1
538	399	159	Dutch Census Data: 7,125,000 males and 8,368,421 females[1]		1980: 2.2 1983: 3.8 1986: 5.6	1980: 0.5 1983: 1.0 1986: 1.9	3:1

of Statistics to estimate the denominator, the authors calculated prevalence of 1.5/100,000 and 0.4/100,000 for MTF and FTM, respectively. The authors acknowledged that their estimates were lower than those reported in other countries and attributed the difference to missing data or cultural factors.

A study in Sweden identified requests for GCS based on data from the National Board of Health and Welfare Statistics (Dhejne et al., 2014). There were 767 applicants (478 MTF and 289 FTM), of which 681 were approved for therapy and underwent the procedure (429 MTF and 252 FTM). Using the Swedish population as of December 2010, the prevalence estimates for applications for GCS were 12.9/100,000 MTF and 7.5/100,000 FTM. The authors calculated the prevalence among those who were approved for therapy and underwent GCS to be 11.6/100,000 MTF and 6.6/100,000 FTM. The authors noted that, over the 50-year study period, there was an increase in the number of people seeking GCS.

Only one study assessing prevalence of surgical gender confirmation was conducted outside of North America and Europe. Tsoi (1988) calculated prevalence of transsexualism by identifying patients in Singapore who had sought GCS and were subsequently diagnosed as transsexuals by psychiatrists. The author reported that, until 1986, 458 (343 MTF and 115 FTM) Singapore-born transsexuals were reported by the Department of Obstetrics and Gynecology and private surgeons. Using the total male and female population of Singapore in 1986, the prevalence was reported as 35.2/100,000 and 12.0/100,000 for MTF and FTM respectively. The author cited cultural acceptance of transgender and more established GCS procedures as possible reasons for the higher-than-previously reported prevalence estimates.

Two studies conducted in the Netherlands at the Free Amsterdam University clinic used the initiation of hormonal therapy (HT) among persons with GD as the definition of transgender (Table 2.1). In 1976, the clinic established a gender team. Based on data collected through 1986, 538 individuals began HT at that facility (Eklund et al., 1988). Of those, 399 were MTF and 139 FTM. Using the Dutch Bureau of Statistics data for population estimates, the prevalence was calculated as 5.6/100,000 MTF and 1.9/100,000 FTM.

In a subsequent study based at the same clinic, the analysis was extended through the end of 1990 (Bakker et al., 1993). By that time, the clinic was providing HT to 713 Netherlands-born transgender patients over the age of 15 years, 507 MTF and 206 FTM. The total population of the Netherlands in 1990 was used to determine prevalence estimates of 8.4/100,000 MTF and 3.3/100,000 FTM. Bakker et al. stated that the prevalence estimates had risen dramatically over the years.

Prevalence of Transgender-Related Diagnoses

Ten studies calculated the prevalence estimate of transgender-related diagnoses using *International Classification of Disease* (ICD) codes for transgender, GID, or GD (Table 2.2). In clinical records these diagnostic codes include: 302.85

GID in adolescent or adult, 302.6 GID not otherwise specified, and 302.5 transsexualism, but application of the ICD codes varied across the studies. The terminology describing this condition and the diagnostic criteria have evolved over the years since the original definition (Benjamin et al., 1966). Spain, Japan, and the United States each contributed two studies and England, Northern Ireland, Ireland, and Iran each contributed one study in this category between 1968 and 2014.

Hoenig and Kenna (1974) conducted a study aiming to identify all patients diagnosed with GID at the University Department of Psychiatry at the Royal Infirmary, Manchester, between 1958 and 1968. The study relied on the referral of patients from other clinics. The clinic identified 66 individuals with GID. Using the population of the Manchester region on June 30, 1970, the prevalence estimates were calculated as 1.9/100,000 total, 2.9/100,000 for MTF, and 0.9/100,000 for FTM.

In a study based in Northern Ireland, O'Gorman (1982) collected information from the Department of Mental Health, Queen's University, Belfast. Twenty-eight individuals diagnosed as transsexual (21 MTF and seven FTM) were identified over an unspecified 14-year period. Using an approximation of the population in Northern Ireland, the prevalence was estimated at 1.9/100,000.

Esteva et al. (2006) estimated the prevalence of GID based on clinic data from the Gender Identity Disorder Unit in Andalucia, Spain. The clinic reported that, from its opening in 1999 until October 2004, 391 individuals with GID, 243 MTF and 148 FTM, had been seen. Using the total population of Andalucia in 2004, the corresponding prevalence estimates were reported as 10.3/100,000 for MTF and 6.5/100,000 for FTM. The authors stated that these prevalence estimates were higher than previously reported and outlined the importance of early detection and integral treatment in order to improve social adaptation.

In another Spanish study, Gomez Gil et al. (2006) estimated the prevalence of transsexualism in Catalonia using ICD-10 diagnostic code of F64.0 (transsexualism) at the Hospital Clinic in Barcelona from 1996 through 2004. The authors identified 161 patients (113 MTF and 48 FTM) who were living in Catalonia. Based on population data from the Regional Institute of Statistics, the prevalence estimates for MTF and FTM were calculated as 4.8/100,000 and 2.1/100,000, respectively. The authors also calculated a Barcelona-specific prevalence of 5.5/100,000 for MTF and 2.5/100,000 for FTM, indicating a higher proportion of transgender people in the urban population. The authors stated that transsexualism had been marginalized in Spain and this may have contributed to the lower-than-previously observed prevalence estimates.

In Japan, the prevalence of GID was determined from the outpatient GID Clinic of Okayama University Hospital between April 1997 and October 2005 (Okabe et al., 2008). Using the *Diagnostic Statistical Manual of Mental Disorders*, fourth edition (DSM-IV) criteria, 579 patients (230 MTF and 349 FTM) constituted the numerator. Assuming a denominator of 40 million people living in western Japan, the prevalence estimate for FTM GD patients was 0.9/100,000.

Table 2.2 Prevalence of transgender-specific diagnoses

Reference	Location, time period	Case definition	Source of numerator	Numerator		
				Total	MTF	FTM
Ahmadzad-Asl et al., 2010	Iran, 2002–2009	GID diagnosis DSM-IV-TR	Tehran Psychiatric Institute	281	138	143
Baba et al., 2011	Hokkaido, Japan, Dec 2003–Jan 2010	GID diagnosis ICD-10 and DSM-IV	Sapporo Medical University Hospital	342	104	238
Blosnich et al., 2013	VA system, USA, 2002–2011	GID diagnosis ICD-9 codes 302.85 (GID) or 302.6 (GID NOS)	Confirmed GID diagnosis in VHA, fiscal year 2000–2011	2002: 569 2011: 1,329		
Esteva et al., 2006	Andalucia, Spain, 1999–2004	GID diagnosis	Regional Gender Identity Disorder Unit		243	148
Gomez-Gil et al., 2006	Catalonia, Spain, 1996–2004	ICD-10 F64.0 (transsexualism)	Psychiatric and Psychology Institute at the Barcelona Hospital, 1996–2004		Catalonia: 113 Barcelona: 100	Catalonia: 48 Barcelona: 45
Hoenig & Kenna, 1974	England and Wales, 1958–1968	GID	Royal Infirmary Manchester at the University Department of Psychiatry	66	49	17
Judge et al., 2014	Ireland, 2005–2014	GID, DSM-IV/V	GD clinic referrals 2005–2014	218		
Kauth et al., 2014	VA system, USA, 2006–2013	GID diagnosis ICD-9 codes 302.85, 302.6, 302.5	Confirmed GID diagnosis VHA, fiscal year 2006–2013	2567		
O'Gorman, 1982	Northern Ireland, dates not specified	GID	Clinic-based, over 14 years	28	21	7
Okabe et al., 2008	Japan, April 1997–October 2005	GID, DSM-IV	GID Clinic, Okayama University Hospital	579	349	230
Ross et al., 1981	Australia, 1976–1978	Transsexual	Questionnaires to registered psychiatrists	243	209	34
Wålinder, 1968	Sweden, as of 1965	GID	Survey of psychiatrists	110		
Wilson et al., 1999	Scotland, 1998	GD	Questionnaires to general medical practices	273	218	55

MTF, male-to-female; FTM, female-to-male; GID, gender identity disorder; DSM-IV-TR, *Diagnostic Statistical Manual of Mental Disorders*, fourth edition, text revision; ICD-10, *International Classification of Disease*, tenth edition; VA, Veterans Administration; GID NOS, gender identity disorder not otherwise specified; VHA, Veterans Health Administration.

[1] Denominator calculated from the numerator from the reported prevalence.

[2] Prevalence calculated using total population as the denominator.

Source and size of denominator	Prevalence (per 100,000)			Ratio
	Overall	*MTF*	*FTM*	*MTF:FTM*
Center of Statistics of Iran, population aged 15–44 39,526,948	0.7	0.69	0.74	0.96:1
Native Japanese Hokkaido residents 5,500,000		3.97	8.2	1:2
Total VHA patients 4,544,353 (2002), 5,795,165 (2011)	2002: 12.5 2011: 22.9			
Regional population: 2,359,223 males and 2,276,923 females[1]		10.3	6.5	1.64:1
Catalonia: 2,376,538 males 2,308,611 females Barcelona: 1,996,708 males 1,776,269 females)		Catalonia: 4.8 Barcelona: 5.5	Catalonia: 2.1 Barcelona: 2.5	2.6:1
Manchester population June 30, 1970: 3,498,700 (1,652,000 males, 1,846,700 females)	1.9	2.9	0.9	3.25:1
2011 census reports: total 3,205,882[1]	6.8	9.9	3.6	2.7:1
VHA enrollees 7,809,269		32.9		
Northern Ireland population 1,500,000	1.9			3:1
Inhabitants of Western Japan, estimated at 40,000,000[2]		0.9		1.5:1
Australia's population on June 31, 1978 10,616,188[1]	2.4	4.2	0.7	6.1:1
Not stated 6,272,886[1]	1.9	2.7	1.0	2.5:1
Registered patients over 15 years of age 3,336,261 (1,622,090 males 1,714,171 females)	8.2	13.4	3.2	4:1

Another Japanese study sought to assess the prevalence of GID based on data collected at the Gender Identity Disorder Clinic at Sapporo Medical University Hospital between December 2003 and January 2010 (Baba et al., 2011). Identification was based on diagnoses using ICD-10 and DSM-IV codes. The study identified 342 patients (104 MTF and 238 FTM). Using the population of Hokkaido as the denominator, the MTF and FTM prevalence estimates were 3.97/100,000 and 8.20/100,000, respectively. The authors concluded that FTM individuals may be more prevalent in Japan than in other parts of the world, which is in agreement with the previous report from that country (Okabe et al., 2008).

Ahmadzad-Asl et al. (2010) aimed to estimate the prevalence of GID in Iran between 2002 and 2009 through a review of the records at the Tehran Psychiatric Institute and the identification of subjects with a diagnosis of GID according to the DSM-IV criteria. A total of 281 individuals (138 MTF and 143 FTM) were identified, yielding prevalence estimates of 0.7/100,000 (0.69/100,000 for MTF and 0.74/100,000 for FTM). The authors postulated that the patriarchal socio-cultural characteristics in Iran explained the roughly equal numbers of MTF and FTM, which contrasted with reports from other countries that have observed a higher MTF:FTM ratio.

Using the DSM-IV/5 criteria, Judge and colleagues (2014) retrospectively collected information on patients diagnosed with GD at the Department of Endocrinology in St. Columcille's Hospital, Dublin, between 2005 and 2014. Among the 218 patients referred to the clinic, 159 were MTF and 59 were FTM. Based on 2011 census data, the prevalence estimates were reported as 6.8/100,000 (9.9/100,000 for MTF and 3.6/100,000 for FTM).

In a recent study conducted in the United States, Blosnich et al. (2013) used Veterans Health Administration (VHA) electronic medical records from 2000 through 2011 to examine the prevalence of GID among veterans. The numerator for the study included individuals who had received an ICD-9 diagnostic code of either 302.85 (GID) or 302.6 (GID not otherwise specified). Using the VHA data and electronic record database to define the denominator, the authors reported prevalence estimates for different years starting in 2002. The 2002 prevalence estimate was 12.52/100,000 and the prevalence reported in 2011 was 22.88/100,000, indicating an almost twofold increase over the 10-year study period. Although the data did not distinguish MTF from FTM, it is important to note that the VHA population is 95% natal male. The prevalence of GID among veterans appeared to be higher than the estimates cited in previous reviews.

In a more recent Veterans Administration-based publication, Kauth et al. (2014) also used the electronic medical records. ICD-9 diagnoses used to identify cases included 302.85 (GID), 302.6 (GID not otherwise specified), and 302.5 (transsexualism), and cases between 2006 and 2013 were identified. Prevalence in 2013 was reported as 32.9/100,000. It is important to keep in mind that this result is not directly comparable to those reported in the Blosnich et al. study due to expanded criteria for the case definition. In addition, the denominator the Kauth et al. study included all VHA enrollees, while Blosnich et al. calculated the prevalence among VHA utilizers.

Table 2.2 includes three additional studies (from Sweden, Australia, and Scotland) which calculated the prevalence of transgender by surveying national clinics specializing in the treatment of transgender patients. All three studies present relatively old data, with publication dates between 1968 and 1999.

Wålinder (1968) attempted to estimate the prevalence of transgender in Sweden in 1968 through a survey of psychiatric clinics. Questionnaires were mailed out to the clinics, requesting information regarding transvestite and transsexual individuals who sought medical attention as of December 1965. Seventy-six percent of the psychiatrists confirmed having provided treatment to transgender people, and 67 such individuals were identified in the responses. After including 43 additional individuals known to the author, the numerator used for calculations was 110. Using census data from Sweden, the prevalence estimates were calculated as 1.9/100,000 total; 2.7/100,000 for MTF and 1/100,000 for FTM.

Prevalence of GD in Australia between June 1976 and June 1978 was estimated through distribution of questionnaires to subscribers of the *Australian and New Zealand Journal of Psychiatry* and the subscribers' responses (Ross et al., 1981). According to the authors, all psychiatrists in Australia receive this journal. A total of 904 questionnaires were distributed and 263 were returned (29.1%). Based on the completed questionnaires, 243 transgender individuals (209 MTF and 34 FTM) were identified. Prevalence estimates were calculated using the population of Australia 15 years of age or older as of June 31, 1978, and were determined to be 2.4/100,000 total, 4.2/100,000 for MTF and 0.7/100,000 for FTM.

Wilson et al. (1999) surveyed senior partners at all general medical practices in Scotland in 1998. The survey asked for information regarding the number of patients registered to the practice as well as the number of patients with GD. Just under three-quarters (73%) of the surveys were completed and returned, identifying 273 patients with GD. The denominator for calculation of the prevalence was based on the number of patients over the age of 15 registered to the respondents' practices, standardized to match the age distribution of the general population in Scotland. The resulting GD population prevalence estimate was 8.2/100,000.

Prevalence of Self-Reported Transgender Identity

Five studies utilized survey-based data to estimate the prevalence of incongruent gender identity and gender non-conformity (Table 2.3). Three of these studies were based in the United States, one in the Netherlands, and one in Belgium.

Conron et al. (2012) analyzed data collected between 2007 and 2009 from the Massachusetts Behavioral Risk Factor Surveillance Study (MA-BRFSS).

Table 2.3 Prevalence of self-reported transgender identity and gender non-conformity

Reference	Location, time period	Case definition	Source of numerator	Numerator			Source and size of denominator	Prevalence (per 100,000)			Ratio MTF:FTM
				Total	MTF	FTM		Overall	MTF	FTM	
Conron et al., 2012	Massachusetts, USA, 2007–2009	Self-identify as transgender	Massachusetts Behavioral Risk Factor Surveillance Survey 2007–2009	131			28,176	500			
Kuyper and Wijsen, 2014	Netherlands, 2013	Incongruent gender identity	Sexual Health Survey		48	16	8,064		600	200	3:1
Gates, 2011	USA	Self-identify as transgender	Massachusetts Behavioral Risk Factor Surveillance Survey in 2007–2009, 2003 CA LGBT Tobacco Survey					300			
Reisner et al., 2014	USA, 2010	Self-identify as transgender	Growing Up Today Study (GUTS)	26	10	16	7,831 (2,605 males, and 5,226 females)	330	380	310	
Van Caenegem et al., 2015	Flanders, Belgium, 2011–2012	Incongruent gender identity	Sexual Health Survey	13	7	6	1,799	722	671	552	1.2:1

MTF, male-to-female; FTM, female-to-male; CA LGBT, California Lesbian, Gay, Bisexual Transgender.

A survey was administered to 28,662 adults aged 18–64 years, reading in part as follows:

> Some people describe themselves as transgender when they experience a different gender identity from their sex at birth. For example, a person born into a male body, but who feels female or lives as a woman. Do you consider yourself to be transgender?

A total of 131 participants responded "yes" to that question, corresponding to a prevalence of 500/100,000 persons. The authors acknowledged that their estimate may have been affected by misclassification bias due to the broad scope of the question. Another limitation of the data was a lack of information on natal sex and current gender identity.

Gates combined information from the MA-BRFSS, as reported by Conron et al., the 2003 California LGBT Tobacco Survey, and the 2009 California Health Interview survey in order to estimate the number of transgender adults in the United States (Conron et al., 2012; Gates, 2011). The MA-BRFSS had reported that 0.5% of adults in Massachusetts identified as transgender. The 2009 California Health Interview Survey estimated that 3.2% of adults in California were LGBT. Based on the 2003 California LGBT Tobacco Survey, 2.4% of LGBT persons self-identified as transgender. With this information, Gates estimated that the prevalence of transgender people among California adults was 0.1%. Gates then stated that the average of the percentages from Massachusetts and California allowed an estimation of a U.S. prevalence of approximately 0.3% or 300 per 100,000 individuals.

Using the Growing Up Today (GUTS) prospective cohort study of U.S. young adults (Reisner et al., 2014), a 2010 survey implemented a two-step approach by inquiring about sex assigned at birth, and asking about the participants' self-described gender identity. The response options were "Female," "Male," "Transgender, "and "Do not identify as female, male or transgender." Of the 7,831 survey respondents, 26 (0.33%) identified as having a gender identity that differed from the assigned (natal) sex. Of those, seven (0.09%) were cross-sex identified, five (0.06%) self-described as transgender, and 14 (0.18%) did not identify as female, male, or transgender. The authors stated that, when assessing gender identity among young adults, it is important to include non-binary measures.

Kuyper and Wijsen (2014) estimated the proportion of transgender people among 15–70-year-old residents of the Netherlands using data from an internet-based sexual health study conducted in 2012. The study aimed to identify individuals with incongruent gender identities and gender-dysphoric feelings. The final sample included 8,064 participants who were asked questions regarding gender identity and gender-dysphoric feelings. The responses were recorded on a Likert scale. The results gave the percentage of natal men or women with ambivalent or incongruent gender identities who also reported both aspects of GD, dislike of natal sex characteristics, and desire for hormone therapy and/or surgery. Although the exact case definition is not clear, among natal men, the reported prevalence was 600/100,000; among natal females, 200/100,000. About 20% of those invited to participate and who met eligibility criteria completed the internet-based survey. The authors acknowledged that the low participation may limit the generalizability of the results to the general Dutch population.

Van Caenegem et al. (2015) estimated prevalence of gender non-conformity and gender incongruence based on a population survey of adolescent and adult (age range 14–80 years) residents of the Flanders region, Belgium. Survey participants were randomly selected from the Belgian National Register. Forty percent of eligible persons completed the survey. The final denominators for prevalence calculations included 1,799 participants (864 natal males and 905 natal females). Responses to questions pertaining to gender identity and gender expression were assessed via a computer-assisted personal interview. Based on a 5-point Likert scale (ranging from 1, totally disagree to 5, totally agree), the participants were asked to score the following statements: "I feel like a woman," and "I feel like a man." A person was considered gender-ambivalent if the same answer (e.g., a 1 or a 2) was given to both statements. Gender incongruence was defined as a lower score assigned to the natal sex than to the opposite sex. Using these definitions, the prevalence of gender incongruence was estimated to be 671/100,000 natal men and 552/100,000 natal women. The corresponding estimates for gender ambivalence among natal men and natal women were 2,200/100,000 and 1,900/100,000, respectively.

Prevalence of Legal Name or Sex Changes

Two studies, one from Germany and another from New Zealand, reported population prevalence of transgender based on documented administrative sex or name change.

Weitze and Osburg (1996) relied on the 1981 German Transsexuals' Act, which allowed applicants to change their first name or their legal sex status. The study examined the decisions rendered during the 10 years following the implementation of the law. Questionnaires were submitted to the courts, and information regarding the number of relevant applications and corresponding court decisions was collected. During the study period, the courts issued 683 decrees on first-name changes and 733 rulings on legal reestablishment of sex. These rulings concerned 1,199 individuals, of whom 1,047 received approval. Using the adult population of West Germany before reunification, the prevalence was estimated at 2.1/100,000. The natal MTF ratio of applicants was approximately 3:1.

A more recent report extended the work of Weitze and Osburg by evaluating change in legal sex status beween 1991 and 2000 in all of Germany (Dhejne et al., 2014). The overall transgender prevalence was estimated as 3.88 per 100,000, using the German population in 2000 as the denominator. The MTF prevalence was reported to be 4.95 per 100,000 and the FTM prevalence was reported as 2.87 per 100,000.

In New Zealand, individuals may request a change of their gender marker from M or F to X. To determine the frequency of this change, Veale (2008) contacted the New Zealand Department of Internal Affairs Passport Office in 2008. A total of 385 such changes were identified. Given the number of passport holders in New Zealand, the prevalence was calculated as 16/100,000. Considering that 49% of passport holders in New Zealand were male and 51% were female, the corresponding prevalence estimates were 27/100,000 for MTF and 4.4/100,000 for FTM, with a sex ratio of 6:1. This study was limited in that the original sex status on the passport was not always known.

Summary and Discussion

Whereas direct comparison of results across studies is difficult due to the geographic, cultural, and methodologic differences, the key determinant of prevalence is the definition of transgender. In several previous reviews (Meier & Labuski, 2013; Zucker & Lawrence, 2009), all studies that reported the proportions of transgender individuals in a population were discussed together, and for this reason, the results appeared to be too inconsistent to provide a basis for overall conclusions. Based on our review, we would argue that, once the studies are sub-classified according to case definition, the results are not as wide-ranging as previously thought.

Studies estimating the prevalence of receipt or requests for hormonal or surgical gender confirmation therapy between 1968 and 2010 have relatively similar results. The prevalence estimates in this category of studies ranged between 1 and 12 per 100,000 individuals, with three exceptions. Horton and Conway both estimated the prevalence of receipt of GCS in the United States to be around 40 per 100,000 (Conway, 2002; Horton, 2008). These two reports fall into the category of "gray literature," which can be defined as any study that is not published in peer-reviewed journals or scientific monographs (Goodman et al., 2014). Both reports suggest that the available data underestimate the true prevalence of GCS; however, the basis for this conclusion, and the methodology used to calculate the prevalence estimates, are not clear. Another study reporting a higher prevalence estimate was conducted in Singapore (Tsoi, 1988). As this was the only study assessing GCS outside of North America or Western Europe, the discrepancy may stem from cultural or medical practice-related differences between Southeast Asia and Western countries (Winter, 2009).

Among studies reporting prevalence of transgender-specific diagnoses, most (10 of 13) estimates ranged from between 1 and 10 per 100,000 individuals. Three studies reported results outside of this range. A study from Iran calculated a prevalence of less than 1 per 100,000 (Ahmadzad-Asl et al., 2010). It has been reported that treatment for GD in Iran, although legal, is heavily regulated (Javaheri, 2010); however, more information is needed to draw conclusions about the differences between Iranian and Western data.

Two U.S.-based studies using the VHA electronic medical records reported higher-than-previously observed prevalence of GID in the 20–30 per 100,000 range (Blosnich et al., 2013; Kauth et al., 2014). The discrepancy between the VHA studies and other reports may have several explanations. It is likely that the availability of high-quality electronic data and a more complete ascertainment of both the numerator and the denominator offer more accurate results. Alternatively, as the VHA analyses were based on comparatively recent data, the higher prevalence of GID reported in those studies may reflect the secular trend of an ever-increasing proportion of persons who acknowledge their transgender status and seek appropriate care. It is also possible, however, that the prevalence among veterans is truly higher than that in the general population, in keeping with the "flight to hypermasculinity" phenomenon, which may disproportionately affect veterans (Brown, 1988).

The prevalence of self-reported transgender status and gender non-conformity appears to be orders of magnitude higher than the corresponding treatment- or diagnosis-based estimates. The results of four survey-based studies ranged from 300 to 700 per 100,000 persons (Conron et al., 2012; Gates, 2011; Kuyper and Wijsen, 2014; Van Caenegem et al., 2015). The four studies used somewhat different methods and all may have been affected by a substantial number of non-responses (Schneider et al., 2012). Nevertheless, the relatively consistent findings in this group of studies indicate that transgender identity and gender non-conformity are far more widespread than what could be expected based on clinical data.

With respect to methodological issues, a particular shortcoming of the extant literature is the lack of good denominator data. Prevalence by definition is a proportion; that is, a ratio in which all observations in the numerator arise from a pre-defined denominator (Gordis, 2004). It is notable that the majority of studies included in this review first quantified the numerator and then used an approximated population size to arrive at a prevalence estimate. With these limitations in mind, future research should employ established, formal methods of prevalence calculations, such as those used in recent studies of U.S. veterans (Blosnich et al., 2013; Kauth et al., 2014). As many transgender people do not receive the diagnosis, future studies should also take advantage of modern informatics tools that go beyond ICD codes and include evaluation of free text available in the electronic medical records. An important prerequisite of an accurate prevalence estimate is outcome validation to decrease misclassification; this may require detailed record abstraction or the use of alternative, preferably independent, data sources.

Another notable finding of this review is the need to consider cultural differences as to how transgender people are perceived and treated in a society. A more definitive weight-of-evidence assessment and a better understanding of the geographic, demographic, and cultural differences in prevalence of transgender and gender non-conformity will be possible when studies conducted in different population groups use the same or similar methodology and strict application of definition within each study in order to better generalize findings.

References

Ahmadzad-Asl M, Jalali A-H, Alavi K, Naserbakht M, Taban M, Mohseninia-Omrani K, et al. 2010. The epidemiology of transsexualism in iran. *J Gay Lesbian Ment Health* 15:83–93.

Baba T, Endo T, Ikeda K, Shimizu A, Honnma H, Ikeda H, et al. 2011. Distinctive features of female-to-male transsexualism and prevalence of gender identity disorder in japan. *J Sex Med* 8:1686–1693.

Bakker A, van Kesteren PJ, Gooren LJ, Bezemer PD. 1993. The prevalence of transsexualism in the Netherlands. *Acta Psychiatr Scand* 87:237–238.

Benjamin H, Lal GB, Green R, Masters RE. 1966. *The Transsexual Phenomenon*. Ace Publishing Company.

Blosnich JR, Brown GR, Shipherd JC, Kauth M, Piegari RI, Bossarte RM. 2013. Prevalence of gender identity disorder and suicide risk among transgender veterans utilizing Veterans Health Administration care. *Am J Public Health* 103:e27–32.

Brown GR. 1988. Transsexuals in the military: Flight into hypermasculinity. *Arch Sex Behav* 17:527–537.

Cahill S, Makadon H. 2014. Sexual orientation and gender identity data collection in clinical settings and in electronic health records: A key to ending LGBT health disparities. *LGBT Health* 1:34–41.

Caldarera A, Pfäfflin F. 2011. Transsexualism and sex reassignment surgery in Italy. *Int J Transgenderism* 13:26–36.

Coleman E, Bockting W, Botzer M, Cohen-Kettenis P, DeCuypere G, Feldman J, et al. 2012. Standards of care for the health of transsexual, transgender, and gender-nonconforming people, version 7. *Int J Transgenderism* 13:165–232.

Conron KJ, Scott G, Stowell GS, Landers SJ. 2012. Transgender health in Massachusetts: Results from a household probability sample of adults. *Am J Public Health* 102:118–122.

Conway L. 2002. How frequently does transsexualism occur? Available at: http://www.conseil-lgbt.ca/wp-content/uploads/2013/12/How-Frequently-Does-Transsexualism-Occur.pdf.

De Cuypere G, Vanhemelrijck M, Michel A, Carael B, Heylens G, Rubens R, et al. 2007. Prevalence and demography of transsexualism in Belgium. *Eur Psychiatry* 22:137–141.

Dhejne C, Oberg K, Arver S, Landen M. 2014. An analysis of all applications for sex reassignment surgery in Sweden, 1960–2010: Prevalence, incidence, and regrets. *Arch Sex Behav* 43:1535–1545.

Eklund PL, Gooren LJ, Bezemer PD. 1988. Prevalence of transsexualism in the Netherlands. *Br J Psychiatry* 152:638–640.

Esteva I, Gonzalo M, Yahyaoui R, Domínguez M, Bergero T, Giraldo F, et al. 2006. Epidemiología de la transexualidad en Andalucía, atención especial al grupo de adolescentes. *C Med Psicosom* 78:65–70.

Esteva I, Gomez-Gil E, Almaraz MC, Martinez-Tudela J, Bergero T, Olveira G, et al. 2012. [Organization of healthcare for transsexual persons in the Spanish national health system.] *Gaceta Sanitaria / SESPAS* 26:203–209.

Gates GJ. 2011. How many people are lesbian, gay, bisexual and transgender? Williams Institute, University of California, Los Angeles School of Law; Los Angeles, CA: Available at: http://williamsinstitute.law.ucla.edu/wp-content/uploads/Gates-How-Many-People-LGBT-Apr-2011.pdf.

Gomez Gil E, Trilla Garcia A, Godas Sieso T, Halperin Rabinovich I, Puig Domingo M, Vidal Hagemeijer A, et al. 2006. [Estimation of prevalence, incidence and sex ratio of transsexualism in Catalonia according to health care demand.] *Actas Esp Psiquiatr* 34:295–302.

Goodman M, Lakind JS, Mattison DR. 2014. Do phthalates act as obesogens in humans? A systematic review of the epidemiological literature. *Crit Rev Toxicol* 44:151–175.

Gordis L. 2004. *Epidemiology*, 3rd ed. Philadelphia, PA: WB Saunders.

Hoenig J, Kenna JC. 1974. The prevalence of transsexualism in England and Wales. *Br J Psychiatry* 124:181–190.

Horton MA. 2008. The incidence and prevalence of SRS among US residents. Available at http://www.tgender.net/taw/thb/THBPrevalence-OE2008.pdf.

Institute of Medicine. 2011. *The Health of Lesbian, Gay, Bisexual, and Transgender People: Building a Foundation for Better Understanding.* Washington, DC:The National Academies Press.

Javaheri F. 2010. A study of transsexuality in Iran. *Iranian Studies* 43:365–377.

Judge C, O'Donovan C, Callaghan G, Gaoatswe G, O'Shea D. 2014. Gender dysphoria – prevalence and co-morbidities in an Irish adult population. *Front Endocrinol (Lausanne)* 5:87. doi: 10.3389/fendo.2014.00087. eCollection 02014.

Kauth MR, Shipherd JC, Lindsay J, Blosnich JR, Brown GR, Jones KT. 2014. Access to care for transgender veterans in the Veterans Health Administration: 2006–2013. *Am J Publ Hlth* 104:S532–S534.

Kuyper L, Wijsen C. 2014. Gender identities and gender dysphoria in the Netherlands. *Arch Sex Behav* 43:377–385.

Meier SC, Labuski CM. 2013. The demographics of the transgender population. In: Baumle AK (Ed.) *International Handbook on the Demography of Sexuality.* New York: Springer, pp. 289–327.

Moher D, Shamseer L, Clarke M, Ghersi D, Liberati A, Petticrew M, et al. 2015. Preferred reporting items for systematic review and meta-analysis protocols (prisma-p) 2015 statement. *Syst Rev* 4:2046–4053.

O'Gorman E. 1982. A retrospective study of epidemiological and clinical aspects of 28 transsexual patients. *Arch Sex Behav* 11:231–236.

Okabe N, Sato T, Matsumoto Y, Ido Y, Terada S, Kuroda S. 2008. Clinical characteristics of patients with gender identity disorder at a Japanese gender identity disorder clinic. *Psychiatry Res* 157:315–318.

Pauly IB. 1968. The current status of the change of sex operation. *J Nerv Ment Dis* 147:460–471.

Reisner SL, Conron KJ, Tardiff LA, Jarvi S, Gordon AR, Austin SB. 2014. Monitoring the health of transgender and other gender minority populations: Validity of natal sex and gender identity survey items in a U.S. national cohort of young adults. *BMC Publ Hlth* 14:1224.

Ross MW, Walinder J, Lundstrom B, Thuwe I. 1981. Cross-cultural approaches to transsexualism. A comparison between Sweden and Australia. *Acta Psychiatr Scand* 63:75–82.

Schneider KL, Clark MA, Rakowski W, Lapane KL. 2012. Evaluating the impact of non-response bias in the behavioral risk factor surveillance system (BRFSS). *J Epidemiol Commun Hlth* 66:290–295.

Tsoi WF. 1988. The prevalence of transsexualism in Singapore. *Acta Psychiatr Scand* 78:501–504.

Van Caenegem E, Wierckx K, Elaut E, Buysse A, Dewaele A, Van Nieuwerburgh F, et al. 2015. Prevalence of gender nonconformity in Flanders, Belgium. *Arch Sex Behav* 15:15.

Veale JF. 2008. Prevalence of transsexualism among New Zealand passport holders. *Aust N Z J Psychiatry* 42:887–889.

Wålinder J. 1968. Transsexualism: Definition, prevalence sex distribution. *Acta Psychiatr Scand* 43:255–258.

Weitze C, Osburg S. 1996. Transsexualism in Germany: Empirical data on epidemiology and application of the German transsexuals' act during its first ten years. *Arch Sex Behav* 25:409–425.

Wilson P, Sharp C, Carr S. 1999. The prevalence of gender dysphoria in Scotland: A primary care study. *Br J Gen Pract* 49:991–992.

Winter S. 2009. Cultural considerations for the World Professional Association for Transgender Health's standards of care: The Asian perspective. *Int J Transgenderism* 11:19–41.

Zucker KJ, Lawrence AA. 2009. Epidemiology of gender identity disorder: Recommendations for the standards of care of the World Professional Association for Transgender Health. *Int J Transgender* 11:8–18.

3 An Overview of the *Standards of Care for the Health of Transsexual, Transgender, and Gender Nonconforming People*

Eli Coleman

Clinicians involved in trans health care should be familiar with the *Standards of Care for the Health of Transsexual, Transgender, and Gender Nonconforming People—Version 7* (*SOC*), which have been produced by the World Association for Transgender Health (Coleman et al., 2012). The World Professional Association for Transgender Health (WPATH) (formerly the Harry Benjamin International Gender Dysphoria Association) is an international association devoted to the understanding and care of transgender, transsexual, and gender non-conforming individuals. Founded in 1979, the organization is composed of physicians, psychologists, allied health care professionals, social scientists, and legal experts, all of whom are engaged in research and/or clinical practice that affect the lives of transsexual, transgender, and gender non-conforming people. One can remain current with the latest clinical approaches by becoming a member of WPATH and attending their biennial symposia, training courses, and certification process, participating in their list serve, and reading their official journal—the *International Journal of Transgenderism*.

The *SOC* are updated regularly, and it is therefore important for clinicians to consult WPATH to make sure one is using the current version.

The main purpose of the *SOC* is to provide universal guidance to clinicians to provide safe and effective pathways for achieving lasting personal comfort with trans persons' gendered selves, to maximize their overall health, psychological well-being, and self-fulfillment.

It is an essential document for any clinician, and access to the *SOC* should be readily available for guidance and as a key reference document. The *SOC* are available to be downloaded from the WPATH website and as a mobile app. The *SOC* have also been translated into a myriad of languages, all of which are freely available on the WPATH website. Additionally, hard copies can be purchased from WPATH.

The *SOC* set a standard which is designed to provide optimal care based upon the best-available science. However, the *SOC* are also designed to be flexible. Clinicians should be able to document reasons for deviations from the accepted *SOC*. While every attempt was made to ensure cultural relevance and universal acceptance, the *SOC* acknowledge the need to modify their use in culturally appropriate ways, without sacrificing the essential principles, and to adjust to resource limitations, particularly in underdeveloped parts of the world.

History of the *Standards of Care*

The current *SOC* represent a significant departure from previous versions, owing to significant cultural shifts, advances in clinical knowledge, and appreciation of the many health care issues that can arise for gender-variant people, beyond hormonal and surgical reassignment. The first version of the *SOC* for the hormonal and surgical sex reassignment of gender-dysphoric persons was published in 1979 (Walker et al., 1979). The aim of the original *SOC* was to set minimal standards for assessment and determination of eligibility for hormonal and surgical reassignment, and to provide guidelines for optimal care for patients. There was a clear subtext that the *SOC* were designed to protect professionals who prescribed hormones or performed surgery from legal, ethical, or moral scrutiny, or liability. They were also established to legitimize medical and surgical procedures and encourage the medical establishment to recognize these as medically viable and promote health care coverage.

There were successive revisions in 1980, 1981, and 1990, which contained minor and yet not insignificant changes. A radical departure in the *SOC* came about in Version 5 (Levine et al., 1998). Reflecting a cultural paradigm shift, Version 5 of the *SOC* acknowledged that many adults with gender dysphoria were finding comfortable, effective ways of self-identification that did not include all the components of what was termed "the triadic treatment sequence" (real-life experience, hormonal treatment, and surgical sex reassignment). There was an important clarification made in this version. Namely, that psychotherapy, while not a requirement for hormonal or sex reassignment, was only strongly recommended. Although no longer a requirement, there was a large section added to describe the potential benefits of psychotherapy, the tasks of the mental health professional, the therapeutic relationship, and the process of psychotherapy (Levine et al., 1998).

Due to a number of concerns that were raised after the publication of Version 5, some significant modifications of eligibility requirements were made in Version 6. In addition, there were further clarifications that allowed for a variety of management options other than the "triadic sequence" (Meyer et al., 2001).

From 2001 to 2012, Version 6 of the *SOC* of the Association continued to be a useful resource for promoting and ensuring high-quality care for transgender persons around the world (Bryant, 2006; Coleman, 2007). The *SOC* were widely referenced to explain the nature of gender dysphoria and treatment options. The *SOC* increased awareness of the need for medical and psychological assistance for individuals with gender issues, and improved access to care (including funding through insurance or government-paid health services), and were constantly used to fight legal battles to ensure transgender rights for equality and access to care, and to recognize a person's gender status as a legitimate marker of an individual's sex identity (Bryant,

2006; Coleman, 2007; Currah, Juang, & Minter, 2006). However, Version 6 was not without its critics. After a significant cultural shift towards greater tolerance and understanding of gender variance and a simultaneous increase in knowledge, a revision became necessary, and was completed in 2012 (Coleman et al., 2012).

For a more complete history of the *SOC* and a description of the process and background papers which were commissioned to help write the new standards, see Coleman (2009a; 2009b; 2009c; 2009d).

WPATH *Standards of Care—Version 7*

While Versions 5 and 6 represented a radical departure from previous versions, Version 7 brought yet another significant shift. This version, more than previous iterations, acknowledged that gender variance is not a disorder and that many people live comfortable lives without seeking therapy or medical interventions. It also recognized that gender-variant persons have unique health care needs, necessary for the promotion of their overall health and well-being. Version 7 clearly articulated that health care needs go well beyond the need for hormonal treatment and/or surgical interventions. Comprehensive care includes the importance of primary care, preventive health care, gynecologic and urologic care, and provision of reproductive options and mental health services.

As stated previously, the *SOC* were designed as international standards. However, there was a clear acknowledgment that much of the standards has evolved from research and experience that comes from a North American and Western European perspective. Adaptations of the *SOC* to other areas of the world are necessary. However, adaptations need to be with adherence to and respect for some fundamental principles. Health professionals throughout the world—even in areas with limited resources and training opportunities— can apply the many core principles that undergird the *SOC*. These principles include the following: exhibit respect for patients with non-conforming gen- der identities (do not pathologize differences in gender identity or expression); provide care (or refer to knowledgeable colleagues) that affirms patients' gender identities and reduces the distress of gender dysphoria, when present; become knowledgeable about the health care needs of transsexual, transgender, and gender non-conforming people, including the benefits and risks of treatment options for gender dysphoria; match the treatment approach to the specific needs of patients, particularly their goals for gender expression and need for relief from gender dysphoria; facilitate access to appropriate care; seek patients' informed consent before providing treatment; offer continuity of care; and be prepared to support and advocate for patients within their families and com- munities (schools, workplaces, and other settings) (Coleman et al., 2012).

Version 7 also advocates for a greater collaborative relationship with gender-variant persons and health care providers. It clearly articulates minimal standards of care but also acknowledges the role of informed decision mak- ing and harm reduction approaches. In addition, this version recognizes and validates various expressions of gender variance that may not necessitate hormonal or surgical treatments.

There is an updated section on treatment of children and adolescents. Here there is a clear statement that "refusing timely medical interventions for adolescents might prolong gender dysphoria and contribute to an appearance that could provoke abuse and stigmatization," and that "withholding puberty suppression and subsequent feminizing or masculinizing hormone therapy is not a neutral option for adolescents" (Coleman et al., 2012). There is a strong statement that:

> treatment aimed at trying to change a person's gender identity and expression to become more congruent with sex assigned at birth has been attempted in the past without success, particularly in the long term. Such treatment is no longer considered ethical. (Coleman et al., 2012)

These statements were tempered with words of caution regarding the encouragement of social transition during childhood without careful assessment and working with systems to accommodate the child's gender expression. Mental health professionals are encouraged to not impose a binary view of gender. They should give ample room for children and adolescents to explore different options for gender expression. Hormonal or surgical interventions are considered appropriate for some adolescents, but not others.

This is a rapidly evolving area with insufficient research and evaluation of protocols. The *SOC* give some overarching considerations of the treatment of children and adolescents, but clinicians should pay considerable attention to new research in this area.

The *SOC* also address the importance of care for trans people in institutional environments. A clear statement was made that access to these medically necessary treatments should not be denied on the basis of institutionalization or housing arrangements (continuing or starting), and that reasonable accommodation be provided to foster a tolerant and positive climate.

A new section contains information about the treatment of gender dysphoria among intersex individuals. While most intersex individuals do not experience gender dysphoria, there are those who do, and the *SOC* provide information and guidance on how to manage these patients.

As a result of the internet and rapidly evolving technologies of telemedicine, there is a new section of the *SOC* on the use of *etherapy*, distance counseling, or online therapy. This is a rapidly evolving area, with ethical and legal considerations. But it provides a vehicle to access care from gender specialists for individuals who might not otherwise have access to care for any number of reasons.

There is a new section on voice and communication therapy, describing the competencies of voice and communication specialists working with transsexual, transgender, and gender non-conforming clients. It includes issues of assessment and treatment considerations, including voice feminization surgery. WPATH has recently completed a companion document to the *SOC*, which more clearly outlines the guidelines for voice and communication therapy (Davies et al., 2015).

In terms of surgical procedures, the *SOC* make explicit that sex reassignment surgery is effective and medically necessary. There is a very useful appendix which summarizes the follow-up studies documenting an undeniable beneficial effect of sex reassignment surgery on postoperative outcomes, including subjective well-being, cosmesis, and sexual function.

Finally, Version 7 of the *SOC* recognizes the social determinants of health. For this reason, there was a call for health care professionals to advocate for public policy and legal reforms that promote tolerance and equity for gender- and sexually diverse people. In addition, clinicians are asked to participate in efforts to eliminate prejudice, discrimination, and stigma.

The *SOC* contain many useful appendices, including a glossary, an overview of medical risks of hormone therapy, a summary of criteria for hormone therapy and surgery, evidence for clinical outcomes of therapeutic approaches, and a description of the development process for creating Version 7 of the *SOC*. Finally, the evidence for supporting these standards is clearly articulated and referenced.

Probably the most significant aspect of Version 7 of the *SOC* is the tone of the document. It emphasizes what professionals need to do, rather than what the client needs to do. It particularly emphasizes that health care for trans individuals is more than just providing hormones and surgery—it is about promoting overall health and well-being.

Conclusion

The *SOC* are an essential resource for health care providers. It is extremely important that health care providers familiarize themselves with the *SOC* and keep up to date with new versions and companion documents produced by WPATH.

The *SOC* Version 7 has been very positively received by health professionals, public policy makers, health care systems and authorities, and trans individuals themselves. It is having an impact on increasing health care access, supporting the need for additional training and certification for gender specialists, and stimulating new research.

WPATH continues to work on developing companion documents and has already embarked on a process of revising Version 7. One cannot overestimate the importance of keeping current with these developments in order to provide optimal, best-practice care.

References

Bryant, K. (2006). Making gender identity disorder of childhood: Historical lessons for contemporary debates. *Sexuality Research & Policy*, 3(3), 23–39.

Coleman, E. (2007). Afterword. In R. Ettner, S. Monstrey, & A. Eyler (Eds.), *Principles of Transgender Medicine and Surgery* (pp. 311–314). New York: Haworth Press.

Coleman, E. (2009a). Toward Version 7 of the World Professional Association for Transgender Health's *Standards of Care*: Medical and therapeutic approaches to treatment. *International Journal of Transgenderism*, 11(4), 215–219.

Coleman, E. (2009b). Toward Version 7 of the World Professional Association for Transgender Health's *Standards of Care*: Hormonal and surgical approaches to treatment. *International Journal of Transgenderism*, 11(3), 141–145.

Coleman, E. (2009c). Toward Version 7 of the World Professional Association for Transgender Health's Standards of Care: Psychological assessment and approaches to treatment. *International Journal of Transgenderism*, 11(2), 69–73.

Coleman, E. (2009d). Toward Version 7 of the World Professional Association for Transgender Health's *Standards of Care*. *International Journal of Transgenderism*, 11(1), 1–7.

Coleman, E., Bockting, W., Botzer, M., Cohen-Kettenis, P., DeCuypere, G., Feldman, J., Fraser, L., Green, J., Knudson, G., Meyer, W., Monstrey, S., Adler, R., Brown, G., Devor, A., Ehrbar, R., Ettner, R., Eyler, E., Garofalo, R., Karasic, D., Lev, A. I., Mayer, G., Meyer-Bahlburg, H., Hall, B. P., Pfaefflin, F., Rachlin, K., Robinson, B., Schechter, L., Tangpricha, V., van Trotsenburg, M., Vitale, A., Winter, S., Whittle, S., Wylie, K., & Zucker, K. (2012). Standards of care for the health of transsexual, transgender, and gender nonconforming people, 7th version. *International Journal of Transgenderism*, 13(4), 165–232.

Currah, P., Juang, R. M., & Minter, S. P. (2006). *Transgender Rights*. Minneapolis, MN: University of Minnesota Press.

Davies, S., Papp, V. G., & Antoni, C. (2015). Voice and communication change for gender nonconforming individuals: Giving voice to the person inside. *International Journal of Transgenderism*, 16(3), 117–159.

Levine, S. B., Brown, G., Coleman, E., Cohen-Kettenis, P. T., Hage, J., Van Maasdam J., et al. (1998). The standards of care for gender identity disorders. *International Journal of Transgenderism*, 2(2). Retrieved November 7, 2015, from http://web.archive.org/web/20070502001025/http://www.symposion.com/ijt/ijtc0405.htm.

Meyer, W., Bockting, W. O., Cohen-Kettenis, P., Coleman, E., DiCeglie, D., Devor, H., et al. (2001). The Harry Benjamin International Gender Dysphoria Association's standards of care for gender identity disorders – Sixth version. *International Journal of Transgenderism*, 5(1). Retrieved November 7, 2015, from http://web.archive.org/web/20070422090725/http://www.symposion.com/ijt/soc_2001/index.htm.

Walker, P., Berger, J., Green, R., Laub, D., Reynolds, C., & Wollman, L. (1979). *Standards of Care: The Hormonal and Surgical Sex Reassignment of Gender Dysphoric Persons.* Minneapolis, MN: World Professional Association for Transgender Health.

4   Primary Medical Care of Transgender and Gender Non-conforming Persons

A. Evan Eyler

Introduction

This chapter is intended for primary care physicians, physician assistants, and nurse practitioners who would like to provide medical care to adults who are transgender, gender-variant, or gender non-conforming.

Many primary care clinicians decide to become knowledgeable about transgender medical care when they are approached by their patients who are planning to transition gender or have already done so. Others seek out information about gender variance when they encounter patients whose gender expression is outside usual male or female norms, or whose personal gender identity is other than fully female or fully male, also referred to as *non-binary* gender or *genderqueer* (Bockting, 2008; Coleman, Bockting, Botzer, Cohen-Kettenis, et al., 2012). The term *transgender* will be used in this chapter to refer to persons whose gender identity or expression differs from expectations based on birth-assigned sex (Bockting, 1999; Coleman et al., 2012). In recent years, transgender care has become a part of routine clinical care in many family medicine, internal medicine, and general practice settings.

Preventive care for transgender adults is the same as care for *cisgender* (i.e., non-transgender) adults in most respects (Eyler, 2007; Feldman, 2007, 2008; Feldman & Goldberg, 2006). Primary care clinicians who lack experience in cross-sex hormonal management can still ensure that their transgender patients receive routine health maintenance services. Some physicians and other clinicians seek consultation with an endocrinologist, or more experienced colleague in internal medicine or family medicine, when they begin providing treatment with masculinizing and feminizing hormones. Many conduct the pre-hormone evaluation and prescribe estrogen and androgen preparations themselves, referring only the complicated cases to endocrinology. Hormone management is fairly straightforward in most cases. This chapter discusses the key principles of routine clinical care and introduces the basic principles of hormonal treatment.

Variation in Gender Identity and Expression

Primary care needs may be somewhat different, depending on the culture and background of the individual patient, and the way in which gender has been experienced. Concepts of gender and sexual orientation have exhibited significant variation over time and in different cultural contexts. Western culture has traditionally assumed that anatomical genital sex (male or female) is concordant with gender, the psychological self-perception of maleness or femaleness (Coleman et al., 2012). Many other cultures have recognized the existence of more than two genders and have different expectations for persons who do not fit either the man's or the woman's role (Ramet, 1996). Throughout ancient and modern history, some individuals have lived cross-gendered and been perceived throughout all or part of their adult life as belonging to, or behaving as, the gender not usually associated with their natal, anatomic sex.

Recent years have seen the recognition in majority American culture of persons who perceive themselves as differently gendered, outside the *gender binary* of women and men, or as possessing significant attributes usually associated with both genders. This was described as *gender blended* by Devor (1989) and more recently as *genderqueer* (Bockting, 2008), especially among adolescents and young adults. Other terms, such as gender-variant, gender non-conforming (Drescher, 2010), and gender diversity, are conceptually similar. Some consider the concept of gender itself as problematic or inapplicable: "Many in the [transgender] community would see themselves as existing outside of gender, of being oppressed by it, but using its icons and signifiers to say who they are" (Whittle, 1996). At a recent theater opening in New York City, Holly Rae Taylor remarked, "Gender is so passé," when a butch woman friend was referred to as male (Thurman, 2015).

Gender identity can be conceptualized as a continuum (Eyler & Wright, 1997), a mobius (Witten, 2002), or patchwork. Some people report having the sense of gender identity different from the birth-assigned sex at a very young age, often age 3 or 4, and may begin living as members of the psychological gender in childhood, using medical services for gender confirmation at later ages. Others identify as members of one gender, but engage in behaviors or expressions of appearance that are strongly associated with another gender, such as men who enjoy cross-dressing as women on a part-time basis, recreationally or sexually, but do not experience any need to alter the body in a permanent way. Historical concepts of sexual orientation (Kinsey, Pomeroy, & Martin, 1948) are difficult to apply to people who are transgender, as these have historically been grounded in anatomic, genital sex rather than gender identity. Killerman (2015) has developed an educational tool called the Genderbread Person which visually represents the difference between physical anatomic sex, gender identity, sexual orientation, and gender role; this can be helpful in discussing variation in each of those domains in a clinical context, such as with gender-variant youth and their parents, or trainees working with transgender adults.

The medical needs of transgender and gender-variant persons always include routine primary care services, delivered in a respectful manner, with full acceptance of gender as defined by the individual. In many cases, hormonal and surgical treatments are also needed. These bring about physical changes that can help internal self-perception and physical attributes to become more congruent, thus increasing gendered self-comfort and social confidence.

Transgender Health Care

Primary Care

People who are transgender have often encountered difficulty in obtaining adequate medical services (Eyler, Witten, & Cole, 1997; Kammerer, Mason, & Connors, 1999; Witten, 2003), though access has been improving in some respects (Nemoto, Opertario, & Keatley, 2005) in recent years, at least in many places. Access to appropriate services remains limited in some geographic areas, such as in the American rural South (Petersen, Sharon, & Karasic, 2015). Many people receive care through transgender programs at universities and lesbian, gay, bisexual, and transgender (LGBT) health centers, but these are usually located in urban areas. Rural family medicine and internal medicine practices play a crucial role in providing care to transgender persons who do not have access to urban specialty care. Many people also prefer to receive their health care through their personal physician's office, rather than in a transgender or LGBT health program, and may receive more personal care at a practice where they are well known.

Information about transgender health care has become much more widely available with the expansion of internet sites maintained by transgender health organizations (e.g., Coleman et al., 2012; Mazzoni Center, 2015; UCSF Center of Excellence for Transgender Health, 2011), and a number of excellent guidelines and reviews are available, as discussed below. Physicians, physician assistants, and nurse practitioners who wish to become expert in transgender health can enter the field by reviewing information about transgender preventive services and hormonal care, attending conferences on transgender medicine, or consulting with colleagues who have more experience in this area of practice.

Case 1. Francine (birth name Francis) is a 24-year-old technical student who resides in a rural area in the Northeastern United States. She struggled against the transgender identity and its implications for years, and came close to suicide when she suddenly admitted to herself that she was female-gendered and needed to change the male body in order to become a woman physically as well. In a panic, she called the physician assistant she had seen for years, who helped her through this emotional crisis and arranged for an urgent psychiatric consultation. When Francine had regained emotional stability, she asked to begin treatment with estrogen. Her physician assistant recommended referral to a transgender clinic in the closest city. Francine declined this advice, asking, "Can't you do this for me? How hard can it be?" Her physician assistant brought this request to the clinic's practice management committee, downloaded hormone-prescribing guidelines from the internet, and arranged for consultation while she learned how to provide good transgender hormonal care.

Providing quality transgender primary care involves hormonal management and preventive services across the lifespan, coordinating referrals to other specialties, and creating an office environment that is welcoming to people who are transgender or gender-variant, one that communicates respect. The details of practice management are often the most difficult aspect of clinical care to change, because of the comprehensive review of existing policies, and sustained effort, that this often entails. Initial steps often include the following:

1. Patients should be asked how they would like to be addressed, including the preferred name and which pronouns to use. If legal name and gender changes have not been finalized, the "memo" or "banner" portion of many electronic records can be used to communicate patient preferences.
2. At least one restroom should be designated gender-neutral.
3. Forms should be updated to offer a write-in option for gender, rather than relying on M/F.
4. Pediatric history forms should be reviewed. "Child's mother" and "child's father" should be replaced by "parents or guardians."
5. Insurance status should be kept current and checked whenever claims are submitted. For example, some transmen defer changing gender designation with their insurers, in order to be able to receive insurance coverage for gynecologic care without administrative complication.
6. Every member of the office staff should receive education about gender identity and transgender.
7. A mechanism for patient feedback should be offered, and concerns about treatment as a transgender person taken seriously and used non-judgmentally to improve the practice.

Multidisciplinary Care and Referrals

Many people who are receiving medical services for the physical aspects of gender transition are seen by a family physician, internist, or endocrinologist who is knowledgeable about hormonal management and general medical care, and by a number of professionals in other fields. These may include urologists, gynecologists, plastic surgeons, speech therapists, and members of the mental health fields. Communication between members of this clinical team is essential, especially whenever a treatment change is planned.

Physicians, physician assistants, and nurse practitioners in the primary care specialties are often in a position to choose consultants in other fields, and establish patterns of referral. Contacting colleagues to ask about their level of interest and expertise in treating patients who are transgender can provide an opportunity for informal professional education, and can be used to avoid referrals that will be unhelpful to the patients who are gender-variant or gender non-conforming.

> Case 2. Kyle, birth name Kylie, is a 28-year-old teacher who started treatment with testosterone 9 months ago. His family physician refers him to a colleague in gynecology due to an episode of fairly severe dysfunctional uterine bleeding. After the clinical visit, he writes a letter describing his humiliation at being persistently addressed as "miss," and describing the obvious discomfort of the receptionist and medical assistant during their interactions with him. The gynecologist schedules an office in-service about transgender health, in which every member of the staff has the opportunity to ask questions and discuss their feelings about caring for transgender men. Together, the members of the practice review office procedures and make revisions that will make providing services to transgender patients easier and better in the future. After the visit, Kyle learns that his insurer has declined the claim for the cytology analysis, and that he now must come out to a large corporation in order to have the claim processed and avoid being charged for this service.

Common Clinical Presentations

Physicians, physician assistants, and nurse practitioners who are known in their communities as empathic sources of transgender medical care will find patients presenting to their practices for a variety of reasons. Patients will seek initiation of hormonal treatment; prescription medications to replace informally obtained (e.g., via the internet or gym) hormonal preparations; and post-transition medical care. Some individuals who are not planning to transition gender, but whose gender presentations or roles are outside societal norms, will also seek care from clinicians who are knowledgeable about variation in gender identity and who are known to treat their "non-traditionally gendered" patients with dignity and respect.

The Patient Who Is Seeking Initiation of Hormonal Treatment

Transgender adults who are beginning hormonal treatment may be referred to the primary care practice by a mental health professional, a colleague who is less experienced in transgender medicine, or may self-refer. Communication between the physical and mental health professionals involved in the patient's care is important, and a release of information should be obtained at the initial visit.

The initial evaluation includes a full health history, a physical examination, and endocrine assessment, as well as discussion of social circumstances and support. This is an excellent opportunity to assess other chronic health conditions and potential medication interactions. Laboratory evaluation is usually obtained at the first visit and the hormone prescription started at a subsequent visit.

There are no randomized controlled trials establishing the superiority of one program of hormonal care over another, though a number of guidelines and reviews have been published (Dahl, Feldman, Goldberg, & Jaberi, 2006; Feldman & Safer, 2009; Hembree et al., 2009; Moore, Wiesniewski, & Dobbs, 2003; UCSF Center of Excellence for Transgender Health, 2011). Many endocrinologists follow the Endocrine Society clinical practice guideline (Hembree et al., 2009) with regard to medication doses and expected physical findings. Clinicians who are in the process of developing proficiency in transgender medicine may wish to review the available literature, especially the World Professional Association for Transgender Health (WPATH) *Standards of Care* (Version 7, Coleman et al., 2012) and consult with a more experienced colleague.

The Patient Who Has Been Using Informally Obtained Hormones, and Who Wishes to Begin Prescription Medications

Some people begin hormone treatment with informally obtained preparations, such as testosterone purchased at a fitness center, non-prescription "botanical" estrogen preparations, or hormonal medications obtained over the internet without prescription. Veterinary hormonal preparations are also sometimes used.

People start hormone use in these ways for many reasons, including economic need, confidentiality concerns, lack of locally available services, the desire to control medication use without "negotiating" with a medical professional, and ambivalence about transitioning gender (Nemoto et al., 2005). Some people wish to use higher doses of estrogen or testosterone than would normally be prescribed, in an effort to achieve physical changes more swiftly. Regardless of reason, transgender persons who are self-treating may decide to begin regular medical care, particularly if a physical problem ensues. Initial evaluation includes the same components as for patients who are beginning hormone use, as well as a comprehensive history regarding the use of non-prescription preparations, obtained in a non-judgmental and welcoming manner.

The use of other unregulated treatments should be sympathetically discouraged. This is particularly important with regard to injections of silicone and other viscous substances, such as mineral oil. These are sometimes used by transwomen to create a more feminine appearance by enhancing lip line, hips, and buttocks, but can be medically dangerous in both the short and long term, often causing complications that are particularly difficult to treat (Hage, Kanhai, Oen, van Diest, & Karim, 2001; Oen, Bergers, Kanhai, Hage, & Manoliu, 2002).

The WPATH *Standards of Care* (Version 7, Coleman et al., 2012, p. 43) also discuss the use of "bridging prescriptions," of 1–6 months' duration, when people who have been using informally obtained hormones present for care. This temporary period can be used to obtain past records, complete a clinical evaluation, refer for mental health or other services if needed, or refer to a colleague who can prescribe transgender hormonal medications if this is not a part of the primary care practice. The latter is an aspect of comprehensive care that will likely not be needed in the future, as more and more family medicine and internal medicine practices offer hormone management services to their patients who are transgender.

The Patient Who Has Completed Medical Transition

Individuals who have completed the gender transition process may change sources of care due to geographic relocation, new health insurance plans (in the United States), and many other reasons. The initial meeting with a new physician, physician assistant, or nurse practitioner can be fraught with anxiety, particularly if the individual's gender history is not known to the new community or employer, or if he or she has not had genital surgery and is nervous about disclosing this to a new clinician. Assurances regarding confidentiality of medical records and a warm, welcoming attitude by all members of the office staff are especially important under these circumstances.

The WPATH *Standards of Care* (Version 7, Coleman et al., 2012, p. 43) distinguish between patients who have had the gonads removed, and those who have not, when discussing maintenance hormone treatment. Doses of hormonal medications can often be reduced after removal of the ovaries or testes, but are usually continued lifelong. Dosage can also often be reduced with age.

The Patient Who Is Not Seeking Transition

Some persons who have physical characteristics usually associated with a different gender, or who consider themselves genderqueer, gender-blended, or as having gender identities other than female or male, prefer to obtain medical care from generalist physicians with many transgender patients in their practices, in order to be more readily accepted and understood. As numerous transmasculine health care survey participants noted, having to "educate" one's physician regarding lifestyle and identity concerns can be tiresome (Eyler et al., 1997). Though time has passed since those data were collected, similar sentiments are still commonly expressed today in many areas.

Family Members of Gender-Transitioning Persons

Gender transition requires a substantial and sustained effort in many domains, including medical treatment, social adjustment, legal document change, and attention to the hundreds of details that accompany living in a gendered world. Transwomen and transmen who are married or partnered sometimes continue these relationships during and after transition. In these cases, the couple may become focused on the transition process and neglect other concurrent difficulties and more routine concerns. It can be helpful to inquire whether the patient's partner is receiving routine medical care and, if not, to invite that person into the clinical practice.

> Case 3. Steve, birth name Stephanie, is a 34-year-old retail worker who has been taking testosterone cypionate that he obtained from the internet for the last 14 months. He chose this course of action because of frustration with being unable to obtain the services he wanted through usual means. He was diagnosed with type 1 diabetes at age 12 and has used insulin for many years. His endocrinologist said that he didn't treat gender dysphoria and referred him to a colleague in another community, but transportation was problematic. He consulted a surgeon about female-to-male chest reconstruction (top surgery) but was told that he needed to use testosterone for a year before he could be considered for surgery. He describes becoming discouraged and giving up on regular medical and mental health services, and deciding just to treat himself. He made this appointment because he has been having pelvic pain and has become afraid to continue on his own. His physician listens non-judgmentally, conveys empathy regarding the situation, and makes arrangements for evaluation of the pain.

> Case 4. Beverly is a 52-year-old accountant whose husband of 31 years came out as a transwoman 2 years ago. The partner is taking estrogen and planning for vulvovaginoplasty next year. They are in couple counseling, are reassessing their finances in order to try to pay for the surgery, and are still renegotiating family relationships in light of the gender transition. Beverly has not had an appointment for any aspect of her own health care for over 3 years. Her spouse's physician asks about her need for preventive services and invites her to make an appointment with his practice partner, which she does with thanks.

Ten Principles of Transgender Medical Care

Family physicians, general practitioners, and internists sometimes initiate transgender medical care by referring their patients to an endocrinologist for hormonal treatment while continuing to provide more routine services. Others prefer to prescribe the hormonal medications themselves, reserving endocrinologic consultation for the more complicated cases. This section offers some basic guidelines for the practice of transgender medicine, including the use of hormonal treatments, in primary care practice.

1. Be prepared to involve other professionals in the treatment of patients who are transgender, and maintain close clinical communication.

The medical aspects of treating people who are transgender or gender-variant can be fairly straightforward, particularly for young adults who are physically and mentally healthy and do not want any genital surgical procedures. Other clinical cases are complex, and may require the services of professionals in multiple disciplines, including the general medical, mental health, and surgical fields. Integrated transgender health programs, such as at LGBT health centers and university medical centers, offer the advantages of convenience and coordinated care, but may not be the best option for many people, including those who wish to remain in the care of a personal physician or psychotherapist.

Solo physicians and primary care clinicians in small practices often develop referral relationships with particular endocrinologists, surgeons, mental health professionals, and members of other specialties. Many seek consultation with colleagues who have more experience in transgender health care when they first begin to see patients who are transgender. In cases involving multi-specialty care, all of the participating professionals should remain in close clinical communication. The WPATH *Standards of Care* (Version 7; Coleman et al., 2012) provide flexible guidelines for primary care, hormonal care, mental health, and surgical services. It can be useful for the physicians and other professionals involved in the care of transgender adults to familiarize themselves with these principles.

Comprehensive care for transgender adults often requires an interdisciplinary approach. Persons seeking full medical gender transition, including genital surgery, will need the services of a family physician, general practitioner, or internist experienced in delivering routine and preventive health care and hormone management, and a surgeon skilled in genital reconstruction procedures. Endocrinologic consultation may be helpful in cases that are more complicated. Breast augmentation, transmasculine chest reconstruction, and facial surgeries can be performed by a plastic surgeon who does not perform genital surgeries, but require familiarity with transgender techniques nonetheless. Insurers in the United States require mental health evaluation prior to scheduling surgical procedures, similar to requirements for bariatric surgery or organ transplantation. Most require evaluation by two mental health professionals (Coleman et al., 2012, pp. 59–60) before genital procedures, and many still require that at least one of these be from a doctoral level professional, i.e., a psychiatrist or psychologist.

It is often helpful to identify local physicians in other specialties who are interested in working with patients who are transgender, and whose office personnel will project a welcoming attitude to individuals who appear somewhat gender-atypical. For example, transgender women early in the transition process may still appear somewhat masculine in demeanor and appearance, despite dressing *en femme*. This can be a time of particular emotional vulnerability, and clinical situations involving nudity can be particularly anxiety provoking. Basic principles of medical ethics, such as respect for persons and prevention of harm, should prompt physicians and other medical clinicians to relate to all patients in a positive and welcoming manner, regardless of gender identity or expression, but this is not always the case. In addition, members of the office staff may not have received any training about gender variation and may not respond well to patients who seem unusual in that respect. It can be reassuring to patients to hear that the consulting physician, such as the urologist, cares for many transgender patients, is sympathetic as well as skilled, and works in a welcoming environment.

2.   Emphasize primary care and preventive medical services.

Many transgender adults experience difficulty in obtaining routine preventive medical care, due to lack of availability of appropriate services, psychological barriers to accessing them, or both. Transgender care is becoming mainstream, and many family medicine and internal medicine practices include transgender patients. However, progress in acceptance is uneven, and, in many places, there is still stigma attached to being transgender or showing any significant difference in gender expression. Transgender older adults have often had very negative experiences with medical, nursing, or mental health care, and avoid health care environments unless they are very ill (Witten & Eyler, 1999, 2012). Many people do not present for routine medical care, due to either a desire to conceal true identity or a fear of exposure. For example, a cisgender man who cross-dresses *en femme* may postpone medical visits in order to allow time for body hair to regrow, so as to avoid explaining his gender expression to his physician. Others postpone medical care involving organs that are not congruent with their true gender identity due to gender dysphoria. A transman who has not had hysterectomy may avoid cervical cancer screening due to privacy concerns and discomfort with the "female" aspects of health care. He may also experience difficulty in obtaining insurance coverage for gynecologic care if he has changed his insurance document gender designation to male (Ippolito & Sampson, 2015).

The initial clinical visit for hormonal care may provide an excellent opportunity for assessing other health risks, need for preventive services, and status of other chronic health conditions. While obtaining the complete health history, physicians can identify conditions needing further evaluation and gaps in preventive care. Undiagnosed chronic illnesses, such as hypertension and type 2 diabetes, may first come to medical attention during the pre-hormone evaluation, especially among persons in middle and older adulthood who have not had routine medical care for many years.

Medical care involving genital anatomy, such as cervical cancer screening or evaluation of pelvic pain, is emotionally difficult for some people who are transgender and not for others, depending on the focus and intensity of gender dysphoria. Having a cervical cytology sample collected may be an emotionally neutral, or positive, experience for a transmasculine or genderqueer young adult who is not planning any "bottom surgeries" (genital reconstruction) and whose sexual activity includes his vagina. The same procedure may be extremely problematic for a transman who is attempting to obtain phalloplasty and is not comfortable still having female genital anatomy.

A relaxed, supportive, and empathic approach is essential in these situations. Helpful messages include the concept that body organs may have little to do with gender identity, and that it is important to take care of the body at all stages of the transition process. Some transgender medical practices employ mottos such as "Love your body while you change it," and "Real men get Pap tests" (Stanley & Eyler, 2000). Patients with high levels of discomfort should be scheduled for longer-than-usual appointments in order to ensure that the visit can proceed in a calm and unhurried manner. Other adaptive measures, such as headphones for listening to music during a cervical examination, or mild sedation prior to an endometrial sampling, can also be offered.

> Case 5. Phyllis (legal name Philip) is a 68-year-old differently gendered departmental manager who lives a double life, Philip at work and Phyllis at home. She has injured her ankle and does not want to let her physician know that the mechanism of injury was tripping on the carpet while wearing high heels. She has also not been to very many appointments in recent years because she does not want him to know that she removes her chest hair. Her physician senses that she is holding something back and states openly that he would be honored by her honesty and will maintain her confidence if she confides private information. She is able to do so, and therefore is able to obtain more comprehensive medical care.

3.   Assess initial expectations and goals.

The transgender communities are diverse, and different people find different means of authentic, satisfying gender expression. Clarifying goals at the beginning of treatment is often helpful, while also communicating understanding of the fact that gender transition is a process; specific goals can evolve with time. Is the patient seeking a comprehensive medical transition that includes genital surgery? Is the primary goal to attain the physical changes that supplementing with estrogen or testosterone can bring about? Is some other treatment needed to address the most important aspect of the gender dysphoria, such as speech therapy for a transwoman with a deep, masculine voice? In some cases, there may be other important concerns that warrant attention along with the physical aspects of gender transition, such as a burden of symptoms due to past traumatic experiences related to gender difference. A referral for mental health services, or for more comprehensive psychiatric evaluation, may be needed along with beginning general medical services and hormonal care.

Discussing the specifics of the transition process can also be important. If the goal is physical transition, has the patient formed a mental "timeline," and is it realistic? The Endocrine Society guidelines (Hembree et al., 2009) provide reasonable estimates of the time needed for the changes in secondary sexual characteristics that treatment with estrogen or testosterone will bring about, and a general dose range for the hormonal medications that are commonly used. Using high doses of hormonal medications in an attempt to obtain more rapid change is usually not very helpful, but will increase the risk of side effects and complications.

> Case 6. Jonas, birth name Janet, is an 18-year-old transman who is just beginning treatment with testosterone cypionate. He states that he needs to use "as much as it will take" for him to masculinize well enough to be consistently "read" as male when he begins his university studies in 2 months. His physician explains that this will likely not occur, and joins with his therapist in exploring with Jonas ways that he can express his masculine identity regardless of the level of physical masculinization that develops in the next few months. Jonas considers deferring his enrollment, but ultimately decides to proceed with his studies, and seeks support at the LGBT Student Programs office.

Discussion of the patient's important relationships, living arrangements, and employment situation is an important aspect of beginning transition-related medical care.

Has the patient discussed the decision to begin hormone treatment with the significant others in his, her, or their life, or more broadly? Is there a partner or other important person who will be involved in the transition process, or who should be contacted in case of medical emergency? If the individual begins hormonal transition prior to full disclosure (coming out) about the gender transition, will she or he be able to conceal the physical changes from public notice, such as in the work environment, or slow down the rate of progress until an announcement can be made? For example, some transwomen continue to present as male in the work environment early in the process of hormonal transition, and wear vests to camouflage the beginnings of breast development. This can be an effective temporary strategy, though it is useful to discuss the process of coming out at work in advance, and to consider means of managing problems that may arise.

Flexibility and open communication are usually the most important aspects of discussion regarding goals and expectations of general medical and hormonal care. Personal goals may change with time, particularly with regard to whether genital surgery is desired, but an early, open discussion regarding treatment expectations can foster a more complete understanding of the patient's personal identity and life experience, and help to avoid miscommunication or ultimate dissatisfaction with treatment. Many people who transition gender remark on the importance that a good relationship with a personal physician, physician assistant, or nurse practitioner held for them at a critical time of their life journey.

4. Define realistic expectations of hormone use at the beginning of the treatment process.

Hormone supplementation fosters the development of secondary sexual characteristics of the other natal sex, but does very little to reverse the secondary sexual development that has already taken place. Androgen use will cause male-pattern hair growth (and, sometimes, male-pattern baldness) and deepening of the voice, but breast atrophy will be minimal. Estrogen use will result in female breast development and some thinning of the facial and body hair, but depilation or electrolysis will still usually be required, and inherent vocal range will not change. (Many transwomen make use of speech therapy to learn vocal techniques that connote femininity, and demonstration videos are widely available on YouTube.) Both estrogens and androgens will cause some degree of body habitus change, but individual results vary greatly, and basic skeletal structure will not be affected.

Sexual changes may or may not occur. Response is quite individual in this regard. Some persons who are transitioning from male to female will experience a lowered libido as serum testosterone levels diminish, but others will find an increase in sex drive, likely due to the erotically powerful psychological experience of (at last!) finding the physical body coming into harmony with the internal self-perception. Some transwomen, who find their male genitalia a burdensome reminder of the natal sex, may experience penile erection only rarely after beginning treatment with estrogens, while their peers who do not experience psychological conflict in continuing to enjoy erection and orgasm during transition sometimes remain able to function sexually even when testosterone production is very low. Some transwomen report that estrogen use changes the quality of orgasm in a pleasurable and affirming way, becoming less "genital" and more "total body," consistent with common expectations regarding female sexuality. Responses and outcomes are individual and difficult to predict; solutions to problems that develop must be individualized as well. For example, a transwoman who has not yet had genital surgery may need treatment with both estrogen supplementation and sildenafil or a similar agent. Most transmen experience an increase in libido with testosterone use; some find that this reduces with time and others do not.

Hormonal changes can affect genital anatomy and reproductive potential. Many transwomen experience some shrinkage of the penis and testes; most transmen experience significant enlargement of the clitoris with testosterone use. The vaginal epithelium often becomes thinner and somewhat atrophic. Some transmen who do not want vaginectomy use intravaginal estrogen preparations to keep the epithelium thicker and the vaginal tissue more flexible, particularly if the vagina is used for sexual participation (Ippolito & Sampson, 2015). Ovulation often resumes if testosterone use is suspended, even for several years; sperm production is less resilient. Transwomen who may be interested in future fertility should be strongly encouraged to bank sperm before beginning treatment with estrogen (Eyler, Pang, & Clark, 2014).

Emotional changes may or may not occur. Emotional experience is generally a result of a mix of factors, including personality structure; previous life experience; medical health and illness, including hormonal status; environmental cues and props, such as the personal enjoyment that can accompany wearing the clothing of the preferred gender; and the response of other persons to self-presentation. Patients who begin treatment with hormones should be informed that, although their basic personality and personhood will not change, the combination of the new social presentation and hormone use can facilitate some shifting of emotional experience.

Some individuals experience a broadening of emotional range even before the initiation of treatment with hormones, or very early in the treatment process. Some cisgender men who are not pursuing gender transition feel more free to laugh, cry, and express affection in feminine ways when dressed *en femme*; some transwomen have similar experiences even before beginning estrogen supplementation. Similarly, some transmen feel more free to act out sexually or aggressively, even before the androgen levels have reached male norms. Patients should be advised that some shifts in emotional experience may occur, but that neither estrogen use nor androgen use will cause, or be an excuse for, inappropriate behavior.

5.   Attempt to foster a therapeutic physician–patient (or clinician–patient) alliance regarding the safe and effective use of hormonal preparations and other medical treatments.

Attempting to hasten the transition process by using very high doses of hormone preparations will not improve the end result but will increase the risk of medical complications, which can interfere with the individual's ultimate physical goals. For example, a transwoman who develops a deep-vein thrombosis while using a very high estrogen dose may need to suspend use of hormones for months while anti-coagulated, or may need to discontinue them entirely. A frank discussion regarding shared goals and medical concerns should be undertaken prior to beginning treatment with estrogens or androgens. The message is one of strong support for the patient's personal identity and the process of transition, *and* a commitment to safe and effective medical treatment.

Though hormonal medications are readily available without prescription in many countries, and can be obtained via the internet and other means, caring for patients without full knowledge of the prescription and non-prescription medications they are using can be both challenging and dangerous. A reasonable condition for treatment is the commitment to taking only prescribed medications, and taking them as directed. This should be discussed openly at the first medical visit, before hormone prescription. Any evidence that the patient has not openly disclosed the use of hormones received through alternate sources should be confronted in the same manner as would a breach of the clinical relationship in the treatment of any other medical condition.

It may be useful to discuss the range of treatments available, and the advantages and disadvantages of pursuing them, early in the treatment process. In addition to hormone supplementation and genital gender-confirming (sex reassignment) surgeries, a variety of other medical procedures are available, particularly for transwomen. Unfortunately, most of these procedures are costly and many are not routinely covered by medical insurance. For instance, obtaining breast augmentation surgery (after maximal breast development has occurred), feminizing facial surgery, and vocal surgery—in addition to the more common aspects of treatment, such as estrogen supplementation, electrolysis or laser depilation, and vulvovaginoplasty—may not be feasible due to the interference with other life activities, and the expense. Most transmen need chest reconstruction surgery but do not need other non-genital procedures.

Although all decisions about physical appearance must ultimately be left to the individual, deciding when to *stop* a physical transition process can present different challenges than those faced when deciding to begin. Spending one's retirement savings on multiple cosmetic surgeries may be regretted later, even if the gender transition has been extremely satisfactory and fulfilling. Ongoing support for the patient's true gender identity, presentation, and new life in the preferred gender may help bring the medical process of transition gently to a close when reasonable goals have been achieved.

6.   Obtain a baseline endocrine laboratory evaluation.

It is useful to know the baseline hormonal status of the patient prior to beginning treatment with supplemental hormones. If serum testosterone and estradiol levels differ significantly from natal sex- and age-expected norms, then additional investigation is usually indicated. (Is an endocrinopathy present? Has the patient already been using hormones obtained informally or through other medical sources?) Other age-appropriate laboratory evaluations, such as screening for hyperlipidemia and glucose intolerance, can be performed concurrently, if these have not already been obtained.

7.   Strongly recommend smoking cessation before hormonal treatment begins, and provide assistance in quitting.

The medical risks associated with hormone use are significantly increased by smoking. Patients who smoke and take estrogens face a higher risk of thromboembolic complications than those who do not. Smoking and testosterone use are risk factors for development of polycythemia (McKean, Ross, Dressler, Brotman, & Ginsberg, 2012) and the risk of polycythemic stroke may be increased by androgen supplementation with concurrent smoking (Darby & Anawalt, 2005). A candid discussion is particularly important for transwomen who are beginning hormonal transition in middle and older adulthood. Some physicians decline to prescribe estrogens to persons who smoke in midlife, regardless of gender or medical reason, though many will prescribe estrogens for transwomen after full informed consent (UCSF Center of Excellence for Transgender Health, 2011) as part of a harm reduction approach that may include using only transdermal estrogen while the patient is still actively smoking (Feldman & Safer, 2009). Some people become interested in smoking cessation after learning that development of a serious smoking-related complication, such as a deep-vein thrombosis, may make use of estrogen more complicated, at least for a time.

The time between the initial presentation for gender transition medical services and the first prescription of estrogens or androgens can be a particularly positive opportunity for smoking cessation. This is often a time of optimism about the future, engagement in medical treatment planning, and justifiable pride in taking steps to improve quality of life. The combination of a strengthened sense of self-efficacy, demonstrated by making the decision to physically confirm his or her authentic gender, and new, personalized information about the risks of smoking can provide a good basis for motivational assessment and behavior change (Bandura, 1997; DiClemente & Velasquez, 2002; DiClemente et al., 1991; Miller & Rollnick, 2012).

> *The U.S. Preventive Services Task Force recommends that clinicians ask all adults about tobacco use and provide tobacco cessation interventions for those who use tobacco products (Grade A) (Siu, for the U.S. Preventive Services Task Force, 2015).*

Patients who decide to stop smoking should be given full support in accordance with current practice, such as brief cognitive behaviorally based education, and pharmacotherapy with nicotine replacement, bupropion, or other agents (Siu, for the U.S. Preventive Services Task Force, 2015; U.S. Preventive Services Task Force, 2009). Counseling is aimed at identifying cues to smoking, breaking the link between triggers and smoking behavior, and management of cravings. Smokefree.gov (2015) offers online resources for smoking cessation and a free texting service for adults and young adults who want support while they quit. Other resources are available through voluntary agencies such as the American Cancer Society. Some LGBT community centers offer smoking cessation support groups.

> Case 7. Janice is a 53-year-old transwoman who has been taking oral estradiol since she began gender transition 23 years ago. She has tried to quit smoking off and on over the years, but finds that her job in management is very stressful and that she always resumes smoking when the workload increases. Her best friend suffered a myocardial infarction 6 weeks ago, and has not been able to return to work. She shares with her nurse practitioner the fear that she is experiencing about having a serious complication from smoking along with estrogen use, as well as the sense of failure that she has not been able to quit already despite numerous attempts. They discuss both medical risks and emotional benefits of smoking, using motivational interviewing techniques and a calm, non-judgmental manner.

Janice first changes her estrogen program to a lower-dose transdermal patch, and then makes another attempt to stop smoking, using nicotine replacement, bupropion, and online support. She resumes smoking twice, but tries again, 6 months later. Two years later, she is still maintaining abstinence from smoking. Her exercise tolerance has improved and she has more energy.

8. Choose the simplest hormonal program that will provide adequate, steady-state serum hormone levels.

Testosterone can be taken through many routes of administration. Androgen supplementation has traditionally been by injection every 1–2 weeks, occasionally every 3 weeks. These programs produce an initial peak in serum testosterone, sometimes to a supraphysiologic level, followed by a gradual diminution over the time preceding the next injection. This pattern is quite different from the usual minor diurnal variations experienced by cisgender males. Also, testosterone injections can be painful.

Many physicians are now prescribing testosterone gel, or patches, for their transmen patients. These preparations provide less variability in serum testosterone levels (Mazur et al., 2005) and are generally well accepted by patients (Feldman, 2005), although some develop skin irritation. In addition, they can be self-administered, without the need for training in injection technique. Unfortunately, insurance coverage for testosterone gel remains incomplete in the United States, and expense can be prohibitive. Injectable testosterone preparations remain the mainstay of hormonal maintenance for many transmen.

Both topical and injection preparations are effective in producing masculinization. Community-based services can make use of injectable testosterone safer and less problematic. For example, the Minnesota Transgender Health Coalition (2015) operates a free Shot Clinic for transmen who have trouble with self-injection and a clean needle exchange.

Administration of estrogens by injection was once the treatment of choice for transwomen, and many transwomen still rely on injectable estrogen, due to cost or convenience. This practice has the same disadvantages as intramuscular androgen administration: variable serum levels, risk of supraphysiologic levels, and the need for the patient to learn good injection technique. Transdermal and oral (sublingual) preparations can provide an alternative when feasible (Feldman & Safer, 2009; Hembree et al., 2009; UCSF Center of Excellence for Transgender Health, 2011). Sublingual, transdermal, and intramuscular preparations offer the advantage of bypassing the first pass of hepatic metabolism and reducing the risk of medication interactions (Feldman & Safer, 2009). Choice of estrogen is also important. The rate of thromboembolic complications in one large group of transwomen patients fell significantly following the change from conjugated equine estrogens to estradiol valerate (van Kesteren et al., 1997). Oral estrogens, especially ethinyl estradiol, are associated with an elevated risk of venous thromboembolism, and transdermal estrogen with a lower risk.

9.   Utilize serum hormone levels to guide hormone dosage.

Significant individual variation exists in pharmacokinetic processing of hormonal medications (Speroff & Fritz, 2005). Two persons of the same age and natal sex can require substantially different doses of the same estrogen or androgen preparation in order to achieve the same serum level. It is important to measure serum estradiol or testosterone levels periodically, in order to guard against under- or overdosing. Patient symptom report is usually not sufficient as a sole criterion to guide dosing of either estrogens or androgens, though careful history and physical examination may be used in cases in which labs are deferred due to cost. However, any report of new adverse symptoms, whether physical (e.g., significant nausea) or emotional (e.g., emotional lability, weepiness, aggressive irritability) should prompt a reassessment of serum hormonal levels.

Although the risks of adverse events due to hormonal medication use have diminished over time, the risk of osteoporosis, thromboembolic and cardio-vascular events, particularly for transwomen, remains significant (Wierckx, Mueller, Weyers, van Caenegem, et al., 2012) and the available evidence favors maintaining serum hormone concentrations in the physiologic range, with min-imal peak-and-trough effects, as much as possible (Meriggiola & Berra, 2013).

10.   Adopt a long-term perspective: gender transition health care encompasses the medical needs of the patient across the lifespan.

During the gender transition process, the focus of the patient and helping professionals often narrows to the immediate medical and social exigencies of the transition itself. (Is adequate physical development being safely achieved? Is it time to inform the employer of the change in identity, and is the client emotionally prepared to do this?) However, once body modification has been accomplished, the focus of both medical care and social development must shift to a more long-term perspective.

Patients should be advised early on that health maintenance is a lifelong pro-cess. Persons who transition have the same need for preventive care as their cisgender peers. In addition, decisions regarding use of hormones will need to be periodically revisited during midlife and older age. Testosterone production declines by about 50% between ages 30 and 80 among natal males (Snyder, 2004), and best practices of androgen supplementation for older men are cur-rently being defined (Bhasin & Basaria, 2011; Bhasin, Cunningham, Hayes, & Matsumoto, 2010; Corona, Rastrelli, & Maggi, 2013; Endocrine Society of Australia, 2013; Merce Fernandez-Balsells et al., 2010). Gradually reducing tes-tosterone dosage as transmen age has intuitive appeal, but evidence regard-ing best practices in this regard is currently lacking. Similarly, optimum use of estrogen following menopause in cisgender women remains an evolv-ing area of research and practice (de Villiers, Gass, Haines, Hall, et al., 2013; Schmidt, 2012) and reduction in estrogen doses over time for transwomen also seems prudent. The evidence base regarding long-term transgender hormone use remains thin. Physicians, physician assistants, nurse practitioners—and transgender persons—will need to reassess the practical aspects of hormonal care in the years ahead, as more transwomen and transmen enter middle and older adulthood, and as better evidence-based practices are defined through longitudinal study.

Conclusion

Gender is a fundamental aspect of human experience. Hormonal and surgical treatments are medically necessary for the treatment of gender dysphoria and can provide enormous relief to transgender persons, with associated benefit to their loved ones.

Providing clinical care for transgender and gender-variant persons can be an intellectually stimulating and emotionally rewarding experience for physicians, physician assistants, nurse practitioners, and other clinical professionals. Accompanying transgender persons on their journeys of physical transformation and personal evolution can be a life-changing experience for the primary care professional and other members of the treatment team. Many clinicians report that working with gender-transitioning persons has profoundly affected their personal beliefs regarding the nature of masculinity and femininity and, indeed, the concept of gender itself.

References

Bandura, A. (1997). *Self-Efficacy: The Exercise of Control*. New York: W. H. Freeman.

Bhasin, S., Basaria, S. (2011). Diagnosis and treatment of hypogonadism in men. *Best Pract Res Clin Endocrinol Metab* 25: 251–270.

Bhasin, S., Cunningham, G. R., Hayes, F. J., Matsumoto, A. M. (2010). Testosterone therapy in men with androgen deficiency syndromes: An Endocrine Society Clinical Practice Guideline. *J Clin Endocrinol Metab* 95(6): 2536–2559.

Bockting, W. O. (1999). From construction to context: Gender through the eyes of the transgendered. *SIECUS Report*, 28(1): 3–7.

Bockting, W. O. (2008). Psychotherapy and the real-life experience: From gender dichotomy to gender diversity. *Sexologies*, 17(4): 211–224.

Coleman, E., Bockting, W., Botzer, M., Cohen-Kettenis, P., et al. (2012). *Standards of Care for the Health of Transsexual, Transgender, and Gender- Nonconforming People.* The World Professional Association for Transgender Health (WPATH). www.wpath. org.

Corona, G., Rastrelli, G., Maggi, M. (2013). Diagnosis and treatment of late-onset hypogonadism: Systematic review and meta-analysis of TRT outcomes. *Best Pract Res Clin Endocrinol Metab* 27: 557–559.

Dahl, M., Feldman, J. L., Goldberg, J. M., Jaberi, A. (2006). Physical aspects of transgender endocrine therapy. *Int J Transgenderism* 9(3): 111–134.

Darby, E., Anawalt, B. D. (2005) Male hypogonadism: An update on diagnosis and treatment. *Treat Endocrinol* 4(5): 293–309.

De Villiers, T. J., Gass, M. L. S., Haines, C. H., Hall, J. E., et al. (2013). Global consensus statement on menopausal hormone therapy. *Climacteric* 16: 203–204.

Devor, H. (1989). *Gender Blending: Confronting the Limits of Duality.* Bloomington, IN: University of Indiana Press.

DiClemente, C. C., Velasquez, M. N. (2002). Motivational interviewing and the stages of change. In Miller, W. R., Rollnick, S. (Eds.) *Motivational Interviewing: Preparing People for Change,* 2nd ed. New York, NY: Guilford Press, pp. 201–216.

DiClemente, C. C., Prochaska, J. O., Fairhurst, S. K., Velicer, W. F., Velasquez, M. N., & Rossi, J. S. (1991). The process of smoking cessation: An analysis of precontemplation, contemplation, and preparation stages of change. *J Consult Clin Psychol* 59(2): 295–304.

Drescher, J. (2010). Queer diagnoses: Parallels and contrasts in the history of homosexuality, gender variance, and the Diagnostic and Statistical Manual. *Arch Sex Behav* 39:427–460.

Endocrine Society of Australia. (2013). Position statement, use and misuse of androgens. http://www.endocrinesociety.org.au/position-statement-androgens.asp.

Eyler, A. E., Pang, S. C., Clark, A. (2014). LGBT assisted reproduction: Current practice and future possibilities. *LGBT Health* 1(3): 151–156.

Eyler, A. E. (2007). Primary medical care of the gender-variant patient. In Ettner, R., Monstrey, S., & Eyler, E. (Eds.) *Principles of Transgender Medicine and Surgery.* Binghamton, NY: Haworth Press, pp. 15–32.

Eyler, A. E., Wright, K. (1997). Gender identification and sexual orientation among genetic females with gender-blended self-perception in childhood and adolescence. *Int J Transgenderism,* 1(1). www.symposion.com/ijt/ijtc0405.htm.

Eyler, A. E., Witten, T. M., Cole, S. S. (1997). Assessing the health care needs of the transgender community: Preliminary survey results [abstract]. XV Harry Benjamin International Gender Dysphoria Association Symposium: The State of Our Art and the State of Our Science. Vancouver, BC, Canada.

Feldman, J. (2005). Masculinizing hormone therapy with testosterone 1 percent topical gel. XIX Biennial Smposium, Harry Benjamin International Gender Dysphoria Association, Universita Degli Studi di Bologna, Bologna, Italy.

Feldman, J. (2007). Preventive care of the transgendered patient. In Ettner, R., Monstrey, S., & Eyler, E. (Eds.) *Principles of Transgender Surgery and Medicine.* Binghamton, NY: Haworth Press, pp. 33–72.

Feldman, J. (2008). Medical and surgical management of the transgender patient: What the primary care clinician needs to know. In: Makadon, H. J., Mayer, K. H., Potter, J., Goldhammer, H. (Eds) *Fenway Guide to Lesbian, Gay, Bisexual and Transgender Health.* American College of Physicians, Philadelphia, PA: American College of Physicians, pp. 365–392.

Feldman, J., Goldberg, J. (2006). Transgender primary medical care. *Int J Transgenderism* 9(3): 3–34.

Feldman, J., & Safer, J. (2009). Hormone therapy in adults: Suggested revisions to the sixth version of the *Standards of Care. Int J Transgenderism* 11(3): 146–182.

Hage, J. J., Kanhai, R. C., Oen, A. L., van Diest, P. J., & Karim, R. B. (2001). The devastating outcome of massive subcutaneous injection of highly viscous fluids in male-to-female transsexuals. *Plast Reconstr Surg* 107(3): 734–741.

Hembree, W. C., Cohen-Kettenis, P., Delemarre-van de Waal, H. A., Gooren, L. J., Meyer III, W. J., Spack, N. P., ... Montori, V. M. (2009). Endocrine treatment of transsexual persons: An Endocrine Society clinical practice guideline. *J Clin Endocrinol Metab* 94(9): 3132–3154.

Ippolito, J., & Sampson, J. (2015). Baby boomers and Gen-X'ers: Exploring aging issues in trans male communities. 14th Philadelphia Trans-Health Conference. A Program of Mazzoni Center. Philadelphia Convention Center, Philadelphia, PA, USA.

Kammerer, N., Mason, T., & Connors, M. (1999). Transgender health and social service needs in the context of HIV risk. *Int J Transgenderism* 3: 1+2, www.symposion.com/ijt/hiv_risk/kammerer.htm.

Killerman, S. (2015). The Genderbread Person, v.3. http://itspronouncedmetrosexual.com/edugraphics-printables/. Downloaded 24 June, 2015.

Kinsey, A., Pomeroy, W., & Martin, C. (1948) *Sexual Behavior in the Human Male*. Philadelphia: Saunders, USA.

Mazur, N, et al. (2005). Comparison of the steady-state pharmacokinetics, metabolism, and variability of a transdermal testosterone patch versus a transdermal testosterone gel in hypogonadal men. *J Sex Med* 2(2): 213–226.

Mazzoni Center. (2015). Resources for Clients. https://mazzonicenter.org/resources. Downloaded 26 June, 2015.

McKean, S. C., Ross, J. J., Dressler, D. D., Brotman, D. J., & Ginsberg, J. S. (2012). *Principles and Practice of Hospital Medicine*. Chapter 173. McGraw-Hill. http://accessmedicine.mhmedical.com/book.aspx?bookid=496.

Merce Fernandez-Balsells, M., Murad, M. H., Lane, M., Lampropulos, J. F., et al. (2010). Adverse effects of testosterone therapy in adult men: A systematic review and meta-analysis. *J Clin Endocrinol Metab* 95(6): 2560–2575.

Meriggiola, M. C., & Berra, M. (2013). Safety of hormonal treatment in transgenders. *Curr Opin Endocrinol Diabetes Obes* 20(6): 565–569.

Miller, W. R., & Rollnick, S. (2012). *Motivational Interviewing: Helping People Change*, 3rd ed. New York, NY: The Guilford Press.

Minnesota Transgender Health Coalition. (2015). http://www.mntranshealth.org. Downloaded 24 June, 2015.

Moore, E., Wisniewski, A., & Dobbs, A. (2003). Endocrine treatment of transsexual people: A review of treatment regimens, outcomes, and adverse effects. *J Clin Endocrinol Metab* 88(8): 3467–3473.

Nemoto, T., Opertario, D., & Keatley, J. (2005). Health and social services for male-to-female transgender persons of color in San Francisco. *Int J Transgenderism* 8(2/3): 5–19.

Oen, A. L., Bergers, E., Kanhai, R., Hage, J. J., & Manoliu, R. A. (2002). Magnetic resonance imaging of injected silicone: Findings in seven male-to-female transsexuals. *Eur Radiol* 12(5): 1221–1227.

Petersen, D., Sharon, N., & Karasic, D. (2015). Transgender in the Bible Belt. 2015 Annual Meeting. American Psychiatric Association. Convention Centre, Toronto, Ontario, Canada.

Ramet, S. P. (Ed.) (1996). *Gender Reversals and Gender Cultures: Anthropological and Historical Perspectives*. New York, NY: Routledge.

Schmidt, P. (2012). The 2012 hormone therapy position statement of the North American Menopause Society. *Menopause* 19(3): 257–271.

Siu, A.L., for the U.S. Preventive Services Task Force. (2015). Behavioral and pharmacotherapy interventions for tobacco smoking cessation in adults, including pregnant women: U.S. Preventive Services Task Force Recommendation Statement. *Ann. Intern. Med.*, 163: 622–634.

Smokefree. (2015). http://smokefree.gov. Downloaded 24 June, 2015.

Snyder, P. J. (2004). Hypogonadism in elderly men – what to do until the evidence comes. *N Engl J Med* 350(5): 440–442.

Speroff, L. & Fritz, M. (2005). *Clinical Gynecologic Endocrinology and Infertility*, 7th ed. Philadelphia, PA: Lippincott Williams & Wilkins, pp. 694–695.

Thurman, J. (2015). The boards: finish line. *The New Yorker*, May 11, p. 22.

UCSF Center of Excellence for Transgender Health. (2011). Primary care protocol for transgender patient care. University of California, San Francisco, Department of Family and Community Medicine, April 2011. http://transhealth.ucsf.edu/trans?page=protocol-00-00.

U.S. Preventive Services Task Force (2009). Tobacco use in adults and pregnant women: Counseling and interventions. http://www.uspreventiveservicestaskforce. org/Page/Topic/recommendation-summary/tobacco-use-in-adults-and-pregnant-women-counseling-and-interventions.

van Kesteren, P. J., et al. (1997). Mortality and morbidity in transsexual subjects treated with cross-sex hormones. *Clin Endocrinol* 47(3): 337–342.

Whittle, S. (1996). Gender fucking or fucking gender? Current cultural contributions to theories of gender blending. In Ekins, R., & King, D. (Eds.) *Blending Genders: Social Aspects of Cross-dressing and Sex-changing*. New York, NY: Routledge.

Wierckx, K., Mueller, S. C., Weyers, S., van Caenegem, E., et al. (2012). Long-term evaluation of cross-sex hormone treatment in transsexual persons. International Society of Sexual Medicine. *J Sex Med* 9: 2641–2651.

Witten, T. M. (2002). *The Tao of Gender: Lao Tzu's Tao Te Ching Adapted for a New Age*. Atlanta, GA: Brumby Holdings.

Witten, T. M. (2003). Transgender aging: An emerging problem and an emerging need. *Rev Sexol* 12(4): 15–20.

Witten, T. M., & Eyler, A. E. (1999). Hate crimes against the transgendered: An invisible problem. *Peace Rev* 11(3): 461–468.

Witten, T. M., & Eyler, A. E. (2012). Transgender aging; beings and becomings. In: Witten, T. M., & Eyler, A. E. (Eds.) *Gay, Lesbian, Bisexual and Transgender Aging: Challenges in Research, Practice and Policy*; Baltimore, MD: Johns Hopkins University Press, pp. 187–269.

5 Preventive Care of the Transgender Patient

An Evidence-Based Approach

Jamie Feldman

Introduction

Preventive care is an essential component of health care for all individuals and critical to the achievement of many national health objectives (for example, Office of Disease Prevention and Health Promotion 2011). Primary and secondary prevention of chronic disease has become increasingly important among the transgender population, especially in light of an aging cohort on long-term transgender hormone therapy and a significant number of patients presenting for hormone therapy at older ages, with risk factors for chronic disease or comorbid conditions (Blanchard 1994; Witten 2003; Nieder et al. 2011). However, transgender people face significant barriers to adequate preventive services, including lack of health insurance, the experience of discrimination in the health care setting, and lack of access to medical personnel competent in transgender medicine (Grant et al. 2011). This chapter will review the preventive care challenges for the transgender population, describe an evidence-based approach to prevention, and present transgender-specific prevention recommendations based on the available evidence.

Challenges in Providing Preventive Care to the Transgender Population

Delivering quality preventive care to transsexual or transgender patients presents several challenges. First, transgender identity and behavior are often socially stigmatized, leading many transgender individuals to maintain a traditional male or female presentation and public role while keeping their transgender health concerns concealed. A Minnesota study of transgender health seminar participants found that 45% had not informed their personal physician of their true gender identity (Bockting 2000). Social stigma, health systems barriers, and, for some patients, discomfort with the body can lead the transgender patient to avoid medical care altogether (Kammerer et al. 1999; Grant et al. 2011; Institute of Medicine 2011). Thus, transgender persons often lack access to preventive health services and timely treatment of routine health problems.

In addition, most physicians and other health care professionals do not receive training in health issues specific to transgender patients, and lack ready access to appropriate information or to a knowledgeable colleague (Institute of Medicine 2011; Obedin-Maliver et al. 2011; Snelgrove et al. 2012). Long-term, prospective studies for most transgender-specific health issues are lacking, thus resulting in variable preventive care recommendations based primarily on expert opinion. However, by utilizing an increasing body of peer-reviewed, scientific research on transgender health, along with relevant data from the general population, one can develop an evidence-based approach to preventive care for patients who are transgender or transsexual.

Evidence-Based Transgender Health Care

Assembling the Evidence: Methodology

The U. S. Preventive Services Task Force (USPSTF) noted that producing a formal systematic review (consisting of a comprehensive literature search, evaluation of the data, and detailed documentation of methods and findings) is not feasible when addressing many topics in preventive care (Harris et al. 2001). Transgender health research consists primarily of many small sample studies with a variety of methodologies, and includes very few randomized trials. Rather than being confined to MEDLINE, the literature on transgender health is spread over many disparate databases.

This chapter follows the USPSTF approach, focusing on a limited number of priority topics, and reviewing the questions and evidence most critical to making recommendations for medical practice based on the best available evidence. A computerized search of the transgender health literature was performed using the following terms: transsexual*, gender dysphoria, gender identity disorder, and sex reassignment. (An asterisk after a search term means that any extension of that word was also searched—i.e., transsexual* also searched the derivative terms "transsexuals" and "transsexualism.") Databases across disciplines were searched to facilitate a comprehensive review. The citation databases that were searched were MEDLINE, PubMed, Science Direct, and Social Sciences Index. The online academic search engine Google Scholar was used to further identify published articles and peer-reviewed presentations. Finally, available abstracts from the World Professional Association for Transgender Health (WPATH)/ Harry Benjamin International Gender Dysphoria Association (HBIGDA) symposia from 1999 to 2013, and all articles published in the *International Journal of Transgenderism* unavailable on searchable databases (prior to 2003), were reviewed. Relevant cisgender studies were identified through MEDLINE searches, focusing on meta-analyses, systematic reviews, and large-scale clinical trials.

Peer-reviewed presentations and publications were prioritized over non-peer-reviewed evidence. Wherever possible, evidence showing that preventive services influenced health status per se (i.e., patient-oriented outcomes) was prioritized over evidence that focused on intermediate markers (i.e., disease-oriented outcomes). Lower-level evidence, such as disease-oriented studies or case reports, was not exhaustively reviewed when stronger evidence was available. The evidence was then graded according to the Strength of Recommendation Taxonomy (SORT).

Assessing the Evidence: The SORT Taxonomy

In 2004, the editors of the principal American family medicine and primary medical care journals (i.e., *American Family Physician, Family Medicine, The Journal of Family Practice, Journal of the American Board of Family Medicine,* and *BMJ-USA*) and the Family Practice Inquiries Network came together to develop a unified system and taxonomy for grading the strength of recommendations based on a body of evidence (Ebell et al. 2004). This system values the patient-oriented outcomes (e.g., fewer strokes) over disease-oriented outcomes (e.g., lower blood pressure). The grade (or strength) of a recommendation for clinical practice is based on a body of evidence, accounting for the level of evidence of individual studies. This includes the type of outcomes; the number, consistency, and coherence of research studies; and the relationship between benefits, harm, and costs. The SORT taxonomy and the algorithm for determining the strength of the recommendation are outlined in Table 5.1 and Figure 5.1. While this algorithm provides a general guideline, in some cases, the strength of recommendation has been adjusted, based on the degree of benefit, risk, and cost of the intervention being recommended.

Recommendations should be based on the highest-quality evidence available. For example, vitamin E was found in some cohort studies (level 2 study quality) to be beneficial for cardiovascular protection, but good-quality randomized trials (level 1 study quality) have not confirmed this effect.

Incorporating Cisgender Evidence into the Transgender Context

Currently, only a few prospective, large-scale studies regarding transgender health care exist. The best-available evidence comes from a Dutch retrospective chart review involving 966 transwomen (male-to-female: MTF) and 365 transmen (female-to-male: FTM) patients, with duration of hormone use ranging from 0.7 to 44.5 years, and with a median follow-up of 18 years (Asscheman et al. 2011). In all, 86.7% of the transwomen and 94% of the transmen underwent sex reassignment surgery. Overall and specific causes of mortality, but not morbidity, were compared to age- and gender-specific statistics in the general Dutch population. A total of 20.6% of transwomen and only 4.4% of transmen in the study were over 40 years of age, and less than 1% of all participants were over 65 years, although 42.8% of transwomen and 40.5% of transmen had taken hormones for over 20 years. As this study did not track a specific cohort over a long period of time, particularly beyond 65 years of age, this study, and several like it, does not provide definitive answers on

Table 5.1 Strength of Recommendation Taxonomy (SORT)

In general, only key recommendations for readers require a grade of the "Strength of Recommendation." Recommendations should be based on the highest quality evidence available. For example, vitamin E was found in some cohort studies (level 2 study quality) to have a benefit for cardiovascular protection, but good-quality randomized trials (level 1) have not confirmed this effect. Therefore, it is preferable to base clinical recommendations in a manuscript on the level 1 studies.

Strength of recommendation	Definition
A	Recommendation based on consistent and good-quality patient-oriented evidence.*
B	Recommendation based on inconsistent or limited-quality patient-oriented evidence.*
C	Recommendation based on consensus, usual practice, opinion, disease-oriented evidence,* or case series for studies of diagnosis, treatment, prevention, or screening.

Use the following table to determine whether a study measuring patient-oriented outcomes is of good or limited quality, and whether the results are consistent or inconsistent between studies.

Study quality	Diagnosis	Treatment/prevention/screening	Prognosis
Level 1—good-quality patient-oriented evidence	Validated clinical decision rule SR/meta-analysis of high-quality studies High-quality diagnostic cohort study†	SR/meta-analysis of RCTs with consistent findings High-quality individual RCT‡ All-or-none study§	SR/meta-analysis of good-quality cohort studies Prospective cohort study with good follow-up
Level 2—limited-quality patient-oriented evidence	Unvalidated clinical decision rule SR/meat-analysis of lower-quality studies or studies with inconsistent findings Lower-quality diagnostic cohort study or diagnostic case-control studya§	SR/meta-analysis of lower-quality clinical trials or of studies with inconsistent findings Lower-quality clinical trial‡ Cohort study Case-control study	SR/meta-analysis of lower-quality cohort studies or with inconsistent results Retrospective cohort study or prospective cohort study with poor follow-up Case-control study Case series
Level 3—other evidence	Consensus guidelines, extrapolations from bench research, usual practice, opinion, disease-oriented evidence (intermediate or physiologic outcomes only), or case series for studies of diagnosis, treatment, prevention, or screening		

Consistency across studies

Consistent	Most studies found similar or at least coherent conclusions (coherence means that differences are explainable)
	or
	If high-quality and up-to-date systematic reviews or meta-analyses exist, they support the recommendation
Inconsistent	Considerable variation among study findings and lack of coherence
	or
	If high-quality and up-to-date systematic reviews or meta-analyses exist, they do not find consistent evidence in favor of the recommendation

*—Patient-oriented evidence measures outcomes that matter to patients: morbidlity, mortality, symptom improvement, cost reduction, and quality of life. Disease-oriented evidence measures intermediate, physiologic, or surrogate end points that may or may not reflect improvements in patient outcomes (e.g., blood pressure, blood chemistry, physlologic function, pathologic findings).
†—High-quality diagnostic cohort study: cohort design, adequate size, adequate spectrum of patients, blinding, and a consisten, well-defined reference standard.
‡—High-quality RCT: allocation concealed, blinding if possible, intention-to-treat analysis, adequate statistical power, adequate follow-up (greater than 80 percent).
§—in an all-or-none study, the treatment causes a dramatic change in outcomes, such as antibiotics for meningitis or surgery for appendicitis, which precludes study in a controlled trial.

SR, systematic review; RCT, randomized controlled trial.

Source: Ebell, M. H. et al. (2004). Strength of Recommendation Taxonomy (SORT): A patient-centered approach to grading evidence in the medical literature. *American Family Physician*, 69(3):548–556. Reprinted with permission.

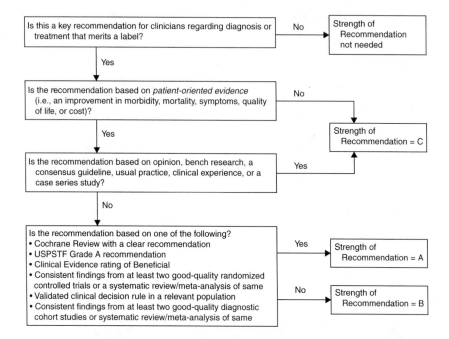

Figure 5.1 Strength of recommendation on a body of evidence. Algorithm for determining the strength of a recommendation based on a body of evidence (applies to clinical recommendations regarding diagnosis, treatment, prevention, or screening). While this algorithm provides a general guideline, authors and editors may adjust the strength of recommendation based on the benefits, harm, and costs of the intervention being recommended. USPSTF, U. S. Preventive Services Task Force. (*Source:* Ebell, M. H., et al. (2004). Strength of Recommendation Taxonomy (SORT): A patient-centered approach to grading evidence in the medical literature. *American Family Physician,* 69(3):548–556. Reprinted with permission.)

long-term health effects of transgender hormone therapy. According to the SORT criteria, this represents level 2 evidence. The medical literature does contains trans-specific studies of smaller scale on particular clinical issues, such as osteoporosis, along with much cisgender-specific evidence (i.e., studies involving cisgender men and women).

Published trans-specific level 1 evidence, particularly regarding transition-related interventions, is rare due to the difficulties with performing randomized controlled trials. Good-quality prospective cohort studies have become more frequent, and strongly support the short-term safety and efficacy of cross-sex hormone therapy (Wierckx et al. 2014). However, level 1 evidence regarding a number of preventive health care issues has been gathered for the general population, allowing clinicians to extrapolate evidence-based recommendations for their transgender patients. When applying knowledge from the general, cisgender population, physicians should look for rigorous studies that are highly relevant to the clinical context. For example, a large prospective study involving cisgender women using postmenopausal hormone therapy may be relevant for transwomen over 50 years of age using similar types of hormones or supplements. Evidence from cisgender studies can be directly applied to similar transgender patients who have not had surgical or hormonal interventions, i.e., conclusions from studies involving cisgender women are probably applicable to people who identify as transmasculine and who have not taken testosterone or had masculinizing surgery. Subtle physiologic differences between transgender people and members of their natal sex may exist prior to the initiation of hormonal therapy, but these principles provide a useful approximation.

In this analysis, cisgender-specific evidence has been incorporated into SORT by ranking it one level of evidence lower when applied in the transgender health context. For example, the Women's Health Initiative Study on cardiovascular disease in women using hormone replacement therapy (Rossouw et al. 2002) represents level 1 evidence for postmenopausal cisgender women, but level 2 evidence for transwomen who are over 50 years of age and using feminizing hormone treatments. The grade of recommendations for transgender health care has not been changed for those areas in which Grade A recommendations have been established for cisgender patients (based on overwhelming level 1 evidence) and these would be unaffected by hormonal or surgical interventions.

Preventive Care Recommendations

Risks and recommendations for screening depend on the patient's hormonal and surgical status. Recommendations specific to particular patient groups are given for the following areas: cancer (breast, cervical, ovarian, uterine, prostate), cardiovascular disease and its risk factors (hypertension, hyperlipidemia, smoking), diabetes, osteoporosis, blood-borne infections (human immunodeficiency virus (HIV) and hepatitis B and C), and other sexually transmitted infections (STIs). Vaccination recommendations are as per cisgender individuals, except for hepatitis A and B.

Cancer

Breast Cancer in Transwomen

PATIENTS WHO HAVE NEVER TAKEN ESTROGEN

- There is no evidence of increased risk of cancer compared to cisgender male patients, in the absence of other known risk factors (e.g., Klinefelter's syndrome).
- Routine screening, in the form of either regular breast exams or mammography, is not indicated for these patients (Grade A).

PATIENTS WITH PAST OR CURRENT ESTROGEN USE

- Transwomen who have taken feminizing hormones may be at increased risk of breast cancer compared to cisgender males, but appear to have significantly decreased risk compared to cisgender females (Grade C).
- Longer duration of feminizing hormone exposure (i.e., number of years taking estrogen preparations), family history of breast cancer, obesity (body mass index (BMI) >35), and the use of progestins may further increase risk (Grade C).
- Screening mammography is advisable every 1–2 years for patients over 50 years of age with additional risk factors (e.g., estrogen use for more than 5 years, use of combined estrogen and progestin preparations, positive family history of breast cancer) (Grade C).
- There is insufficient evidence for annual clinical breast exams for cancer screening, but these may serve an educational purpose (Grade C).

Currently, there are no long-term, prospective studies of the risk of breast cancer among transwomen who have taken feminizing hormones. There is one prospective case-control study, showing no difference in breast (or any other cancer) (Wierckx et al. 2013a). However, the study was relatively short for a cancer study, with follow-up over an average of 7.4 years, and the average age of transwomen at start of study was 43.7 years. Two large retrospective studies indicate a relatively low breast cancer rate, similar to those found in cisgender male populations (Gooren et al. 2013; Brown & Jones 2015). The Dutch mortality study (Asscheman et al. 2011) revealed no breast cancer deaths, but did not examine non-fatal cancer cases. The limitation to all of these studies is that the study populations may not have been old enough or followed long enough to detect a significant difference. Numerous published case reports (level 3) exist regarding breast cancer among transwomen using feminizing hormone therapy (summarized in Gooren et al. 2013, 2015; Sattari 2015).

Multiple prospective studies have demonstrated an increased risk of breast cancer among menopausal women using hormone replacement therapy (level 2 evidence when applied in the transgender health care context). In these studies, risk appears increased, but not limited to combined estrogen and progestin use, and with length of therapy greater than 5 years. Longer-term use is associated with the highest risk, while the effects of different estrogens, different progestins, and different doses of estrogen are unknown (Chen et al. 2014). Additional risk factors relevant to a transgender population include older age, family history, obesity (defined as BMI ≥ 30 kg/m^2), alcohol, and smoking (Costanza & Chen 2012). Among transwomen, the length of time exposed to exogenous estrogens may be most important, given the relative lack of endogenous estrogen production.

Annual screening with mammography has shown a demonstrated significant benefit for cisgender women of 50 years of age and above, and a lesser benefit for women from ages of 40 to 50 years (level 2 applied in the transgender health care context) (Olsen & Gotzsche 2001; Humphrey et al. 2002; Smith et al. 2003). Mammography among transwomen may be complicated by the relatively high prevalence of breast augmentation as well as the use of silicone injections (Deapen et al. 2000; Phillips et al. 2014). Nevertheless, mammography appears to be both technically feasible and acceptable in this population (Weyers et al. 2010a; Maglione et al. 2014; Phillips et al. 2014). However, the risk of breast cancer among the transwomen population appears substantially lower, with the accompanying increased risk of false-positive findings resulting in potential harm (e.g., emotional distress, biopsies, and expense). The benefits of mammography may outweigh the risks and costs for patients over 50 years of age without additional risk factors. However, decisions regarding whether or not to pursue cancer screening are both weighty and personal, and should be made by the transwoman herself, in consultation with her physician.

Annual physician breast exams have not been shown to decrease breast cancer morbidity or mortality in the natal female population (Calonge et al. 2009). However, this intervention has little associated risk or cost, and provides an opportunity for education regarding breast health.

PATIENTS WITH A HISTORY OF BREAST AUGMENTATION

- Breast augmentation does not appear to increase the risk of breast cancer, although it may impair the accuracy of screening mammography (Grade B).

There are no studies on the long-term effects of saline or silicone breast implants in transgender patients. Studies of cisgender women do not suggest an increased risk of breast cancer (Bryant & Brasher 1995), but implants may impair the accuracy of mammography (Deapen et al. 2000).

Breast Cancer in Transmen

PATIENTS WHO HAVE NOT HAD CHEST SURGERY, WITH OR WITHOUT TESTOS-TERONE USE

- Breast exams and screening mammography are recommended as for cisgender women (Grade A as applied to transmen not using testosterone; Grade B for those with testosterone use).

There is no strong evidence of increased risk of breast cancer for transmen as compared to cisgender women with intact breasts. However, there are case reports of breast cancer among transmen aged 20–50 years with varying doses and years of hormone therapy (Shao et al. 2011; Gooren et al. 2013, 2015). Seven cases were identified among transmen in a U.S. cohort of 5,135 transgender veterans, but most had not received any testosterone therapy within the veterans' health system (Brown & Jones 2015). It is unclear what, if any risk factors, including possible supraphysiologic doses of testosterone, link these cases. Level 3 evidence from multiple studies involving low doses of androgen use among postmenopausal cisgender women are mixed, as many also include estrogen replacement therapy. Most indicate no increased risk for breast cancer (Dimitrakakis et al. 2004; Davis et al. 2009; Jick et al. 2009; van Staa & Sprafka 2009), while studies evaluating the use of oral testosterone have indicated an increased risk (Tamimi et al. 2006; Ness et al. 2009).

PATIENTS WHO HAVE HAD CHEST SURGERY, WITH OR WITHOUT
TESTOSTERONE USE

- The risk of breast cancer is reduced with chest surgery, but may be higher among transmen than cisgender men (Grade B).
- Risk is affected by the amount of breast tissue removed (Grade C).
- Pre-chest surgery mammography is not recommended unless the patient meets usual recommendations for cisgender women (Grade B).
- Consider yearly chest wall and axillary exams, along with education regarding the small but still possible risk of breast cancer (Grade C).

Transmen who undergo breast reduction or masculinizing chest surgery (usually subcutaneous mastectomy) must retain some degree of underlying breast tissue for good cosmetic results. A plurality of transmen in the United States, Canada, and a majority in many European countries undergo some form of masculinizing chest surgery (Forshee 2008; Asscheman et al., 2011; Grant et al. 2011; Kreukels et al. 2012), but there are currently no long-term prospective studies on the risk of breast cancer in this population. There is one prospective case-control study, showing no difference in breast (or any other) cancer (Wierckx et al. 2013a). However, the study was relatively short for a cancer study, with follow-up over an average of 7.4 years, and the average age of transmen at start of study was 37.5 years. A large retrospective study indicated a relatively low breast cancer rate, similar to that found in cisgender male populations (Gooren et al. 2013; Brown & Jones 2015) and the Dutch mortality study (Asscheman et al., 2011) revealed no breast cancer deaths, but did not examine non-fatal cancer cases. The limitation to all of these studies is that the study populations may not have been old enough or followed long enough to detect a significant difference. However, the literature contains numerous case reports of breast cancer among transmen post chest surgery (Eyler & Whittle 2001; Burcombe et al. 2003; Nikolic et al. 2012; Brown 2015; Gooren et al. 2015).

Multiple observational and large retrospective studies of cisgender women after breast reduction surgery show reduced risk of breast cancer, directly related to the amount of tissue removed—anywhere from 30 to 90% (Boice et al. 1997, 2000; Brinton et al. 2001; Fryzek et al. 2006). Presurgical mammography does not appear to significantly improve detection of occult cancers in these patients (Netscher et al. 1999).

Given the uncertainty regarding the degree of risk reduction, a yearly examination for chest masses and axillary adenopathy is a low-cost and low-risk intervention which provides an opportunity for education regarding breast cancer recognition.

Cervical/Vaginal Neoplasia in Transwomen With a History of Vaginoplasty

- In the absence of other risk factors for cancer, screening vaginal Pap smears are not indicated (Grade B).
- Following penile inversion vaginoplasty, consider vaginal Pap smear for immunosuppressed patients with a history of genital warts or human papillomavirus (HPV) positivity (Grade C).

There are only two published case reports of vaginal dysplasia in this population, and disease-oriented evidence suggests that the risk of neoplasia is extremely small (Lawrence 2001; Fernandes et al. 2014). In addition, the USPSTF recommends against screening cisgender women after hysterectomy for benign disease (Moyer 2012a). Multiple case reports of neovaginal condyloma in transwomen, especially those with HIV, are noted in the literature (Fiumara & Di Mattia 1973; van Engeland et al. 2000; Liguori et al. 2004; Weyers et al. 2010b; Matsuki et al. 2015), and physicians may consider additional evaluation and ongoing screening of these patients if high-risk HPV and immunosuppression are present.

Cervical Cancer in Transmen

TRANSMEN WITH AN INTACT CERVIX (NO HYSTERECTOMY OR WITH SUBTOTAL HYSTERECTOMY), WITH OR WITHOUT HISTORY OF TESTOSTERONE USE

- Pap smears, or other cervical cytology sampling, should follow the recommended guidelines for cisgender women (Grade A).
- There is no evidence that testosterone increases or reduces the risk of cervical cancer (Grade B).
- Transmen demonstrate a higher rate of unsatisfactory or inadequate Pap smears compared to cisgender women, associated with length of time on testosterone. To improve accuracy of the reading, the pathologist should be informed of the patient's hormonal status (Grade B).
- Total hysterectomy should be considered in patients with persistent high-risk HPV, especially in the presence of high-grade dysplasia, in those patients unable to tolerate appropriate surveillance/treatment measures, unless the patient wishes to preserve the option for pregnancy or health would be adversely affected by surgery (Grade C).

Pap smears may be traumatic for many transmen, particularly in patients who do not engage in penetrative vaginal sexual activities. While no evidence exists to guide the risk stratification of need for cervical screening based on sexual behavior history, a sample of 50 lesbians with no history of penile sexual contact revealed a high-risk HPV prevalence rate of only 2% (Marrazzo et al. 2001). Given this, it may be reasonable to have an informed discussion with patients regarding the realistic risks of deferral of Pap screening. The USPSTF recommends cervical cytology sampling at least once every 3 years from ages 21 until 65, for all persons with an intact cervix, and who are at low risk for cervical dysplasia (Moyer 2012a), with more intensive screening for those at higher risk. There is no evidence that testosterone increases or reduces the risk of cervical cancer, either among transmen (Gooren et al. 2008; Asscheman et al. 2011; Wierckx et al., 2013a) or cisgender women utilizing testosterone.

One large comparison study involving 233 transmen demonstrated a higher rate of unsatisfactory or inadequate Pap smears compared to cisgender women at the same clinic, associated with length of time on testosterone therapy (Peitzmeier et al. 2014). This may be related to androgen therapy causing significant atrophy in the cervical epithelium, mimicking dysplasia on the Pap smear (Miller et al. 1986). However, these changes are not well characterized in literature, and colposcopy may be indicated for patients at increased cancer risk. For patients otherwise at low risk of cervical cancer, atypical squamous cells of undetermined significance and low-grade squamous intraepithelial lesion Pap smears are unlikely to represent precancerous lesions, especially in the absence of high-risk strains of HPV (Melnikow et al. 1998; Sherman et al. 2003). In 2014, the Food and Drug Administration approved the Cobas HPV test without cytology as a primary cervical cancer screening test for patients aged 25 and older. Professional societies and national guidelines have not yet incorporated this screening approach, which still would require collection of cervical cells with a swab by a clinician. Several studies are in the process of evaluating the efficacy of self-collection of cervical samples for HPV testing in a variety of populations (Racey et al. 2013; Igidbashian et al. 2014).

Transmen with cervical dysplasia requiring frequent Pap smears or colposcopy may find it difficult to adhere to adequate cervical cancer screening on a long-term basis. Options for treating dysplasia or improving comfort with procedures should be discussed with the patient. In those patients with persistent high-risk HPV, especially in the presence of high-grade dysplasia, total hysterectomy should be considered, unless the patient wishes to preserve the option for pregnancy or health would be adversely affected by surgery

TRANSMEN WHO HAVE HAD TOTAL HYSTERECTOMY (CERVIX COMPLETELY REMOVED)

- If there is no prior history of high-grade cervical dysplasia or cervical cancer, no future Pap smears or other cytological examinations are needed (Grade A).

- If there is prior history of high-grade cervical dysplasia or cervical cancer, patients should have periodic Pap smears of the vagina, as recommended for cisgender women (Grade B).

As noted previously, the USPSTF recommends against screening cisgender women after hysterectomy for benign disease (Moyer 2012a). The risk of cervical cancer among transmen after hysterectomy is thus similarly low, even with testosterone therapy. There are no studies involving transmen post total hysterectomy with a past history of cervical high-grade dysplasia. Guidelines developed for cisgender women in this category recommend that patients should continue to undergo periodic surveillance (Massad et al. 2013).

Ovarian Cancer

TRANSMEN WITH INTACT OVARIES/UTERUS (NO HYSTERECTOMY), WITH OR WITHOUT A HISTORY OF TESTOSTERONE USE

- Recommend screening patients for symptoms and signs of polycystic ovarian syndrome (PCOS) (Grade C).
- Consider periodic pelvic examinations for patients over 50 years of age with a family history of breast or ovarian cancer or if PCOS is present (Grade C).
- Consider bilateral oophorectomy if there are ongoing concerns regarding ovarian cancer, particularly if maintenance of fertility is not desired, the patient is more than 50 years old, and the patient's health will not be adversely affected by surgery, or the patient is unable to tolerate pelvic exams/evaluations (Grade C).

There are no long-term studies on the incidence of ovarian cancer among transmasculine patients on testosterone, as the largest studies of transmen involve patients who have undergone hysterectomy and oophorectomy within a few years of commencing testosterone therapy. Case reports of ovarian cancer do exist among transmen (Hage et al. 2000; Dizon et al. 2006; Mueller & Gooren 2008; Urban et al. 2011).

Increased incidence of hyperandrogenism and PCOS has been noted among transmen, even in the absence of testosterone use (Bosinski et al. 1997; Baba et al. 2007, 2011; Mueller et al. 2008). PCOS is a hormonal syndrome complex characterized by some or all of the following: failure to ovulate, absent or infrequent menstrual cycles, multiple cysts on the ovaries, hyperandrogenism, hirsuitism, acne, hidradenitis suppurativa, acanthosis nigricans, obesity, and glucose intolerance or diabetes. PCOS is associated with infertility as well as increased risk of cardiac disease, high blood pressure, and endometrial cancer (Cibula et al. 2000). There is mixed evidence for an increased risk of ovarian cancer among persons with PCOS (Chittenden et al. 2009; Barry et al. 2014;

Gottschau et al. 2015), with a trend towards increased risk. There is significant debate as to whether administration of exogenous testosterone induces histologic changes in the ovary similar to PCOS (Pache et al. 1991; Ikeda et al. 2013). While the ovarian cancer is rare, the risk is also increased by age over 50 and genetic risk.

There is no USPTF-recommended screening test for ovarian cancer. The American College of Obstetrics and Gynecology currently recommends annual pelvic exams, including palpation for adnexal masses, although their sensitivity is low (Padilla et al. 2000; Committee on Gynecologic Practice 2012), while other American and European medical organizations do not. Given the life-threatening nature of ovarian cancer, providers may consider screening for ovarian cancer with a history and bimanual pelvic exam periodically for transmen at increased risk who are over age 50. Transmen with known or suspected genetic mutations increasing their risk should be referred for genetic counseling regarding testing and cancer prevention options. An oophorectomy may be a reasonable consideration for patients concerned about ovarian cancer, unable to tolerate pelvic exams, when maintenance of fertility is not desired, and if the patient's health will not be adversely affected by surgery.

Uterine (Endometrial) Cancer

- Recommend screening patients for symptoms and signs of PCOS (Grade C).
- Consider periodic pelvic examinations for patients over 50 years of age at risk, including a family history of uterine cancer or if PCOS is present (Grade C).
- Consider hysterectomy if there are ongoing concerns regarding uterine cancer, the patient is unable to tolerate pelvic exams or evaluation for dysfunctional uterine bleeding, and if maintenance of fertility is not desired and the patient's health will not be adversely affected by surgery (Grade C).

There are no long-term studies on the incidence of uterine cancer among transmasculine patients on testosterone, as the largest studies of transmen involve patients who have undergone hysterectomy and oophorectomy within a few years of commencing testosterone therapy. Case reports of endometrial cancer do exist among transmen (Grynberg et al. 2010; Urban et al. 2011), and while testosterone therapy results usually in either atrophic or proliferative endometrium, hyperplasia occurs. As noted above, there appears to be an increased incidence of hyperandrogenicity and/or PCOS among transmen, and the risk of endometrial cancer is significantly increased in this setting (Barry et al. 2014). The risk of uterine cancer also increases with age over 50.

There is no USPTF-recommended screening test for endometrial cancer. The American College of Obstetrics and Gynecology currently recommends annual pelvic exams, although their sensitivity for uterine abnormalities is low (Padilla et al. 2000; Committee on Gynecologic Practice 2012), while other American and European medical organizations do not. Providers may consider screening for endometrial cancer with a history and bimanual pelvic exam periodically for transmen at increased risk who are over age 50. Providers should evaluate unexplained uterine bleeding with appropriate modalities, including transvaginal ultrasound, pelvic ultrasound, and/or endometrial biopsy if bleeding is prolonged. As with ovarian pathology, a total hysterectomy should be considered if patients cannot tolerate ongoing pelvic exams or procedures, particularly if fertility is not desired, the patient is over 50 years old, and the patient's health will not be adversely affected by surgery.

Prostate Cancer

TRANSWOMEN WITH PAST OR CURRENT ESTROGEN USE, WITH OR WITHOUT GENITAL FEMINIZING SURGERIES

- Feminizing endocrine therapy appears to decrease the risk of prostate cancer, but the degree of reduction is unknown (Grade C).
- Routine prostate-specific antigen (PSA) screening in any usual risk population, including transwomen, is not currently supported by evidence (Grade A).
- PSA levels may be falsely low in transwomen who have had medical or surgical interventions (an androgen-deficient setting) even in the presence of prostate cancer (Grade B).
- Consider screening in high-risk patients (as per guidelines for cisgender men) at age 50 and older (Grade C).
- Recommend education for all patients starting at age 50 regarding the small but present risk of prostate cancer even after genital surgeries (Grade C).

Currently, there are no long-term, prospective studies of the risk of prostate cancer among transwomen who have taken feminizing hormones. A large case-control study revealed no cases of prostate cancer (Wierckx et al. 2012), while the largest retrospective study identified three cases out of 2,236 transwomen (Gooren et al. 2008). The prostate is not removed in feminizing genital surgery, and cases of prostate cancer have been reported among patients on feminizing therapy, both before and after gender reassignment surgery (Markland 1975; Thurston 1994; van Kesteren et al. 1997; van Haarst et al. 1998; Spritz 2003; Miksad et al. 2006; Dorff et al. 2007; Molokwu et al. 2008; Turo et al. 2013; Gooren & Morgentaler 2014). Feminizing hormone therapy appears to decrease the risk of prostate cancer, but the degree of reduction is unknown (Mueller & Gooren 2008).

Routine PSA screening in any usual risk population is not currently supported by evidence (Moyer 2008). PSA levels may be falsely low in an androgen-deficient setting (Morgentaler et al. 1996; Morgentaler & Rhoden 2006), even in the presence of prostate cancer. It is unclear how this compares to that of transwomen, who have reduced gonadal function as a result of exogenous estrogen use. Spritz (2003) found that PSA levels >7 correlated with clinical pathology, but did not distinguish between benign prostatic hypertrophy and cancer. The risk of prostate cancer is increased with age 50 and older, among those of African ethnicity, and with a strong family history.

Prostate cancer screening with PSA and digital rectal exam is thus not recommended in an average-risk transwoman, but may be considered in those at high risk starting at age 50. Education regarding the small, but present, risk of prostate cancer even after genital reassignment surgery is recommended starting at age 50 for all transwomen. If a digital rectal exam is performed as part of rectal cancer screening or other preventive care, the prostate should also be palpated at that time.

Other Cancers

Currently, there is no evidence that transgender people are at either increased or decreased risk of other cancers, independent of other known risk factors. Screening recommendations for other cancers (including colon cancer, lung cancer, and anal cancer) are the same as for cisgender patients.

Cardiovascular Disease

All Patients

- Recommend screening and treatment of modifiable cardiovascular risk for all transgender patients, regardless of hormonal status (Grade A).
- Recommend that modifiable cardiovascular risk factors be reasonably controlled before initiating feminizing or masculinizing endocrine therapy (Grade B).
- Patients with cardio- or cerebrovascular symptoms should be thoroughly evaluated before initiating endocrine therapy (Grade C).
- Transgender patients at high risk for coronary artery disease (CAD) should follow the same guidelines regarding daily aspirin therapy as cisgender patients (Grade A).

Assessing and treating cardiovascular risk factors is an essential primary care intervention for transgender patients. Regardless of hormone status, the transgender population as a whole has several risk factors for cardiovascular disease, while feminizing or masculinizing hormone therapy may increase cardiovascular risks. Smoking is a concern for both transmen and transwomen (Grant et al. 2010). Transwomen tend to present for transition-related care at an older age (Blanchard 1994; Nieder et al. 2011), with an associated increase in comorbidities of hypertension, diabetes, and hyperlipidemia (Feldman et al. 2014; Gooren et al. 2014) prior to commencing hormone therapy. Transmen who present with PCOS are at increased risk for hypertension, insulin resistance, and hyperlipidemia (Barbieri & Ehrmann 2015). It is likely that cardiovascular risk factors are often undiagnosed or undertreated among transgender patients, due to their relative lack of primary care, similar to other underserved populations (Cooper et al. 2000; Mensay et al. 2005). Prompt identification and management of cardiovascular risk factors may decrease the hazards associated with long-term hormone therapy in these patients. As with cisgender patients, daily aspirin therapy may be considered, according to current recommendations for primary or secondary prevention of CAD and stroke. Insufficient evidence exists to support screening electrocardiography in asymptomatic patients (Moyer 2012b), but symptomatic patients should be appropriately evaluated prior to use of cross-sex hormone therapy.

Coronary Artery Disease, Cerebrovascular Disease (CVD), and Hormonal Therapies

Transwomen, Using Estrogen

- Use of estrogen therapy appears to increase the risk of cardiovascular and cerebrovascular events in transwomen over age 50, and with other risk factors for CAD/CVD (Grade C).
- Risk of events may be reduced by omitting the use of progestins, avoiding ethinyl estradiol, reducing estrogen dose, and using transdermal estradiol (Grade C).
- Transwomen over the age of 50 with known cardiovascular risk factors should be closely monitored at the start of feminizing hormone therapy (Grade C).

Retrospective studies of long-term use of feminizing hormones suggest a possible increase in cardiovascular risk over time. The largest retrospective studies have been mixed in terms of detecting any elevations in cardiovascular morbidity or mortality (Gooren et al. 2008), but more recent retrospective and cross-sectional data involving a greater proportion of older patients who smoke and had other comorbidities showed excessive mortality and morbidity (Asscheman et al. 2011; Feldman 2011; Wierckx et al. 2012, 2013a). An age-matched case-control study (using both cisgender male and female controls for each group) indicated that transwomen had an increased incidence of cerebrovascular events compared to control men, and a higher prevalence of myocardial infarction than the control women (but similar to that exhibited by the control men). Of note, in this study, the majority of transwomen participants who had cardiac or cerebrovascular events were over 50 years of age, had one or more risk factors (mainly smoking), and had undergone cross-sex hormone therapy for a short duration (Wierckx et al. 2013a). Finally, there are several case reports of myocardial infarction and ischemic stroke among transgender patients taking estrogen (Cumming & Godfrey 2013).

Studies of postmenopausal hormone replacement therapy in cisgender women, such as the Women's Health Initiative and Heart and Estrogen/

Progestin Replacement Study trials, are also suggestive of adverse cardiovascular and cerebrovascular effects. These studies indicate that the excess cardiovascular risk appears to be confined to older, postmenopausal women, or those who are >10 years postmenopause, and that progestins are an important (but not the only) component in this risk (Martin & Rosenson 2015). In a meta-analysis of randomized trials, oral estrogen therapy, with or without a progestin, was associated with an increase in ischemic stroke (odds ratio 1.29, 95% confidence interval 1.06–1.56 for ischemic stroke) (Bath & Gray 2005). Among all women who had a stroke, there was a trend towards more fatal stroke in those who were taking oral estrogen therapy. Low-dose (≤ 50 mcg) transdermal estrogen therapy does not appear to increase the risk of stroke in postmenopausal women, based on a population-based nested case-control study that included approximately 16,000 cases of stroke and 60,000 controls (Renoux et al. 2010). However, this dose is significantly less than seen in most feminizing hormone regimens. These findings support screening for atherosclerotic risk factors, as well as a high degree of vigilance for the signs and symptoms of CAD/CVD among transwomen on hormone therapy.

Transmen, Using Testosterone

- Recommend clinical monitoring for cardiac events and symptoms in patients at moderate-to-high risk for CAD, including patients with PCOS (Grade C).
- Supraphysiologic doses of testosterone may increase the risk of future cardiovascular events (Grade C).

The effect of testosterone on cardiovascular events among transmen is unclear. Retrospective studies have not seen an increase in cardiovascular events (Asscheman et al. 2011; Gooren et al. 2008, 2014; Wierckx et al. 2012, 2013a), although the populations may not have been old enough or followed long enough to detect any difference. There are case reports of myocardial infarction among patients on testosterone therapy (Inoue et al. 2007; Elamin et al. 2010). Masculinizing hormone therapy increases lipid parameters associated with increased cardiovascular risk (Feldman & Safer 2009; Hembree et al. 2009), but its effects on other cardiovascular risk factors, such as blood pressure and insulin sensitivity, are inconclusive or minimal in average-risk persons (Elamin et al. 2010). While hyperandrogen states among cisgender women increase several cardiac risk factors, current evidence of any increase in cardiac morbidity or mortality with PCOS is limited, but tends to support an increased risk independent of BMI (de Groot et al. 2011; Cobin 2013; Barbieri & Ehrmann 2015). The serum testosterone levels achieved in masculinization therapy usually exceed those occurring with PCOS, and may exceed those achieved in testosterone replacement. Retrospective studies of testosterone replacement therapy in hypogonadal cisgender men have raised concerns about possible increased cardiovascular risk; however, confounding issues include prior CAD and lack of data indicating actual prior hypogonadism (Snyder et al. 2012). Supraphysiologic levels (i.e., those sometimes achieved by male athletes using androgen supplementation) also increase cardiac risk, and sometimes result in premature death (Parssinen & Seppala 2002). Transmen on testosterone therapy with cardiovascular risk factors or preexisting CAD should have their risk factors well controlled and be monitored for any signs and symptoms.

Hypertension

All Patients, not Currently on Hormone Therapy

Hypertension screening and treatment should follow recommended guidelines for cisgender patients, consistent with the guidelines established by the Eighth Joint National Committee (JNC-8) (James et al. 2014), with goals of systolic blood pressure <140 mmHg and diastolic blood pressure <90 mmHg for all patients under 60 years of age, and systolic blood pressure <150 mmHg and diastolic blood pressure <90 mmHg for patients 60 years and older. Ideally, blood pressure should be well controlled prior to initiating feminizing or masculinizing hormone therapy.

Transwomen, Currently Using Estrogen

- Monitor blood pressure periodically, although evidence as to the optimal interval is insufficient (Grade B).
- Consider using spironolactone (an antiandrogen with antihypertensive effects) as part of the patient's antihypertensive regimen (Grade B).

Studies on the effects of feminizing therapy on blood pressure among transwomen are generally neutral. A systematic review and meta-analysis of multiple studies did not identify any significant blood pressure changes, although the quality of studies was low (Elamin et al. 2010). Short-term (6–12-month) prospective studies show no significant change with testosterone therapy in a young, healthy population (Deutsch et al. 2015; Wierckx et al. 2014), though 22% of patients in one study who had been on feminizing hormones for an average of 10 years had elevated blood pressure or treated hypertension (Wierckx et al. 2012). Providers should monitor blood pressure periodically during the course of feminizing hormone therapy, and blood pressure should be well controlled in accordance with JNC-8 guidelines. However, the use of the antiandrogen spironolactone may be considered as part of an antihypertensive regimen in patients desiring feminizing therapy. The antiandrogen spironolactone is a diuretic, and can therefore lower blood pressure (Asscheman & Gooren 1992; Steinbeck 1997; Futterweit 1998; Feldman & Bockting 2003). One study reported a significant reduction of systolic blood pressure when spironolactone was added to the regimen of patients who had been using high-dose estrogen therapy, with a decrease from a baseline of 127.8 mmHg (SD 13.6) to 120.5 mmHg after 1 year ($p < 0.05$) (Prior et al. 1989).

Transmen, Currently Using Testosterone

*   Monitor blood pressure periodically, although evidence as to the optimal interval is insufficient (Grade B).
*   Consider more frequent monitoring in patients with PCOS (Grade C).

Studies on the effects of testosterone therapy on blood pressure among transmen are generally neutral. A systematic review and meta-analysis of multiple studies did not identify any significant blood pressure changes, although the quality of studies was low (Elamin et al. 2010). Large, retrospective studies (Gooren & Giltay 2008; Gooren et al. 2008) have similarly shown little to no change in systolic or diastolic pressure. Short-term (6–12-month) prospective studies show no significant change with testosterone therapy in a young, healthy population (Wierckx et al. 2014; Deutsch et al. 2015), though 28% of patients in one study who had been on testosterone for an average of 10 years had elevated blood pressure or treated hypertension (Wierckx et al. 2012). Cisgender women with PCOS are at increased risk of hypertension (Cibula et al. 2000; Joham et al. 2014). The effects of exogenous testosterone use among patients with known hypertension are not well addressed in the literature. Hypertension screening and treatment should follow recommended guidelines for cisgender patients, consistent with the guidelines established by the JNC-8 (James et al. 2014).

Lipids

All Patients, Not Currently on Hormone Therapy

*   Screen for and treat hyperlipidemia according to guidelines for cisgender patients (Grade A).

Screening for and treatment of hyperlipidemia should follow guidelines for cisgender patients. Ideally, lipids should be well controlled prior to initiation of either feminizing or masculinizing hormones. The USPSTF recommends periodic screening of anyone over the age of 20 at increased risk of cardiovascular disease, including diabetes, personal history of atherosclersosis or CAD, a family history of cardiovascular disease before age 50 in male relatives or age 60 in female relatives, tobacco use, hypertension, and obesity (BMI ≥30) (U.S. Preventive Services Task Force 2014a). In November, 2013, the American College of Cardiology/American Heart Association Task Force on Practice Guidelines published new recommendations for managing lipids as a means of reducing cardiovascular risk (Stone et al. 2014). One key element of this guideline includes the recommendation of statin therapy for individuals without clinical atherosclerotic cardiovascular disease or diabetes with low-density lipoprotein (LDL) cholesterol 70–189 mg/dL and estimated 10-year atherosclerotic CVD risk >7.5%. Unfortunately, the risk calculators used to estimate atherosclerotic CVD risk in this guideline do not account for transgender individuals on current or past masculinizing or feminizing hormone therapy. Providers may choose to calculate risk using both gender markers, and base treatment decisions in consultation with their patient (Stone et al. 2014).

Transwomen, Using Estrogen Therapy

- Recommend transdermal estrogen for patients with hyperlipidemia, particularly hypertriglyceridemia (Grade B).
- Consider increased frequency of lipid screening (< 5 years) for patients on estrogen therapy (Grade C).

Short-term (6–12-month) prospective studies of estrogen therapy among transwomen tend to show increase in high-density lipoprotein (HDL) cholesterol and triglycerides (Wierckx et al. 2014; Deutsch et al. 2015), a finding reinforced in cross-sectional and retrospective cohort studies (Elamin et al. 2010; Ott et al. 2011; Wierckx et al. 2012). Similar outcomes are seen in cisgender women on estrogen replacement therapy (Gooren et al. 2008). Oral estrogen therapy, through increasing triglycerides, has precipitated pancreatitis in the setting of postmenopausal hormone replacement therapy (Glueck et al. 1994; Goldenberg et al. 2003). Transdermal estrogen is preferred for patients with hyperlipidemia, particularly hypertriglyceridemia, as it decreases triglycerides and is either neutral or beneficial with regard to levels of HDL and LDL (Erenus et al. 2001; Sanada et al. 2004; Ott et al. 2011). While the USPSTF screening guidelines suggest lipid screening every 5 years, providers may consider more frequent screening in transwomen on estrogen therapy, due to effects on triglycerides as well as estrogen effects on cardiovascular risk overall. As noted, initial treatment for most patients will consist of therapeutic lifestyle changes, such as exercise, smoking cessation, and dietary modification, rather than lipid-lowering pharmacotherapy, or alteration in hormonal preparation or dose.

Transmen, Currently Using Testosterone

- Consider increased frequency of lipid screening (< 5 years) (Grade C).
- Avoid supraphysiologic testosterone levels, particularly for patients with hyperlipidemia. Daily topical or weekly intramuscular testosterone regimens are preferable to biweekly, or less frequent, intramuscular injection regimens (Grade C).

Short-term (6–12-month) prospective studies of testosterone therapy among transmen on testosterone tend to show a less favorable lipid profile, with decreases in HDL cholesterol, increases in triglycerides, and no change or increase in LDL cholesterol (Pelusi et al. 2014; Wierckx et al. 2014; Deutsch et al. 2015). Cross-sectional and retrospective cohort studies, as well as a systematic literature review, support these findings (Elamin et al. 2010; Ott et al. 2011; Wierckx et al. 2012; Goodrum 2015). Cisgender women with PCOS are at increased risk for dyslipidemia as well. A prospective study compared transmen without PCOS to cisgender women with PCOS, before and after 1 year of testosterone treatment. Before testosterone use, triglycerides and HDL cholesterol levels did not differ between the two groups, cisgender women with PCOS and transmen, but after 1 year of treatment, triglycerides were higher and HDL cholesterol levels lower in transmen than in cisgender PCOS women. Adjustments for age and BMI did not affect these differences (Cupisti et al. 2010). Transmen with PCOS may respond to testosterone therapy differently. Supraphysiologic doses of testosterone may increase the risk of lipid abnormalities, which may be mitigated by transdermal administration or by weekly intramuscular dosing (Rhoden & Morgentaler 2004). As previously noted, initial treatment for most patients will consist of therapeutic lifestyle changes, such as exercise, smoking cessation, and dietary modification, rather than lipid-lowering pharmacotherapy, or alteration in hormonal preparation or dose.

Smoking

All Transgender People

- Recommend screening, by history, of all transgender patients for past and present tobacco use (Grade A).
- Recommend including smoking cessation as part of comprehensive transgender medical care, particularly in association with hormone therapy (Grade C).

The transgender population in the United States experiences a higher prevalence of smoking than the population as a whole. Among a national sample of over 7,000 transgender respondents, 30% reported smoking daily or occasionally, compared to 20.6% of U.S. adults (Grant et al. 2011). Among the transgender population, there are common, multiple-identified risk factors for smoking, including poverty, stressful living and work environments, and social marginalization. The trans-specific risks associated with smoking include an increased risk of venous thromboembolic events with estrogen therapy and genital surgeries, possible increased risk of cardiovascular disease with both feminizing and masculinizing hormone therapy (especially over age 50), and delayed healing following surgery. Providers should screen all transgender patients for past and present tobacco use.

While little is known about cessation patterns in the transgender population, inclusion of smoking cessation as part of comprehensive transgender care appears successful, particularly in association with hormone therapy (Feldman et al. 2003). Bupropion, nicotine replacement, and behavioral modification techniques are also likely to be appropriate. A comprehensive approach involves consistent smoking cessation messages from all staff, frequent supportive follow-up of cessation efforts, and direct communication of the limitations and risks that smoking imposes on hormone therapy (Feldman & Bockting 2003).

Diabetes Mellitus

All Transgender People, Not Currently on Hormone Therapy

- Recommend screening for and treatment of diabetes mellitus as for the cisgender population (Grade A).

Providers should follow diabetes screening and management guidelines as for the cisgender population. Additionally, providers should consider screening (by patient history) all transmen for PCOS and perform diabetes screening if PCOS is present.

Transwomen, Currently on Feminizing Hormone Therapy

- Feminizing hormone therapy may increase the risk of type 2 diabetes among patients with a family history of diabetes or other risk factors for this illness (Grade C).
- Consider annual fasting glucose testing or HgbA1c for transwomen on estrogen and/or androgen-blocking medications (Grade C).
- Recommend annual fasting glucose testing or HgbA1c for patients with risk factors for diabetes, particularly those with a family history and weight gain >5 kg (Grade C).
- Manage diabetes according to guidelines for cisgender patients, but insulin-sensitizing agents are recommended if medications are used (Grade C).

There are no long-term prospective studies assessing the risk of diabetes with feminizing hormone therapy. One cross-sectional study compared transwomen with age-matched cisgender controls, and found a higher prevalence of type 2 diabetes among transwomen, but all but one diagnosis was in place prior to the start of hormone therapy (Wierckx et al. 2013b). Retrospective cohort studies have not shown increased prevalence of diabetes, though it is unclear whether it was an outcome of interest (van Kesteren et al. 1997; Gooren et al. 2008; Asscheman et al. 2011). Feminizing hormone therapy does appear to increase insulin resistance, which may be due to reduction in androgens as much as use of estrogen (Gooren et al. 2014). Transwomen on feminizing hormones experience a modest weight gain (4 kg) (Elbers et al. 1999, 2003) and as much as 21% increase in body fat (Elbers et al. 2003), both of which contribute to diabetes risk (Resnick et al. 2000; Koh-Banerjee et al. 2004). An annual diabetes screening test (HgbA1c or fasting glucose) is recommended in patients at risk for diabetes including age of 45 years or older, overweight or obese, or a first-degree relative with diabetes, and racial/ethnic minorities who are known to be at increased risk. Diabetes should be managed according to guidelines for cisgender patients, but insulin-sensitizing agents are recommended if medications are indicated, given the underlying mechanism of insulin resistance associated with hormonal therapy.

Transmen, with Testosterone Use

- Screen for and treat diabetes mellitus as for the cisgender population (Grade A).
- Diabetes screening is indicated if PCOS is present (Grade B).

As noted above, individuals with PCOS, which may be increased among transmen, have an increased risk of glucose intolerance. Retrospective studies do not indicate an altered risk of type 2 diabetes among transmen on testosterone as a whole, however. In prospective studies, masculinizing testosterone therapy increases visceral fat and decreases fasting glucose, with little effect on insulin resistance (Elbers et al. 2003; Gooren et al. 2008, 2014). An annual diabetes screening test (HgbA1c or fasting glucose) is recommended in patients 45 years or older, overweight or obese, with a first-degree relative with diabetes, and those with a history of gestational diabetes or PCOS. Racial/ethnic minorities who are known to be at increased risk of diabetes should also be screened annually. Guidelines for managing diabetes mellitus are the same as for the cisgender population (Feldman & Spencer 2015).

Osteoporosis

TRANSWOMEN, WITHOUT ESTROGEN USE OR GENDER REASSIGNMENT SURGERY

- There is no evidence of increased risk, and no screening is recommended except as indicated by additional risk factors (Grade A).

TRANSWOMEN, WITH CURRENT OR PAST ESTROGEN USE, WITHOUT ORCHIECTOMY

- No current evidence of increased risk of osteoporosis, and no screening is recommended, except as indicated by additional risk factors (Grade C).
- May recommend calcium and vitamin D supplementation for patients with deficient diets or little sun exposure (Grade C).
- Adequate weight-bearing exercise as recommended for cisgender women for osteoporosis prevention (Grade C).
- Treat low bone density and osteoporosis as recommended for cisgender women (Grade A).

TRANSWOMEN, AFTER ORCHIECTOMY

- Recommend for lifelong estrogen therapy to reduce the risk of osteo-porosis, unless significant contraindications to estrogen use are present (Grade A).
- Dual X-ray absorptiometry (DEXA) scan screening is recommended for patients aged 50–65 who have been off estrogen therapy for longer than 5 years and all patients over age 65 (Grade C).
- If there are contraindications to estrogen therapy, supplemental calcium (1200 mg daily) and vitamin D (800–1000 units daily) are recommended to limit bone loss (Grade C).
- Consider calcium or vitamin D supplementation in patients with diets deficient in calcium and/or vitamin D, or in patients with little sun exposure (Grade C).
- Adequate weight-bearing exercise as recommended for cisgender women for osteoporosis prevention (Grade C).
- Treat low bone density and osteoporosis as recommended for cisgender women (Grade A).

Prospective studies suggest that many transwomen may begin feminizing hormone therapy with lower bone mineral density compared to age-matched cisgender male controls, likely due to decreased physical activity from childhood onward (van Caenegem et al. 2015). Current studies on the effects of feminizing hormone therapy on bone mineral density are mixed, with some studies finding increases, while others finding fairly dramatic decreases, especially at the lumbar spine (Jones et al. 2009; Wierckx et al. 2012). There are no long-term studies of fracture risk, especially in an older adult transgender population, and routine screening is not currently recommended for pre-orchiectomy patients, except as indicated by additional risk factors. Weight-bearing activity and calcium and vitamin D supplementation, if diet is inadequate, are recommended.

It is unclear how much estrogen is needed following gonadal removal to protect against bone loss, but studies in postmenopausal women suggest that very low-dose estrogen (0.025 mg transdermal estradiol, for example) may be sufficient (Dören & Samsioe 2000). Loss of bone density is most likely after orchiectomy in patients with other risk factors (e.g., Caucasian or Asian ethnicity, smoking, family history, high alcohol use, hyperthyroidism) and in those who are not fully adherent to hormone therapy. In general, estrogen therapy is advised to reduce the risk of osteoporosis. If there are contraindications to estrogen therapy, weight-bearing exercise and adequate calcium (1200 mg daily) and vitamin D (800–1000 units daily) are recommended to limit bone loss, as recommended for postmenopausal women (National Osteoporosis Foundation 2010). DEXA scan screening is recommended for patients aged 50–65 who have been off estrogen therapy for longer than 5 years, and all patients over age 65 (Feldman 2008). Calcium, vitamin D supplementation, and weight-bearing exercises are indicated for all transgender patients using hormonal therapies who are at risk for osteoporosis. DEXA screening may be indicated for patients at an increased risk of osteoporosis, although normative data for transgender persons have not been established. Regardless of hormonal or surgical status, if a transgendered individual shows significant bone loss compared to birth sex norms, further intervention is warranted.

TRANSMEN, NOT USING TESTOSTERONE, WITHOUT SURGERY

- Recommend for screening and treatment for osteoporosis as for cisgender women (Grade A).

TRANSMEN, PAST OR PRESENT TESTOSTERONE USE, WITHOUT SURGERY

- No current evidence of increased risk of osteoporosis, and no screening is recommended except as indicated by additional risk factors (Grade C).
- Consider bone density screening for transmen on long-term testosterone therapy over the age of 60 years with additional risk factors for osteoporosis, including significant interruptions in testosterone therapy (Grade C).
- Treat low bone density and osteoporosis as recommended for cisgender men (Grade A).

TRANSMEN WITH CURRENT OR PREVIOUS TESTOSTERONE USE, AND POSTOOPHERECTOMY OR TOTAL HYSTERECTOMY

- There is an increased risk of bone density loss after oophorectomy, particularly if testosterone supplementation is reduced or discontinued (Grade C).
- Recommend lifelong testosterone therapy to reduce the risk of bone density loss, if there are no significant contraindications (Grade B).
- DEXA scan screening is recommended for patients aged 50–65 who have been off testosterone therapy for longer than 5 years and all patients over age 65.
- Recommend weight-bearing exercise, supplemental calcium (1,200 mg daily), and vitamin D (800–1000 units daily) to maintain bone density (Grade B).
- Treat low bone density and osteoporosis as recommended for cisgender men (Grade A).

The USPSTF (2011) recommends bone density screening for all cisgender women over the age of 65 years and younger cisgender women with a similar level of risk. Transmen begin with an average of 10–12% less bone density than natal males, prior to any hormonal or surgical intervention (Campion & Maricic 2003). Prospective and case-control studies have found that uninterrupted testosterone therapy maintains or increases bone density among transmen (Haraldsen et al. 2007; Mueller et al. 2007; van Caenegem et al. 2012), with the most recent study following subjects an average of 8.7 years post reassignment surgery. It is unclear what testosterone level is needed following gonad removal to protect against bone loss. Prospective studies of transgender patients with oophorectomy indicate that bone mineral density may decrease even with testosterone supplementation, particularly if testosterone use is interrupted or the dose is inadequate to suppress luteinizing hormone (Goh & Ratnam 1997; van Kesteren et al. 1998; Turner et al. 2004).

Overall, loss of bone density is most likely in those patients with other risk factors (e.g., Caucasian or Asian ethnicity, smoking, family history, high alcohol use, hypothyroidism) and those who are not fully adherent to hormone therapy, especially after oophorectomy. In general, testosterone therapy is advised to reduce the risk of osteoporosis. If there are contraindications to testosterone, weight-bearing exercise, and adequate calcium (1200 mg daily) and vitamin D (800–1000 units daily) are recommended to limit bone loss (National Osteoporosis Foundation 2010). DEXA scan screening is recommended for patients aged 50–65 who have been off testosterone therapy for longer than 5 years, and all patients over age 65 (Feldman 2008). Calcium, vitamin D supplementation, and weight-bearing exercises are indicated for all transgender patients using hormonal therapies who are at risk for osteoporosis. DEXA screening may be indicated for patients at an increased risk of osteoporosis, although normative data for transgender people have not been established. Regardless of hormonal or surgical status, if a transgender individual shows significant bone loss compared to birth sex norms, further intervention is warranted.

Sexual Health: Sexually Transmitted Infections

- Perform an individualized sexual health history, including concerns associated with increased risk among transgender people (Grade B).
- Screen for HIV, hepatitis B and C, and STIs according to recommended guidelines (USPSTF 2014b; Workowski & Bolan 2015) and individualized assessment.
- Recommend hepatitis A and B vaccination to all sexually active patients who are not already immune (Grade B).
- Screening modalities for STIs should account for the variable anatomy and comfort of transgender patients, such as self- or clinician-collected vaginal swabs, or first-catch urine specimens (Grade A).

Transgender individuals share many of the same concerns regarding STIs, hepatitis B and hHIV as do individuals in the lesbian, gay, and bisexual communities (Feldman 2008). There are a few transgender-specific considerations, however. Transgender individuals (of any gender) who have sex with men (TSM) can be considered at increased risk for STIs (Feldman et al. 2014). Sexual practices among transgender individuals vary greatly, and no assumptions should be made about the gender of a patient's sexual partner(s), sexual activities, or individual risks (Bauer et al. 2012). Cofactors related to unsafe sex, such as depression, suicidal ideation, and physical or sexual abuse, are increased among the transgender population. Studies indicate that the need to affirm one's gender identity can drive high-risk sexual behaviors (Bockting et al. 1998; Nemoto et al. 2004; Crosby & Pitts 2007; Melendez & Pinto 2007; Sausa et al. 2007). Finally, because needle sharing with injectable hormones (or silicone) is a trans-specific potential risk factor for transmission of HIV and hepatitis B/C, patients need to be educated regarding the risks as well as safe handling of needles and syringes.

STI prevention strategies should be appropriately targeted to each individual patient's anatomy and specific sexual practices. For example, non-penetrative sexual activities with appropriate barrier protection (latex gloves, dental dams, non-microwaveable plastic wrap) or penetration with a dildo (covered by a condom) can be recommended for patients who are taking feminizing hormones and are unable to sustain an erection sufficiently firm for condom use. To prevent condom breakage, supplemental lubrication should be recommended for transwomen who have had vaginoplasty (as the neovagina is not self-lubricating) and transmen who take testosterone (as decreased estrogen can result in vaginal atrophy and dryness). Water-based lubricants only should be used with latex barriers, as oil-based products degrade latex, and therefore may result in inadvertent transmission of infectious agents (Feldman & Spencer 2015).

The variable anatomy of transgender people can affect screening for STIs. A self- or clinician-collected vaginal swab is the recommended sample type. A first-catch urine specimen is acceptable, but might detect up to 10% fewer infections when compared with vaginal and endocervical swab samples (Centers for Disease Control and Prevention 2014). However, this test can be used regardless of anatomy, providing an acceptable alternative testing method when a vaginal, endocervical, or urethral swab is not appropriate. Rectal and pharyngeal samples should be used in patients based on symptoms or on a history of high-risk oral or anal sex. Hormone therapy does not affect treatment of STIs in the transgender individual. Some HIV medications increase or decrease serum estrogen levels, but there is no evidence that cross-sex hormones interfere with the effectiveness of HIV medication or negatively affect the progression of HIV/acquired immune deficiency syndrome (AIDS). Little has been published regarding the risks of genital reassignment surgery among those with HIV/AIDS. HIV-infected persons have an increased risk of infection with any major surgery, with the number and severity of complications related to CD4 count. Genital surgery outcomes appear to be good with adequate patient selection and preoperative preparation (Kirk 1993).

Conclusion

Due to a variety of factors, including lack of access to routine medical services, transgender patients may be at an increased risk for common, chronic medical conditions. Research evidence regarding preventive care for transgender people is limited, but evidence-based recommendations can be made by systematically incorporating information from the best-available transgender and relevant general population studies.

Preventive care is often neglected during the process of gender transition, when the individual is focused on obtaining hormonal and surgical care. Family physicians, general practitioners, and internists can play a crucial role in improving the health of these patients, by recommending appropriate screening for chronic conditions and other health risks before, during, and after gender transition.

Preventive health care recommendations must account for the current hormonal and surgical status of the patient, as well as the effects of the years spent with the hormonal physiology of the natal sex. Finally, continued research is needed to improve our understanding of transgender health, including the impact of long-term treatment with estrogen and testosterone.

References

Asscheman, H. and L. J. Gooren (1992). Hormone treatment in transsexuals. *J. Psychol. Hum. Sex.* 5(4): 39–54.

Asscheman, H., et al. (1994). Serum testosterone level is the major determinant of the male-female differences in serum levels of high-density lipoprotein (HDL) cholesterol and HDL2 cholesterol. *Metabolism* 43(8): 935–939.

Asscheman, H., et al. (2011). A long-term follow-up study of mortality in transsexuals receiving treatment with cross-sex hormones. *Eur. J. Endocrinol.* 164:635–642.

Baba, T., et al. (2007). Association between polycystic ovary syndrome and female-to-male transsexuality. *Hum. Reprod.* 22(4):1011–1016.

Baba, T., et al. (2011). Distinctive features of female-to-male transsexualism and prevalence of gender identity disorder in Japan. *J. Sex. Med.* 8(6): 1686–1693.

Barbieri, R. L., and D. A. Ehrmann. (2015). Clinical manifestations of polycystic ovary disease in adults. *UpToDate* 17. Accessed March 3, 2015.

Barry, J.A., M. M. Azizia, and P. J. Hardiman. (2014). Risk of endometrial, ovarian and breast cancer in women with polycystic ovary syndrome: A systematic review and meta-analysis. *Hum. Reprod. Update* 20(5): 748–758.

Bath, P. M. J., and L. J. Gray. (2005). Association between hormone replacement therapy and subsequent stroke: A meta-analysis. *BMJ* 330(7487): 342.

Bauer, G. R., et al. (2012). High heterogeneity of HIV-related sexual risk among transgender people in Ontario, Canada: A province-wide respondent-driven sampling survey. *BMC Public Health* 12: 292.

Blanchard, R. (1994). A structural equation model for age at clinical presentation in nonhomosexual male gender dysphorics. *Arch. Sex Behav.* 23(3): 311–320.

Bockting, W. O. (2000). All gender health: HIV/STD prevention in the context of transgender-specific, comprehensive sexuality education. Paper presented at the Fifth International Congress on Crossdressing, Sex, and Gender Issues, Philadelphia, PA.

Bockting, W. O., Robinson, B. B. E., and Rosser, B. R. S. (1998). Transgender HIV prevention: A qualitative needs assessment. *AIDS Care* 10, 505–526.

Boice, J. D., Jr., et al. (1997). Cancer following breast reduction surgery in Denmark. *Cancer Causes Control* 8(2): 253–258.

Boice, J. D., Jr., et al. (2000). Breast cancer following breast reduction surgery in Sweden. *Plast. Reconstr. Surg.* 106(4): 755–762.

Bosinski, H. A., et al. (1997). A higher rate of hyperandrogenic disorders in female-to-male transsexuals. *Psychoneuroendocrinology* 22(5): 361–380.

Brinton, L. A., et al. (2001). Breast cancer risk in relation to amount of tissue removed during breast reduction operations in Sweden. *Cancer* 91(3): 478–483.

Brown, G. R. (2015). Breast cancer in transgender veterans: A ten-case series. *LGBT Health* 2(1): 77–80.

Brown, G. R., and K. T. Jones. (2015). Incidence of breast cancer in a cohort of 5,135 transgender veterans. *Breast Cancer Res.* 149:191–198.

Bryant, H. and P. Brasher. (1995). Breast implants and breast cancer: Reanalysis of a linkage study. *N. Engl. J. Med.* 332(23): 1535–1539.

Burcombe, R. J., et al. (2003). Breast cancer after bilateral subcutaneous mastectomy in a female-to-male transsexual. *Breast* 12(4): 290–293.

Calonge, N., et al. (2009). Screening for breast cancer: U.S. Preventive Services Task Force recommendation statement. *Ann, Intern. Med.* 151: 716–726.

Campion, J. M. and M. J. Maricic. (2003). Osteoporosis in men. *Am. Fam. Physician* 67(7): 1521–1526.

Centers for Disease Control and Prevention. (2014). Recommendations for the laboratory-based detection of *Chlamydia trachomatis* and *Neisseria gonorrhoeae*. *MMWR* 63(0): 1–19.

Chen, W. Y. et al. (2014). Menopausal hormone therapy and the risk of breast cancer. *Up to Date* [online].

Chittenden, B. G., et al. (2009). Polycystic ovary syndrome and the risk of gynaecological cancer: A systematic review. *Reprod. BioMed. Online* 19(3): 398–405.

Cibula, D., et al. (2000). Increased risk of non-insulin dependent diabetes mellitus, arterial hypertension, and coronary artery disease in perimenopausal women with a history of the polycystic ovary syndrome. *Hum. Reprod.* 15(4): 785–789.

Cobin, R. H. (2013). Cardiovascular and metabolic risks associated with PCOS. *Int. Emerg. Med.* 8(1) Suppl.: 61–64.

Committee on Gynecologic Practice. (2012). Committee opinion no. 534: Well-woman visit. *Obstet. Gynecol.* 120(2) Pt. 1: 421–424.

Cooper, R., et al. (2000). Trends and disparities in coronary heart disease, stroke, and other cardiovascular diseases in the United States: Findings of the National Conference on Cardiovascular Disease Prevention. *Circulation* 102(25): 3137–3147.

Costanza, M. E., and W. Y. Chen. (2012). Factors that modify breast cancer risk in women. *Up to Date* [online].

Crosby, R. A., and N. L. Pitts. (2007). Caught between different worlds: How transgendered women may be "forced" into risky sex. *J. Sex. Res.* 44(1): 43–48.

Cumming, G., and J. Godfrey. (2013). Acute ischaemic stroke in a male-to-female transsexual using high dose oestrogen therapy. In: *Cerebrovascular Diseases, Vol. 35.* Basel, Switzerland: Karger.

Cupisti, S., et al. (2010). The impact of testosterone administration to female-to-male transsexuals on insulin resistance and lipid parameters compared with women with polycystic ovary syndrome. *Fertil. Steril.* 94(7): 2647–2653.

Davis, S. R., et al. (2009). The incidence of invasive breast cancer among women prescribed testosterone for low libido. *J. Sex. Med.* 6(7): 1850–1856.

Deapen, D., et al. (2000). Breast cancer stage at diagnosis and survival among patients with prior breast implants. *Plast. Reconstr. Surg.* 105(2): 535–540.

de Groot, P. C. M., et al. (2011). PCOS, coronary heart disease, stroke and the influence of obesity: A systematic review and meta-analysis. *Hum. Reprod. Update* 17(4)): 495–500.

Deutsch, M. B., V. Bhakri, and K. Kubicek. (2015). Effects of cross-sex hormone treatment on transgender women and men. *Obstet. Gynecol.* 125(3): 605–610.

Dimitrakakis, C., et al. (2004). Breast cancer incidence in postmenopausal women using testosterone in addition to usual hormone therapy. *Menopaus.* 11(5): 531–535.

Dizon, D. S., et al. (2006). Ovarian cancer associated with testosterone supplementation in a female-to-male transsexual patient. *Gynecol. Obstet. Invest.* 62(4): 226–228.

Dorff, T. B., et al. (2007). Successful treatment of metastatic androgen-independent prostate carcinoma in a transsexual patient. *Clin. Genitourinary Cancer* 5(5): 344–346.

Ebell, M. H., et al. (2004). Strength of Recommendation Taxonomy (SORT): A patient-centered approach to grading evidence in the medical literature. *Am. Fam. Phys.* 69(3): 548–556..

Elamin, M. B. et al. (2010). Effect of sex steroid use on cardiovascular risk in transsexual individuals: A systematic review and meta-analyses. *Clin. Endocrinol.* 72(1): 1–10.

Elbers, J. M., et al. (1999). Effects of sex steroid hormones on regional fat deposits as assessed by magnetic resonance imaging in transsexuals. *Am. J. Physiol* 276(2) Pt 1: E317–E325.

Elbers, J. M. H., et al. (2003). Effects of sex steroids on components of the insulin resistance syndrome in transsexual subjects. *Clin. Endocrinol.* 58(5): 562–571.

Erenus, M., B. Karakoc, and A. Gurler. (2001). Comparison of effects of continuous combined transdermal with oral estrogen and oral progestogen replacement therapies on serum lipoproteins and compliance. *Climacteric.* 4(3): 228–234.

Eyler, A. E. and S. Whittle. (2001). FTM breast cancer: community awareness and illustrative cases. Paper presented at 17th Biennial Symposium of the Harry Benjamin International Gender Dysphoria Association, Galveston, TX, November 2001.

Feldman, J. (2008). Medical and surgical management of the transgender patient: What the primary care clinician needs to know. In H. J. Makadon, K. H. Mayer, J. Potter, and H. Goldhammer (Eds.), *Fenway Guide to Lesbian, Gay, Bisexual, and Transgender Health*. Philadelphia, PA: American College of Physicians, pp. 365–392.

Feldman, J. L. (2011). Initiating feminizing hormone therapy over age 50: Results and challenges. Paper presented at World Professional Association for Transgender Health Biennial Symposium; September 27, 2011; Atlanta, GA.

Feldman, J. and W. Bockting. (2003). Transgender health. *Minn. Med.* 86(7): 25–32.

Feldman, J. and J. Safer (2015). Hormone therapy in adults: suggested revisions to the sixth version of the standards of care. *Int. J. Transgender* 11: 146–182.

Feldman, J. and K. Spencer (2015). Medical and surgical management of the transgender patient: What the primary care clinician needs to know. In H. J. Makadon, K. H. Mayer, J. Potter, and H. Goldhammer (Eds.), *The Fenway Guide to Lesbian, Gay, Bisexual, and Transgender Health*. Philadelphia, PA: American College of Physicians, pp. 479–516.

Feldman, J., et al. (2003). Smoking cessation among transgender persons receiving hormone therapy. Paper presented at the 18th Biennial Symposium of the Harry Benjamin Gender Dysphoria Association, Kloster Irsee, Germany, September 10.

Feldman, J., F. Ettner, and R. Ettner. (2014). Cross-sex hormone treatment in transgender subjects and somatic co-morbidity in a United States sample. WPATH Symposium, Bangkok, Thailand, February 14–28.

Feldman, J., R. Swinburne Romine, and W. O. Bockting. (2014). HIV risk behaviors in the U.S. transgender population: Prevalence and predictors in a large internet sample. *J. Homosex.* 61(11): 1558–1588.

Fernandes, H. M., T. P. Manolitsas, and T. W. Jobling. (2014). Carcinoma of the neovagina after male-to-female reassignment. *J. Lower Genital Tract Dis.* 18(2): E43–E45.

Fiumara, N. J. and Di Mattia, A. (1973). Gonorrhoea and condyloma acuminata in a male transsexual. *Br. J. Vener. Dis.* 49(5): 478–479.

Forshee, A. S. (2008). Transgender men: A demographic snapshot. *J Gay Lesbian Soc. Serv.* 20(3): 221–236.

Fryzek, J. P., et al. (2006). A nationwide epidemiologic study of breast cancer incidence following breast reduction surgery in a large cohort of Swedish women. *Breast Cancer Res. Treat.* 97(2): 131–134.

Futterweit, W. (1998). Endocrine therapy of transsexualism and potential complications of long-term treatment. *Arch. Sex Behav.* 27(2): 209–226.

Glueck, C. J., et al. (1994). Severe hypertriglyceridemia and pancreatitis when estrogen replacement therapy is given to hypertriglyceridemic women. *J. Lab Clin. Med.* 123(1): 59–64.

Goh, H. H., and S. S. Ratnam. (1997). Effects of hormone deficiency, androgen therapy and calcium supplementation on bone mineral density in female transsexuals. *Maturitas* 26(1): 45–52.

Goldenberg, N. M., P. Wang, and C. J. Glueck. (2003). An observational study of severe hypertriglyceridemia, hypertriglyceridemic acute pancreatitis, and failure of triglyceride-lowering therapy when estrogens are given to women with and without familial hypertriglyceridemia. *Clin. Chim. Acta* 332(1–2): 11–19.

Goodrum, B. A. (2015). The effects of long-term testosterone use on lipid-related cardiovascular risk factors among FtM patients. *Int. J. Transgenderism* 15(3–4): 164–172.

Gooren, L. J., and E. J. Giltay. (2008). Review of studies of androgen treatment of female-to-male transsexuals: Effects and risks of administration of androgens to females. *J. Sex. Med.* 5(4): 765–776.

Gooren, L. J., and A. Morgentaler. (2014). Prostate cancer incidence in orchidectomised male-to-female transsexual persons treated with oestrogens. *Andrologia* 46(10): 1156–1160.

Gooren, L. J., E. J. Giltay, and M. C. Bunck. (2008). Long-term treatment of transsexuals with cross-sex hormones: Extensive personal experience. *J. Clin. Endocrinol. Metab.* 93(1):19–25.

Gooren, L. J., et al. (2013). Breast cancer development in transsexual subjects receiving cross-sex hormone treatment. *J. Sex. Med.* 10(12): 3129–3134.

Gooren, L. J., K. Wierckx, and E. J. Giltay. (2014). Cardiovascular disease in transsexual persons treated with cross-sex hormones: Reversal of the traditional sex difference in cardiovascular disease pattern. *Eur. J. Endocrinol.* 170: 808–819.

Gooren, L., et al. (2015). Five new cases of breast cancer in transsexual persons. *Andrologia* 47: 1202–1205.

Gottschau, M., et al. (2015). Risk of cancer among women with polycystic ovary syndrome: A Danish cohort study. *Gynecol. Oncol.* 136(1): 99–103.

Grant, J. M., et al. (2010). National Transgender Discrimination Survey Report on Health and Health Care. Washington, DC: National Center for Transgender Equality and National Gay and Lesbian Task Force.

Grant, J. M., et al. (2011). Injustice at Every Turn: A Report of the National Transgender Discrimination Survey. Washington, DC: National Center for Transgender Equality and National Gay and Lesbian Task Force.

Grynberg, M., et al. (2010). Histology of genital tract and breast tissue after long-term testosterone administration in a female-to-male transsexual population. *Reprod. BioMed. Online* 20(4): 553–558.

Hage, J. J., et al. (2000). Ovarian cancer in female-to-male transsexuals: Report of two cases. *Gynecol. Oncol.* 76(3): 413–415.

Haraldsen, I. R., et al. (2007). Cross-sex pattern of bone mineral density in early onset gender identity disorder. *Horm. Behav.* 52(3): 334–343.

Harris, R., et al. (2001). Current methods of the U.S. Preventive Services Task Force: A review of the process. *Am. J. Prev. Med.* 20(suppl 3): 21–35.

Hembree, W. C., P. Cohen-Kettenis, H. A. Delemarre-van de Waal, et al. (2009). Endocrine treatment of transsexual persons: an Endocrine Society clinical practice guideline. *J. Clin. Endocrinol. Metab.* 94:3132–3154.

Humphrey, L. L., et al. (2002). Breast cancer screening: A summary of the evidence for the U.S. Preventive Services Task Force. [See comment] [Summary for patients in *Ann. Intern. Med.* 2002 Sep 3; 137(5 Part 1):I47; PMID: 12204048]. *Ann. Intern. Med.* 137(5 Part 1): 347–360.

Igidbashian, S. et al. (2014). Performance of self-sampled HPV test in comparison with liquid based cytology. *Eur. J. Obstet. Gynecol. Reprod. Biol.* 177: 72–76.

Ikeda, K., et al. (2013). Excessive androgen exposure in female-to-male transsexual persons of reproductive age induces hyperplasia of the ovarian cortex and stroma but not polycystic ovary morphology. *Hum. Reprod.* 28(2): 453–461.

Inoue, H., et al. (2007). The sudden and unexpected death of a female-to-male transsexual patient. *J. Forensic Legal Med.* 14(6): 382–386.

Institute of Medicine. (2011). *The Health of Lesbian, Gay, Bisexual, and Transgender People: Building a Foundation for Better Understanding.* Washington, DC: National Academies Press.

James, P. A., S. Oparil, and B. L. Carter. (2014). Evidence-based guideline for the management of high blood pressure in adults. Report From the Panel Members Appointed to the Eighth Joint National Committee (JNC 8). *JAMA* 311(5): 507–520.

Jick, S. S., et al. (2009). Postmenopausal estrogen-containing hormone therapy and the risk of breast cancer. *Obstet. Gynecol.* 113(1): 74–80.

Joham, A. E., et al. (2014). Hypertension in reproductive-aged women with polycystic ovary syndrome and association with obesity. *Am. J. Hypertens.* 28(7): 847–851.

Jones, R. A., C. G. Schultz, and B. E. Chatterton. (2009). A longitudinal study of bone density in reassigned transsexuals. *Bone* 44: S126–S126.

Kammerer, N., Mason, T., Connors, M., and Durkee, R. (1999). Transgender health and social service needs in the context of HIV risk. *Int. J. Transgenderism* 3(1+2). Retrieved January 1, 2005, from http://www.symposion.com/ijt/hiv_risk/kammerer.htm.

Kirk, S. (1993). Guidelines for selecting HIV positive patients for genital reconstructive surgery. *Int. J. Transgenderism* 3(1).

Koh-Banerjee, P., et al. (2004). Changes in body weight and body fat distribution as risk factors for clinical diabetes in U.S. men. *Am. J. Epidemiol.* 159(12): 1150–1159.

Kreukels, B. P. C., et al. (2012). A European Network for the Investigation of Gender Incongruence: The ENIGI initiative. *Eur. Psychiatry* 27(6): 445–450.

Lawrence, A. (2001). Vaginal neoplasia in a male-to-female transsexual: Case report, review of the literature, and recommendations for cytological screening. *Int. J. Transgenderism* 5(1).

Liguori, G., et al. (2004). Condylomata acuminata of the neovagina in a HIV-seropositive male-to-female transsexual. *Urol. Int.* 73(1): 87–88.

Maglione, K. D., et al. (2014). Breast cancer in male-to-female transsexuals: Use of breast imaging for detection. *Am. J. Roentgenol.* 203(6): W735–W740.

Markland, C. (1975). Transexual surgery. *Obstet. Gynecol. Annu.* 4: 309–330.

Marrazzo, J. M., et al. (2001). Papanicolaou test screening and prevalence of genital human papillomavirus among women who have sex with women. *Am. J. Publ. Hlth* 91(6): 947–952.

Martin, K., and R. Rosenson. (2015). Menopausal hormone therapy and cardiovascular risk. *Up to Date [online]*. Accessed Feb. 24, 2015.

Massad, L. S., et al. (2013). 2012 Updated consensus guidelines for the management of abnormal cervical cancer screening tests and cancer precursors. *Obstet. Gynecol.* 121(4): 829–846.

Matsuki, S., et al. (2015). Condylomata acuminata in the neovagina after male-to-female reassignment treated with CO2 laser and imiquimod. *Int. J. STD AIDS* 26(7): 509–511.

Melendez, R. M., and R. Pinto. (2007). 'It's really a hard life': Love, gender and HIV risk among male-to-female transgender persons. *Cult. Health. Sex.* 9(3): 233–245.

Melnikow, J., et al. (1998). Natural history of cervical squamous intraepithelial lesions: A meta-analysis. *Obstet. Gynecol.* 92(4) Pt 2: 727–735.

Mensay, G. A., et al. (2005). State of disparities in cardiovascular health in the United States. *Circulation* 111(10): 1233–1241.

Miksad, R. A., et al. (2006). Prostate cancer in a transgender woman 41 years after initiation of feminization. *JAMA* 296(19): 2312–2317.

Miller, N., et al. (1986). Histological changes in the genital tract in transsexual women following androgen therapy. *Histopathology* 10(7): 661–669.

Molokwu, C. N., J. S. Appelbaum, and R. A. Miksad. (2008). Detection of prostate cancer following gender reassignment. *BJU Int.* 101(2): 259–259.

Morgentaler A., and E. L. Rhoden. (2006). Prevalence of prostate cancer among hypogonadal men with prostate-specific antigen levels of 4.0 ng/mL or less. *Urology* 68(6): 1263–1267.

Morgentaler, A., C. O. Bruning, III, and W. C. DeWolf. (1996). Occult prostate cancer in men with low serum testosterone levels. *JAMA* 276(23): 1904–1906.

Moyer, V. A. (2008). Screening for prostate cancer: U. S. Preventive Services Task Force recommendations statement. *Ann. Intern. Med.* 149(3): 185–191.

Moyer, V. A. (2012a). Screening for cervical cancer: U. S. Preventive Services Task Force recommendation statement. *Ann. Intern. Med.* 156(12): 880–891.

Moyer, V. A. (2012b). Screening for coronary heart disease with electrocardiography: U. S. Preventive Services Task Force recommendation statement. *Ann. Intern. Med.* 157(7): 512–518.

Mueller, A., and L. Gooren (2008). Hormone-related tumors in transsexuals receiving treatment with cross-sex hormones. *Eur. Soc. Endocrinol.* 159: 197–202.

Mueller, A., et al. (2007). Long-term administration of testosterone undecanoate every 3 months for testosterone supplementation in female-to-male transsexuals. *J. Clin. Endocrinol. Metabol.* 92(9): 3470–3475.

Mueller, A., et al. (2008). Prevalence of polycystic ovary syndrome and hyperandrogenemia in female-to-male transsexuals. *J. Clin. Endocrinol. Metab.* 93(4): 1408–1411.

National Osteoporosis Foundation. (2010). *Clinician's Guide to Prevention and Treatment of Osteoporosis*. Washington, DC: National Osteoporosis Foundation.

Nemoto, T., Keatley, J., and Operario, D. (2002). Implementing HIV prevention, drug abuse treatment, and mental health services in the transgender community in San Francisco. Poster presented at XVI International AIDS Conference, Barcelona, Spain.

Nemoto, T., et al. (2004). HIV risk behaviors among male-to-female transgender persons of color in San Francisco. *Am. J. Publ. Hlth* 94(7): 1193–1199.

Ness, R. B., et al. (2009). Influence of estrogen plus testosterone supplementation on breast cancer. *Arch. Intern. Med.* 169(1): 41–46.

Netscher, D. et al. (1999). Mammography and reduction mammaplasty. *Aesthetic Surg. J.* 19(6): 445–451.

Nieder, T. O., et al. (2011). Age of onset and sexual orientation in transsexual males and females. *J. Sex. Med.* 8(3): 783–791.

Nikolic, D. V., et al. (2012). Importance of revealing a rare case of breast cancer in a female to male transsexual after bilateral mastectomy. *World J. Surg. Oncol.* 10(280): 2–4.

Obedin-Maliver, J., et al. (2011). Lesbian, gay, bisexual, and transgender-related content in undergraduate medical education. *JAMA* 306(9): 971–977.

Office of Disease Prevention and Health Promotion. (2011). *US Department of Health and Human Services: Healthy People 2020*. Washington, DC: Office of Disease Prevention and Health Promotion, US Department of Health and Human Services.

Olsen, O., and P. C. Gotzsche. (2001). Screening for breast cancer with mammography. *Cochrane Database Systemat. Rev.* (4): CD001877.

Ott, J., et al. (2011). Cross-sex hormone therapy alters the serum lipid profile: A retrospective cohort study in 169 transsexuals. *J. Sex. Med.* 8(8): 2361–2369.

Pache, T. D., et al. (1991). Ovarian morphology in long-term androgen-treated female-to-male transsexuals. A human model for the study of polycystic ovarian syndrome? *Histopathology* 19(5): 445–452.

Padilla, L. A., D. M. Radosevich, and M. P. Magdy. (2000). Accuracy of the pelvic examination in detecting adnexal masses. *Obstet. Gynecol.* 96(4): 593–598.

Parssinen, M., and T. Seppala (2002). Steroid use and long-term health risks in former athletes. *Sports Med.* 32: 83–94.

Peitzmeier, S. M., et al. (2014). Female-to-male patients have high prevalence of unsatisfactory paps compared to non-transgender females: Implications for cervical cancer screening. *J. Gen. Int. Med.* 29(5): 778–784.

Pelusi, C., et al. (2014). Effects of three different testosterone formulations in female-to-male transsexual persons. *J. Sex. Med.* 11(12): 3002–3011.

Phillips, J., et al. (2014). Breast imaging in the transgender patient. *Am. J. Roentgenol.* 202(5): 1149–1146.

Prior, J. C., Y. M. Vigna, and D. Watson. (1989). Spironolactone with physiological female steroids for presurgical therapy of male-to-female transsexualism. *Arch. Sex. Behav.* 18(1): 49–57.

Racey, C. S., D. R. Withrow, and D. Gesink. (2013). Self-collected HPV testing improves participation in cervical cancer screening: A systematic review and meta-analysis. *Can. J. Publ. Hlth* 104(2): e159–e166.

Renoux, C., S. Dell'Aniello, E. Garbe, and S. Suissa. (2010). Transdermal and oral hormone replacement therapy and the risk of stroke: A nested case-control study. *BMJ* 340: c2519.

Resnick, H. E., et al. (2000). Relation of weight gain and weight loss on subsequent diabetes risk in overwieght adults. *J. Epidemiol. Commun. Hlth* 54(8): 596–602.

Rhoden, E. L., and A. Morgentaler. (2004). Risks of testosterone-replacement therapy and recommendations for monitoring. *N. Engl. J. Med.* 350(5): 482–492.

Rossouw, J. E., et al. (2002). Risks and benefits of estrogen plus progestin in healthy postmenopausal women: Principal results from the Women's Health Initiative randomized controlled trial. *JAMA* 288(3): 321–333.

Sanada, M., et al. (2004). Substitution of transdermal estradiol during oral estrogen-progestin therapy in postmenopausal women: Effects on hypertriglyceridemia. *Menopause* 11(3): 331–336.

Sattari, M. (2015). Breast cancer in male-to-female transgender patients: A case for caution. *Clin. Breast Cancer* 15(1): e67–e69.

Sausa, L. A., J. Keatley, and D. Operario. (2007). Perceived risks and benefits of sex work among transgender women of color in San Francisco. *Arch. Sex. Behav.* 36(6): 768–777.

Shao, T., M. L. Grossbard, and P. Klein. (2011). Breast cancer in female-to-male transsexuals: Two cases with a review of physiology and management. *Clin. Breast Cancer* 11(6):417–419.

Sherman, M. E., et al. (2003). Baseline cytology, human papillomavirus testing, and risk for cervical neoplasia: A 10-year cohort analysis. *J. Natl. Cancer Inst.* 95(1): 46–52.

Smith, R. A., et al. (2003). American Cancer Society guidelines for breast cancer screening: Update 2003. *CA Cancer J. Clin.* 53(3): 141–169.

Snelgrove, J. W., et al. (2012). "Completely out-at-sea" with "two-gender medicine": A qualitative analysis of physician-side barriers to providing heathcare for transgender patients. *BMC Hlth Serv. Res.* 12: 110.

Snyder, P. J, A. M. Matsumoto, and K. A. Martin. (2012). Testosterone treatment of male hypogonadism. *UpToDate [online].* Accessed March 2, 2015.

Spritz, M. (2003). Effects of cross gender hormonal therapy on prostates in 20 postoperative patients. Paper presented at the Eighteenth Biennial Symposium of the Harry Benjamin Gender Dysphoria Association, Gent, Belgium.

Steinbeck, A. (1997). Hormonal medication for transsexuals. *Venereology* 10(3): 175–177.

Stone, N. J., et al. (2014). ACC/AHA guideline on the treatment of blood cholesterol to reduce atherosclerotic cardiovascular risk in adults. *Circulation* 129: S1–S45.

Tamimi, R. M., et al. (2006). Combined estrogen and testosterone use and risk of breast cancer in postmenopausal women. *Arch. Intern. Med.* 166(14): 1483–1489.

Thurston, A. V. (1994). Carcinoma of the prostate in a transsexual. *Br. J. Urol.* 73(2): 217.

Turner, A., et al. (2004). Testosterone increases bone mineral density in female-to-male transsexuals: A case series of 15 subjects. *Clin. Endocrinol.* 61(5): 560–566.

Turo, R., et al. (2013). Metastatic prostate cancer in transsexual diagnosed after three decades of estrogen therapy. *Can. Urol. Assoc. J.* 7(7–8): E544–E546.

Urban, R. R., N. N. H. Teng, and D. S. Kapp. (2011). Gynecologic malignancies in female-to-male transgender patients: The need of original gender surveillance. *Am. J. Obstet. Gynecol.* 204(5): e9–e12.

U. S. Preventive Services Task Force. (2005). *The Guide to Clinical Preventive Services.* AHRQ Pub. No. 05–0570. Washington, DC: Agency for Health Care Research and Quality.

U. S. Preventive Services Task Force. (2011). Screening for osteoporosis: US Preventive Services Task Force recommendation statement. *Ann. Intern. Med.* 154(5): 356–364.

U. S. Preventive Services Task Force (2014a). *Final Recommendation Statement: Lipid Disorders in Adults (Cholesterol, Dyslipidemia): Screening.* Available at http://www.uspreventiveservicestaskforce.org/Page/Document/RecommendationStatementFinal/lipid-disorders-in-adults-cholesterol-dyslipidemia-screening#consider.

U. S. Preventive Services Task Force (2014b). USPSTF Recommendations for STI Screening. Available at: http://www.uspreventiveservicestaskforce.org/Page/Name/ uspstf-recommendations-for-sti-screening.

van Caenegem, E., et al. (2012). Bone mass, bone geometry, and body composition in female-to-male transsexual persons after long-term cross-sex hormonal therapy. *J. Clin. Endocrinol. Metab.* 97(7): 2503–2511.

van Caenegem, E., et al. (2015). Preservation of volumetric bone density and geometry in trans women during cross-sex hormonal therapy: A prospective observational study. *Osteoporos. Int.* 26(1): 35–47.

van Engeland, A. A., et al. (2000). Colpectomy after vaginoplasty in transsexuals. *Obstet. Gynecol.* 95(6) Pt 2: 1006–1008.

van Haarst, E. P., et al. (1998). Metastatic prostatic carcinoma in a male-to-female transsexual. *Br. J. Urol.* 81(5): 776.

van Kesteren, P. J., et al. (1997). Mortality and morbidity in transsexual subjects treated with cross-sex hormones. *Clin. Endocrinol.* 47(3): 337–342.

van Kesteren, P., et al. (1998). Long-term follow-up of bone mineral density and bone metabolism in transsexuals treated with cross-sex hormones. *Clin. Endocrinol.* 48(3): 347–354.

van Staa, T. P, and J. M. Sprafka. (2009). Study of adverse outcomes in women using testosterone therapy. *Maturitas* 62(1): 76–80.

Weyers, S., et al. (2010a). Mammography and breast sonography in transsexual women. *Eur. J. Radiol.* 74(3): 508–513.

Weyers, S., et al. (2010b). Cytology of the 'penile' neovagina in transsexual women. *Cytopathology* 21(2): 111–115.

Wierckx, K., et al. (2012). Long-term evaluation of cross-sex hormone treatment in transsexual persons. *J. Sex. Med.* 9(10): 2641–2651.

Wierckx, K., et al. (2013a). Prevalence of cardiovascular disease and cancer during cross-sex hormone therapy in a large cohort of trans persons: A case-control study. *Eur. J. Endocrinol.* 169(4): 471–478.

Wierckx, K., et al. (2013b). Cross-sex hormone therapy related adverse events: Data from a large gender identity unit. *Endocrine Abstracts* 32: P969.

Wierckx, K., et al. (2014). Cross-sex hormone therapy in trans persons is safe and effective at short-time follow-up: Results from the European Network for the Investigation of Gender Incongruence. *J. Sex. Med.* 11(8): 1999–2011.

Witten, T. M. (2003). Transgender aging: An emerging population and an emerging need. *Rev. Sex.* 12(4): 15–20.

Workowski, K. A., and G. A. Bolan (2015). Sexually transmitted diseases treatment guidelines, 2015. *MMWR* 64.RR-03:1.

6   Mental Health Issues

Griet De Cuypere

Introduction

In discussing the mental health issues of transgender people, it is key to explore how transgenderism is conceptualized and how this conceptualization has changed over the last decades. Already in 1969, in their book *Transsexualism and Sex Reassignment*, Green and Money (1969), through their research in history, mythology, and cultural anthropology, emphasized that "transsexualism" is a long-standing, widespread, and pervasive phenomenon. Gender-variant people exist all over the world and are considered in many different cultures as merely natural variants. Sometimes trans people are seen as more gifted individuals, even having a position between god/goddess and the people (Coleman et al., 1992). In contrast with these cultures, where gender non-conforming behavior is not stigmatized and accepted, the Western world in the mid 20th century has conceptualized transsexualism as a psychotic symptom of a psychiatric disorder that should be treated accordingly. From that moment trans people and their wishes were addressed by medicine properly; the diagnosis of transsexualism made an appearance in the *Diagnostic and Statistical Manual of Mental Disorders,*—third edition (DSM-III) (American Psychiatric Association, 1980) under the diagnostic class of "psychosexual deviations," as a separate, independent psychiatric disorder (Gijs et al., 2014). At that time, gender-confirming medical treatment started to become accepted as the treatment of choice for people suffering from incongruence between their body sex and soul sex. Although the DSM-III criteria contained the exclusion criterion "not due to another mental disorder, such as schizophrenia," it was assumed that individuals with transsexualism generally had a "moderate to severe coexisting personality disturbance" (American Psychiatric Association, 1980).

Thirty years later, a tremendous paradigm shift occurred. Gender variance is no longer considered as a symptom of psychopathology. In 2010, the World Professional Association of Transgender Health (WPATH) released a statement urging the de-psychopathologization of gender variance worldwide:

> The expression of gender characteristics, including identities that are not stereotypically associated with one's assigned sex at birth, is a common

and culturally diverse human phenomenon which should not be judged as inherently pathological or negative. The psychopathologization of gender characteristics and identities reinforces or can prompt stigma, making prejudice and discrimination more likely, rendering transgender and transsexual people more vulnerable to social and legal marginalization and exclusion, and increasing risks to mental and physical well-being. WPATH urges governmental and medical professional organizations to review their policies and practices to eliminate stigma toward gender-variant people.

Although it has been debated whether a diagnosis of "gender identity disorder" should be retained in the new version of the DSM manual, DSM-5 still classifies the diagnosis "gender dysphoria" as a psychiatric disorder (American Psychiatric Association, 2013). The World Health Organization (WHO) proposes, for the upcoming new *International Classification of Diseases* (ICD-11) diagnoses (publication expected in 2017), regarding trans people, that the new diagnoses should be "gender incongruence of adolescence and adulthood" and "gender incongruence of childhood," and that they should be removed from the Mental and Behavioral Disorder chapter, placed in a chapter entitled Conditions Related to Sexual Health (World Health Organization, under continuing revision). With this proposal, WHO acknowledges that the combined stigmatization of being transgender and of having a psychiatric condition is a double burden for transgender people (Drescher et al., 2012).

Although the debate regarding the classification of gender dysphoria or gender incongruence as a psychiatric diagnosis is still ongoing, there is more consensus concerning the effectiveness of the gender-confirming therapies. Also, the benefit for gender-dysphoric individuals of counseling for exploring their gender identity, role, and expression and for making decisions about the gender-confirming therapeutic options is acknowledged. Care for mental health remains a rather important topic in the guidance of gender-dysphoric individuals in the assessment procedure and during the transition, as well as in the referral for hormonal and surgical treatment and of course in the treatment of co-existing mental health concerns (Coleman et al., 2011).

Relationship Mental Health Issues—Transcare

Historical Notes

When, in the 1980s, transgenderism started to be medicalized and gender-confirming medical therapies became accepted, professionals were very cautious in selecting the right person for this kind of irreversible therapy, with the aim of preventing postoperative regret (Cohen-Kettenis & Pfäfflin, 2010). Hormonal and surgical reassignment therapy was only meant for those with extreme gender dysphoria, called "transsexuals." In DSM-III, "transsexualism" was very narrowly defined and there was a direct link to therapy (American Psychiatric Association, 1980). Partial sex reassignment treatment (e.g., only hormonal treatment) was not allowed. The mental health provider was a gate-keeper who screened his/her patient very carefully concerning the degree of gender dysphoria, his/her wish to undergo a total physical and social transition, his/her psychological-psychiatric status to exclude any other psychiatric diagnosis, social functioning, and social support, and other well-documented negative prognostic factors for postoperative failure (Wålinder et al., 1978). The applicant was asked to live in the role of the desired gender without hormones, to evaluate how he/she was coping with the consequences of the social role change. Only after achieving this "real-life test" could the applicant receive hormone treatment (Cohen & Gooren, 1999).

For clinical purposes, a subdivision was made between primary and secondary transsexualism (in transwomen) (Person & Ovesey, 1974a, 1974b). Individuals with primary transsexualism were considered to be asexual without fetishistic arousal in adolescence, in contrast to individuals with secondary transsexualism who experience their cross-gender wishes only after puberty, usually evolving from transvestitism. Many authors at that time recommended that individuals with secondary transsexualism should undergo psychotherapy before having gender-confirming therapy (at that time called sex reassignment therapy) to convince the mental health professional as well as to be convinced themselves that the transgender wish was genuine and remained stable (e.g., Dolan, 1987; Levine & Lothstein, 1981).

A rather similar typology was described in transwomen by Blanchard when describing the "homosexual transsexual" (gender-dysphoric individual who is sexually attracted to individuals of the same sex) and the "non-homosexual transsexual" (gender-dysphoric individual attracted to individuals of the opposite sex) (Blanchard, 1985; Blanchard et al., 1987). According to Blanchard, these different categories have different etiologies. The "non-homosexual transsexual" is an individual who is aroused by thoughts or images of himself as a woman, which can be considered a paraphilia. He seeks gender-confirming surgery to actualize his autogynephilic desires. He wants to "become what he finds sexually desirable," and that is a woman (Lawrence, 2007). Usually he seeks gender-confirming therapy later in life, has to deal with more loss (marriage, family, friends, work), and has more difficulties with social acceptance in the new role after transition (Lawrence, 2003). The "homosexual transsexual" (the androphilic transwoman), on the contrary, has another trajectory. Mostly he is very feminine as a child and has gender dysphoria from childhood on.

Concerning the different typology in transmen, it was believed in the past that they were all attracted to women (Blanchard et al., 1987). This idea has been abandoned since, although as a group transwomen are still considered more homogeneous. Most, but not all, transwomen are indeed gynephilic, applying for gender-confirming therapy at a younger age, with fewer psychological problems and having less postoperative regrets than transwomen (Dolan, 1987; Levine & Lothstein, 1981).

Present ideas

The most important shift in the 21st century is that gender diversity is more accepted, that a variety of treatment options is offered, and that the mental health professional has left behind the gate-keeper's role in working with persons with gender dysphoria.

Although hormone therapy and surgery are considered to be medically necessary to alleviate gender dysphoria in many people (WPATH, 2008), some individuals need only one of these treatment options, and some even need only psychological support and counseling (Bockting, 2008). The individual seeking help for gender dysphoria can find an ally in the mental health professional. Together they can explore the cross-gender feelings and the different ways of expressing these feelings, how to align gender role and gender identity (e.g., partial or full-time), how to make a choice between the different medical treatment options for alleviating gender dysphoria, how to address the negative impact of gender dysphoria and stigma, and how to help to cope with the effects of the transition (Coleman et al., 2011). The diagnosis is nowadays more an all-round joint (trans individual and the mental health professional) exploration/assessment and the decision about the treatment options tailored to the individual needs of the gender-dysphoric client.

Some transgender organizations even voice that mental health professionals are not needed anymore, and are promoting the informed consent model for hormone therapy (Radix & Deutsch, 2015). Still, these protocols are consistent with the guidelines of the *Standards of Care (SOC)* of WPATH, version 7. The requirement is that the health professional (not necessarily mental health professional) who recommends or prescribes hormones should have the necessary knowledge and experience to assess gender dysphoria. The health professional should also inform clients of the effects, limitations, and risks of hormone therapy (Coleman et al., 2011). Individuals without any particular mental health problem, functioning well, with good family support, experiencing no opposition in their transition can indeed transition without the help of any mental health professional. But the *SOC*, version 7, in contrast to these informed consent models, stresses the important role the mental health professional can play in the psychosocial adjustment of individuals who encounter more difficulties in their choice. One of the criteria for hormone therapy as well as for gender-confirming surgery in the *SOC*, version 7, is "if significant medical or mental health concerns are present, they must be reasonably well controlled." It is well documented that clients with gender dysphoria have mental health concerns more often than the general population (Gómez-Gil et al., 2009; Heylens et al., 2014b; Hoshiai et al., 2010) and that the suicide risk in this population is higher (Dhejne et al., 2011; Haas et al., 2011; Liu & Mustanski, 2012). In this context the psychological functioning and mental health concerns of the patient, whether they are related to gender dysphoria and minority stress or not, must be addressed.

The difference in typology of the transpopulation is nowadays less important for clinical-therapeutic purposes and is no longer used in the evaluation of eligibility for gender-confirming therapy. In the *SOC* version 7, for example, description of typologies is omitted and also specifiers are eliminated from the DSM-5 (sexual attraction was a specifier in DSM-IV: American Psychiatric Association, 2000). The two different developmental trajectories described in the DSM-5 are early- versus late-onset trajectory. This division is more used for research purposes. In a recent paper, authors have questioned the adequacy of this categorization within the field of transsexual developments, and called this categorization rather simplistic (Nieder et al., 2011).

Etiological Issues

In medicine the general rule is that diagnosis should precede treatment. If possible the etiology of the diagnosis should be traced to allow a causal treatment. Concerning gender dysphoria, in former times psychoanalytic-trained mental health professionals gave gender-reparative therapy, starting from the idea that the transgender wish was a symptom of supposedly unresolved, unconscious conflicts and could be "cured" by psychotherapy (Pfäfflin, 2007). Psychotherapy intending to alter a person's gender identity is nowadays no longer considered as ethical (Coleman et al., 2011). The literature provided overwhelming evidence that gender-confirming therapy and surgery help to alleviate the distress from gender dysphoria and the accompanying minority stress (Gijs & Brewaeys, 2008; Pfäfflin & Junge, 1998) whatever the etiology of gender dysphoria.

Besides, in the research on the etiology of gender dysphoria there is more evidence indicating biological grounds to explain the development of an atypical gender identity. In fact, genetic research (gene-mapping and twin studies), magnetic resonance imaging studies and post-mortem studies point that way. In the future, interaction between genetic predisposition and environmental factors should be investigated more frequently, as well as the period in which this interaction is situated (age × gene × environment) (De Vries et al., 2013; Steensma et al., 2013).

Co-morbidity

Since gender dysphoria (formerly called gender identity disorder in DSM-IV) is considered as a separate diagnosis, the term used to name the occurrence of other mental health issues is generally "co-morbidity," and in former DSM editions (DSM-III and DSM-IV) was diagnosed on Axes I and II of the DSM. In the general assessment of a client, attending for hormonal or surgical therapy, this evaluation of co-morbidity is of great importance, as one of the criteria for these therapies is that "mental health concerns, if present, must be well controlled" (*SOC* version 7). Severe psychiatric co-morbidity is known as a negative prognostic feature and can lead towards postoperative regret (Gijs & Brewaeys, 2007; Pfäfflin & Junge, 1998).

The prevalence of co-morbid Axis I problems varies across different studies (from 6% to 80%), depending mainly on the methodology applied (à Campo et al., 2003; Heylens et al., 2014b; Lawrence & Zucker, 2012) and on the time point of assessing the co-morbidity. More recent studies from Gómez-Gil et al. (2009) and two Japanese studies (Hoshiai et al., 2010; Terada et al., 2011) described a rate of only 12–20% of the transpopulation with Axis I co-morbidity, mostly depression, anxiety problems, and substance abuse. Psychotic disorders, eating disorders, and body-dysmorphic disorders are not more frequently diagnosed in the trans population compared to the general population (Hepp et al., 2005).

A recent major multicenter European study, including data from 721 transgender individuals attending gender clinics from four different countries at the time of assessment, found that 38% of clients suffered from an affective and anxiety disorder. In particular, the lifetime prevalence of co-morbid Axis I disorder was almost 70%, a figure that is in contrast with the 25% of lifetime prevalence for mental disorders in the general population of Belgium, Germany, the Netherlands, and Norway (Heylens et al., 2014b). Research on lifetime prevalence of Axis I co-morbid problems and comparison with the general population is interesting to untangle the relationship between gender dysphoria and psychiatric co-morbidity.

Another alarming feature is that many studies report a high risk of suicidal ideation, attempts, and suicides in the transgender population, before as well as after gender-confirming therapy (Dhejne et al., 2011; Haas et al., 2011; Hoshiai et al., 2010; Liu & Mustanski, 2012; Motmans et al., 2012; Terada et al., 2012). Discrimination, stigmatization, and psychiatric problems have been identified as provoking factors (Haas et al., 2011). In their study, Terada et al. (2011) demonstrated that the suicidal ideation rate cannot be explained entirely by psychiatric co-morbidity, as in this study 72% of gender-dysphoric individuals without psychiatric co-morbidity had suicidal ideation at some point in their life.

Concerning co-morbidity on Axis II in individuals with gender dysphoria, Lawrence and Zucker (2012) concluded from different studies that the rate varies between 20% and 70%. This high range proves that it is difficult to make comparisons between the different studies. In the large study of Heylens et al. (2014b), only 15% of individuals at the time of attending the gender clinic had a personality disorder; this rate is comparable to the prevalence rate in the general population. Replication of these results would be interesting to eliminate the idea that individuals with gender dysphoria have a personality disorder.

We can conclude that individuals with gender dysphoria both in their lifetime and at the time of attending a gender clinic are suffering more often from mental problems, such as depression and anxiety.

Attention to the co-occurrence of gender dysphoria and autism spectrum disorder is rather new and has started with some case reports (Kraemer et al., 2005; Landén & Rasmussen, 1997). De Vries et al. (2010), some years later, conducted their own research, using a systematic approach. They found that the incidence of autism spectrum disorder is higher (7.8%) in gender-dysphoric children and adolescents than in the general population. Some authors, conceptualizing gender as a component of identity formation that is salient when applied to autism spectrum disorder, advocate that individuals with autism spectrum disorder should have equal rights with regard to treatment for gender dysphoria (van Schalkwyk et al., 2015). Unfortunately, up to the present, only one systematic study in adults has been published. The authors came to the same conclusion as the child psychiatrists, namely that there is a higher prevalence rate of autism spectrum disorder in individuals with gender dysphoria (Pasterski et al., 2014).

How can the interaction between gender dysphoria and mental disorders be explained? There are four models of co-morbidity (Gijs et al., 2014; Lawrence & Zucker, 2012; Links et al., 2012):

1. Gender dysphoria is a symptom of an underlying or more pervasive psychiatric disorder. As pointed out above, this model is outdated in the field of gender dysphoria (psychoanalytic conceptualization) and has only a few followers.
2. The development of "other" psychiatric disorders is due to social stigma as a result of an atypical gender identity: we call this "minority stress." Studies in the homosexual, lesbian, and transgender population prove that minority stress is an important negative determinant in the mental health of these individuals (Meijer, 2007).
3. Common risk factors, biological as well as social, make an individual vulnerable for the development of various psychiatric problems and gender dysphoria (e.g., emotional neglect, sexual abuse, autism spectrum disorder). Although this model can be accepted on theoretical and also on clinical grounds, solid evidence is lacking because prospective longitudinal research on this topic is nearly non-existent.
4. Gender dysphoria in itself, especially the distress and insecurity caused by the experienced gender dysphoria, can lead to psychological problems, and even psychiatric disorders. In this context, some studies noticed (Smith et al., 2005) that individuals with late-onset gender dysphoria had more psychiatric co-morbidity than those with early-onset gender dysphoria. However, this result could not be replicated by Heylens and colleagues (2014b).

The evaluation of co-morbidity and the link between co-morbidity and gender dysphoria is important in the decision-making process of the therapeutic guidance of the patient (Gijs et al., 2014). When the patient is psychotic and gender dysphoria is thought to be a psychotic symptom, the treatment will first focus on the psychotic condition of the individual, and psychotropic medication will be under consideration. When the psychiatric condition is considered more as a consequence of the gender dysphoria (e.g., depression, eating disorder), gender dysphoria should be the focus of the therapy. From clinical experience it is well known that hormonal treatment can be effective also for the co-morbidity. In a recent prospective study on the effects of different steps in gender-confirming therapy on psychopathology it has been proven that the initiation of hormone therapy induces a marked reduction in psychopathology (Heylens et al., 2014a).

Sexual Functioning

Sexuality is an important aspect of human nature and sexual health is a substantial part of mental well-being. Individuals with gender dysphoria usually suffer from genital distress. This has an impact on sexual contacts and partnerships. Sexual desire and sexual organs are targeted by gender-confirming therapy (especially hormone treatment and genital surgery) and consequently also sexuality and sexual functioning. In this context more attention has been drawn nowadays to sexual functioning of gender-dysphoric individuals (Elaut et al., 2010), both before and after gender-confirming therapy (hormone therapy and surgery), in research and in clinical care.

In 2005, Lawrence showed, in contrast with the longstanding idea of gender dysphoria being a "hyposexual condition," that the number of sexual partners in transwomen before gender-confirming therapy was comparable to the number of sexual partners in men in a general American population. Cerwenka et al. (2014) researched sexual health aspects in partnered gender-dysphoric individuals at the start of gender-confirming treatment. Transwomen were frequently found to have androphilic female partners, which is considered non-complementary with their female gender identity. Transmen also often had androphilic female partners, but this is complementary with their male gender identity. In both genders, though, complementary partnership constellations were associated with more negative sexual experiences. This finding may be of clinical interest during the psychological guidance of the gender-dysphoric client.

In some follow-up studies of gender-confirming therapy, sexual outcome has been the focus of research. Klein and Gorzalka (2009) did an extensive review and found that, in transwomen, the rate of hyposexual desire disorder was comparable to the rate in the general female population and that in transmen sexual desire was higher than before treatment, due to testosterone treatment. The ability to reach orgasm was not affected, and both transwomen and transmen reported moderate to high rates of orgasmic functioning. The authors concluded that more research has to be done to understand the effect of the varying types and dosages of cross-sex hormones and the different surgical techniques on sexual functioning.

Tasks of the Mental Health Professional (See in More Detail SOC *Version 7*)

The *SOC* recommend that the mental health professional who is competent to work with gender-dysphoric adults, besides the assessment and treatment of gender dysphoria, should have the clinical competence in the assessment, diagnosis, and treatment of mental health concerns. The mental health professional should have documented credentials from a licensing board or equivalent for that country. Knowledge about the community and public policy issues relevant to the gender-dysphoric client and family is a plus factor (Coleman et al., 2011).

The role of the mental health professional can be multiple: assessor, counselor, psychotherapist, educator, or advocate, depending on the client's needs. The assessment includes an evaluation of the client's gender identity and gender dysphoria, history and development of gender-dysphoric feelings, the impact of the gender-variant feelings on the client's mental health, the support or rejection of family, friends, and peers and the client's coping mechanisms. As a counselor and educator it is also the task of the mental health professional to inform clients regarding the diversity of gender identities and expressions and to discuss and explore the various options available to alleviate gender dysphoria (Coleman et al., 2011). The goal is to find a gender role and gender expression that comfort the client, and to discuss the different possibilities and medical interventions if needed. Sometimes psychotherapy (without the intention of altering a person's gender identity) can help to improve psychological well-being and self-fulfillment. If the decision is a change in gender role, implications for different life aspects need to be discussed (Bockting et al., 2006).

As mentioned above, also the present co-existing mental health concerns need to be evaluated, whether related or not to the gender dysphoria and/or minority stress, and treated. Sometimes psychotropic medications are recommended to control psychic symptomatology. If the client wants feminizing/masculinizing hormonal therapy, the mental health professional can help and guide the client to take fully informed decisions with realistic expectations. The referral letter, according to the *SOC* a requirement for starting hormone therapy, can be drafted by the mental health professional. Although the decision to take hormones to alleviate gender dysphoria is first and foremost the decision of the client, the mental health professional recommending hormonal therapy shares the ethical and legal responsibility for that decision together with the physician who prescribes the hormones (Coleman et al., 2011).

Another task of the mental health professional is to prepare clients who are considering breast/chest surgery and genital surgery (gender-confirming surgery) psychologically and practically to undergo these surgeries. Again, the mental health professional should help to take decisions after ample information about the consequences on different levels, discussing the reproductive options, insuring that the expectations of surgery are realistic, including family and community if needed and as appropriate. Regarding surgical treatments for gender dysphoria, the *SOC* require one referral letter from a qualified mental health professional for breast/chest surgery (e.g., mastectomy, chest reconstruction, or augmentation mammoplasty) and two referrals from two different mental health professionals, who have independently assessed the client, for genital surgery. For transmen these surgeries are hysterectomy and salpingo-oophorectomy, metoidioplasty or phalloplasty and for transwomen, orchiectomy and vaginoplasty. The second referral letter should be from a mental health professional, who has no close psychotherapeutic relationship with the client, but has only an evaluative role. The need for two referral letters for hysterectomy and salpingo-oophorectomy is nowadays under discussion (Bouman et al., 2014; Colebunders et al., 2015).

The mental health professional can have a supportive psychotherapeutic role during the whole process, from exploration of gender identity and gender expression through possible transition, whether a psychological, social transition or a physical transition, towards the postoperative phase. Sometimes, and if the mental health professional and the client feel comfortable with it and it is appropriate, family therapy or group therapy is also an option.

Effectiveness of Gender-Confirming Therapy

As gender-confirming medical therapy was rather controversial in the 1970s, a number of follow-up studies since then have been conducted initially to find support for the hormonal and surgical treatment of individuals with gender dysphoria and afterwards to detect the negative prognostic features and to refine the treatment procedures. A first big review article covering the international follow-up literature of the years 1961–1991 was published in 1998 by Pfäfflin and Junge. They concluded that gender-confirming surgery was effective and that predominantly interdisciplinary treatment approaches were favorable. The regret rate was less than 1% in transmen and 1–1.5% in transwomen. The factors that were contributing to a positive outcome were: living in the desired gender role congruent with clients' gender identity, cross-hormone therapy, counseling and psychotherapy, (quality of) surgery, and legal sex change (Pfäfflin, 2007). Another review paper from Green and Fleming (1990) covering 11 follow-up studies confirmed that gender-confirming therapy reduces the gender dysphoria and enhances the overall well-being of gender-dysphoric individuals.

The authors added that another predictor of successful sex reassignment surgery outcome was "an adequate understanding of what surgery can and cannot do," which is a useful topic of concern in the counseling of clients. It has been demonstrated that clients operated on after 1986 did better than those before 1986 due to a decrease in surgical complications (Eldh et al., 1997).

The results of more recent research and reviews, giving the outcome data from some thousand clients, show that most people are very satisfied after gender-confirming therapy: their gender dysphoria is alleviated, psychological functioning and body satisfaction have improved, and their quality of life has increased. In these follow-up studies psychiatric co-morbidity is diminished, and individual sexual health is increased (Asscheman et al., 2011; De Cuypere et al., 2005; Gijs & Brewaeys, 2007; Murad et al., 2010; Smith et al. 2005).

In general, transmen are doing better than transwomen in these studies, although the difference is not very convincing. The clients who regret having undergone gender-confirming therapy are between 0.5% and 1.5% (Gijs

& Brewaeys, 2008). Lower quality-of-life scores are measured in transgender individuals who are older, less educated, unemployed, who have a low household income, and who are isolated (Motmans et al., 2012). From these different retrospective studies and one prospective study (De Cuypere et al., 2006; Gijs & Brewaeys, 2008; Murad et al., 2010; Smith et al., 2005), the conclusion can be drawn that the worst postoperative outcome is related to psychiatric co-morbidity. This observation has led to the establishment of one of the following criteria in version 7 of the *SOC*: "if significant (medical or) mental health concerns are present, they must be well controlled," a criterion for hormone treatment as well as for gender-confirming surgery.

Although most outcome studies of the last two decades are very positive, there are nevertheless some worrisome papers. The first is from Newfield et al. (2006), reporting lower scores on quality of life for transmen than for the general population. Looking into more detail, one-third of subjects had received no treatment at all. Those transmale participants who had received testosterone reported statistically significant higher quality-of-life scores than those who had not received hormone therapy.

The other paper is a Swedish retrospective study from Dhejne et al. (2011), giving data from more than 10 years after surgery. The authors found that, in comparison with the general population, the trans population reported significantly more admissions to psychiatric clinics, more suicide attempts, and also more suicides. These results were even more striking for transwomen than transmen. Unfortunately, this cohort study gave results only concerning the comparison of mental health with the general population. The study did not compare the pre- and post-surgery prevalence of mental health issues, nor was there a control group who had not received treatment or received treatment other than genital surgery.

Also, in a large Dutch study on trans people after gender-confirming therapy taking hormone treatment, with an average postoperative period of 18.5 years, the mortality due to suicide was more than six times the expected rate (Asscheman et al., 2011). This research has the same drawbacks as the previous one. So no conclusion can be drawn from these studies about the efficacy of gender-confirming treatment. These results do show that individuals, even after physical transition, can remain psychologically vulnerable, and that mental care should be available if needed or wanted (Coleman et al., 2011).

Even if gender-confirming hormonal and surgical therapy has become the gold standard for treating individuals with gender dysphoria for a number of years, the research on effectiveness of gender-confirming therapy has some weaknesses. Randomized controlled studies are very difficult, if not impossible, to perform on ethical grounds. Until recently prospective studies were also scarce. As a consequence, the American Psychiatric Association (APA) Task Force on treatment of gender identity disorder, evaluating follow-up studies on the treatment of gender dysphoria using their "evidence coding system," came to the conclusion that the quality of evidence concerning most aspects of treatment is low and situated in level C (cohort or longitudinal research) (Byne et al., 2012). The report nevertheless recommends that the APA issues a position statement regarding the medical necessity of treatment for gender identity disorder.

Another weakness in research is the lack of investigations on the efficacy of the different treatment procedures: which part of the transition and/or the treatment has the most effect on gender dysphoria and psychological well-being? Recent publications try to give an answer to these questions. Heylens et al. (2014a) in a prospective study have reported that the initiation of hormone treatment had the largest impact on the decrease in psychoneurotic symptoms, more than gender-confirming surgery. This finding can be important to optimize the guiding of clients. Further research is needed.

Clinical Care

Clinical mental care of gender-dysphoric individuals, consisting of: (1) assessment of gender dysphoria and related mental health concerns; (2) providing information about treatment options and possible medical intervention; (3) psychotherapy (during the whole transition process and beyond); and (4) referral for hormone and surgical treatment are very widely described in the *SOC*, version 7 (Coleman et al., 2011). The task of the mental health provider is also discussed above. In this section, although many issues have already been mentioned, we give an outline of the more concrete procedure.

Assessment

Some individuals with gender dysphoria may visit the mental health professional because they want to explore their gender identity and the stress they experience due to gender incongruence, and other related mental health concerns, as well as the various options of gender expression and the feasibility of a possible transition. Other gender-dysphoric individuals may come to the mental health professional with a self-diagnosis and a well-determined goal and treatment wish. Although both kinds of individuals need a different approach, the core task of the mental health professional remains the same.

First of all attention should be drawn to the fact that the relationship between client and mental health professional should be a "working" relationship and that the partners can consider themselves more as allies than as evaluator–client. Only in an atmosphere of understanding, dignity, respect, trust, and safety can clients express themselves without fear, reveal hidden histories and doubts, and come to balanced decisions. Sometimes, there is a lack of confidence between the mental health professional and the client and the work alliance remains strained. In these cases, a separation between assessment and counseling/psychotherapy is recommended (Bockting et al., 2006).

The assessment is based on the client's self-reported history of psychosexual development. The nature and severity of the gender-dysphoric feelings are discussed as well as the importance and connotation of cross-dressing and body-image issues. If a more objective assessment of the degree of gender dysphoria is needed, the validated Utrecht Gender Dysphoria Scale can be used (Kreukels et al., 2012; Steensma et al., 2013) as well as the Gender Identity/ Gender Dysphoria Questionnaire for Adolescents and Adults (Deogracias et al., 2007). A psychological evaluation must reveal whether the client has mental health concerns and how these relate to the gender dysphoria (see above). This is crucial in the decision-making process about the sequence and the kind of treatment. For example, psychotic individuals need psychiatric treatment first. Only if the psychosis is under control, and the gender dysphoria remains, can further treatment options regarding the gender dysphoria be considered. The impact of stigma and of keeping the gender-dysphoric feelings silent for a lifetime is another issue to be discussed. Mental health problems, such as depression, anxiety, addiction, and anorexia, can be due to this (Gijs et al., 2014). Further topics of concern are physical and/or sexual abuse, child–parent relationship, sexuality, and coping mechanisms during the client's lifetime.

An evaluation of the client's social support (family, friends, colleagues, and peers) is also recommended in order to tailor the therapeutic program; for example, isolation is known to be a negative prognostic feature.

Sometimes the assessment can be short. A few sessions can be sufficient if the client has a clear-cut lifelong gender dysphoria, and the treatment wishes are clear. If the client is more hesitant about the nature of his/her feelings, wants to explore different psychological domains, and has more mental health concerns, more time and reflection are needed.

Providing Information

Although the decision of a gender transition (be it social and/or bodily transition) is first and foremost the client's decision, the mental health provider should help the client to make fully informed decisions and discuss other topics, such as implications of the process of coming out, grief and loss, sexual concerns, fertility concerns, and spiritual issues.

Educational sessions about the different possibilities of alleviating gender dysphoria can be important in guiding clients. If a client, together with the mental health professional, comes to the conclusion that he/she is gender-dysphoric, the next step is to come to terms with the diagnosis, to search to alleviate the gender-dysphoric feeling, to question if a gender transition is the best solution, which gender transition should be chosen (social and/or physical), and how to transition. Only after being fully informed of the numerous consequences (psychological, social, physical, sexual, occupational, financial, and legal) (Bockting et al., 2006) of these different possibilities will the client have realistic expectations and be able to make deliberate decisions. When it comes to the information and discussion about physical consequences of medical procedures (e.g., consequences of hormone therapy on fertility), the information is best given by the medical doctors providing these treatments. In contrast with a decade ago, treatment options are far more flexible and tailored to the client's need. Clients do not need to go "the whole way," and should be informed of this.

Psychotherapy

Although *SOC* version 7, in contrast with the previous versions, no longer requires a number of psychotherapy sessions prior to hormone therapy or surgery, psychotherapy is still recommended by the *SOC*. Especially when mental health concerns or relational tensions are noted, psychotherapy can be very helpful. Psychotherapy is about "maximizing a person's overall psychological well-being, quality of life, and self-fulfillment. It can help the individual to explore gender concerns and find ways to alleviate gender dysphoria" (Coleman et al., 2011). Psychotherapy does not aim to alter the individual's gender identity, but to find the gender expression and gender role that gives the best fit and the greatest relief to the individual, taking into account the familial, social, and professional context. Most mental health professionals have in their sessions two parallel foci: first, the strict gender-related care (as well as the consequences of minority stress), and second, the care of other mental health problems (if present).

In the ideal scenario, assessment and psychotherapy can be covered by the same mental health professional and in the same sessions. The precondition for this merge of tasks of the mental health professional is that the assessment, as previously mentioned, can take place in the spirit of an alliance, with respect and trust as the most salient ingredients. Assessment as well as psychotherapy can benefit from this merge.

Sometimes therapy other than individual therapy is needed. In long-term follow-up research it has been demonstrated that individuals who have good familial and social support as well as an adequate professional life have a higher quality of life (Motmans et al., 2012). In this context involving the partner and/or family can be very useful to enhance the familial connections. In some cases it can even be fruitful to give informative sessions at the workplace. This approach can only be considered after thorough discussion and with the consent of the client.

The goal of group psychotherapy of connecting peers with the same life issues (e.g., bereavement) or mental health issues is experiencing the feeling of "not being alone" (universality), learning from each other (interpersonal learning), receiving and giving advice on diverse issues, and feeling supported (Lieberman & Yalom, 1992). These therapeutic factors are also valid for individuals with gender dysphoria, for whom group psychotherapy or peer support group sessions (without a psychotherapist) sometimes can be the first step in socializing.

The psychological guidance does not always (have to) end at the moment the gender-confirming therapy is done and the transition is realized. It has been proven that the client can still benefit from psychotherapy after gender-confirming therapy (Coleman et al., 2011; Rehman et al., 1999). When the body has been adjusted to the gender identity, some clients can find the psychological freedom to do more introspective work and are keen to continue the sessions. Other individuals need to be further supported in the stigma they encounter or for other issues concerning the new gender (e.g., outing in a romantic relationship, intimacy-related concerns, sexuality). After transition, though, most individuals stop the sessions with the mental health professional, and do not want to be considered as "sick or weak." But, by treating the gender dysphoria through gender-confirming therapy, mental health issues are not always solved, and the individual sometimes remains vulnerable (Dhejne et al., 2011).

Referral for Hormone and Surgical Treatment (See Also SOC *Version 7)*

Besides the assessment, education, and psychotherapy, mental health professionals usually prepare the client for hormone and surgical treatment and draft the referral letters.

For hormone treatment, as defined by the *SOC*, the referral letter (only one letter is needed) can also be written by a health professional who is appropriately trained in behavioral health and competent in the assessment of gender dysphoria. The referral letter (or, if the provider is a member of a multidisciplinary gender team, documentation in the client's chart is sufficient) should contain the psychosocial assessment, treatment history, eligibility, and a statement that informed consent has been obtained. As some consequences of hormone treatment can be radical (e.g., affecting reproductive capacity, irreversible lowering of the voice), the mental health professional should check if the client is well informed of these consequences, has realistic expectations, is psychologically prepared to cope with the psychosocial implications, and has been evaluated by a physician to address medical contraindications to hormone use. The co-existing mental concerns, if present, "must be reasonably well controlled" (one of the four criteria for hormone therapy according to the *SOC* version 7), and this is the responsibility of the mental health professional. The presence of psychological co-morbidity does not necessarily preclude hormone therapy, but should at least be managed concurrently with the treatment of the gender dysphoria.

The preparation for surgery is even more thorough, as surgery, especially genital surgery, is totally irreversible. The client can only give informed consent after being fully informed of the consequences of surgery on different domains, about the different surgical procedures, as well as about the different surgeons performing these kinds of surgery. The mental health provider can stimulate, guide, and support the client in his/her research. The prerequisites for surgery are well described in the *SOC* (version 7). The *SOC* provide different criteria for breast/chest surgery (mastectomy, chest reconstruction, or augmentation mammoplasty) than for genital surgery. For breast/chest surgery only one referral letter is needed. Also the criteria for hysterectomy/salpingo-oophorectomy in transmen and orchiectomy in transwomen are different from the criteria used for metoidioplasty or phalloplasty in transmen and vaginoplasty in transwomen. For these latter procedures, "twelve months of living in a gender role that is congruent with their gender identity" is required (Coleman et al., 2011), based on expert clinical consensus that genital gender-confirming surgery without social transition provokes a stressful feeling of incongruence. Living in the gender-congruent role for a whole year gives the client the opportunity to experience the pros and cons of living in the wished gender, and to cope with potential critiques. For genital surgery the *SOC* require two referral letters.

The *SOC* stress that these criteria are only clinical guidelines which can be adapted if needed, according to the uniqueness of a client and of a context.

The *SOC* is also a living document, an exponent of the evolving world. There are now two criteria for surgery under discussion—the "age of majority in a given country" for genital surgery and the necessity for two referral letters for hysterectomy/salpingo-oophorectomy (Bouman et al., 2014; Colebunders et al., 2015).

Conclusion

Although gender dysphoria should not be considered as a mental disorder, the mental health of persons with gender dysphoria can be under threat as the experience of the incongruence between gender and physical appearance can be disturbing in itself, and the expression of transgender feelings can be met with stigma and rejection. There is indeed evidence that individuals with gender dysphoria have more mental health problems. In view of this, clinical care of trans persons consists not only of an assessment of gender dysphoria but also of the related mental health concerns, informing clients about treatment options, psychotherapy (if needed and/or wanted), and referral for hormone and surgical treatment. The mental health professional should establish a respectful working relationship with the client to assist him/her in the decisions necessary to alleviate the gender dysphoria and the feeling of "dysphoria" in general.

References

A Campo, J.M., Nijman, H., Merckelbach, H., & Evers, C. (2003). Psychiatric comorbidity of gender identity disorders: a survey among Dutch psychiatrists. *American Journal of Psychiatry*, 160(7), 1332–1336.

American Psychiatric Association. (1980). *Diagnostic and Statistical Manual of Mental Disorders* (3rd ed.). Washington, DC: American Psychiatric Association.

American Psychiatric Association. (2000). *Diagnostic and Statistical Manual of Mental Disorders* (4th ed., text rev.). Washington, DC: American Psychiatric Association.

American Psychiatric Association. (2013). *Diagnostic and Statistical Manual of Mental Disorders* (5th ed.). Washington, DC: American Psychiatric Association.

Asscheman, H., Giltay, E.J., Megens, J.A.J., de Ronde, W., van Trotsenburg, M.A.A., & Gooren, L.J.G. (2011). A long-term follow-up study of mortality in transsexuals receiving treatment with cross-sex hormones. *European Journal of Endocrinology*, 164(4), 635–642.

Blanchard, R. (1985). Typology of male to female transsexualism. *Archives of Sexual Behavior*, 14(3), 247–258.

Blanchard, R., Clemmensen, L.H., & Steiner, B.W. (1987). Heterosexual and homosexual gender dysphoria. *Archives of Sexual Behavior*, 16(2), 139–152.

Bockting, W.O. (2008). Psychotherapy and the real-life experience: From gender dichotomy to gender diversity. *Sexologies*, 17(4), 211–224.

Bockting, W.O., Knudson, G., & Goldberg, J.M. (2006). Counseling and mental health care for transgender adults and loved ones. *International Journal of Transgenderism*, 9(3/4), 35–82.

Bouman, W.P., Richards, C., Addinall, R.M., Arango de Montis, I., Duisin, D., Esteva, I., et al. (2014). Yes and yes again: Are standards of care which require two referrals for genital reconstructive surgery ethical? *Sexual and Relationship Therapy*, 29(4), 377–389.

Byne, W., Bradley, S., Coleman, E., Eyler, A.E., Green, R., Menvielle, E.J., Meyer-Bahlburg, H.F.L., Pleak, R.R., & Tompkins, D.A. (2012) Report of the APA Task Force on treatment of gender identity disorder. *Archives of Sexual Behavior*, 41(4), 759–796.

Cerwenka, S., Nieder, T. O., Briken, P., Cohen-Kettenis, P. T., Cuypere, G. D., Haraldsen, I. R., Kreukels, B. P. C., & Richter-Appelt, H. (2014). Intimate partnerships and sexual health in gender-dysphoric individuals before the start of medical treatment. *International Journal of Sexual Health*, 26(1), 52–65.

Cohen-Kettenis, P.T., & Gooren L.J.G. (1999). A review of etiology, diagnosis and treatment. *Journal of Psychosomatic Research*, 46(4), 315–333.

Cohen-Kettenis, P.T., & Pfäfflin, F. (2010). The DSM diagnostic criteria for gender identity disorder in adolescents and adults. *Archives of Sexual Behavior*, 39(2), 499–513.

Colebunders, B., De Cuypere, G., & Monstrey, S. (2015). New criteria for sex reassignment surgery: WPATH *Standards of Care* version 7 revisited. *International Journal of Transgenderism*, 16(4), 222–233.

Coleman, E., Colgan, P., & Gooren, L. (1992). Male cross-gender behaviour in Myanmar (Burma): A description of the acault. *Archives of Sexual Behavior*, 21(3), 313–21.

Coleman, E., Bockting, W., Botzer, M., Cohen-Kettenis, P., De Cuypere, G., Feldman, J., et al. (2011). Standards of care for the health of transsexual, transgender, and gender nonconforming people, 7th version. *International Journal of Transgenderism*, 13(4), 165–232.

De Cuypere, G., T'Sjoen, G., Beerten, R., Selvaggi, G., De Sutter, P., Hoebeke, P., Monstrey, S., Vansteenwegen, A., & Rubens, R. (2005). Sexual and physical health after sex reassignment surgery. *Archives of Sexual Behaviour*, 34, 6(6), 679–690.

De Cuypere, G., Elaut, E., Heylens, G., Van Maele, G., Selvaggi, G., T'Sjoen, G., Rubens, R., Hoebeke, P., & Monstrey, S. (2006). Long-term follow-up: Psychosocial outcome of Belgian transsexuals after sex reassignment surgery. *Sexologies*, 15(2), 126–133.

Deogracias, J.J., Johnson, L.L., Meyer-Bahlburg, H.F.L., Kessler, S.J., Schober, J.M., & Zucker, K.J. (2007). The gender identity/gender dysphoria questionnaire for adolescents and adults. *Journal of Sex Research*, 44(4), 370–379.

De Vries, A.L.C., Noens, I.L.J., Cohen-Kettenis, P.T., van Berckelaer-Onnes, I.A., & Doreleijers, T.A. (2010). Autism spectrum disorders in gender dysphoric children and adolescents. *Journal of Autism and Development Disorders*, 40(8), 930–936.

De Vries, A.L.C., Kreukels, B.P.C., Steensma, T.D., & McGuire, J.K. (2013). Gender identity development: a biopsychosocial perspective (pp. 53–80). In: *Gender Dysphoria and Disorders of Sex Development: Progress in Care and Knowledge* (Eds. Kreukels, B.P.C., Steensma, T.D., & de Vries, A.L.C.). New York: Springer.

Dhejne, C., Lichtenstein, P., Boman, M., Johansson, A., Langstrom, N., & Landen, M. (2011). Long-term follow-up of transsexual persons undergoing sex reassignment surgery: Cohort study Sweden. *PLosS One*, 22 e16885.

Dolan, J.O. (1987). Transsexualism: Syndrome or symptom? *Canadian Journal of Psychiatry*, 32(8), 666–673.

Drescher, J., Cohen-Kettenis, P., & Winter, S. (2012). Minding the body: Situating gender identity diagnoses in the ICD-11. *International Review of Psychiatry*, 24(6), 568–577.

Elaut, E., Bogaert, V., De Cuypere, G., Weyers, S., Gijs, L., Kaufman, J-M., & T'Sjoen, G. (2010). Contribution of androgen receptor sensitivity to the relation between sexual desire and testosterone: an exploration in male-to-female transsexuals. *Journal of Endocrinological Investigation*, 33(1), 37–41.

Eldh, J., Berg, A., & Gustafsson, M. (1997). Long-term follow-up after sex reassignment surgery. *Scandinavian Journal of Plastic and Reconstructive Surgery and Hand Surgery*, 31(1), 39–45.

Gijs, L., & Brewaeys, A. (2007). Surgical treatment of gender dysphoria in adults and adolescents: Recent developments, effectiveness, and challenges. *Annual Review of Sex Research*, 18(1), 178–224.

Gijs, L., van der Putten-Bierman, E., & De Cuypere, G. (2014). Psychiatric comorbidity in adults with gender identity problems. In: *Gender Dysphoria and Disorders of Sex Development: Progress in Care and Knowledge* (Eds. Kreukels, B.P.C., Steensma, T.D., & de Vries, A.L.C.). New-York: Springer.

Gómez-Gil, E., Trilla, A., Salaremo, M., Godás, T., & Valdés, M. (2009). Socio-demographic, clinical, and psychiatric characteristics of transsexuals from Spain. *Archives of Sexual Behavior*, 38(3), 378–392.

Green, R., & Fleming, D. (1990). Transsexual surgery follow-up: Status in the 1990s. *Annual Review of Sex Research*, 1(1), 163–174.

Green, R., & Money, J. (1969). *Transsexualism and Sex Reassignment*. Baltimore: Johns Hopkins Press.

Haas, A.P., Eliason, M., Mays, V.M., Mathy, R.M., Cochran, S.D., D'Augelli, A.R., et al. (2011). Suicide and suicide risk in lesbian, gay, bisexual, and transgender populations: Review and recommendations. *Journal of Homosexuality*, 58(1), 10–51.

Hepp, U., Kraemer, B., Schnyder, U., Miller, N., & Delsignore, A. (2005). Psychiatric comorbidity in gender identity disorder. *Journal of Psychosomatic Research*, 58(3), 259–61.

Heylens, G., Verroken, C., De Cock, S., T'Sjoen, G., & De Cuypere, G (2014a). Effect of different steps in gender reassignment therapy on psychopathology: A prospective study of persons with a gender identity disorder. *Journal of Sexual Medicine*, 11(1), 119–126.

Heylens, G., Elaut, E., Kreukels, B.P., Paap, M.C., Cerwenka, S., Richter-Appelt, H., Cohen-Kettenis, P.T., Haraldsen, I.R., & De Cuypere, G. (2014b). Psychiatric characteristics in transsexual individuals: Multicentre study in four European countries. *British Journal of Psychiatry*, 204(2), 151–6.

Hoshiai, M., Matsumoto, Y., Sato, T., Ohnishi, M., Okabe, N., Kishimoto, Y., Terada, S., & Kuroda, S. (2010). Psychiatric comorbidity among patients with gender identity disorder. *Psychiatry and Clinical Neurosciences*, 64(5), 514–519.

Klein, C., & Gorzalka, B.B. (2009). Sexual functioning in transsexuals following hormone therapy and genital surgery: A review. *Journal of Sexual Medicine*, 6(11), 2922–2939.

Kraemer, B., Delsignore, A., Gundelfinger, R., Schnyder, U, & Hepp, U. (2005). Comorbidity of Asperger syndrome and gender identity disorder. *European Child and Adolescent Psychiatry*, 14(5), 292–296.

Kreukels, B.P.C., Haraldsen, I.R., De Cuypere, G., Richter-Appelt, H., Gijs, L., & Cohen-Kettenis, P.T. (2012). A European network for the investigation of gender incongruence: the ENIGI initiative. *European Psychiatry*, 27(6), 445–450.

Landén, M., & Rasmussen, P. (1997). Gender identity disorder in a girl with autism – a case report. *European Child and Adolescent Psychiatry*, 6(3), 170–173.

Lieberman, M.A., & Yalom, I. (1992). Brief group psychotherapy for the spousally bereaved: A controlled study. *International Journal of Group Psychotherapy*, 42(1), 117–132,

Links, P., Ansari, J., Fazalullasha, F., & Shah, R. (2012). The relationship of personality disorders and Axis I clinical disorders (pp. 237–259). In: *The Oxford Handbook of Personality Disorders* (Ed. Widiger, T.). Oxford: Oxford University Press.

Liu, R.T., & Mustanski, B. (2012). Suicidal ideation and self-harm in lesbian, gay, bisexual, and transgender youth. *American Journal of Preventive Medicine*, 42(3), 221–8.

Lawrence, A. (2003). Factors associated with satisfaction or regret following male-to-female sex reassignment surgery. *Archives of Sexual Behavior*, 32(4), 299–315.

Lawrence, A.A. (2005). Sexuality before and after male-to-female sex reassignment surgery. *Archives of Sexual Behavior*, 34(2), 147–166.

Lawrence, A.A. (2007). Becoming what we love: Autogynephilic transsexualism conceptualized as an expression of romantic love. *Perspectives in Biology and Medicine*, 50(4), 506–520.

Lawrence, A., & Zucker, K. (2012). Gender identity disorders (pp. 601–635). In *Adult Psychopathology and Diagnosis* (6th ed.) (Eds. Hersen, M., Beidel, D.). London: Wiley.

Levine, S.B., & Lothstein, L.M. (1981). Transsexualism or the gender dysphoria syndromes. *Journal of Sex & Marital Therapy*, 7(2), 85–113.

Meijer, I. (2007). Prejudice and discrimination as social stressors (pp. 222–267). In: *The Health of Sexual Minorities: Public Health Perspectives on Lesbian, Gay, Bisexual and Transgender Populations* (Eds. Meijer, I., & Northridge, M.). New York: Springer.

Motmans, J., Meier, P., Ponnet, K., & T'Sjoen, G. (2012). Female and male transgender quality of life: socioeconomic and medical differences. *Journal of Sexual Medicine*, 9(3), 743–750.

Murad, M.H., Elamin, M.B., Garcia, M.Z., Mullan, R.J., Murad, A. Erwin, P.J., & Montori, V.M. (2010). Hormonal therapy and sex reassignment: A systematic review and meta-analysis of quality of life and psychosocial outcomes. *Clinical Endocrinology*, 72(2), 214–231.

Newfield, E., Hart, S., Dibble, S., & Kohler, L. (2006). Female-to-male transgender quality of life. *Quality of Life Research*, 15(9), 1447–1457.

Nieder, T. O., Herff, M., Cerwenka, S., Preuss, W. F., Cohen-Kettenis, P. T., De Cuypere, G., Haraldsen, I., & Richter-Appelt, H. (2011). Age of onset and sexual orientation in transsexual males and females. *Journal of Sexual Medicine*, 8(3), 783–791.

Pasterski, V., Gilligan, L., & Curtis, R. (2014). Traits of autism spectrum disorders in adults with gender dysphoria. *Archives of Sexual Behavior*, 43(2), 387–393.

Person, E., & Ovesey, L. (1974a). The transsexual syndrome in males. Primary transsexualism. *American Journal of Psychotherapy*, 28(4), 4–20.

Person, E., & Ovesey, L. (1974b). The transsexual syndrome in males. Secondary transsexualism. *American Journal of Psychotherapy*, 28(4), 174–193.

Pfäfflin, F. (2007). Mental health issues (pp. 169–184). In: *Principles of Transgender Medicine and Surgery* (Eds. Ettner, R., Monstrey, S., & Eyler, A.E.). New York: The Haworth Press.

Pfäfflin, F., & Junge, A. (1998). Sex reassignment. Thirty years of international follow-up studies after sex reassignment surgery: A comprehensive review, 1961–1991. *International Journal of Transgenderism. Book Section.* Accessed 4 June, 2015; http://web.archive.org/web/.

Radix, A., & Deutsch, M. (2015). Transgender health program protocol at the Callen Lorde Community Health Center: the informed consent model of care. Paper presented at Transgender Health Care in Europe. First biennial conference of EPATH, Ghent, Belgium.

Rehman, J., Lazer, S., Benet, A., Schaeffer, L., & Melman, A. (1999). The reported sex and surgery satisfaction of 28 postoperative male-to-female transsexual patients. *Archives of Sexual Behavior*, 28(1), 71–89.

Smith, Y.L.S., Van Goozen, S.H.M., Kuiper A.J., & Cohen-Kettenis, P.T. (2005). Sex reassignment: Outcomes and predictors of treatment for adolescent and adult transsexuals. *Psychological Medicine*, 35(1), 89–99.

Steensma, T.D., Kreukels, B.P.C., de Vries, A.L.C., & Cohen-Kettenis, P.T. (2013). Gender identity development in adolescence. *Hormones & Behaviour*, 64(2), 288–297.

Terada, S., Matsumoto, Y., Sato, T., Okabe, N., Kishimoto, Y., & Uchitomi, Y. (2011). Suicidal ideation among patients with gender identity disorder. *Psychiatry Research*, 190(1), 159–162.

van Schalkwyk, G.I., Klingensmith, K., & Volkmar, F.R. (2015). Gender identity and autism spectrum disorders. *Yale Journal of Biology and Medicine*, 88(1), 81–83.

Wålinder, J., Lundström, B., & Thuwe, I. (1978). Prognostic factors in the assessment of male transsexuals for sex reassignment. *British Journal of Psychiatry*, 132(1), 16–20.

World Health Organization (under continuing revision). ICD-11 Beta Draft. Retrieved April 15th 2015, from http://apps.who.int/classifications/icd11/browse/l-m/en.

World Professional Association of Transgender Health. (2008). WPATH clarification on medical necessity of treatment, sex reassignment and insurance coverage for transgender and transsexual people worldwide. Retrieved February 16th 2016, from http:/www.wpath.org.

World Professional Association of Transgender Health. (2010). WPATH de-psychopathologisation statement. Retrieved February 16th 2016, from http:/www.wpath.org.

7 Psychotherapy with Transgender People

Lin Fraser and Griet De Cuypere

Introduction

Who Comes to Therapy

People with transgender issues seeking transgender health care can be subdivided more or less into two categories: those who have made their self-diagnosis of being "gender-dysphoric" and wanting a medical treatment to alleviate the gender dysphoria without specific psychological needs, and those who come to the mental health provider/psychotherapist with questions such as: "Who am I? And where do I fit in this world?" People in this group typically want to explore questions having to do with who they are as a gendered person and how they can relate to others as their authentic gendered self, whether those others be partners, family members, their work environment, communities, or in their spiritual life. For the latter group, psychotherapy can be useful.

Invisibility, Stigma, and the Importance of the Therapy Relationship

For trans people, good mental health may be impeded by the following factors that can lead to psychological issues later addressed in therapy. First, many recognize a mismatch between the sex they were assigned at birth and the gender they know themselves to be (gender/body incongruence) (De Cuypere et al., 2013). The development of a comfortable gender identity is impaired because they have not received the requisite social feedback necessary for healthy identity development in their authentic gender (Fraser, 2009a). The true gendered self is often invisible to others and develops in secret. Second, as they seek to express (emotionally and physically) who they experience themselves to be, they are exposed to stigma and rejection (Bockting, 2014; Fraser, 2009a).

The therapy environment and relationship with the therapist may initially be the only safe place clients have ever known where they can sort out who they are and where they fit in the world. It may be the first place they have ever talked about their unease experienced by the incongruence between body and gender and then had the opportunity to express and then listen to their own words without shame and in the presence of a compassionate other. The therapy relationship may serve as a psychosocial corrective for their initial gendered invisibility and provide a safe harbor from the ensuing stigma. Therefore, the value of therapy and the therapy relationship cannot be overestimated.

Introductory Basic Concepts

Sexual Identity and Gender Identity

When working with trans people, it is important to realize that one is working with identity, specifically gender identity, which is not to be confused with sexual orientation or even biologic sex, although the latter are important.

The four components of sexual identity (Shively & DeCecco, 1977) include biologic sex, gender identity, gender role, and sexual orientation, but it is important not to conflate gender identity with the other factors, even though all will be discussed in therapy. The work primarily is a search for *who am I* in a *gendered* sense. For example, the overall goal of the *Standards of Care* is:

> to provide clinical guidance for health professionals to assist transsexual, transgender, and gender nonconforming people with safe and effective pathways to achieving lasting personal comfort with their **gendered** selves, in order to maximize their overall health, psychological well being, and self-fulfillment (Coleman et al., 2011).

People come to therapy to sort out the questions of who am I? How do I express who I am and, adjunctively, who do I love and also, who will love me? And what does my sexed body have to do with it? The therapist needs to be aware that these questions will be explored repeatedly, and there is much repetition in the work. Therapy provides a safe place to explore these questions. Since it takes time to form, develop, and consolidate a coherent gendered self, capable of healthy emotional and physical relationships, therapy can also be long-term.

Paradigm Shift

Another important concept is that our understanding has evolved from a binary (man, woman, boy, girl) to a spectrum perspective of gender (Bockting, 2008; Ekins & King, 2006; Fraser & Knudson, 2015). The history of trans health and the *Standards of Care* have evolved in parallel from a sex change model to one of overall health and individualized care, where gender is seen as diverse, and may be experienced in multiple ways (Coleman et al., 2011).

The clinician needs to hold both binary and spectrum perspectives in mind, as clients differ regarding their understanding of gender in general and their own gender identity specifically. Younger people coming to the clinician's office may now identify outside the gender binary and the clinician can expect to see potentially more complex configurations of sex and gender, pronoun use, more fluidity of sex and gender identities and body images than those who operate in the binary

(Bockting, 2008; Katz-Wise et al., 2015; Nestle et al., 2002; Nieder et al., 2014; Siebler, 2012). Many, however, still hold the binary gender self-concept and plan on a full medical transition.

The clinician needs to hold the space for multiple outcomes, a possible changing sense of identity and sexual orientation over time regardless of the paradigm. People may also settle into a sexual identity only to have it evolve as life events and circumstances change.

Care Over the Lifespan

Another thing to keep in mind is that the therapist's job may be lifelong. People return to therapy over the years with issues that may or may not have anything to do with gender. Although not so true today, there is still a dearth of knowledgeable practitioners available. The earliest *Standards of Care* (Walker et al., 1979) noted that clinicians in this field do far more than might be expected in other endeavors. Most people feel that working in the field is a calling requiring more than the normal commitment expected of health care providers.

Therapeutic Approach

Theories and Therapies

Therapy with trans people addresses concerns related to finding, strengthening, and expressing one's authentic gendered self and then learning to be in relationships as that self.

Many theories and systems of psychotherapy may be useful in helping trans people develop their authentic gender identity. For example, narrative therapy (Lev, 2004; White, 2007) may be useful in helping people construct a narrative that makes sense over time, to re-author and construct a storyline that gives meaning to their lives about who they are and how they got to be that way. For psychodynamic therapists, working with trans people involves a focus on the development of a coherent identity, on the importance of relationships, on the sense of connectedness, including the development of empathy, on how early patterns and self-representations continue over time, and how relational therapy based on insight, empathy, and compassion can modify unconscious or painful processes (Westen, 1998).

Jungian depth therapy may be useful because psychotherapy from a Jungian perspective is about fostering individuation, "being who the person is meant to be" (Wheelwright, 1982), and addresses questions of meaning and expansion of consciousness (Stein, 1998). The goal is to help clients develop a healthy self and find meaning in relation to their own ego (the self with a small "s"); to others (e.g., intimate partner, family, friends, and community); to work; and to the Self (with a big "S," which some call God or Higher Self).

Individuation is uniquely challenging for transgender people because in order to be who they were meant to be, they must challenge societal norms, expectations of family and loved ones, and what others tell them they are meant to be. They must challenge the generally accepted certainty of the stability of biological sex and gender that most believe to be fixed and immutable. A Jungian perspective works well with transgender people, however, because it is not as concerned with cultural rules and conformity as other perspectives and is about developing who one uniquely is in the larger world (Fraser, 2009a).

Any theories and therapies concerned with the development of a self (Kohut, 1971, 1977, 1982) and identity formation may be useful—for example, the concepts of mirroring (Devor, 2004; Lacan, 1949; Winnicott, 1971,) and attachment theory (Ainsworth et al., 1978; Bowlby, 1969, 1973), the ideas of good-enough mothering (Winnicott, 1958, 1965), stages of healthy identity development (Erickson, 1950), and relational psychotherapies (Duncan et al., 2010). Even early sociology theory on psychosocial processes to develop a self based on the reflections of others (Cooley, 1902), and newer theories on relational intersubjective psychotherapies (Kahn, 1997), may also be helpful. Other therapies such as cognitive behavioral therapy may provide useful tools and methods to cope with some of the co-occurring conditions that may emerge as a result of invisibility and stigma.

As in any good therapy, the most important practice is to listen empathically to clients, to listen carefully to the story they are telling you, to believe that they are the architect of their own narrative, and to trust in one's clinical training. Because our understanding of gender is rapidly changing, trans narratives may provide a laboratory for ongoing and continued understanding about what it means to be a gendered person (Pula, 2015) and the clinician needs to maintain an attitude of flexibility and willingness to let go of old paradigms (Coleman, 2003).

Compassionate Neutrality

The therapist's stance of compassionate neutrality is the same as in any good therapy. The therapist needs to be mindful that the relationship in the room, no matter the excitement or upheaval in the outside world, the dramatic changes in the culture, or the tumult of the individual client's life, remains an anchor and an oasis. A hospitable, welcoming, quiet, and liminal space creates the environment where change can occur (Nouwen, 1975).

Power of Words

With trans people, it is especially important to help people put into words and articulate feelings that are often inchoate, deeply personal, and mysterious. What is gender anyway and what is my gender? The recognition of hearing one's own words about gender can be quite powerful. The power of saying them repeatedly cannot be overestimated. Often there are no words to describe what people are feeling, and then it is important to sit in silence as they struggle to articulate their experience of gender.

Patience

One of the biggest challenges involves the complexity of what might be seen, the multiple iterations and fluidity of identity, and its changes over time that may occur. The clinician needs to maintain a respect for variation, differences in cultural understanding of gender, where the person stands in history and in relationships, and the pushes and pulls in multiple directions. Hence the importance of good clinical training and appreciation for one's own story, the importance of being a patient anchor over time in a shifting internal and external landscape, maintaining space for multiple, changing, and moving parts of sexual identity, gender identity, gender role, and sexual orientation, with the most important being gender identity, should not be underestimated.

Awareness of Potential Blind Spots

Potential blindness may occur on either side of the political spectrum. For example, an experienced clinician has the capacity to recognize potential countertransference that might be overly affirming and identify with the movement on the one hand, or be uncomfortable with medical interventions on apparently healthy tissue on the other, either of which can interfere with good therapy and compassionate neutrality. People who have difficulty with mystery and complexity with a desire for simple answers and an inability to challenge preconceived ideas may need a good deal of mentoring to feel comfortable in the field.

Therapy with the Whole Person

Like anyone who comes to therapy, trans people bring a multiplicity of issues and identities aside from gender to the consulting room. It is important to keep in mind that therapy involves interplay between gender-related issues and whatever else comes up for discussion. Race, class, and cultural identities intersect with gender and sexuality and their interplay may come up as part of the work. The clinician may be selected for his or her knowledge of gender identity, but the therapy itself may be only tangentially related to that area of expertise. For others, gender may be the primary focus, especially in the beginning stages, and then may expand over time to address other concerns.

A Developmental Model of Transgender Identity

The core of the work is to help the person find, build, and express the authentic gendered self as it emerges in therapy, to develop a coherent narrative in the presence of a compassionate other, and then to sort out how best to express that self in the world with dignity and without shame. For some this may include masculinizing and feminizing medical interventions. A description of a composite trans person is given, growing up from childhood through old age. Critical times in development (childhood, adolescence, coming out, moving into a more stable identity, integration and consolidation of a gendered presentation, and, finally, aging) will be described along with examples of issues that emerge at each stage and how they may be addressed later in therapy. Keep in mind that this is a general composite picture and therapy is individualized. The descriptions do not apply to everyone.

Childhood

The key developmental tasks of childhood have to do with first attachment, the development of basic trust, followed by separation and identification as a gendered self. For the trans person, it is often experienced as the development of what feels like a false self and what some term a shell identity, as mostly no trans person is able to express the core authentic gendered self.

As the trans child grows, resolution is often along dual lines of development, a core inchoate but true gendered self and a false self, the latter mirrored by society and the former often a shameful secret (Fraser, 2009a).

In thinking about clients' childhood, it may be helpful for the clinician to address the following questions to help guide the therapy over time:

- In terms of attachment, how is that happening? How do they separate in a gendered way and from whom? How is that impacting the therapeutic relationship?
- How have they been mirrored in terms of a construction of self and what should the clinician be doing to strengthen that construction now?

Some potential concerns that may emerge as a result of these developmental deficits related to gender identity might include the following attributes that are often seen in therapy:

- shy, isolated, introverted, depressed;
- mistrustful, a good actor, reactive, lonely;
- rich internal fantasy world;
- compartmentalization and self-sufficiency;
- difficulty locating core sense of self;
- mistrust of one's own feelings;
- shameful internalized transphobia.

Adolescence and Pre-Transition

Adolescence can be a time of a betrayal of the body but also confusion about the body.

Adolescents may report experiencing a dissociation and lack of feeling in their gendered parts as puberty erupts. Many have had a fantasy that they would have the puberty that they had imagined. The reality can be a huge disappointment. They report identity issues and "not fitting in," feeling separate and isolated from others their age. They have no one to talk to and many feel guilty and shameful. Many report depression and suicidality (Haas et al., 2011; Heylens et al., 2014).

For some, there is no understanding of their feelings and this confusion may continue until they come to, and even during much of, therapy. The feeling has no name, as many just know they feel "not male" or "not female," but don't necessarily identify with being trans, although some do. Some develop identification with characters from science fiction that are not fully human, such as androids or cyborgs. Variations on the term "weird" may be used a lot and many say, "I'm the only one." Some report starting to spend time with machines and having a comfort with technology rather than with people. These patterns of working with computers, for example, may be lifelong. Many are quite concrete and spend a good deal of time alone.

If they start wearing clothing in their preferred gender, many spend time in front of the mirror trying to see themselves in their own image, rather than the image reflected back by society. The development of sexuality can be quite confusing, especially for those assigned male, as there can be an erotic component to the time spent in front of the mirror. Masturbatory fantasies may not include other people in these cases and be more about imagining themselves a woman. The question of "who am I attracted to?" for anyone on the spectrum can be confusing because they are asking, "who is my gendered self that is feeling the attraction?" Or the attraction is beginning to be split, toward an inner image of self as the preferred gender as well as toward others.

Gender identity and sexuality can also be fluid and for those experiencing numbness, they can also feel asexual. Imagining being touched in the wrong anatomy can be repulsive. Some, particularly those assigned female at birth, report sexual abuse which they speculate might at least partially have a connection to the development of their trans feelings (Kersting et al., 2003). Although there is little evidence of a psychological precursor to most trans feelings, it is important to pay attention to all narratives, including those with seemingly psychological components, to help make sense of a life. Understanding the how and why of a story line can be useful for many.

Finally, adolescence can be a very painful time and many of these feelings continue into adulthood. Many fear being in intimate relationships and experience continued shame and confusion about their body and identity.

Adulthood—Paths to Trans and Other Related Identities

For adults who come to therapy, the clinician can expect to see a wide range of gender identities, from the more stable to the more fluid, as there are many variations on a spectrum. They may come in at any age and position on the transition path and may have multiple other issues besides gender identity. In terms of gender and sexuality, however, the clinician may expect to see the following:

- Those with paths that are rather straightforward gender identities are stable over time, and they report feeling trans from earliest memories, with a fixed gender identity, and sexual orientation always in a certain direction. Many report their identities as having a strong biogenetic component.
- Others have a stable transgender identity from earliest memory but have a more fluid sexual orientation, especially after transition.
- Others have a more fluid gender identity with an inchoate and fluctuating development and recognition of their trans identity, which may have a late onset and late transition, but, once recognized, the trans outcome is fixed.
- Others are quite complex. Their identity is more fluid and may have a fluctuating gender identity, one that is waxing and waning due to sometimes-identifiable stressors and life events. The person doesn't know which direction, if any, the psyche wants to go and the outcome is unknown. For some, fluidity itself seems to be the outcome. Some may not want to transition but may have cross-gender genital and sexual eroticism, but may still want to explore various medical interventions.
- More recently, people are identifying on a trans masculine or trans feminine spectrum. Large numbers of non-binary or gender non-conforming people are presenting for therapy and may want to explore a menu of possible medical interventions. People in this group may have a multitude of terms that they use to describe their experience of gender.
- Still others don't identify as trans but may elect to see a gender specialist. Some may identify as eunuchs or a variation thereof and may want therapy or medical interventions (Johnson, 2010; Johnson & Irwig, 2014; Vale et al., 2010).
- Some may be uncomfortable with their gendered body parts but report being comfortable with their gender identity. They may want to explore these feelings and/or receive referrals for surgeries.
- Some will come in because they are sexually attracted to trans people with a mix of self-gendered images themselves.

Adulthood: Co-Occurring Conditions

It is important to remember that most people come to therapy with more than one issue and some have dual or multiple diagnoses (American Psychiatric Association, 2013; Rachlin & Lev, 2011). These diagnoses may be connected to their gender issues or they may be independent but they should be addressed in tandem with their gender concerns.

Some of the more common ones, as discussed in Chapter 6, include depression, suicidality, anxiety, obsessive-compulsive disorder, post-traumatic stress disorder (PTSD), dissociation, and autism spectrum.

Trauma, PTSD, and Dissociation

Numerous reports suggest that painful upbringing, minority stress (Bockting, 2014), and repeated micro aggressions (Nadal, 2012) contribute to trauma symptoms and PTSD in many trans clients. Some are victims of repeated sexual abuse that may also contribute to the development of dissociative identity disorder in some cases. Dissociation is a common symptom.

Autism Spectrum

More recent research suggests a possible overlap between autism spectrum disorder and gender dysphoria in a number of cases (De Vries et al., 2010; Jacobs et al., 2014; Robinow, 2009). Although the reasons are poorly understood for this overlap, the parallels of difficulty putting thoughts and feelings into words are notable. Others have difficulty with symbolization and are quite concrete, as noted earlier.

In addition, as noted by Rachlin and Lev (2011), therapy can be complicated when people present with issues of substance abuse (Institute of Medicine, 2011), severe psychiatric and cognitive conditions, relational difficulties, or severe Axis II disorders.

Some co-occurring conditions will be alleviated as gender dysphoria decreases, especially anxiety and depression. Substance abuse may be directly related to the degree of dysphoria, as some people use substances as a way to deal with gender dysphoria. Once treated, the use of substances may decrease, although this is not always the case. Rarely does the dysphoria decrease once the person gets substance abuse treatment.

Co-morbidity has been discussed extensively in Chapter 6.

Adulthood: Concerns Raised During This Phase

Issues described in the sections on childhood and adolescence continue into adulthood. The clinician may hear variations on themes about identity, bodily discomfort, and sexuality, concerns about relationships, and especially worries about rejection at home and work.

For example, many feel extreme intrapsychic pressure to transition but also experience worries about coming out to family and friends. Although they may not be ambivalent about the direction they want to go, they may worry about how to negotiate relationships and work, imagining potential rejection. Many still feel guilt and shame about their identity and experience much-internalized transphobia. In therapy, many report oscillation, paralysis, and sometimes even hopelessness. The impact of stigma and minority stress over the lifespan cannot be overemphasized.

Whether they plan on transitioning or not, many struggle with the ongoing issue of authenticity, asking, "What do I really feel? What else may be going on? Am I really trans? I know I'm trans but does that mean I should transition?

I'm not sure I'm trans but I am uncomfortable with my body and am not sure what to do about it. Where do I best fit on the gender spectrum?"

Others have complications with sorting out sexuality and feel much bodily discomfort. Sexuality can be complicated and they wonder what will happen over time. Some people assigned male at birth are concerned and feel shame about the role of sexuality in the development of their gender identity.

Those who go on hormones often report feeling like they are having a second adolescence. They may experience the hormonal feelings of a younger person finally having the "right" hormones in their bodies combined with the life experience of an older person. Some experience dramatic changes, for example, a trans man on testosterone, which may include having a stronger sex drive. Trans women are often relieved not to be reminded of unwanted body parts, as many no longer have early-morning erections.

Adulthood: Clinician's Role

1. The task of the therapist is to create a welcoming, hospitable space, to provide a safe harbor for developing trust and safety in the midst of stigma. For many, the therapist's job is to help build a self that may be initially quite vulnerable (which may involve a certain degree of reparenting) and to provide an emotional corrective for parts of the psyche that have been invisible, unmirrored, and/or stigmatized so that a coherent self may emerge. Ideally, the therapy relationship itself may provide an antidote to some of the shame.

2. Another job of the therapist is, without agenda, to help people imagine potential multiple possibilities or outcomes. There is no one right path for everyone and the therapist can help clarify what factors might need to be taken into account when making decisions about next steps. Some people have quite complex gender identities and sexualities, as noted earlier, and may need time sorting out the ramifications of transition on all they have built before or whether they might be better suited for other outcomes. Some can't imagine life with the potential impending losses, as they have built quite comfortable lives prior to coming to therapy, but also feel compelled to transition due to the degree of dysphoria. People who identify as gender non-conforming may need help deciding if medical interventions are right for them. Others might feel ready to transition but need guidance.

   The therapist guides the individuation process and the expansion of consciousness, which includes understanding all parts of one's psyche so that better and more conscious choices can be made.

3. For those who decide to start hormones, part of the work involves providing information and then monitoring the psychological and physical impact of hormones on identity development. The same is true for surgery, which also involves writing letters of referral. This process has been described in detail in Chapter 6.

4. In some situations it may be appropriate to bring other family members into the consulting room, as the client is not the only one affected by his or her trans identity and transitions. Whether the clinician refers to another clinician for family or couples counseling needs to be addressed in therapy, with a description of the pros and cons of each approach.

Another important aspect to consider is that family members are also going through a shift in identity (Emerson & Rosenfeld, 1996). It can be a major change for partners to be seen in the eyes of the world as newly straight or gay if their identity is not fluid, or if they hadn't known their partner's trans status before making a commitment to marriage or otherwise. Issues of betrayal can be paramount in couples therapy, but even more prominent are the partner's questions about his or her own identity, how the partner's potential or actual transition impacts not only the relationship but also their personal sense of self. Children, depending on their age, are impacted more or less; younger children seem to be less affected by a parent's transition. Family members may benefit from individual therapy as they sort out their feelings.

Adulthood: Identity Integration, Consolidation, and Presentation

For those who do transition, this next phase typically involves consolidating a sense of self with bodily integrity. Many people report feeling happier than they could have imagined initially, feeling a sense of wholeness for the first time in their lives. The research on outcomes (Carroll, 1999; De Cuypere et al., 2005; Gijs & Brewaeys, 2008; Pfafflin & Junge, 1998) is generally quite positive. The literature on outcome has been reviewed in Chapter 6.

Clients generally report feelings of great relief, although some are disappointed that the inner image of the hoped-for transitioned self does not completely mesh with reality. Those obviously trans may be experiencing discrimination for the first time. This may be especially true for those assigned male, usually Caucasian, who had successful careers as men and are now experiencing sexism and stigma as trans women. On the other hand, trans men, who do tend to pass, may have been discriminated against as masculine women and are now experiencing male privilege. Black trans men, however, are learning to negotiate being a black man in the world, an often-difficult experience, as people tend to fear them. Many are also dealing with relational issues if they have a partner, who also may be going through unwanted or unfamiliar transitions.

Later, they tend to be more realistic as they learn that living in their affirmed gender is not exactly what they thought it would be, but few have regrets. For some, it can be challenging to lose a lifelong and possibly exaggerated and ideal fantasy of what life might be in the affirmed gender. Some describe it as "giving up the dream." Some report missing escaping into the familiar fantasy of being the preferred gender because it is no longer a fantasy.

Nevertheless, most appreciate finally being able to "be myself," "to live in my own skin," to finally see themselves reflected back by other people and instead of seeing a stranger there, "to see myself in the mirror" for the first time, being able to give up internalized transphobia. Others find that their relationships improve, for they can be themselves fully and they no longer have a "secret."

For those who transition fully and have surgery, sexual issues and shifting sexual orientation can be more complicated than once imagined. The new body image may have issues, postoperative body parts may not have as much sensitivity as once hoped for, and orgasm may be elusive, at least in the short run. This is also a time when people are exploring their sexual orientation, which may change as they experience themselves in their appropriate gender. Clients are typically thrilled with no longer having to deal with disliked, even repulsive, secondary sex characteristics which are almost never missed. They are relieved that their genitals match their internal representation. Few have regrets although for most, dysphoria never completely disappears. Quite a few will tell clinicians concerns that they may not tell others, particularly given the oft-romanticized online culture, which, although supportive, may not provide accurate information.

Some report continued feelings of inauthenticity/fraudulence if they are secretive or "stealth" about their former identity. A familiar refrain is: "Have I gone from one closet into another?"

More recently, some people are moving toward celebrating their unique transgender identities and have less interest in passing or blending into heteronormative society. Hence, they do not experience the same issues regarding secrecy and inauthenticity, although they still face stigma.

The clinician's role is to continue to see and mirror in the appropriate gender, to guide the individuation process, and to provide information about normative transgender identity development, particularly during periods of internalized transphobia. The therapist can help build resilience and develop pride in the client's unique transgender identity. As before, many of the tasks are repetitive, as the client continues to stabilize and consolidate identity.

Aging and Returning to Therapy

Transgender people experience the same issues as they age as anyone else and then have unique concerns that may also be addressed in therapy.

The universal tasks of aging are generativity, legacy, meaning, spirituality, mortality, and acceptance (Erickson, 1950). Difficulties include grief, loss, and regret, no longer feeling needed, feeling useless, medical concerns and decline of the body, isolation and loneliness, loss of gender markers and sexuality. Aging transgender people may experience additional difficulties, including the following examples: continued experience of earlier loss; if they transition late, they may grieve a lost youth in the affirmed gender; ongoing effects of stigma; potential continuation of difficulties with earlier life stages, as described in earlier sections of this chapter (e.g., trust, identity, intimacy issues). They also may worry about credibility in their affirmed gender; isolation from family; lack of community; and financial concerns due to earlier problems at work.

They may have difficulty finding medical providers in both gerontology and transgender medicine and have fears of assisted living and nursing homes and being presumed mentally ill. They may be denied equal care or denied care; and when they receive such care, they may experience erasure of their affirmed identity; disrespectful end-of-life care in the "wrong" body; being "outed"; being maligned and/or not seen or respected in the affirmed transitioned body. They may have difficulty finding an accepting spiritual home as they deal with mortality and may be buried in the wrong gender. Other concerns include sadness about the loss of hard-won gender markers with aging, particularly for transwomen, unexpected aspects of life in the affirmed gender, or occasional regrets about transition.

Finally, people may come to therapy in later life after their children have grown, or a spouse has died, so that the time is finally right to explore transition. The clinician's task is one of helping people with acceptance, and being comfortable with not only trans issues but also grief and loss. It can be useful to consider the similarities and differences that trans people face as they age from anyone else. The point is to make sense of a life, coming to terms with choices made over the lifespan. Most aging transgender people feel affirmed by the decisions they made and experience integrity and wholeness in their gender despite much loss over the lifespan.

In terms of individuation, the transgender person has consciously, often at great cost, chosen his or her path and can reflect upon a life lived with the utmost truth and integrity.

Finally, some people may return to therapy to talk about issues that emerge over the lifespan, and can return many years after completion of transition-related care. Old issues about gender may re-emerge or have never left, or issues having nothing to do with gender may be the reason for returning to therapy. Rather than start with a new therapist, many people prefer to return to the original witness of their story, the person who understands the arc and meaning of their personal narrative. Some come back to talk about the ongoing consolidation of their gender identity or new unexpected challenges that have emerged. The therapist may be able to follow up with reminders of their strengths and patterns worked on in the original therapy and, at the very least, serve as a compassionate witness to their life over the lifespan.

Other Topics

Assessment and Letter Writing as Part of the Therapy

Documentation may be a major part of the mental health professional's responsibility and is described in detail elsewhere (Coleman et al., 2011; Lev, 2009).

As part of long-term therapy, surgery letters are a collaborative process. The therapist may write the letter and the client provide feedback during the process or they may write it together.

Technology and E-Therapy

E-Therapy

Online or e-therapy has been shown to be particularly useful for people who have difficulty accessing competent in-person psychotherapeutic treatment and who may experience isolation and stigma (Derrig-Palumbo & Zeine, 2005; Fenichel et al., 2004; Fraser, 2009a; Maheu et al., 2005). "By extrapolation, e-therapy may be a useful modality for psychotherapy with transsexual, transgender, and gender-nonconforming people. E-therapy offers opportunities for potentially enhanced, expanded, creative and tailored delivery of services" (Coleman et al., 2011). However, the complexities, ethics, and legalities have not yet been sorted out. Hence, e-therapy may carry unknown, unexpected risks. More evidence-based, long-term data concerning its use are needed. Until then caution is advised.

Conclusion

In conclusion, psychotherapy is primarily about helping transgender individuals find, build, and express their authentic gendered self as it emerges in therapy, to develop a coherent narrative in the presence of a compassionate other, and then to sort out how best to express that self in the world with dignity and without shame. The initial process may take a long time and the client may also return to therapy over the lifespan to continue the original work or pursue other concerns. During the entire therapeutic process the relationship between the therapist and transgender person is key, more than any psychotherapeutic theory, to guide the trans person in finding and expressing his or her authentic gendered self.

References

Ainsworth, M. D., Blehar, M. C., & Waters, E. (1978). *Patterns of Attachment*. Hillsdale, NJ: Lawrence Erlbaum.

American Psychiatric Association. (2013). *Diagnostic and Statistical Manual of Mental Disorders DSM-5* (5th ed., text rev.). Washington, DC: Author.

Bockting, W. O. (2008). Psychotherapy and the real-life experience: From gender dichotomy to gender diversity. *Sexologies*, 17(4), 211–224.

Bockting, W. O. (2014). The impact of stigma on transgender identity development and mental health. In Kreukals, B. P. C., Steensma, T.D., & de Vries, A. L. C. (Eds.). *Gender Dysphoria and Disorders of Sex Development*. New York, NY: Springer, pp. 319–330.

Bowlby, J. (1969). *Attachment and Loss. Vol. I: Attachment*. New York: Basic Books.

Bowlby, J. (1973). *Attachment and Loss. Vol. II: Separation, Anxiety and Anger.* New York: Basic Books.

Carroll, R. (1999). Outcomes of treatment for gender dysphoria. *Journal of Sex Education and Therapy*, 24, 128–136.

Coleman, E. (2003). Presidential Address, HBIGDA XVIII International Symposium, Ghent, Belgium, 10–13 September.

Coleman, E., Bockting, W., Botzer, M., Cohen-Kettenis, P., De Cuypere, G., Feldman, J., et al. (2011). Standards of care for the health of transsexual, transgender, and gender nonconforming people, 7th version. *International Journal of Transgenderism*, 13(4), 165–232.

Cooley, C. H. (1902). *Human Nature and the Social Order.* New York: Scribners.

De Cuypere, G., T'Sjoen, G., Beerten, R., Selvaggi, G., De Sutter, P., Hoebeke, P., Monstrey, S., Vansteenwegen, A., & Rubens, R. (2005). Sexual and physical health after sex reassignment surgery. *Archives of Sexual Behavior*, 34(6), 679–690.

De Cuypere, G., Knudson, G., & Green, J. (2013). WPATH Consensus Process regarding transgender and transsexual related diagnoses in ICD-11. Available online at: http://www.wpath.org/uploaded_files/140/files/ICD Meeting Packet-Report-Final-sm.pdf, retrieved July 20, 2015.

Derrig-Palumbo, K., & Zeine, F. (2005). *Online Therapy: A Therapist's Guide to Expanding your Practice.* New York, NY: W. W. Norton.

Devor, A. H. (2004). Witnessing and mirroring: A fourteen-stage model. *Journal of Gay and Lesbian Psychotherapy*, 8(1/2), 41–67.

De Vries, A. L. C., Noens, I. L. J., Cohen-Kettenis, P. T., van Berckelaer-Onnes, I. A., & Doreleijers, T. A. (2010). Autism spectrum disorders in gender dysphoric children and adolescents. *Journal of Autism and Developmental Disorders*, 40(8), 930–936.

Duncan, B. L., Miller, S. D., Wampold, B. E., & Hubble, M. A. (2010). *The Heart and Soul of Change*, Washington, DC: American Psychological Association.

Ekins, R., & King, D. (2006). *The Transgender Phenomenon.* Thousands Oaks, CA: Sage.

Emerson, S., & Rosenfeld, C. (1996). Stages of adjustment in family members of transgender individuals. *Journal of Family Psychotherapy*, 7(3), 1–12.

Erickson, E. (1950). *Childhood and Society.* London: W. W. Norton.

Fenichel, M., Suler, J., Barak, A., Zelvin, E., Jones, G., Munro, K., ... Walker-Schmucker, W. (2004). Myths and realities of online clinical work, observations on the phenomena of online behavior, experience, and therapeutic relationships. A 3rd-year report from ISMHO's clinical case study group. Retrieved from https://www.ismho.org/myths_n_realities.asp.

Fraser, L. (2009a). Depth psychotherapy with transgender people. *Sexual and Relationship Therapy*, 24(2), 126–142.

Fraser, L. (2009b). E-therapy: Ethical and clinical considerations for version 7 of The World Professional Association for Transgender Health's Standards of Care. *International Journal of Transgenderism*, 11(4), 247–263.

Fraser, L. (2009c). Psychotherapy in The World Professional Association for Transgender Health's *Standards of Care*: Background and recommendations. *International Journal of Transgenderism*, 11(2), 110–126.

Fraser, L., & Knudson, G. (2015). Gender dysphoria and transgender health. In: Wylie, K. (Ed.). *ABC of Sexual Health.* West Sussex: Wiley Blackwell.

Gijs, L., & Brewaeys, A. (2008). Surgical treatment of gender dysphoria in adults and adolescents: Recent developments, effectiveness, and challenges. *Annual Review of Sex Research*, 18, 178–224.

Haas, A. P., Eliason, M., Mays, V. M., Mathy, R. M., Cochran, S. D., D'Augelli, A. R., et al. (2011). Suicide and suicide risk in lesbian, gay, bisexual, and transgender populations: Review and recommendations. *Journal of Homosexuality*, 58(1), 10–51.

Heylens, G., Elaut, E., Kreukels, B. P., Paap, M. C., Cerwenka, S., Richter-Appelt, H., Cohen-Kettenis, P. T., Haraldsen, I. R., & De Cuypere, G. (2014). Psychiatric characteristics in transsexual individuals: Multicentre study in four European countries. *British Journal of Psychiatry*, 204(2), 151–156.

Institute of Medicine. (2011). *The Health of Lesbian, Gay, Bisexual, and Transgender People: Building a Foundation for Better Understanding*. Washington, DC: The National Academies Press.

Jacobs, L. A., Rachlin, K., Erickson-Schroth, L., & Janssen, A. (2014). Gender dysphoria and co-occurring autism spectrum disorders: Review, case examples, and treatment considerations. *LGBT Health*, 1, (4). 277–282.

Johnson, V. K. (2010). The development of standards of care for individuals with a male-to-eunuch gender-identity disorder. *International Journal of Transgenderism*, 12(1), 40–51.

Johnson, T. W., & Irwig, M. S. (2014). The hidden world of self-castration and testicular self-injury. *Nature Reviews Urology*, 11, 297–300.

Kahn, M. (1997). *Between Therapist and Client*. New York: Holt.

Katz-Wise, S. L., Reisner, S. L., Hughto, J. W. & Keo-Meier, C. L. (2015). Differences in sexual orientation diversity and sexual fluidity in attractions among gender minority adults in Massachusetts. *Journal of Sex Research*, DOI: 10.1080/00224499.2014.1003028.

Kersting, A., Reutemann, M., Gast, U., Ohrmann, P., Suslow, T., Michael, N., & Arolt, V. (2003). Dissociative disorders and traumatic childhood experiences in transsexuals. *Journal of Nervous and Mental Disease*, 191, 182–189.

Kohut, H. (1971). *The Analysis of the Self*. New York: International Universities Press.

Kohut, H. (1977). *The Restoration of the Self*. New York: International Universities Press.

Kohut, H. (1982). Introspection, empathy and the semi-circle of mental health. *International Journal of Psychoanalysis*, 63, 395–407.

Lacan, J. (1949). Le stade du miroir. Paper presented at XVI Congres International de Psychanalyse, Zurich.

Lev, A. I. (2004). *Transgender Emergence: Therapeutic Guidelines for Working with Gender-Variant People and their Families*. Binghamton, NY: Haworth Clinical Practice Press.

Lev, A. I. (2009). The ten tasks of the mental health provider: Recommendations for revision of the World Professional Association for Transgender Health's standards of care. *International Journal of Transgenderism*, 11(2), 74–99.

Maheu, M. M., Pulier, M. L., Wilhelm, F. H., McMenamin, J. P., & Brown-Connolly, N. E. (2005). *The Mental Health Professional and the New Technologies: A Handbook for Practice Today*. Mahwah, NJ: Lawrence Erlbaum.

Nestle, J., Wilchins, R. A., & Howell, C. (2002). *Genderqueer: Voices from Beyond the Sexual Binary*. Los Angeles, CA: Alyson Publications.

Nieder, T., T'Sjoen, G., Motmans, J., & Bowers, M. (2014). Pluralistic identities, queer bodies, multidisciplinary perspectives on increasing clinical needs. Papers presented at the WPATH 2014 Biennial International Symposium, Bangkok.

Nouwen, H. J. M. (1975). *Reaching Out, The Three Movements of the Spiritual Life*. New York: Doubleday, p. 51.

Pfafflin, F., & Junge, A. (1998). *Sex Reassignment Thirty Years of International Follow-up Studies SRS: A Comprehensive Review, 1961–1991*. Düsseldorf, Germany: Symposium Publishing.

Pula, J. (2015). Understanding gender through the lens of transgender experience. *Journal of Psychoanalytic Inquiry*, 35: 809–822.

Rachlin, K., & Lev, A. I. (2011). Challenging cases for experienced therapists. *Journal of Gay & Lesbian Mental Health*, 15(2), 180–199.

Robinow, O. (2009). Paraphilia and transgenderism: A connection with Asperger's disorder? *Sexual and Relationship Therapy*, 24(2), 143–151.

Shively, M. G., & DeCecco, J. P. (1977). Components of sexual identity. *Journal of Homosexuality*, 3, (1).

Siebler, K. (2012). Transgender transitions: Sex/gender binaries in the digital age. *Journal of Gay & Lesbian Mental Health*, 16, 74–99.

Stein, M. (1998). *Jung's Map of the Soul*. Chicago, IL: Open Court.

Vale, K., Johnson, T. W., Jansen, M., Lawson, K., Leiberman, T., Willette, K., & Wassersug, R. (2010). Development of *Standards of Care* with a male-to-eunuch GID. *IJT*, 12(1):40–51.

Walker, P. A., Berger, P. C., Green, R., Laub, D. R., Reynolds, C. L., & Wollman, L. (1979) *Standards of Care*. The hormonal and surgical sex-reassignment of gender dysphoric persons. Available online at: http://www.wpath.org.

Westen, D. (1998). Lecture 5, Is anyone really normal? *Perspectives on Abnormal Psychology. Contemporary Psychodynamic Thinking*. Springfield, VA: The Teaching Company.

Wheelwright, J. (1982). *St George and the Dandelion: 40 Years of Practice as a Jungian Analyst*. San Francisco, CA: CG Jung Institute of San Francisco.

White, M. (2007). *Maps of Narrative Practice*. New York: W.W. Norton.

Winnicott, D. W. (1958). The capacity to be alone. *International Journal of Psychoanalysis*, 39(5), 416–420.

Winnicott, D. W. (1965). *The Maturational Process and the Facilitating Environment*. New York: International Universities Press.

Winnicott, D. W. (1971). Mirror-role of mother and family in child development. In: Lomas, P. (Ed.), *The Predicament of the Family: A Psycho-analytical Symposium*. London: Hogarth Press and the Institute of Psychoanalysis, pp. 1–6.

8 Developmental Stages of the Transgender Coming-Out Process

Toward an Integrated Identity

Walter Bockting and Eli Coleman

Introduction

Since the term *transgender* was coined in the early 1980s (Feinberg 1996), much has changed in our understanding of transgenderism and the clinical management of gender dysphoria. The paradigm has shifted from a binary understanding of gender toward recognition of greater gender diversity (Bockting 1999, 2008). The distinction between transsexualism and transvestism has made room for the unified concept of transgenderism, albeit with the acknowledgment of different developmental processes of coming out. An increasing number of transgender individuals define their gender identity outside of the boundaries of boy/man or girl/woman, using such terms as "genderqueer" and "gender non-conforming" to describe their gender-diverse identities (Harrison et al. 2012). A human rights approach to health increasingly informs transgender-specific health care (Drescher et al. 2012).

Specifically, "transsexualism" was defined as "a strong and persistent cross-gender identification" (women trapped in men's bodies, and men trapped in women's bodies), whereas "transvestism" was defined as "an erotic desire to wear women's clothes." Although several types of transvestites and transsexuals were identified, as well as syndromes that combined features of both transvestism and transsexualism (Benjamin 1966; Blanchard et al. 1987; Person & Ovesey 1974a, 1974b), until recently, the distinction between the two remained paramount. Gender identity was either male or female. The clinical management of transsexualism focused on helping males to become women and females to become men, whereas transvestites were not eligible for medical intervention to feminize the body but were encouraged to episodically cross-dress with less shame (Bockting 1997a, 1997b). For many transvestites, this meant compartmentalizing identity into "two names, two wardrobes, two personalities" (Money 1974), a male self, and a female self, leading a double life, thereby also conforming to a binary conceptualization of sex and gender.

With the advent of the transgender movement, these distinctions began to shift. Transsexuals and transvestites united to affirm their unique *transgender* identities "from outside the boundaries of gender, beyond the constructed" male versus female (Stone 1991). Clinical management followed suit by adopting a *transgender coming-out* model, which we describe below. Recent revisions of the diagnosis of gender dysphoria in the *Diagnostic Statistical Manual of Mental Disorders* (American Psychiatric Association 2013) and the *Standards of Care for the Health of Transgender, Transsexual, and Gender Nonconforming People* (Coleman et al. 2012) further reflect this shift toward affirmation of a spectrum of gender-diverse identities.

Through reading this chapter, clinicians will gain an understanding of the psychological and social issues involved in the coming-out process, an understanding that is essential to delivering sensitive and effective health care to this client population.

Coming Out as a Developmental Process

Stage models of coming out have been extensively used to describe the development of a homosexual identity (e.g., Cass 1979; Coleman 1981/82, 1982; Minton & McDonald 1984). Stage models have also been applied to transgender coming out (Devor 2004; Gagne et al. 1997; Lev 2004; Lewins 1995). Gagne and colleagues (1997) defined four stages based on a qualitative study of male-to-female transgender persons: (1) early transgender experiences; (2) coming out to one's self; (3) coming out to others; and (4) resolution of identity. Lewins (1995) described six stages of becoming a woman for male-to-female transsexuals: (1) abiding anxiety; (2) discovery; (3) purging and delay; (4) acceptance; (5) surgical reassignment; and (6) invisibility. Emerson and Rosenfeld (1996) described five stages of adjustment for family members of transgender individuals on the basis of Kubler-Ross's (1970) stages of grief: (1) denial; (2) anger; (3) bargaining; (4) depression; and (5) acceptance. Devor (2004) defined 14 possible stages of transsexual identity formation based on sociological field research and in-depth interviews with female-to-male transsexuals. Finally, Lev (2004) described six stages of transgender *emergence:* (1) awareness; (2) seeking information/reaching out; (3) disclosure to significant others; (4) exploration, identity and self-labeling; (5) exploration, transition issues/possible body modification; and (6) integration, acceptance, and post-transition issues.

We adapted Coleman's (1981/82) model of developing a homosexual identity to the development of a transgender identity (Bockting & Coleman 2007). Our model identifies five developmental stages: (1) pre-coming out; (2) coming out; (3) exploration; (4) intimacy; and (5) identity integration. It is based upon Erikson's concepts of social development (Erikson 1956). It posits that identity development is greatly influenced by social interaction (Erikson 1956; Plummer 1975) and is shaped according to the nature of interpersonal relationships (Sullivan 1953). It is not only consistent with the models previously described, but also reflects our particular insights and clinical experience, and accounts for a wide diversity of transgender identities.

The use of stages may suggest that identity development is a linear process; however, the developmental tasks organized into the five stages are often not completed in any particular order. Rather, individuals may cycle through tasks across the stages, depending on their psychosocial challenges and the assets available at a particular time in their development.

While this model posits that identity development is shaped by social interaction forces, the process may be limited or altered by physical disease, genetic disorders, and/or psychiatric conditions. Or it may be assisted through medical interventions such as hormone therapy or surgery. The model is further limited by the fact that it was constructed within the context of the dominant North American/Western European culture, without accounting for processes that exist in other cultures. The Western cultural context includes a binary conceptualization of sex and gender, as well as social stigmatization of gender non-conformity, while cross-cultural and historical accounts are more consistent with the affirmation of a spectrum of gender identities (e.g., Feinberg 1996).

In order to foster identity development, the clinician must address all biopsychosocial factors. This chapter will focus on, and limit its discussion to, how the clinician can promote transgender individuals' mental and sexual health by facilitating normal processes of identity development.

Pre-Coming Out

The first stage, pre-coming out, refers to the time during which the individual experiences cross-gender or transgender feelings, but is not naming these feelings as such. Early in life, children are taught about the values and norms of family and culture, and incorporate these external rules while structuring self-identity. When children do not conform to societal rules regarding gender, they learn that something is wrong with them. They feel different and experience alienation from others. They have a sense of aloneness, fear, and confusion, and a feeling of being inherently defective or of shame (Kaufman 1992). This is a profound existential experience that the child does not understand and is rarely able to articulate.

The social stigma associated with gender non-conformity plays an important role. The parallel with homosexuality is striking. Gay, lesbian, bisexual, and transgender individuals are all stigmatized for varying degrees of visible gender non-conformity. Individuals who are outwardly gender non-conforming may experience this stage somewhat differently and more dramatically than individuals who are not.

Children who do not conform to their assigned gender role (i.e., visibly feminine boys and masculine girls) cannot hide their "true selves." As a result, they experience actual rejection and discrimination, and face the challenge of how to cope with shame and isolation from a very early age. Others may label their stigmatized identity and force them to "come out of the closet." Such circumstances require these children to address their gender identity *differentness* with peers, parents, teachers, religious leaders, and, in some cases, clinicians hired to address the "problem." This occurs when cognitive abilities and attachments are forming; developmental processes of separation, individuation, attachment, and psychosexual development are at critical stages (Bowlby 1969; Erikson 1956; Freud & Brill 1995), and they are still highly dependent upon their parents and authorities. These outwardly gender non-conforming children usually proceed to the next stage of coming out early in life.

In contrast, those who are less outwardly gender non-conforming unconsciously hide their "true" selves to avoid rejection and discrimination, and attempt to conform by presenting a false self to the world. Secrecy becomes a way of life as they suffer in silence. Hence, outwardly gender-conforming transgender individuals usually proceed through the developmental stages of coming out later in life, often following a long period of pre-coming out when years of hiding their cross-gender feelings impose a different kind of toll. They take the risk when they are older and have more autonomy, and when they are naturally going through stages of individuation. With increasing visibility of transgender people in society, however, outwardly gender-conforming transgender individuals are also coming out at earlier ages (e.g., in mid-adolescence).

Whether outwardly gender non-conforming or not, the actual or perceived stigma challenges the person's mental health (Bockting et al. 2013; Hendricks & Testa 2012). Shame, low self-esteem, loneliness, and isolation are common. The child fears abandonment because of gender non-conformity, and forms anxious attachments to others (Bowlby 1969). The experience of alienation and aloneness is enough to preclude further healthy psychosexual development in many children. The situation worsens if the child grows up in a dysfunctional family environment with general neglect, physical abuse, or sexual abuse. On the other hand, psychosexual damage can be mitigated by positive factors such as a loving family environment. Gender non-conforming girls may have an easier time than gender non-conforming boys since, in our culture, being a "sissy" may be more stigmatized than being a "tomboy." Facing the existential crisis of being different would be a healthy resolution of this stage. This means breaking through fear of abandonment and risking rejection by others.

Children in the pre-coming-out stage may be brought by parents to see a clinician due to concern about gender non-conformity, or about isolation, depression, or difficulties in academic performance as a result of teasing at school (Vignette A). A gender-conforming adult may present with a concern about something other than gender dysphoria, such as chemical dependency or depression (Vignette B). The health care provider can create an environment which allows the client to move toward the next stage of development (coming out) by acknowledging transgender feelings, first to oneself and then to others.

Vignette A

Ben (aged 7 years) presented with crying spells, sadness, and tension headaches. At the intake session, he stated, "Nobody likes me." His parents expressed concern about Ben's gender non-conformity. People regularly mistook him for a girl. Ben identified with Dorothy from *The Wizard of Oz*. At Christmas, he asked for ruby slippers. Recently, he had insisted on wearing a red headband to school. The parents were afraid that this would lead to teasing. Ben was a loner and only had one friend, a girl.

In therapy, Ben revealed that he felt different from other boys of his age. Although he had dreamed in the past about being a girl, he denied any current wish for this. He was averse to rough-and-tumble play. Rather, Ben loved reading and theater. His interest and talent in the arts were encouraged in therapy, and Ben was able to develop pride in his differentness, his sensitivity, and his creativeness.

Vignette B

A 35-year-old female was referred for treatment of depression after completing a chemical dependency program. During the assessment, she revealed past difficulties in romantic relationships with women. After initiation of antidepressant medication and the development of a trusting therapeutic relationship, the client shared that she had never really felt a part of the lesbian community. Rather, her feelings of identity differed from those of her lesbian friends. She had felt like an outsider, isolated for as long as she could remember. Her depression seemed to date back to childhood, when she felt she did not fit in with her peers. When she discussed her sexual feelings and fantasies in therapy, she realized that her gender identity might not be that of a woman.

Coming Out

The second stage, coming out, involves the acknowledgment to oneself, and then to others, of persistent cross-gender or transgender feelings. Such acknowledgment is challenging because the individual risks abandonment and feeling more isolated through rejection or taking on a stigmatized identity. This stage is usually fraught with trepidation and confusion. The developmental task to be mastered is the resolution of confusion and the achievement of self-acceptance. This can be made more difficult by rigidity of the social climate, poor quality of the individual's interpersonal relationships, or the existence of psychiatric disorders. Failure to master the task may exacerbate psychiatric disorders, contribute to further intimacy dysfunction, and delay or preclude healthy psychosexual development.

At this juncture, the response of others is critical. If positive, it can challenge the individual's low self-esteem. If negative, it can confirm feelings of alienation, aloneness, fear, confusion, shame, and being defective. A negative reaction can also foreclose or delay a healthy resolution of this stage. Suicide is a particular risk at this stage and this needs to be carefully monitored (Clements-Nolle et al. 2006; Grossman & D'Augelli 2007).

The sociocultural environment is also critical. Recognition of transgender identities and acceptance of gender diversity certainly vary within our culture. While there have been tremendous gains in societal acknowledgment of gay and lesbian identities in the last several decades, the positive recognition of transgender identities is a more recent phenomenon. Validation of transgender identity and expression within society and the media is having a positive effect on individuals with emerging transgender identities. As the culture relaxes its views on gender non-conformity, coming out is occurring at even earlier ages, including childhood and adolescence. However, we still see many individuals entering this stage well into adulthood and old age.

The health care provider may be the first person to whom a client discloses transgender feelings or a transgender identity. The clinician must remember that coming out is a very critical stage, and it should go without saying that an open and accepting attitude about gender diversity is essential in order to assist the individual with resolution. To date, most clinicians have not been sufficiently educated or trained to address this type of situation in a positive and helpful way.

The client should be encouraged to take calculated risks. This means disclosing the transgender feelings first to those most likely to accept. The clinician can provide assistance in deciding whom to tell. Additionally, the clinician can help the client anticipate the variety of reactions that might occur. Because of the stigma associated with being transgender, immediate acceptance cannot be expected. Support from family and peers is critical, but they may go through their own coming-out process, and need time to adjust to the news. Support at this early stage is often easier to find from transgender peers than from family and friends. Moreover, transgender peers have first-hand experience with coming out to family and friends, and can help put initial negative reactions into perspective.

Usually, transgender individuals have kept the secret for so long that they are hungry for acceptance and emotionally vulnerable. When acceptance does not immediately follow disclosure, the client may be tempted to discontinue communication with family; however, keeping the lines of communication open will facilitate the family's coming-out process and lead it toward eventual acceptance. The provider can play an important role here by counseling and guiding the transgender client, by offering group therapy with peers, and by encouraging the client to include family and friends in therapy (Vignettes C and D).

Vignette C

After calling our office several times over a 4-year period, Robert (aged 52 years) finally made an appointment with a therapist. When asked what brought him to therapy, Robert stated, "I think I am a woman." He had cross-dressed since the age of 10 years, only in the privacy of his home, and initially found it sexually arousing. One factor that had kept Robert from coming forward earlier was his fear that he would not be able to make a "convincing woman."

Robert had never told anyone about his feelings, not even his wife and children. He described his fears of being discovered, his social isolation, and his depression that included suicidal ideation.

After exploring his history in individual therapy, Robert, with assistance from the therapist, decided to come out to his wife by writing her a letter. The first draft of the letter beat around the bush, as Robert tried to "soften the blow." It also contained self-defeating messages, such as, "I will understand if you want nothing to do with me any more. Just tell me and I will disappear." In subsequent drafts, Robert learned to clearly state the facts, assertively describe his own feelings, and ask for what he wanted: to be heard by her and get the space he needed to explore his identity. The letter also included an invitation for his wife to join him in a session with the therapist. After several renditions, Robert eventually shared the letter with his wife at home.

Initially, the wife reacted with shock, some denial, and fear ("Can't we just continue the way we have been? Nobody needs to know"), and feelings of anger and betrayal ("Why did you not tell me earlier?" and "Why does this have to happen to me?"). In couples therapy, Robert gradually shared more of his feelings. Attempting to understand, she asked questions of both Robert and the therapist. She was referred to another therapist at our clinic for support in working through her feelings and issues.

Robert joined group therapy with other transgender individuals. This was particularly important to him because his wife had been his best friend. Upon disclosure, they had briefly become closer, but she later needed space and distance (e.g., they decided to sleep in separate bedrooms). The group also helped to support Robert when he came out to his children.

Robert told both children at the same time with his wife present. They took it well, although his son-in-law expressed moral concerns and initially did not want Robert to be around the grandchildren, particularly in the female role. Robert's daughter, feeling caught between her dad and her husband, broke off contact with Robert for a period of time. However, Robert kept the lines of communication open. When the daughter saw the improvement in Robert's mood and level of happiness, she confronted her husband and, gradually, the situation improved. She and her brother came in for a family therapy session.

Coming out to friends and to his faith community followed. Most friends required time to adjust to the news, but supported Robert as best as they could. His closest male friend joined Robert in therapy, received answers to his questions, and became a great source of support, especially in Robert's struggle with his wife. Finally, to Robert's surprise, his minister was supportive and helped Robert deal with his fear that giving in to his transgender feelings in general, and feminizing his body in particular, was against the will of God.

Eventually, Robert and his wife divorced, but they were able to preserve a friendship. Other relationships were altered, and he lost some friends as he changed his gender. But he also developed new friendships, including with transgender peers.

Vignette D

Rhonda (aged 22 years) was referred by a counselor from her eating disorder program. She had insisted that she was different from all the other women in the program. After prompting, Rhonda had revealed issues relating to her "sexual identity."

At the sexual health clinic, we were able to help Rhonda articulate her particular sexual identity issues. A very visceral discomfort with her body, particularly with her primary and secondary sex characteristics, surfaced. She took showers in the dark, as she could not tolerate looking at her body. Refusing to eat was an effort to stop her menstrual periods.

Rhonda had once told an online friend that she felt like a man, but had never told anyone else. She had been confused by a concurrent attraction to other men. Online chatting revealed other female-to-male transgender individuals who were attracted to men and identified as gay. Rhonda concluded, "I am a transfag."

Rhonda lived alone and was socially quite isolated. She joined a therapy group for transgender individuals. The group encouraged Rhonda to come out to her parents and brother. Her father was also gay, although not openly so, which made coming out even more difficult for her, as this appeared to be against the family rules. Eventually, she conquered her fear and came out to her father, who then came to us for family therapy. He accepted Rhonda's transgender feelings, but adamantly opposed her plans to have chest surgery. He also opposed Rhonda coming out to the extended family, as he feared this would risk exposure of other family secrets, including his homosexuality.

When Rhonda came out to her mother, she joined them in therapy. She expressed concerns about Rhonda's mental health, suggesting that the transgender feelings might be just another obsession. Ultimately, Rhonda and her parents agreed to a comprehensive treatment plan that addressed her coexisting psychological problems (i.e., eating disorder, obsessive-compulsive disorder) before initiating masculinizing hormone therapy or transgender surgery.

In time, Rhonda was able to develop a small group of friends that included a transgender man and a non-transgender gay man. Rhonda also came out to her brother, who became her biggest supporter.

Exploration

Exploration is the stage of learning as much as possible about expressing one's transgender identity now that the secret has been revealed. The first developmental task, to learn about oneself and one's community, is experimentation. It involves ending social isolation, meeting and socializing with similar individuals, and developing interpersonal skills through the newly adopted identity with peers, friends, and family.

Sometimes, exploration precedes coming out to family and old friends. The internet provides ample opportunity for transgender individuals to connect with peers and resources. Offline resources are available as well, mostly in major metropolitan areas. Transgender or gay, lesbian, or bisexual community organizations offer a safe space for initial as well as ongoing exploration of the new identity. Positive social experiences breed self-confidence, security, and skills in communicating with others.

Exploration includes explicit experimentation with gender roles and expression. This allows the transgender individual to find both identity (who am I?) and the most comfortable way to express it (how can I best actualize or express my gender identity?), often through trial and error. Options for identity management range from integrating cross-gender feelings into a gender role that is consistent with the sex assigned at birth, to living in another gender role part- or full-time without any medical interventions, to hormone therapy and various surgical procedures (Bockting 1997a, 2013; Bockting & Coleman 1992). Sometimes, in an attempt to end many years of ambiguity, turmoil, and pain, the individual demands (rather than requests) hormone therapy or surgery. The drive to resolve the discrepancy between sex and gender identity may be exacerbated by anxiety, fear, and loneliness, and take on obsessive-compulsive characteristics.

The second developmental task is to create a sense of personal attractiveness and sexual competence. For many transgender individuals, this is complicated by an aversion to their body and genitals, precluding any feeling of personal attractiveness or willingness to become sexually intimate. Some go through the motions of sexual activity but lack any feeling of comfort and authenticity, usually in an attempt to fulfill societal or spousal expectations. For many, this stage of exploration means a second adolescence. For those who did not have many adolescent experiences because of their gender dysphoria, it can mean a first adolescence. Some individuals delay this exploration until they can present themselves in accordance with their authentic gender identity through cross-dressing, or living in the desired gender role, or until they have begun hormone therapy or completed breast/chest and/or genital reconstructive surgery.

Because society generally struggles to acknowledge a legitimate transgender identity, exploration may not take place until late adolescence, early adulthood, or later. Limited access to hormone therapy or surgery may also delay this stage. As a result, exploration sometimes includes behaviors that may be considered inappropriate for the client's chronological age. For example, a 45-year-old transgender woman may experiment with clothing, makeup, and accessories in a way that reminds one of a 14-year-old. The clinician can be helpful by giving the client permission to be an "adolescent" without getting into trouble or neglecting adult responsibilities (e.g., as a parent or on the job). Finding comfort and learning boundaries are as much a part of this stage as they are of any adolescence.

Also like adolescence, this stage is characterized by ambiguity, intensity, and defiance. Because our society offers only two real gender choices, individuals often feel pressured to live in one gender role or the other. Ambiguity is not well tolerated in our culture, and it is often not well tolerated by the individual, who may try to mask conflict about gender identity and expression by attempting to shed natal sex characteristics and adopt highly stereotyped sex role behaviors of the other gender. Doing so is an important step in exploration of gender identity and part of normal gender identity development. During this stage, the clinician must help the individual explore, rather than rush to a premature identity consolidation.

The individual is responsible for deciding how to express or manage gender identity. But according to the *Standards of Care for the Health of Transsexual, Transgender, and Gender Nonconforming People* (Coleman et al., 2012), access to hormone therapy or surgery requires the support of one or more specialized health professionals. Those who are anxious to finally obtain congruity between body, gender identity, and gender role may perceive the mental health professional as an unwelcome "gatekeeper" (Pollack 1997; Stryker 1997). However, transitioning, and finding ways to successfully cope with a stigmatized identity, are part of an intensive, challenging process which requires careful planning and support. The therapist's guidance and participation can help pace the coming-out process and encourage exploration of aspects of identity management that, left unaddressed, could block future identity development.

The *Standards of Care* require living for 1 year, full-time, in the desired gender role prior to genital reconstructive surgery. In the past, this was interpreted to mean living for 1 year, fully and continuously, as a member of the "opposite" sex. If the client's decision as to identity management is to change his or her sex as completely as possible, this could still be the goal. However, there is a continuum of gender expression, rather than only two discrete binary categories of male or female. In our clinical practice, consistent with a model of transgender coming out, we interpret the period of living 1 year in the desired gender role as a time during which the client lives as a woman, a man, both (bigender), neither (gender-neutral), or any other type of authentic transgender identity that incorporates or defies binary conceptualizations of gender (e.g., genderqueer). Consistent with the *Standards of Care*, we believe that experiencing (and experimenting with) gender expression is a necessary developmental step toward an integrated transgender identity.

During preparation for the change in gender role, the therapist can provide invaluable guidance with regard to coming out and gender role transitioning at work. Like family and friends, co-workers will need time to come to terms with the news that their colleague is transgender and will change gender expression on the job. A range of feelings and reactions can be expected. Consistent with general equal-opportunity and sexual harassment policies, conduct tending to create a hostile work environment for the transgender person or any other employee should not be tolerated.

Gendered bathrooms are frequently the place around which fear, anxiety, and ignorance are expressed. Although the transgender person is entitled to use the restroom facilities assigned to his or her authentic gender role, we often recommend an agreement to temporarily use a designated bathroom. This gives co-workers time to adjust to the new gender role, and eases anxiety and tension. Within a period of 6 months or so, the transgender employee can usually use the desired bathroom comfortably.

Completion of the developmental tasks of the exploration stage is signified by the transformation of shame into pride in self and in identity. Such pride is often expressed in enhanced participation and activism in the transgender community and in the prominence the transgender identity takes on in one's life and self-definition. In order to foster identity pride, the therapist may need to assist the client in confronting internalized transphobia (i.e., discomfort with one's own transgenderism stemming from society's normative gender expectations). Internalized transphobia may be expressed in an overemphasis on passing as a member of the other sex. Certainly, the desire to blend in with non-transgender women or men is what often defines gender dysphoria for transgender individuals with a strong conflict between their core gender identity and their sex assigned at birth. However, when passing means keeping a secret (i.e., that one is transgender), stigma will be internally felt, and the secret eventually is likely to undermine relationships with friends and peers, as well as intimacy in primary relationships.

For those who grew up gender role-conforming, the emphasis on passing may be reinforced by an identity split between the "false" self they presented to the world and the inner self expressed in isolation (including through cross-dressing, sexual fantasy, and/or fetishistic behavior). In the exploration stage of coming out, they may seek to realize the part of the split self that has been hidden for all these years, which oftentimes takes the form of an idealized, hyperfeminine presentation. In the course of coming out, however, these individuals will learn that realizing the imagined cross-gender self will mean letting go of the split and integrating the two selves into a transgender identity. The clinician can facilitate this by encouraging the client to grieve and let go of the fact that one was not born and raised as a member of the desired gender, and by introducing the concept and affirmation of a transgender identity.

Psychiatric problems can complicate resolution of the exploration stage. Reasoning, education, and encouragement of further exploration are not effective for an individual who is highly anxious, depressed, personality-disordered, or chemically dependent. The clinician should examine these issues carefully, and address them appropriately, while encouraging the client to pursue the developmental tasks of exploration. Successful resolution of this stage can be accomplished if decisions about identity management are made thoughtfully and deliberately, without any obsessive or compulsive drive to end confusion. Comprehensive treatment can help individuals meet the difficult developmental challenges of this stage (Bockting 1997a, 2013; Bockting & Coleman 1992).

Vignette E

John (aged 35 years) had been too fearful and depressed to focus on his transgenderism. After alleviating the depression with medication, John joined a therapy group for individuals exploring their transgender identity. He was able to relate to several of the group members, which helped reduce his shame. He began to read about transgender issues on the internet, and he accompanied one of the group members to a local transgender organization meeting.

John then gave himself permission to fully explore his transgender identity. As a result, he started to come cross-dressed to the group and began to spend time in public in the female gender role. He experimented with different styles of clothing and accessories. Gradually, he became less self-conscious and learned to enjoy his newfound freedom of expression.

One evening, John came to the group and described a close call with some young men who had ridiculed him with sexual comments. The group told him that they were not surprised, given the way he sometimes dressed. Several months earlier, such a response would have hurt his feelings and could have caused him to retreat into suppression. But now, John was ready to listen. The group members explained that experimenting at the right time and place was critically important, and acknowledged that he deserved to have fun. They encouraged him to nevertheless be careful in public, more careful than he had needed to be in the male role.

Now identifying as Ellen, she began exploration of her identity, which included flirting with men in the female gender role. Previously, sex had been confined to relations with women, during which John assumed a stereotypical male role (i.e., taking the initiative and focusing on penile–vaginal intercourse in the missionary position). Now, the roles were reversed: Ellen assumed a stereotypical female role during sex with men (i.e., being rather passive and focusing on pleasing her partner). However, she eventually recognized that, while flirting and having sex with men affirmed her sense of femininity and appeal, she was more attracted to women than to men.

After a year of cross-dressing only on weekends, Ellen began to pursue a full-time gender role transition. She decided to become as complete a woman as possible, as soon as possible. She laid out her plans for hormone therapy and facial, voice, and genital reconstructive surgery. When the therapist reviewed the *Standards of Care* with her, Ellen became impatient, threatening to leave the clinic and find another which might provide hormone therapy and surgery sooner. The group encouraged her to slow down and focus on the various steps involved in making a full-time gender role change. For example, Ellen had not come out to her parents or co-workers. The group suggested that it might be easier for them to accept her transgender identity if she informed them before starting hormone therapy or undergoing feminizing surgery. Then they challenged Ellen's plans for extensive facial surgery, inquiring as to her expectations. They helped her see that, no matter what she did, she would never become a non-transgender woman. Ellen experienced profound sadness, and the group members and her transgender friends empathized. This led to a deeper acceptance of herself as a transgender person.

After coming out to her parents, Ellen developed a plan for coming out at work. Her company brought in a consultant (an expert in transgenderism) to facilitate the on-the-job transition. Ellen informed her co-workers of her pending gender change. Her boss immediately expressed the company's support. Human resources reviewed the sexual harassment policy and a transgender sensitivity training took place. After an anxious first day, Ellen felt liberated and excited about going to work in the female role. Supportive co-workers complimented Ellen on her appearance.

When colleagues inquired about the transition process, Ellen described virtually her entire life story. An eavesdropping associate complained about Ellen's disclosures. Ellen felt wronged and wanted to fight back. However, Ellen's therapy group helped her see that she needed to observe appropriate boundaries on the job. If she expected others to keep negative judgments to themselves so as to not create a hostile environment for her, she, in turn, had to exercise privacy. She learned to share her excitement only with selected co-workers and only outside of work.

After having lived 1 year in the female gender role, Ellen announced to the group that she no longer felt the need to have feminizing facial surgery. Moreover, she had developed a sexual relationship with another woman and, for now, suspended her plans for genital reconstructive surgery.

Vignette F

At her intake interview, Carolyn (aged 24 years) stated, "I feel like a freak." She explained that she had realized that her gender identity was that of a man. Carolyn joined a therapy group for transgender individuals (with both male-to-female and female-to-male spectrum participants). She eventually came out to her friends and family, changed her name to Carl, and bound her breasts. Carl joined a social group for transgender men. He became very active on the internet, sharing his experience of transitioning with others like him.

After meeting the guidelines of the *Standards of Care*, Carl had chest surgery and underwent masculinizing hormone therapy. His personality quickly changed to that of a very cocky adolescent. Once a group member providing helpful feedback and able to express empathy, he now appeared uninterested. He even fell asleep during one of the sessions.

Carl's favorite subject became the girlfriends he met via the internet, and his ability to persuade each of them that he was "the only one." The group challenged Carl's behavior, reminding him of his previous activism in the lesbian feminist community, and pointing out that he was now displaying some of the attitudes and conduct he had previously protested against. The therapist gave Carl permission to be an adolescent, but also set limits when he displayed inappropriate behavior in the group. These limits eventually carried over into his life outside of group.

Masculinizing hormone therapy helped Carl to let go of his shame about his transgenderism. He recognized and accepted the limitations of female-to-male genital reconstructive surgery. While this initially had been a major concern, he now realized that he could live in a manner true to himself, be desirable, and function sexually as a man without a penis. Although his primary attraction was toward women, in order to satisfy his curiosity about male sexuality, he experimented with sex with men. Having decided against genital reconstructive surgery at this time, Carl did have his ovaries and uterus removed. He also reduced his hormones to sustain his masculine appearance while minimizing the negative effects of testosterone (e.g., acne, hair loss, increased aging, and cardiovascular disease).

Carl still follows the advancements in female-to-male genital reconstructive surgery. He said he might be interested in undergoing such surgery if the outcomes improve.

Intimacy

Once pride in self and in identity, and a sense of belonging with the transgender community, have developed, a desire for intimacy in the new gender role emerges. Intimacy (and facing the fear of being unlovable) becomes a crucial developmental task. This is challenging for those who developed varying degrees of anxious attachments to others in childhood, adolescence, and early adulthood. The lack of trust and fear of abandonment can be deep-seated and rather unconscious. Fear of abandonment is a present as well as a past issue, since the newly adopted transgender identity is, to some degree, still stigmatized by society. The fear is understandable and realistic.

Transgender men appear to have an easier time developing intimacy than transgender women. The factors that account for this difference are not exactly clear, but one possibility is that transgender men have better intimacy skills because they were socialized as women. In addition, the majority of transgender men develop relationships with women who are generally more accepting of diversity than men. Nevertheless, transgender men may encounter prejudice and a lack of understanding in women, particularly within the lesbian community. This reaction usually relates to alteration of the body through hormone therapy and chest surgery. Many transgender men fear that heterosexual women would not want to be with men who do not have a penis, but in reality, this rarely interferes with the development of intimate relationships.

The difficulty or ease of establishing and maintaining intimate relationships is affected by the transgender person's sexual orientation. Those who partner with a member of the other gender form heterosexual relationships and enjoy the approval of society. Those who partner with a member of the same gender form homosexual relationships and carry a double stigma: that of being transgender and that of being homosexual (Bockting et al. 2009; Coleman & Bockting 1989; Coleman et al. 1993; Feinbloom et al. 1976). As a result, they often experience another coming out, not only as transgender but also as gay, lesbian, or bisexual. This complicates the task of developing an integrated identity. Transgender individuals have often found support among gay men and lesbian women. But many people are confused, unable to understand why one would change sex in order to become gay or lesbian. Therefore, acceptance within both the larger society and the gay and lesbian community can be challenging. Finally, it is also not uncommon for transgender individuals to develop intimate relationships with other transgender individuals, enabling them to immediately assume a level of mutual understanding and acceptance of transgender identity. This situation provides perhaps more freedom and certainly the opportunity to explore transgender sexuality as distinct from male and female sexuality (Bockting 1999; Bockting et al., 2009).

It has been hypothesized that negative societal constraints, lack of family support, the absence of positive role models, and the lack of their own consolidated identity have caused many gay men and lesbians to experience difficulty in forming and maintaining intimate relationships (Coleman & Rosser 1996). Similar dynamics make this developmental task difficult for the individual who is making a gender role transition. Therefore, it is no wonder that new or first relationships are extra challenging for transgender individuals. Of course, relationships are a process of trial and error, and healthy relationships develop through learning by trial and error. The clinician can be helpful by normalizing many of these struggles and providing information on developing intimate relationships within the context of living with a stigmatized identity.

A pattern frequently observed among transgender men is a quickly forming, intense involvement with a heterosexually identified woman (often with children) who is needy. This situation provides the opportunity for newly transitioned transgender men to find acceptance and to affirm their manhood by assuming the role of rescuer. As is common with first relationships, these relationships usually do not last, leaving the transgender man feeling used after he has done too much for his partner in an effort to avoid abandonment. Because of the intensity of these relationships, attempts to protect the client from such a pattern often fall on deaf ears. All that a clinician might be able to do is to be there for the client, help to put the experience in the perspective of the transgender coming-out process, and help the client make different choices in subsequent relationships.

Like non-transgender people, transgender individuals often approach sexual relationships within paradigms prevailing in our culture. This becomes extra important as they seek to affirm their gender identity. Along with economic necessity, this is why transgender individuals are especially vulnerable to participation in sex work: initially, the attention from men can serve as a powerful affirmation of being a woman or a gay man. For gay transgender men, the emphasis on sexual performance and promiscuity in the gay community can interfere with getting intimacy needs met and increases their vulnerability to human immunodeficiency virus (HIV) infection. However, like bisexual individuals, transgender individuals have an opportunity to move beyond the confines and pitfalls of normative heterosexuality and homosexuality; indeed, some have begun to define a transgender sexuality distinct from male and female, gay/lesbian, and straight sexuality (Alexander & Yescavage 2004; Bockting et al. 2009).

Vignette G

Alex (aged 36 years) was married when he presented with a desire for sex reassignment. In the course of therapy, it became clear that his marriage would not survive the gender role transition. Coming from a place of guilt, he almost transferred all of his assets to his wife without adequately taking care of himself. The therapist and his transgender therapy group helped him to stand up for himself and negotiate a more equitable arrangement. After grieving the loss of his marriage, and now living in the female gender role, she identified as Lisa and began dating. At first, she dated men, feeling very affirmed by them, particularly as the receptive partner during anal intercourse. However, Lisa learned that many of these men were primarily interested in sex, which, after a while, was no longer satisfying for her. She wanted more.

Lisa longed for love and affection. As she had previously experienced such intimacy with women, she was encouraged not to limit herself to male partners. Lisa had to adjust to the idea of dating a woman as a woman, recognizing that people would probably perceive their relationship as lesbian. She began to identify as bisexual and joined a bisexual support group in the community. There, she fell head over heels in love with a female group member. They had an intense relationship for 3 months. When it ended, Lisa was devastated. The therapist commended her for her courage in having allowed herself, for the first time, to have such strong feelings as a woman for a woman, and empathized with the rejection she felt now that it was over.

After a brief period, Lisa resumed dating. Eventually, she met her current partner, also a transgender woman. Both Lisa and her partner had genital reconstructive surgery. In the safety of their relationship, they explored their sexuality, including the sexual functioning of their genitals following surgery. Most importantly, Lisa had found her soul mate. When asked to define their relationship, Lisa responded, "This relationship is more than I ever expected. I can truly say that I am happy. Is our relationship heterosexual? No. Is our relationship homosexual? No. We are simply two people proud to be transgender and in love with one another."

Vignette H

Jack (aged 24 years) is a transsexual man who had just completed chest surgery when he came to the clinic. He described a history of relationships with women while identifying as a lesbian until he met his current partner, Angie (aged 31 years), a heterosexual woman. Angie had never been with a female-bodied person. She was previously married and had two children, a 5-year-old boy and a 3-year-old girl. She had financial difficulties; her ex-husband had not paid child support since losing his job. Even though Jack's therapy group expressed concern over his taking on too much, 3 months into the relationship, Jack decided to move in with Angie. Jack talked about how much better this relationship felt than his previous relationships with lesbian-identified women.

She made him "feel like a man." In addition, Jack got along beautifully with Angie's children, enjoying the role of father figure.

Five months later, the "honeymoon" was over. Jack had paid more than his share of the rent, and had spent additional money to support the family. His savings account was depleted. Moreover, Jack had caught Angie flirting with another man, and had become furious. Nevertheless, it was extremely difficult for Jack to end the relationship. When he did, several months later, his parents took him in and consoled him. The group empathized and, after the immediate grief was processed, encouraged Jack to take inventory of what had happened, and learn to take better care of himself in subsequent relationships.

Identity Integration

In the final stage, integration, the individual incorporates public and private identities into an integrated and positive self-image. Having formed a comfortable gender and sexual identity, the individual can now integrate into the rest of the social fabric, find social support, and experience intimate relationships. In this final stage, being transgender is no longer the most important signifier of one's identity but, rather, one of several. A hallmark of this stage is that there is less preoccupation with identity labels. During the stages of coming out, exploration, and intimacy, labels defining one's identity, such as transgender, bigender, genderqueer, cross-dresser, gay, and lesbian, are an important part of developing a positive sense of self. During the stage of integration, these labels are less important. The individual's overall identity as a person becomes more important for self-definition than gender or sexual identity.

Integration implies a deeper level of self-acceptance. Passing becomes less and less important. Rather than insisting on being recognized as a woman or a man, the individual tolerates ambiguity. While the use of appropriate pronouns was previously all-important, during the integration stage misuse of pronouns is no longer perceived as a failure (to pass) or a sign of disrespect (you know I am transgender, but you refuse to employ the right pronouns because you do not approve of transgender people). Similarly, while being transgender was previously first and foremost on the individual's mind, now days go by without it being given much thought. One is living life, and if situations arise in which being transgender is relevant, one is comfortable addressing it. Ignorance is no longer taken as personal rejection but, rather, as a characteristic of the person exhibiting it. The transgender individual is willing to inform this person in order to complete the social transaction, if necessary. The individual no longer leads with shame or with pride, but leads instead with self-acceptance and confidence. Exuding this confidence, and displaying comfort and openness with one's transgenderism when necessary, often has a positive impact on others. Indeed, research has shown that personal contact with a transgender person is the best predictor of a positive and accepting attitude (Kendel et al. 1997).

Individuals in this stage face other developmental tasks and stages of adulthood, such as midlife and aging. They may continue to experience some of the issues of the previous stages of development, and continue the process of consolidation and integration. In some ways, coming out becomes an everyday experience, whether looking in the mirror, meeting a new person, applying for a job, or seeing a new health care provider. Relationships may be quite stable, or new relationships may begin. The individual in this stage manages crises or difficulties with growing confidence, self-esteem, pride, and wisdom.

Vignette I

Anne (aged 31 years), a transgender woman, returned to our clinic about 7 years after successfully coming out and having genital reconstructive surgery. The experience had been positive. She had the advantage of being young (less lost time and fewer lost opportunities) and the privilege of passing extremely well. She was indistinguishable from a non-transgender woman.

Ironically, Anne's success was at the heart of her presenting problems. Anne explained that she had become increasingly isolated. She had pushed herself to date, and had actually met some nice men who were interested in her, but two recent experiences had triggered shame and anxiety. In the first such experience, she felt a mutual attraction with a man who was "marriage material." In the second, she received a promotion at work. Both of these events triggered feelings of unworthiness, and she wondered if they would have happened if people knew of her transgender identity. Anne's ability to easily pass had protected her from confronting her shame and self-hatred. Now, it was interfering with feeling authentic and feeling that she deserved the good things that life was bringing her.

Anne realized that she needed to reconnect with the transgender community. She joined a support group for transgender people who had completed sex reassignment, and began to confront her internalized transphobia. She reached a deeper level of acceptance of her transgender identity. The group gave Anne permission to enjoy her ability to easily pass, but encouraged her to disclose her transgender identity at appropriate times, in appropriate ways, with people who mattered. Anne did so with the man she was dating and with her supervisor on the job. Both reacted with interest and support.

Subsequently, Anne discussed her sexuality and sexual response with the women in the group, gaining insights that helped her in the relationship with her newly found boyfriend. No longer was she preoccupied with figuring out how a woman is supposed to function sexually. She was able to relax and surrender in the relationship, now that her partner knew and accepted her transsexuality. Anne had managed to give transgenderism a proper place in her life: no longer something to be ashamed of, but something that she could address, if necessary.

Vignette J

Carl (the same individual described in Vignette F, now aged 29) lived life "like any other man." But the longer he lived in the male role, the more he reclaimed some of the things he had learned in the lesbian feminist community prior to transitioning. He decided to stop engaging in the same chauvinist behaviors that he used to decry. He asked his therapy group and friends to let him know when he was crossing the line. Carl valued his connection with the transgender community, but it was not his only or even his main social venue; he had developed a diverse circle of friends and affiliations.

Previously, Carl's relationship with his family had been strained as a result of some acting-out during adolescence. But closeness developed after he came out and resolved his gender identity conflict. Although his mother initially struggled due to her religious beliefs, she witnessed how the gender role change had made her child blossom. She simply could not deny that it appeared right for him.

Carl entered into a committed relationship with a woman. The couple enjoyed sexual intimacy that incorporated his transgender anatomy. Carl consulted with an attorney to determine how best to legally protect himself and his partner when they made plans to adopt a child. He made sure to amend the sex on his birth certificate before getting married.

Conclusion

We want to reiterate that people will not necessarily go through these steps in a linear fashion. Individuals do not progress neatly from stage to stage. We have presented a general model, which does not always fit individual experiences. Life is more idiosyncratic than the model suggests. However, the model has been useful for us and for our clients in understanding the development of an integrated identity.

In addition, completion of some of the developmental tasks embedded in these stages of development may take a long time, or even a lifetime. For example, it is not uncommon for those who undergo transition to take a break from therapy after surgery. They may return later to work on intimacy and on examination and acceptance of a transgender identity on a deeper level.

Too many others remain stuck in early stages because of a variety of biopsychosocial factors. They never experience an integrated identity. Such an identity seems to be reserved for those who are extremely resilient or happen to live and work in an environment that is more tolerant of diversity. Society will require further changes in order to become more tolerant of diversity, provide proper education, and provide access to transgender-sensitive care to give transgender individuals a greater opportunity to achieve integrated identities. It will take a broader public health approach to promote sexual health for all citizens (Coleman 2002).

The most important message is that coming out is, first and foremost, a psychosocial process, and the role of psychotherapy in facilitating this process can be very powerful (Bockting 2008, 2013; Coleman et al. 2012; Fraser 2009). Many individuals may have found an integrated identity without the assistance of psychotherapy; there are many resilient people and adaptable environments. However, given the complexities of the process, many can benefit from the assistance of transgender-affirmative psychotherapy. In the past, psychotherapy was viewed with suspicion by many transgender individuals because its aim was to "cure" them, or because the professional was mainly perceived as a "gatekeeper." We hope that we have suggested a way to manage this dynamic and offer the best psychological support possible to assist transgender individuals affected by stigma to develop resilience and a positive sense of self and identity.

References

Alexander, J., and Yescavage, K. (Eds.) (2004). *Bisexuality and Transgenderism: Intersexions of the Others*. Binghamton, NY: The Haworth Press.

American Psychiatric Association. (2013). *Diagnostic and Statistical Manual of Mental Disorders (DSM-5*)*. Washington: American Psychiatric Association.

Benjamin, H. (1966). *The Transsexual Phenomenon*. New York: Julian Press.

Blanchard, R., Clemmensen, L.H., and Steiner, B.W. (1987). Heterosexual and homosexual gender dysphoria. *Archives of Sexual Behavior*, 16(2): 139–152.

Bockting, W.O. (1997a). The assessment and treatment of gender dysphoria. *Directions in Clinical and Counseling Psychology*, 7(11): 1–23.

Bockting, W.O. (1997b). Transgender coming out: Implications for the clinical management of gender dysphoria. In B. Bullough, V.L. Bullough, and J. Elias (Eds.), *Gender Blending* (pp. 48–52). Amherst, NY: Prometheus Books.

Bockting, W.O. (1999). From construction to context: Gender through the eyes of the transgendered. *SIECUS Report*, 28(1): 3–7.

Bockting, W.O. (2008). Psychotherapy and the real-life experience: From gender dichotomy to gender diversity. *Sexologies*, 17.4 211–224.

Bockting, W.O. (2013). Transgender identity development. In D. L. Tolman, & L. Diamond (Eds.), *American Psychological Association's Handbook of Sexuality and Psychology* (pp. 739–758). Washington, DC: American Psychological Association.

Bockting, W.O., and Coleman, E. (1992). A comprehensive approach to the treatment of gender dysphoria. *Journal of Psychology and Human Sexuality*, 5(4): 131–155.

Bockting, W., and Coleman, E. (2007). Developmental stages of the transgender coming out process: Toward an integrated identity. In R. Ettner, S. Monstrey, & E. Eyler (Eds.), *Principles of Transgender Medicine and Surgery* (pp. 185–208). New York: The Haworth Press.

Bockting, W., Benner, A., and Coleman, E. (2009). Gay and bisexual identity development among female-to-male transsexuals in North America: Emergence of a transgender sexuality. *Archives of Sexual Behavior*, 38, (5): 688–701.

Bockting, W.O., Miner, M.H., Swinburne Romine, R.E., Hamilton, A., and Coleman, E. (2013). Stigma, mental health, and resilience among an online sample of the U.S. transgender population. *American Journal of Public Health*, 103(5): 943–951.

Bowlby, J. (1969). *Attachment and Loss: Attachment (Vol. 1)*. London: Hogarth Press.

Cass, V.C. (1979). Homosexual identity formation: A theoretical model. *Journal of Homosexuality*, 4(3): 219–235.

Clements-Nolle, K., Marx, R., and Katz, M. (2006). Attempted suicide among transgender persons: The influence of gender-based discrimination and victimization. *Journal of Homosexuality*, 51(3): 53–69.

Coleman, E. (1981/82). Developmental stages of the coming out process. *Journal of Homosexuality*, 7(2/3): 31–43.

Coleman, E. (2002). Promoting sexual health and responsible sexual behavior: An introduction. *Journal of Sex Research*, 39(1): 3–6.

Coleman, E. and Bockting, W.O. (1989). "Heterosexual" prior to sex reassignment – "homosexual" afterward: A case study of a female-to-male transsexual. *Journal of Psychology and Human Sexuality*, 1(2): 69–82.

Coleman, E. and Rosser, B.R.S. (1996). Gay and bisexual male sexuality. In R.P. Cabaj, and T.S. Stein (Eds.), *Textbook on Homosexuality and Mental Health* (pp. 707–721). Washington, DC: American Psychiatric Press.

Coleman, E., Bockting, W.O., and Gooren, L. (1993). Homosexual and bisexual identity development in female-to-male transsexuals. *Archives of Sexual Behavior*, 22(1): 37–50.

Coleman, E., Bockting, W., Botzer, M., Cohen-Kettenis, P., DeCuypere, G., Feldman, J., Fraser, L. et al. (2012). Standards of Care for the health of transsexual, transgender, and gender-nonconforming people, version 7. *International Journal of Transgenderism*, 13(4): 165–232.

Devor, A.H. (2004). Witnessing and mirroring: A fourteen-stage model of transsexual identity formation. *Journal of Gay and Lesbian Psychotherapy*, 8(1/2): 41–67.

Drescher, J., Cohen-Kettenis, P., and Winter, S. (2012). Minding the body: Situating gender identity diagnoses in the ICD-11. *International Review of Psychiatry* 24(6): 568–577.

Emerson, S., and Rosenfeld, C. (1996). Stages of adjustment in family members of transgender individuals. *Journal of Family Psychotherapy*, 7(3): 1–12.

Erikson, E. (1956). The problem of ego identity. *Journal of the American Psychoanalytic Association*, 4(1): 56–121.

Feinberg, L. (1996). *Transgender Warriors: Making History from Joan of Arc to RuPaul*. Boston, MA: Beacon Press.

Feinbloom, D.H., Fleming, M., Kijewski, V., and Schulter, M. (1976). Lesbian/feminist orientation among male-to-female transsexuals. *Journal of Homosexuality*, 2(1): 56–71.

Fraser, L. (2009). Depth psychotherapy with transgender people. *Sexual and Relationship Therapy*, 24(2): 126–142.

Freud, S., and Brill, A.A. (Eds.) (1995). *The Basic Writings of Sigmund Freud: Psychopathology of Everyday Life/The Interpretation of Dreams/Three Contributions to the Theory of Sex*. New York: Modern Library Edition.

Gagne, P., Tewksbury, R., and McGaughey, D. (1997). Coming out and crossing over: Identity formation and proclamation in a transgender community. *Gender and Society*, 11(4): 478–508.

Grossman, A.H., and D'Augelli, A.R. (2007). Transgender youth and life-threatening behaviors. *Suicide and Life-Threatening Behavior*, 37(5): 527–537.

Harrison, J., Grant, J., and Herman, J. L. (2012). A gender not listed here: Genderqueers, gender rebels, and otherwise in the National Transgender Discrimination Survey. *LGBTQ Public Policy Journal at the Harvard Kennedy School*, 2(1): 13–24.

Hendricks, M.L., and Testa, R.J. (2012). A conceptual framework for clinical work with transgender and gender nonconforming clients: An adaptation of the Minority Stress Model. *Professional Psychology: Research and Practice*, 43(5): 460–467.

Kaufman, G. (1992). *Shame: The Power of Caring* (3rd ed.). Rochester, NY: Schenkman Books.

Kendel, M., Devor, H., and Strapko, N. (1997). Feminist and lesbian opinions about transsexuals. In B. Bullough, V. Bullough, and J. Elias (Eds.), *Gender Blending* (pp. 146–159). Amherst, NY: Prometheus.

Kubler-Ross, E. (1970). *On Death and Dying*. London: Tavistock Publications.

Lev, A. (2004). *Transgender Emergence*. Binghamton, NY: The Haworth Press.

Lewins, F. (1995). *Transsexualism in Society: A Sociology of Male-to-Female Transsexuals*. South Melbourne: MacMillan Education, Australia.

Minton, H.L., and McDonald, G.J. (1984). Homosexual identity formation as a developmental process. *Journal of Homosexuality*, 9(2/3): 91–104.

Money, J. (1974). Two names, two wardrobes, two personalities. *Journal of Homosexuality*, 1(1): 65–70.

Person, E., and Ovesey, L. (1974a). The transsexual syndrome in males. I. Primary transsexualism. *American Journal of Psychotherapy*, 28: 4–20.

Person, E., and Ovesey, L. (1974b). The transsexual syndrome in males. II. Secondary transsexualism. *American Journal of Psychotherapy*, 28: 174–193.

Plummer, K. (1975). *Sexual Stigma: An Interactionist Account*. London: Routledge Kegan Paul.

Pollack, R. (1997). What is to be done? A commentary on the recommended guidelines. In G.E. Israel, and D.E. Tarver II (Eds.), *Transgender Care* (pp. 229–235). Philadelphia, PA: Temple University Press.

Stone, S. (1991). The empire strikes back: A posttranssexual manifesto. In J. Epstein and K. Straub (Eds.), *Body Guards: The Cultural Politics of Gender Ambiguity* (pp. 280–304). New York: Routledge.

Stryker, S. (1997). Over and out of academe: Transgender studies come of age. In G.E. Israel, and D.E. Tarver II (Eds.), *Transgender Care* (pp. 241–247). Philadelphia, PA: Temple University Press.

Sullivan, H.S. (1953). *The Interpersonal Theory of Psychiatry*. New York: Norton.

9 Sexual Function in the Transgender Population

Kevan Wylie, Edward Wootton, and Sophie Carlson

Introduction

This chapter is a focus on sexual function and dysfunction in transgender patients before and after surgical intervention. It explores an area of quite limited research and brings to light some of the key issues faced by this specific population.

The literature confirms that in the vast majority of cases sex reassignment surgery (SRS) improves the lives of transgender people overall, although this does not necessarily extend to sexual functioning (De Cuypere et al., 2005; Lawrence, 2003). Weyers et al. (2009) found that the general health of patients improved following SRS based on self-perception and that both self- and peer-perceived body image also improved. However, the research also found that inadequate sexual functioning caused patients difficulty postsurgery. Particular problems highlighted were reduced arousal, inadequate lubrication, and a painful experience of sex. With SRS being such an extensive and invasive option it is understandable, though not ideal, that there is a high chance of functional loss. Patients must be suitably assessed, informed, and supported throughout the process, but levels of postsurgical regret are extremely low (De Cuypere et al., 2006; Lobato et al., 2006; Royal College of Psychiatrists, 2013). Rehman et al. (1999) found that all 28 of the male-to-female (MTF) patients in their study felt better after surgery than they did before surgery. A total of 25/28 reported no medical problems post-SRS; however, a quarter did complain of lack of vaginal depth. This was most often due to patients failing to dilate their vaginoplasty adequately to keep it open throughout the complete length.

More so than many medical conditions, the key to treating people with gender dysphoria is a multidisciplinary team approach. The main reason for this is the significant emotional and psychological unrest associated with the treatment process. In cisgender populations, although psychotherapy is used, the management of sexual dysfunction is mainly focused on physical treatments. In transgender people there is much more emphasis on psychological therapy alongside the physical management. This is not to say that psychotherapy is a requirement in the transition process, but it certainly has a big part to play in many cases. Unfortunately, studies have shown that the understanding of sexuality in transgender patients is inadequately discussed between health care professionals, despite the recognition that sexuality is an area which is vital to self-esteem, mental health, and quality of life (World Association for Sexual Health, 2008).

Transgender people face distinct issues that the majority of the general population do not encounter. In the transgender population there is very clear distinction between satisfaction and sexual function, whereas in the cisgender population these two outcomes usually come hand in hand (Klein & Gorzalka, 2009). A number of studies have shown that, although many transgender patients are less sexually functional in a physical sense after surgery, they are still more satisfied (De Cuypere et al., 2005; Sørensen, 1981). For example, Lief and Hubschman (1993) found that eight of 14 MTF transgender people reported decreased ability to orgasm, but increased satisfaction. In the female-to-male (FTM) group of the same study, both ability to orgasm and satisfaction improved after SRS. This highlights that, while sexual function is of course important, there is more value in SRS than sexual function alone.

For many transgender patients, sexual dysfunction is an issue prior to surgery and the opportunity to participate sexually as a member of their desired gender is an overwhelming driver to opt for SRS (Lief & Hubschman, 1993). People report various problems with sexual function before surgical intervention. In particular incongruence between physical sexual satisfaction and psychological sexual dissatisfaction is an important issue (Doorduin & Van Burlo, 2014). In one piece of research, a patient describes his experience: "I'm being touched in one spot and it feels pleasant, but on the other hand I do not want it to feel pleasant, because I associated that with an organ I didn't really want to have" (Doorduin & Van Burlo, 2014). Some participants' distress at intercourse in a body with which they felt gender dysphoria was so great that they likened it to "a feeling of being raped," not by their partners, but by the situation. In one study, some participants were reluctant to have sexual relations until "they were complete," i.e., had undergone phalloplasty (Devor, 1993). This highlights the important point that sexual function has both mental and physical components. It also shows that gender identity itself is a core component which intertwines with sexual attraction to make up sexual identity. The mind *and* the body must react positively and in unity for an individual to experience pleasurable sexual function.

The discordance of mind and body of transgender people prior to surgery can be a barrier to fully exploring their sexuality. It is likely that in transgender patients there is a fear of rejection. Studies have reported the frustration of transmen who are rejected by their gay male lovers because of a lack of a penis (Colton Meier et al., 2013; Rowniak & Chesla, 2013). However, this is not to say that all transmen require a penis for complete satisfaction with their transition, as Bockting et al. (2009) have found. For some transmen, their gender role is integral to the act of intimacy. Coping mechanisms may be used to achieve this gender role during sex, such as imagining themselves as a man during the sexual act (Doorduin & Van Burlo, 2014). Another technique is "recoding" of the body parts. For example, transmen may recode genitalia which were once associated with being feminine and give them a masculine name instead (Bettcher, 2014; Schilt & Windsor, 2014).

The placation of gender dysphoria after surgical intervention often comes with a stage of sexual experimentation, often termed "the second puberty" (Doorduin & Van Burlo, 2014). Many transgender people miss essential stages of sexual development before transition, despite many engaging in sexual encounters at this time. Participants report a pressure to conform to social expectations and explain that this made it harder to identify their true desires and communicate these desires to their partners (Doorduin & Van Burlo, 2014). The rediscovery of sexuality may in turn lead to the rediscovery of sexual preferences, in terms of both orientation and activities. From this fluidity of sexuality, new sexual preferences can arise in the transgender patient. There may be a shift in the objects of attraction, such as MTF shifting from a preference for women to a preference for men (Daskalos, 1998).

In the literature, sexual function is measured in a number of ways, including the desire for sex and the ability to orgasm (Lief & Hubschman, 1993; Wierckx et al., 2014). It should be considered that some factors affecting desire are not related to SRS but may still impact the results of studies: sexual desire decreasing with age, for example (Eplov et al., 2007), and also the fact that hormone therapy, particularly testosterone, will be affecting desire (Bancroft, 2005). Research suggests that in FTM transitions libido tends to increase, whereas in the MTF populations libido decreases (Doorduin & Van Burlo, 2014; Wierckx et al., 2014). This is very likely due to the hormonal changes within the body. The authors of one such study commented that, while the transwomen did experience a loss of libido, this was not necessarily distressing (Wierckx et al., 2014). The researchers suggest that other factors such as "an increasingly positive self-image due to the transition and a boosted self-esteem from being recognized as female" may compensate for the loss of libido (Wierckx et al., 2014). Another study investigating FTM transgender people found that sexual desire was increased in three-quarters of their patients after SRS (Wierckx et al., 2011). The study involved 45 FTM transgender people and explored desire using a self-report questionnaire. The authors theorized that the increased desire might be due to a number of factors, including relief of gender dysphoria and more satisfactory sexual relationships after SRS (Wierckx et al., 2011). It is worth mentioning that one paper investigated the prevalence of hypoactive sexual desire disorder (HSDD) in transwomen and found that, although one-third of transwomen experienced HSDD, this was not statistically significant compared to the control group (Elaut et al., 2008). Klein and Gorzalka (2009) summarized the results of a number of papers regarding sexual desire. An adapted version of their data is shown in Table 9.1.

Other papers investigate sexual function by looking at orgasmic changes. This involves both the ability to orgasm and the changes that have occurred between orgasm before surgery and orgasm after SRS. De Cuypere et al. (2005) conducted a study which focused on sexual and physical health postsurgery.

Table 9.1 Evidence of sexual desire in studies of postsurgical transgender people

Study	MTF/FTM	n	Outcome measure	Overall result
Elaut et al., 2008	MTF	62	Incidence of HSDD in MTFs compared to natal women	No significant difference
			Relationship between testosterone levels and sexual desire in MTFs	No significant relationship
Weyers et al., 2009	MTF	50	Sexual desire in MTFs compared to natal women without sexual complaints	Lower desire in MTFs
Rehman et al., 1999	MTF	28	Sexual desire over time	No change
Mate-Kole et al., 1990	MTF	20	Sexual desire following SRS	Increased
Lief & Hubschman, 1993	MTF	14	Sexual activity following SRS	Increased
Lawrence, 2005	MTF	232	Incidence of masturbation in MTFs compared to male and female comparison groups	Higher in MTFs
Cohen-Kettenis & Van Goozen, 1997	MTF	5	Frequency of masturbation following SRS	Decreased
Smith et al., 2001	MTF	7	Frequency of masturbation following SRS	Decreased
De Cuypere et al., 2005	MTF	32	Frequency of masturbation following SRS	No change
Sørensen, 1981	MTF	23	Frequency of masturbation	Infrequent to never
Schroder & Carroll, 1999	MTF	17	Frequency of sexual desire	Low
Lobato et al., 2006	MTF/FTM	18	Sexual activity following SRS	Increased
Lief & Hubschman, 1993	FTM	9	Sexual activity following SRS	Increased
De Cuypere et al., 2005	FTM	23	Frequency of masturbation following SRS	Increased
Cohen-Kettenis & Van Goozen, 1997	FTM	14	Frequency of masturbation following SRS	Increased or unchanged
Smith et al., 2001	FTM	13	Frequency of masturbation following SRS	Increased or unchanged

MTF, male-to-female; FTM, female-to-male; HSDD, hypoactive sexual desire disorder; SRS, sex reassignment surgery.

They followed up 32 MTF patients and 23 FTM transgender people. Results from the study showed that FTM patients experienced greater sexual excitement and reached orgasm more easily than MTF patients. They also described the sensation of orgasm as becoming shorter but more powerful (an outcome that was also noted in a separate study: Doorduin & Van Burlo, 2014). Of these transmales, the ones with an erection prosthesis reported meeting sexual expectations more so than those without the prosthesis. They also suffered more pain during intercourse, however. In the MTF population, secretion of lubricating fluid was reported during sexual excitation and the opposite effect from FTM patients was noticed with the feeling of orgasm: people described a "more intense, smoother and longer" orgasmic sensation. The authors also commented that the types of sexual acts people involved themselves in changed after SRS. FTM transgender people moved from mainly clitoral stimulation to penetrative vaginal sex with their new penis while MTF transgender people moved to predominantly vaginal intercourse as opposed to both vaginal and anal intercourse preoperatively. Again, Klein and Gorzalka (2009) summarized the results of papers regarding orgasm in transgender patients. An adapted version of their data is shown in Table 9.2. The summarized findings paint a mixed picture of how likely patients are to be able to orgasm post-SRS. Although the majority of studies show a high percentage of patients able to achieve orgasm, a number also show worryingly low outcomes. There are any number of reasons for these results. Patients who are particularly satisfied or dissatisfied with surgery will likely have high or low ability to orgasm respectively. Furthermore, surgery has come a long way in recent years so the more recent procedures are likely to result in better functionality than older operations.

There are a number of patients for whom surgery is not the desired final outcome of transitional therapy. One study investigated this and questioned patients on their views of body modification and SRS (Schilt & Windsor, 2014). The authors interviewed 74 transmen, the majority of whom underwent only hormone therapy and chest surgery. They received very varied responses from patients but a message that was repeated was that patients were more interested in feeling comfortable in their body than they necessarily were with having all male genitals. One patient who was not considering genital surgery made the comment, "I like what I've got now. I have a penis that works. I have many penises that work!" referring to his non-surgical, detachable penises (Schilt & Windsor, 2014). Another study showed that, for some FTM patients who began hormone therapy, their external appearance as male made them feel comfortable enough to incorporate their vagina into sexual practice, meaning that surgery was not a necessary step to take (Bockting et al., 2009).

In summary, SRS is a procedure that is becoming increasingly common. The surgical techniques used are constantly improving and, as a result, so are functional outcomes of surgery. It is key to remember that sexual satisfaction and function are closely related but are not the same thing and that many transgender people may compromise to an extent on functionality if it means greater sexual satisfaction.

Table 9.2 Orgasmic capacity in studies of post-surgical transgender people

Study	MTF/FTM	n	Able to orgasm post-SRS
Soli et al., 2008	MTF	26	27%
Lief & Hubschman, 1993	MTF	14	29%
Brotto et al., 2005	MTF	15	40%
Lindemalm et al., 1986	MTF	13	46%
Schroder & Carroll, 1999	MTF	17	66%
Eldh et al., 1997	MTF	33	67%
Eicher et al., 1991	MTF	50	70–80%
Rehman et al., 1999	MTF	28	79%
Hage & Karim, 1996	MTF	59	80%
Stein et al., 1990	MTF	10	80%
Perovic et al., 2005	MTF	89	82%
Van Noort & Nicolai, 1993	MTF	22	82%
Freundt et al., 1993	MTF	19	84%
Lawrence, 2005	MTF	232	85%
Ross & Need, 1989	MTF	14	85%
Rehman & Melman, 1999	MTF	10	90%
Rubin, 1993	MTF	13	92%
Eldh, 1993	MTF	20	100%
De Cuypere et al., 2005	MTF/FTM	32	65%
Lief & Hubschman, 1993	FTM	9	78%
Sørensen, 1981	FTM	8	100%
De Cuypere et al., 2005	FTM	23	78–95%

MTF, male-to-female; FTM, female-to-male; SRS, sex reassignment surgery.

References

Bancroft, J., 2005. The endocrinology of sexual arousal. *Journal of Endocrinology*, 186(3), pp.411–27.

Bettcher, T., 2014. When selves have sex: What the phenomenology of transsexuality can teach about sexual orientation. *Journal of Homosexuality*, 61(5), pp.605–20.

Bockting, W., Benner, A., & Coleman, E., 2009. Gay and bisexual identity development among female-to-male transsexual people in North America: Emergence of a transgender sexuality. *Archives of Sexual Behaviour*, 38, pp.688–701.

Brotto, L., et al., 2005. Psychophysiological and subjective sexual arousal to visual sexual stimuli in new women. *Journal of Psychosomatic Obstetrics & Gynaecology*, 26(4), pp.237–44.

Cohen-Kettenis, P., & Van Goozen, S., 1997. Sex reassignment of adolescent transsexual people: A follow-up study. *Journal of the American Academy of Child & Adolescent Psychiatry*, 36(2), pp.263–71.

Colton Meier, S., Pardo, S.T., Labuski, C., & Babcock J., 2013. Measures of clinical health among female-to-male transgender persons as a function of sexual orientation. *Archives of Sexual Behaviour*, 42, pp.463–74.

Daskalos, C.T., 1998. Changes in sexual orientation of six heterosexual male-to-female transsexual people. *Archives of Sexual Behaviour*, 27, pp.605–14.

De Cuypere, G., et al., 2005. Sexual and physical health after sex reassignment surgery. *Archives of Sexual Behaviour*, 34(6), pp.679–90.

De Cuypere, G., et al., 2006. Long-term follow-up: psychosocial outcome of Belgian transsexual people after sex reassignment surgery. *Sexologies*, 15(2), pp.126–33.

Devor, H., 1993. Sexual orientation identities, attractions and practices of female-to-male transsexual people. *Journal of Sex Research*, 30, pp.303–15.

Doorduin, T., & Van Burlo, W., 2014. Trans people's experience of sexuality in the Netherlands: A pilot study. *Journal of Homosexuality*, 61(5), pp.654–72.

Eicher, W., Schmitt, B., & Berger, C., 1991. Transfomationsoperation bei Mann-zu-Frau-Transexuellen: Darstellung der Method und Nachuntersuchung von 50 Operierten. *Zeitschrift Sex Forschung*, 4, pp.119–32.

Elaut, E., et al., 2008. Hypoactive sexual desire in transsexual women: Prevalence and association with testosterone levels. *European Journal of Endocrinology*, 158, pp.393–99.

Eldh, J., 1993. Construction of a neovagina with preservation of the glans penis as a clitoris in male transsexual people. *Plastic & Reconstructive Surgery*, 91(5), pp.895–900.

Eldh, J., Berg, A., & Gustafsson, M., 1997. Long-term follow up after sex reassignment surgery. *Scandinavian Journal of Plastic & Reconstructive Surgery & Hand Surgery*, 31(1), pp.39–45.

Eplov, L., et al., 2007. Sexual desire in a nationally representative Danish population. *Journal of Sexual Medicine*, 4(1), pp.47–56.

Freundt, I., et al., 1993. Long-term psychosexual and psychosocial performance of patients with a sigmoid neovagina. *American Journal of Obstetrics & Gynecology*, 169(5), pp.1210–14.

Hage, J., & Karim, R., 1996. Sensate pedicled neoclitoroplasty for male transsexual people: Amsterdam experience in the first 60 patients. *Annals of Plastic Surgery*, 36(6), pp.621–4.

Klein, C., & Gorzalka, B., 2009. Sexual functioning in transsexual people following hormone therapy and genital surgery: a review. *Journal of Sexual Medicine*, 6(11), pp.2922–39.

Lawrence, A., 2003. Factors associated with satisfaction or regret following male-to-female sex reassignment surgery. *Archives of Sexual Behaviour*, 32(4), pp.299–315.

Lief, H., & Hubschman, L., 1993. Orgasm in the postoperative transsexual. *Archives of Sexual Behaviour*, 22(2), pp.145–55.

Lindemalm, G., Körlin, D., & Uddenburg, N., 1986. Long-term follow-up of "sex change" in 13 male-to-female transsexual people. *Archives of Sexual Behaviour*, 15(3), pp.187–210.

Lobato, M., et al., 2006. Follow-up of sex reassignment surgery in transsexual people: A Brazillian cohort. *Archives of Sexual Behaviour*, 35(6), pp.711–15.

Mate-Kole, C., Freschi, M., & Robin, A., 1990. A controlled study of psychological and social change after surgical gender reassignment in selected male transsexual people. *British Journal of Psychiatry*, 157, pp.261–64.

Perovic, S., Stanojevic, D., & Djordjevic, M., 2005. Vaginoplasty in male to female transsexual people using penile skin and urethral flap. *International Journal of Transgenderism*, 8, pp.43–64.

Rehman, J., & Melman, A., 1999. Formation of neoclitoris from glans penis by reduction glansplasty with preservation of neurovascular bundle in male-to-female gender surgery: Functional and cosmetic outcome. *Journal of Urology*, 161(1), pp.200–6.

Rehman, J., et al., 1999. The reported sex and surgery satisfactions of 28 postoperative male-to-female transsexual patients. *Archives of Sexual Behaviour*, 28(1), pp.71–89.

Ross, M., & Need, J., 1989. Effects of adequacy of gender reassignment surgery on psychological adjustment: A follow-up of fourteen male-to-female patients. *Archives of Sexual Behaviour*, 18(2), pp.145–53.

Rowniak, S., & Chesla, C., 2003. Coming out for a third time: trans men, sexual orientation and identity. *Archives of Sexual Behaviour*, 42, pp.449–61.

Royal College of Psychiatrists, 2013. *Good Practice Guidelines for the Assessment and Treatment of Adults with Gender Dysphoria*. College Report CR181. London: Royal College of Psychiatrists.

Rubin, S., 1993. Sex-reassignment surgery male-to-female. Review, own results and report of a new technique using the glans penis as a pseudoclitoris. *Scandinavian Journal of Urology & Nephrology. Supplementum*, 154, pp.1–28.

Schilt, K., & Windsor, E., 2014. The sexual habitus of transgender men: negotiating sexuality through gender. *Journal of Homosexuality*, 61(5), pp.732–48.

Schroder, M., & Carroll, R., 1999. New women: Sexological outcomes of male-to-female gender reassignment surgery. *Journal of Sex Education & Therapy*, 24(3), pp.137–46.

Smith, Y., Van Goozen, S., & Cohen-Kettenis, P., 2001. Adolescents with gender identity disorder who were accepted or rejected for sex reassignment surgery: A prospective follow-up study. *Journal of the American Academy of Child & Adolescent Psychiatry*, 40(4), pp.472–81.

Soli, M., et al., 2008. Male to female gender reassignment: Modified surgical technique for creating the neoclitoris and mons veneris. *Journal of Sexual Medicine*, 5(1), pp.210–16.

Sørensen, T., 1981. A follow-up study of operated transsexual females. *Acta Psychiatrica Scandinavica*, 64(1), pp.50–64.

Stein, M., Tiefer, L., & Melman, A., 1990. Followup observations of operated male-to-female transsexual people. *Journal of Urology*, 143(6), pp.1188–92.

Van Noort, D., & Nicolai, J., 1993. Comparison of two methods of vagina construction in transsexual people. *Plastic & Reconstructive Surgery*, 91(7), pp.1308–15.

Weyers, S., et al., 2009. Long-term assessment of the physical, mental and sexual health among transsexual women. *Journal of Sexual Medicine*, 6(3), pp.752–60.

Wierckx, K., et al., 2011. Sexual desire in female-to-male transsexual persons: exploration of the role of testosterone administration. *European Journal of Endocrinology*, 165(2), pp.331–7.

Wierckx, K., et al., 2014. Sexual desire in trans persons: associations with sex reassignment treatment. *Journal of Sexual Medicine*, 11(1), pp.107–18.

World Association for Sexual Health, 2008. *Sexual Health for the Millennium. A Declaration and Technical Document*. Minneapolis, MN: World Association for Sexual Health.

10 Hormone Treatment of Adult Transgender People

Louis J. Gooren

Introduction

As described elsewhere in this book, transsexualism is the condition in which a person with apparently normal somatic sexual differentiation is convinced that he or she is actually a member of the other sex. This conviction is accompanied by the irresistible urge to live in that preferred gender: hormonally, anatomically, legally, and psychosocially. The principles of hormone treatment of this population will be discussed herein.

General Principles of Treatment

The administration of cross-sex hormones to transgender people is, from the viewpoint of endocrinology, seemingly unorthodox. The indication is not based on technical endocrine grounds, such as a deficiency or excess of hormone action. Therefore, cross-sex hormone treatment has met with some reservations in professional circles, although acceptance is growing. For instance, the Endocrine Society has issued guidelines for treatment (Hembree et al. 2009).

The indication for treatment is the conclusion that sex reassignment will bring relief to an individual suffering from gender dysphoria—the extreme feeling often described as being "trapped in the wrong body." Although endocrine treatment is recommended by mental health professionals, it is the prescribing physician who retains responsibility for the intervention and the quality of care. It is important to maintain a close collaboration with the mental health professional. Medical practitioners are encouraged to follow the *Standards of Care* drafted by the international organization committed to professional assistance to transgender and transsexual people (Coleman et al. 2011). The major purpose of the *Standards of Care* is to articulate this organization's professional consensus opinion and available evidence about the psychological, medical, and surgical management of gender non-conforming conditions. These *Standards* provide guidance to professionals practicing in this area, around the world, many of whom work in isolation, far from mainstream medicine or endocrinology. The *Standards* may also be useful in issues involving legal medicine, if it becomes necessary to identify professional standards. Persons with gender identity conditions and their families, as well as social institutions, can turn to the *Standards of Care* to understand the current thinking of professionals in this field. Before initiating hormonal or surgical treatments, the physician should counsel the patient regarding the following issues.

Realistic Expectations of Treatment

The only benefit that sex reassignment can confer is relief of gender dysphoria; all human problems outside the arena of gender dysphoria will remain, although overall well-being usually improves (Ettner & Wylie 2013). Unrealistic expectations that persons may harbor concerning the impact of hormonal and surgical treatment on transition must therefore be addressed. Also, the limitations of cross-sex hormone administration in adult, and certainly elderly, patients, should be frankly discussed. After years of silent suffering and loneliness, fantasy can often supersede reality. Contact with others who are in the process of transition, or who have completed this process, can be quite helpful in shaping a person's expectations of what can be reasonably achieved with hormonal and surgical treatment. Likewise, the problems—personal, professional, and social—that may arise, both initially and long-term, can often be averted. It is important to realize that somatic treatment of transgender patients—both endocrinological and surgical—is rehabilitative rather than curative. Consequently, quality of life for reassigned persons will definitely improve, but will be characterized by certain limitations, similar to the medical treatment of many congenital conditions.

Hormonal Gender-Affirming Therapy

The acquisition of the secondary sex characteristics of the other gender, to the fullest extent possible, is fundamental to sex reassignment for the transsexual patient. Obviously, acquisition of these secondary sex characteristics is contingent on sex steroids. There is no known essential difference in sensitivity to the biological action of sex steroids on the basis of genetic configurations or gonadal status. Adults undergoing sex reassignment have the disadvantage that, by adulthood, several years of hormonal masculinization or feminization have already occurred.

Unfortunately, the elimination of these hormonally induced natal sex characteristics is rarely complete. In male-to-female transsexual patients, the previous effects of androgens on the skeleton (average greater height; size and shape of hands, feet, and jaw; and pelvic structure) cannot be reversed by hormone treatment. Conversely, the relatively short stature in female-to-male patients as compared to natal males (on average 12 cm), and the often broader hip configuration, will not change with androgen treatment. These features, however, show considerable overlap between the sexes, more so in some races than in others. Thus, for some individuals, characteristics of the natal sex will be comparatively less visible than for others.

The typical adult requesting treatment is a young to middle-aged healthy person and, therefore, there are few absolute or relative contraindications against cross-sex hormone administration. Relative contraindications for estrogen use are a strong family history of breast cancer, personal history of thromboembolic disease, or the presence of a prolactin-producing pituitary tumor. Relative contraindications for androgen use are hormone-dependent cancers or severe lipid disorders with cardiovascular complications. Caution must be used with sex steroid administration when there is serious cardiovascular, cerebrovascular, or thromboembolic disease, or with marked obesity, poorly controlled diabetes mellitus, or serious liver disease (Gooren 2011; Hembree et al. 2009).

It is advisable to discontinue sex steroid administration 3–4 weeks prior to any elective surgical intervention. Immobilization is a thrombogenic risk factor, and sex steroids may aggravate the risk of thromboembolism. Like other patients on sex steroid replacement, once fully mobilized following the surgical procedure, the patient may resume hormone therapy.

Treatment of Male-to-Female Patients

For the male-to-female transsexual individual, elimination of body hair growth, induction of breast formation, and a more female fat distribution are essential. To accomplish these goals, a near-complete reduction of the biological effects of androgens is required. Administration of estrogens alone will suppress gonadotropin output and therefore androgen production, but dual therapy with a compound that suppresses androgen secretion or action, and a second compound that supplies estrogen, is more effective.

For suppression of androgen secretion or action, several agents are available. In Europe, the most widely used drug is cyproterone acetate (usually 50 mg twice daily), a progestational compound with antiandrogenic properties. If that is not available, then medroxyprogesterone acetate, 5–10 mg/day, is a less effective alternative. Spironolactone (up to 200 mg twice daily, if tolerated), a diuretic with antiandrogenic properties, has similar effects, and is widely available. Long-acting gonadotropin-releasing hormone agonists, injected monthly, also inhibit gonadotropin secretion. Finasteride (5 mg/day), a 5-alpha-reductase inhibitor, might also be considered (Gooren 2011; Hembree et al. 2009) on the basis of its pharmacological action—inhibition of the conversion of testosterone to 5-alpha-testosterone. This is less useful when testosterone is already profoundly suppressed by other pharmacological interventions such as combined antiandrogens plus estrogens.

Estrogen

A wide range of estrogens is available. Oral ethinyl estradiol (50–100 μg/day) is a potent and inexpensive estrogen, but may cause venous thrombosis, particularly in those over 40 years of age (Asscheman et al. 2014; Toorians et al. 2003). Furthermore, it has been implicated in elevated cardiovascular mortality (Asscheman et al. 1989). Ethinyl estradiol should not be used any more. Oral estradiol, 2–4 mg/day, or transdermal 17β-estradiol, 100 μg delivered continuously per day changed once or twice a week, are the treatments of choice, and are much less thrombogenic than ethinyl estradiol (Toorians et al. 2003). Many people prefer injectable estrogens as they generate high levels of circulating estrogens. However, they have the potential risk of overdose and, if an emergency were to occur that required discontinuation of estrogens, it would be impossible to get rid of the long-lasting effects of depot estrogen injections. Injections of estradiol may be considered if circulating estradiol levels cannot be achieved despite reaching maximal doses of oral estradiol.

No evidence suggests that progestogens (progestins) add to the feminization process. In female reproductive endocrinology, progesterone prepares the uterus for conception, and the breasts for lactation. Some patients strongly believe that progestogens are a necessary addition to estrogens in their feminization (Wierckx et al. 2014). They should be informed not only that this is not the case, but also that progestogens may have side effects, such as salt/water retention, leading to elevated blood pressure or venous varicoses. In a large-scale study of postmenopausal hormone use in women, the combination of estrogens and progestagons appeared to be associated with a higher incidence of breast cancer and cardiovascular disease (Gooren et al. 2014), providing yet another reason to advise against their use.

Results of Hormone Therapy for Male-to-Female People

Results of hormonal therapy are as follows.

BODY HAIR

There is a reduction in body hair growth; hair becomes thinner and loses its pigment. But adult male beard growth is very resistant to inhibition, even with the combined hormonal intervention of antiandrogens plus estrogens. In Caucasian individuals, additional measures to eliminate facial hair are necessary, such as electrolysis or laser treatment. Hair growth on other parts of the body responds more favorably to hormonal intervention, and will usually be markedly reduced after 1 or 2 years of cross-sex hormone treatment (Giltay & Gooren 2000). Some Asian subjects have little or no secondary sexual hair and administration of antiandrogens may not be necessary (Gooren 2014).

BREAST DEVELOPMENT

Breast formation starts almost immediately after initiation of cross-sex hormone administration and proceeds with periods of growth and plateau (Wierckx et al. 2014). As androgens have an inhibitory effect on breast formation, estrogens will be most effective in a low-androgen milieu, which is usually achieved with the combination of cyproterone acetate or spironolactone and estrogens. After 2 initial years of full hormone administration, no further development can be expected (Wierckx et al. 2014). Older age also impedes full breast formation. About 50–60% of the hormone-treated subjects report satisfaction with breast volume, while the remaining 40–50% judge their breast development as insufficient. The attained size, in itself a measure of success of cross-sex hormone administration, is often disproportional to the greater height and dimension of the chest of adult male-to-female transsexual individuals. The latter group will often seek surgical breast augmentation.

SKIN

Androgen deprivation leads to a decreased activity of sebaceous glands, which may result in dry skin or brittle nails, sometimes requiring protection from detergents and/or local application of hydrating creams (Giltay & Gooren 2000).

BODY COMPOSITION

Following androgen deprivation, there is an increase in subcutaneous fat, and a decrease in lean body mass. Body weight usually increases but can be controlled with dietary measures.

TESTES

Lacking gonadotropic stimulation, the testes become atrophic. In rare cases, they may enter the inguinal canal, and cause discomfort.

PROSTATE

Androgen deprivation leads to atrophy of the prostate and a change in the anatomical condition of the bladder neck, which may produce transient dribbling following micturition. This complaint usually disappears in the course of 1 year.

VOICE

Antiandrogens and estrogens have no effect on the properties of the voice. Some individuals may wish to consult a specialized phoniatric center for speech therapy. Maleness of the voice is not so much determined by the pitch of the voice as by chest resonance and volume. Speech therapy may lead to more feminine speech and speech patterns (Cosyns et al. 2014). Laryngeal surgery may change the pitch of the voice, but will also reduce the range.

LONG-TERM THERAPY

After reassignment surgery, including orchiectomy, hormone therapy must be continued. Some patients still exhibit male-pattern hair growth, and experience teaches that antiandrogens may remain effective in reducing it, although the dose may be lowered. Continuous estrogen therapy is required to avoid symptoms of hormone deprivation and, most importantly, to prevent osteoporosis (Van Caenegem et al. 2012). We have found that estrogens alone, adequately dosed, are capable of maintaining bone mass in male-to-female transsexuals. There was an inverse relationship between serum luteinizing hormone concentrations and bone mineral density, suggesting that serum luteinizing hormone may serve as an indicator of the adequacy of sex steroid administration (Van Kesteren et al. 1998). There is, as yet, no consensus as to the age until which cross-sex hormone must be continued. Transgender patients usually favor maintenance of hormones throughout the later years. There are no data to support or dismiss this treatment policy (Gooren & Lips 2014). Perhaps a parallel can be drawn with women who receive postmenopausal estrogen replacement, but that regimen rarely extends beyond the late 50s.

Treatment of Female-to-Male Patients

The goal of treatment in the female-to-male patient is to induce virilization (including a deepening of the voice), production of male-pattern body hair growth and physical contours, and cessation of menses. The principal hormonal treatment used to accomplish these goals is a testosterone preparation. The most commonly used preparations are testosterone esters, an injectable that is administered intramuscularly in doses of 200–250 mg every 2 weeks. In some countries, testosterone undecanoate (1,000 mg) is available, and injections may be spaced at 10–12 weeks. Some clinicians favor weekly injections of lower doses of testosterone in order to avoid the variation in serum testosterone levels that can occur with other programs. Use of androgen gel or transdermal patches can also provide good, steady-state levels, and can be used by the patient at home.

Regardless of the vehicle of administration, serum testosterone levels should be evaluated periodically to guard against prolonged administration of supraphysiologic doses, known to have deleterious effects in men. Occasionally, menstrual bleeding does not cease, and the addition of a progestational agent is necessary. If a transdermal or oral testosterone preparation is used, addition of a progestational agent is nearly always required to stop menstrual bleeding, which is experienced by patients as an unpleasant reminder of the sex they wish to relinquish.

Results of Hormone Therapy for Female-to-Male People

The many results of hormonal therapy in this population are as follows.

HAIR

The development of body hair essentially follows the pattern observed in pubertal boys, appearing first on the upper lip, then the chin, then the cheeks (Giltay & Gooren 2000). The degree of facial and body hair can usually be predicted by the extent and pattern existing in their male family members. This also applies to the occurrence of androgenetic alopecia, which will affect approximately 50% of the patients to some degree. There is no association between type of androgen used, be it injections, transdermal, or oral agents, and this outcome.

ACNE

Acne occurs in approximately 40% of those treated, and usually appears more pronounced on the back than the face. This has also been observed in hypogonadal men who start androgen treatment past the age of normal puberty. This can usually be remedied with conventional antiacne treatment.

VOICE

Deepening of the voice starts after 6–10 weeks of androgen administration and is irreversible.

FAT

Androgen administration leads to a reduction of subcutaneous fat, but an increase in abdominal fat. The increase in lean body mass is, on average, 4 kg, and the increase in body weight is usually greater (Elbers et al. 1999). Although weight gain is associated with androgen use, it is certainly possible to control it with dietary measures.

CLITORAL ENLARGEMENT

Clitoral enlargement occurs in all transmen, but the degree varies. In approximately 5–8%, the size becomes sufficiently large for vaginal intercourse.

LIBIDO

Most patients report an increase in libido, and this is rarely experienced as bothersome or disruptive.

OVARIES

Ovaries show polycystic changes (Ikeda et al. 2013), and androgen administration may decrease glandular activity of the breasts (Slagter et al. 2006). It does not, however, reduce breast size.

After bilateral oophorectomy, androgen therapy must be continued to maintain virilization and prevent osteoporosis (Van Caenegem et al. 2012). Suppression of the serum luteinizing hormone concentration to within normal range can be used as an indication of the efficacy of androgen administration.

Side Effects of Hormonal Sex Reassignment

Administration of cross-sex hormones may have side effects, with hormone-dependent tumors being of particular concern. Overall, cross-sex hormone treatment is acceptably safe (Meriggiola & Berra 2012). A study in 2011 reported on the Amsterdam (the Netherlands) gender clinic on 966 transwomen and 365 transmen treated with cross-sex hormones for 1–20 years (Asscheman et al. 2011). In the group of transwomen, total mortality was 51% higher than in the general population, mainly from increased mortality rates due to suicide, acquired immunodeficiency syndrome, cardiovascular disease, drug abuse, and unknown cause. No increase was observed in total cancer mortality, but lung and hematological cancer mortality rates were elevated. Current, but not past, ethinyl estradiol use was associated with an independent threefold increased risk of cardiovascular death. In the group of transmen, total mortality and cause-specific mortality were not significantly different from those of the general population (Asscheman et al. 2011). Another study noted increased cardiovascular disease as well as decreased bone mineral density in transwomen (Wierckx et al. 2012).

Venous Thromboembolism

The incidence of side effects of this nature was 2–6% in male-to-female people treated with oral ethinyl estradiol (Asscheman et al. 2014; Van Kesteren et al. 1997). In vitro studies show that this thrombogenic effect is typical of oral ethinyl estradiol but not of oral 17β-estradiol valerate or transdermal estrogens (Toorians et al. 2003). Because immobilization is also a risk factor for venous thromboembolic events, estrogen admnistration should be discontinued for 3–4 weeks before elective surgical interventions. Once patients are fully mobilized following these procedures, estrogen therapy may be resumed (Asscheman et al. 2014).

Atherosclerosis

Although the considerable sex difference in the prevalence of cardiovascular disease between men and women would lead one to expect an effect of hormonal treatment, the actual risk remains to be established. The effects of estrogen administration in transwomen and androgen administration in transmen on biochemical risk markers have been studied (Gooren & Giltay 2014). It appears that estrogen administration has more negative effects on these risk markers than do androgens (Gooren et al. 2014). Genetic factors may play a role (Gooren et al. 2014). But long-term studies with clinical endpoints are needed to fully assess the effects of cross-sex hormones on cardiovascular risk. In our study, cardiovascular disease became more manifest as transpeople age (Gooren et al. 2014), and cardiovascular risks should be treated aggressively in elder transgender people. Smoking should be strongly discouraged.

It should be noted that dosages used in transgender individuals are often much higher than those used in hormone replacement for hypogonadal patients (Gooren et al. 2014; Wierckx et al. 2012).

Lactotroph Adenoma

Several cases of lactotroph adenoma (prolactinoma) following high-dose estrogen administration have been reported in patients with normal serum prolactin concentrations before therapy (Cunha et al. 2015). A case of a pituitary microprolactinoma developed in a transwoman after 14 years of normal-dose estrogen treatment (Bunck et al. 2009). Although causality has not been established, we recommend that serum prolactin levels continue to be monitored long-term in estrogen-treated transwomen at 1–2-year intervals.

Breast Cancer

The number of cases of breast cancer in transsexual people is increasing. A new aspect is that transmen may develop breast cancer as well, even though they have had breast ablation. Cancer may occur in residual mammary tissue (Gooren et al. 2013). Fortunately, prevalence remains rather low. In Veterans Health Administration data from 5,135 transgender veterans in the United States from 1996 to 2013, ten breast cancer cases were confirmed. Seven were in transmen and three in transwomen veterans. Breast cancer in transgender people may occur at a relatively young age and after a relatively short period of exposure to cross-sex hormones. Even though relatively rare, patients should be taught self-examination of the breasts, particularly when there is a family history of breast cancer. Increased risk of breast cancer due to, e.g., *BRCA1* or *BRCA2* mutations may be present in these individuals, and ablation of breast tissue before hormone therapy may be considered (Colebunders et al. 2014).

Benign Prostate Hyperplasia

The prostate is not removed with sex reassignment surgery. Prostatectomy is a surgically cumbersome operation, with possible complications, such as urinary incontinence. As expected, the prostate volume shrinks after androgen deprivation. Estrogen exposure does not induce signs of hyperplasia or (pre) malignancy (Van Kesteren et al. 1996). One case of benign prostate hyperplasia, requiring transurethral prostate resection, has been described (Brown & Wilson 1997). Epidemiological studies have shown that orchiectomy before the age of 40 years prevents the development of prostate cancer and benign prostate hyperplasia. The individual in this case was over 40 years of age when starting cross-sex hormones. One case of obstructive enlargement of the verumontanum, appearing 25 years after initiation of cross-sex hormones and requiring resection of the verumontanum, has also been reported (Goodwin & Cummings 1984). Urological problems after sex reassignment of transwomen have been reviewed (Hoebeke et al. 2005). In transmen who have undergone genital surgery, urethral fistulae, urethral strictures, and meatal stenosis with an incidence of >30% have been observed, requiring surgical treatment (Lumen et al. 2011).

Prostate Cancer

Prostate cancer in transwomen has recently been reviewed (Gooren & Morgentaler 2014). It is not clear whether these cancers are estrogen-sensitive, or whether they were present prior to beginning estrogen administration and then subsequently de-differentiated to become androgen-independent. These patients were each beyond 50 years of age when they initiated cross-sex hormone treatment (resulting in total androgen ablation). As previously indicated, epidemiological studies have shown that orchiectomy before the age of 40 prevents the development of prostate cancer and benign prostate hyperplasia (Wilson & Roehrborn 1999), and the aforementioned cases do not contradict this notion. In most clinics, screening for the development of levels of prostate-specific antigen is not routinely done, but it may be in those with a family history of prostate cancer, starting at the age of 50 years. Due to antiandrogen treatment, the cut-off level for prostate-specific antigen should be set at the much lower level of 1 ng/mL.

Ovarian Cancer

We recently observed two cases of ovarian carcinoma in long-term, testosterone-treated transmen. The ovaries of female-to-male patients taking androgens resemble polycystic ovaries (Spinder et al. 1989), which are also more prone to develop malignancies. Therefore, it seems reasonable to remove the ovaries of androgen-treated female-to-male patients after transition. In several countries, sex reassignment treatment is not covered by health insurance schemes. This may delay the surgical removal of ovaries, thereby increasing the risk of malignant degeneration.

Sexual Function After Surgery

Little attention has been given to the subject of sexual functioning in the postoperative person, and the scant available research has been largely based on self-reports. As expected, there is a correlation between sexual function and the quality of the neovagina, neoclitoris, or neophallus (Klein & Gorzalka 2009). While not all postoperative patients are orgasmic, many report sexual satisfaction.

A hormonal factor to consider in sexual health may be the almost complete, pharmacologically induced androgen depletion that occurs in transwomen. The circulating androgen levels are lower in these cases than in cases involving non-transgender women. It is becoming clear that low levels of androgens in women are important for female libido and sexual enjoyment. Occasionally, the drug for postmenopausal women, tibolone, can be successfully employed, but this information is anecdotal. Low-dose testosterone therapy was shown to be successful (Kronawitter et al. 2009). By contrast, transmen receiving androgen therapy usually experience an increase in sexual interest (Costantino et al. 2013; Wierckx et al. 2011). More research is needed to shed light on the sexual functioning of postoperative individuals, and how to maximize sexual health and pleasure.

Regrets After Surgery

Given the irreversibility of sex reassignment surgery and, to a lesser degree, of cross-sex hormone administration, it is very valuable to have insight into factors that foretell success or failure. Prospective controlled studies specifically designed to assess outcome and its prognostic factors are methodologically difficult, and absent in the literature. It has been estimated that 1–2% of those undergoing reassignment will have regrets (Pfafflin 1992). Some of these individuals have experienced gender dysphoria late in adult life, without strong manifestations in childhood; others have difficulty in transitioning to the preferred gender because of their appearance or limited social skills.

Therefore, the importance of social role transition cannot be overemphasized. People must be encouraged to discuss their doubts and ambivalence with a mental health professional. Celebrating successes in the adaptation process also encourages a consolidation of identity in the postoperative period and beyond. The quality of the surgical construction of the genitalia is extremely important in successful postsurgical satisfaction. Indeed, this factor alone, whether the surgery is aesthetically and functionally sound, often differentiates those who regret having undergone sex reassignment from those who thrive in their new status (Lawrence 2003).

References

Asscheman, H., L. J. Gooren and P. L. Eklund (1989) Mortality and morbidity in transsexual patients with cross-gender hormone treatment. *Metabolism.* 38(9): 869–873.

Asscheman, H., et al. (2011) A long-term follow-up study of mortality in transsexuals receiving treatment with cross-sex hormones. *Eur J Endocrinol.* 164(4): 635–642.

Asscheman, H., et al. (2014) Venous thrombo-embolism as a complication of cross-sex hormone treatment of male-to-female transsexual subjects: A review. *Andrologia.* 46(7): 791–795.

Brown, J. A. and T. M. Wilson (1997) Benign prostatic hyperplasia requiring transurethral resection of the prostate in a 60-year-old male-to-female transsexual. *Br J Urol.* 80(6): 956–957.

Bunck, M. C., et al. (2009) Autonomous prolactin secretion in two male-to-female transgender patients using conventional oestrogen dosages. *BMJ Case Reports.* doi: 10.1136/bcr.02.2009.1589. pii: bcr02.2009.1589. Epub 2009 Aug 10.

Colebunders, B., et al. (2014) Hormonal and surgical treatment in trans-women with BRCA1 mutations: A controversial topic. *J Sex Med.* 11(10): 2496–2499.

Coleman, E., et al. (2011) *Standards of Care* (SOC) for the health of transsexual, transgender, and gender nonconforming people. *Int J Transgend.* 13: 165–232.

Costantino, A., et al. (2013) A prospective study on sexual function and mood in female-to-male transsexuals during testosterone administration and after sex reassignment surgery. *J Sex Marital Ther.* 39(4): 321–335.

Cosyns, M., et al. (2014) Voice in female-to-male transsexual persons after long-term androgen therapy. *Laryngoscope.* 124(6): 1409–1414.

Cunha, F. S., et al. (2015) Diagnosis of prolactinoma in two male-to-female transsexual subjects following high-dose cross-sex hormone therapy. *Andrologia.* 47(6): 680–684.

Elbers, J. M., et al. (1999) Effects of sex steroid hormones on regional fat depots as assessed by magnetic resonance imaging in transsexuals. *Am J Physiol.* 276(2 Pt 1): E317–325.

Ettner, R. and K. Wylie (2013) Psychological and social adjustment in older transsexual people. *Maturitas.* 74(3): 226–229.

Giltay, E. J. and L. J. Gooren (2000) Effects of sex steroid deprivation/administration on hair growth and skin sebum production in transsexual males and females. *J Clin Endocrinol Metab.* 85(8): 2913–2921.

Goodwin, W. E. and R. H. Cummings (1984) Squamous metaplasia of the verumontanum with obstruction due to hypertrophy: Long-term effects of estrogen on the prostate in an aging male-to-female transsexual. *J Urol.* 131(3): 553–554.

Gooren, L. J. (2011) Clinical practice. Care of transsexual persons. *N Engl J Med.* 364(13): 1251–1257.

Gooren, L. J. (2014) Should cross-sex hormone treatment of transsexual subjects vary with ethnic group? *Asian J Androl.* 16(5): 809–810.

Gooren, L. J. and E. J. Giltay (2014) Men and women, so different, so similar: observations from cross-sex hormone treatment of transsexual subjects. *Andrologia.* 46(5): 570–575.

Gooren, L. and P. Lips (2014) Conjectures concerning cross-sex hormone treatment of aging transsexual persons. *J Sex Med.* 11(8): 2012–2019.

Gooren, L. and A. Morgentaler (2014) Prostate cancer incidence in orchidectomised male-to-female transsexual persons treated with oestrogens. *Andrologia.* 46(10): 1156–1160.

Gooren, L. J., et al. (2013) Breast cancer development in transsexual subjects receiving cross-sex hormone treatment. *J Sex Med.* 10(12): 3129–3134.

Gooren, L. J., K. Wierckx and E. J. Giltay (2014) Cardiovascular disease in transsexual persons treated with cross-sex hormones: Reversal of the traditional sex difference in cardiovascular disease pattern. *Eur J Endocrinol.* 170(6): 809–819.

Hembree, W. C., et al. (2009) Endocrine treatment of transsexual persons: An Endocrine Society clinical practice guideline. *J Clin Endocrinol Metab.* 94(9): 3132–3154.

Hoebeke, P., et al. (2005) Impact of sex reassignment surgery on lower urinary tract function. *Eur Urol.* 47(3): 398–402.

Ikeda, K., et al. (2013) Excessive androgen exposure in female-to-male transsexual persons of reproductive age induces hyperplasia of the ovarian cortex and stroma but not polycystic ovary morphology. *Hum Reprod.* 28(2): 453–461.

Klein, C. and B. B. Gorzalka (2009) Sexual functioning in transsexuals following hormone therapy and genital surgery: A review. *J Sex Med.* 6(11): 2922–2939; quiz 2940–2921.

Kronawitter, D., et al. (2009) Effects of transdermal testosterone or oral dydrogesterone on hypoactive sexual desire disorder in transsexual women: results of a pilot study. *Eur J Endocrinol.* 161(2): 363–368.

Lawrence, A. A. (2003) Factors associated with satisfaction or regret following male-to-female sex reassignment surgery. *Arch Sex Behav.* 32(4): 299–315.

Lumen, N., et al. (2011) Urethroplasty for strictures after phallic reconstruction: A single-institution experience. *Eur Urol.* 60(1): 150–158.

Meriggiola, M. C. and M. Berra (2012) Long-term cross-sex hormone treatment is safe in transsexual subjects. *Asian J Androl.* 14(6): 813–814.

Pfafflin, F. (1992) Regrets after sex reassignment surgery. *J Psychol Human Sex.* 5: 69–85.

Slagter, M. H., et al. (2006) Effects of long-term androgen administration on breast tissue of female-to-male transsexuals. *J Histochem Cytochem.* 54(8): 905–910.

Spinder, T., et al. (1989). The effects of long term testosterone administration on pulsatile luteinizing hormone secretion and on ovarian histology in eugonadal female to male transsexual subjects. *J Clin Endocrine Metab.* 88(12): 5723–5729.

Toorians, A. W., et al. (2003) Venous thrombosis and changes of hemostatic variables during cross-sex hormone treatment in transsexual people. *J Clin Endocrinol Metab.* 88(12): 5723–5729.

Van Caenegem, E., et al. (2012) Bone mass, bone geometry, and body composition in female-to-male transsexual persons after long-term cross-sex hormonal therapy. *J Clin Endocrinol Metab.* 97(7): 2503–2511.

Van Kesteren, P., et al. (1996) Effects of estrogens only on the prostates of aging men. *J Urol.* 156(4): 1349–1353.

Van Kesteren, P. J., et al. (1997) Mortality and morbidity in transsexual subjects treated with cross-sex hormones. *Clin Endocrinol (Oxf).* 47(3): 337–342.

Van Kesteren, P., et al. (1998) Long-term follow-up of bone mineral density and bone metabolism in transsexuals treated with cross-sex hormones. *Clin Endocrinol (Oxf).* 48(3): 347–354.

Wierckx, K., et al. (2011) Sexual desire in female-to-male transsexual persons: Exploration of the role of testosterone administration. *Eur J Endocrinol.* 165(2): 331–337.

Wierckx, K., et al. (2012) Long-term evaluation of cross-sex hormone treatment in transsexual persons. *J Sex Med.* 9(10): 2641–2651.

Wierckx, K., L. Gooren and G. T'Sjoen (2014) Clinical review: Breast development in trans women receiving cross-sex hormones. *J Sex Med.* 11(5): 1240–1247.

Wilson, J. D. and C. Roehrborn (1999) Long-term consequences of castration in men: Lessons from the Skoptzy and the eunuchs of the Chinese and Ottoman courts. *J Clin Endocrinol Metab.* 84(12): 4324–4331.

11 Gender Dysphoria in Children and Adolescents

Annelou L. C. de Vries and Peggy T. Cohen-Kettenis

Introduction

Knowledge of and care for children and adolescents with gender dysphoria (GD), the diagnostic term used in the *Diagnostic Statistical Manual of Mental Disorders*, fifth edition (DSM-5: American Psychiatric Association, 2013), have increased considerably over the last few decades. This is likely due to substantial media attention and a rapid spread of information through the internet, the emancipation of the lesbian, gay, bisexual, and transgender population in general, an increasing number of clinicians who provide care, and the fact that medical interventions have become available for gender-dysphoric minors. Thirty years ago, families attending the few specialized gender identity clinics almost always learned of the phenomenon by chance. Nowadays, children, adolescents, and parents are usually well aware of its existence. Still, they are uncertain, have questions, may suffer from co-existing emotional or behavioral problems, or request medical interventions, thus causing them to come to these specialized clinics.

Gender Variance Versus Gender Dysphoria

Long before children have a sophisticated understanding of gender, they display female and male gender role behavior. While babies are not born with a crystallized self-awareness of their sex and gender, such self-awareness evolves gradually over time. While growing up, children increasingly develop knowledge of the various aspects of gender. They first learn to *label* the differences between males and females, then recognize that gender does not change over time, and finally, they realize that gender does not change if someone's appearance or activities change. The primary difference is generally ascribed to one's genitalia (see Ruble et al., 2006, for an overview of typical gender development). Gender identity not only is the ability to classify oneself and others as male or female but also has strong affective components (Egan & Perry, 2001).

During the pre-school years, most children develop a core sense of self as male or female, a gender identity, which is largely congruent with their gender role behaviors and their natal sex. However, in the same period, some children will show a different gender development. This is often called a *gender-atypical,* *gender non-conforming,* or *gender-variant* development.

Gender role behavior is shaped by nature as well as nurture. Adults and children influence gender development directly by reinforcing or discouraging gender-typical behaviors, and indirectly by offering role models. Sex hormones also play a significant role in the development of gender-typical behavior and characteristics (Hines, 2011). It is less clear to what extent these factors influence gender identity, although presumably biological, psychological, and social factors all play a role as well (de Vries et al., 2014).

Classification

The distress resulting from an incongruence between gender identity and sex of assignment is often referred to as GD. For gender-dysphoric youngsters, DSM-5 makes a distinction between GD in childhood and GD in adolescence (or adulthood: American Psychiatric Association, 2013). Compared to the earlier DSM-IV version (American Psychiatric Association, 2000), some changes were made.

The first change concerned the name of the diagnosis. Instead of gender identity disorder, the term *gender dysphoria* is now used. The change of name was meant to reduce stigma attached to a diagnosis that is used by mental health professionals.

For children, the criteria have become stricter, and a stated wish or desire to be another gender is now required. In earlier editions of the DSM it was assumed that some children may not be verbal or self-conscious enough to express their desire explicitly and, therefore, it was not a required criterion. However, this likely leads to false positives. Therefore, it is no longer included in DSM-5.

In the DSM-5 the criteria for adults and adolescents have been broadened compared to the child criteria, acknowledging that a dichotomous division in two gender categories, male or female, does not reflect the experience of some individuals. They may feel they are somewhere between male and female on a more continuous gender spectrum or even outside the male–female spectrum. The criteria for adolescents and adults also include a specifier to indicate whether the individual has transitioned to full-time living in the desired gender. This provides a classification code for individuals who continue to need medical treatment (e.g., hormones) but are no longer gender-dysphoric after gender-affirming treatment. The specifier of sexual orientation was removed in the DSM-5 because the distinction is no longer considered clinically useful.

In contrast to the DSM-IV, intersexuality is no longer an exclusion criterion but "with or without a disorder of sex development (DSD)" is now a specifier in the DSM-5. Individuals with somatic DSDs (that is, discrepancies between their sex chromosomes, gonads, and/or genitals) may show behaviors, interests, and identifications that are not in line with their sex of assignment at birth.

They may also show anatomic dysphoria. In the DSM-5 they can be given a GD diagnosis.

For children, the DSM-5 criteria have been criticized for being in the DSM at all. It is questioned whether GD should be regarded as a psychiatric disorder, because in most children GD will fade in late childhood and medical interventions are not necessary. It appears that these children display gender-variant behavior as part of the normal variation. Critics also condemn the use of dysphoria in the name of the child diagnosis, because it psychopathologizes and stigmatizes childhood gender non-normative behavior.

With regard to the upcoming newest version of the World Health Organization's *International Classification of Diseases* (ICD-11), there is an ongoing debate with arguments for and against retaining a separate diagnosis of gender incongruence (the proposed term for the ICD-11) for children (Drescher et al., 2012). Children may not suffer from distress related to their gender incongruence, therefore it should not be pathologized. One of the most important arguments against retention is that there is no medical necessity for a childhood diagnosis. Children do not need hormone therapy or surgical procedures, no matter how much gender incongruence, with or without distress, they may have. Opponents of a childhood diagnosis fear that the proposed diagnosis may be potentially harmful and could lead to attempts to change the children's gender variance into gender-typical development and may exacerbate stigma and discrimination for children and their families. Proponents of a childhood diagnosis, however, argue that a diagnosis is necessary to access care, to bring recognition and increased tolerance (e.g., in schools), to conduct research and move the field forward, and to promote the developing training and education curricula.

Epidemiology

No epidemiological studies of the prevalence of childhood GD exist. Studies with the Child Behavior Checklist, a parent-report questionnaire on emotional and behavioral problems with two items concerning gender variance (cross-gender behavior and cross-gender wish), show that cross-gender behavior in children is more common than the stated wish to be of the other gender. For example, in a large Dutch twin study, 3.4% of the 7-year-old boys and 5.2% of the 7-year-old girls were reported to behave like the opposite gender, while only 1.0% and 1.7% respectively had stated the wish to be of the opposite gender (van Beijsterveldt et al., 2006). At age 10 years, these percentages had decreased, although less so for the stated wish. This shows that cross-gender behaviors seem to diminish when children reach their teenage years. In a behavioral genetic study of 314 child and adolescent twins, it was estimated that the prevalence is 2.3% (Coolidge et al., 2002). One should bear in mind that most prepubertal children with GD will more likely be homosexual than transgender as they enter adolescence or adulthood (see below). This means that the 2.3%

figure almost certainly overstates the percentage of children with GD who will be "persisters" in adulthood.

Presumably, only a small number of the children in these studies with gender-variant behavior fulfill the criteria for a GD diagnosis. Prevalence estimates of *transsexualism* among adults are usually based on either the number of transsexuals treated at major centers, or on survey responses from mental health professionals. The numbers from studies vary widely. In the first years of transsexual treatment, very low prevalences were reported (between 1: 100,000 and 1: 400,000). More recent studies indicated higher prevalences (between 1: 3,000 and 1: 30,000) (see Zucker & Lawrence, 2009, for a review). These discrepancies probably reflect variations in methodology, differences between countries in treatment availability, and differing criteria for treatment eligibility. The most recent studies, among the general population, report much higher prevalence rates. One Dutch study revealed that 0.6% of natal men experience gender incongruence, body dislike, and a wish for hormones or surgery, while this percentage was 0.2% for natal women (Kuyper & Wijsen, 2014). In a large survey among high school students in New Zealand asking, "do you think you are transgender?," 94.7% reported being non-transgender, 1.2% reported being transgender, 2.5% reported being not sure about their gender, while 1.7% did not understand the question (Clark et al., 2014).

Sex Ratio

The majority of prepubertal children attending gender clinics are boys. The boy–to–girl ratios are about 6:1 in Canada (n = 358), 3:1 in the Netherlands (n = 130; Cohen-Kettenis et al., 2003) and 4:1 in the United Kingdom (n = 53; Di Ceglie et al., 2002). The higher rates of boys seen in childhood in the United Kingdom and Canada may reflect greater parental anxiety about male effeminacy. This idea is supported by a study showing that Canadian children with gender identity disorder are seen at significantly younger ages than Dutch children (Cohen-Kettenis et al., 2003).

For many years, the sex ratio of adolescents at three gender clinics (Toronto, Amsterdam, and London) approached a 1:1 relationship (boys to girls: 1.2:1, n = 133, Cohen-Kettenis, unpublished; 1.4: 1, n = 43, Zucker & Bradley, 1995; 1.4: 1, n = 69, Di Ceglie et al., 2002). Recent analyses of data of consecutive referrals to two gender identity clinics in Toronto and Amsterdam not only showed a sharp increase in number, but also an inverse sex ratio: more natal females compared to natal males were referred since 2006 (Aitken et al., 2015). Sociocultural factors may play a role in this reversal of the sex ratio. Perhaps the greater visibility and acceptance of gender variance over the last decade resulted in less stigmatization and social ostracism in general, but more so in females than in males. This would make it easier for transgender natal women to come out and seek medical care. Other clinics also report this reversal in referrals (Kaltiala-Heino et al., 2015).

Predicting Persistence of Childhood GD Into Adolescence and Adulthood

Most children with GD will no longer be gender-dysphoric by adolescence or adulthood. GD in childhood seems a better predictor of future sexual orientation than of persisting GD into adolescence or adulthood. Prospective studies of children with GD show that, at follow-up, the proportion of participants with a homosexual or bisexual sexual orientation is substantially higher than the rates in the general population. In one longitudinal general population study of 879 Dutch boys and girls, gender-variant behavior was measured in childhood by the Child Behavior Checklist, while sexual orientation was assessed 24 years later, when participants were 27–36 years of age (Steensma et al., 2013). The prevalence rates of homosexuality were, depending on the sexual orientation domain, 8.4–15.8 times higher in the childhood gender-variant subgroup, as compared to the childhood non-gender-variant subgroup. None of the gender-variant children showed GD in adulthood. In follow-up studies into adolescence or young adulthood of children with GD who were assessed at specialized gender identity clinics, the prevalence rates of a bisexual or homosexual orientation varied from 24% (Drummond et al., 2008) of 25 no longer gender-dysphoric natal girls to 56% (Wallien & Cohen-Kettenis, 2008) of 25 no longer gender-dysphoric natal boys.

Persistence rates of childhood GD differ between the various studies (2–27%); Steensma (2013) showed in a review of 246 described child cases with GD that feelings of GD persisted into adolescence in only 39 of the children (15.8%). Therefore, clinicians who work with adolescents should realize that childhood GD and adolescent/adult GD are not necessarily linked.

For persistence or desistance of childhood GD, the period between 10 and 13 years of age seems crucial. During this period, the segregation between boys and girls tends to increase, which raises more awareness of the experienced GD. Further, the (anticipated) bodily changes of puberty become a reality. Finally the first experiences of romantic feelings and relationships may either confirm or question the cross-gender identification (Steensma et al., 2011).

There is now some evidence that persistence of childhood GD is associated with more extreme gender-variant behavior and a higher intensity of GD (Drummond et al., 2008; Wallien et al., 2007). In addition, being a natal girl, older age, and having socially transitioned in childhood are associated with higher probability of persistence (Steensma et al., 2013). However, for an individual child, it is not yet possible to predict who will or will not appear to be a transgender person in adulthood.

In contrast to prepubertal children, it is recognized that, once puberty has started, GD rarely changes or desists (Cohen-Kettenis & Pfäfflin, 2003; Zucker, 2006). Indeed, in a study on youth who underwent puberty suppression at an average age of 14.75 years (to enable them to explore their GD and treatment wish), they remained gender-dysphoric nearly 2 years later. Around age 16, they all initiated the first steps of their actual gender reassignment trajectory, the cross-sex hormones (de Vries et al., 2011b).

Clinical Picture of Gender-Dysphoric Youth

Children

As soon as children are able to talk, they may repeatedly state that they are, or will later become, members of the other gender, show gender-variant preferences and behavior, and show unhappiness if not allowed to act on these preferences. As they grow older, they often stop talking about their gender-variant feelings and may, out of shame, display fewer gender-variant behaviors. Children can also show a strong preference for cross-dressing, choose cross-gender roles in fantasy play, and prefer toys, games, and activities usually associated with the other gender. Children may express a strong desire for the primary and/or secondary sex characteristics that match their experienced gender and show an aversion to their genitalia and to stereotypical activities and clothes associated with their assigned gender.

Vignette Paul

Paul is a 7-year-old boy. As far back as his parents can remember, he had a strong interest in girls' toys, games, and activities. He disliked rough-and-tumble play. In fantasy play, he always took the role of princess. Paul never played with other boys. When he entered elementary school, he had a few girlfriends, but was frequently teased and sometimes bullied. As a result, he became anxious and developed learning problems. A few times, he told his mother that he would cut off his penis. His mother often saw him hiding his genitals when he showered. Paul always urinated in a sitting position. When he was younger, he believed that his penis would automatically fall off, and he would grow breasts like his mother when he became an adult.

Vignette Anne

According to her mother, Anne (9 years old) never was a "real" girl. She disliked typically feminine clothing and jewelry, and started refusing to wear dresses at age 4. She had a short haircut and was regularly mistaken for a boy. Anne was fond of playing with cars and construction toys. She loved ball games, especially soccer, and roughhousing. Usually, she played outside with male friends. Like boys without GD, her friendships seemed to be focused more on sharing activities and interests than on sharing feelings. At school, Anne was quite popular, especially with the boys. She showed typical male motor behavior and tried to speak in a low-pitched voice. For some time, Anne put rubber balls in her underpants to simulate male genitals. She never wanted to discuss her physical development after puberty.

Adolescents

Adolescents with extreme forms of GD have usually been children with GD. Some of the adolescents have socially transitioned in the last grades of elementary school and some start high school in the other gender role. A number of them (natal girls more often than natal boys) date and have sexual relationships with same-sex peers as they grow older. Sexually active youngsters usually avoid involvement of their primary sex characteristics during lovemaking.

Other adolescents with GD, who might have shown more openly gender-variant behavior when they were younger, try to adjust to gender-typical norms due to the increased peer pressure or because they want to experiment to see if they can fit in with their natal gender once puberty has started. They wear gender-neutral or gender-typical clothing, have a gender-typical hairstyle, and behave as inconspicuously as possible. In fearful and cautious youngsters, GD may be difficult to detect.

Vignette Jack

Jack is a 12-year-old young adolescent with a history of gender-variant behavior from a young age. Jack liked to play with girls and Barbies. He has always insisted that he should have been born a girl. At school he was accepted as one of the girls. Jack started wearing dresses and other girls' clothes and let his hair grow long. When his parents realized that this was more than a "phase," they went to a mental health provider with a transgender specialization. During the last year of primary school, after discussions with the specialist, Jack socially transitioned. People started to use the girl's name Jacky and the female pronoun. Jacky then expressed more clearly how much she disliked her male genitalia and wanted to have breasts "like the other girls." She worried about possible puberty development, started asking for puberty blockers, and wanted to know how they work. Her parents had never prohibited any gender-variant behavior, although they had slowed her down in her desire to be called Jacky and "her." When entering the clinic, they felt that it was time to find out whether the use of gonadotropin-releasing hormone (GnRH) analogs would indeed be helpful for Jacky.

Vignette Sophie

Sophie is a 15-year-old natal girl. She had shown tomboyish behavior when she was in preschool, and, according to her parents, at age 4 she had expressed a desire to be a boy. During later school years she became a shy and insecure girl with few friends and she behaved in a gender-neutral manner. In high school, she has become increasingly socially isolated. While watching a documentary on TV about transgender kids, she recognized how much aversion she felt to her female body and how strongly she identified with boys. It took a year before she dared to tell this to her parents. They were quite surprised but also relieved as they could now better understand why Sophie was so unhappy. They sought specialized transgender care and supported Sophie in buying male clothes, cutting her hair, and showing more male behavior. Sophie's mood improved, and the family considered medical interventions.

Variability of GD in Children and Adolescents

Adolescents with gender concerns are a heterogeneous group. Although some seek hormones and surgery, others may be ambivalent about medical treatment, be confused about their gender feelings, or have gender concerns that are secondary to other psychopathology.

It has been repeatedly proposed that adults with GD be divided into two categories. One category has been described as early-onset, core, primary, nuclear, attracted to persons of the same natal sex; the other category as late-onset, non-core, secondary, fetishistic, not attracted to persons of the same natal sex. Indeed, there is evidence that transgender individuals can be divided into at least two types with different developmental routes. The early-onset group has been extremely gender-variant from early in life, has never had any sexual interest in cross-dressing, is attracted to same-sex heterosexual partners, and pursues gender-affirming medical treatment relatively early in life. The other group has been more stereotypical with regard to gender role behaviors as a child, is (or used to be) sexually aroused when cross-dressing, and is attracted to partners of the other natal sex. This group pursues gender-affirming treatment after having tried to live for a relatively long period of time in the social role of their natal sex (Lawrence, 2010).

Like adults, children also vary in type and intensity of gender variance. As noted above, most children with GD will not pursue gender-affirming medical treatment later in life, but a substantial minority do. Therefore, one would expect that children with GD could be classified into at least two subgroups: the pre-homosexual children and the pre-transgender children.

Most likely, adolescents who present with a request for medical intervention have shown extreme gender-variant behavior and a wish to be the other gender from a young age on. Increasingly, however, it is recognized that not every transgender adolescent wishes a "complete" gender-affirming medical treatment (that is, cross-sex hormones and surgeries), because of the non-binary character of gender identity. As previously noted, some youth may identify not as male or female, but as genderqueer, gender-fluid, agender, or other-gendered (e.g., Vance et al., 2014). Not every adolescent may desire all parts of medical gender-affirming treatments, but may seek either cross-sex hormone treatment or some type of surgery.

Co-Occurring Psychopathology

While many children and adolescents with GD are well-functioning healthy individuals, several studies have shown that co-occurring psychopathology may be present.

Using the Child Behavior Checklist to measure behavioral and emotional problems reported by parents, 12.5–89% of the gender-dysphoric children aged 4–12 years showed total problem behavior in the clinical range (for a review, see Zucker et al., 2014). In the two largest samples, these percentages were 47.2% and 59.3% respectively. In a study that used a diagnostic interview to assess DSM diagnoses, 52% of the prepubertal gender-dysphoric children suffered from one or more psychiatric disorders, with internalizing disorders (anxiety, depression) being more prevalent than externalizing, disruptive disorders (attention-deficit hyperactivity disorder, oppositional defiant disorder) (Wallien et al., 2007).

In gender-dysphoric adolescents referred to a specialized gender identity clinic, two medical chart studies report significant psychiatric histories of, e.g., self-mutilation (20.6%) and suicide attempts (9.3%) (Spack et al., 2012) and mood and anxiety disorders (35% and 24%, respectively: Khatchadourian et al., 2014). In a study that used a diagnostic interview to establish DSM classifications, 67.6% of the adolescents had no concurrent psychiatric disorder. Anxiety disorders occurred in 21%, mood disorders in 12.4%, and disruptive disorders in 11.4% of the adolescents (de Vries et al., 2011a). Using the Child Behavior Checklist to measure behavioral and emotional problems reported by the parents, 55–77% of the transgender adolescents aged 13–18 years showed total problem behavior in the clinical range (de Vries et al., 2015). When using the same instrument, and adolescent reports (Youth Self Report), these percentages ranged from 39.7% to 48% in three gender identity clinics (de Vries et al., 2015; Skagerberg et al., 2013).

An overrepresentation compared to the general population of autism spectrum disorders (ASD) in gender-dysphoric children and adolescents has been reported, with 6.4% of assessed gender-dysphoric children and 9.4% of gender-dysphoric adolescents assessed at a specialized gender identity clinic having a co-occurring ASD diagnosis (de Vries et al., 2010). Other studies using instruments measuring autistic traits in children and adolescents with GD support this overrepresentation (van der Miesen et al., 2016).

The relationship between co-occurring psychopathology and gender issues remains a matter of debate. Gender-variant behavior may sometimes primarily be a component of another disorder (e.g., ASD). Other disorders, such as Tourette syndrome, may be entirely unrelated to the GD. However, such disorders can undermine a boy's social status and make him more prone to flee into the less-threatening girls' world. Finally, certain disorders or problems may be a consequence of the GD (e.g., depression). Especially social ostracism and peer victimization may make gender non-conforming children and adolescents prone to develop emotional and behavioral problems. In three studies using the Child Behavior Checklist, the Youth Self Report, and the Teacher Report Form in children and adolescents with GD, poor peer relations were the strongest predictor of co-occurring emotional and behavioral problems (Cohen-Kettenis et al., 2003; de Vries et al., 2015; Steensma et al., 2014). Treatment will depend on the assumed relationship between the GD and the co-occurring psychological problems. Societal interventions and school-based programs that lead to greater acceptance of gender non-conformity in children and adolescents may also be important. Although not a direct measure of psychopathology, in one large population-based study a lesbian, gay, bisexual, and transgender-positive school climate was related to decreased school absenteeism, particularly for youth who identify as transgender (Greytak et al., 2013).

Diagnosis in Children

When a child with gender identity problems is referred for diagnosis, clinicians must first assess whether the child actually meets the criteria for GD. In extreme cases, this will not be a very difficult task. However, children may fall anywhere between "typical for boys" and "typical for girls" on various dimensions, such as identity statements, identification figures, the desire for opposite-sex characteristics, rough-and-tumble play, peer preference, cross-dressing, role and fantasy play, toy preference, games and activities preference, and mannerisms and speech.

When one looks beyond the current situation, the picture can grow even more complex. Gender non-conforming profiles may shift over time because of true changes or as a result of the maturing child's growing awareness of the social undesirability of cross-gender behavior. When children do not state they want to be of the other gender and do not report an aversion to the sex characteristics of their body, it can be particularly hard to know whether their gender-variant behaviors and preferences are manifestations of GD or just part of the normally distributed gender non-conforming variance.

Clinicians should put information about the child's gender development and behavior in a broader perspective. This means that general aspects of the child's functioning, such as cognitive level, social-emotional functioning, and school performance, also have to be evaluated. Poor functioning in these areas may help the clinician to interpret certain gender-variant behaviors. For instance, a boy who often plays with younger girls and girls' toys and games may do so not as a result of a gender problem, but rather as a result of limited cognitive abilities and immaturity that make play with boys too daunting.

The broader perspective includes family functioning as well as the child's functioning. Family functioning may have a direct impact on the child's gender feelings and behavior, and could possibly generate negative feelings in the child. For instance, parental conflicts due to differences in emotional reactions to the child's gender-variant behavior may cause feelings of guilt in the child. Similarly, it is relevant to know about attitudes of the broader environment towards the gender-variant behavior of the child.

In sum, proper understanding of the extent of the gender incongruence, the child's development and current functioning, the family dynamics, and the attitudes of the child's broader environment is necessary when making a decision as to what type of interventions will benefit the child (for an overview of the clinical management, see Cohen-Kettens & Pfäfflin, 2003 and de Vries & Cohen-Kettenis, 2012).

Diagnostic Procedure

The information needed to make a treatment plan can be assembled in four to five sessions, but may take longer in complex cases. After the first session, where parents and child are seen together and separately, sessions with the child alone and each parent alone are necessary.

At the first session, the motive for coming to the clinic is discussed. Parents are briefly interviewed concerning the development and behavior of the child, and their responses to this behavior. Also, the parents' expectations of the assessment and possible treatment are discussed, and procedures are explained. The child is asked what the assessment means to him or her, a working alliance is created, and some preliminary information regarding the gender concerns is gathered.

In the following sessions, the (gender) development and current functioning of the child are discussed in depth with the parents. The child's behaviors, preferences, and statements are addressed in relation to the DSM-5 criteria. Specific attention is paid to the parents' own family history and any gender issues that may have played a role in their lives. Furthermore, the parents' feelings about their child's gender-variant behavior, their child-rearing practices, and marital or family conflicts regarding the gender-variant behavior are explored. If family dynamics seem to impact on the gender concerns, a family therapist should also see the family. Psychological testing is part of the process, as it yields information that is useful and that cannot otherwise easily be gathered.

Instruments

In addition to the clinical interview, a few instruments are available to assess the extent of the child's cross-genderedness (for an overview, see Cohen-Kettenis & Pfäfflin, 2003; Zucker, 2006). For young children with GD, who tend to be more cognitively confused about gender than children without GD, tasks can be used to test their knowledge of the gender concept. When assessing playmate preference, it may be helpful to use photographs for younger children, because these tasks do not require advanced verbal skills. One should be aware that play and games questionnaires are rather culturally sensitive.

Play observation creates an opportunity to observe the child's mannerisms and gestures. If a boy makes many feminine gestures, it explains why he is an easy target for teasing, even if he does not reveal his gender-variant preferences to other children.

When drawing a person, children with GD tend to draw opposite-sex persons first. They also tend to draw the opposite-sex person taller and with greater detail than the same-sex person. However, this is not always the case, and the value of this measure lies more in the qualitative than in the quantitative information.

Interventions in Children

Ethics of Intervention; Models of Care for Children with GD

In recent years, various guidelines on clinical management of gender-dysphoric children and adolescents have been published. The American Academy of Child and Adolescent Psychiatry published a "Practice Parameter on Gay, Lesbian, or Bisexual Sexual Orientation, Gender Nonconformity, and Gender Discordance in Children and Adolescents" that includes children and adolescents with GD (Adelson, 2012). The American Psychological Association also published "Guidelines for Psychological Practice With Transgender and Gender Nonconforming People" (American Psychological Association, 2015). The Endocrine Society developed a clinical practice guideline that included, in addition to guidelines for hormone treatment for adolescents, more general comments on the management of GD in children and adolescents (Hembree et al., 2009). Finally, the World Professional Association for Transgender Health (WPATH) published its seventh edition of the *Standards of Care* (*SOC*) with a more extensive section on children and adolescents (Coleman et al., 2012). These recent publications all reflect the quest for clinical guidance now that increasing numbers of families with gender-dysphoric youth seek care.

The care for prepubertal children with GD is subject to various controversies. Different underlying ideological, theoretical, and moral motives and, as a consequence, different approaches exist. Although these approaches share as an overarching goal the well-being of the child and optimal psychological adjustment (Drescher & Byne, 2012b), how this goal is reached is uncertain. Studies on the effectiveness of the different treatment options are lacking. The gold standard of a randomized controlled trial is not ethical or feasible (Drescher & Byne, 2012a). Therefore it is important that clinicians are at least aware of these controversies and are well informed of the limited evidence on effectiveness of the various interventions.

There is agreement in the various recently published professional guidelines against moral or religious motives that have led some therapists to treat gender-variant children in an effort to prevent homosexuality. More dispute exists around the issue of whether it may be possible and ethical to prevent the need for future medical gender-affirming interventions in young children. Dreger (2009) recognizes the dilemma that parents might experience when they have a young gender-dysphoric child. She describes three models of care, depending on the clinicians' views on the etiology and malleability of GD at a young age. First, according to what she calls the "therapeutic model," GD at a young age may be malleable in interaction with the child's personality and the functioning of the parents and the extended family. Clinicians who consider GD to be the result of an underlying developmental psychopathology, and/or a defense to deal with distress generated by early-life experiences, aim at modifying the supposed causal and/or perpetuating factors. In so doing, they will try to effect a gender identity change. If they regard GD as a result of inappropriate learning experiences, their goal will be to extinguish gender-variant behaviors and reinforce same-gender behaviors and skills (e.g., athletic skills in boys), assuming that these behaviors imply a cross-gender identity. Therapists adhering to this model acknowledge that, once puberty has started, the chance of remittance of gender incongruence is small, and medical interventions might be an option.

Second, Dreger recognizes the "accommodation model." A child with GD, a term best not used according to this model, should be allowed to express him- or herself. The child should be enabled to fully explore his or her gender identity and be free in gender expression. The social environment, not the child, should be the focus of attention. This way, the child is fully free to develop according to his or her own developmental pathway. If this results in a persistence of GD when puberty starts, puberty blockers and consecutive cross-sex hormones and gender-affirming surgery are provided.

The third model of care might be called the "pragmatic approach." This approach acknowledges that not only the GD of the child needs attention, but this can only be assessed in the context of a child's complete psychological and social functioning. Co-occurring psychopathology and dysfunctional family functioning are addressed. With regard to the GD itself, this approach provides the child and the family with current knowledge on gender identity development, explains the uncertainty of the future outcome, and helps the families to endure this uncertainty. Treatment is focused on guidance and supporting conscious choices on how and when to allow or to limit certain gender-variant behaviors, clothing, hairstyle, preferences, and expression. During prepubertal years a "watchful waiting" approach is followed. When the child and the family feel comfortable with the existing gender incongruence and psychosocially the child is functioning well, no specific focus of treatment is thought necessary. Only if GD persists and increases at puberty does the child need to be referred for assessment for eligibility for puberty suppression and possible consecutive medical treatment. These different approaches are described by various authors in different publications (e.g., Cohen-Kettenis et al., 2011; de Vries & Cohen-Kettenis, 2012; Di Ceglie, 2010; Ehrensaft, 2012; Menvielle, 2012; Zucker et al., 2012).

Independently of theoretical background, most clinicians will agree that GD may lead to severe distress for parents and child. Such distress may come from social ostracism, co-occurring psychiatric or family problems, or intense unhappiness about one's sex characteristics and being a boy or a girl. The suffering should be alleviated under all circumstances.

Parent Organizations

In various European countries and U.S. states, parent organizations exist. They organize educational or supportive meetings for parents, and offer information through the internet. Because the threshold for these meetings is low, many parents seek contact with such organizations before going to a clinic. They offer services for parents and families and have contacts with schools. As a result of their activities (often reported in the national media), teachers are now more aware of the phenomenon and feel more comfortable handling the daily matters that they encounter. Some schools now have developed "anti-teasing programs" to prevent teasing and bullying of gender-atypical children.

Early-Childhood Social Transition

During the last decade, more children have made a social gender role transition, sometimes as early as 4 or 5 years of age. This is generally supported by parents and the wider social environment. The social transition may be partial, with a change of clothing and hairstyle, or complete, with a change of name and use of pronouns (Steensma & Cohen-Kettenis, 2011). Whether clinicians should actively promote and support or limit and advise against early transition is a controversial issue. Mental health professionals diverge in their views on when and how social transitioning should occur (see also *Standards of Care* version 7, Coleman et al., 2012, and above). Although there is some evidence that more intense GD increases the chance of persistence in adolescence and young adulthood (Steensma et al., 2013), it remains impossible to predict whether a given child will be a transgender adult in need of medical interventions. Mental health professionals can help parents make an informed decision while balancing the positive direct relief that a young child with a strong desire to live in the gender role experiences against the potential of the highly stressful experience of transition back to the natal gender some adolescents experience in cases of desistence of GD (Steensma et al., 2011).

To solve this difficult dilemma, in-between solutions or compromises, such as socially transitioning at some occasions (e.g., a dress on holidays or another name and pronoun use during vacations) may be considered. In the case where a child has socially transitioned, it should be made clear that there is always a way back, and that, in the case that a child wants to transition back, it is good to have tried at least. In all cases, it should be supported to keep all developmental possibilities as open as possible. Independently of the clinician's view, a supportive approach that addresses the complete functioning of the child and the family is most helpful. At present, in young children it is unknown in what respect the social transitioning itself influences later gender identity development, specifically the likelihood of either diminishing or aggravating gender incongruence in adolescence.

Treatment Effectiveness

Considering the absence of sound studies providing support for any physical and psychosocial treatment for childhood GD, and the ethical problems that accompany such treatment, clinicians should be very cautious with interventions aimed at treating GD per se. Even well-meaning therapists can hurt the child and hinder gender identity development.

Diagnosis in Adolescents

Adolescents with gender concerns may have a straightforward wish for gender-affirming medical treatment, but may also have more open questions regarding their identity.

For adolescents, the recommended procedure in the WPATH *SOC* is usually followed (Coleman et al., 2012). The decision to initiate medical treatment is largely similar to the procedure that is followed for adults, but a definite decision regarding medical gender-affirmative treatments can be postponed by providing puberty suppression before initiation of cross-sex hormones and surgery, with their irreversible physical effects. Also, mental health involvement is considered more important in youth than in adults.

Compared to earlier versions of the *SOC*, the seventh edition adheres more closely to an informed-consent model, in which the task of the clinical professionals involved is to support the transgender individual with making the best informed choice in each individual's case. A specific section of the *SOC* is dedicated to care for children and adolescents with gender incongruence. How informed consent in minors should be interpreted is not part of the *SOC*. In medicine and society in general, informed consent in children and adolescents is a matter of debate and varies in different countries, cultures, and contexts. It is also dependent on the type of decision to be made. In some countries, there is a legal age when children are allowed to make medical informed-consent decisions. For example, in the Netherlands, until the child is 12, parents make the decision for the child; between 12 and 15, both parents and adolescent must consent; and from age 16 on, the adolescent can make independent decisions. Therefore, ages 12 and 16 were originally chosen as the ages to start fully reversible treatment (with puberty blockers) or partially irreversible treatment (with cross-sex hormones) respectively (de Vries & Cohen-Kettenis, 2012). Increasingly, it is acknowledged that psychological maturity and the ability to weigh the pros and cons of medical intervention and reflect on long-term consequences may be better indicators of capacity of consent than strict age limits.

The Initial Phase; Creating a Working Alliance and Assessing Gender Dysphoria

When working with gender-dysphoric adolescents and their families, it is important to create a good working alliance. An open attitude by the clinician that acknowledges the possibility of medical interventions is most helpful. Within this alliance, the adolescent and the family are most likely to openly explore the gender-dysphoric feelings. Also, if medical interventions are provided, many years of medical and mental health follow-up will ensue. In most services, the mental health professional on the team will have the main role initially, but it can be helpful if the pediatric endocrinologist is involved at an early stage.

To assess GD and psychological and social functioning, information is obtained from both the adolescent and the parents or guardians on various aspects of the general and psychosexual development of the adolescent (Cohen-Kettenis & Pfäfflin, 2003). Present gender-variant feelings and behavior, school functioning, peer relations, and family functioning are assessed. With regard to sexuality, the subjective meaning of cross-dressing, the type of cross-dressing, sexual experiences, sexual behavior and fantasies, sexual attractions, and body image should be explored.

To prevent unrealistic expectations of medical interventions, the adolescent should be thoroughly informed about the possibilities and limitations of the various available interventions. This information is best provided soon after the first session if a strong wish for hormones and surgery is present. If the adolescent seems confused or ambivalent about this kind of medical treatment, delivery of this information is postponed until it becomes a more realistic option. The adolescent's understanding of the reality of medical treatment can also be diagnostically informative.

It is important to realize that even extremely gender-dysphoric adolescents may lack the support or psychological resilience to handle the drastic life changes that accompany medical treatment. Thus, one should take potential psychological and social risk factors into account when making decisions regarding the appropriateness of early interventions.

Most instruments that measure aspects of GD that have been developed for adults can also be used for adolescents with GD.

Differential Diagnosis

As previously noted, not all transgender adolescents have a clear and explicit wish for hormones and surgery. Some may simply be confused regarding aspects of their gender. For example, young *homosexuals* may have a history of gender-variant interests and behavior. In some cases, they may have difficulties in distinguishing sexual orientation issues from gender concerns. If the homosexuality is ego-dystonic, it is not confusion, but rather lack of acceptance of the homosexuality, that may lead one to consider medical treatment as a solution to their problem. Individuals who experience *transient stress-related cross-dressing*, or *compulsive cross-dressing*, for sexual or other reasons, may mistake their interest in cross-dressing for a need for medical gender-affirming treatment. This may also occur in persons suffering from *severe psychiatric conditions* (e.g., schizophrenia), accompanied by delusions of belonging to the other (or another) gender.

Some youngsters with GD try to *integrate masculine and feminine aspects* of the self. In such cases, hormones or some form of surgery may be sought to minimize existing masculine or feminine physical characteristics (rather than to promote other-sex development). In the experience of most clinicians, such a treatment wish is rare in younger adolescents but occurs more frequently from age 16 and older. This may be because people who experience GD onset at earlier ages typically have more severe and extreme forms of GD. As the normal developmental process of adolescence often involves experimentation relating to self-expression, more caution seems indicated if an adolescent presents at an early age seeking partial change.

Treatment in Adolescents

The Desirability of Medical Interventions for Adolescents

The desirability of medical treatment as a resolution for the psychological suffering of transgender persons, irrespective of age, has been controversial since the first gender-affirming operations were performed. Some psychotherapists may still believe that one should try to help transgender individuals resolve emotional conflicts underlying the wish for sex change by psychotherapy alone. However, the existing case reports do not provide convincing evidence for complete and long-term reversal of a complete cross-gender identity by means of psychotherapy.

The absence of evidence that psychotherapy is the treatment of choice has led clinicians to opt for the adaptation of the sex characteristics to the experienced gender identity. This solution was supported by the results of numerous studies showing no apparent psychological disturbance in transgender persons which would render gender-affirming treatment a hazardous enterprise (for an overview, see Cohen-Kettenis & Gooren, 1999).

Currently, clinicians are faced with increasing numbers of youngsters who powerfully express that they find their lives unbearable without hormonal interventions (Wren, 2002). Physicians working in adolescent medicine and pediatric endocrinology in the United States increasingly report feeling comfortable and having experience with treating transgender adolescents, although they also report insufficient training and a lack of qualified mental health professionals as barriers (e.g., Simons et al., 2014; Vance et al., 2014). In Europe, the availability of multidisciplinary care including medical interventions for transgender youth differs strongly between countries. Some countries have multidisciplinary teams with a long history of providing this care, whereas other countries are just starting, or still lack such services. With the exception of Japan, services for transgender minors hardly exist in non-Western countries.

An argument in favor of early hormone treatment in adolescents with GD is that an eventual arrest in emotional, social, and intellectual development can be successfully warded off when the ultimate cause of this arrest has been addressed. Another argument is that early hormone treatment provides lifelong benefits for adolescents as their secondary sex characteristics have not yet fully developed. Young natal males identifying as females will, as adults, pass much more easily as females if they have never grown a beard or developed a low voice. If the bodily changes of puberty are not interrupted, and an adolescent still wants gender-affirming treatment in adulthood, major physical interventions will be required to remove the unwanted physical characteristics. Yet, despite these obvious advantages, early hormone treatment for adolescents with GD touches sensitive strings. In the absence of evidence that gender incongruence can be treated in adolescence by psychotherapy alone, or is necessarily associated with severe psychopathology, and in view of arguments favoring early treatment, many centers now offer hormonal therapy, both puberty suppression and cross-sex hormones, prior to adulthood (e.g., Fisher et al., 2014; Hsieh & Leininger, 2014; Khatchadourian et al., 2014; Nakatsuka, 2012).

Psychological Interventions

Psychotherapeutic interventions can be helpful both for adolescents who are unsure about their identity as well as for those who have a clear wish to pursue medical interventions. As there are numerous possible underlying problems, the range of treatment goals is equally large (see also de Vries et al., 2007).

For those who pursue medical treatment, the process is lengthy and intensive. Even the diagnostic phase contains therapeutic elements. Adolescents with GD need time to reflect on any unresolved personal issues or doubts regarding their treatment wish before embarking on somatic treatment. It is imperative that any form of psychotherapy offered to adolescents who are considering medical treatment be supportive. This means that the clinician makes clear to the adolescent that any outcome of therapy (ranging from acceptance of living in the social role congruent with the natal sex to medical gender-affirming treatment) is acceptable, as long as it ultimately contributes to the individual's well-being. For many gender-dysphoric adolescents, some form of psychotherapy and psychotherapeutic techniques are often helpful to address issues such as self-esteem, body image, identity, social relationships, and expectations of the future. This is true not only for those with co-occurring mental health difficulties, but also for those who seem to be well-functioning. Therefore, some form of psychotherapy is often recommended (e.g., Tishelman et al., 2015).

Therapists need to be knowledgeable about the different treatment options in order to explain all the consequences of gender-affirming medical treatment. They also should be accustomed to working with this age group and comfortable discussing sensitive topics, such as sexuality. Views and experiences of the adolescent often change over time and will have to be repeatedly addressed. One such example is the lifelong impact of transitioning. Adolescents who have been fortunate to have supportive parents, a protective school, early treatment, and have no unwanted secondary sex characteristics do not always realize that life may be more challenging in adulthood. Conversely, adolescents who have been teased and bullied, or who have a non-accepting family, may feel shameful about their GD and overestimate the negative impact of transitioning on their lives. Adolescents will profit most from having a balanced view of the short- and long-term costs and benefits of the treatment. Therapists may be helpful in establishing such a balanced view.

Adolescents who are eligible for hormones and surgery, as well as those who are not, may need psychotherapy to address the impact of teasing, bullying, violence, and social isolation. These life experiences may seriously hamper the development of a healthy self-esteem or ability to trust other people. In severe cases, clinicians may have to reduce the negative impact of these experiences before they can continue with the diagnostic work.

Family therapy may, in some instances, help to resolve conflicts between family members. For example, some adolescents want to be more open about transgender feelings or express their gender in ways that family members are not comfortable with. Conversely, if an adolescent has already socially transitioned, parents may fear aggressive reactions when uninformed friends discover the adolescent's history of transition.

Another common source of conflict is that family members find it hard to distinguish between what is related to GD and what is not. Family therapists or family counselors may try to help parents determine realistic demands, and work on the development of healthy boundaries and limits.

Inpatient treatment in psychiatric hospitals may be needed for adolescents suffering from severe psychiatric conditions. If the psychiatric disorder has been treated properly (by medication or otherwise), the request for gender-affirming treatment will have to be re-evaluated. In the case of adolescents with severe psychiatric comorbidity, hormone therapy will only be prescribed before adulthood if the psychiatric illness is managed. Careful assessment or medical treatment of the GD should not be hindered by the psychiatric problems. The efficacy of all these interventions, however, has not been investigated in formal outcome studies.

An overrepresentation of adolescents with a co-occurring ASD present at gender identity clinics (de Vries et al., 2010). They may pose a difficult diagnostic challenge for the clinician. It can be difficult to disentangle whether the gender-dysphoric feelings are part of the rigid thinking of autism or exist as a separate co-occurring experience. If medical intervention is considered, it is extremely important, although difficult, to work on realistic expectations, as some adolescents with ASD have idealized notions on the effects of medical treatment. When adolescents with ASD are considered eligible for medical intervention, including puberty suppression, treatment has to be introduced very carefully, and each step should take place in close consultation with the mental health clinicians involved in the adolescent's treatment or counseling.

Even after surgery, psychotherapy can be useful. Some people will face loss or negative reactions from the environment. Others can work on certain personal issues only after they no longer need to worry about their physical treatment. For these reasons, some clinics offer postsurgical psychotherapy. Whether one participates is largely dependent on the youngster's needs and the quality of the earlier therapist–adolescent relationship.

Social Transition in Adolescence

Most adolescents with GD choose to live permanently in the role of the experienced gender during the treatment with puberty suppression, or sometimes even during the latter years of elementary school. By then, it has become clear for most whether their childhood GD has faded or become stronger and persistent. Through social transition with change of name and use of pronoun, they have ample opportunity to appreciate in vivo the familial, interpersonal, educational, and legal consequences of a gender role change.

For some adolescents who have not been very open about their GD because they were too shy or ashamed, coming out about their transgender feelings and social transition is difficult. In these cases, it may be necessary to treat social anxiety first, until there is enough self-confidence to take this step. Parents may have difficulty accepting and adapting to their child's GD. As social support and a positive family climate are important for every adolescent, it may be necessary to make the social transition slowly. Meeting other transgender adolescents and sharing the experience of social transitioning can be very helpful for both the adolescents and their parents (e.g., Menvielle, 2012). After social transition, the adolescent's feelings about this experience are a major focus of the discussions.

For adolescents seeking medical treatment, social transitioning includes informing family, friends, school, and other social contacts about the wish for treatment and the intention to undergo a gender role change. Usually, a new name, congruent with the adolescent's gender identity, is chosen, and there is a concurrent switch in gender pronouns. There may also be a change in clothing, hairstyle, and gender-specific behaviors (including the use of the boys' washroom for transboys and the girls' washroom for transgirls). The expectation is that the adolescent live in the desired gender role when cross-sex hormones are introduced, as that will result in physical characteristics of the new gender. Since puberty suppression does not lead yet to such physical changes, a gender role change is not a prerequisite for adolescents who start them, although most do socially transition.

Physical Interventions

A formal diagnosis of GD is one of the eligibility criteria to start the treatment phase of puberty suppression or cross-sex hormones. Despite the fact that DSM or ICD criteria are applicable to an individual patient, the actual severity of the GD may vary. With regard to adolescents, most will have shown signs of GD from an early age (toddlerhood) with a clear and extreme cross-gender identification in all social environments. They want to transition socially and pursue gender-affirming medical treatment. However, even extremely gender-dysphoric youngsters may not be able to handle the drastic life changes that accompany treatment. Thus, one should take potential risk factors into account when making individual decisions about eligibility for, and timing of, early interventions.

For adolescents, the guidelines of the WPATH *SOC* distinguish between three stages of physical interventions: (1) fully reversible interventions—pubertal delay; (2) partially reversible interventions—cross-sex hormone treatment; and (3) irreversible interventions—surgery.

Fully Reversible Interventions

As soon as pubertal changes have begun, adolescents with extreme forms of GD may be eligible for GnRH treatment to delay puberty. However, they should be able to make an informed decision about pubertal delay, having received and understood the accurate information provided. Experiencing the onset of puberty is considered important diagnostically and it is preferable if they experience puberty at least to the second phase of pubertal development, Tanner stage 2. Desisters report that their experience of the early treatment phases often made them aware that they no longer desired to change gender (Steensma et al., 2011).

Allowing adolescents with GD to take puberty-delaying hormones is justified by two goals. The first is to gain time to further explore the gender identity and other developmental issues in psychotherapy. The second is to make passing easier if the adolescent continues to pursue reassignment.

Adolescents with GD eligible for any form of hormone treatment are required to meet the following criteria:

- throughout childhood, the adolescent has demonstrated an intense pattern of cross-gender behaviors and identity;
- gender discomfort has significantly increased with the onset of puberty;
- co-occurring psychopathology or social problems are addressed or have been resolved so as not to interfere with careful assessment and medical treatment of gender dysphoria;
- the adolescent is able to give informed consent; and
- there is support from parents or other adults, preferably those who can give informed consent and participate in the therapy.

Puberty-delaying hormone treatment should not be viewed as a first step of the cross-sex treatment, but as a diagnostic aid. Therefore, formal social transitioning is not required during puberty suppression, but only when cross-sex hormones are taken.

Adolescents who have gone into puberty at a very young age, or have started with GnRH analogs at a relatively late age, have already developed certain secondary sex characteristics. Some cannot be reversed by hormone treatment. Because facial hair growth is very resistant to antiandrogen therapy, additional mechanical hair-removal techniques may be necessary. Speech therapy is sometimes needed, as the vocal cords will not shorten once they have grown, and the transgirl has to learn to use the voice in a female fashion. Surgical techniques to shorten the vocal cord exist, but are rarely employed, as concerns remain about the safety and effectiveness of such voice modification procedures.

Partially Reversible Interventions

Adolescents eligible for cross-sex hormone therapy (estrogens for transfemales or androgens for transmales) are usually about 16 years of age. In many countries, 16-year-olds are legally considered adults for medical decision-making purposes. Although parental consent is not required, it is preferred, as adolescents need the support of their parents in this complex phase of their lives. Some clinics may start cross-sex hormones earlier in adolescents with extreme and very early-onset GD who have been treated for several years with puberty suppression. However, even when GnRH analogs are provided, adolescents should not receive cross-sex hormones automatically but only after careful reevaluation of their functioning and their treatment wish, and after having been provided with very specific information on the irreversible consequences of cross-sex hormones. In particular, infertility and (with transgirls) the possibility of preservation of sperm must be discussed. Sperm preservation, however, is only possible if the adolescent is already capable of producing fertile sperm. This is not the case for those adolescents who have started early with puberty suppression. For transboys, the conservation of oocytes is not yet possible, but medical techniques are rapidly advancing so at some time this may become available. A relatively new desire of some older adolescent transboys is to carry and give birth to a child. Such desires obviously need careful counseling.

Irreversible Interventions

Genital surgery is not carried out prior to adulthood. There is international clinical consensus that the risks of early surgical intervention far outweigh the potential benefits in virtually all cases. Breast surgery is sometimes considered, and may be provided at age 16, according to the WPATH's *SOC*. The ages of 16 and 18 years respectively should be seen as an eligibility criterion and not an indication in itself for active intervention.

Results of Gender-Affirming Treatment

Numerous studies of transgender adults have shown that gender-affirming medical treatment resolves GD and improves quality of life and psychological functioning (for a review, see Murad et al., 2010). There are far fewer studies that have investigated whether gender-affirming treatment leads to the same results for adolescents.

In the first few follow-up studies on adolescents with GD, none of the participants had regrets; GD had virtually disappeared; and, psychologically and socially, the adolescents functioned fairly favorably (Cohen-Kettenis & van

Goozen, 1997; Smith et al., 2001, 2002). This is likely due to the ability to pass relatively easily in the new social role and because adolescents with severe psychopathology and/or very poor social support were, at the time, not allowed to start treatment before adulthood. In these studies, cross-sex hormones were provided before legal adulthood, but after the age of 16, and surgeries occurred after age 18.

The first study on gender-dysphoric adolescents who received puberty suppression between the ages of 12 and 18 showed improved psychological functioning with regard to behavioral and emotional problem behavior and general functioning, and no remittance of GD during those years (de Vries et al., 2011a, b). All the adolescents who had started puberty suppression in this cohort continued with cross-sex hormones between age 16 and 17 and had genital surgery after age 18. The first study following these procedures showed positive results in their psychological functioning, quality of life and GD, comparable to same-age peers of the general population (de Vries et al., 2014).

Another study on psychological functioning and treatment satisfaction 3–27 years (mean 9.7 years) after initial evaluation at a gender identity clinic and possibly psychotherapy showed satisfaction with treatment in most individuals (who had not all yet received gender-affirming medical treatment). Most participants reported little psychopathology, and infrequent, supportive treatment appeared sufficient to obtain safe judgment on hormonal or surgical treatment (Meyenburg et al., 2015).

Conclusion

GD in children and adolescents is rapidly receiving increasing attention from society and media, as well as clinicians and researchers. Numbers of referrals to specialized gender identity clinics are rising, and new transgender youth care services have come into existence in many areas and countries. Children, adolescents, and their parents arrive with many different issues and need various forms of help. Parents may want to know if their prepubertal child has GD, and how to address it. Co-occurring social anxieties or autistic behavior may need to be treated. How and when should a child make a social gender role transition? Adolescents may seek psychotherapeutic help while exploring their gender identity or support while coming out. Family therapy can be helpful when controversies and misunderstanding exist about the gender identity experience and expression in an adolescent, or when parents may disagree with one another. For a carefully assessed group of adolescents, medical interventions may be helpful. Puberty suppression, with supposedly fully reversible effects, may provide the time and rest until a more definite decision is reached regarding cross-sex hormones and the resulting irreversible physical changes. Early research evidence and convincing clinical experience prove the usefulness of this approach and make medical interventions at a young age a promising tool in the management of the transgender adolescent. However, long-term results do not yet exist and the side effects on bone development, for example, are unknown (Klink et al., 2015). Within the near future, results from other clinics and longer-term evidence may further support and refine treatment guidelines for transgender children and adolescents.

References

Adelson, S. L. (2012). Practice parameter on gay, lesbian, or bisexual sexual orientation, gender nonconformity, and gender discordance in children and adolescents. *Journal of the American Academy of Child and Adolescent Psychiatry*, 51(9), 957–974.

Aitken, M., Steensma, T. D., Blanchard, R., VanderLaan, D. P., Wood, H., Fuentes, A., … Zucker, K. J. (2015). Evidence for an altered sex ratio in clinic-referred adolescents with gender dysphoria. *Journal of Sexual Medicine*, 12(3), 756–763.

American Psychiatric Association. (2000). *Diagnostic and Statistical Manual of Mental Disorders* (4th ed., text rev.). Washington, DC: American Psychiatric Association.

American Psychiatric Association. (2013). *Diagnostic and Statistical Manual of Mental Disorders* (5th ed.). Washington, DC: American Psychiatric Association.

American Psychological Association. (2015). *Guidelines for Psychological Practice With Transgender and Gender Nonconforming People*. American Psychologies, 70(9), 832–864.

Clark, T. C., Lucassen, M. F., Bullen, P., Denny, S. J., Fleming, T. M., Robinson, E. M., & Rossen, F. V. (2014). The health and well-being of transgender high school students: Results from the New Zealand adolescent health survey (Youth'12). *Journal of Adolescent Health*, 55(1), 93–99.

Cohen-Kettenis, P. T., & Gooren, L. J. (1999). Transsexualism: A review of etiology, diagnosis and treatment. *Journal of Psychosomatic Research*, 46(4), 315–333.

Cohen-Kettenis, P. T., & Pfäfflin, F. (2003). *Transgenderism and Intersexuality in Childhood and Adolescence* (Vol. 46). Thousand Oaks, CA: SAGE Publications.

Cohen-Kettenis, P. T., & van Goozen, S. H. (1997). Sex reassignment of adolescent transsexuals: A follow-up study. *Journal of the American Academy of Child and Adolescent Psychiatry*, 36(2), 263–271.

Cohen-Kettenis, P. T., Owen, A., Kaijser, V. G., Bradley, S. J., & Zucker, K. J. (2003). Demographic characteristics, social competence, and behavior problems in children with gender identity disorder: A cross-national, cross-clinic comparative analysis. *Journal of Abnormal Child Psychology*, 31(1), 41–53.

Cohen-Kettenis, P. T., Steensma, T. D., & de Vries, A. L. (2011). Treatment of adolescents with gender dysphoria in the Netherlands. *Child and Adolescent Psychiatric Clinics of North America*, 20(4), 689–700.

Coleman, E., Bockting, W., Botzer, M., Cohen-Kettenis, P., DeCuypere, G., Feldman, J., … Zucker, K. (2012). Standards of care for the health of transsexual, transgender, and gender-nonconforming people, version 7. *International Journal of Transgenderism*, 13(4), 165–232.

Coolidge, F. L., Thede, L. L., & Young, S. E. (2002). The heritability of gender identity disorder in a child and adolescent twin sample. *Behavior Genetics*, 32(4), 251–257.

de Vries, A. L., & Cohen-Kettenis, P. T. (2012). Clinical management of gender dysphoria in children and adolescents: The Dutch approach. *Journal of Homosexuality*, 59(3), 301–320.

de Vries, A. L., Cohen-Kettenis, P. T., & Delemarre-van de Waal, H. A. (2007). Clinical management of gender dysphoria in adolescents. *International Journal of Transgenderism*, 9(3–4), 83–94.

de Vries, A. L., Noens, I. L., Cohen-Kettenis, P. T., van Berckelaer-Onnes, I. A., & Doreleijers, T. A. (2010). Autism spectrum disorders in gender dysphoric children and adolescents. *Journal of Autism and Developmental Disorders*, 40(8), 930–936.

de Vries, A. L., Doreleijers, T. A., Steensma, T. D., & Cohen-Kettenis, P. T. (2011a). Psychiatric comorbidity in gender dysphoric adolescents. *Journal of Child Psychology and Psychiatry, and Allied Disciplines*, 52(11), 1195–1202.

de Vries, A. L., Steensma, T. D., Doreleijers, T. A., & Cohen-Kettenis, P. T. (2011b). Puberty suppression in adolescents with gender identity disorder: A prospective follow-up study. *Journal of Sexual Medicine*, 8(8), 2276–2283.

de Vries, A. L., Kreukels, B. P., Steensma, T. D., & McGuire, J. K. (2014). Gender identity development: A biopsychosocial perspective. In B. P. Kreukels, A. B. Steensma, & A. L. C. de Vries (Eds.), *Gender Dysphoria and Disorders of Sex Development* (1st ed., pp. 53–83). New York: Springer.

de Vries, A. L., Steensma, T. D., Cohen-Kettenis, P. T., VanderLaan, D. P., & Zucker, K. J. (2015). Poor peer relations predict parent- and self-reported behavioral and emotional problems of adolescents with gender dysphoria: A cross-national, cross-clinic comparative analysis. *European Child and Adolescent Psychiatry* (epub ahead of print). doi: 10.1007/s00787-015-0764-7.

Di Ceglie, D. (2010). Gender identity and sexuality: What's in a name? *Diversity in Health and Care*, 7, 83–86.

Di Ceglie, D., Freedman, D., McPherson, S., & Richardson, P. (2002). Children and adolescents referred to a specialist gender identity development service: Clinical features and demographic characteristics. *International Journal of Transgenderism*, 6(1), [np].

Dreger, A. (2009). Gender identity disorder in childhood: Inconclusive advice to parents. *The Hastings Center Report*, 39(1), 26–29.

Drescher, J., & Byne, W. (2012a). Gender dysphoric/gender variant (GD/GV) children and adolescents: Summarizing what we know and what we have yet to learn. *Journal of Homosexuality*, 59(3), 501–510.

Drescher, J., & Byne, W. (2012b). Introduction to the special issue on "The treatment of gender dysphoric/gender variant children and adolescents". *Journal of Homosexuality*, 59(3), 295–300.

Drescher, J., Cohen-Kettenis, P., & Winter, S. (2012). Minding the body: situating gender identity diagnoses in the ICD-11. *International Review of Psychiatry*, 24(6), 568–577.

Drummond, K. D., Bradley, S. J., Peterson-Badali, M., & Zucker, K. J. (2008). A follow-up study of girls with gender identity disorder. *Developmental Psychology*, 44(1), 34–45.

Egan, S. K., & Perry, D. G. (2001). Gender identity: A multidimensional analysis with implications for psychosocial adjustment. *Developmental Psychology*, 37(4), 451–463.

Ehrensaft, D. (2012). From gender identity disorder to gender identity creativity: True gender self child therapy. *Journal of Homosexuality*, 59(3), 337–356.

Fisher, A. D., Ristori, J., Bandini, E., Giordano, S., Mosconi, M., Jannini, E. A., … Maggi, M. (2014). Medical treatment in gender dysphoric adolescents endorsed by SIAMS-SIE-SIEDP-ONIG. *Journal of Endocrinological Investigation*, 37(7), 675–687.

Greytak, E. A., Kosciw, J. G., & Boesen, M. J. (2013). Putting the "T" in "resource": The benefits of LGBT-related school resources for transgender youth. *Journal of LGBT Youth*, 10(1–2), 45–63.

Hembree, W. C., Cohen-Kettenis, P., Delemarre-van de Waal, H. A., Gooren, L. J., Meyer, W. J., 3rd, Spack, N. P., … Montori, V. M. (2009). Endocrine treatment of transsexual persons: An Endocrine Society clinical practice guideline. *Journal of Clinical Endocrinology and Metabolism*, 94(9), 3132–3154.

Hines, M. (2011). Gender development and the human brain. *Annual Review of Neuroscience*, 34, 69–88.

Hsieh, S., & Leininger, J. (2014). Resource list: Clinical care programs for gender-nonconforming children and adolescents. *Pediatric Annals*, 43(6), 238–244.

Kaltiala-Heino, R., Sumia, M., Työläjärvi, M., & Lindberg, N. (2015). Two years of gender identity service for minors: Overrepresentation of natal girls with severe problems in adolescent development. *Child and Adolescent Psychiatry and Mental Health*, 9.

Khatchadourian, K., Amed, S., & Metzger, D. L. (2014). Clinical management of youth with gender dysphoria in Vancouver. *Journal of Pediatrics*, 164(4), 906–911.

Klink, D., Caris, M., Heijboer, A., van Trotsenburg, M., & Rotteveel, J. (2015). Bone mass in young adulthood following gonadotropin-releasing hormone analog treatment and cross-sex hormone treatment in adolescents with gender dysphoria. *Journal of Clinical Endocrinology and Metabolism*, 100(2), E270–275.

Kuyper, L., & Wijsen, C. (2014). Gender identities and gender dysphoria in the Netherlands. *Archives of Sexual Behavior*, 43(2), 377–385.

Lawrence, A. A. (2010). Sexual orientation versus age of onset as bases for typologies (subtypes) for gender identity disorder in adolescents and adults. *Archives of Sexual Behavior*, 39(2), 514–545.

Menvielle, E. (2012). A comprehensive program for children with gender variant behaviors and gender identity disorders. *Journal of Homosexuality*, 59(3), 357–368.

Meyenburg, B., Kroger, A., & Neugebauer, R. (2015). [Gender dysphoria in children and adolescents – treatment guidelines and follow-up study.] *Zeitschrift fur Kinder- und Jugendpsychiatrie und Psychotherapie*, 43(1), 47–55.

Murad, M. H., Elamin, M. B., Garcia, M. Z., Mullan, R. J., Murad, A., Erwin, P. J., & Montori, V. M. (2010). Hormonal therapy and sex reassignment: A systematic review and meta-analysis of quality of life and psychosocial outcomes. *Clinical Endocrinology*, 72(2), 214–231.

Nakatsuka, M. (2012). [Adolescents with gender identity disorder: Reconsideration of the age limits for endocrine treatment and surgery.] *Seishin Shinkeigaku Zasshi = Psychiatria et Neurologia Japonica*, 114(6), 647–653.

Ruble, D. N., Martin, C. L., & Berenbaum, S. A. (2006). Gender development. In N. Eisenberg, W. Damon, & R. M. Lerner (Eds.), *Handbook of Child Psychology: Vol. 3, Social, Emotional, and Personality Development (6th ed.)* (pp. 858–932). Hoboken, NJ: John Wiley.

Simons, L. K., Leibowitz, S. F., & Hidalgo, M. A. (2014). Understanding gender variance in children and adolescents. *Pediatric Annals*, 43(6), e126–131.

Skagerberg, E., Davidson, S., & Carmichael, P. (2013). Internalizing and externalizing behaviors in a group of young people with gender dysphoria. *International Journal of Transgenderism*, 14(3), 105–112.

Smith, Y. L., van Goozen, S. H., & Cohen-Kettenis, P. T. (2001). Adolescents with gender identity disorder who were accepted or rejected for sex reassignment surgery: A prospective follow-up study. *Journal of the American Academy of Child and Adolescent Psychiatry*, 40(4), 472–481.

Smith, Y. L., Cohen, L., & Cohen-Kettenis, P. T. (2002). Postoperative psychological functioning of adolescent transsexuals: A Rorschach study. *Archives of Sexual Behavior*, 31(3), 255–261.

Spack, N. P., Edwards-Leeper, L., Feldman, H. A., Leibowitz, S., Mandel, F., Diamond, D. A., & Vance, S. R. (2012). Children and adolescents with gender identity disorder referred to a pediatric medical center. *Pediatrics*, 129(3), 418–425.

Steensma, T. D. (2013). *From Gender Variance to Gender Dysphoria; Psychosexual Development of Gender Atypical Children and Adolescents*. (PhD). Amsterdam: VU University Medical Center.

Steensma, T. D., & Cohen-Kettenis, P. T. (2011). Gender transitioning before puberty? *Archives of Sexual Behavior*, 40(4), 649–650.

Steensma, T. D., Biemond, R., Boer, F. D., & Cohen-Kettenis, P. T. (2011). Desisting and persisting gender dysphoria after childhood: A qualitative follow-up study. *Clinical Child Psychology and Psychiatry*, 16(4), 499–516.

Steensma, T. D., McGuire, J. K., Kreukels, B. P., Beekman, A. J., & Cohen-Kettenis, P. T. (2013). Factors associated with desistence and persistence of childhood gender dysphoria: A quantitative follow-up study. *Journal of the American Academy of Child and Adolescent Psychiatry*, 52(6), 582–590.

Steensma, T. D., Zucker, K. J., Kreukels, B. P. C., VanderLaan, D. P., Wood, H., Fuentes, A., & Cohen-Kettenis, P. T. (2014). Behavioral and emotional problems on the teacher's report form: A cross-national, cross-clinic comparative analysis of gender dysphoric children and adolescents. *Journal of Abnormal Child Psychology*, 42(4), 635–647.

Tishelman, A. C., Kaufman, R., Edwards-Leeper, L., Mandel, F. H., Shumer, D. E., & Spack, N. P. (2015). Serving transgender youth: Challenges, dilemmas, and clinical examples. *Professional Psychology: Research and Practice*, 46(1), 37–45.

van Beijsterveldt, C. E., Hudziak, J. J., & Boomsma, D. I. (2006). Genetic and environmental influences on cross-gender behavior and relation to behavior problems: A study of Dutch twins at ages 7 and 10 years. *Archives of Sexual Behavior*, 35(6), 647–658.

Vance, S. R., Jr., Ehrensaft, D., & Rosenthal, S. M. (2014). Psychological and medical care of gender nonconforming youth. *Pediatrics*, 134(6), 1184–1192.

van der Miesen, A. I., Hurley, H., & De Vries, A. L. (2016). Gender dysphoria and autism spectrum disorder: A narrative review. *International Review of Psychiatry*, 28(1), 70–80.

Wallien, M. S., & Cohen-Kettenis, P. T. (2008). Psychosexual outcome of gender-dysphoric children. *Journal of the American Academy of Child and Adolescent Psychiatry*, 47(12), 1413–1423.

Wallien, M. S., Swaab, H., & Cohen-Kettenis, P. T. (2007). Psychiatric comorbidity among children with gender identity disorder. *Journal of the American Academy of Child and Adolescent Psychiatry*, 46(10), 1307–1314.

Wren, B. (2002). 'I can accept my child is transsexual but if I ever see him in a dress I'll hit him': Dilemmas in parenting a transgendered adolescent. *Clinical Child Psychology and Psychiatry. Special Issue: Sexual Identity and Gender Identity*, 7(3), 377–397.

Zucker, K. J. (2006). Gender identity disorder. In D. A. Wolfe & E. J. Mash (Eds.), *Behavioral and Emotional Disorders in Adolescents: Nature, Assessment, and Treatment* (pp. 535–562). New York, NY: Guilford Publications.

Zucker, K. J., & Bradley, S. (1995). *Gender Identity Disorder and Psychosexual Problems in Children and Adolescents*. New York: Guilford.

Zucker, K. J., & Lawrence, A. A. (2009). Epidemiology of gender identity disorder: Recommendations for the *Standards of Care* of the World Professional Association for Transgender Health. *International Journal of Transgenderism*, 11, 8–18.

Zucker, K. J., Wood, H., Singh, D., & Bradley, S. J. (2012). A developmental, biopsychosocial model for the treatment of children with gender identity disorder. *Journal of Homosexuality*, 59(3), 369–397.

Zucker, K. J., Wood, H., & VanderLaan, D. P. (2014). Models of psychopathology in children and adolescents with gender dysphoria. In B. P. C. Kreukels, T. D. Steensma & A. L. C. de Vries (Eds.), *Gender Dysphoria and Disorders of Sex Development: Progress in Care and Knowledge* (pp. 171–192). New York: Springer.

12 Transgender Youth
Endocrine Management

Stephen M. Rosenthal

Introduction

An increasing number of gender non-conforming/transgender pre-adolescents and adolescents are seeking medical services to enable the development of physical characteristics consistent with their experienced gender. Such services, including use of agents to block endogenous puberty at Tanner stage 2 and subsequent use of cross-sex hormones, are based on longitudinal studies demonstrating that those individuals who were first identified as gender-dysphoric in early or middle childhood and continue to meet the mental health criteria for being transgender at early puberty are likely to be transgender as adults. Furthermore, onset of puberty in transgender youth is often accompanied by increased "gender dysphoria"—clinically significant distress related to the incongruence between one's "affirmed" or "experienced gender" and one's "assigned (or natal) gender." Studies have shown that such distress may be ameliorated by a "gender-affirming" model of care. The goals of this chapter are to review terms and definitions applicable to gender non-conforming youth (and adults), and review the natural history of transgenderism, current clinical practice guidelines for transgender youth, and limitations and challenges to optimal care.

Background

Terms and Definitions

While a person's "sex" refers to the physical attributes that characterize biologic maleness or femaleness (e.g., the genitalia), "gender identity" refers to a person's fundamental, inner sense of self as male or female (and is not always binary). At birth, most children are assigned a "sex of rearing" based on genital anatomy, and with that assignment comes societal expectations of gender roles, behaviors, and expressions, which are sometimes referred to as a child's "assigned gender" or "natal gender" (Vance et al., 2014). While "sex of rearing" can be assigned at birth, "gender identity" can only be assumed, and not, in fact, known until an individual achieves a particular level of psychological development and self-awareness. An individual for whom gender identity and physical sex characteristics are in alignment may be referred to as "cisgender."

Some youths' internal gender identity is not consistent with their gender, implied by their birth sex assignment. Such youth are sometimes referred to as "gender non-conforming" (Vance et al., 2014). More specifically, "transgender," as defined by the American Psychiatric Association, refers to a person who transiently or persistently identifies with a gender different from his or her "natal gender" (American Psychiatric Association, 2013). As defined in the *Standards of Care* (*SOC*) from the World Professional Association for Transgender Health (WPATH), "transgender" (adjective) describes "a diverse group of individuals who cross or transcend culturally defined categories of gender" (Coleman et al., 2011). In the WPATH *SOC*, "transsexual" (adjective) describes "individuals who seek to change or have changed their primary and/ or secondary sex characteristics through feminizing or masculinizing medical interventions (hormones and/or surgery), typically accompanied by a permanent change in gender role" (Coleman et al., 2011). "Transsexual" has also been used to describe a person who identifies as a member of the gender opposite to that assigned at birth (Hembree et al., 2009; Meyer-Bahlburg, 2013), but who has not necessarily sought medical and/or surgical interventions.

Defined more narrowly, "transgender" refers to an individual whose gender identity is the "opposite" of their "assigned" or "natal gender." A person with a female gender identity and male assigned sex would be referred to as a "transgender girl/woman" or male-to-female (MTF); a person with a male gender identity and female assigned sex would be referred to as a "transgender boy/man" or female-to-male (FTM) (Sherer et al., 2015).

Some youth state that their gender identities are neither male nor female, and others accept the genders assigned to them but not the cultural expectations for those genders; these youth may be referred to as "genderqueer," "gender-variant," "gender-expansive," "gender-creative," or "gender-independent." "Gender-fluid" refers to an individual whose gender identity changes over time or is not a fixed binary (Sherer et al., 2015).

"Gender behavior" (sometimes referred to as "gender role") is not equivalent to gender identity (Hembree et al., 2009; Meyer-Bahlburg, 2013). In fact, the majority of youth with gender non-conforming behavior will not turn out to have a transgender identity (Drummond et al., 2008; Wallien & Cohen-Kettenis, 2008). Previously referred to as "gender identity disorder" in the *Diagnostic and Statistical Manual of Mental Disorders*, fourth edition (DSM-IV: American Psychiatric Association, 1994) this term was replaced with "gender dysphoria" in DSM-5, with distinct diagnostic criteria for "gender dysphoria in children" and "gender dysphoria in adolescents and adults" (specifying with or without a disorder of sex development) (American Psychiatric Association, 2013). Replacing "disorder" with "dysphoria" depathologizes the transgender identity, and instead, focuses on dysphoria as the clinical problem (American Psychiatric Association, 2013). It should be noted that the majority of patients with "gender dysphoria" do not have a disorder of sex development. Whether in children or adolescents, a core feature of "gender dysphoria" is "a marked incongruence between one's experienced/expressed gender and assigned gender" of at least 6 months' duration (American Psychiatric Association, 2013). While prevalence data for younger transgender adolescents are lacking, multidisciplinary clinics for transgender youth and adolescents in Europe and North America have seen a steadily increasing demand for services in recent years (de Vries & Cohen-Kettenis, 2012; Sherer et al., 2012; Spack et al., 2012; Zucker et al., 2008), with a ratio of phenotypic males to females close to 1:1 (Spack et al., 2012).

"Sexual identity" (or "sexual orientation") is often confused with "gender identity." Both are distinct aspects of human development. While the former refers to those to whom one is sexually attracted, the latter refers to who one "is," as male, female, or somewhere on the gender continuum. Gender non-conforming/transgender individuals may have a heterosexual, homosexual, or bisexual orientation.

Psychiatric Co-Morbidities and Impact of Family Support

Life-threatening behaviors represent a significant risk for transgender youth and adolescents. A study of transgender youth in New York City (n = 55: MTF = 31; FTM = 24) demonstrated that 45% had experienced suicidal ideation while 26% had attempted suicide (Grossman & D'Augelli, 2007). The impact of the degree of parental support on mental health outcomes was reported in a cohort of transgender youth and young adults aged 16–24 years (n = 84) from Ontario, Canada. Satisfaction with life and self-esteem were significantly greater in transgender youth whose parents were "very supportive" vs. those whose parents were "somewhat to not at all supportive" (Travers et al., 2012). In addition, depression and suicide attempts were significantly decreased in transgender youth whose parents were supportive in comparison to those whose parents were not supportive (Travers et al., 2012). Yet, even with supportive parents, transgender youth still have a significant risk for depression (Travers et al., 2012), perhaps in part from their experience of transphobia from members of their communities and feelings of rejection and social isolation.

Natural History of Transgenderism in Youth/Adolescents

Longitudinal studies have demonstrated that, once puberty has begun, the majority of gender-dysphoric pre-pubertal youth will no longer meet the mental health criteria for gender dysphoria (Drummond et al., 2008; Wallien & Cohen-Kettenis, 2008). While gender "fluidity" may be a contributing factor, the lack of persistence of gender dysphoria in the majority of gender-dysphoric pre-pubertal youth likely reflects the heterogeneous nature of this group. In fact, many such individuals will turn out to be homosexual (natal males, in particular) rather than transgender (American Psychiatric Association, 2013; Drummond et al., 2008; Wallien & Cohen-Kettenis, 2008; Zucker, 2008). Recent studies have attempted to identify factors that predict gender dysphoria "persisters" versus "desisters" (Steensma et al., 2013).

Persisters reported relatively greater degrees of gender dysphoria and were more likely to have experienced social transition (to their affirmed gender) during childhood (Steensma et al., 2013). Furthermore, persisters believed they "were" the other sex, while desisters "wished they were" the other sex (Steensma et al., 2013). The limitations in prediction of persistence, coupled with the observation that most gender-dysphoric children will not become transgender adolescents or adults, have led some investigators and/or practitioners to promote efforts to encourage gender-dysphoric children to accept their natal gender (Zucker et al., 2012). In contrast, a model of care that "affirms" a child's gender expression is thought to have a more optimal mental health outcome (Hidalgo et al., 2013; Vance et al., 2014). Long-term outcome studies are needed to resolve these differences in approach to the care of gender-dysphoric pre-pubertal youth.

Clinical Practice Guidelines for Transgender Youth

Assessment

While the symptoms of gender dysphoria will decrease or disappear in the majority of gender-dysphoric youth following initiation of puberty, persistence of gender dysphoria implies a very high likelihood that such individuals will be transgender as adults; in fact, the emergence or worsening of gender dysphoria with onset of puberty is thought to have significant diagnostic value in the determination of being transgender (Cohen-Kettenis et al., 2008). It is noteworthy, however, that with the availability of gender-affirming medical interventions (as detailed below), awareness of such treatment options may positively impact and, thus, limit the degree of dysphoria that might otherwise accompany the onset of puberty in a transgender individual. It is therefore essential that gender-dysphoric youth undergo a thorough psycho-diagnostic evaluation by a qualified mental health provider. An important role of the mental health/gender specialist is not only to determine the presence or absence of gender dysphoria, but to also evaluate for other mental conditions. For example, while there is an increased prevalence of autism spectrum disorder in clinically referred gender-dysphoric children in comparison to the general population (de Vries et al., 2010) (and, conversely, increased "gender variance" in referred children with autism spectrum disorder: Strang et al., 2014), the majority of gender-dysphoric children and adolescents do not have an underlying severe psychiatric illness (Cohen-Kettenis et al., 2008).

Management

Early Pubertal Transgender Youth

The strategy of pubertal suppression with a gonadotropin-releasing hormone (GnRH) agonist (classically used for the treatment of precocious puberty) in early/mid-pubertal gender-dysphoric adolescents was first described in studies from the Netherlands (Cohen-Kettenis & van Goozen, 1998; Cohen-Kettenis et al., 2011; Delemarre-van de Waal & Cohen-Kettenis, 2006; de Vries et al., 2011). This fully reversible treatment allows additional time for gender exploration without the pressure of ongoing pubertal development. Once completed, the physical changes of puberty cannot be reversed (by means other than surgical or, for voice, other than by voice training)—e.g., low voice, Adam's apple, and facial features in phenotypic males and breast development in phenotypic females. Theoretically, preventing pubertal development that does not match a person's gender identity can lead to decreased distress, and can ultimately enable the individual to more easily "blend" in society as an adult. Subsequently, if the individual continues to identify as transgender, cross-sex hormones can be added while continuing GnRH agonist suppression of endogenous puberty, enabling the individual to experience only the physical changes of puberty that match the person's experienced/affirmed gender identity (Coleman et al., 2011; Hembree et al., 2009). The Endocrine Society (ES) guidelines and WPATH SOC endorse the use of pubertal blockers (using GnRH agonists) at Tanner stage 2/3 in individuals experiencing a significant increase in gender dysphoria with onset of puberty (Coleman et al., 2011; Hembree et al., 2009). While age-specific guidelines for subsequent interventions are not delineated in the WPATH SOC, the ES guidelines suggest that cross-sex hormones can be initiated at about the age of 16 years (the legal age for medical decision making in some countries), while surgical procedures (with the exception of mastectomy) should be deferred until the individual is at least 18 years of age (Hembree et al., 2009). Despite the recommendation that cross-sex hormone treatment not be initiated before age 16 years, delaying such treatment until that age could not only be detrimental to bone health, but, by keeping someone in a pre-pubertal state until this age, would isolate the individual further from age-matched peers, with potentially negative consequences for emotional well-being. Therefore, gender centers at our institution and elsewhere are studying the impact of cross-sex hormone treatment initiation at 14 years of age (which approximates the upper end of the age range for normal pubertal onset in natal males and 1 year beyond the upper end of the age range in natal females). In this group, sex steroids are increased gradually over the course of 2–3 years (Rosenthal, 2014).

Limited available outcomes data support the above-noted ES and WPATH recommendations. A prospective follow-up study from the Netherlands assessed 70 gender-dysphoric adolescents (33 MTF, 37 FTM), average age 13.65 years (range 11.1–17 years) at initial assessment, who were Tanner stage 2–3, had "lifelong gender dysphoria" that increased with puberty, had stable psychological function, and were supported by their environment (Delemarre-van de Waal & Cohen-Kettenis, 2006; de Vries et al., 2011). These adolescents were studied at the initiation of GnRH agonist treatment and approximately 2 years later, just before starting cross-sex hormones (de Vries et al., 2011). While gender dysphoria persisted, depressive symptoms decreased, general mental health functioning improved, no subjects withdrew from pubertal suppression, and all went on to cross-sex hormone treatment (de Vries et al., 2011). A subsequent report from this initial cohort in the Netherlands assessed mental health outcomes in 55 transgender adolescents/young adults (22 MTF, 33 FTM) at three time points: before the start of GnRH agonist treatment, at initiation of cross-sex hormones (average 16.7 years at start of treatment), and at least 1 year after "gender reassignment surgery" (average age 20.7 years) (de Vries et al., 2014). Despite a decrease in depression and an improvement in general mental health functioning, gender dysphoria persisted during the period of pubertal suppression (as noted in earlier reports); however, following cross-sex hormone treatment and "gender reassignment surgery," gender dysphoria was resolved and psychological functioning steadily improved (de Vries et al., 2014). Furthermore, "well-being" was found to be similar to or better than that in age-matched young adults from the general population, and none of the study participants regretted treatment (de Vries et al., 2014). This study represents the first long-term follow-up of patients managed according to currently existing clinical practice guidelines for transgender youth, and underscores the benefit of the multi-disciplinary approach pioneered in the Netherlands.

Potential Adverse Effects of GnRH Agonists in Transgender Youth

The primary risks of pubertal suppression in gender-dysphoric youth treated with GnRH agonists include adverse effects on bone mineralization (which can theoretically be reversed with cross-sex hormone treatment), compromised fertility, and unknown effects on brain development (Cohen-Kettenis et al., 2008; Delemarre-van de Waal & Cohen-Kettenis, 2006).

With respect to bone mineral density (BMD), studies of the lumbar spine, femoral neck, and total body were initially carried out in a small number of gender-dysphoric adolescents during 2 years of GnRH agonist alone and for an additional 2 years of combination treatment with GnRH agonist and cross-sex hormones (Delemarre-van de Waal & Cohen-Kettenis, 2006). BMD (g/cm^2) did not change significantly during treatment with GnRH agonist alone, though z-scores decreased; during combination therapy with GnRH agonist and cross-sex hormones, absolute BMD increased, as did z-scores (Delemarre-van de Waal & Cohen-Kettenis, 2006). A 22-year follow-up of the first described gender-dysphoric adolescent treated with GnRH agonist and cross-sex hormones was recently reported (Cohen-Kettenis et al., 2011). In this individual, GnRH agonist was begun at age 13.7 years (Tanner stage 3); at 18.6 years, testosterone was initiated and GnRH agonist was discontinued. At age 35 years, BMD was assessed and found to be within the normal range for both sexes (Cohen-Kettenis et al., 2011).

A more recent 6-year longitudinal, observational study assessed BMD in 34 transgender adolescents (15 MTF, 19 FTM) who had received GnRH agonist beginning at an average age of 14.9–15 years (individuals were mid-late pubertal at study onset by testicular volume or breast stage), had initiation of cross-sex hormones at 16.4–16.6 years, followed by gonadectomy with discontinuation of GnRH agonist at a minimum age of 18 years (Klink et al.,

2015). BMD was assessed at onset of GnRH treatment, initiation of cross-sex hormone treatment, and at age 22 years (Klink et al., 2015). Over the 6-year observation period, areal BMD z-scores decreased significantly in MTF individuals with a trend for a decrease in FTM individuals, suggesting either a delay in attainment of peak bone mass, or an attenuation of peak bone mass, itself (Klink et al., 2015). The authors acknowledge potential limitations of their study, including a relatively small *n*, the fact that individuals were already late pubertal at the time of GnRH agonist initiation, the possibility that relatively low doses of cross-sex hormones were used during the initial period of that phase of treatment, and that information was not available regarding dietary calcium intake, vitamin D levels, and weight-bearing exercise, all of which can influence BMD (Klink et al., 2015). Particularly during the GnRH agonist treatment phase, it would seem important to ensure adequate intake of calcium and vitamin D, with routine monitoring of 25-OH vitamin D levels (Rosenthal, 2014).

It is essential that any use of pubertal blockers and cross-sex hormones includes an informed-consent process and a discussion about implications for fertility. Transgender adolescents may wish to preserve fertility, which may be otherwise compromised if puberty is suppressed at an early stage and the patient completes phenotypic transition with the use of cross-sex hormones (Rosenthal, 2014). While full in vitro maturation of germ cells has not yet been achieved in humans, promising studies have been carried out in mice. For example, recent reports describe in vitro production of functional sperm from neonatal mice (Sato et al., 2011). Micro-insemination following full in vitro spermatogenesis resulted in healthy, reproductively competent offspring (Yokonishi et al., 2014).

Little is currently known regarding potential adverse effects of GnRH agonists (and cross-sex hormones) on brain. A recent study investigated whether GnRH agonist treatment of gender-dysphoric adolescents would impair executive functioning (reasoning, problem solving, etc.), thought to reflect pre-frontal brain activation, and to have significant development during puberty (Staphorsius et al., 2015). No significant detrimental effects of GnRH agonist treatment on executive functioning were observed (Staphorsius et al., 2015).

A retrospective review of gender-dysphoric youth receiving multi-disciplinary care in a university-based clinic in Vancouver, Canada, also assessed potential adverse effects of GnRH agonist treatment in this population (Khatchadourian et al., 2014). Relatively few adverse effects were observed: of 27 patients receiving GnRH agonist, one developed a sterile abscess at the injection site, one developed transient leg pains and headaches, and one developed significant weight gain (though body mass index was > 85th perecentile prior to initiation of GnRH agonist treatment: Khatchadourian et al., 2014).

Late Pubertal Transgender Youth

Some transgender adolescents first come to medical attention when they are late pubertal (Tanner stage 4/5). MTF individuals are optimally treated with estrogen with concurrent use of an agent that blocks testosterone secretion and/or action, while FTM individuals can be treated with testosterone alone (Coleman et al., 2011; Gooren, 2011; Hembree et al., 2009; Spack, 2013). While too late to block endogenous pubertal development, GnRH agonists can be used to suppress the hypothalamic–pituitary–gonadal axis, potentially enabling use of lower doses of cross-sex hormones to induce phenotypic transition to the affirmed gender, thereby decreasing potential toxicities associated with cross-sex hormone treatment. In this older cohort (having already experienced the full or near-full puberty associated with their physical sex), cross-sex hormone regimens may be increased to full replacement doses over a shorter interval than used for the younger cohort that had been initially treated with pubertal blockers at Tanner stage 2/3 (Rosenthal, 2014). While GnRH agonists are the preferred option for pubertal suppression in both the early and late pubertal individuals, this treatment is costly and often inaccessible (Rosenthal, 2014). Options for pubertal suppression and cross-sex hormone treatment are listed in Table 12.1 (Rosenthal, 2014).

Regarding estrogen treatment, 17β-estradiol (transdermal, oral, or parenteral) is preferred to conjugated (e.g., Premarin) or synthetic estrogens (e.g., ethinyl estradiol), given that conjugated and synthetic estrogen levels cannot be monitored in the serum and that ethinyl estradiol (in comparison to 17β-estradiol) is associated with an increased risk for venous thromboembolic disease and death from cardiovascular causes (Asscheman et al., 2011; Toorians et al., 2003).

As previously described, MTF individuals treated with estrogen may have impaired insulin sensitivity and hyperprolactinemia (Hembree et al., 2009). Principal risks associated with testosterone treatment in FTM individuals include cystic acne, polycythemia, hypertension, an atherogenic lipid profile, and possible decreased insulin sensitivity (Hembree et al., 2009). Surveillance recommendations for desired as well as adverse effects during treatment with pubertal blockers alone and in combination with cross-sex hormones are adapted from the current ES guidelines (Drummond et al., 2008) and are summarized in Table 12.2 (Rosenthal, 2014).

Of note, some Tanner stage 4/5 transgender adolescents present for medical services before 16 years of age. As with the group treated with GnRH agonists at early puberty, we and others are studying the consequences of cross-sex hormone treatment at 14 years of age (Rosenthal, 2014). Occasionally, some gender-dysphoric youth first come to medical attention when they are Tanner stage 4/5, but < 14 years of age. Such individuals would be candidates for pubertal blockers (e.g., to stop menses in an FTM adolescent), but without supportive outcomes data, they are not currently candidates for cross-sex hormone use under most circumstances (Rosenthal, 2014).

Controversies and Areas of Uncertainty/Barriers to Ideal Practice

Areas of uncertainty, controversies, and barriers to state-of-the art practice limit the ability to provide optimal health care to gender-dysphoric/transgender youth. Limited safety and efficacy data currently exist; there are virtually no

Table 12.1 Hormonal interventions for transgender adolescents (all currently off-label for gender non-conforming/transgender youth)

A.   **Inhibitors of gonadal sex steroid secretion or action**

   1.   **GnRH analogs: Inhibition of the hypothalamic–pituitary–gonadal (HPG) axis (FTM and MTF)**

      a.   Leuprolide acetate IM (1- or 3-month preparations) or SC (1-, 3-, 4-, or 6-month preparations) at dose sufficient to suppress pituitary gonadotropins and gonadal sex steroids

      b.   Histrelin acetate SC implant (once-yearly dosing, though may have longer effectiveness)

      c.   Other options: goserelin acetate SC implant (4- or 12-week preparations), triptorelin (1-, 3, and 6 month preparations), nafarelin acetate intranasal (multiple daily doses) also available, but no reported use in this population

   2.   **Alternative approaches**

      a.   Medroxyprogesterone acetate orally (up to 40 mg/day) or IM (150 mg q 3 months): Inhibition of HPG axis and direct inhibition of gonadal steroidogenesis (FTM and MTF)

      b.   Spironolactone (25–50 mg/day with gradual increase to 100–300 mg/day orally, divided into BID dosing): Inhibition of testosterone synthesis and action (MTF)

      c.   Cyproterone acetate (gradual increase up to 100 mg/day orally; not available in the United States): Inhibition of testosterone synthesis and action (MTF)

      d.   Finasteride (2.5–5 mg/day orally): Inhibition of type II 5 α-reductase, blocking conversion of testosterone to 5 α-dihydrotestosterone (MTF)

B.   **Cross-sex hormones**

   1.   **MTF: Estrogen: 17β-estradiol**

      a.   Transdermal: twice-weekly patches (6.25 mcg (achieved by cutting a 25 mcg patch) with gradual increase to full adult dose)

      b.   Oral/sublingual: daily (0.25 mg with gradual increase to full adult dose of 6–8 mg/day)

      c.   Parenteral IM (synthetic esters of 17β-estradiol): estradiol valerate (5–20 mg up to 30–40 mg q 2 weeks) or estradiol cypionate (2–10 mg q 1 week)

   2.   **FTM: Testosterone**

      a.   Parenteral IM or SC (synthetic esters of testosterone): testosterone cypionate or enanthate (12.5 mg q week or 25 mg q 2 weeks, with gradual increase to 50–100 mg q week or 100–200 mg q 2 weeks)

      b.   Transdermal (consider once full adult testosterone dose has been achieved parenterally): patch (2.5–7.5 mg/day) or 1% gel (2.5–10 g/day of gel = 25–100 mg/day of testosterone)

GnRH, gonadotropin-releasing hormone; MTF, male-to-female; FTM, female-to-male; IM, intramuscularly; SC, subcutaneously; BID, twice a day.

Reprinted with permission from the Endocrine Society: Rosenthal SM. Approach to the patient: transgender youth: endocrine considerations. *J Clin Endocrinol Metab* 2014; 99:4379–4389.

Table 12.2 Monitoring during pubertal suppression and during cross-sex hormone treatment[1]

A. Pubertal suppression

Measure	Frequency
1. Physical exam: height, weight, Tanner staging	T0 and q 3 months
2. Hormonal studies: ultrasensitive LH, FSH, estradiol/ testosterone	T0 and q 3 months
3. Metabolic: Ca, phos, alk phos, 25-OH vitamin D (see also Coleman et al., 2011)	T0 and q 1 year
4. Bone density: DEXA	T0 and q 1 year
5. Bone age	T0 and q 1 year

B. Cross-sex hormone treatment in previously suppressed patients or in late pubertal patients not previously suppressed

Measure	Frequency
1. Physical exam: height, weight, Tanner staging	T0 and q 3 months[2] BP (for FTM, in particular); monitor for adverse reactions
2. Hormonal studies: ultrasensitive LH, FSH, estradiol/ testosterone	T0 and q 3 months[2]
If MTF: also monitor prolactin	T0 and q 1 year
3. Metabolic: Ca, phos, alk phos, 25-OH vitamin D, complete blood count, renal and liver function, fasting lipids, glucose, insulin, glycosylated hemoglobin	T0 and q 3 months[2]
If MTF on spironolactone: serum electrolytes (potassium)	T0 and q 3 months[2]
4. Bone density: DEXA (if puberty previously suppressed)	T0 and q 1 year[3]
5. Bone age (if puberty previously suppressed)	T0 and q 1 year[3]

[1] Modified from Hembree WC, Cohen-Kettenis P, Delemarre-van de Waal HA, Gooren LJ, Meyer WJ 3rd, Spack NP, Tangpricha V, Montori VM; Endocrine Society. Endocrine treatment of transsexual persons: An Endocrine Society clinical practice guideline. *J Clin Endocrinol Metab* 2009; 94:3132–3154.

[2] q 3–12 months after first year.

[3] Until puberty is completed.

LH, luteinizing hormone; FSH, follicle-stimulating hormone; Ca, calcium; phos, phosphate; alk phos, alkaline phosphatase; 25-OH vitamin D, 25-hydroxy vitamin D; DEXA, dual X-ray absorptiometry; BP, blood pressure; FTM, female-to-male; MTF, male-to-female. Reprinted with permission from the Endocrine Society: Rosenthal SM. Approach to the patient: transgender youth: endocrine considerations. *J Clin Endocrinol Metab* 2014; 99:4379–4389.

published data on the use of pubertal blockers in gender-dysphoric individuals < 12 years of age or cross-sex hormones in transgender youth < 16 years of age. In addition, randomized controlled trials for hormonal interventions in gender-dysphoric youth have not been considered feasible or ethical (Drescher & Byne, 2012). The clinical practice guidelines that currently exist are based on best-available evidence, with significant reliance on expert opinion. The need for prospective, longitudinal safety and efficacy studies of medical interventions in gender non-conforming/transgender youth has been endorsed by a report from the Institute of Medicine of the National Academies in the United States (Institute of Medicine (US) Committee on Lesbian, Gay, Bisexual, and Transgender Health Issues and Research Gaps and Opportunities, 2011). Challenges to implementation of current clinical practice guidelines in the United States include the fact that pubertal blockers and cross-sex hormone treatments are off-label for gender-dysphoric youth, are expensive, and coverage is often denied by insurance companies. In addition, while an increasing number of clinical programs have emerged in recent years, there are many geographic regions in which such services do not exist, limiting access to care and often requiring patients and families to travel long distances. Furthermore, lack of training of providers and prejudice and misunderstanding on the part of family, community, and medical and mental health professionals may limit access to optimal care. A report surveying the memberships of the Pediatric Endocrine Society and the Society for Adolescent Health and Medicine explored providers' clinical experiences, comfort, and confidence with and barriers to providing care to transgender youth (Vance et al., 2015). Of the respondents, 66.5% had provided care to transgender youth, 62.4% felt comfortable with providing medical therapy, and 47.1% felt confident doing so (Vance et al., 2015). Principal barriers to provision of transgender-related care included lack of the following: training, exposure to transgender patients, available qualified mental health providers, and insurance reimbursement (Vance et al., 2015).

Conclusions

While there have been significant advances in our understanding of gender non-conforming/transgender youth, many gaps in knowledge remain. Compelling studies have demonstrated that gender identity is not simply a psychosocial construct, but likely reflects a complex interplay of biologic, environmental, and cultural factors (Rosenthal, 2014). The recent replacement of "disorder" with "dysphoria" in DSM-5 removes the connotation that a transgender identity, itself, is pathologic, and instead, focuses on dysphoria as the clinical concern (American Psychiatric Association, 2013). A landmark study from the Netherlands indicates that mental health concerns in gender-dysphoric youth significantly diminish or resolve when such individuals are subject to a gender-affirming model of care, optimally delivered in a multi-disciplinary clinical setting (de Vries et al., 2014). Optimization of medical and mental health care for transgender youth will require further prospective studies focused on long-term safety and efficacy.

References

American Psychiatric Association. *Diagnostic and Statistical Manual of Mental Disorders.* 4th ed. Arlington, VA: American Psychiatric Association; 1994.

American Psychiatric Association. *Diagnostic and Statistical Manual of Mental Disorders.* 5th ed. Arlington, VA: American Psychiatric Association; 2013.

Asscheman H, Giltay EJ, Megens JA, de Ronde WP, van Trotsenburg MA, Gooren LJ. A long-term follow-up study of mortality in transsexuals receiving treatment with cross-sex hormones. *Eur J Endocrinol* 2011; 164:635–642.

Cohen-Kettenis PT, van Goozen SH. Pubertal delay as an aid in diagnosis and treatment of a transsexual adolescent. *Eur Child Adolesc Psychiatry* 1998; 7:246–248.

Cohen-Kettenis PT, Delemarre-van de Waal HA, Gooren LJ. The treatment of adolescent transsexuals: Changing insights. *J Sex Med* 2008; 5:1892–1897.

Cohen-Kettenis PT, Schagen SE, Steensma TD, de Vries AL, Delemarre-van de Waal HA. Puberty suppression in a gender-dysphoric adolescent: A 22-year follow-up. *Arch Sex Behav* 2011; 40:843–847.

Coleman E, Bockting W, Botzer M, Cohen-Kettenis P, DeCuypere G, Feldman J, Fraser L, Green J, Knudson G, Meyer WJ, Monstrey S, Adler RK, Brown GR, Devor AH, Ehrbar R, Ettner R, Eyler E, Garofalo R, Karasic DH, Lev AI, Mayer G, Meyer-Bahlburg H, Hall BP, Pfaefflin F, Rachlin K, Robinson B, Schechter LS, Tangpricha V, van Trotsenburg M, Vitale A, Winter S, Whittle S, Wylie KR, Zucker K. Standards of care for the health of transsexual, transgender, and gender-nonconforming people, version 7. *Int J Transgenderism* 2011; 13:165–232.

Delemarre-van de Waal HA, Cohen-Kettenis PT. Clinical management of gender identity disorder in adolescents: A protocol on psychological and paediatric endocrinology aspects. *Eur J Endocrinol* 2006; 155:S131–S137.

de Vries AL, Cohen-Kettenis PT. Clinical management of gender dysphoria in children and adolescents: The Dutch approach. *J Homosex* 2012; 59:301–320.

de Vries AL, Noens IL, Cohen-Kettenis PT, van Berckelaer-Onnes IA, Doreleijers TA. Autism spectrum disorders in gender dysphoric children and adolescents. *J Autism Dev Disord* 2010; 40:930–936.

de Vries AL, Steensma TD, Doreleijers TA, Cohen-Kettenis PT. Puberty suppression in adolescents with gender identity disorder: A prospective follow-up study. *J Sex Med* 2011; 8:2276–2283.

de Vries ALC, McGuire JK, Steensma TD, Wagenaar ECF, Doreleijers TAH, Cohen-Kettenis PT. Young adult psychological outcome after puberty suppression and gender reassignment. *Pediatrics* 2014; 134:1–9.

Drescher J, Byne W. Gender dysphoric/gender variant (GD/GV) children and adolescents: Summarizing what we know and what we have yet to learn. *J Homosex* 2012; 59: 501–510.

Drummond KD, Bradley SJ, Peterson-Badali M, Zucker KJ. A follow-up study of girls with gender identity disorder. *Dev Psychol* 2008; 44:34–45.

Gooren LJ. Clinical practice. Care of transsexual persons. *N Engl J Med* 2011; 364:1251–1257.

Grossman AH, D'Augelli AR. Transgender youth and life-threatening behaviors. *Suicide Life Threat Behav* 2007; 37:527–537.

Hembree WC, Cohen-Kettenis P, Delemarre-van de Waal HA, Gooren LJ, Meyer WJ 3rd, Spack NP, Tangpricha V, Montori VM; Endocrine Society. Endocrine treatment of transsexual persons: An Endocrine Society clinical practice guideline. *J Clin Endocrinol Metab* 2009; 94:3132–3154.

Hidalgo MA, Ehrensaft D, Tishelman AC, Clark LF, Garofalo R, Rosenthal SM, Spack NP, Olson J. The gender affirmative model: What we know and what we aim to learn. *Hum Dev* 2013; 56:285–290.

Institute of Medicine (US) Committee on Lesbian, Gay, Bisexual, and Transgender Health Issues and Research Gaps and Opportunities. *The Health of Lesbian, Gay, Bisexual, and Transgender People: Building a Foundation for Better Understanding.* Washington, DC: National Academies Press (US); 2011, p. 347. Available from: http://www.ncbi.nlm.nih.gov/books/NBK64806/.

Khatchadourian K, Amed S, Metzger DL. Clinical management of youth with gender dysphoria in Vancouver. *J Pediatr* 2014; 164:906–911.

Klink D, Caris M, Heijboer A, van Trotsenburg M, Rotteveel J. Bone mass in young adulthood following gonadotropin-releasing hormone analog treatment and cross-sex hormone treatment in adolescents with gender dysphoria. *J Clin Endocrinol Metab* 2015; 100:E270–275.

Meyer-Bahlburg HF. Sex steroids and variants of gender identity. *Endocrinol Metab Clin North Am* 2013; 42:435–452.

Rosenthal SM. Approach to the patient: Transgender youth: Endocrine considerations. *J Clin Endocrinol Metab* 2014; 99:4379–4389.

Sato T, Katagiri K, Gohbara A, Inoue K, Ogonuki N, Ogura A, Kubota Y, Ogawa T. In vitro production of functional sperm in cultured neonatal mouse testes. *Nature* 2011; 471:504–507.

Sherer I, Rosenthal SM, Ehrensaft D, Baum J. Child and adolescent gender center: A multidisciplinary collaboration to improve the lives of gender nonconforming children and teens. *Pediatr Rev* 2012; 33:273–275.

Sherer I, Baum J, Ehrensaft D, Rosenthal SM. Affirming gender: Caring for gender atypical children and adolescents. *Contemp Pediatr* 2015; 32:16–19.

Spack NP. Management of transgenderism. *JAMA* 2013; 309:478–484.

Spack NP, Edwards-Leeper L, Feldman HA, Leibowitz S, Mandel F, Diamond DA, Vance SR. Children and adolescents with gender identity disorder referred to a pediatric medical center. *Pediatrics* 2012; 129:418–425.

Staphorsius AS, Kreukels BPC, Cohen-Kettenis PT, Veltmanc DJ, Sarah M. Burke SM, Schagend SEE, Woutersd FM, Delemarre-van de Waale HA, Bakker J. Puberty suppression and executive functioning: An fMRI-study in adolescents with gender dysphoria. *Psychoneuroendocrinology* 2015; 56:190–199.

Steensma TD, McGuire JK, Kreukels BP, Beekman AJ, Cohen-Kettenis PT. Factors associated with desistence and persistence of childhood gender dysphoria: A quantitative follow-up study. *J Am Acad Child Adolesc Psychiatry* 2013; 52:582–590.

Strang JF, Kenworthy L, Dominska A, Sokoloff J, Kenealy LE, Berl M, Walsh K, Menvielle E, Slesaransky-Poe G, Kim KE, Luong-Tran C, Meagher H, Wallace GL. Increased gender variance in autism spectrum disorders and attention deficit hyperactivity disorder. *Arch Sex Behav* 2014; 43:1525–1533.

Toorians AW, Thomassen MC, Zweegman S, Magdeleyns EJ, Tans G, Gooren LJ, Rosing J. Venous thrombosis and changes of hemostatic variables during cross-sex hormone treatment in transsexual people. *J Clin Endocrinol Metab* 2003; 88:5723–5729.

Travers R, Bauer G, Pyne J, Bradley K for the Trans PULSE Project, Gale L, Papadimitriou M. Impacts of strong parental support for trans youth: A report prepared for Children's Aid Society of Toronto and Delisle youth services. *Trans Pulse* 2012:1–5.

Vance SR, Ehrensaft D, Rosenthal SM. Psychological and medical care of gender nonconforming youth. *Pediatrics* 2014; 134:1184–1192.

Vance SR, Halpern-Felsher BL, Rosenthal SM. Health care providers' comfort with and barriers to care of transgender youth. *J Adolesc Health* 2015; 56:251–253.

Wallien MS, Cohen-Kettenis PT. Psychosexual outcome of gender-dysphoric children. *J Am Acad Child Adolesc Psychiatry* 2008; 47:1413–1423.

Yokonishi T, Sato T, Komeya M, Katagiri K, Kubota Y, Nakabayashi K, Hata K, Inoue K, Ogonuki N, Ogura A, Ogawa T. Offspring production with sperm grown in vitro from cryopreserved testis tissues. *Nature Commun* 2014; 5:4320.

Zucker KJ. On the "natural history" of gender identity disorder in children. *J Am Acad Child Adolesc Psychiatry* 2008; 47:1361–1363.

Zucker KJ, Bradley SJ, Owen-Anderson A, Kibblewhite SJ, Cantor JM. Is gender identity disorder in adolescents coming out of the closet? *J Sex Marital Ther* 2008; 34:287–290.

Zucker KJ, Wood H, Singh D, Bradley SJ. A developmental, biopsychosocial model for the treatment of children with gender identity disorder. *J Homosex* 2012; 59:369–397.

13 Disorders of Sex Development (DSD)

Definition, Syndromes, Gender Dysphoria, and Differentiation from Transsexualism

Tom Mazur, Melissa Gardner, Aden M. Cook, and David E. Sandberg

Introduction

Since the first publication of this chapter, a number of conceptual changes have occurred regarding issues of gender and intersexuality. *Diagnostic and Statistical Manual of Mental Disorders*, fifth edition (DSM-5) has replaced DSM-IV-TR, gender identity disorder (GID) has been replaced by gender dysphoria (GD), and intersex has been replaced by disorders of sex development (DSD). Persons with a DSD who are experiencing a gender identity incongruent with the one announced or assigned to them at birth can now receive the same DSM-5 diagnosis as persons with GD who do not carry a DSD diagnosis. In addition, interest in DSD research, care, and follow-up has grown. National registries of persons with DSD conditions have been created in Europe and the United States (Sandberg et al., 2015). The U.S. National Institutes of Health funded the creation of a clinical research network (the Disorders of Sex Development Translational Research Network: dsdtrn. genetics.ucla.edu) that includes a patient registry and biobank and otherwise fosters research in DSD through sponsorship of workshops (http://www. nichd.nih.gov/about/meetings/2014/Pages/032714.aspx) and funding opportunities (Research on the Health of LGBTI Populations; http://grants. nih.gov/grants/guide/pa-files/PA-12-111.html). Advocacy and peer support groups have also grown internationally (Baratz et al., 2014). Legislatures in several countries have passed laws accommodating those born with a DSD and who identify as other than male or female (Schmall, 2012). Greater emphasis on "patient-centeredness" in health care delivery (Institute of Medicine, 2001) and increased awareness of DSD have been accompanied by controversy, especially about the utility of elective genital surgery in infancy or early childhood. Legal questions have been raised and there is currently an ongoing lawsuit regarding the legality of surgical intervention in the management of a child with a DSD (Saussar, 2015). The purpose of this chapter is to bring the reader up to date by providing an overview of DSD and recent changes in the field.

A New Classification System and New Terminology: Intersex Out— Disorders of Sex Development In

In 2005, under the auspices of pediatric endocrinology societies in North America and Europe, international health care experts, researchers, and patient advocates convened in Chicago to formulate a consensus document on the clinical management of individuals born with intersex conditions. The outcome of this consensus conference (Lee et al., 2006) was: (1) the recommendation to eliminate traditional descriptive terms like "intersex," "pseudohermaphroditism," "hermaphroditism," "sex errors of the body," "ambiguous genitalia," and "sex reversal," because they were considered confusing and stigmatizing by professionals, parents, and the individual; and (2) the creation of a new all-inclusive term, "disorders of sex development" (DSD), with subcategories of various DSD classified according to genotype. Thus, "DSD," defined as "congenital conditions in which development of chromosomal, gonadal, or anatomic sex is atypical," created a new classification system supplanting the one formulated by Klebs in 1876 based on the nature of the gonads. The full report was published in 2006 under the title, "Consensus Statement on Management of Intersex Disorder," in *Pediatrics* (Lee et al., 2006).

The three DSD subcategories based on genotype are: (1) variations in numbers of sex chromosomes (e.g., Klinefelter syndrome and Turner syndrome); (2) 46,XX DSD (including disorders of ovarian development and excessive androgen); and (3) 46,XY DSD (including disorders of testicular development and insufficient androgen). Formation of a combination of ovarian and testicular tissue—ovotestes—can be either an XX or an XY condition. Conditions not fitting these categories are classified as "other." Lack of precise medical codes precludes collection of accurate population statistics for DSD, rare conditions, but in the aggregate has an estimated incidence of 0.1–0.5% of live births (Arboleda et al., 2013). Approximately one in 4,000 infants is born with atypical external genitalia and will receive a DSD diagnosis (Lee et al., 2006).

Typical Sexual Differentiation Process

Development of the sexual reproductive system involves the internal (Figure 13.1) and external (Figure 13.2) sex organs. These organs develop through a series of steps. At the outset, sex determination occurs when either a Y- or an X-bearing sperm fertilizes the ovum. If the resulting genetic sex is XY, then the undifferentiated and bipotential gonad develops as a testis. A single gene located on the short arm of the Y chromosome, referred to as the sex-determining region of the Y chromosome, or SRY, is responsible for this event. Testes develop approximately in the sixth to seventh week of pregnancy in an XY embryo. The bipotential gonad develops into an ovary in the absence of SRY (i.e., XX sex chromosomes) (Grumbach et al., 2003).

The process of sexual differentiation begins once the Leydig cells of the testes secrete two hormones, testosterone and anti-Müllerian hormone (AMH), at

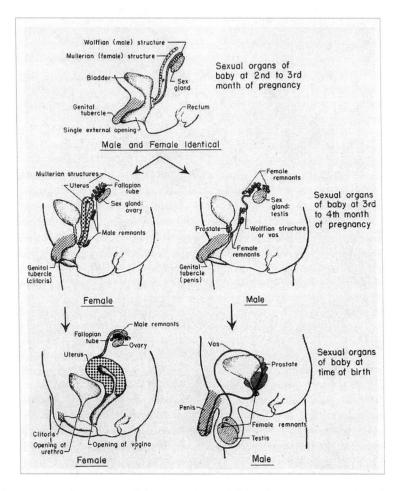

Figure 13.1 Differentiation of the internal genital ducts. (*Source:* Money, J. (1994). *Sex Errors of the Body and Related Syndromes: A Guide to Counseling Children* (2nd ed., p. 32). Baltimore, MD: Paul H. Brookes. Reprinted with permission of the estate of John Money.)

weeks 8–9 of pregnancy. Testosterone causes the Wolffian (male) duct to differentiate into the epididymis, vas deferens, seminal vesicles, and ejaculatory ducts. AMH suppresses Müllerian (female) duct development: fallopian tubes, uterus, cervix, and upper third of the vagina. Müllerian duct differentiation unfolds in the absence of hormonal stimulation (i.e., the ovary is quiescent during this stage of development). In the absence of testosterone exposure, the Wolffian duct regresses.

After completion of the internal sexual reproductive structures, differentiation of the external genitalia begins (week 10). The external genitalia, male

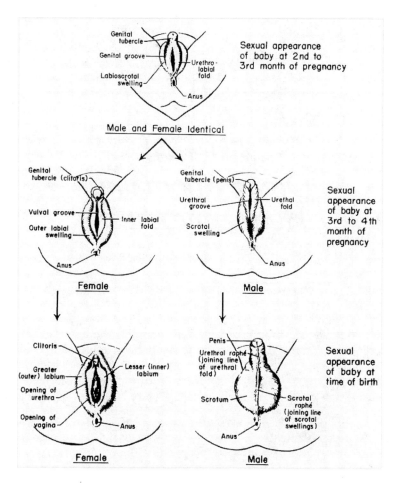

Figure 13.2 Differentiation of external genitalia. (*Source:* Money, J. (1994). *Sex Errors of the Body and Related Syndromes: A Guide to Counseling Children* (2nd ed., p. 36). Baltimore, MD: Paul H. Brookes. Reprinted with permission of the estate of John Money.)

and female, are created from a single set of structures, in contrast to the internal genitalia, which differentiate from a double system, Wolffian and Müllerian. Thus, the external genitalia, like the gonads, are bipotential, differentiating and developing into either male or female external sex organs.

Dihydrotestosterone (DHT), the 5-alpha-reduced metabolite of testosterone, is responsible for differentiation of the genital tubercle into a penis in an XY fetus (Conte & Grumbach, 2004). The labioscrotal swellings fuse to form the scrotum. Urethral-labia folds form the shaft and foreskin of the penis. Male external genital differentiation is complete by weeks 12–14 of pregnancy. Penile enlargement continues during the second and third trimesters of pregnancy.

In an XX fetus, the ovary secretes no masculinizing hormones. The genital tubercle becomes a clitoris. The labioscrotal swellings become the labia majora. The urethral-labia folds become the labia minora and the clitoral hood. DSD occur as a consequence of disorders of androgen biosynthesis or action, partial or complete, in genetic males, or excess androgen exposure in genetic females.

DSD Syndromes and Related Conditions

Atypical sexual development occurs in multiple syndromes and related conditions; commonly encountered DSD are summarized in the following section, which uses the new classification and the old classification in parentheses for historical continuity and to make clear to the reader the association between the new and old nomenclature. The reader is also referred to Conte and Grumbach (2004) for a more thorough endocrine review; for brief descriptions of the behavioral characteristics of persons diagnosed with these conditions, see Cohen-Kettenis and Pfafflin (2003).

Sex Chromosome DSD (Formerly Disorders of Gonadal Differentiation)

Klinefelter Syndrome

Klinefelter syndrome is a non-heritable genetic condition in which an extra X chromosome is present (Zurenda & Sandberg, 2003a). The most commonly found chromosomal pattern is a single extra X (47,XXY), but other variations (e.g., 48,XXYY) and mosaicism (e.g., 46,XY/47,XXY) have been documented. Incidence is estimated at 1:600 live male births (Nielsen & Wohlert, 1991). Klinefelter syndrome is typically diagnosed during puberty when small, firm testicles are palpated on physical exam. Additional features, which assist in making the diagnosis, include tall stature and disproportionately long legs (Ratcliffe et al., 1990). Infertility is almost certain because the testes do not produce a normal volume of sperm. However, assisted reproductive technologies such as intracytoplasmic sperm injection are helping men with Klinefelter syndrome to father children with a normal karyotype (Denschlag et al., 2004).

Additional features of Klinefelter syndrome may include unilateral or bilateral breast development (gynecomastia), incomplete masculine body build, and social and/or cognitive-educational problems (Grumbach & Conte, 1998). Puberty may also be delayed (Nielsen & Wohlert, 1991), and individuals will need testosterone replacement in adolescence and adulthood to prevent osteoporosis and maintain physical energy, sexual function, and a general sense of well-being (Zurenda & Sandberg, 2003a). Neurocognitively, individuals with Klinefelter syndrome characteristically achieve a full-scale IQ that falls in the average range, but verbal IQ is typically significantly lower than performance IQ. This profile is associated with language and reading problems, speech and language delays in childhood, and poor school performance. Many individuals with Klinefelter syndrome are described as having a passive personality and a tendency to internalize problems, and exhibit chronic difficulties with peer relationships (Sandberg & Barrick, 1995). Psychosexually, men with Klinefelter syndrome, on average, exhibit decreased interest in women, less dating, and limited sexual experience (Mazur & Dobson, 1995). A 20-year-long follow-up study showed that 59% of Klinefelter syndrome individuals were married or involved in a longstanding heterosexual relationship (Nielsen & Pelsen, 1987). While most persons with Klinefelter syndrome establish a male gender identity, there are reports of GD in individuals who transition to live fully as female (Cossey, 1991; Seifert & Windgassen, 1995).

Turner Syndrome

Turner syndrome is the consequence of a chromosomal genetic abnormality in females characterized by a missing or partially deleted X chromosome (Fennell, 2003). Incidence is estimated at 1:2,500 live female births (Fennell, 2003; Hook & Warbuton, 1983). Several dysmorphic features characterize the physical appearance of those with Turner syndrome, including low-set ears and hairline, high-arched palate, webbed (thick) neck, broad chest, and short stature (Fennell, 2003; Sybert & McCauley, 2004). The number and degree of physically dysphoric features are variable in individuals with Turner syndrome. Additionally, hearing problems, malformed kidneys, and cardiovascular abnormalities may be present. The Wolffian ducts regress and the Müllerian ducts differentiate normally in Turner syndrome; individuals with Turner syndrome typically have streak (non-functioning) gonads resulting in infertility. For most women, the external genitalia are normal in appearance. For the majority, endocrinological intervention includes hormone replacement therapy to initiate puberty and to maintain secondary sexual characteristics. Growth hormone is used to treat marked short stature. Various assisted reproductive techniques are now available for achieving pregnancy. For those women who do not have functional ovaries, oocyte or embryo donation can be used to achieve pregnancy (Saenger et al., 2001).

Neurocognitively, individuals with Turner syndrome characteristically achieve a full-scale IQ that falls in the average range, but performance IQ is typically significantly lower than verbal IQ. Turner syndrome is associated with a variety of learning problems, such as poor math skills, which may be related to poor visual-perceptual abilities (Mazur & Dobson, 1995; Sandberg & Barrick, 1995; Sybert & McCauley, 2004). Hyperactivity and inattentiveness in childhood are noted in the literature (Sandberg & Barrick, 1995). Women with Turner syndrome exhibit difficulties in establishing satisfying long-term social relationships and are at risk for having low self-esteem (Sandberg & Barrick, 1995; Sybert & McCauley, 2004). Psychosexually, gender identity in Turner syndrome is unambiguously female. To our knowledge, there are no reports of a woman with Turner syndrome transitioning to live in the male gender.

Ovotesticular Disorder of Sex Development (formerly True Hermaphroditism) (OT)

OT is associated with a number of chromosomal patterns: 46,XX (most common), combined 46,XX/46,XY chimerism, or 46,XY (rare). Stated to be "uncommon," but "reported in more than 400 individuals," the incidence of OT is unknown (Grumbach et al., 2003). OT is defined by the presence of both testicular and ovarian tissue in the same individual (Grumbach et al., 2003). The internal reproductive ducts differentiate in accordance with the gonad on that side of the body, i.e., female internal reproductive structures if an ovary is present. The external genitalia in these individuals may range from typical male to typical female. Breast development is common and menses may occur in more than half of individuals with OT. Clinical management depends on the age at diagnosis and functional capacity of the reproductive structures. Individuals diagnosed with OT have been assigned to either the male or the female gender. Comprehensive reviews of long-term psychosocial or psychosexual outcomes in OT have not been performed (Meyer-Bahlburg, 2005a).

46,XX DSD (Formerly Female Pseudohermaphroditism)

Congenital Adrenal Hyperplasia (CAH)

CAH is the result of an enzyme deficiency (most commonly 21-hydroxylase) that occurs in both males and females. CAH is inherited as an autosomal-recessive disorder and has an estimated incidence of 1:15,000 live births (Speiser & White, 2003), with considerable variation between ethnic/racial populations. Genetic males with CAH show no ambiguity of their external sex organs at birth. In contrast, the prenatal androgen excess in genetic females results in varying degrees of masculinization of the external genitalia. In the most extreme form (Prader stage 5), the genitalia of the 46,XX infant look typically male, with the urethral meatus terminating at the tip of an enlarged phallic structure and fused labia which resemble a scrotum. There are no gonads in the scrotum, as the internal genital ducts are typically female, with ovaries and uterus in the typical position. CAH is associated with excess of adrenal androgen production in utero and, sometimes, an accompanying deficiency in the salt-retaining hormone, aldosterone. Depending upon the degree of aldosterone deficiency, an electrolyte imbalance due to salt loss can occur, which can be life-threatening. Endocrine intervention is lifelong cortisol replacement which controls excess androgen production. If needed, mineralocorticoid treatment is added to control salt loss.

Neurocognitively, individuals with CAH characteristically achieve a full-scale IQ that falls in the average range; however, some affected individuals may demonstrate decreased global IQ or specific cognitive deficits resulting from salt-wasting crises during infancy (Zurenda & Sandberg, 2003b). Females with CAH represent the most systematically studied of all DSD, with emphasis on behaviors that show significant gender-related variation. Some 46,XX CAH infants have been gender-assigned male, but current medical consensus recommends a female gender assignment. However, there have been recent reports of 46,XX CAH adults with Prader stage 4/5 successfully living as males with a male gender identity (Lee & Houk, 2010). Based on these data, the authors believe that some consideration should be given to recommending a male gender assignment. For those assigned female, gender identity is characteristically female, gender role behavior is often masculine or "tomboyish," and there is a higher likelihood of experiencing bisexual or homosexual erotic/romantic dreams, fantasies, and sexual attraction when compared to unaffected women (Zurenda & Sandberg, 2003b). Dessens et al. (2005) reviewed the extensive literature on CAH and found that the majority (94.8%) of 46,XX CAH-reared females established a female gender identity with no dysphoria. However, 13 of 250 (5.2%) individuals had "serious problems" of gender identity. This percentage is higher than the prevalence of transmen in the general population of 46,XX females. They also reported that four of 33 46,XX CAH individuals (12.1%) assigned male at birth, and reared as male, had serious gender problems: one identified as female and the other three experienced GD. Meyer-Bahlburg (2014) has written the most thorough summary of the psychoendocrinology of CAH to date.

46,XY DSD (Formerly Male Pseudohermaphroditism)

Androgen Insensitivity Syndrome (AIS)

AIS is an X-linked disorder which occurs as a result of a mutation of the androgen receptor (AR) gene, making the tissue completely or partially unresponsive to the influence of androgens, although testes form and synthesize androgens normally. In complete AIS (CAIS), the external genitalia have a typical female appearance because of the lack of tissue responsiveness to androgens. Likewise, the Wolffian ducts fail to develop but the Müllerian ducts regress, due to the action of AMH. Breasts develop under the influence of androgens that are metabolized into estrogen. The diagnosis is usually made at puberty when lack of menstruation becomes a concern. Gender assignment is always female, gender identity is unambiguously female, gender role is feminine, and sexual orientation in both overt behavior and fantasy is typically heterosexual (Cohen-Kettenis & Pfafflin, 2003). A literature review (Mazur, 2005) of gender identity stability in individuals diagnosed with CAIS confirmed that no individuals with a CAIS diagnosis changed to live as a male. However, since that summary review there have been two reports, one a letter (Kulshreshtha et al., 2009) and one a confirmed case report (T'Sjoen et al., 2011), about individuals with CAIS changing to live as males. Estimated incidence of CAIS is 1:20,400 (Bangsboll et al., 1992).

Partial AIS (PAIS) results in an individual born with ambiguous external genitalia. The genital tubercle is enlarged but is not typically of normal male size, a partially fused labia/scrotum may be present, and severe hypospadias is often present. Infants with PAIS have been gender-assigned as males and as females (Conte & Grumbach, 2004). The incidence of PAIS is unknown. Mazur (2005) reported that self-initiated gender change was observed among those with PAIS, and the change occurred in both directions. Cadet (2011) wrote about her own gender change, from male to female. AR gene mutations were documented in PAIS individuals who changed gender and in those who did not. A specific AR gene mutation was not associated with gender identity outcomes. This finding is similar to Wilson's (2001) finding that gender change is not related to the severity of the AR mutation.

5-Alpha-Reductase Deficiency (5-ARD) and 17β-Hydroxysteroid Dehydrogenase-3 Deficiency (17β-HSD-3)

5-ARD is an enzyme deficiency secondary to a gene deletion or mutation in 46,XY individuals. It is an autosomal-recessive disorder, which results in an inability of testosterone to be converted to DHT by peripheral tissue in utero. DHT is required for the development of external male genitals and prostate. Consequently, infants with 5-ARD are born with ambiguous external genitalia. The underdeveloped penis resembles a clitoris and the scrotum appears as labia majora; as such, infants may have been announced or assigned either a female or a male gender at birth. The natural course of this condition is a virilizing puberty with voice deepening, phallic enlargement, increased muscle mass, and the development of male-pattern facial and body hair growth. This masculinization is probably due to increase in an enzyme that converts pubertal testosterone into DHT (Wilson, 2001).

A second autosomal-recessive disorder similar to 5-ARD is 17β-HSD-3. External genitals appear ambiguous or not completely masculinized and either male or female gender may be assigned. The prevalence in the general population for both of these autosomal-recessive disorders is unknown (Cohen-Kettenis, 2005; Conte & Grumbach, 2004). There has been considerable controversy over the stability of gender identity and gender role behavior of these individuals, especially as they transition through puberty. Cohen-Kettenis (2005) reviewed the world literature on this topic. Fifty-six percent (62 of 110) of those individuals diagnosed with 5-ARD changed gender from female to male and 39% (19 of 49) of those diagnosed with 17β-HSD-3 changed from female to male. Gender change in those initially assigned as female who did gender reassign could not be explained by prenatal exposure to androgens or to the degree of external masculinization. Cohen-Kettenis (2005) also identified 28 individuals diagnosed with either 5-ARD or 17β-HSD-3 who were assigned and reared as male. None of them changed to the female gender or appeared to have any wish to do so.

Other (Formerly Unclassified Forms of Abnormal Development)

Hypospadias

Hypospadias refers to the positioning of the urinary meatus (opening) at some point on the undersurface of the penis, rather than at its tip. Hypospadias is a feature of many malformation syndromes, but it can also occur alone (i.e., isolated hypospadias). A multifactor etiological model has been proposed for hypospadias. The exact cause of isolated hypospadias, which occurs in 1:300 newborn males (Conte & Grumbach, 2004), remains unknown in most cases. Classified according to the position of the urinary meatus, the mildest and most common form (85%) is glandular or coronal hypospadias (Grumbach et al., 2003). Research indicates that hypoandrogenization associated with hypospadias does not interfere with developing gender-typical (masculine) behavior in boys during middle childhood (Sandberg et al., 1995). Individuals with hypospadias report relatively normal sexual behavior and function and, as a group, they do not report any more behavioral/emotional problems than comparison groups (Mureau, 1995).

Micropenis

Micropenis refers to a completely formed penis, with the urethral meatus at the tip of the glans, that measures at or below 2.5 sp in length for age and stage of puberty when stretched from the pubis ramus to the tip of the glans (i.e., a penis <1.9 cm in a newborn or <9.3 cm in an adult qualifies as a micropenis) (Lee et al., 1980). Micropenis can result from a heterogeneous group of disorders, the most common of which is fetal testosterone deficiency (Conte & Grumbach, 2004). A micropenis does not necessarily occur as part of a syndrome; rather, it can occur in isolated form or be associated with a number of other conditions. For this reason, the incidence is not known. Using the Adjustment Self-Report Questionnaire, Lee and Houk (2004) reported no significant differences between a small group of adult males with isolated micropenis and controls regarding psychosocial and psychosexual functioning. They also failed to identify any differences in psychiatric symptoms between these two groups using the Hopkins Symptoms Checklist. Money and Norman (1988) found an association between micropenis and central nervous system impairments in four cases, all with CHARGE syndrome (coloboma, heart disease, atresia choanae, retarded growth/development or central nervous system anomalies, genital hypoplasia, and ear anomalies). Newborns with a micropenis have been assigned at birth to either the female or the male gender. In a review of extant literature with respect to gender stability in individuals with a micropenis reared as male or female, there was not a single documented case of gender change among the 89 individuals studied, ten of whom were assigned to the female gender (Mazur, 2005). However, those reared female were young and follow-up of these individuals is needed.

Mayer–Rokitansky–Küster–Hauser (MRKH)

MRKH, marked by the absence of the vagina with abnormal or absent Müllerian structures, is a congenital syndrome that occurs in genetic females. The incidence is estimated at between 1:4,000 (Rock & Breech, 2003) and

1:5,000 (Evans et al., 1981; Grumbach et al., 2003) female births. Associated features include amenorrhea with normal ovarian function. Renal and skeletal abnormalities may be present. Hearing loss occurs in approximately 25% of women with MRKH (Grumbach et al., 2003). Follow-up studies describing the psychological health of women with MRKH are limited. With psychological support and proper medical intervention to create a vagina, a normal sexual life can be expected (Bean, 2003). Gender identity is firmly established as female with no known published reports of gender change.

Penile Agenesis

Penile agenesis (or aphallia) refers to complete absence of the penis as part of a developmental pelvic field defect (Cendron, 2001). The incidence of penile agenesis is not known. There may be associated anomalies such as failure of one or both testes to descend, renal abnormalities, and pulmonary problems. In the most pure form, there is absolutely no penile tissue in the normal position, two testes in a fully formed scrotum, and the urethral opening on or in the anus (Cendron, 2001). To our knowledge, there are no psychosexual or neurocognitive studies of a group of these individuals due to the rarity of the condition.

Meyer-Bahlburg (2005b) reported on individuals assigned female or male with penile agenesis. There were 16 individuals assigned at birth as female or reassigned to female in early childhood. Of these 16 individuals, 12 were living as females, two were living as females with possible GD, and two were living as males. Only four were 18 years old or older. There were 17 assigned male. None of the 17 individuals with penile agenesis assigned and living as male had changed gender at the time of the report. Only six of the 17 were adults. There was a "highly significant" statistical difference between these two groups.

Penile Ablation

Penile ablation is not the result of an anomaly of genital development, like penile agenesis, but refers to traumatic loss of the penis resulting from, for example, an accident during circumcision. Thus penile ablation is not a DSD per se; however, research conducted on those with penile ablation has historically been used to inform clinical decision making for those with DSD. Meyer-Bahlburg (2005b) reported on seven individuals who had traumatic loss of the penis in childhood or infancy. All had "physician-imposed re-assignment to female." Four (one child, two adolescents, and one adult) were living as females. The fifth was living as a female with GD. The sixth and seventh individuals (one adolescent and one adult) were living as males.

Cloacal Exstrophy of the Bladder (CE)

Affecting both genetic males and genetic females, CE is a severe variant of a defect to multiple organ systems involving, among others, the bladder complex, abdominal wall, and pubic bones (Gearhart, 2001). It appears the bladder and abdominal wall are turned inside out, thus exposing the bladder. In males, the penis is often aplastic and split into halves. Classical bladder exstrophy is less severe than CE, but severe malformations can occur in this condition as well. Exstrophy of the bladder is a rare, congenital anomaly occurring in live births in a 1:25,000 to 1:40,000 ratio. There is a male predominance over female in a ratio of about 2:1 (Dominguez, 2003).

Meyer-Bahlburg (2005b) reported a "highly significant" difference in gender outcome between those living as females and those living as males. In his literature review, Meyer-Bahlburg also reported on individuals with classical bladder exstrophy. Of the three assigned as females, two were living as males, and one, an adolescent, as a female. Of the 279 individuals reared as males, and now adults, 279 were living as males, although one, a 12-year-old, had "possible" GD. Meyer-Bahlburg's overall conclusion was that there is "clearly an increased risk of later gender change to male in persons with non-hormonal genital defects after female assignment," but this does not indicate that the etiology is prenatal androgens. Furthermore, the absence of childhood GD does not mean that gender change will not happen later in life.

DSD Syndromes and Adult Gender Identity Outcomes

Data on gender stability and change in those DSD conditions reviewed in the world literature are summarized in Table 13.1. Several conclusions (Meyer-Bahlburg, 2005a) can be drawn by inspecting this table: (1) self-initiated gender change occurs in DSD and related conditions; (2) the prevalence of individuals who change gender varies by syndrome; (3) self-initiated gender change is not universal for any one syndrome or condition; (4) gender change is more frequent in XY persons than in those with an XX chromosomal pattern; (5) self-initiated gender change occurs in both directions, that is, male-to-female and female-to-male, although it more frequently occurs in the direction of female-to-male, as exemplified in Meyer-Bahlburg's (2005b) review of penile agenesis, classical and cloacal exstrophy, and penile ablation; and (6) there are no published reports of gender change in micropenis regardless of whether the person was assigned and reared as male or female. However, the small number of individuals assigned and reared as girls ($n = 10$) were all prepubertal.

Events Post-2005 Consensus Meeting

It has been 10 years since the Consensus meeting in Chicago. While scientific and medical communities rapidly adopted the new nomenclature, some vocal elements of the patient community strongly opposed the word "disorder"— experiencing it as unnecessary pathologization of atypical bodies that contributes to potentially harmful surgical "normalization" procedures. Some affected individuals prefer "differences" to "disorders"; i.e., "differences of sex development" and others rejecting DSD entirely, still preferring the

Table 13.1 Gender identity stability in disorders of sex development

Study	Diagnosis	n	Initial assignment	Gender reassignment		
				n	%[1]	Direction
Cohen-Kettenis (2005)	5-ARD	110	F	62	56	F → M
	17β-HSD-3	49	F	19	39	F → M
Dessens et al. (2005)	CAH (46,XX)	250	F	4	2	F → M
	CAH (46,XX)	33	M	0[2]	0	N/A
Mazur (2005)	CAIS	157	F	1[3]	0	F → M
	PAIS	100		10[4]	10	F → M (3) M → F (7)
	Micropenis	79	M	0	0	N/A
	Micropenis	10	F	0	0	N/A
Meyer-Bahlburg (2005b)	Penile agenesis	16	F	2	13	F → M
	Penile agenesis	17	M	0	0	N/A
	Penile ablation	7	F	2	29	F → M
	Cloacal exstrophy	51	F	11	22	F → M
	Cloacal exstrophy	15	M	0	0	N/A
	Classical exstrophy	3	F	2	67	F → M
	Classical exstrophy	279	M	0	0	N/A

5-ARD, 5-alpha-reductase deficiency; 17β-HSD-3, 17β-hydroxysteroid dehydrogenase-3 deficiency; CAH, congenital adrenal hyperplasia; CAIS, complete androgen insensitivity syndrome; PAIS, partial androgen insensitivity syndrome.

[1] Percentages rounded to the nearest whole number.

[2] Four of 33 (12.1%) were reported to have "serious gender problems; one individual lived as a male, but was convinced he was a woman starting at age 26 when he began to menstruate."

[3] T'Sjoen, G., De Cuypere, G., Monstrey, S., Hoebeke, P., Freedman, K. F., Appari, M., et al. (2011). Male gender identity in complete androgen insensitivity syndrome. *Archives of Sexual Behavior, 40*, 635–638.

[4] Cadet, P. (2011). Androgen insensitivity syndrome with a male sex-of-living. *Archives of Sexual Behavior, 40*, 1101–1102.

term "intersex"—referring to an identity, rather than a diagnosable medical condition. Currently, there is a global initiative to address a number of issues since the 2005 Consensus meeting. One issue is the term DSD. It will come as no surprise if this term is replaced by another. There also remains disagreement whether conditions like Turner syndrome, Klinefelter syndrome, and hypospadias constitute a DSD (Vilain & Sandberg, 2009). Lee et al. (2014) documented a number of changes that have occurred, some of which have been influenced by the 2006 Consensus report.

Improvements in Genetic Diagnoses

Diagnosis of patients with a DSD has traditionally been through the assessment of the patient's phenotype, including physical examination of external genitalia, imaging of the internal reproductive structures, endocrine assessment in basal and stimulated states, and molecular analysis of a small number of genes known to cause DSD. Modern technology along with increasingly wide availability and decreasing prices has allowed genetic investigation to be utilized earlier in the diagnostic process. Potential benefits of new genetic diagnostic tools include a shorter diagnostic time, improved genetic counseling and understanding of reproductive options for the family, and improved monitoring (Baxter & Vilain, 2013).

Major Controversies

Unnecessary Medical Surgery

Performing surgery on infants that is not medically necessary for survival, but rather is cosmetic, is questioned and remains a major controversy. Research on benefits of such surgery is lacking and there is no evidence that advanced surgical techniques have resulted in improvements for the individual. On the other hand, there is evidence that operations to create the appearance of typical male or female genitals have been shown in some individuals to impair sexual function and sensation. Furthermore, such operations to create sex-typical genitals can be damaging should a child's eventual gender identity not match the birth assignment. This controversy has prompted surgeons to improve their surgical techniques, but whether or not these will result in benefits to the individual remains to be proven. A second controversial issue is the timing of cosmetic surgery. Some surgeons believe healing is superior if performed in early childhood, preferably within the first 2 years of life, while others advise waiting until the child can participate in the decision-making process. It is an important aspect of care that parents be fully informed of the current controversy so that they feel knowledgeable, know that nothing is kept from them, and trust their providers to work with them in giving their child the best possible care.

Global Legislation on DSD and Lawsuits

Over the past several years, a number of legislative changes regarding assignment to a gender of rearing and DSD status have occurred. In 2012, Argentina passed the Gender Identity Law, which allows for name and sex changes on official documents without proof of surgical reconstruction or other medical or psychiatric treatment. This law was the first to allow gender reassignment based solely on individual proclamation and is applicable to both DSD and transsexual cases (Schmall, 2012). In 2013, the Australian Senate passed the Sex Discrimination Amendment Bill that introduced legislation prohibiting discrimination on the basis of DSD status. The new guidelines on gender recognition state that individuals should be given the option of selecting male, female, or intersex on their personal documents. In the same year, Germany introduced an "indeterminate" sex option on birth certificates. Also in 2013, the Council of Europe adopted a resolution on the protection of children's rights to physical integrity, demanding no one be "subjected to unnecessary medical or surgical treatment that is cosmetic rather than vital for health during infancy or childhood."

While there have been lawsuits brought by individuals with a DSD, or their parents, regarding unnecessary medical surgery, these have largely been settled out of the public eye (Tamar-Mattis, 2014). The first public lawsuit challenging early sex assignment surgery on a child with a DSD was filed in the United States. The child was diagnosed with ovotesticular DSD, assigned a female gender, and received feminizing genital surgery at 16 months of age, after obtaining parental consent. Shortly thereafter, the biological parents abandoned their child, who then came under the care of the South Carolina Department of Social Services, and was later adopted. Despite the feminizing surgery, the child eventually identified as male, and the adoptive parents alleged that the medically unnecessary early genital surgery which occurred without the child's consent violated the child's constitutional rights.

In Germany, a woman with 46,XX CAH successfully sued the surgeon who removed her fully intact female internal organs when she was 18 years old. Her diagnosis of CAH occurred following an appendectomy in which a uterus and ovaries were discovered; she had previously been reared as a male and undergone surgery to correct hypospadias in childhood. She sought 100,000 euros in damages for pain and suffering, claiming the surgeon failed to fully inform her about the consequences of the operation or about possible alternatives (Lee et al., 2014). In both cases, the issue of informed consent with regard to elective surgery appears to lie at the heart of the matter.

Advocacy

Since Hermaphrodites with Attitude, the first advocacy group in North America, numerous advocacy organizations have formed for the purpose of advocating for individuals with DSD and their families. These different advocacy organizations hold meetings to provide support as well as to allow individuals to meet others, voice concerns, and educate themselves and others on their conditions. The link http://www.accordalliance.org/ is a portal through which one can access many of these advocacy/support groups.

Global Networks, Research, and Registries

National registries provide a large database for research and clinical purposes. Categorization and standardization of information allow for improved clinical care, research, and general understanding. While there have been registries for a number of medical conditions for years (e.g., cancer), only recently has there been creation of national registries for DSD. There are two, International DSD (I-DSD) in Europe and Disorders of Sex Development-Translational Research Network (DSD-TRN) in the United States. In addition to creating a large database for research purposes, the DSD-TRN is also designed to delineate the process of clinical care with the hope of providing a more standardized non-categorical (Sandberg & Mazur, 2014) approach to patient and family care, thus improving outcomes.

In addition to these two registries, there are currently two ongoing research projects. The one in the United States (Short-Term Outcomes of Genitoplasty) is a prospective study of the short-term outcomes of feminizing or masculinizing surgeries for children under the age of 2. The one in Europe (Comprehensive European Clinical Outcome Study) is focusing long-term on the outcome of adults with various DSD diagnoses.

Clinical Management

For years, the clinical research and management of persons with DSD focused on the relationship between gender identity, gender role, sexual orientation, sexual functioning, and pre- and post-natal hormones because there was evidence from animal research that hormones, primarily androgens, affected sexual behavior. This approach was categorical, meaning that the focus was on investigating and managing psychosexual development and hormones to the exclusion of other variables of human development (i.e., quality-of-life variables, in addition to psychosexual status and hormones). Recently, Sandberg and Mazur (2014) outlined an approach which encompasses psychosexual development in persons with a DSD in a broader, non-categorical approach to clinical care. This non-categorical approach guides theory development and clinical care by taking into account a growing body of evidence that successful developmental trajectories of persons with chronic medical conditions are influenced as much by psychosocial environment, supports, and organization of health care delivery as by the specific nature of the person's medical condition (Stein, 2011; Stein & Jessop, 1982). Such an approach holds the potential to systematically account for variability in DSD patient quality-of-life outcomes and lead to translating clinical interventions, proven effective in the management of other chronic conditions, to the circumstances faced by those affected by DSD.

DSM-5: Gender Dypshoria In; Gender Identity Disorders Out

After a lengthy process involving feedback from various experts and the public, the Gender Identity Disorders sub-workgroup proposed 11 changes to DSM-IV-TR which would be incorporated in DSM-5 (Zucker et al., 2013). Only two of these 11, #1and #10, are discussed here because of their relevance to DSD.

The first (#1) of the 11 proposed changes was to "change the name of the diagnosis from Gender Identity Disorder (GID) to Gender Dysphoria (GD)." The reason for the change was that GID was stigmatizing. The term "gender incongruence" was first proposed, but many expressed anxiety that this term could "easily be misread as applying to individuals with gender-atypical behaviors who had no gender identity problem." Many suggested "gender dysphoria" to indicate the "aversive emotional component" to this condition. It was accepted, and GD replaced GID in the DSM-5. Members of the sub-workgroup believed that GD will: (1) signal a conceptual change in the formulation of the diagnosis; that is, an emphasis on the distress or dysphoria a person experiences and not on identity per se; and (2) satisfy critics worried about the stigmatizing use of the word "disorder" in GID, which is not found in DSM-5.

The second change (#10) pertains directly to DSD. It reads, "Inclusion of a subtype pertaining to the presence (or absence) of a disorder of sex development (DSD). A DSD includes (but covers more than) what, in the past, were termed physical intersex conditions."

DSD was an exclusionary criterion for GID in DSM-IV-TR. The reason it is now included in DSM-5 is "considerable additional evidence has accumulated that some individuals with a DSD experience GD and may wish to change their assigned gender." The evidence referred to here is found in Table 13.1. Zucker et al. (2013) also pointed out that persons with GD and a DSD have similarities and differences from persons with GD with no known DSD and can have different developmental trajectories. The final rationale is that persons with GD and DSD may suggest a "specific causal mechanism" not seen in persons with GD who are not affected by DSD.

Prior to the publication of DSM-5, there were individuals who made a case for not merging DSD with a GID (i.e., transsexualism) even though persons with a DSD could experience GD (Mazur et al., 2007). Richter-Appelt and Sandberg (2010) argued that the natural history and response to treatment of individuals with a DSD diagnosis and experiencing GD were quite different from a person with no DSD diagnosis and GD. The etiology may be different. Commenting on proposed revisions to GID diagnoses in DSM-5, Lawrence (2010) noted that one of the proposed changes was to replace the term "sex" with "assigned gender" in order to make the criteria applicable to individuals with a DSD. Lawrence continued, stating, "it would be inadvisable to allow persons with a DSD to be eligible for the diagnosis of GID/GI; GI referring to gender incongruence, the first term proposed to replace GID," which Lawrence noted is "merely a euphemism for GID." Lawrence wrote that "The Sub-workgroup would have been better advised to follow Meyer-Bahlburg's (1994) original recommendation and make persons with a DSD ineligible for any GID/GI diagnosis." In the final version of DSM-5, GD replaced GID/GI.

Post-publication, Lawrence criticized DSM-5, calling it:

> a major disappointment. In many respects it is a significant step backwards from the diagnosis of Gender Identity Disorder (GID) in the DSM-IV-TR

(APA, 2000), and the members of the GID Sub-workgroup (Zucker et al., 2013) have done a disservice to both patients with GD and the clinicians who treat them (Lawrence & Zucker, 2014).

Lawrence said the

> rationale for emphasizing assigned gender—making the same diagnosis applicable to persons with and without a disorder of sex development (DSD; see Zucker et al., 2013, p. 903)—was clearly a smokescreen, because such an outcome was actually undesirable, as several international experts (Mazur et al., 2007; Meyer-Bahlburg, 1994, 2009; Richter-Appelt & Sandberg, 2010; Zucker, 2010)—including two sub-workgroup members themselves—have repeatedly and persuasively argued (Lawrence & Zucker, 2014).

Lawrence also believes that the paradigm shift (in DSM-5) to an incongruence between gender identity and assigned gender suggests to professionals and others that GD in persons with a DSD diagnosis is a "prevalent phenomenon of significant clinical importance, which it actually is not."

Gender Dysphoria in DSD and Non-DSD

Clinical investigators have been unable to determine whether the etiology of GD is biological, psychological/environmental, or both. However, there are several factors associated with GD in individuals with and without DSD (Cohen-Kettenis & Pfafflin, 2003; Zucker, 2004). While there are some overlapping features (Tables 13.2 and 13.3) in the putative etiology of GD in persons with DSD diagnosis and non-DSD conditions, the presence of factors unique to those with DSD suggests the possibility that the pathway to GD differs between groups. This is acknowledged by the DSM-5 sub-workgroup (Zucker et al., 2013).

Meyer-Bahlburg (1994) reported that GD in individuals without DSD conditions appears quite early in life, that is, before the age of 6 years; in contrast, most marked gender problems appear for individuals with DSD during adolescence. With regard to the sex ratio, in persons without DSD, boys far outnumber girls; in those with DSD, there are more reports of individuals initially assigned female who change to male than the reverse (Table 13.1). As such, Meyer-Bahlburg concluded that it is unlikely that GD is the same entity for persons with a DSD as those without such a condition.

While terms have changed and now individuals with a DSD diagnosis and experiencing GD can be given the same DSM-5 diagnosis as a person experiencing GD without a DSD, there remains recognition that differences exist. Lawrence and Zucker (2014) underscored these differences by advising that the recommendation for evaluation and treatment made by Mazur et al. (2007) "still seems advisable" (see next section).

Table 13.2 Putative etiologic factors in gender dysphoria: disorders of sex development (DSD) and non-DSD

Feature	DSD	Non-DSD
Biologic	1. Prenatal hormones 2. Puberty discordant for assigned sex	1. Prenatal hormones 2. Handedness 3. Sibling sex ratio/ birth order 4. Birth weight
Psychosocial	1. Late correction or uncorrected genitalia 2. Stigmatization regarding genitalia 3. Parental tolerance/encouragement of cross-gender behavior secondary to doubt about assigned gender 4. Parental psychopathology	1. Social reinforcement 2. Prenatal sex preference 3. Parental relationship and attachment

Adapted from: Zucker, K. J. (2004). Gender identity development and issues. *Child and Adolescent Psychiatric Clinics of North America*, *13*, 551–568.

Table 13.3 Comparison of disorders of sex development (DSD) and non-DSD features

Feature	DSD	Non-DSD
1. Reproductive anatomy	Atypical/discordant	Typical/concordant
2. Gender assignment at birth	Delayed or reassigned	Unambiguous and immediate
3. Medical care associated with DSD		
a. Contact with health care professionals (e.g., endocrinologist, urologist)	Routine contact throughout lifetime	No routine contact
b. Surgical decisions and procedures	During infancy and childhood	None
c. Medication	May begin during infancy and continue throughout lifetime	None
d. Puberty	May be induced by exogenous hormones	Induced by endogenous hormones
4. Gender dysphoria		
a. Age of onset	Adolescence or later	Early childhood
b. Sex ratio	More common in those assigned female at birth	More common in males
5. Self-initiated gender change	May occur	May occur

Evaluation and Treatment Strategies

Despite the fact that individuals with a DSD diagnosis who are experiencing distress because of a discordance between their assigned gender and their experienced gender identity are now included, according to DSM-5, in the same category as such a person without a DSD, the approach to evaluation and initial treatment strategies should not be the same. One of our main concerns with this change is that professionals will approach the person with a DSD just like a person without a DSD. The chairman of the Sexuality and Gender Section of the DSM-5, and a member of the sub-workgroup, along with Lawrence (2014), acknowledged this in an article after publication of the DSM-5. They stated:

> In some cases, persons with various disorders of sex development (DSDs [sic]; formerly known as intersex conditions) experience distress due to incongruence between their gender identity and their assigned gender. These individuals can be given the principal diagnosis of GD in the DSM-5, with the assignment of the newly added DSD specifier...Notwithstanding this change, the recommendation made by Mazur, Colsman and Sandberg (2007) still seems advisable: Because of the probable but still incompletely understood differences in the etiology and presentation of GD "in physically typical persons (i.e., transsexuals) and in those with intersex conditions...it would be prudent to consider them as separate entities when initiating and evaluation" (Lawrence & Zucker, 2014, p. 236).

Whether or not the changes to DSM-5 will have the effect on the professional community that Dr. Lawrence suggests, only time will tell. The question of how many individuals with a DSD have GD is still open. A survey (Mazur et al., 2005) of World Professional Association of Transgender Health members, then called the Harry Benjamin International Gender Dysphoria Association, indicated that 40% of respondents provided services to individuals with a DSD. Table 13.1 shows that there is gender change in individuals with a DSD diagnosis. However, the histories of individuals with a DSD diagnosis are significantly different than those of individuals without DSD. Regardless of changes in the DSM-5, these differences have clinical significance and relevance to clinical service.

While the final etiological explanation of GD in both groups awaits further research, it must be emphasized that persons with a DSD condition experiencing GD have different histories from those born without a diagnosed DSD condition (Tables 13.2 and 13.3). DSD, from the very moment of birth, triggers a series of events that are not experienced by either non-DSD individuals or their parents. These events relegate the affected individual and that person's parents, at least through infancy, childhood, and adolescence, to monitoring by health care professionals, much like a person with a chronic illness. For individuals born with genitalia that is neither clearly male nor female, the question parents and health care providers immediately face is which gender of rearing to assign to the infant. The history may even include a change of the initial gender of announcement, with parents having to reannounce the gender of their child to siblings, grandparents, and friends. There may also be an immediate necessity for lifesaving medication, as in the case of infants with salt-wasting CAH (46,XX DSD). Eventually, there are issues surrounding surgical reconstruction of the genitals, hormone treatment to induce puberty, and general state of good health (i.e., continued hormone replacement to maintain physical health).

As a consequence, the context within which a child with a DSD condition grows and develops is much different from that for a child without a somatic DSD condition. Therefore, the clinician needs to obtain a thorough history, including chromosomal pattern, diagnosis, etiology (if known), surgeries, hormone treatment, pubertal development, and history of medications taken (up to and including current prescriptions). When obtaining a medical history, particular attention should be paid to factors believed to be associated with gender change in persons with a DSD. Questions to ask might include the following: Did the person have late (after age of 3 years) or no genital surgery? If the person is an adolescent or adult, is puberty (secondary sexual characteristics) discordant with assigned gender? Is the person sexually attracted to individuals of the same gender, meaning the gender to which the person with DSD was initially assigned?

Cohen-Kettenis (2005) hypothesized three factors as a possible explanation of self-generated gender change from female to male in 5-ARD or 17β-HSD-3 individuals. A masculine appearance in childhood coupled with masculine (tomboyish) behavior due, "perhaps," to prenatal androgen exposure influences a gender change with the onset of physical changes brought about by puberty; pubertal development intensifies an "already existing gender discomfort" (dysphoria). This combination of masculinized appearance, atypical gender-role behavior, and pubertal hormones precipitates a self-initiated gender change in a subgroup of these individuals.

It has also been suggested that uncorrected or late-corrected genital appearance may lead to parental confusion over or rejection of the gender of rearing, as well as to the child's own confusion (Meyer-Bahlburg et al., 1996; Money et al., 1986). A discordant puberty may then exacerbate this confusion and, in some, contribute to the development of GD (Cohen-Kettenis, 2005). There is, thus, a developmental sequence of events that may result in a "crystallized" gender dysphoria with the wish to self-reassign gender. Part of obtaining a detailed history of the condition is ascertaining what the person has been told (or not told) by parents and physicians about the person's medical history. More important than *what* has been told is how the person *understands* the DSD condition. For example, a patient who states, "I was told that I really was born a boy but reared as a girl," demonstrates a lack of specific knowledge about the diagnosis and sequelae of the condition.

Adults born with a DSD or related condition are at risk for misunderstanding their medical history if accurate information about their birth circumstances and the rationale for the medical treatment in childhood are either not provided or withheld. Consequently, gender confusion, even GD, may result. Also, consider that due to the complexity of the information involved, a person may misinterpret accurately provided information. Therefore, a main difference between assessing a person with a possible GD, who also has a DSD condition, and assessing one who does not, is in discerning to what degree the presenting gender problem is associated with possible confusion or lack of information about the person's somatic condition. Such an assessment requires that the clinician understand what is known etiologically about DSD conditions, know how and why the somatic discordance occurs, and, most importantly, be able to provide this information to the client, who is likely to have gaps in knowledge or misinformation.

An important distinction between the clinical management of individuals with a GD who have a DSD and the management of those who do not have a DSD is *psychoeducation* about their medical history and the known associated behavior. Such information may help resolve a person's gender concerns and/or clarify the history. Several helpful resources are available for clinician and patient use and can be accessed through http://www.accordalliance.org.

In the event the patient wants to proceed with reassignment, a comprehensive understanding of the medical condition and treatment history is essential, not only to increase self-knowledge but, in certain cases, to ensure prolonged good health (i.e., the rationale for endocrine life-sustaining intervention in salt-wasting CAH, pubertal induction, or maintaining bone strength) and to make the person aware of the possible limitations of hormonal and surgical interventions given the person's specific DSD diagnosis (e.g., lack of or limited testosterone response in a person with CAIS or PAIS, both 46,XY DSD). Therefore, the first step in managing GD diagnosed in a person with a DSD condition, regardless of age, is not to implement therapeutic support for a change of gender, but rather to obtain the medical history and make sure that the person has a thorough and accurate understanding of the condition. In children and adolescents, this includes parental understanding as well.

Discussion

A number of changes have occurred worldwide regarding DSD. Prompted by the 2005 Consensus meeting, DSD is a superordinate term encompassing congenital conditions in which chromosomal, gonadal, or anatomic sex development is atypical and in which between one in 200 and one in 1,000 people are born with some degree of atypical sex development. Although the adopting of the term DSD was meant to be a decision based on inclusivity, it is not without controversy. Some (particularly within patient advocacy communities) prefer terms like "differences of sex development," "intersex," or "variations of sex anatomy" due to concerns that the word "disorder" may foster stigma and cause physicians to insist on unnecessary, risky, and sometimes harmful "normalization" procedures like cosmetic genital surgeries (Davis, 2013; Feder,

2014). Clinicians, meanwhile, generally prefer "disorder" due to concerns that speaking of sex atypicality, as if it always involves benign variation, may lead parents, patients, or medical professionals to ignore serious health risks that attend some forms of DSD, such as gonadal dysgenesis or CAH, which entail elevated risk of morbidity and mortality (Hollenbach et al., 2014).

Further confounding the terminology for DSD is that, while some adults with these conditions apply the identity label "intersex" to themselves, others do not wish to be so defined by their biological histories and/or want to distance themselves (or their affected children) from any terminology that might be understood as a condition being associated with atypical sexuality or gender. Additionally, while individuals born with DSD may identify as lesbian, gay, bisexual, or transgender (LGBT), many will identify as heterosexual and accept the gender category of boy/man or girl/woman announced at birth or assigned shortly thereafter. While making it convenient to identify subgroups of society facing similar types of discrimination, the increasingly common attachment of "I" (for intersex) to the acronym LGBT creates the perception that these groups are homogeneous and that individuals under these umbrella acronyms have parallel or even identical health care needs and concerns. However, as explicated in this chapter, important differences exist between groups that need to be addressed in clinical care and research.

While the change in nomenclature has been a major stepping stone in regard to awareness and inclusivity, there have been other more recent changes that have added to perception of individuals who have been diagnosed with a DSD. Advocacy organizations have emerged to provide social support and education for individuals with a DSD diagnosis as well as their family members. These support groups have prompted professionals to reexamine how they care for and listen to their DSD patients. Such awareness has generated constructive controversy, especially around surgery. Other changes that have occurred during the last decade are the incorporation of diverse language and action in the legal setting. Legislation in several countries has allowed a third possibility of "sex indeterminate" or "intersex" in addition to "male" and "female" on legal documents. Court systems have also been used more often in a public manner to address issues around perceived failure to gain full informed consent to genital surgeries deemed not medically necessary. There are national registries in the United States and in Europe and there is beginning to be cross-collaboration as well. Another significant collaboration is the advent of professionals working with patient advocate groups. Patients are now actively participating in providing support in some DSD clinics which have recently been created in a number of children's hospitals in the United States and in Europe. All of these changes and the awareness that they bring will produce a better standard of care in the years ahead.

Acknowledgment

We thank Dr. Anne Lawrence for reviewing the section on DSM-5 to make sure it accurately reflects her position.

References

American Psychiatric Association. (2000). *Diagnostic and Statistical Manual of Mental Disorders*. IV-Text Revision. Washington, DC: American Psychiatric Association.

Arboleda, V., Lee, H., Sanchez, F., Delot, E., Sandberg, D., Grody, W., … Vilain, E. (2013). Targeted massively parallel sequencing provides comprehensive genetic diagnosis for patients with disorders of sex development. *Clinical Genetics*, 83(1), 35–43.

Bangsboll, S., Qvist, I., Lebech, P. E., & Lewinsky, M. (1992). Testicular feminization syndrome and associated gonadal tumors in Denmark. *Acta Obstetrica et Gynecologica Scandinavica*, 71, 63–66.

Baratz, A. B., Sharp, M. K., & Sandberg, D. E. (2014). Disorders of sex development peer support. In O. Hiort & S. Ahmed (Eds.), *Understanding Differences and Disorders of Sex Development (DSD)* (pp. 99–112). Basel: Karger.

Baxter, R. M., & Vilain, E. (2013). Translational genetics for diagnosis of human disorders of sex development. *Annual Review of Genomics and Human Genetics*, 14:371–92.

Bean, E. (2003). Mayer–Rokitansky–Kuster–Hauser syndrome. In T. H. Ollendick & C. S. Schroder (Eds.), *Encyclopedia of Pediatric and Clinical Child Psychology* (pp. 360–362). New York: Kluwer Academic/Plenum Publishers.

Cadet, P. (2011). Androgen insensitivity syndrome with a male sex-of-living. *Archives of Sexual Behavior*, 40, 1101–1102.

Cendron, M. (2001). Disorders of the penis and scrotum. In J. P. Gearhart, R. C. Rink, & P. D. E. Mouriquar (Eds.), *Pediatric Urology* (pp. 729–737). Philadelphia: W. B. Saunders.

Cohen-Kettenis, P. T. (2005). Gender change in 46,XY persons with 5α-reducatase-2 deficiency and 17β-hydroxysteroid dehydrogenase-3 deficiency. *Archives of Sexual Behavior*, 34, 399–410.

Cohen-Kettenis, P. T., & Pfafflin, F. (2003). *Transgenderism and Intersexuality in Childhood and Adolescence: Making Choices*. Thousand Oaks, CA: Sage Publications.

Conte, F. A., & Grumbach, M. M. (2004). Abnormalities of sexual determination and differentiation. In F. S. Greenspan & D. G. Gardner (Eds.), *Basic and Clinical Endocrinology* (pp. 564–607). New York: Lange Medical Books/McGrawHill.

Cossey, C. (1991). *My Story*. London: Faber and Faber.

Council of Europe: Resolution 1952. (2013). Children's right to physical integrity. Retrieved on February 17, 2016 from: http://www.assembly.coe.int/nw/xml/XRef/X2H-Xref-ViewPDF.asp?FileID=20174&lang=en.

Davis, G. (2013). The power in a name: Diagnostic terminology and diverse experiences. *Psychology & Sexuality*, 5(1), 15–27.

Denschlag, D., Tempfer, C., Kunze, M., Wolff, G., & Keck, C. (2004). Assisted reproductive techniques in patients with Klinefelter's syndrome: A critical review. *Fertility and Sterility*, 82, 775–779.

Dessens, A. B., Slijper, F. M., & Drop, S. L. (2005). Gender dysphoria and gender change in chromosomal females with congenital adrenal hyperplasia. *Archives of Sexual Behavior*, 34, 389–397.

Dominguez, C. E. (2003). Surgical conditions of the vagina and urethra. In J. A. Rock & H. W. Jones, III (Eds.), *Te Linde's Operative Gynecology*, 9th ed. (pp. 893–924). Nashville, TN: Lippincott Williams and Wilkins.

Evans, T. N., Poland, M. L., & Boving, R. L. (1981). Vaginal malformations. *American Journal of Obstetics and Gynecology*, 141, 910–920.

Feder, E. K. (2014). *Making Sense of Intersex: Changing Ethical Perspectives in Biomedicine.* Bloomington, IN: Indiana University Press.

Fennell, E. (2003). Turner syndrome. In T. H. Ollendick & C. S. Schroeder (Eds.), *Encyclopedia of Clinical Child and Pediatric Psychology* (pp. 687–689). New York: Kluwer Academic/Plenum Press.

Gearhart, J. P. (2001). The bladder exstrophy–epispadias–cloacal exstroph complex. In J. P. Gearhart, R. C. Rink, & P. D. E. Mouriquar (Eds.), *Pediatric Urology* (pp. 511–546). Philadelphia: W.B. Saunders.

Grumbach, M. M., & Conte, F. A. (1998). Disorders of sexual differentiation. In J. W. Wilson & D. W. Foster (Eds.). *Williams Textbook of Endocrinology,* 9th ed. (pp. 1400–1405). Philadelphia: W. B. Saunders.

Grumbach, M. M., Hughes, I., & Conte, F. A. (2003). Disorder of sex differentiation. In P. R. Larsen, H. M. Kronenberg, S. Melmed, & K. S. Polonsky (Eds.), *Williams Textbook of Endocrinology,* 10th ed. (pp. 842–1002). Philadelphia: W.B. Saunders.

Hollenbach, A. D., Eckstrand, K. L., & Dreger, A. D. (2014). *Implementing Curricular and Institutional Climate Changes to Improve Health Care for Individuals who are LGBT, Gender Nonconforming, or Born with DSD.* Washington, DC: Association of American Medical Colleges.

Hook, E. B., & Warburton, D. (1983). The distribution of chromosomal genotypes associated with Turner's syndrome: Live birth prevalence rates and evidence for diminished fetal mortality and severity in genotypes associated with structural X abnormalities or mosaicism. *Human Genetics, 64,* 24–27.

Institute of Medicine. (2001). Crossing the quality chasm: a new health system for the 21st century. Retrieved on February 17, 2016 from: https://iom.nationalacademies. org/~/media/Files/Report%20Files/2001/Crossing-the-Quality-Chasm/Quality%20 Chasm%202001%20%20report%20brief.pdf.

Klebs, E. (1876). *Handbuch der pathologischen Anatomie [Handbook of Pathological Anatomy].* Berlin: A. Herschwald.

Kulshreshtha, B., Philibert, P., Eunice, M., Khandelwal, S. K., Mehta, M., Audran, F., … Ammini, A.C. (2009). Apparent male gender identity in a patient with complete androgen insensitivity syndrome [letter to the editor]. *Archives of Sexual Behavior, 38,* 873–875.

Lawrence, A. A. (2010). Proposed revisions to gender identity disorder diagnoses in the DSM-5. *Archives of Sexual Behavior, 39,* 1253–1260.

Lawrence, A. A. (2014). Gender assignment dysphoria in the DSM-5. *Archives of Sexual Behavior, 43,* 1263–1266.

Lawrence, A. A., & Zucker, K. J. (2014). Gender dysphoria. In M. Hersen & D. C. Beidel (Eds.), *Adult Psychopathology Diagnosis,* 7th ed. (pp. 603–639). Hoboken, NJ: John Wiley.

Lee, P. A., & Houk, C. P. (2004). Outcome studies among men with micropenis. *Journal of Pediatric Endocrinology and Metabolism, 17,* 1043–1053.

Lee, P. A., & Houk, C. P. (2010). Review of outcome information in 46,XX patients with congenital adrenal hyperplasia assigned/reared male: What does it say about gender assignment? *International Journal of Pediatric Endocrinology, 982025.*

Lee P. A., Mazur, T., Danish, R., Amrhein, J. A., Blizzard, R. M., Money, J., & Migeon, C. J. (1980). Micropenis I: Criteria, etiologies, and classification. *Johns Hopkins Medical Journal, 146,* 156–163.

Lee, P. A., Houk, C. P., Ahmed, S. F., Hughes, I. A., & Participants in the International Consensus Conference on Intersex. (2006). Consensus statement on management of intersex disorders. International Consensus Conference on Intersex. *Pediatrics*, 118(2): e488–e500.

Lee, P. A., Wisniewski, A., Baskin, L., Vogiatzi, M. G., Vilain, E., Rosenthal, S., & Houk, C. (2014). Advances in diagnosis and care of persons with DSD over the last decade. *International Journal of Pediatric Endocrinology*, 19. doi: 10.1186/1687-9856-2014-19.

Mazur, T. (2005). Gender dysphoria and gender change in androgen insensitivity or micropenis. *Archives of Sexual Behavior*, 34, 411–421.

Mazur, T., & Dobson, K. (1995). Psychologic issues in individuals with genetic, hormonal, and anatomic anomalies of the sexual system: Review and treatment considerations. In G. A. Rekers (Ed.), *Handbook of Child and Adolescent Sexual Problems* (pp. 101–134). New York: Lexington Books.

Mazur, T., Cohen-Kettenis, P. T., Meyer, W. J., Meyer-Bahlburg, H. F. L., & Zucker, K. J. (2005). Survey of HBIGDA membership: Intersex. *International Journal of Transgenderism*, 10(2):99–108.

Mazur, T., Colsman, M., & Sandberg, D. E. (2007). Intersex: Definition, examples, gender stability, and the case against merging with transsexualism. In R. Ettner, D. Monstrey, & A. E. Eyler (Eds.), *Principles of Transgender Medicine and Surgery* (pp. 235–259) Binghamton, NY: Haworth Press.

Meyer-Bahlburg, H. F. L. (1994). Intersexuality and the diagnosis of gender identity disorder. *Archives of Sexual Behavior*, 23, 21–40.

Meyer-Bahlburg, H. F. L. (2005a). Introduction: Gender dysphoria and gender change in persons with intersexuality. *Archives of Sexual Behavior*, 34, 371–373.

Meyer-Bahlburg, H. F. L. (2005b). Gender identity outcome in female-raised 46XY persons with penile agenesis, cloacal exstrophy of the bladder or penile ablation. *Archives of Sexual Behavior*, 34, 423–438.

Meyer-Bahlburg, H. F. L. (2009). Concerns regarding the change to male in 46, XY with complete androgen insensitivity syndrome: Comment on Kulshreshtha et al. (2009). *Archives of Sexual Behavior*, 38(6), 876–877.

Meyer-Bahlburg, H. F. L. (2014). Psychoendocrinology of congenital adrenal hyperplasia. In M. A. New, O. Lekarev, A. Parsa, T. Yuen, D. O'Malley, & G. Hammer (Eds.), *Genetic Steroid Disorders* (pp. 285–300). London: Academic Press.

Meyer-Bahlburg, H. F. L., Gruen, R. S., New, M. I., Bell, J. J., Morishima, A., Shimshi, M., … Baker, S. W. (1996). Gender change from female to male in classical congenital adrenal hyperplasia. *Hormones and Behavior*, 30, 319–332.

Money, J., & Norman, B. F. (1988). Pedagogical handicap associated with micropenis and other CHARGE syndrome anomalies of embryogenesis: Four 46XY cases reared as girls. *American Journal of Psychotherapy*, XLII, 354–379.

Money, J., Devore, H., & Norman, B. F. (1986). Gender identity and gender transposition: Longitudinal outcome study of 32 male hermaphrodites assigned as girls. *Journal of Sex and Martial Therapy*, 12, 165–181.

Mureau, M. (1995). *Psychosexual and Psychosocial Adjustment of Hypospadias Patients*. Molenaarsgraaf, The Netherlands: Optima Druk.

Nielsen, J., & Pelsen, B. (1987). Follow-up 20 years later of 34 Klinefelter males with karyotype 47XXY and 16 hypogonadal males with karyotype 46XY. *Human Genetics*, 77, 188–192.

Nielsen, J., & Wohlert, M. (1991). Chromosome abnormalities found among 34,910 newborn children: Results from a 13-year incidence study in Arhus, Denmark. *Human Genetics*, 87, 81–83.

Ratcliffe, S. G., Butler, G. E., & Jones, M. (1990). Edinburgh study of growth and development of children with sex chromosome abnormalities. *Birth Defects: Original Article Series*, 26, 1–44.

Richter-Appelt, H., & Sandberg, D. E. (2010). Should disorders of sex development be an exclusion criterion for gender identity disorder in DSM-5? *International Journal of Transgenderism*, 12, 94–99.

Rock, J. A., & Breech L. L. (2003). Surgery for anomalies of the Müllerian ducts. In J. A. Rock and H. W. Jones, III (Eds.), *Te Linde's Operative Gynecology*, 9th ed. (pp. 705–724). Nashville, TN: Lippincott Williams and Wilkins.

Saenger, P., Wikland, K. A., Conway, G. S., Davenport, M., Gravholt, C. H., Hintz, R., … Fifth International Symposium on Turner Syndrome. (2001). Recommendations for the diagnosis and management of Turner syndrome. *Journal of Clinical Endocrinology and Metabolism*, 86, 3061–3069.

Sandberg, D. E., & Barrick, C. (1995). Endocrine disorders in childhood: A selective survey of intellectual and educational sequelae. *School Psychology Review*, 24, 146–170.

Sandberg, D. E., & Mazur, T. (2014). A noncategorical approach to the psychological care of persons with DSD and their families. In B. P. C. Kreukels, T. D. Steensma, & A. L. C. de Vries (Eds.), *Gender Dysphoria and Disorders of Sex Development: Progress in Care and Knowledge* (pp. 93–114). New York, NY: Springer.

Sandberg, D. E., Meyer-Bahlburg, H. F. L., Yager, T. J., Hensle, T. W., Levitt, S. B., Kogan, S. J., & Reda, E. F. (1995). Gender development in boys born with hypospadias. *Psychoneuroendocrinology*, 20, 693–709.

Sandberg, D. E., Callens, N., & Wisniewski, A. B. (2015). Disorders of sex development (DSD): Networking and standardization considerations. *Hormone and Metabolic Research*, 47(5):387–93.

Schmall, E. (2012). Transgender advocates hail law easing rules in Argentina. *The New York Times*, pp. A8. Retrieved from http://www.nytimes.com/2012/05/25/world/americas/transgender-advocates-hail-argentina-law.html?_r=0.

Seifert, D., & Windgassen, K. (1995). Transsexual development of a patient with Klinefelter's syndrome. *Psychopathology*, 28, 312–316.

Sex Discrimination Amendment (Sexual Orientation, Gender Identity, and Intersex Status) Bill 2013 (Australia). Retrieved from http://www.aph.gov.au/Parliamentary_Business/Bills_Legislation/Bills_Search_Results/Result?bId=r5026.

Speiser, P. W., & White, P. C. (2003). Congenital adrenal hyperplasia. *New England Journal of Medicine*, 349, 776–788.

Stein, R. K. (2011). The 1990s: A decade of change in understanding children with ongoing conditions. *Archives of Pediatrics and Adolescent Medicine*, 165, 880–883.

Stein, R. E. K., & Jessop, D. J. (1982). A noncategorical approach to chronic childhood illness. *Public Health Reports*, 97, 354–362.

Sybert, V. P., & McCauley, E. (2004). Medical progress: Turner's syndrome. *New England Journal of Medicine*, 351, 1227–1238.

Tamar-Mattis, A. (2014). *Lecture. Personal Collection of Anne Tamar-Mattis*. Phoenix, AZ: Phoenix Meeting on DSD, May 1–4.

T'Sjoen, G., De Cuypere, G., Monstrey, S., Hoebeke, P., Freedman, K. F., Appari, M., … Cools, M. (2011). Male gender identity in complete androgen insensitivity syndrome. *Archives of Sexual Behavior*, 40, 635–638.

Vilain, E., & Sandberg, D. E. (2009). Disorders of sex development: nomenclature. *Growth, Genetics, and Hormones*, 25, 9–10.

Wilson, J. D. (2001). Androgens, androgen receptors, and male gender role behavior. *Hormones and Behavior*, 40, 358–366.

Zucker, K. J. (2010). Reports from the DSM-V work group on sexual and gender identity disorders. *Archives of Sexual Behavior*, 39, 217–220.

Zucker, K. J. (2004). Gender identity development and issues. *Child and Adolescent Psychiatric Clinics of North America*, 13, 551–568.

Zucker, K. J., Cohen-Kettenis, P. T., Drescher, J., Meyer-Bahlburg, H. F. L., Pfafflin, F., & Womack, W. M. (2013). Memo outlining evidence for change for gender identity disorder in the DSM-5. *Archives of Sexual Behavior*, 42, 901–914.

Zurenda, L., & Sandberg, D. E. (2003a). Klinefelter syndrome. In T. H. Ollendick and C. S. Schroeder (Eds.), *Encyclopedia of Clinical Child and Pediatric Psychology* (pp. 331–333). New York: Kluwer Academic/Plenum Press.

Zurenda, L., & Sandberg, D. E. (2003b). Congenital adrenal hyperplasia. In T. H. Ollendick & C. S. Schroeder (Eds.), *Encyclopedia of Clinical Child and Pediatric Psychology* (pp. 134–136). New York: Kluwer Academic/Plenum Press.

14 Male-to-Female Gender Reassignment Surgery

Britt Colebunders, Wim Verhaeghe, Katrien Bonte,
Salvatore D'Arpa, and Stan Monstrey

History of Transwomen Surgery

Abraham was the first to describe an intentional sex change operation in a transsexual patient in 1931; however, this was certainly not the first use of surgery to relieve the agony of persons with irreversible gender dysphoria (Abraham 1931; Edgerton 1974). Already in ancient times people have witnessed the methods and effects of animal castration and, therefore, self-castration must have been one of the most rudimentary attempts to employ surgical solutions. Eunuchs often underwent the procedure by force in order to remove their sexuality but it is unknown to what extent their castrations were voluntary. It is quite likely that hundreds or thousands of transsexuals have sought and undergone surgeries far riskier and more dramatic in effect than mere castration. It is unknown when such practices first occurred, but such surgeries were recorded in ancient Greece and particularly in Rome, known for being sexually permissive. The Roman emperor Elagabalus (204–222), a young successor to Marcus Aurelius, and a documented transvestite, was one of the first to undergo some form of sex change surgery at the hands of the skillful Roman doctors practicing in that era. It remains unclear if this procedure was successful, as little is known about Elagabalus other than that he was killed at age 18 (Wikipedia.org/wiki/Elagabalus).

Two rather crude, self-inflicted operations were described in 17th-century personal diaries as providing great and lasting subjective relief of gender dysphoria. These emasculating tactics were suppressed in the Christian world (with the exception of the castration of boys to maintain voice quality), but in Asia they have continued to the present times, notably in Southeast Asia, India and surrounding countries where young transwomen joined the Hijra caste and voluntarily underwent emasculating surgery under rather primitive conditions.

The development of modern gender reassignment surgery began in earnest in the 20th century when, following rapid advances in the fields of endocrinology and plastic surgery after World War II, comprehensive medical and surgical treatments for transsexualism started to become available.

In 1952, the Danish plastic surgeon Paul Fogh-Andersen initiated the modern era of sex reassignment surgery (SRS) by using penile skin as a full-thickness graft to line the neovagina of Christine Jörgensen (Fogh-Andersen 1956). This "change of sex" of a U.S. citizen was widely reported by the media, and Ms. Jorgensen became world-famous. In the United States, these surgeries were still widely unknown by then. Under intense pressure from religious groups, and in response to the publicity generated by the Jörgensen case, most U.S. hospitals enacted policies that expressly prohibited such operations. During that time, a number of severely gender-dysphoric individuals in the United States resorted to auto-castration in an attempt to feminize and bypass hospital regulations. If one rid oneself of the testicles, a hospital might complete SRS, provided the patient had the available funds.

In most countries, the laws defining sex remained hazy, and the legality of changing sex was even more obscure. Moreover, surgeons were afraid that patients might come to regret surgery, lapse into psychosis, and sue the surgeon for mayhem.

Things began to change in the United States and beyond, during the late 1950s, when several hundred transsexuals came under the care of Dr. Harry Benjamin, a compassionate endocrinologist. Benjamin was the first physician to elucidate the nature of gender dysphoria. Rather than perceiving transsexuals as mentally ill deviants, as did most psychiatrists of that era, he understood that transsexuals suffered from an authentic "misgendering" condition of unknown origin. In an effort to ease suffering, he prescribed estrogen to selected patients. He monitored the results of the few transsexual surgeries being performed and referred the most severely dysphoric patients to reconstructive surgeons.

Benjamin was aware that operations were being performed furtively in the United States, and occasionally in Mexico (e.g., by José Jesus Barbosa) and Italy. However, for the majority of transsexuals seeking surgery, the Clinique du Parc in Casablanca, Morocco, was the place of last resort. There, Dr. Georges Burou (1910–1987), a French gynecologist, invented and applied the anteriorly pedicled penile skin flap inversion technique in 1956 (Benjamin 1964, 1966; Burou 1973; Pauly & Edgerton 1986; Van Dis 1988). Modern variations of his inversion technique are still in use. From 1958 on, Burou operated on several well-known and very beautiful young transwomen from Le Carrousel club in Paris, including Coccinelle and April Ashley.

By the mid-1960s, centers in the United States were becoming interested in SRS (Benjamin 1964; Burou 1973). This was largely the result of Harry Benjamin's persistence in enlisting competent surgeons to operate on his patients (Benjamin 1966; Pauly & Edgerton 1986).

In 1966, surgeons at the Johns Hopkins Medical Center began performing a limited number of male-to-female (MTF) SRS operations at its new gender identity clinic. Announcement of the Johns Hopkins Clinic confirmed that Benjamin was the world's foremost authority on transsexualism, as did a textbook he authored, *The Transsexual Phenomenon* (Benjamin 1966). Shortly after the first sex reassignment procedures were performed at Johns Hopkins, hospitals at Stanford, Chicago, and Colorado followed suit (Laub & Fisk 1974; Pandya & Stuteville 1973).

The surgeons at Johns Hopkins initially used partial-thickness skin grafts to line the neovaginal cavity, but later used penile skin, applied as a full-thickness skin graft, much as the technique employed in Copenhagen. The *posteriorly* pedicled penile skin flap inversion technique for vaginoplasty—a variation of Burou's method—was introduced by Edgerton and Bull at Johns Hopkins between 1968 and 1970 (Edgerton 1974). Beginning in 1967, the Chicago group used the *anteriorly* pedicled penile skin flap to line the vagina, and scrotal skin to form the labia (Pandya & Stuteville 1973).

In Europe, beginning in the 1970s, the University Hospital of the Free University of Amsterdam became the leading center for medical and surgical treatment of patients with severe gender dysphoria. By the end of the 20th century many centers of excellence employed a multidisciplinary approach for transsexual individuals, providing state-of-the-art treatment, including surgical therapy, for both transwomen and transmen. With the recent increase in number of individuals seeking treatment for gender dysphoria, the quantity and quality of the multidisciplinary teams have substantially increased worldwide, with the largest number of vaginoplasties probably still being performed in Thailand.

Criteria of Male-To-Female Gender Reassignment Surgery

Standards of Care *for Surgery*

The 7th version of *Standards of Care* (*SOC*) of the World Professional Association of Transgender Health (WPATH) offers flexible guidelines for the treatment of people experiencing gender dysphoria and put forth the following criteria for surgical treatments (Coleman et al. 2012).

For breast augmentation with implants or lipofilling (one referral):

- persistent, well-documented gender dysphoria;
- capacity to make a fully informed decision and to give consent for treatment;
- age of majority in a given country;
- if significant medical or mental health concerns are present, they must be well controlled.

Although not an explicit criterion, it is recommended that transwomen undergo feminizing hormone therapy (minimum 12 months) prior to breast augmentation surgery. The purpose is to maximize breast growth in order to obtain better surgical (aesthetic) results.

For genital surgery, two referrals are recommended and specifically for orchiectomy the following criterion is added to the list above:

- 12 continuous months of hormone therapy as appropriate to the patient's gender goals (unless hormones are not clinically indicated for the individual). The aim of hormone therapy prior to gonadectomy is primarily to introduce a period of reversible testosterone suppression, before a patient undergoes irreversible surgical intervention.

For vaginoplasty one additional criterion is recommended:

- 12 continuous months of living in a gender role that is congruent with their gender identity (formerly called "real-life experience").

Prior to any surgical procedure, the surgeon should have all medical conditions appropriately monitored, and the effects of the hormonal treatment upon the liver and other organ systems adequately investigated. This is usually done in conjunction with the medical colleagues prescribing the hormones.

Typically, the patient is advised to stop all hormonal therapy at least 2 weeks prior to any surgical procedure; estrogens, in particular, can cause an increased risk of thromboembolic complications.

Experience of Living in an Identity-Congruent Gender Role (the Former "Real-Life Experience")

As mentioned above, the *SOC* only recommend a 12-month experience of living in the identity-congruent gender role prior to a vaginoplasty procedure. The rationale for this additional criterion in the case of genital surgery is based on expert clinical consensus that this experience provides ample opportunity for patients to experience and socially adjust in this desired gender role before undergoing irreversible genital surgery.

Hormonal treatment can greatly facilitate this experience. Transwomen treated with estrogens can realistically expect breast growth, some redistribution of body fat to approximate a female body habitus, decreased upper-body strength, softening of the skin, decrease in body hair, and slowing or cessation of loss of scalp hair. Hormonal therapy, however has no effect on voice, hand, feet, or shoulder dimensions. Also, beard density is not significantly affected by cross-sex hormone administration. Removal of facial hair, via electrolysis, laser, or intense pulsed-light epilation can be an additional manner to facilitate the experience of living in the new gender role. It is a generally safe but costly and time-consuming process. Formal medical or psychological approval for hair removal procedures is not required; it can be initiated whenever the patient deems it prudent. For most patients, 2 years of regular treatment are required to effectively eradicate facial hair.

A number of feminizing surgical procedures may also assist in living the identity-congruent gender role. These can include liposuction of abdomen and waist, reduction rhinoplasty, otoplasty, maxillofacial feminizing surgery (reduction of mandible angles and frontal bossing, genioplasty), and facial rejuvenation (face and/or brow lift, and blepharoplasty). None of these feminizing interventions require letters of recommendation from mental health professionals.

A reduction thyroid-chondroplasty can be performed early on, although certain techniques in voice modification and surgery affecting the vocal cords are best postponed until after all other surgery requiring general anesthesia with intubation, in order to protect the vocal cords. However, in the case of too-low voice pitch, living in the female gender role is difficult. In these cases the laryngeal framework surgery (cricothyroid approximation and/or anterior commissure webbing) to elevate the vocal pitch can be done at an early stage.

Facial Feminization Surgery and Voice Surgery

Facial Feminization Surgery

In most human interactions, the face communicates vital social information. First impressions are largely based upon a person's facial features and expressions. A face reflects aspects of one's personality and emotions, and serves as a vehicle to convey verbal and non-verbal communication. The head and face are commonly considered to be the location of the "self." In initial contacts, it is most often the face that provides the cues about the person, including gender. For the transsexual patient, nothing is more important than to appear externally congruent with the internal and emotional self. While many patients undergo surgery to feminize the face, there is a paucity of literature on these procedures (Hage et al. 1997).

Facial form is composed of many elements, including skeletal foundation and the overlying soft tissue. Although defining the bony foundation is of great importance, it is the soft tissue and the skin envelope that is observable and measurable, as it is encompassed within the frame created by hairdo and neck and shoulder configuration. According to Tessier (1987), "Harmony or disharmony does not lie within angles, distances, lines, surfaces, or volumes; they arise from proportion." Indeed, our perception of shape results from the response of light to depressions and prominence, i.e., highlights and shadows. Lines, insofar as shape is concerned, really do not exist, except as edges of a shape; more important than angles and lines are the texture, shape, light, and anatomic units, which are often accentuated with makeup in females. Several authors have investigated the nature of differences between the male and female face. But even measurement of dimensions such as facial height, bitragion width, bitragion frontal arch, and bitragion gnathion arc leads to differing conclusions among authors. And the variations between ethnic groups create more confounding variables, making generalizations impossible.

Farkas (1987) stated that:

> the relatively small average differences between the sexes suggest that, in
> general, the facial proportions do not differ noticeably between the sexes

although some proportion differences in anatomical area sensitive for a visual perception (lips, nose, orbits) may be apparent.

Although the face, like most physical attributes, varies considerably in projection and form, there is an overlap of masculine and feminine forms and few remarkable differences between the two. Yet it is relatively easy to distinguish between female and male faces. Therefore, some basic attributes of what are commonly perceived to be masculine and feminine features have been set forth. These are the standards which facial surgery addresses as part of an overall SRS.

Typically, the female face is oval and heart-shaped with smooth lines, in contrast to the square and angulated male face. Females have a more pointed chin, more pronounced zygomatic processes, less pronounced mandibular angles, and less nasal prominence than males. Additionally, females have a less angular nasal tip. It is generally accepted that female profiles with smaller noses are more aesthetically pleasing. The forehead is quite different in males from females, particularly the areas of the brows and the mid-forehead, and the shape of the skull affects the drape and contour of the skin. Changing the shape of the skull will assist in changing one feature from distinctly male to female. The techniques used and the areas modified are always individualized. Obviously, some MTF transsexual patients have more feminine-appearing features than others have. Typically, when facial feminizing surgery is under consideration, a preoperative computer simulation is generated to provide a preview of the eventual postoperative result.

Forehead

The forehead covers a large portion of the face and is different in males and females. Consequently, the forehead may be one of the most important areas to surgically modify. Spiegel (2011) investigated the determinants of female gender and discovered a strong association between facial femininity and attractiveness more specifically attributed to the upper third of the face and the interplay of the glabellar prominence of the forehead, along with the eyebrow shape and position and the hairline shape and position.

Males have brow bossing, with a flat area in between the bossing, while females tend to have a completely convex skull in all planes. Based on differences in anthropological measurements, the size of the frontal sinus (in the mid-lower forehead above the eyes and nose), and the general contour of the orbits and forehead, three different ways of modifying the forehead shape have been developed. These vary from simple bony contouring to the more complex procedure, wherein the anterior wall of the frontal sinus is placed into a more posterior position, or in combination with filling of the concavity superior to the frontal bossing with bone cement. Orbital rim contouring may be helpful to make the orbit look bigger, and is completed at the same time. If indicated, a bilateral brow lift can be simultaneously performed.

The female brow is not positioned at the level of the supraorbital rim but just a little above. The female eyebrow has an arch shape with the highest point at one-third laterally, in contrast with the male brow, that is straight. Scalp advancement can reduce the distance from the brows to the hairline, which is on average 5 cm for women, in comparison to 7 cm for men. Forehead and/or scalp advancement is generally performed under general anesthesia, but local anesthesia and sedation can be used in selected cases. The surgical approach to these various procedures is all basically the same, via an incision in the scalp either in front of the hair-bearing area (so the surplus of skin can easily be excised) or within it if no scalp advancement is necessary.

Cheeks

The cheekbones are more prominent in women and malar augmentation makes the face more heart-shaped. Moreover, lack of cheek prominence is not considered attractive. Cheek augmentation is therefore often effective in feminizing the face. Usually this is done with an implant or with soft-tissue filling, but certain bone cuts (zygoma osteotomies) and bone segment repositioning may be useful in some cases. The bilateral partial removal of the buccal fat pads of Bichat at the same time can help to accentuate the cheekbones by creating a sub-malar hollowing.

Nose

The nose is a feature that varies tremendously from individual to individual, and may be quite masculine-appearing. The noses of men are usually larger than those of women and naso-labial and naso-glabellar angles are sharper. If a patient has a thick skin, a significant size reduction can be undertaken. If not, as is often the case in biological males, the contour can still be markedly improved, but there will be a definite limitation to the extent of reduction possible. However, contour changing alone greatly feminizes the basic nasal appearance. In a reduction rhinoplasty mostly dorsum and tip will have to be made smaller and the tip needs to be lifted. The volume of the nostrils can be reduced by alar base excision. Correction of the frontal bossing and tip lifting make the naso-glabellar angle and naso-labial angle more obtuse and more feminine. If a breathing difficulty happens to coexist, this can often be improved at the time of surgery.

Chin

The chin can vary markedly between male and female. The male chin is generally wide and vertically high, while the female chin tends to be more pointed, narrow, and vertically shorter. The chin, therefore, is a significant marker of gender. The chin can be modified in numerous ways to improve facial appearance and feminize the lower face. This may only require a small implant or little shaving, but it is often necessary to perform extensive bone cuts, with removal of excess of bone and repositioning of the chin to make the chin shorter and narrower. Modifications to the chin will depend on individual anatomy of the patient and the desired outcome.

Angle of the Mandible

Males tend to have a more obvious mandible angle, with thicker muscles and resulting fullness, than females. The angle contour in the male is usually due to a heavy masseter muscle and, as a result, a lateral and posterior flaring of the bony angle occurs. The female tends to have a smaller muscle with a more gradual curve or even a straight line along the lateral border from the posterior border of the mandible to the chin. Modifications of the lower face can reduce this obvious aspect of masculinity, thereby creating a feminine appearance. This lower-jaw-contouring procedure is completed under general anesthesia through incisions in the mouth, and usually does not require external skin incisions. The masseter muscle is reduced on its internal surface, i.e., the portion adjacent to the bone. The bone is then significantly reduced laterally, softening the bony angle. When there is a significant mandibular angle present, the angle is osteotomized to give this area a more rounded and smoother appearance. Botulin toxin can also be used to decrease the volume of the masseter muscle.

Upper Lip

Lip lift is regularly used in facial feminization. Its aim is to shorten the upper lip in the area between the alar bases of the nose, making the maxillary tooth crowns more visible. Also techniques making the upper lip more voluminous can help in making the face look more feminine. This can be done by fillers, but the use of dermis grafts has few complications. The dermis graft can be harvested from the coronal flap.

Orthognatic Surgery

Using the Le Fort 1 and bilateral sagittal ramus osteotomy, a combination of feminizing effects can be obtained. A clockwise rotation of the bimaxillary complex with posterior impaction of the maxilla gives more volume to the midface, making the face look rounder. It also makes the gonial angles more obtuse, makes the chin less pronounced, and gives more show to the maxillary tooth crowns.

Hair Transplantation

Hair transplantation, or scalp shifting, is very helpful in transwomen who have considerable balding. There are many ways to approximate a female hair pattern. Major procedures like scalp flap or tissue expansion may be required in some cases but, more often, plugs or micro-grafts are employed. Scalp reductions are useful in certain individuals. For those with extensive baldness, there is no choice but to use a hairpiece.

Chondrolaryngoplasty and Voice Surgery

The secondary sex characteristics of the larynx with its vocal function remain a major obstacle to achieving gender congruency for many. Unlike hormonal therapy for transmen, estrogen does not have any substantial or lasting influence on voice pitch, and speech therapy alone often does not produce satisfactory results. Even after transition, an individual may be identified as a man because of voice, most often on the telephone. This can cause social and psychological problems. Surgical procedures to raise the patient's voice pitch are performed with the aim of assisting social integration, and can greatly improve self-esteem in some cases.

Various authors have described operative techniques to raise voice pitch. Basically, this can be achieved by reducing the vibrating vocal cord length (shortening the vocal cords) or increasing the vocal cord tension. The most frequently used technique is the one described by Isshiki (1989). In this technique, the cricoid cartilage is approximated to the lower edge of the thyroid cartilage, causing an increase in vocal cord tension. The cricoid and thyroid cartilages are then fixed to each other with sutures. A modification consists of twisting the fixing wire sutures over titanium, or absorbable miniplates (Neumann et al. 2002). This obviously eliminates the possibility of rupture of cartilages or loosening of the sutures over time.

While this technique extends the vocal cords, it does not cause a narrowing of the glottis. This obviates the necessity of future operations under intubation anesthesia where placement of the tube might be difficult due to a surgically narrowed glottis.

When choosing between local and general anesthesia, the advantage of local anesthesia is that acoustic checking of the voice rise intraoperatively is possible, and thus, over-approximation can be avoided. However, since most patients want the maximum rise, many surgeons perform this procedure using general anesthesia.

A reduction of the prominent thyroid cartilage can be performed in the same procedure. During this intervention, the thyroid cartilage is exposed, perichondrial flaps are raised, and a resection of the upper limit of the thyroid cartilage is performed. A mild, transient voice weakness can be observed postoperatively, and lasts a few weeks. This is probably due to prolonged edema. According to literature, surgical outcomes of voice pitch raising are very good, and the cosmetic benefit of the reduction of the Adam's apple contributes greatly to the patient's psychological well-being (Wolfort et al. 1990).

If cricothyroid approximation is not resulting in sufficient raise of voice pitch, anterior commissure webbing is performed to reduce the length of the vibrating vocal cord, which provides an additional feminization of the voice.

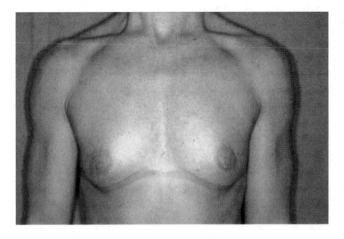

Figure 14.1 Breast augmentation with prostheses: preoperative view.

Breast Augmentation

Introduction

For most transwomen, breast augmentation (or breast "reconstruction") greatly increases subjective feelings of femininity. Mammoplasty provides a more feminine profile, facilitating adjustment. In a prospective, non-comparative, cohort study it has been shown that the gains in breast satisfaction, psychosocial well-being, and sexual well-being after transwomen have undergone breast augmentation are statistically significant and clinically meaningful to the patient shortly after surgery as well as in the long term (Weigert et al. 2013). The presence of breasts significantly increases the factors involved in passability (Figures 14.1 and 14.2). The augmentation mammoplasty may be performed at the same time as genital surgery, or as a preliminary or subsequent procedure.

Breast Development After Hormonal Therapy

While some breast formation occurs after hormonal therapy, for many, it is insufficient. Unfortunately there are no studies looking in detail at what is the optimum delay after start of hormonal treatment. As mentioned above, the current version of the WPATH *SOC* (version 7) does not explicitly indicate a minimum period of hormone therapy that must be completed before breast surgery may be performed. However, most surgeons recommend a 12-month period of feminizing hormone therapy prior to breast augmentation surgery in order to maximize breast growth and obtain better surgical (aesthetic) results.

Mammogenesis in transwomen receiving estrogens follows a pattern similar to female pubertal mammogenesis, as described by Tanner (Marshall & Tanner 1969). As breast development, it is not exclusively dose-responsive—67–75%

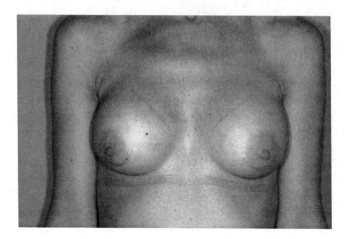

Figure 14.2 Breast augmentation with prostheses: postoperative view.

of transwomen require an augmentation mammoplasty (Kanhai et al. 1999a) because hormonal treatment only results in softly pointed breasts, as seen in young girls, or the small conical form seen in young adolescents (Tanner stage 2 or 3).

Surgical Techniques

Since breast prostheses are implanted in transsexuals with "young adolescent" breast development, the patient should be informed that the complex feminine form and age-related changes of the breast cannot be imitated by using symmetric hemispherical prostheses. Therefore, the result of an augmentation mammoplasty in a transwoman with minimal hormone-induced mammogenesis may be poor (Kanhai et al. 1999b).

Other anatomical differences, which should be taken into consideration in transwomen, are the wider male chest; a stronger pectoral fascia and a more developed pectoralis muscle, and a smaller dimension of nipple and areola. Usually a larger volume of breast prostheses is chosen by transwomen than that chosen for breast augmentation by a female patient, but even with a larger prosthesis, it is often impossible to avoid an abnormally wide cleavage between the breasts. The nipple areola should always overlie the prosthesis centrally and a very medial position of these prostheses could result in a divergent nipple position with an unacceptable breast appearance (Laub & Fisk 1974). In our personal experience we have used lipofilling as an adjunct to make the prosthesis less visible and palpable, as well as to narrow the wide cleavage between the breasts. Lipofilling is a technique where fat is harvested by liposuction of the abdomen or thighs. Subsequently the fat is prepared as described by Coleman and Saboeiro (2015) and injected in the subcutaneous plane. In transwomen

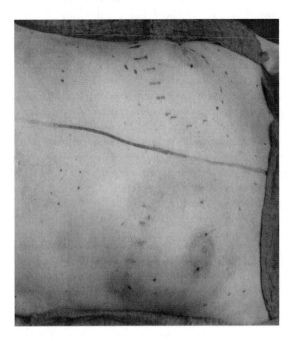

Figure 14.3 Lipofilling (left breast only here) can be used for a moderate augmentation without prostheses.

who already have some breast volume due to hormone treatment, lipofilling can be a good option to provide a moderate augmentation of the breast, therefore avoiding the need for an implant (Figure 14.3). Patients should be informed that a variable percentage of the injected fat is resorbed.

Despite some sexual differences in chest wall and mammary anatomy, the implantation of mammary prostheses is not essentially different from breast augmentation in a female patient, except that, usually, larger prostheses are used. The same choices apply as to the kind of prostheses, the position of the pocket, and the surgical approach. Patient and surgeon can choose between a silicone gel-filled prosthesis and a saline-filled prosthesis. In most cases, a textured prosthesis is chosen to reduce the chance of capsular contraction. When a more cohesive gel-filled prosthesis is chosen, it can be a round prosthesis or a so-called anatomical prosthesis, resulting in additional filling of prominence in the lower part of the breast.

The incision can be made axillary, inframammary, or even periareolar, although the latter is less popular in transwomen because of the smaller size of the areola. If an inframammary incision is used, it should be positioned lower than the preoperative inframammary fold, as the distance between the inferior areolar margin and the inframammary fold will expand after augmentation mammoplasty, likely due to the recruitment of the inframammary or even abdominal skin (Kanhai et al. 1999a).

The pocket for the prosthesis can be created behind the glandular tissue or behind the pectoralis muscle. Some authors (Kanhai et al. 1999a) recommend implanting the prostheses in a subglandular position. This is especially indicated in patients who have more subcutaneous and glandular tissue to start with (Tanner stage 4 or 5). The surgical procedure is easier to perform and less painful. Many surgeons, however, prefer to put the prostheses in a retropectoral position. In this case, the lower portion (as well as part of the medial origin) of the pectoralis muscle should be detached from the thoracic cage (Monstrey et al. 2001). In the retropectoral position, the prosthesis is covered with more soft tissue (important in the case of thin patients), and a lower risk of capsular contraction has also been reported.

Complications

Kanhai et al. (1999b) reported the main (but rarely occurring) complications after breast augmentation: hematoma, symmastia, capsular contracture, a decreased sensation in the nipple and/or part of the breast, leakage of the prostheses (more obvious in saline-filled prostheses than in cohesive silicone gel-filled prostheses), and malposition of the prostheses. Although it is very rare in these patients, mastopexy can be the treatment of choice to correct (substantial) mammary ptosis, but usually an augmentation is sufficient to fill out the (slightly) ptotic breasts.

Galactorrhea is another rare condition that can occur pre- or postoperatively. It requires an extensive hormonal evaluation with particular attention to the pituitary gland. Apart from hormonal causes, excessive prolactin secretion causing galactorrhea may also result from a peripheral stimulus such as breast manipulation or intercostal nerve stimulation. Galactorrhea in the latter case is associated with chest incisions or inflammation of the chest wall and thus may also be caused by mammary implants. In many patients, however, no cause for the galactorrhea can be found and the condition remains idiopathic.

Postoperative follow-up is mandatory in all patients undergoing breast augmentation. Gooren et al. (2013) performed a cohort study documenting the occurrence of breast cancer in 2,307 transgender persons with an exposure to cross-sex hormones between 5 and 30 years and reported 10 cases of breast cancer in transwomen. All patients received oral estrogens for prolonged periods to maintain secondary female characteristics. Three out of these 10 were not estrogen-dependent breast carcinomas. The study by Gooren et al. suggested that cross-sex hormone administration does not increase the risk of breast cancer development in transwomen. Breast carcinoma incidences were comparable to male breast cancers, and thus lower than in the female population. However, the historical use of cross-sex hormones may have been too short for malignancies to develop. Therefore good screening and follow-up are imperative. Moreover, since breast exams are also very well accepted by transwomen, transgender persons should be encouraged to participate in relevant cancer screening protocols, which for breast cancer screening are the same as for cisgender women (Weyers et al. 2010).

Routine preoperative investigation of family history is imperative. Screening for genetic predisposition (such as *BRCA* mutations) should be considered in patients with multiple breast and/or ovarian cancers within their family (often diagnosed at an early age); two or more primary breast and/or ovarian cancers in a single family member; and/or cases of male breast cancer within their family. Psychological counseling about bilateral prophylactic mastectomy and consecutively primary reconstruction with either autologous tissue (such as a deep inferior epigastric perforator flap) or prosthesis should be offered in patients with a genetic predisposition for breast cancer (Colebunders et al. 2014).

Orchiectomy

General Considerations

Orchiectomy can be performed simultaneously with a vaginoplasty or as a first-stage procedure prior to the vaginal reconstruction. If an orchiectomy is performed as a preliminary procedure, it will not compromise the possibility of a vaginoplasty at a later stage, as the testicles can be accessed via a short 5-cm incision at the raphe, leaving very little scar tissue. Androgen-blocking treatment can usually be stopped or reduced after the orchiectomy. In most countries an orchiectomy is mandatory for a transwoman in order to legally become a woman, but this may change in the near future as several countries no longer require any surgery at all.

Reproductive Options

Attention should be given to reproductive possibilities and restrictions after orchiectomy. A majority of transwomen has been reported to desire having children (Wierckx et al. 2012). Transwomen should be given the option of sperm preservation in sperm banks, prior to initiating hormones. If patients have already initiated hormones, there are data that report eventual recuperation of sperm count after a hormone-free period. So these patients can be given the option to stop hormonal therapy temporarily to bank their sperm. There is a reasonable chance of a live birth from transwomen's sperm storage, in contrast to transmen, who have approximately a 4–13, 6% chance of a live birth from cryopreservation of their gametes (Richards & Seal 2014).

Vaginoplasty

Introduction

As affirmed by Karim et al. (1996), the goal of genital reassignment surgery in MTF transsexuals is to create a perineo-genital complex as feminine in appearance and function as possible and free of poorly healed areas, scars, and neuromas. The urethra should be shortened in such a way that the direction of the urinary stream is downward in the sitting position and it should be free of stenosis or fistulas. The neovagina should, ideally, be lined with moist, elastic, and hairless epithelium. Its depth should be at least 10 cm and its diameter 30 mm. The sensation should be sufficient to provide satisfactory erogenous stimulus during sexual intercourse. Ideally, all these requirements should be met without major surgical intervention necessitating long and distressful postoperative treatment, and addressing them should not create new lesions or donor area malfunction.

The major steps in a vaginoplasty are an orchiectomy (if not previously performed), amputation of the penis, creation of the neovaginal cavity, the lining of this cavity, reconstruction of a urethral meatus and, finally, construction of the labia and clitoris.

In order to obtain a functional and aesthetic outcome, most authors advise to construct a wide and deep vaginal cavity, and to perform a near-complete resection of the corpus spongiosum, an eversion of the urethral mucosa, and the construction of clitoris/clitoral prepuce, labia minora/majora. Several refinements of vaginoplasty (mostly using the inverted penile-scrotal skin flap technique in combination with skin grafts) have been described (Karim et al. 1995; Selvaggi et al. 2005). These include preoperative epilation of the area at the base of the penis and posterior scrotum; preoperative bowel preparation; the use of a drape with a rectal condom; blunt dissection of the vaginal cavity; and the use of double-silicone prosthesis to create and maintain a vaginal cavity of adequate dimension.

Vaginal Lining

Methods for lining the neovagina can be classified into six categories: (1) non-genital skin grafts; (2) penile or scrotal skin grafts; (3) penile-scrotal skin flaps; (4) non-genital skin flaps; (5) pedicled intestinal transplants; and (6) recent developments.

Non-Genital Skin Grafts

Laub and Fisk (1974) reported the first series of transwomen in whom a *split-skin* graft pulled over a plastic mold was applied in a one-stage vaginoplasty. The use of a *full-thickness* skin graft, harvested from the region of a (mini) abdominoplasty, has been described by Hage and Karim (1998). It is generally known that full-thickness skin grafts contract less than their thinner counterparts. Abdominal skin grafts are usually used if there is insufficient penile and scrotal skin available or if transwomen request an abdominoplasty procedure. The advantages of non-genital skin grafts are that they are non-hair-bearing, and they carry a low risk of complications (Hage 1995). The disadvantages include the tendency of the skin graft to shrink (postoperative daily dilation is required), suboptimal sensation, and the absence of any natural lubrication (McGregor 1989).

Penile or Scrotal Skin Grafts

Fogh-Andersen was the first to report the use of a full-thickness skin graft harvested from the *penile* skin to line the neovagina (Fogh-Andersen 1956). The advantage of using penile skin is that it is non-hair-bearing, compared to scrotal skin. However the use of penile skin as a graft for vaginoplasty is rarely, if ever, performed as it is usually preserved to be used as a (pedicled) penile flap undergoing less contraction postoperatively. On the other hand, in most vaginoplasty operations the excess of *scrotal* skin is used as a full-thickness graft to line the deepest part of the vaginal cavity, since the amount of skin provided by the penile skin flap is often insufficient to provide a neovagina of adequate dimensions. This redundant skin must be thinned in order to facilitate the ingrowth of the skin graft and also to eliminate all the hair follicles, avoiding postoperative hair growth in the vagina.

Penile-Scrotal Skin Flaps: The Technique of Choice

As previously discussed, Burou has been credited with inventing the anteriorly pedicled penile skin flap inversion technique, and it became (and still is) the technique of choice for vaginoplasty in transwomen. However, in 1957, Gillies and Millard were the first to report on the use of penile skin as a pedicled flap for vaginoplasty. Several modifications of this technique were subsequently described. These can be classified into the following three groups (Bouman 1989):

1. The inverted penile skin is used solely on an abdominal pedicle as an inside-out skin tube (Eicher 1989; Gillies & Millard 1957); this penile skin flap can be augmented with a small triangular scrotal skin flap to "break" the circular introitus (Bouman 1988; Karim et al. 1995). Variations of this technique are used by most surgeons who perform SRS in transwomen today and this technique is therefore considered "the gold standard in vaginoplasty" (Figures 14.4, 14.5, and 14.6).
2. The pedicled penile skin tube can also be split open to form a rectangular flap which is augmented by a rectangular, posteriorly pedicled scrotal skin flap comparable in size (Jones et al. 1968).
3. The inverted penile skin tube may be applied based on an inferior pedicle (Edgerton & Bull 1970). Perovic et al. (2000) described a modification of the technique wherein a long, vascularized urethral flap is harvested and embedded in the penile skin tube flap. They also described the suspension of the neovagina to the sacrospinous ligament to prevent vaginal prolapse, a complication that is rarely, if ever, experienced by others.

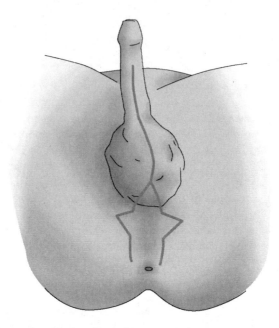

Figure 14.4 Inverted penile skin flap technique with dorsal scrotal flap.

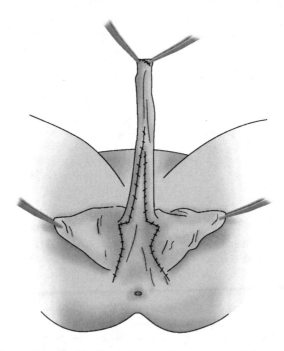

Figure 14.5 Inverted penile skin flap technique after resection of all erectile tissue.

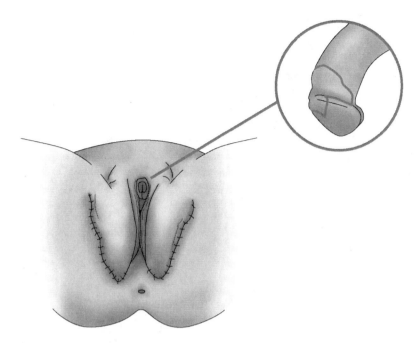

Figure 14.6 Inverted penile skin flap technique: immediate postoperative result with clitoroplasty.

There are several advantages to penile skin flaps. They demonstrate fewer tendencies to contract (McGregor 1989). In the event of inadvertent damage to the rectum, correction is easier, as it is immediately covered with vascularized tissue (Karim et al. 1995). Local innervation is provided and the flap is virtually hairless. Although flaps have much less tendency to contract than grafts, patients are still required to use a dilator postoperatively for 6 months. The disadvantages of penile skin flaps are that a limited amount of penile skin may be available (Van Noort & Nicolai 1993), and that this technique might results in widening of the anterior commissure, which can leave the clitoris more exposed (Bouman 1988; Karim et al. 1995).

Combining an abdominally pedicled penile skin flap with a wide posteriorly based scrotal skin flap produces an ideal anatomically located introitus and favorable dimensions of the neovagina (Van Noort & Nicolai 1993). However, this technique will introduce hair-bearing scrotal skin within the posterior lining of the vagina if epilation has not been performed prior to surgery. Moreover, it leads to a transverse appearance of the vaginal introitus if a wide flap is used (Turner et al. 1978), which is less aesthetically pleasing.

Non-Genital Skin Flaps

In 1980, Cairns and De Villiers reported the use of a medial thigh flap for vaginoplasties in four patients who had previously undergone penile skin inversion vaginoplasty with inadequate results. Huang (1995) used two inguino-pudendal flaps, sutured to one another in the midline and then to the penile flap, forming a single large flap. The use of distant free flaps for vaginoplasties in transsexuals has never been reported.

The advantages of using non-genital flaps are that they have less risk of contraction and a reduced period of postoperative dilation. The disadvantages are donor site morbidity and scarring, technical complexity (in some cases the flaps are unreliable) (Wee & Joseph 1989), and their tendency to be bulky as compared to genital skin flaps. This added bulk can decrease the functional dimensions of the neovagina, which is particularly disadvantageous in transwomen, as the male pubic arch is narrower than the female (Karim et al. 1996). Again, these flaps have no natural source of lubrication. Non-genital skin flaps should be reserved as a choice of last resort, after all other options have been exhausted.

Pedicled Intestinal Transfer

Intestinal vaginoplasty is a good alternative technique in cases where insufficient skin is available. A lack of penile and scrotal skin is often present in young transwomen who started hormonal therapy at an early age. Transwomen who had a previous failed vaginal reconstruction with skin flaps and/or grafts can also benefit from this procedure (Kim et al. 2003). A pedicled intestinal transfer can also be used to elongate the vagina in transwomen requiring more depth after a previous vaginal reconstruction.

Both small as well as large intestinal segments have been used for vaginal reconstruction (Bouman et al. 2014). For vaginoplasty with a large intestinal segment, the sigmoid is most commonly the first choice. Where the small intestines are used, the ileum is mainly chosen. Harvest of the bowel can be performed through a median or Pfannenstiel laparotomy, a laparoscopy-assisted laparotomy, or totally laparoscopic. Laparoscopic harvest of bowel has been described by Wedler et al. in 2004 and has been more widely used since. Zhang et al. (2014) showed that laparoscopic-assisted vaginoplasty using pedicled ileum or sigmoid segment are both effective in reconstructing a vagina.

The advantages of using a rectosigmoid transplant are not only the length it provides, but also the texture and appearance, which is more similar to vaginal lining, and of course its natural lubrication (Dalton 1981; Kim et al. 2003). Although the natural lubrication with the production of mucus is usually regarded as an advantage, it may lead to excessive discharge (Hage et al. 1995), especially when ileum is used, compared to colon.

Neovaginal length after an intestinal transfer usually is significantly longer compared to other vaginoplasty techniques. However, if the intestinal segment is taken too long, it can lead to stasis and dehydration of mucus in the deepest portion of the vagina. An intestinal transfer itself has little or no tendency to shrink but dilation remains important to avoid introital stenosis, which is the most common reported complication of intestinal vaginoplasty (Bouman et al. 2014; Davies & Creighton 2007).

Bouman et al. (2014) performed a review of the literature focusing on clinical outcomes of intestinal vaginoplasty, including 21 studies. Prevalence and severity of procedure-related complications were low. Diversion colitis (inflammation that occurs in the bypassed colonic tissue related to diversion of the fecal stream) was very rare. Severe complications were incidental and included necrosis of the intestinal segment, necrotizing fasciitis, bilateral lower-extremity compartment syndrome, an intraluminal abscess, and intestinal obstruction (Bouman et al. 2014). The colonic mucosa is thought to be more vulnerable, and hence, more accessible to sexually transmitted diseases, including human immunodeficiency virus (HIV) infection (Hage & Laub 1995). A limited number of cancers in both sigmoidal and ileal grafts have been observed (Schober 2007).

Recent Developments

AUTOLOGOUS BUCCAL MUCOSA

In 2003 Lin et al. were the first to describe vaginoplasty with autologous buccal mucosa as graft material in eight cases of vaginal agenesis, such as Mayer–Rokitansky–Küster–Hauser syndrome (MRKHS). They used buccal mucosal grafts of approximately 2.5×7 cm^2 in size and sutured them into a newly created vaginal cavity (Lin et al. 2003). Later, Li et al. (2014) modified this technique by using micro-grafts of the buccal mucosa, minimizing donor site morbidity, and enlarging the possible surface area to be grafted. Dessy et al. (2014) reduced donor site morbidity even further by taking a 2-cm^2 full-thickness oral biopsy and culturing it into fully differentiated mucosal tissue. They used these cultured autologous oral epithelial cells for SRS in transwomen in a three-step procedure: first, they took the mucosal biopsy; second, they created a vaginal cavity with autologous mucosal lining; and third, they constructed the clitoris and labia using the glans of the penis and the scrotum. Although autologous mucous tissue is not yet widely used in SRS, it might become a treatment of choice in the future as it has potential advantages. Grafted mucosa has a high survival rate and low incidence of contracture. Moreover mucosa has a secretory function, which can play a role of lubrication during sexual intercourse, reducing the rate of dyspareunia.

ACELLULAR DERMAL MATRIX

To date there are no reports using acellular dermal matrix as vaginal lining in transwomen. However its use has been described for vaginal reconstruction in patients with MRKHS. Ding et al. (2015) reported successful use of acellular porcine small intestinal submucosa graft in MRKHS patients. In future it may become a choice for transsexual patients who have previously undergone

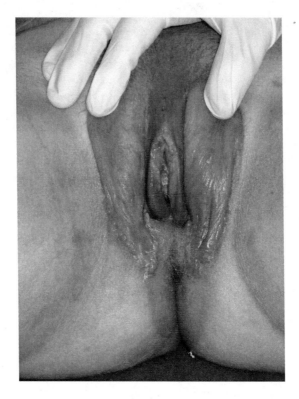

Figure 14.7 Vaginoplasty: early postoperative result (2 weeks) with still-swollen smaller and greater labia.

penectomy and orchiectomy. The main drawback of using acellular dermal matrix, however, is the high cost.

CLITORO-LABIOPLASTY (VULVOPLASTY)

In order to achieve the physiologic and aesthetic equivalent of female external genitalia, it is imperative to create labia majora and minora, a clitoris, and a clitoral hood (Figures 14.7 and 14.8). The creation of the labia majora is dependent on the use of either a penile flap or a graft, and the amount of scrotal skin remaining after resection. Usually, creating aesthetically acceptable labia majora is not a problem. However, secondary corrections may be needed, since changes in appearance may occur during the first year postsurgery (Hage et al. 2000). A common secondary correction is symmetrization of the labia majora and sometimes a commisuroplasty with recreation of the anterior commissure covering the neoclitoris (Hage et al. 2000; Selvaggi et al. 2005).

Little has been written specifically about the labia minora. Perovic et al. (2000) described using the base of the penile skin to form the labia minora,

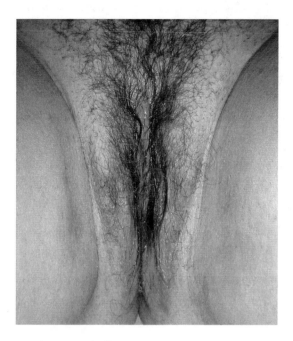

Figure 14.8 Vaginoplasty—result after 3 months.

which are then sutured to the deepithelialized area of the neoclitoris. Thus, the neoclitoris is hooded with labia minora. We have used penile foreskin (in continuity with the glans flap for clitoral reconstruction—see below) in order to construct the labia minora and the clitoral hood.

The first person to describe the construction of a neoclitoris was Brown, in 1976. He reported the creation of a functional clitoris using the reduced glans, which remained attached to its dorsal penile neurovascular pedicle (Brown 1976, 1978). The high percentage of clitoral necrosis (33%) that Brown reported prompted some surgeons to search for new techniques. These have included the free composite graft of the tip of the penile glans to cover the shortened dorsal neurovascular bundle, a small bud of corpus cavernosum covered by penile skin, and the corpus spongiosum as the vascular pedicle of the neoclitoris, preserving the glans (Hage et al. 1994; Malloy et al. 1976; Meyer & Kesselring 1980; Rubin 1980). At present, most surgeons performing a clitoroplasty in transsexual patients use the dorsal portion of the glans penis in a horseshoe or W-pattern with the dorsal neurovascular pedicle (Eldh 1993; Giraldo et al. 2004; Karim et al. 1995; Rubin 1993; Selvaggi et al. 2005). Dissection of the pedicle can be performed in a plane just above the tunica albuginea of the corpora cavernosa, or in a plane just posterior to this tunica. The latter is a more rapid dissection, but may result in a bulky pedicle and thus an elevated mons pubis.

The clitoral hood and the labia minora can be constructed using a thin inner layer of penile foreskin, which is harvested in continuity with the glans flap. This is the only manner in which the very delicate features of the anterior commissure of the vulva, where the clitoris is located and where the labia minora start from the clitoral hood, can be reconstructed in a natural way (Figures 14.9, 14.10, and 14.11).

The neoclitoris has the ability to swell and cause a climax on erogenous stimulation. In order to achieve swelling of the labia minora as well, we have designed an extended clitoroplasty in which two lateral extensions of the glans penis are placed in the base of the labia minora (unpublished data). Anatomically, this extended neoclitoris mimics better the female clitoral apparatus. The extensions simulate the female corpora cavernosa—cylindrical organs, made of cavernous erectile tissue, which are the "hidden" part of the clitoris (Puppo 2011).

Selvaggi et al. (2005) described the use of the penile urethra to construct the region between the urethral opening and the neoclitoris. The urethra is incised longitudinally along its ventral aspect, folded open, and sutured just inferior to the neoclitoris. This produces a natural appearance, in both color and texture.

Postoperative Care

When an anteriorly pedicled penile skin flap technique has been used in combination with a posterior scrotal flap and skin grafts, the patient usually remains in bed for 4–5 days, with the dilator firmly in place. Fractionized heparin is provided subcutaneously.

After 5 days, the dilator is removed, and the patient is allowed to ambulate. The neovaginal cavity is cleansed daily with an iso-Betadine solution and the patient starts to dilate according to a strict protocol. The following day, the urethral catheter is removed and spontaneous voiding is started.

The patient is usually discharged on the seventh or eighth postoperative day, and is instructed in the care of the neovagina. This consists of progressive removal of the dilator and irrigation of the vaginal cavity with iso-Betadine. The period of time that the dilator remains out is gradually increased over the following 3–6 months. Later, if the patient is having regular sexual intercourse, no further dilation is required. Otherwise, routine dilation should continue once or twice per week, especially if a full-thickness skin graft has been used in addition to the pedicled penile skin flap.

Complications

Although the surgical techniques for vaginoplasty have evolved and improved significantly, patients have to be informed that both medical and surgical treatments are rarely perfect. Revisional surgery is sometimes required to optimize aesthetic results.

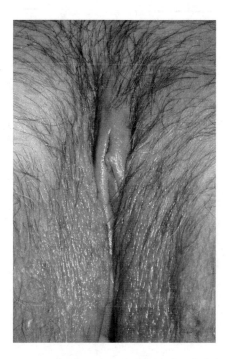

Figure 14.9 Vaginoplasty—result after 3 months with a detail of the clitoral hood.

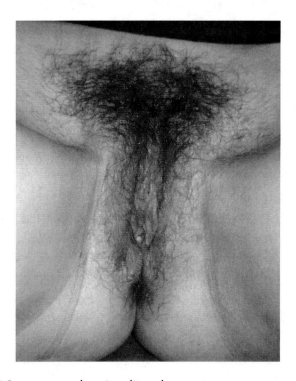

Figure 14.10 Long-term result vagino-clitoroplasty.

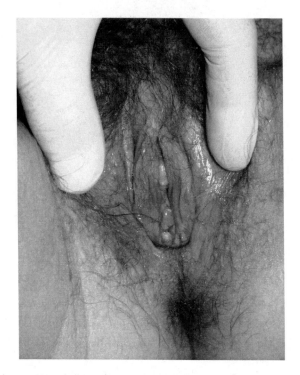

Figure 14.11 Long-term result vagino-clitoroplasty.

Early (but rare) postoperative complications include bleeding (usually resolved by applying some pressure), lower-extremity compartment syndrome, infection, or impaired wound healing. One specific complication related to the vaginoplasty procedure is the development of a rectovaginal fistula, as the vaginal cavity needs to be created between the prostate urethra anteriorly and the rectum posteriorly. The rectum has a rather thin wall, and care must be taken to avoid a perforation. If a rectal injury occurs during the dissection of the neovagina, a double-layer closure should be performed. This usually heals without problem since a preoperative bowel preparation is routinely performed.

Possible late complications include stenosis of the new urethral meatus, which is rare with the eversion flap of the urethral mucosa.

Lifelong vaginal hygiene and dilatation are recommended, especially in operated transwomen undergoing limited or no penetrative sex. Most patients are able to reach an orgasm after the operation (clitoral in most cases), and despite the fact that they often experience some moistening of the vulva during sexual excitation, most transwomen require lubrication for sexual intercourse. Until the first uterine transplantation in a transwoman, pregnancy is of course not possible.

References

Abraham, F. (1931). Genitalumwandlung an zwei mannlichen Transvestiten. *Sexwiss Sexpol* 18: 223–226.

Benjamin, H. (1964). Nature and Management of Transsexualism, with a Report of Thirty-one Operated Cases. *Western J Surg* 72: 105.

Benjamin, H. (1966). Conversion Operation. In *The Transsexual Phenomenon*. New York: Julian Press, pp. 100–118.

Bouman, F.G. (1988). Sex Reassignment Surgery in Male-to-female Transsexuals. *Ann Plast Surg* 21: 526–531.

Bouman, F.G. (1989). Vaginoplasty with Abdominally Pedicled Penis Skin in Male-to-female Transsexuals. In Eicher, W., Kubli, F., & Herms, V. (Eds.), *Plastic Surgery in the Sexually Handicapped*. Berlin: Springer-Verlag, pp. 7–90.

Bouman, M.B., Van Zeijl, M., Buncamper, M.E., Meijerink, W., Van Bodegraven, A.A., & Mullender, M.G. (2014) Intestinal Vaginoplasty Revised: A Review of Surgical Techniques, Complications, and Sexual Function. *J Sex Med* 11(7):1835–1847.

Brown, J. (1976). Creation of a Functional Clitoris and Aesthetically Pleasing Introitus in Sex Conversion. In Marchac, D., & Hueston, J.T. (Eds.), *Transactions of the Sixth International Congress of Plastic and Reconstructive Surgery*. Paris: Masson, pp. 654–655.

Brown, J. (1978). A Single-stage Operative Technique for Castration, Vaginal Construction, and Perineoplasty in Transsexuals. *Arch Sex Behav* 4: 313–323.

Burou, G. (1973). Male-to-female Transformation. In: Laub, D.R. & Gandy, P. (Eds.), *Proceedings of the Second Interdisciplinary Symposium on Gender Dysphoria Syndrome*. Palo Alto, CA: Stanford University Press, pp. 188–194.

Cairns, T.S., & De Villiers, W. (1980).Vaginoplasty. *S Afr Med J* 57: 50–55.

Colebunders, B., T'Sjoen, G., Weyers, S., & Monstrey, S. (2014). Hormonal and Surgical Treatment in Trans-Women with BRCA1 Mutations: A Controversial Topic. *J Sex Med* 11, 2496–2499.

Coleman, S.R., & Saboeiro, A.P. (2015) Primary Breast Augmentation with Fat Grafting. *Clin Plast Surg* 42(3):301–306, vii.

Coleman, E., Bockting, W., Botzer, M., et al. (2012). Standards of Care for the Health of Transsexual, Transgender, and Gender-Nonconforming People, Version 7. *International Journal of Transgenderism*, 13(4): 165–232.

Dalton, J.R. (1981). Use of Sigmoid Colon in Sex Reassignment Operations. *Urology* 17: 223–227.

Davies, M.C., & Creighton, S.M. (2007). Vaginoplasty. *Curr Opin Urol* 17: 415–418.

Dessy, L.A., Mazzocchi, M., Corrias, F., Ceccarelli, S., Marchese, C., & Scuderi, N. (2014). The Use of Cultured Autologous Oral Epithelial Cells for Vaginoplasty in Male-to-female Transsexuals: A Feasibility, Safety, and Advantageousness Clinical Pilot Study. *Plast Reconstr Surg* 133(1): 158–161.

Ding, J.X., Chen, L.M., Zhang, X.Y., Zhang, Y., & Hua, K.Q. (2015). Sexual and Functional Outcomes of Vaginoplasty Using Acellular Porcine Small Intestinal Submucosa Graft or Laparoscopic Peritoneal Vaginoplasty: A Comparative Study. *Hum Reprod* 30(3): 581–589.

Edgerton, M.T. (1974). The Surgical Treatment of Male Transsexuals. *Clin Plast Surg* 1: 285.

Edgerton, M.T., & Bull, J. (1970). Surgical Construction of the Vagina and Labia in Male Transsexuals. *Plast Reconstr Surg* 46: 529–539.

Eicher, W. (1989). The Inverted Penis Skin Technique in Male-to-Female Transsexuals. In: Eicher, W., Kubli, F., & Herms, V. (Eds.), *Plastic Surgery in the Sexually Handicapped*. Berlin: Springer-Verlag, pp. 91–112.

Eldh, J. (1993). Construction of a Neovagina with Preservation of the Glans Penis as a Clitoris in Male Transsexuals. *Plast Reconstr Surg* 91: 895–903.

Farkas, L.G. (1987). Age- and Sex-related Changes in Facial Proportions. In Farkas, L.G., & Munro, I.R. (Eds.), *Anthropometric Facial Proportions in Medicine*. Springfield, IL: Charles C. Thomas, p. 29.

Fogh-Andersen, P. (1956). Transvestism and Transsexualism: Surgical Treatment in a Case of Autocastration. *Act Med Leg Soc* 9: 33.

Gillies, H., & Millard, R.D. Jr. (1957). Genitalia. In *The Principles and Art of Plastic Surgery*. London: Butterworth, pp. 368–388.

Giraldo, F., Esteva, I., Bergero, T., Cano, G., Gonzalez, C., Salinas, P., Rivada, E., Lara, J.S., & Soriguer, F. (2004). Corona Glans Clitoroplasty and Urethropreputial Vestibuloplasty in Male-to-Female Transsexuals: Vulval Aesthetic Refinement by the Andalusia Gender Team. *Plast Reconstr Surg* 114: 1543–1550.

Gooren, L.J., van Trotsenburg, M.A., Giltay, E.J., & van Diest, P.J. (2013) Breast Cancer Development in Transsexual Subjects Receiving Cross-Sex Hormone Treatment. *J Sex Med* 10(12): 3129–3134.

Hage, J.J. (1995). The Use of a Tissue Expander as a Vaginal Stent in Vagina Reconstruction. *Br J Obstet Gynaecol* 102: 1020.

Hage, J.J. & Karim, R.B. (1998). Abdominoplastic Secondary Full-thickness Skin Graft Vaginoplasty for Male-to-Female Transsexuals. *Plast Reconstr Surg* 101(6): 1512–1515.

Hage, J.J., & Laub, D.R. (1995). Debate: Penile Inversion Versus Rectosigmoid Vaginoplasty. *Presented at the XIV Harry Benjamin International Gender Dysphoria Symposium*. Kloster Irsee, Bavaria, Germany, September 8, 1995.

Hage, J.J., Karim, R.B., Bloem, J.J., Suliman, H.M., & van Alphen, M. (1994). Sculpturing the Neoclitoris in Vaginoplasty for Male-to-female Transsexuals. *Plast Reconstr Surg* 93: 358–365.

Hage, J.J., Karim, R.B., Asscheman, H, Bloemena, E. & Cuesta, M.A. (1995). Unfavorable Long-term Results of Rectosigmoid Neocolpopoiesis. *Plast Reconstr Surg* 95: 842–848.

Hage, J.J., Becking, A.G., de Graaf, F.H., & Tuinzing, D.B. (1997). Gender-Confirming Facial Surgery: Considerations on the Masculinity and Femininity of Faces. *Plast Reconstr Surg* 99: 1799–1807.

Hage, J.J., Goedkoop, A.Y., Karim, R.B., & Kanhai, R.C. (2000). Secondary Corrections of the Vulva in Male-to-Female Transsexuals. *Plast Reconstr Surg* 106(2): 350–359.

Huang, T.T. (1995). Twenty Years of Experience in Managing Gender Dysphoric Patients: I. Surgical Management of Male Transsexuals. *Plast Reconstr Surg* 96(4): 921–934.

Isshiki, N. (1989). *Phonosurgery – Theory and Practice*. Berlin: Springer, pp. 141–155.

Jones, H.W. Jr., Schrimer, H.K., & Hoopes, J.E. (1968). A Sex Conversion Operation in Males with Transsexualism. *Am J Obstet Gynecol* 10: 101–109.

Kanhai, R.C.J., Hage, J.J., Asscheman, H., & Mulder, J.W. (1999a). Augmentation Mammaplasty in Male-to-female Transsexuals. *Plast Reconstr Surg* 104: 542–549.

Kanhai, R.C.J., Hage, J.J., Karim, R.B., & Mulder, J.W. (1999b). Exceptional Presenting Conditions and Outcome of Augmentation Mammaplasty in Male-to-Female Transsexuals. *Ann Plast Surg* 43: 476–483.

Karim, R.B, Hage, J.J., Bouman, F.G., de Ruyter, R., & Van Kesteren, P.J.M. (1995). Refinements of Pre, Intra, and Postoperative Care to Prevent Complications of Vaginoplasty in Male Transsexuals. *Ann Plast Surg* 35: 279–284.

Karim, R.B., Hage, J.J., & Mulder, J.W. (1996). Neovaginoplasty in Male Transsexuals: Review of Surgical Techniques and Recommendations Regarding their Eligibility. *Ann Plast Surg* 37(6): 669–675.

Kim, S.K., Park, J.H., Lee, K.C., Park, J.M., Kim, J.T., & Kim, M.C. (2003). Long-term Results in Patients after Rectosigmoid Vaginoplasty. *Plast Reconstr Surg* 112(1): 143–151.

Laub, D.R., & Fisk, N. (1974). A Rehabilitation Program for Gender Dysphoria Syndrome in Surgical Sex Change. *Plast Reconstr Surg* 53: 388–403.

Li, F.Y., Xu, Y.S., Zhou, C.D., Zhou, Y., Li, S.K., Li, Q. (2014). Long-term Outcomes of Vaginoplasty with Autologous Buccal Micromucosa. *Obstet Gynecol* 123(5): 951–956.

Lin, W.C., Chang, C.Y., Shen, Y.Y., & Tsai, H.D. (2003). Use of Autologous Buccal Mucosa for Vaginoplasty: A Study of Eight Cases. *Hum Reprod* 18: 604–607.

Malloy, T.R., Noone, R.B., & Morgan, A.J. (1976). Experience with the One-stage Surgical Approach for Constructing Female Genitalia in Male Transsexuals. *J Urol* 116: 335–337.

Marshall, W.A., & Tanner, J.M. (1969). Variations in pattern of pubertal changes in girls. *Arch Dis Child* 44(235): 291–303.

McGregor, I.A. (1989). *Fundamental Techniques of Plastic Surgery and their Surgical Applications*, 8th ed. Edinburgh: Churchill Livingstone, pp. 39–63.

Meyer, R., & Kesselring, U.K. (1980). One-stage Reconstruction of the Vagina with Penile Skin as an Island Flap in Male Transsexuals. *Plast Reconstr Surg* 66: 401–406.

Monstrey, S., Hoebeke, P., Dhont, M., De Cuypere, G., Rubens, R., Moerman, M., Hamdi, M., Van Landuyt, K., & Blondeel, P.H. (2001). Surgical Therapy in Transsexual Patients: A Multidisciplinary Approach. *Acta Chir Belg* 101: 200–209.

Neumann, K., Welzel, C., & Berghaus, A. (2002). Operative Voice Pitch Raising in Male-to-female Transsexuals. *Eur J Plast Surg* 25:209–214.

Pandya, N.J., & Stuteville, O.H. (1973). A One-stage Technique for Constructing Female External Genitalia in Male Transsexuals. *Br J Plast Surg* 26: 277.

Pauly, I.B., & Edgerton, M.T. (1986). The Gender Identity Movement: A Growing Surgical-psychiatric Liaison. *Arch Sex Behav* 15: 315.

Perovic, S.V., Stanojevic, D.S., & Djordjevic, M.L. (2000).Vaginoplasty in Male Transsexuals using Penile Skin and a Urethral Flap. *BJU Int* 86(7): 843–850.

Puppo, V. (2011). Embryology and Anatomy of the Vulva: The Female Orgasm and Women's Sexual Health. *Eur J Obstet Gynecol Reprod Biol* 154: 3–8.

Richards, C., & Seal, L. (2014). Trans People's Reproductive Options and Outcomes. *J Fam Plan Reproduct Health Care* 40: 245–247.

Rubin, S.O. (1980). A Method of Preserving the Glans Penis as a Clitoris in Sex Conversion Operations in Male Transsexuals. *Scand J Urol Nephrol* 14: 215–217.

Rubin, S.O. (1993). Sex-reassignment Surgery Male-to-Female. Review, Own Results and Report of a New Technique Using the Glans Penis as a Pseudoclitoris. *Scand J Urol Nephrol Suppl* 154, 1–28.

Schober, J.M. (2007). Cancer of the Neovagina. *J Pediatr Urol* 3:167–70.

Selvaggi, G., Ceulemans, P., De Cuypere, G., Van Landuyt, K., Blondeel, P., Hamdi, M., Bowman, C., & Monstrey, S. (2005). Gender Identity Disorder: General Overview and Surgical Treatment for Vaginoplasty in Male-to-Female Transsexuals. *Plast Reconstr Surg* 116.

Spiegel, J. H. (2011). Facial determinants of female gender and feminizing forehead cranioplasty. *Laryngoscope*, 121: 250–261.

Tessier, P. (1987). Foreword, in Farkas, L.G., & Munro, I.R. (Eds.), *Anthropometric Facial Proportions in Medicine*. Springfield, IL: Charles C Thomas, p. ix.

Turner, U.G., Edlich, R.F., & Edgerton, M.T. (1978). Male Transsexualism – A Review of Genital Surgical Reconstruction. *Am J Obst Gynecol* 132: 119–133.

Van Dis, A. (1988). Casablanca. In: *Casablanca – Schetsen en verhalen*. Amsterdam: Meulenhoff. Pocket, pp. 7–34.

Van Noort, D.E., & Nicolai, E.J.P.A. (1993). Comparison of Two Methods of Vagina Reconstruction in Transsexuals. *Plast Reconstr Surg* 91(7): 1308–1315.

Wedler, V., Meuli-Simmen, C., Guggenheim, M., Schneller-Gustafsson, M., & Kunzi, W. (2004). Laparoscopic Technique for Secondary Vaginoplasty in Male-to-female Transsexuals using a Modified Vascularized Pedicled Sigmoid. *Gynecol Obstet Invest* 57(4): 181–185.

Wee, J.T, & Joseph, V.T. (1989). A New Technique of Vaginal Reconstruction using Neurovascular Pudendal-thigh Flaps: A Preliminary Report. *Plast Reconstr Surg* 83: 701–709.

Weigert, R., Frison, E., Sessiecq, Q., Al Mutairi, K., & Casoli, V. (2013). Patient Satisfaction with Breasts and Psychosocial, Sexual, and Physical Well-being after Breast Augmentation in Male-to-female Transsexuals. *Plast Reconstr Surg* 132: 1421–1429.

Weyers, S., Villeirs, G., Vanherreweghe, E., Verstraelen, H., & Monstrey, S. (2010). Mammography and Breast Sonography in Transsexual Women. *Eur J Radiol* 74(3): 508–513.

Wolfort, F.G., Dejerine, E.S., Ramos, D.J., & Parry, R. G. (1990). Chondrolaryngoplasty for Appearance. *Plast Reconstr Surg* 86: 464–470.

Zhang, D., Zhang, J., Wang, H., Li, B., Zhu, X., Wang, L., & Wu, J. (2014). Comparative Study on Laparoscopic Vaginoplasty Using Pedicled Ileal and Sigmoid Colon Segment Transfer. *Zhonghua fu Chan ke za zhi* 49(3): 172–175.

15 Female-to-Male Gender Reassignment Surgery

Britt Colebunders, Salvatore D'Arpa, Steven Weijers, Nicolaas Lumen, Piet Hoebeke, and Stan Monstrey

History of Transmen Surgery

In surgery, particularly in plastic and reconstructive surgery, it is generally easier to resect tissue than to add it. This explains why a phalloplasty is considered a much more complex surgical procedure than a penectomy, with or without vaginoplasty. It also explains why so little is known about the history of penile reconstruction in transmen. Also, virtually no data exist on the number of transgenders who underwent mastectomy, hysterectomy, and/ or bilateral salpingo-oophorectomy (BSO) to relieve severe gender dysphoria prior to the 20th century.

The term "phalloplasty" was first used in 1858 by Sprengler to indicate the reconstruction of the integument after décollement (separation of the superficial tissue layers) of the penis (Biemer 1988a). Bogoras, the first to report on the reconstruction of the entire penis, labeled his procedure "penis plastica totalis" (Bogoras 1936). He was also the first to use a single abdominal tube, a technique that was later applied by others. Subsequently, "phalloplasty" was used to describe penile reconstruction.

Following World War II, some leading plastic surgeons showed an interest in the penile reconstructive procedure. In 1948, McIndoe improved the abdominal tube flap by constructing a neourethra while raising the pedicle tube, employing an inlay skin graft. Maltz (1946) and Gillies and Millard (1957) popularized the technique when they added a costal cartilage graft as a rigidity prosthesis. Gillies was the first to report the use of this technique in a transsexual patient. The Stanford team (Biber 1979; Laub et al. 1989) refined the procedure, tubing an infra-umbilical abdominal flap outside-in in order to create a skin-lined tunnel as a future urethral conduit. This method reduced the number of stages previously required for phalloplasty.

Snyder described a phalloplasty technique incorporating a preconstructed superficial skin-lined conduit for intersex patients employing a single-pedicled infra-umbilical skin flap (Snyder & Browne 1977). Hester performed a penile reconstruction in one stage using a vertical, superficial inferior epigastric artery flap with a subcutaneous pedicle, in a male born with ambiguous genitalia (Hester et al. 1984). However, after McGregor introduced the groin flap in 1972 (McGregor & Jackson 1972), Hoopes (1974) commented, "the groin flap may prove to be the method of choice for phallus reconstruction." Orticochea (1972) used a gracilis myocutaneous flap in a five-stage phalloplasty procedure, and claimed that it produced cosmetically and functionally superior results. The Norfolk team also used a unilateral gracilis myocutaneous flap for phalloplasty (Horton et al. 1977). Sometimes, a combination of flaps was used. Exner (1992) implanted a ridigity prosthesis in a rectus abdominis muscular flap and used bilateral groin flaps to cover the neophallus.

More recently, however, microsurgical free flaps have been considered state of the art in penile reconstruction (Hage et al. 1996; Monstrey 2009). The most frequently used free flap is the radial forearm flap, or Chinese flap, first described by Song et al. in 1982. However, different flaps have been described since then (Felici & Felici 2006; Hage & De Graaf 1993; Santanelli & Scuderi 2000). The fact that so many techniques for penile reconstruction still exist is evidence that no technique is considered ideal.

Criteria for Sex Reassignment Surgery

Surgical therapy in transmen can consist of facial masculinization, surgical lowering of the voice pitch (rarely indicated after hormonal therapy), subcutaneous mastectomy (SCM), hysterectomy, and/or BSO, vaginectomy, reconstruction of the fixed part of the urethra (if isolated, metoidioplasty), scrotoplasty, phalloplasty, insertion of testicular prostheses, and/or erection prosthesis. However, the two major surgical interventions are SCM and phalloplasty with testicular/erection prosthesis.

Standards of Care

The seventh version of *Standards of Care* (SOC) of the World Professional Association of Transgender Health (WPATH) offers flexible guidelines for the treatment of people experiencing gender dysphoria and puts forth the following criteria for surgical treatments (Coleman et al. 2012).

Criteria for mastectomy and creation of a male chest are:

- persistent, well-documented gender dysphoria;
- capacity to make a fully informed decision and to give consent for treatment;
- age of majority in a given country;
- if significant medical or mental health concerns are present, they must be well controlled.

For "internal" genital surgery (hysterectomy and salpingo-oophorectomy) the following criterion is added to the above list:

- 12 continuous months of hormone therapy as appropriate to the patient's gender goals (unless hormones are not clinically indicated for the individual). The aim of hormone therapy prior to gonadectomy is primarily to introduce a period of reversible estrogen suppression, before a patient undergoes irreversible surgical interventions.

For "external" genital surgery (metoidioplasty or phalloplasty), one additional criterion is recommended:

- 12 continuous months of living in a gender role that is congruent with their gender identity.

Gender Binaries

Until recently medical professionals have considered gender to be binary. A person was considered to be either man or woman, nothing in between. This idea of dichotomy forced transgenders to seek out therapy to correctly align their bodies with the opposite of their biologic gender. Partial surgeries were thought to create abnormal bodies and even a "freakish" phenomenon. However, the concept of gender fluidity has existed probably since the beginning of time. The medical profession has been catching up with this concept of gender fluidity. Version 7 of the *SOC* focuses more on gender variance, considering gender as a spectrum instead of a dichotomy. Yerkea and Mitchella (2011) showed in a cohort study that some participants were satisfied with their gender identity after chest surgery alone. They concluded that genital surgery is not a necessary final step of transition for all transmen. A person can be perfectly satisfied with his body somewhere in the spectrum between man and woman. It is obvious that the medical world nowadays has a more fluid view on gender identity beyond the binary. However, empirical data on genderqueer individuals and their quality of life are still lacking today.

Referral Letter

The WPATH *SOC* state that, in order to proceed with any type of genital surgery ("internal" or "external"), two referrals from qualified mental health professionals who have independently assessed the patient for suitability and readiness are required, while for breast/chest surgery, only one letter is required. Recently, several articles (Bouman et al. 2014; Rachlin et al., 2010; Weiss & Green 2014) have questioned this recommendation for two referrals in order to undergo genital surgery and especially in the case of "internal" genital surgery (hysterectomy and salpingo-oophorectomy). It has been demonstrated that, especially for a hysterectomy, the majority of patients in the community will not have two letters (unless maybe when evaluating for a phalloplasty at the same time) (Rachlin et al., 2010; Weiss & Green 2014). Weiss and Green (2014) suggest in a letter to the editor moving the WPATH guidelines to a single mental health letter requirement for hysterectomy, helping patients face fewer barriers to care. This recommendation is supported by Bouman et al. (2014). In their paper they also advocate a single signature of approval from a qualified mental health professional before genital reconstructive surgery, if sufficient safeguards are in place, including assessment within a multidisciplinary team. We have evolved to a more "patient-centered" medicine where it should be simply accepted that a transperson who seeks gender reassignment surgery for a persistent, well-documented gender dysphoria and has taken hormone treatment for 12 continuous months has had enough time to reflect about the benefits and risks of the surgery and can decide by himself if genital surgery is required or not. In this perspective it is difficult to sustain the rationale for the two written qualified mental health professional opinions rule, concerning the prevention of harm to the patient (Bouman et al. 2014).

It could be argued that for external genital surgery still two letters are appropriate, but less imperative for internal genital surgery (BSO and hysterectomy). Adequate preparation and assessment, and this especially within a multidisciplinary team, are much more important than the simple safety measure of requiring two signatures for genital surgeries.

Facial Masculinization Surgery

In most aesthetic operations, patients like to improve their looks but above all continue to look like themselves. In facial feminization and masculinization surgery, the patient wishes to change dramatically. As described in Chapter 14 about facial feminization surgery, the face communicates vital social information. In initial contacts, it is most often the face that provides cues about the person, including gender. For transpeople, nothing is more important than to appear externally congruent with the internal and emotional self. In order to avoid immediate identification as transgender it is essential that facial features are adjusted in such a way that the face will be recognized as belonging to, in this case, the male gender. The male facial skeleton is larger, squarer and more angulated with sharp lines and a strong jaw. Facial masculinization procedures in transmen are exceedingly less common than facial feminization procedures in transwomen. Consistent with these observations, very few studies focusing explicitly on these procedures are found during a literature search. Douglas Ousterhout has published some articles about facial masculinization procedures in male patients, concluding that the areas generally to be considered in masculinization of the male face are the forehead, chin, and angle of the mandible (Ousterhout 2011). These techniques could also be used for facial masculinization surgery in transmen. Like in phalloplasty, these procedures require tissue to be added instead of resected.

Forehead

The forehead is one of the most important areas to surgically modify. Males have brow bossing, with a flat area in between. It is the bossing anterior to both of the frontal sinuses but also at the superior lateral orbital angle that makes the male forehead look as it does. The supraorbital rim can be augmented with methyl methacrylate by a coronal approach. The methyl methacrylate can be contoured easily. The most important thing is to determine preoperatively with the patient how much augmentation he wants.

Angle of the Mandible

In males the angle of the mandible is more pronounced vertically and posteriorly. Also the lateral flaring makes the angle of the mandible look masculine. Augmentation of this region can thus be desired in transmen. There are two methods for augmenting the mandibular angle. The easiest and most common method is to use a mandibular angle implant. These implants can be custom-made and are placed through an intra-oral approach avoiding visible scars. The other technique is to use a bone graft. The bone graft can be calvarial or iliac crest and is placed in between the outer cortex of the mandibular angle and the spongious bone after sagitally splitting the mandibular angle. This prevents resorption of the bone graft. This can be the result if the bone graft is placed in between the lateral cortex and the masseter muscle. The thickness of the bone graft depends upon the desired augmentation.

Chin

The chin in males is vertically higher and laterally there is a fullness that makes the chin more masculine. Also a more anterior prominence is common in men. When the chin is small in whatever dimension, augmentation can be performed as desired. The desired vertical augmentation is very difficult to obtain with an implant. Osteotomies of the chin can augment the chin in vertical, anterior, and lateral directions. The advancement of the chin through an osteotomy can also have a substantial effect on the submental tissues and the submental cervical angle. Chin implants will not have this effect as the bony chin itself is not advanced. After repositioning of the bony segments, they are held in place with multiple plates and screws. The space created by the expansion and repositioning of the bone can be filled with hydroxyapatite granules.

Cheekbones

Prominent cheeks generally are attractive in both genders. So malar augmentation may be a desirable procedure. It is not necessary for increasing masculinization but it can be an individual desire.

Subcutaneous Mastectomy

Introduction

Because hormonal treatment has little influence on breast size, the first (and, arguably, most important) surgery performed in transmen is the creation of a male chest by means of SCM. This procedure allows the patient to live more easily in the male role (Eicher 1992; Hage & Bloem 1995; Lindsay 1979) and thereby facilitates the "real-life experience," which is a prerequisite for external genital surgery.

A large body of literature concerning the optimal technique for performing SCM exists, but most of it focuses on women with breast disease or men with gynecomastia. There is a paucity of information regarding removal of the breasts in transmen.

Obviously, the male chest and the female chest are anatomically different (Hage & Kesteren 1995). The female chest has excess skin, excess glandular tissue, and a surrounding surplus of subcutaneous fat. With regard to the inferior confinement of the breast, in the female, the inframammary fold is well defined. In the average male, the chest does not show an inframammary fold and the inferior margin of the pectoralis muscle (often somewhat squared by rudimentary breast tissue and nipple) represents the dim inferior margin of the chest. The importance of obliterating the inframammary fold while contouring the male chest has been stressed by several authors (Edgerton 1984; Gilbert et al. 1988).

From a purely anatomical viewpoint, SCM in transmen is virtually identical to that of mastectomy for breast disease or prophylaxis. However, the goals for transmen differ, as they include aesthetic contouring of the chest wall by removal of breast tissue and excess skin; reduction and proper positioning of the nipple and areola; obliteration of the inframammary fold; and minimization of chest wall scars (Hage and Kesteren 1995)—in short, the creation of an aesthetically pleasing male chest. Many of the techniques for the treatment of gynecomastia have been used or modified in SCM for transmen, and the methods and indications for each have been discussed in the literature (Eicher 1992; Hage & Kesteren 1995; Lindsay 1979). The reports describe liposuction, semicircular circumareolar techniques, concentric circular techniques, transareolar incisional techniques, and more radical procedures such as breast amputation with a free nipple graft (Davidson 1979; Dolsky 1990; Letterman & Schurter 1972; Pitanguy 1966; Webster 1946).

Poor aesthetic outcomes following in transsexual patients include contour abnormalities (breast, inframammary fold, and nipple); issues relating to the nipple–areola complex (NAC) (size, placement, and viability); skin redundancy; and poor scarring (Hage and Kesteren 1995; Simon & Hoffman 1976). Secondary corrections often are the rule rather than the exception.

Indeed, performing SCM in transmen is more difficult than in a male with gynecomastia since, in most cases, transmen will usually have more breast volume and a greater degree of skin excess and ptosis. According to Hage and Kesteren (1995), skin excess, not breast volume, is the factor that should determine the appropriate SCM technique. Based on more than 400 SCMs we have performed for transmen over the past 15 years, we agree that skin quality—specifically, skin "elasticity"—also is a key factor. It can make the difference between a good aesthetic outcome and a poor one, especially with a less experienced

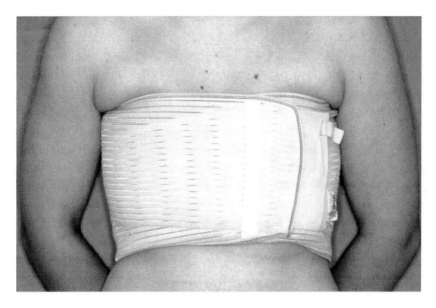

Figure 15.1 Breast binding to camouflage a feminine-looking chest.

surgeon. It is important to be aware that, in this patient population, poor skin quality can be exacerbated when the patient has engaged in years of "breast binding" (Figures 15.1 and 15.2).

Surgical Techniques

The difficulty with SCM lies less in the procedure itself (although it is wrongly considered an "easy" procedure), and more in the choice of technique. Therefore we have developed an algorithm which helps us to choose from five techniques, resulting in an aesthetically pleasing male chest (Monstrey et al. 2008). Preoperative parameters to be evaluated include breast volume; degree of excess skin; NAC size and position; and skin elasticity.

If the patient is a smoker, the surgeon should discuss the effects of the habit on the skin quality, wound healing, and vascularity, and encourage the patient to stop smoking. This is especially important if a free-flap phalloplasty is to be performed later. Hormonal therapy is stopped 2–3 weeks preoperatively.

Early in our series, we carried out each patient's complete sex reassignment surgery in a single stage. SCM, hysterectomy, and oophorectomy, vaginectomy with scrotoplasty, and phalloplasty, including reconstruction of the fixed part of the urethra, were all performed in one operation. Many of these procedures were carried out simultaneously by different surgical teams. However, the combination proved too lengthy, especially for a patient with larger breasts. Until 1 year ago we combined the SCM procedure with a laparoscopic hysterectomy

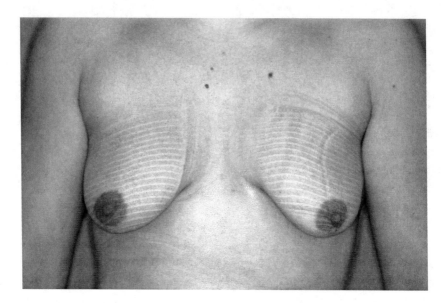

Figure 15.2 Breast binding can result in a ptotic breast with poor skin elasticity.

and oophorectomy in the first stage. Vaginectomy, scrotoplasty, and phallo-plasty with reconstruction of the fixed part of the urethra were later carried out in a second stage. More recently, we consider performing the SCM first, then the hysterectomy with BSO and reconstruction of the fixed part of the urethra with vaginectomy and scrotoplasty (in fact, a metoidioplasty operation), and only 6 months later a phalloplasty.

Regardless of the technique, it is extremely important to preserve all subcuta-neous fat when dissecting the glandular tissue from the flaps. This ensures thick flaps that produce a pleasing contour and do not subsequently become tethered to the chest wall. For the same reason, we preserve the pectoralis fascia. We do not perform liposuction at the anterior aspect of the breast. However, a judi-cious use of liposuction can occasionally be indicated laterally, or to attain com-plete symmetry at the end of the procedure. The inframammary fold is always released, an especially important maneuver for patients with large breasts. This is done by extending the inferior flap on to the abdomen and, where a tight band exists, incising it with multiple transverse cuts. Postoperatively, a circum-ferential elastic bandage is placed around the chest wall and maintained for a total of 4–6 weeks.

The *semicircular technique* (Figure 15.3) is essentially the same procedure as that described by Webster in 1946 for the correction of gynecomastia. It is useful for individuals with smaller breasts. The resulting scar will be con-fined to the lower half of the periphery of the areola (infra-areolar). A suffi-cient amount of glandular tissue should be left in situ beneath the NAC in

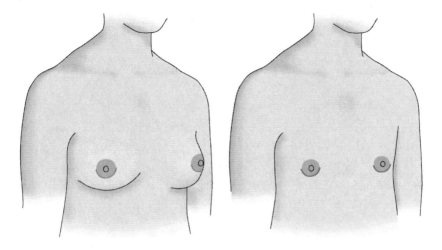

Figure 15.3 Semicircular technique: incisions and scars.

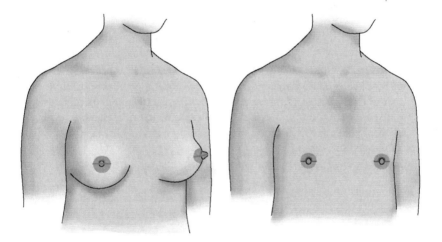

Figure 15.4 Transareolar technique: incisions and scars.

order to avoid a depression. The advantage of this technique is the small and well-concealed scar, which is confined to the NAC. The major drawback is the small window through which to work, making excision of breast tissue and hemostasis more challenging. Care must be taken to avoid overzealous traction on the skin edges with retractors, which could result in wound dehiscence or marginal skin necrosis.

In cases of smaller breasts with large prominent nipples, the *transareolar technique* (Figure 15.4) is used. This is similar to the procedure described by

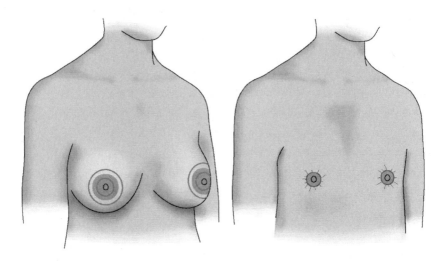

Figure 15.5 Concentric circular technique: incisions and scars.

Pitanguy in 1966. It allows for a subtotal resection of the nipple and usually incorporates the upper aspect, which tends to ameliorate the downward effect of gravity. The resulting scar traverses the areola horizontally and passes around the upper aspect of the nipple. The additional advantage of this technique is that it allows an immediate nipple reduction. The disadvantage is the same as with the semicircular technique, i.e., it is more difficult to excise breast tissue and achieve hemostasis. Additionally, the transareolar scar is usually somewhat more apparent.

The *concentric circular technique* was described by Davidson in 1979 (Figures 15.5, 15.6, and 15.7). It is used for breasts with a medium-sized skin envelope (B cup), or smaller breasts with poor skin elasticity. The resulting scar will be confined to the circumference of the areola. The concentric incision can be drawn as a circle or ellipse, enabling deepithelialization of a calculated amount of skin in the vertical or horizontal direction (Hage & Kesteren 1995). Access is gained via an incision in the inferior aspect of the outer circle. Glandular tissue is carefully dissected off the overlying NAC, leaving it widely based on a dermal pedicle. In this case, it is not necessary to leave excess glandular tissue beneath the NAC, as the folded deepithelialized dermis surrounding the areola provides sufficient NAC projection and prevents nipple–chest wall tethering. A permanent purse-string suture is placed and set to the desired areolar diameter (usually ±20 mm). The advantage of this technique is that it allows for reduction and/or repositioning of the areola, where required, and for the removal of excess skin. It also affords good exposure for glandular excision and hemostasis. It does, however, require experience in determining the amount of skin to be deepithelialized.

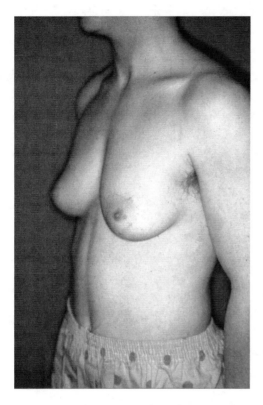

Figure 15.6 Concentric circular technique: preoperative view.

The *extended concentric circular technique* (Figure 15.8) is similar to the concentric circular technique, but includes one or two additional triangular excisions of skin and subcutaneous tissue, which may be inferior and lateral, or medial and lateral. Access for excision of the glandular tissue is provided through these additional skin excisions. This technique is useful for correcting skin excess and wrinkling produced by large differences between the inner and outer circles. On the few occasions where a single vertical triangular excision inferior to the NAC was utilized, the results were suboptimal. Subsequently, this technique was abandoned. Here too, a permanent purse-string suture is placed and set to the desired areolar diameter. The resulting scars will be around the areola, with horizontal extensions on to the breast skin, depending on the degree of excess skin. The advantages of this technique are the wide exposure for glandular excision and hemostasis, NAC reduction and repositioning, and tailoring of excess skin resulting in fewer wrinkles around the areola. The major drawbacks are that the residual scarring is no longer confined to the NAC, and experience is required in planning the amount of tissue to be excised and/or deepithelialized.

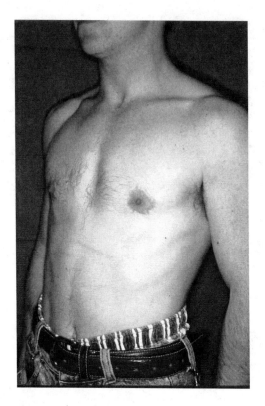

Figure 15.7 Concentric circular technique: postoperative view.

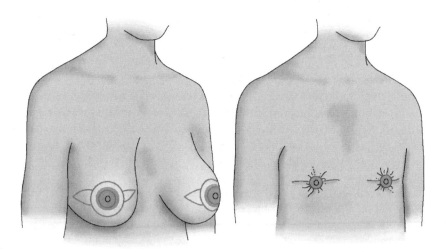

Figure 15.8 Extended concentric circular technique: incisions and scars.

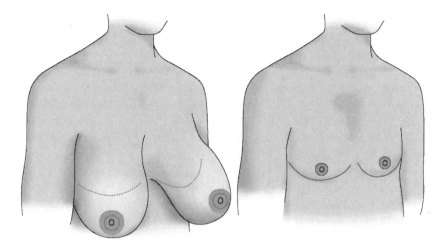

Figure 15.9 Free nipple graft technique: Incisions and scars.

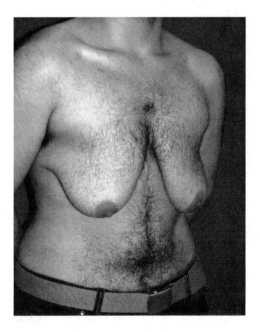

Figure 15.10 Free nipple graft technique: preoperative view.

The *free nipple graft technique* has been proposed by several authors for patients with large and ptotic breasts (Eicher 1992; Hoopes 1974; Kenney & Edgerton 1989; Kluzak 1968; Lindsay 1979) (Figures 15.9, 15.10, and 15.11).

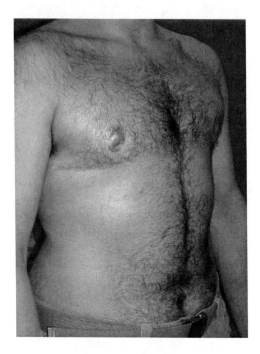

Figure 15.11 Free nipple graft technique: postoperative view.

It consists of harvesting the NAC as a full-thickness skin graft; amputating the breast; and grafting the NAC on to its new location on the chest wall. Our preference is to place the incision horizontally 1–2 cm above the inframammary fold, and then move upward laterally below the lateral border of the pectoralis major muscle. The incisions should not cross the midline. Following breast amputation, the superior flap is pulled downward to eliminate skin redundancy. At this stage, judicious defatting or liposuction may be performed laterally and medially to avoid "dog-ear" formation and ensure symmetric contouring. Again, care should be taken to leave the fat on the undersurface of the breast flaps. Following closure, the NAC is grafted on to the desired position on the chest wall.

Regarding ideal placement of the NAC, we feel that the use of absolute measurements can be misleading. We agree with the recommendations of many authors who position the NAC according to the patient's own anatomical landmarks (Beckenstein et al. 1996; Beer et al. 2001). In our series, the nipples were placed along the existing nipple line and the height was adjusted to approximately 2 cm above the lower border of pectoralis major. In a typical patient, this will correspond to the fourth or fifth intercostal space. Clinical judgment is most important, however, and we always sit the patient up intraoperatively to check final nipple position.

The diameter of the NAC is 20–25 mm and is cut while the area is stretched circumferentially. The resulting scars will include a line on the inferior aspect of the new male breast, in addition to one around the areola. The advantages of the free nipple graft technique are excellent exposure and more rapid resection of tissue, as well as nipple reduction, areola resizing, and repositioning. The disadvantages are the long residual scars, NAC pigmentary, and sensory changes, and the possibility of incomplete graft take.

Complications

The overall postoperative complication rate in our series—around 10%—is similar to that in most other series described in the literature. A hematoma was the most frequent complication. As one might expect, the frequency of hematoma decreases as one moves from the first periareolar technique to the extended concentric and free nipple graft technique in which wider access is provided. Some of the other complications were associated with hematoma: (partial) nipple necrosis and abscess formation. Drains and compression bandages did not necessarily prevent the occurrence of this troublesome complication. This underscores the importance of achieving good hemostasis intraoperatively. Smaller hematomas and seromas can be evacuated through puncture. However, in about half of the cases, surgical evacuation was required.

A significant complication includes simple skin slough of the NAC, which can be left to heal by conservative means. The exceptional cases of partial or total nipple necrosis may require a secondary nipple reconstruction.

Unlike Hage, we rarely planned a two-stage procedure. Nevertheless, despite a rather low complication rate, about one-third of patients required an additional procedure to improve the aesthetic results. The likelihood of an additional aesthetic correction should be discussed with the patient in advance (Beer et al. 2001).

Sometimes, the secondary procedure is performed as part of a planned two-stage event. In the first stage, the skin initially is left oversized to enable it to shrink fully without stretching the scars and areola. This may somewhat reduce the length of the ultimate scar (depending upon the elasticity of the skin). Obviously, the secondary procedure is always necessary.

Recommendations

For a breast with a small envelope and good skin elasticity, a semicircular technique is suitable. The same breast with an oversized nipple is well suited to a transareolar technique. The same breast with moderate to poor elasticity, or a breast having a larger envelope (cup B, grade 1 or 2 ptosis), will require a concentric circular technique. A moderate-sized breast (cup B–C, grade 1 or 2 ptosis) with poor skin elasticity will require an extended concentric circular technique. Finally, a large-volume breast (cup C or larger) with substantial skin excess and little or no skin elasticity will likely require a breast amputation with free nipple grafting. Inevitably, this involves more incisions and longer scars. However, when having to choose between scar and contour, we have noticed that the majority of our patients prefer a better contour above a shorter scar: for this reason we have performed many more free nipple graft technique SCMs in recent years.

It is important to note that there have been reports of breast cancer after bilateral SCM in this population (Burcombe et al. 2003; Secreto et al. 1984; Symmers 1968). Preservation of the NAC after SCM leaves behind insensate ductal tissue at risk for malignant transformation. Residual breast tissue persists even after the most radical prophylactic mastectomy, and a regular SCM never removes all glandular tissue. Although the precise causative role of androgens in breast cancer etiology is unclear, the association between high androgen levels and breast cancer risk is well documented. Apparently, high-circulating androgen in postmenopausal women may increase estrogens via peripheral aromatization of dihydroepiandrostenedione to estradiol and estrone in breast and adipose tissue. This prolonged and unopposed estrogenic stimulation could increase breast cancer. Additionally, family history of breast cancer may play a role in this scenario. Lifelong follow-up of these patients is, therefore, required.

Hysterectomy and Salpingo-Oophorectomy

Transpeople who are searching for information concerning their decisions to have reproductive organ surgery will only find anecdotal material on the internet and a limited amount of information, much of it conflicting, in the medical literature. They will not find any large study of transmen that addresses the subjective experience of hysterectomy, issues of postoperative hormone treatment, sexual satisfaction, or the potential for regret.

Kaiser et al. (2011) conclude that the vaginal hysterectomy with bilateral vaginal adnexectomy after performing a total colpectomy is the optimal choice for reassignment surgery. Other researchers state that a total laparoscopic hysterectomy also offers appropriate surgical outcomes and even is the method of choice for hysterectomy in transmen (O'Hanlan et al. 2007; Weyers et al. 2008). Laparotomy results in a stigmatizing (Pfannenstiel) incision and should be avoided. Laparotomy should only be performed on special indications due to relevant intra-abdominal morbidity or to solve surgical complications (Van Trotsenburg 2009). In a Dutch study conversion from laparoscopy to laparotomy was necessary in one patient (1/32; 3.1%), which was considered an adverse event. None of the patients required reoperation or readmission to hospital (Ott et al. 2010).

There is unanimity in the literature that adequate counseling on the topic of fertility preservation within a multidisciplinary team is very important. The irreversible nature of the surgery as well as its impact on reproduction should be emphasized. Transmen can consider oocyte or embryo cryopreservation (De Sutter 2009). However, more research is needed to enhance fertility options for transmen (Wierckx et al. 2012).

Phalloplasty

Introduction

The goals of a phalloplasty include reconstructing an aesthetically pleasing penis, with erogenous and tactile sensation, which enables the patient to void while standing and have sexual intercourse like a man, in a one-stage procedure (Gilbert et al. 1987; Hage et al. 1993). The reconstructive procedure should also provide a normal scrotum and be predictably reproducible without functional loss in the donor area, and leave the patient with minimal scarring or disfigurement.

Since the first penile reconstruction performed in 1936 by Bogoras with a tubed abdominal flap, the development of phalloplasty has paralleled the overall evolution and advances in plastic and reconstructive surgery. Historically, phallic reconstruction required complex multistage procedures using tubed skin flaps or pedicled myocutaneous flaps (Hoopes 1974; Horton 1973; Orticochea 1972). More recently, microsurgical techniques have allowed for the selection of distant flaps with the transfer of free vascularized tissue and the coaptation of nerves from the donor flap to recipient nerves in the perineum (Biemer 1988b; Chang & Hwang 1984; Hage & De Graaf 1993; Harashima et al. 1990; Gilbert et al. 1987; Koshima et al. 1986; Meyer & Daverio 1987; Sadove et al. 1993; Santanelli & Scuderi 2000; Upton et al. 1987). Despite the multitude of free flaps that have been employed and described (often as case reports), the radial forearm is universally considered the "gold standard" in penile reconstruction (Chang & Hwang 1984; Fang et al. 1999; Gilbert et al. 1987; Hage et al. 1993; Monstrey et al. 2009).

This chapter will describe to what degree the radial forearm flap has been able to meet the criteria for ideal penile reconstruction as well as provide an overview of the different other phalloplasty techniques.

Requirements for an Ideal Penile Reconstruction

According to Hage et al. (1993), to achieve the ideal phalloplasty one should aim for: (1) a one-stage procedure that can be predictably reproduced; (2) creation of a competent neourethra to allow for voiding while standing; (3) return of both tactile and erogenous sensibility; (4) enough bulk to tolerate the insertion of a prosthetic stiffener facilitating sexual intercourse; (5) an aesthetically pleasing phallus; (6) minimal morbidity; and (7) no functional loss and minimal scarring in the donor area.

A "One-Stage" Procedure

In our opinion genital reassignment surgery in transmen, which attempts to even partially meet the desired outcome, can never be achieved in a "one-stage" procedure. Genital surgery is usually performed 1 year after the patient underwent SCM and hysterectomy and BSO. For logistic reasons and to further reduce the complication rate, we nowadays even consider performing an SCM alone in a first operation, then a metoidioplasty (including vaginectomy and scrotoplasty) and only 6 months later a phalloplasty. Combining these procedures in an "all-in-one" procedure is inadvisable as it would result in lengthy operations (more than 10 hours) with considerable blood loss. In addition, early SCM greatly facilitates the real-life experience, which is required for genital reassignment surgery and is important to the patient. For implantation of testicular and/or erection prostheses, an additional operative procedure is required, usually 1 year after the phalloplasty. This delay is necessary to allow nerves to regenerate, as a return of sensation to the top of the phallus is essential to prevent implant complications.

Voiding While Standing

In 2009 a retrospective review of 287 radial forearm phalloplasties was performed at our center, showing that all patients were ultimately able to void while standing (Monstrey et al. 2009). Since that report about 300 more phalloplasties have been performed by the same team of surgeons with similar good (or even slightly better) results. This is in contrast to the results for patients who underwent other phalloplasty techniques (Baumeister et al. 2011; Felici & Felici 2006; Sengezer et al. 2004). For transmen seeking phalloplasty, the ability to void while standing is generally a high priority. However, many surgeons prefer no longer to reconstruct a neourethra because of the high incidence of urological complications.

In our first series urologic complications were seen in 41% of patients (119 of 287), with a fistula in 72, a stricture in 21, and a combination of both in 26. The majority of the fistulas (51 of 72) closed spontaneously, and many strictures (especially at the meatus) could be managed with dilatation. Although this complication rate may seem high, it is low in comparison to other reports (Biemer 1988; Davies & Matti 1988; Fang et al. 1999; Gilbert et al. 1987). In those cases where the fistula did not close spontaneously, a secondary procedure was required. It consisted of a simple closure of the fistula, and/or an open approach with longitudinal incisions closed transversely or, in the case of longer and recurrent strictures, local skin flaps. Since 2009 we have not performed a more recent review of our (about 300 additional) radial forearm phalloplasties, but we have the subjective feeling that the complication rate has been stable.

We have demonstrated that the long-term effects on urinary tract function are minimal after phalloplasty combined with reconstruction of the fixed part of the urethra (Hoebeke et al. 2003). However, it is unknown how the new urethra—a 16-cm skin tube—affects bladder function over the long term. Therefore, from a urological point of view, lifelong follow-up is always required. This underscores the importance of a close collaboration between the reconstructive surgeon and the urologist.

Tactile and Erogenous Sensation

The extent of the recovery of tactile and erogenous sensation in the reconstructed penis is crucial. Of the various donor flaps used for penile reconstruction, the forearm flap has the greatest sensitivity (Gilbert et al. 1987). The medial and lateral antebrachial nerves are easily identified at the beginning of the flap elevation, and dissected an additional 5 cm proximal to the skin paddle to facilitate the anastomosis to the nerves in the groin area. In all patients in our series, one forearm nerve was connected to the ilio-inguinal nerve for protective sensation, while the other antebrachial nerve was connected with one of the two dorsal clitoral nerves. The other clitoral dorsal nerve was left unharmed. The denuded clitoris was always left directly below the phallic shaft. Consequently, manipulation of the neophallus can further stimulate the still-innervated clitoris. This explains why several patients were able to masturbate a few months (or even weeks) after phalloplasty.

In a long-term follow-up study of our patients' sexual and physical health after sex reassignment surgery, more than 80% reported improvement in sexuality. Transmen reported masturbating significantly more often than transwomen and experiencing greater sexual satisfaction, more sexual excitement, and greater ease in reaching orgasm (De Cuypere et al. 2005).

Sexual Intercourse

When using skin flaps for penile reconstruction, a rigidity prosthesis is required in order to engage in sexual intercourse postoperatively. After phalloplasty and scrotoplasty the phallus is flaccid and the scrotum is empty (Hoebeke et al. 2010; Selvaggi et al. 2009). In order to make the new constructed genital look and function as natural as possible, scrotal and penile implants are needed (Hoebeke et al. 2003). Most often these implant procedures are the last stage of reconstruction, preferably 1 year after phalloplasty. At that time most urethral complications will be resolved, sensitivity will be installed, and vascular integration of the phallus will be maximal, decreasing the risk of vascular complications during implantation.

Obtaining rigidity after phalloplasty remains however a real challenge and many complications are reported (Hage et al. 1993; Hoebeke et al. 2010; Leriche et al. 2008).

Different possibilities are available to obtain rigidity. When the phallus is constructed by use of a fibular flap or a radial forearm flap, theoretically part of the fibula or the radius could be transplanted with the flap, thus allowing for rigidity. Unfortunately, the limited amount of bone that can be taken from the distal radius or fibula can never function as a real rigidity device, and the risk of donor site complications is greatly increased (Biemer 1988b; Cavadas 2008; Koshima et al. 1986). In addition, bone or cartilage grafts may absorb or render a pointed deformity to the distal part of the penis, where the extra skin can glide around the end of the bone. Moreover, a permanently erected phallus can be an embarrassment that cannot be easily concealed.

Some centers use two myocutaneous gracilis flaps for penile reconstruction in order to achieve some erectile function when contracting both muscles (S. Suominen personal communication).

Commercially available erectile implants have the advantage of being readily available in many formats, lengths, and sizes and their use in biological males has been very successful for survival and for quality of life of the patients after implantation.

One of the major complications while implanting an erectile device is infection. With antibiotic-impregnated prostheses the infection rate in large groups of biological males has been reduced to around 1% (Carson et al. 2011). However there is an important difference when comparing the implantation in biological males to implantation in a neophallus. In biological males the prosthesis is implanted in the corporal bodies which serve as extra protection against protrusion and in which some blood flow is preserved, enhancing the effect of the local antibiotics. In neophallus the prosthesis is implanted in fatty tissue with low blood supply and without corporal bodies to protect. Many authors describe ways to overcome the lack of corporal bodies by inserting the devices in either Gore-Tex (W.L. Gore and Associates, Newark, DE) or Dacron (DuPont, Wilmington, DE) covers. Furthermore these covers are used to anchor the prosthesis to the pubic bone (Garaffa et al. 2011).

Other options for rigidity are the use of external devices like silicone condoms which can be used over the phallus; however, no studies have been published on the use of these devices.

In our center we have a large experience with erectile devices. The strategies have changed with time based on experience.

In general we experienced that inflatable devices have a limited survival time. There are many reasons why they tend to fail more than the series that have been published in biological males. Biological males receive their implant to treat erectile dysfunction so in general they are older, have in general lower libido, and thus lower frequency of using their implants. Transmen are younger, receive testosterone, and in general have high libido, so they tend to use the prosthesis more often and of course much longer as they are younger. Next to the frequency of use there is also the unlimited space for expansion of the prosthesis as they are not contained in the corporal bodies.

Initially a one-piece hydraulic prosthesis (Dynaflex, AMS Minnetonka, Minnesota) fully covered with Dacron was used, usually in combination with two testicular prostheses. In that series we could see a high amount of leakage due to the rubbing of the silicone against the Dacron, causing wearing of the silicone sheath of the cylinder and leak (Hoebeke et al. 2003). When this implant became unavailable, we switched to the three-piece AMS CX prosthesis. In this device, the pump replaced one testicular prosthesis. Good results were initially reported with this three-piece prosthesis; however we encountered an increase in technical failure due to leakage, probably because there was no limit to the amount of fluid that can be pumped into the cylinders. In a three-piece system there is a reservoir containing 65 mL of saline. We therefore shifted to the two-piece device (Ambicor, AMS), a system that limits the amount of fluid available as the reservoir is integrated in the pump and thus contains less saline. With this two-piece system the initial results were good but after longer follow-up the problem of leakage and malposition was observed, as well as a problem of lack of rigidity. In a first long-term follow-up study, re-intervention in about one in four patients was observed. However, more than 80% of patients were able to have normal sexual intercourse with penetration (Hoebeke et al. 2003).

In an observational study on quality of sexual life it was observed that patients with erection prostheses were more able to attain their sexual expectations than those without prostheses, although the group with prostheses more often reported pain during intercourse (De Cuypere et al. 2005).

In 2010 we reported a longer follow-up on erectile implants. A total of 129 transmen implanted between March 1996 and October 2007 were evaluated. The mean follow-up was 30.2 months (range: 0–132 months). Dynaflex prosthesis was implanted initially in 9 patients, a three-piece hydraulic device (AMS CX or AMS CXM) in 50 patients, and a CX Inhibizone, Ambicor, and Coloplast/Mentor prosthesis in 17, 47, and 6 patients, respectively. Of 129 patients, 76 patients (58.9%) still had their original implant in place. Fifty-three patients (41.1%) needed to undergo either removal or revision of the prosthesis due to infection, erosion, dysfunction, or leak. Forty-one patients underwent a replacement of the prosthesis, 9 needed a second revision, 5 needed a third revision, and 1 patient needed a fourth revision of prosthesis. Malposition of prosthesis was corrected by surgical repositioning so that removal or revision could be avoided. Of 185 prostheses used in 129 patients, 108 (58.4%) still remain in place, with a total infection rate of 11.9%, a total protrusion rate of 8.1%, a total prosthesis leak rate of 9.2%, a total dysfunction rate of 13%, and a total malposition rate of 14.6% (Hoebeke et al. 2010).

With the last observation of higher complication rates with longer follow-up we started to propose the use of semi-rigid implants in transmen. We use a Spectra semi-rigid prosthesis (AMS Minitonka USA) in a Gore-Tex sleeve. This is a titanium-based prosthesis which has the advantage that it is concealed when bent downwards. The results of this prosthesis have not yet been evaluated but malfunction due to leakage is impossible with this device. We observed some infection problems and some malposition but in general it is our impression that the semi-rigid device is more durable.

An Aesthetically Pleasing Phallus and Scrotum

A plethora of techniques for penile reconstruction implies that none is yet considered to be ideal. Most surgeons agree that only microsurgical free-flap techniques lead to optimal functional and aesthetic results in phallic reconstruction (Chang & Hwang 1984; Fang et al. 1994; Gilbert et al. 1987;

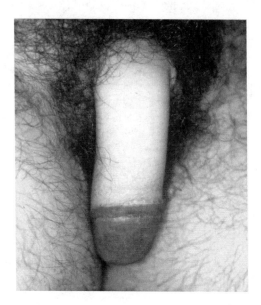

Figure 15.12 Late result after tattooing of the glans to imitate a circumcised penis.

Gottlieb & Levine 1993; Hage et al. 1993; Koshima et al. 1986; Sadove et al. 1993; Young et al. 1992).

The radial forearm flap, modified by Chang and Hwang (1984), has been widely accepted as the best donor site for penile reconstruction. It was used in up to 85% of the published phalloplasty cases.

The flap is thin and pliable, thus allowing the reconstruction of a tube (the urethra) within a tube (the penis). The flap is easy to dissect, is predictably well vascularized and, most uniquely, has easily identifiable sensory nerves. The ulnar aspect of the flap is often hairless and can, therefore, be used as a lining for the urethra. There have been many reports of other free flaps for phallic reconstruction: the lateral arm flap (Shenaq & Dinh 1989; Young et al. 1992), the deltoid flap (Harashima et al. 1990), the dorsal foot flap (Cheng et al. 1995), the parascapular flap (Liang personal communication), the anterolateral thigh (ALT) flap (Felici & Felici 2006), the fibular osteocutaneous flap (Sadove et al. 1993), and the tensor fasciae latae myocutaneous flap (Santanelli & Scuderi 2000), but none have gained wide acceptance.

To achieve an aesthetic phallic reconstruction, it is essential to perform a procedure that can be replicated with minimal complications. Features which increase the aesthetic aspect of the reconstructed penis are preoperative epilation of the forearm, reconstruction of a corona, and a glans of the penis, and tattooing of the glans (Figure 15.12).

The cosmetic outcome of a phalloplasty procedure with a radial forearm flap is a subjective determination, but the ability of most transmen to shower with other men or to go to the sauna naked is the usual cosmetic barometer. Another major aesthetic concern is the aspect of the grafted donor site on the forearm. These results might be related to a suprafascial dissection of the flap sparing the paratenon as well as advancing the skin edges after harvesting of the flap and putting extra attention towards obtaining a flat contour of the underlying muscle surface with careful graft placement to avoid additional wrinkling and scarring.

Drawbacks of the radial forearm flap are the need for rigidity prosthesis and the potential for the flap to become softer and shrink over time, resulting in loss of more than 20% in circumference. This seems to be related to an unexplained degree of atrophy of subcutaneous fat.

The goal of creating natural-appearing genitals also applies to the scrotum. As the labia majora are the embryological counterpart of the scrotum, many scrotoplasty techniques have used this hair-bearing skin. Previous approaches left the labia in situ, with midline closure and prosthetic implant filling, or brought the scrotum in front of the legs using a V-Y plasty. These techniques were aesthetically unappealing and reminiscent of the female genitalia.

Full-thickness skin grafts taken from the groin area have been used to cover the donor defect on the forearm, making the donor site somewhat better aesthetically, but the resulting additional tension after excision of these grafts made the reconstruction of a scrotum much more difficult. Several patients required a secondary expansion of the former labia majora before testicular prostheses could be implanted.

We employ a scrotoplasty technique, which combines a V-Y plasty with a 90° turning of the labial flaps. In this procedure, additional labial skin is transposed forward to enlarge an anteriorly located scrotum. Compared to the outcomes of the earlier procedures, the aesthetic results of this scrotoplasty are excellent (Figures 15.13 and 15.14). Erogenous sensation is increased by scrotoplasty and the recent refinement of preserving the clitoral hood. The functional advantage of fewer urological complications and easier implantation of testicular prostheses make this the technique of choice.

Testicular implants after phalloplasty do not differ from those used in biological males. Most often silicone gel-filled implants are used and they are available off the shelf in different sizes—small, medium, and large. The size used depends on the available space. If an inflatable erectile device is chosen there needs to be extra space for the pump of the erectile device. The pump often is large enough to fill one scrotal part, so most patients who choose an inflatable erectile device will need only one testicular prosthesis. With semi-rigid erectile devices two testicular prostheses will be implanted, one along the incision used for the erectile implant and one via a contralateral inguinal incision. An inguinal incision to place the testicular prosthesis is indeed preferred as the scrotum has often many scars related to the reconstruction, and reopening a scarred area increases the risk of wound infection and delayed or poor wound healing in general. Indeed, the risks of implantation of testicular prosthesis are infection and perforation. The space for the prosthesis is developed bluntly,

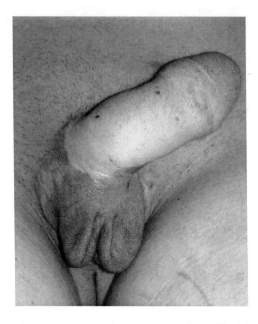

Figure 15.13 Scrotal reconstruction with transposition flaps of the labia before insertion of prostheses.

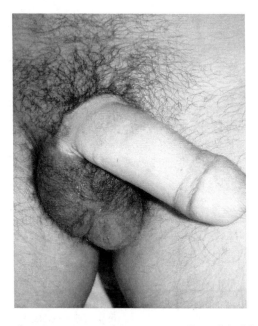

Figure 15.14 Scrotal reconstruction with transposition flaps of the labia after insertion of prostheses.

starting at the inguinal incision. Testicular implants can dislocate from their original position, especially if too large a size is chosen for the area. Capsule formation and retraction are rare but can happen.

There is only little published information on testicular implants in transmen. Some plastic surgeons tend to use tissue expanders in the labia majora in order to create space for implants (Sengezer & Sadove 1993). In the technique of scrotoplasty described by Selvaggi et al. (2009), the scrotal reconstruction aims at bringing the scrotum in front of the legs. When the labia are preserved in their anatomical position and just closed in the midline, then the patient will have problems with the testicular implants while sitting and the chance of dislocation of the implants will increase.

Minimal Morbidity

As in all cases of gender reassignment surgery, hormonal therapy was stopped 2–3 weeks prior to phalloplasty.

Complications following phalloplasty included the general complications attendant to any surgical intervention, such as bleeding, infection, and delayed wound healing. Vaginectomy, which is a particularly difficult operation, carries a potentially high risk of postoperative bleeding. In our series, revision for bleeding in the vaginal cavity was required in 3 patients. Fortunately, none of the patients in this series suffered a rectal perforation during the rather delicate vaginectomy procedure.

About 15% of patients needed additional dressings for minor wound-healing problems in the groin area. These problems were all resolved with conservative measures. Two early patients displayed symptoms of nerve compression in the lower leg, due to prolonged restraint in a gynecological lithotomy position. Subsequently, we limited the length of the restraint to under 2 hours, and this complication no longer occurred.

Apart from the urinary fistulas and stenoses which have been previously described, most complications of the radial forearm phalloplasty stem from the fact that the free vascularized tissue transfer necessitates a microsurgical connection of small blood vessels. Jacques Baudet (1997), an authority in this field, claimed that microvascular flap transfer in penile reconstruction involved more complications than did other free-flap transfers.

In our experience, surgical reintervention due to early vascular compromise of the flap was required in a rather high percentage of cases (12%). In one-third of patients, there was an arterial thrombosis; in two-thirds, a combination of both arterial and venous thrombosis. Treatment consisted of thrombectomy and the reconstruction of an arterial-venous fistula at the end of the penis by anastomosing the distal end of the radial artery to the cephalic vein to improve venous outflow. Still, the total flap failure in this series of radial forearm flap phalloplasties was surprisingly low, less than 1% ($n = 2/287$).

In contrast, about 7.5% of patients demonstrated a minor degree of skin slough or partial necrosis. This was often the case for those who insisted on a large-sized penis, which requires a larger flap, involving almost the entire circumference of the lower arm.

As in all cases of (free) flap failure, smoking was a significant risk factor. Under our present policy, patients who fail to quit smoking 1 year prior to surgery do not qualify for phalloplasty.

None of our patients demonstrated complications due to general anesthesia. Despite the fact that all patients received fractioned heparin subcutaneously, and elastic stockings were routinely used, 2 patients developed a (minor) pulmonary embolism.

No Functional Loss and Minimal Scarring in the Donor Area

Although the radial forearm flap is indeed the gold standard, the major drawback has always been the highly visible and unattractive donor site scar on the forearm (Figure 15.15). As seen in the treatment of burns, full-thickness skin grafts leave a more attractive scar, compared to split-thickness skin grafts. For this reason a full-thickness skin graft taken from the groin area was used in the first 50 patients in our series. However, due to consequential tension in the groin area, the reconstruction of the scrotum became more difficult. Therefore, we switched to split-thickness skin grafts taken from the anterior and medial thigh. Indeed, the average transman would prefer an aesthetically pleasing scrotum over a slightly less unattractive forearm donor site. For 6–12 months following radial forearm phalloplasty, the patient must wear a pressure garment and/or silicone on the forearm, as would a patient with a severe extremity burn.

We conducted a long-term follow-up study (Selvaggi et al. 2006) to assess the degree of functional loss and aesthetic impairment after harvesting a large radial forearm flap. (While small and moderately sized flaps are often used for head and neck reconstruction, in penile construction, the flap involves the complete circumference of the forearm, including all superficial nerves and veins.) Surprisingly, the rate of complications, ranging from hematoma to incomplete graft, was extremely low. We had expected increased morbidity, but we found that neither early nor late complications differed from the rates reported in the literature for smaller flaps. No major or long-term problems (such as functional limitation, chronic pain, cold intolerance, or evidence of vascular compromise) were identified.

With regard to the aesthetic outcome of the donor site, we found that the patients were very accepting of the donor site scar, viewing it as a worthwhile trade-off for the creation of a phallus.

The Radial Forearm Flap

At the University Hospital of Ghent, Belgium, the same team of surgeons has performed phallic reconstruction using a radial forearm flap on more than 600 consecutive transmen. The following section will describe our current

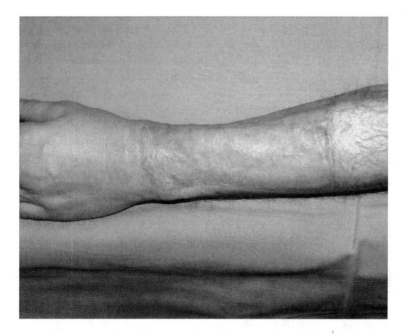

Figure 15.15 Aspect of the donor site on the arm after a phalloplasty procedure.

technique and the refinements we have introduced to improve the results, both functionally and cosmetically.

Two surgical teams operate at the same time, and the patient is first placed in a gynecological position. In the perineal area, the urologist performs a vaginectomy, and lengthens the urethra with mucosa between the minor labiae. The vaginectomy is a mucosal culpectomy in which the mucosal lining of the vaginal cavity is removed. After excision, a pelvic floor reconstruction is always performed to prevent possible later conditions such as cystocele or rectocele. The levator ani muscle is reconstructed, as in a colporrhaphy. This reconstruction of the fixed part of the urethra is combined with a scrotal reconstruction by means of two transposition flaps of the greater labia, resulting in a very natural-looking bifid scrotum (Selvaggi et al. 2009).

Simultaneously, the plastic surgeon dissects the free vascularized flap of the forearm (Figures 15.16 and 15.17). The creation of a phallus with a tube-in-a-tube technique is performed with the flap still attached to the forearm by its vascular pedicle (Figure 15.18). A small skin flap and a skin graft are used to create a corona and simulate the glans of the penis (Figure 15.19).

Once the urethra is lengthened and the vessels are dissected in the groin area, the patient is put into a supine position. The free flap can be transferred to the pubic area after the urethral anastomosis. Usually, the radial artery is microsurgically connected to the common femoral artery in an end-to-side fashion.

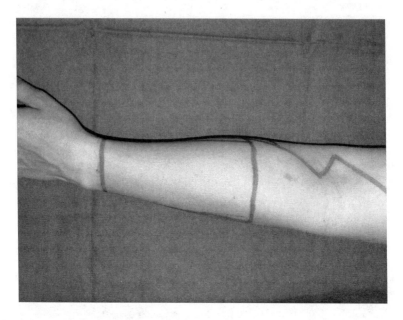

Figure 15.16 Phalloplasty with a radial forearm flap: design of the flap on the forearm.

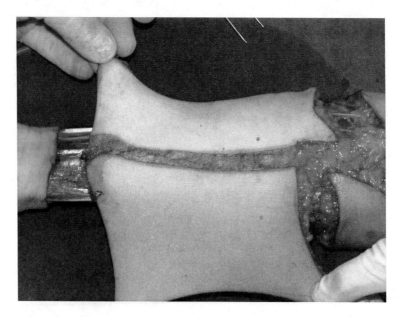

Figure 15.17 Phalloplasty with a radial forearm flap: urethral (longer) and penile part of the forearm flap are dissected.

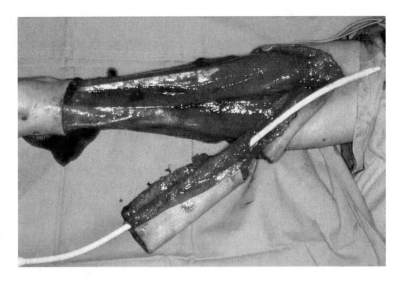

Figure 15.18 Phalloplasty with a radial forearm flap: creation of a urethral tube within a penile tube.

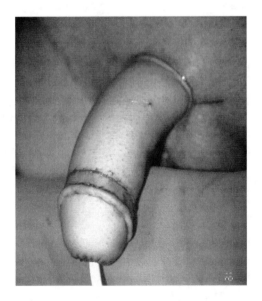

Figure 15.19 Phalloplasty with a radial forearm flap: immediate postoperative results.

The venous anastomosis is performed between the cephalic vein and the greater saphenous vein. One forearm nerve is connected to the ilio-inguinal nerve for protective sensation and the other nerve of the arm is anastomosed to one of the dorsal clitoral nerves for erogenous sensation. The clitoris is usually denuded and buried underneath the penis, thus keeping the opportunity to be stimulated during sexual intercourse with the neophallus.

The defect on the forearm is covered with split-thickness skin grafts harvested from the medial and anterior thigh.

All patients receive a suprapubic urinary diversion postoperatively. The patients remain in bed for a 1-week postoperative period, after which the transurethral catheter is removed. At that time, the suprapubic catheter is clamped, and voiding is begun. Effective voiding may not be observed for several days. Before removal of the suprapubic catheter, a bladder scan is performed after voiding to make sure there is no residue.

The average hospital stay for the phalloplasty procedure is 2½ weeks. Tattooing of the glans can be performed after a 2–3-month period, before sensation returns to the penis (Figure 15.12).

Implantation of the testicular prostheses can be performed after 6 months, but it is typically done in combination with the implantation of penile erection prosthesis. Before these procedures are undertaken, sensation must have returned to the top of the penis. This usually does not occur for at least a year.

Pedicled Anterolateral Thigh Flap

Although the radial forearm flap is considered as the "gold standard" in penile reconstruction, the major drawback remains the wide circumferential scar on the forearm which, for transsexual individuals, can be pathognomic for their condition. We currently consider the ALT flap as the best alternative for patients who want to avoid a scar on the forearm (Figures 15.20 and 15.21). The ALT flap is a skin flap based on a perforator from the descending branch of the lateral circumflex femoral artery, which is a branch from the femoral artery. This flap has been used both as a free flap (Felici 2005) and as a pedicled flap (Ceulemans 2005).

The donor site is less conspicuous as it can be hidden underneath short pants and secondary corrections at that site are easier to make. In order to make the donor scar even less visible, tissue expanders can be used on both sides of the flap design prior to the phalloplasty procedure, enabling primary closure after harvesting the flap. However, since the ALT flap is not as thin or pliable as the radial forearm flap, a tube-within-a-tube construction is not possible. Therefore, a second flap is usually required for urethral reconstruction.

There are five options for urethral reconstruction:

1. a tube-within-a-tube technique (only to be used in extremely thin patients);
2. a pedicled groin or superficial circumflex iliac artery perforator flap (donor area can be closed primarily) (Figures 15.20 and 15.21);

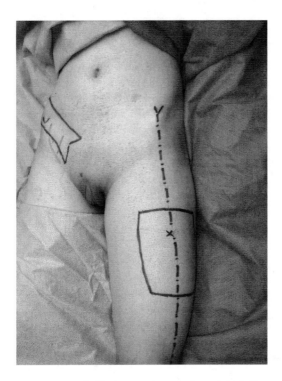

Figure 15.20 Phalloplasty with anterolateral thigh flap and superficial circumflex iliac artery perforator/groin flap: preoperative view.

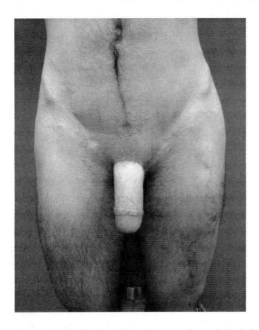

Figure 15.21 Phalloplasty with anterolateral thigh flap and superficial circumflex iliac artery perforator/groin flap: postoperative view.

3. a small radial forearm flap (leaving a scar only on the inner, less exposed side of the forearm);
4. a prefabricated flap, using a skin graft on the inner site of the ALT, which then can be tubed and covered by the ALT flap as an outer tube;
5. tubed tissue of a previous, not functional phalloplasty.

Surgical Technique

Perforators are located using a preoperative angiocomputed tomography. They are usually located within a 3-cm radius circle at the midpoint of the line from the superior iliac spine to the lateral side of the patella. The flap is designed around these perforator vessels. After harvesting, the flap is tunneled underneath the rectus femoris muscle and transferred to the pubic area. The lateral femoral cutaneous nerve is transected after the flap has been harvested and reanastomosed to the clitoral/penile nerve and the ilio-inguinal nerve. The ALT flap is subsequently wrapped around the reconstructed urethra. The donor site of the ALT flap is closed with split-thickness skin grafts.

Alternative Techniques

Metoidioplasty

Metoidioplasty uses the clitoris to reconstruct the microphallus in a way that is comparable to the correction of chordee and lengthening of the urethra in a male pseudohermaphrodite, or in cases of severe hypospadias. Eicher (1989) prefers to call this intervention "the clitoris penoid." Care must be taken to avoid injury to the internal erectile tissues during removal of the fibrous bands, so as not to lose that important function.

In metoidioplasty, the clitoral hood is lifted and the suspensory ligament of the clitoris is detached from the pubic bone, allowing the clitoris to extend out further. When the tissues have been primed with testosterone, the clitoral head begins to resemble an adolescent glans penis. An embryonic urethral plate is divided from the underside of the clitoris to permit outward extension and a visible erection. The more developed the clitoris, the better the outcome of the metoidioplasty.

During metoidioplasty, the urethra is advanced to the tip of the new penis (Figure 15.22). This technique is very similar to the reconstruction of the horizontal part of the urethra in a normal phalloplasty procedure. Overweight patients may achieve greater length with pubic lipectomy, which will recess the body surface line.

During this same procedure, we usually perform a scrotal reconstruction, with a transposition flap of the labia majora (as previously described). In our hospital, this surgical intervention is also combined with a vaginectomy.

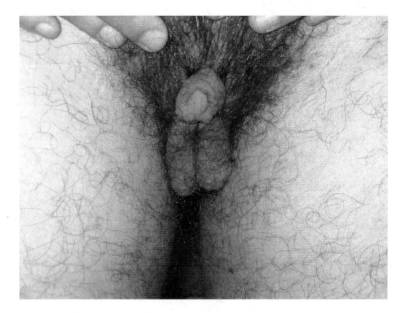

Figure 15.22 Result of a metoidioplasty procedure.

Transmen interested in this procedure should be informed preoperatively that voiding while standing cannot be guaranteed, and sexual intercourse will not be possible.

The major advantage of metoidioplasty is the complete lack of scarring outside the genital area. Another advantage is that its cost is substantially lower than that of phalloplasty. Therefore, many patients opt for this procedure. Complications of a metoidioplasty may include urethral obstruction and/or urethral fistula.

It is always possible to perform a regular phalloplasty (e.g., with a radial forearm flap) at a later stage, and with substantially less risk of complications and operation time.

Fibular Flap

There have been several reports on penile reconstruction with the fibular flap based on the peroneal artery and the peroneal vein (Hage et al. 1996; Sadove et al. 1993). This consists of a piece of fibula which is vascularized by its periosteal blood supply and connected through perforating vessels to an overlying skin island at the lateral site of the lower leg. The advantage of the fibular flap is that it makes sexual intercourse possible without a penile prosthesis. The disadvantages are a pointed deformity to the distal part of the penis where the extra skin can glide around the end of fibular bone, and that a permanently erected phallus is impractical. However, there have also been some reports on the use of a fibular flap without bone to reconstruct a penis (D'Arpa personal communication; Schaff & Papadopulos 2009).

Many authors seem to agree that the fibular osteocutaneous flap is an optimal solution for penile reconstruction in a natal male (Sengezer et al. 2004).

Other Perforator Flaps

Other perforator flaps than the ALT flap include the thoraco-dorsal perforator artery flap and the deep inferior epigastric perforator artery flap. The latter might be an especially good solution for transmen who have been pregnant in the past. Using the perforator flap as a pedicled flap can be very attractive, both financially and technically.

External Prosthesis

For transmen who do not want any donor site morbidity, an external penile prosthesis can be a good alternative (Selvaggi et al. 2015). Although an external prosthesis has no functional benefit for voiding or sensation, it can result in a very satisfying aesthetic result.

The Future

Animal studies have shown the potential implementation of tissue engineering for penile reconstruction. Bioengineered tissue has been used for penile reconstruction in rabbits, who subsequently were able to successfully impregnate females (Chen et al. 2010; Yoo et al. 1999). Kim et al. (2002) suggest the future use of tissue-engineered human cartilage rods as penile prostheses.

Zhang et al. (2015) reported their experience with the use of vaginal mucosa in prefabricating the urethra in penile reconstruction. Due to its histological similarities, the vaginal mucosa can be a good substitute material for urethral reconstruction in total phalloplasty. Further research on this topic is necessary.

The Importance of a Multidisciplinary Approach

Gender reassignment, particularly reassignment surgery, requires close cooperation between the different surgical specialties. In phalloplasty, collaboration between the plastic surgeon, the urologist, and the gynecologist is essential (Monstrey et al. 2001). In the long term, the urologist's role may be the most important one for patients who have undergone penile reconstruction, especially because the complication rate is rather high, particularly with regard to the number of urinary fistulas and urinary stenoses. The urologist also reconstructs the fixed part of the urethra, and is likely the best choice for implantation of the penile and/or testicular prostheses. Later, the urologist must also address sequelae, including stone formation. The surgical complexity of adding an elongated conduit (skin tube urethra) to a biological female bladder, and the long-term effects of evacuating urine through this skin tube, demand lifelong urological follow-up.

It bears repeating that the experience and skill of the surgeon who performs the erection prosthesis account for the resultant adequacy of sexual intercourse in more than 80% of cases (Hoebeke et al. 2003). Long-term follow-up is an absolute requirement, as the prosthesis is often implanted in a relatively young patient.

Therefore, professionals who unite for the purpose of creating a gender reassignment program should be aware of the necessity for a strong alliance between the plastic surgeon, the urologist, and the gynecologist. In turn, the surgeons must commit to the extended care of this unique population, which, by definition, will protract well into the future.

References

Baudet, J. (1997). Personal Communication. 24th Alpine Workshop on Plastic and Reconstructive Surgery, Arabba, Italy.

Baumeister, S., Sohn, M., Domke, C., & Exner, K. (2011). Phalloplasty in Female-to-male Transsexuals: Experience from 259 Cases. *Handchir. Mikrochir. Plast. Chir.* 43(4): 215–221.

Beckenstein, M.S., Windle, B.H, & Stroup, R.T. Jr. (1996). Anatomical Parameters for Nipple Position and Areolar Diameter in Males. *Ann. Plast. Surg.* 36(1): 33–36.

Beer, G.M., Budi, S., Seifert, B., Morgenthaler, W, Infanger, M., & Meyer, V. (2001). Configuration and Localization of the Nipple–areola Complex in Man. *Plast. Reconstr. Surg.* 108(7): 1947–1953.

Biber, S.H. (1979). A Method for Constructing the Penis and Scrotum. Presented at the VIth International Symposium on Gender Dysphoria, San Diego.

Biemer, E. (1988a). Bedeutung und Fortschritte der chirurgischen Geslechtsumwandlung. *Münich Med. Wochenschr.* 130: 480–482.

Biemer, E. (1988b). Penile Construction by the Radial Arm Flap. *Clin. Plast. Surg.* 15(3): 425–430.

Bogoras, N. (1936). Über die volle plastische Wiederherstellung eines zum Koitus fähigen Penis (Peniplastica totalis). *Zentralbl. Chir.* 22: 1271–1276.

Bouman, W.P., Richards, C., Addinall, R.M., Arango de Montis, I., Duisin, D., Esteva, I., et al. (2014). Yes and Yes Again: Are Standards of Care Which Require two Referrals for Genital Reconstructive Surgery Ethical? *Sex. Relat. Ther.* 29: 377–389.

Burcombe, R.J., Makris, A., Pittam, M., & Finer, N. (2003). Breast Cancer after Bilateral Subcutaneous Mastectomy in a Female-to-Male Transsexual. *The Breast* 12: 290–293.

Carson, C.C., 3rd, Mulcahy, J.J., & Harsch, M.R. (2011). Long-term Infection Outcomes After Original Antibiotic Impregnated Inflatable Penile Prosthesis Implants: Up to 7.7 Years of Followup. *J. Urol.* 185(2): 614–618.

Cavadas, P.C. (2008). Secondary Free Fibular Flap for Providing Rigidity in a Radial Forearm Phalloplasty. *Plast Reconstr Surg* 122(2): 101e–102e.

Ceulemans, P. (2005). *The Pedicled Antero-lateral Thigh (ALT) Perforator Flap: A New Technique for Phallic Reconstruction.* XIX Biennial Symposium of the Harry Benjamin International Gender Dysphoria (HBIGDA) Association, Bologna, Italy, April 2005.

Chang, T.S., & Hwang, W.Y. (1984). Forearm Flap in One-stage Reconstruction of the Penis. *Plast. Reconstr. Surg.* 74(2): 251–258.

Chen, K.L., Eberli, D., Yoo, J.J., & Atala, A. (2010). Bioengineered Corporal Tissue for Structural and Functional Restoration of the Penis. *Proc. Natl Acad. Sci. U. S. A.* 107(8): 3346–3350.

Cheng, K.X., Hwang, W.Y., Eid, A.E., Wang, S.L., Chang, T.S., & Fu, K.D. (1995). Analysis of 136 Cases of Reconstructed Penis Using Various Methods. *Plast. Reconstr. Surg.* 95(6): 1070–1080.

Coleman, E., Bockting, W., Botzer, M., et al. (2012). Standards of Care for the Health of Transsexual, Transgender, and Gender-Nonconforming People, Version 7. *Int. J. Transgenderism* 13(4): 165–232.

Davidson, B.A. (1979). Concentric Circle Operation for Massive Gynecomastia to Excise the Redundant Skin. *Plast. Reconstr. Surg.* 63(3): 350–354.

Davies, D.M., & Matti, B.A. (1988). A Method of Phalloplasty using the Deep Inferior Epigastric Flap. *Br. J. Plast. Surg.* 41: 165–168.

De Cuypere, G., T'Sjoen, G., Beerten, R., Selvaggi, G., De Sutter, P., Hoebeke, P., Monstrey, S., Vansteenwegen, A., & Rubens, R. (2005). Sexual and Physical Health after Sex Reassignment Surgery. *Arch. Sex. Behav.* 36(6): 679–690.

De Sutter, P. (2009). Reproductive Options for Transpeople: Recommendations for Revision of the WPATH's Standards of Care. *Int. J. Transgenderism* 11: 183–185.

Dolsky, R.L. (1990). Gynecomastia. Treatment by Liposuction Subcutaneous Mastectomy. *Dermatol. Clin.* 8(3): 469–478.

Edgerton, M.T. (1984). The Role of Surgery in the Treatment of Transsexualism. *Ann. Plast. Surg.* 13(6): 473–476.

Eicher, W. (1989). Surgical Treatment of Female-to-Male Transsexuals. In Eicher, W. (Ed.), *Plastic Surgery in the Sexually Handicapped*. Berlin: Springer, pp. 106–112.

Eicher, W. (1992). *Transsexualismus*. Stuttgart: Fisher Verlag, pp. 120–123.

Exner, K. (1992). Penile Reconstruction in Female-to-Male Transsexualism: A New Method of Phalloplasty. Xth International Congress on Plastic and Reconstructive Surgery, Madrid, 1992.

Fang, R.H., Lin, J.T., & Ma, S. (1994). Phalloplasty for Female Transsexuals with Sensate Free Forearm Flap. *Microsurgery* 15: 349–352.

Fang, R.H., Kao, Y.S., Ma, S., & Lin, J.T. (1999). Phalloplasty in Female-toMale Transsexuals using Free Radial Osteocutaneous Flap: A Series of 22 Cases. *Br. J. Plast. Surg.* 52(3): 217–222.

Felici, N. (2005). Phalloplasty with Free Anterolateral Thigh Flap. XIX Biennial Symposium of the Harry Benjamin International Gender Dysphoria (HBIGDA) Association, Bologna, Italy, April 2005.

Felici, N., & Felici, A. (2006). A New Phalloplasty Technique: The Free Anterolateral Thigh Flap Phalloplasty. *J. Plast. Reconstr. Aesth. Surg.* 59: 153–157.

Garaffa, G., Raheem, A.A., & Ralph, D.J. (2011). Penile Fracture and Penile Reconstruction. *Curr. Urol. Rep.* 12(6): 427–431.

Gilbert, D.A., Horton, C.E., Terzis, J.K., Devine, C.J. Jr., Winslow, B.H., & Devine, P.C. (1987). New Concept in Phallic Reconstruction. *Ann. Plast. Surg.* 18(2): 128–136.

Gilbert, D.A., Winslow, B.H., Gilbert, D.M., Jordan, G.H., & Horton, C.E. (1988). Transsexual Surgery in the Genetic Female. *Clin. Plast. Surg.* 15(3): 471–487.

Gillies, H., & Millard, D.R. Jr. (1957). *The Principles and Art of Plastic Surgery*, Vol. 2. London: Butterworth, pp. 368–384.

Gottlieb, L.J., & Levine, L.A. (1993). A New Design for the Radial Forearm Free Flap Phallic Reconstruction. *Plast. Reconstr. Surg.* 92(2): 276–284.

Hage, J.J., & Bloem, J.J. (1995). Chest Wall Contouring for Female-to-Male Transsexuals: Amsterdam Experience. *Ann. Plast. Surg.* 34(1): 59–66.

Hage, J.J., & De Graaf, F.H. (1993). Addressing the Ideal Requirements by Free Flap Phalloplasty: Some Reflections on Refinements of Technique. *Microsurgery* 14: 592–598.

Hage, J.J., & Kesteren, P.J.M. (1995). Chest-wall Contouring in Female-to-Male Transsexuals: Basic Considerations and Review of the Literature. *Plast. Reconstr. Surg.* 96(2): 386–391.

Hage, J.J., Bouman, F.G., de Graaf, F.H., & Bloem, J.J. (1993). Construction of the Neophallus in Female-to-Male Transsexuals: The Amsterdam Experience. *J. Urol.* 6: 1463–1468.

Hage, J.J., Winters, H.A., & Van Lieshout, J. (1996). Fibula Free Flap Phalloplasty: Modifications and Recommendations. *Microsurgery* 17: 358–365.

Harashima, T., Ionque, T., Tanaka, I., Imai, K., & Hatoko, M. (1990). Reconstruction of Penis with Free Deltoid Flap. *Br. J. Plast. Surg.* 43: 217–222.

Hester, T.R. Jr., Nahain, F., Beeglen, P.E., & Bostwick, J. III. (1984). Blood Supply of the Abdomen Revisited, with Emphasis on the Superficial Inferior Epigastric Artery. *Plast. Reconstr. Surg.* 74(5): 657–666.

Hoebeke, P., De Cuypere, G., Ceulemans, P., & Monstrey, S. (2003). Obtaining Rigidity in Total Phalloplasty: Experience with 35 Patients. *J. Urol.* 169: 221–223.

Hoebeke, P.B., Decaestecker, K., Beysens, M., Opdenakker, Y., Lumen, N., & Monstrey, S.M. (2010) Erectile Implants in Female-to-male Transsexuals: Our Experience in 129 Patients. *Eur. Urol.* 57(2):334–340.

Hoopes, J.E. (1974). Surgical Construction of the Male External Genitalia. *Clin. Plast. Surg.* 1(2): 325–334.

Horton, C.E. (1973). *Plastic and Reconstructive Surgery of the Genital Area.* Boston, MA: Little, Brown, pp. 117–161.

Horton, C.E., McCraw, J.B., Devine, C.J. Jr., & Devine, P.C. (1977). Secondary Reconstruction of the Genital Area. *Urol. Clin. N. Am.* 4: 133–141.

Kaiser, C., Stoll, I., Ataseven, B., Morath, S., Schaff, J., & Eiermann, W. (2011). Vaginal Hysterectomy and Bilateral Adnexectomy for Female-to-male Transsexuals in an Interdisciplinary Concept. *Handchir. Mikrochir. Plast. Chir.* 43: 240–245.

Kenney, J.G., & Edgerton, M.T. (1989). Reduction Mammoplasty in Gender Dysphoria. In Billowitz, A. (Ed.), *Abstract Book of the 11th Symposium of the Harry Benjamin International Gender Dysphoria Association.* Cleveland, Ohio, 1989.

Kim, B.S., Yoo, J.J., & Atala, A. (2002). Engineering of Human Cartilage Rods: Potential Application for Penile Prostheses. *J. Urol.* 168(4 Pt 2):1794–1797.

Kluzak, R. (1968). Sex Conversion Operation in Female Transsexualism. *Acta Chir. Plast.* 10: 188.

Koshima, I., Tai, T., & Yamasaki, M. (1986). One-stage Reconstruction of the Penis Using an Innervated Radial Forearm Osteocutaneous Flap. *J. Reconstr. Microsurg.* 3: 19–26.

Laub, D.R., Eicher, W., Laub, D.R. II, & Hentz, V.R. (1989). Penis Construction in Female-to-Male Transsexuals. In Eicher, W. (Ed.), *Plastic Surgery in the Sexually Handicapped.* Berlin, MA: Springer, pp. 113–128.

Leriche, A., Timsit, M.O., Morel-Journel, N., Bouillot, A., Dembele, D., & Ruffion, A. (2008). Long-term Outcome of Forearm Free-flap Phalloplasty in the Treatment of Transsexualism. *BJU Int.* 101(10): 1297–1300.

Letterman, G., & Schurter, M. (1972). Surgical Correction of Massive Gynecomastia. *Plast. Reconstr. Surg.* 49(3): 259–262.

Lindsay, W.R.N. (1979). Creation of a Male Chest in Female Transsexuals. *Ann. Plast. Surg.* 3(1): 39.

Maltz, M. (1946). Maltz Reparative Technic for the Penis. In Maltz, M. (Ed.), *Evolution of Plastic Surgery.* New York: Froben Press, pp. 278–279.

McGregor, I.A., & Jackson, I.T. (1972). The Groin Flap. *Br. J. Plast. Surg.* 25: 3–16.

McIndoe, A. (1948). Deformities of the Male Urethra. *Br. J. Plast. Surg*, 1, 29–47.

Meyer, R., & Daverio, P.J. (1987). One-stage Phalloplasty without Sensory Deprivation in Female Transsexuals. *World J. Urol.* 5: 9–13.

Monstrey, S., Hoebeke, P., Dhont, M., De Cuypere, G., Rubens, R., Moerman, M., Hamdi, M., Van Landuyt, K., & Blondeel, P.H. (2001). Surgical Therapy in Transsexual Patients: A Multidisciplinary Approach. *Acta Chir. Belg.* 101: 200–209.

Monstrey, S., Selvaggi, G., Ceulemans, P., Van Landuyt, K., Bowman, C., Blondeel, P., Hamdi, M., & De Cuypere, G. (2008). Chest-wall Contouring Surgery in Female-to-male Transsexuals: A New Algorithm. *Plast. Reconstr. Surg.* 121(3): 849–859.

Monstrey, S., Hoebeke, P., Selvaggi, G., Ceulemans, P., Van Landuyt, K., Blondeel, P., Hamdi, M., Roche, N., Weyers, S., & De Cuypere, G. (2009). Penile Reconstruction: Is the Radial Forearm Flap Really the Standard Technique? *Plast. Reconstr. Surg.* 124(2): 510–518.

O'Hanlan, K.A., Dibble, S.L., & Young-Spint, M. (2007). Total Laparoscopic Hysterectomy for Female-to-male Transsexuals. *Obstet. Gynecol.* 110: 1096–1101.

Orticochea, M. (1972). A New Method of Total Reconstruction of the Penis. *Br. J. Plast. Surg.* 25: 347–366.

Ott, J., van Trotsenburg, M., Kaufmann, U., Schrögendorfer, K., Haslik, W., Huber, J.C., & Wenzl, R. (2010). Combined hysterectomy/salpingo-oophorectomy and mastectomy is a safe and valuable procedure for female-to-male transsexuals. *J. Sex. Med.* 7, 2130–2138.

Ousterhout, D.K. (2011). Dr. Paul Tessier and Facial Skeletal Masculinization. *Ann. Plast. Surg.* 67: S10–S15.

Pitanguy, I. (1966). Transareolar Incision for Gynecomastia. *Plast. Reconstr. Surg.* 38(5): 414–419.

Rachlin, K., Hansbury, G., & Pardo, S.T. (2010). Hysterectomy and Oophorectomy Experiences of Female-to-Male Transgender Individuals. *Int. J. Transgenderism* 12, 155–166.

Sadove, R.C., Sengezer, M., McRobert, J.W., & Wells, M.D. (1993). One-stage Total Penile Reconstruction with a Free Sensate Osteocutaneous Fibula Flap. *Plast. Reconstr. Surg.* 92(7): 1314–1325.

Santanelli, F., & Scuderi, N. (2000). Neophalloplasty in Female-to-Male Transsexuals with the Island Tensor Fascia Lata Flap. *Plast. Reconstr. Surg.* 105(6): 1990–1996.

Schaff, J., & Papadopulos, N.A. (2009). A New Protocol for Complete Phalloplasty with Free Sensate and Prelaminated Osteofasciocutaneous Flaps: Experience in 37 Patients. *Microsurgery* 29(5): 413–419.

Secreto, G. et al. (1984). Increased Androgenic Activity and Breast Cancer Risk in Premenopausal Women. *Cancer* 44(12–1): 5902–5905.

Selvaggi, G., Monstrey, S., Hoebeke, P., Ceulemans, P., Van Landuyt, K., Hamdi, M., Cameron, B., & Blondeel, P. (2006). The Donor Site Morbidity of the Radial Forearm Free Flap after 125 Phalloplasties in Gender Identity Disorder. *Plast. Reconstr. Surg.* 118(5): 1171–1177.

Selvaggi, G., Hoebeke, P., Ceulemans, P., Hamdi, M., Van Landuyt, K., Blondeel, P., De Cuypere, G., & Monstrey, S. (2009). Scrotal Reconstruction in Female-to-male Transsexuals: A Novel Scrotoplasty. *Plast. Reconstr. Surg.* 123(6): 1710–1718.

Selvaggi, G., Branemark, R., Elander, A., Liden, M., & Stalfors, J. (2015). Titanium-bone-anchored Penile Epithesis: Preoperative Planning and Immediate Postoperative Results. *J. Plast. Surg. Hand Surg.* 49(1): 40–44.

Sengezer, M., & Sadove, R.C. (1993). Scrotal Construction by Expansion of Labia Majora in Biological Female Transsexuals. *Ann. Plast. Surg.*31(4): 372–376.

Sengezer, M., Ozturk, S., Deveci, M., & Odabasi, Z. (2004). Long-term Follow-up of Total Penile Reconstruction with Sensate Osteocutaneous Free Fibula Flap in 18 Biological Male Patients. *Plast. Reconstr. Surg.* 114(2): 439–450.

Shenaq, S.M., & Dinh, T.A. (1989). Total Penile and Urethral Reconstruction with an Expanded Sensate Lateral Arm Flap: Case Report. *J. Reconstr. Microsurg.* 5: 245.

Simon, B.E., & Hoffman, S. (1976). Correction of the Gynecomastia. In Goldwyn, R.M. (Ed.), *Plastic and Reconstructive Surgery of the Breast*. Boston, MA: Little Brown, pp. 305–327.

Snyder, C.C., & Browne, E.Z. Jr. (1977). Intersex Problems and Hermaphroditism. In Converse, J.M. (Ed.), *Reconstructive Plastic Surgery*, 2nd ed. Philadelphia, PA: Saunders, pp. 3941–3949.

Song, R., Gao, Y., Song, Y., Yu, Y., & Song, Y. (1982). The Forearm Flap. *Clin. Plast. Surg.* 9(1): 21–26.

Symmers, W.S. (1968). Carcinoma of Breast in Transsexual Individuals after Surgical and Hormonal Interference with the Primary and Secondary Sex Characteristics. *Br. Med. J.* 2(597): 82–85.

Upton, J., Mutimer, K.L., Loughlin, K., & Richtie, J. (1987). Penile Reconstruction Using the Lateral Arm Flap. *J. R. Coll. Surg. Edinb.* 32: 97.

Van Trotsenburg, M.A.A. (2009). Gynecological Aspects of Transgender Healthcare. Special Issue: Toward Version 7 of the World Professional Association for Transgender Health's Standards of Care: Medical and Therapeutic Approaches to Treatment. *Int. J. Transgenderism* 11: 238–246.

Webster, J.P. (1946). Mastectomy for Gynecomastia Through a Semicircular Intraareolar Incision. *Ann. Surg.* 124: 557.

Weiss, E., & Green, J. (2014). Transgender Patients' Care. *Am. J. Obstet. Gynecol.* 211: 185–186.

Weyers, S., Monstrey, S., Hoebeke, P., De Cuypere, G., & Gerris, J. (2008). Laparoscopic Hysterectomy as the Method of Choice for Hysterectomy in Female-to-male Gender Dysphoric Individuals. *Gynecol. Surg.* 5: 269–273.

Wierckx, K., Van Caenegem, E., Pennings, G., Elaut, E., Dedecker, D., Van de Peer, F., Weyers, S., De Sutter, P., & T'Sjoen, G. (2012). Reproductive Wish in Transsexual Men. *Hum. Reprod.* 27, 483–487.

Yerkea, A. F., & Mitchella, V. (2011). Am I Man Enough Yet? A Comparison of the Body Transition, Self-Labeling, and Sexual Orientation of Two Cohorts of Female-to-Male Transsexuals. *Int. J. Transgenderism* 13: 64–76.

Yoo, J.J., Park, H.J., Lee, I., & Atala, A. (1999). Autologous Engineered Cartilage Rods for Penile Reconstruction. *J. Urol.* 162(3 Pt2): 1119–1121.

Young, V.L., Khouri, R.K., & Lee, G.W. (1992). Advances in Total Phalloplasty and Urethroplasty with Microvascular Free Flaps. *Clin. Plast. Surg.* 19(4): 927–938.

Zhang, Y.F., Liu, C.Y., Qu, C.Y., Lu, L.X., Liu, A.T., Zhu, L., Wang H., Lin, Z.H., Zhao, Y.Z., Zhu, X.H., & Hua-Jiang. (2015). Is Vaginal Mucosal Graft the Excellent Substitute Material for Urethral Reconstruction in Female-to-male Transsexuals? *World J. Urol.* 33(12): 2115–2123.

16 Understanding Sexual Health and HIV in the Transgender Population

Kevan Wylie and James Woodcock

What is Sexual Health?

Sexual health is a broad concept, and can be thought of as a "state of physical, emotional, mental, and social well-being in relation to sexuality" and not just "the absence of disease, dysfunction, or infirmity" (WHO 2006). The report by the World Health Organization (WHO) details the complex nature of sexual health, and the influence of both sexuality and gender identity on an individual's sexual health. As shown by Melendez and Pinto (2007), sexual health for transwomen can be complicated by the need for affirmation as a transwoman or a need to feel loved. For a clinician involved in the promotion of sexual health it will be important to promote positive affirmation of sexuality and gender identity and to ensure patients understand their sexual rights (WHO 2006).

It is worth noting that gender identity influences an individual's sexual health and within the transgender population there are different expressions and experiences of gender identity which collectively challenge the traditional binary concept of sex as male or female (Kozee et al. 2012; WHO 2006). Kozee et al. showed that transgender individuals with positive gender congruence (perception that their external gender expression represents their own gender identity) have higher levels of life satisfaction and lower rates of depression. They also found the same patterns for individuals who experience gender identity acceptance ("the extent to which they accept their gender identity and hold pride in this identity"). Whether an individual's gender congruence and gender identity acceptance may have an effect on their risk of human immunodeficiency virus (HIV) infection is explored. Also, HIV infection is noted as resulting in sexual ill health, and we will look at this in the transgender population, focussing on male-to-female (MTF) trans people and their associated risk factors for its acquisition.

Prevalence of HIV in Trans People

It is established that there are high rates of HIV infection in the MTF transgender population (De Santis 2009) worldwide. A systematic review by Baral et al. (2013) found the global HIV prevalence in the MTF population to be 19.1%.

When broken down, this was found to be 21.6% in higher-income countries, and 17.7% in lower-income countries. The majority of data used was from countries where the male population made up the majority of the HIV infection burden, and there was little or no data for countries with generalized HIV epidemics.

Taking a look at the rates in individual countries, Herbst et al. (2008) considered HIV prevalence and associated risk factors. In their review laboratory, confirmed HIV infection was averaged at 27.7% across the United States in MTF people. The highest rates of infection were found in African-American people, at 56.3%, with the lowest rates in White individuals and Hispanic individuals, at 16.7% and 16.1% respectively. These results differ from the self-reported average of 11.8%. In terms of other sexually transmitted infections (STIs) averaged from the studies, in the MTF population there was a self-reported rate of 21.1% previous STI (Herbst et al. 2008). An earlier U.S. study by Clements-Nolle et al. (2001) had found the HIV prevalence to be higher, at 35% in the MTF population. Again, African-American people were found to be at greater risk, along with those people with a history of injecting drugs, low education, and multiple sexual partners.

In 2004 Nemoto et al. (2004a) undertook a study specifically in San Francisco where they found 98% of participants had undergone HIV testing, and of those, 26% reported testing positive, 4% were unsure, and 1% refused to give their status. In addition to this, 14% reported testing positive for an STI in the previous 12 months, with the highest rates being herpes simplex virus (HSV), at 5%. Nemoto et al. focussed on MTF people of color and did not include the Caucasian population, but, as seen in previous studies, found the highest rates of HIV infection to be in the African-American population.

However, another study by Stephens et al. (2011) in San Francisco found HIV rates of 11.2% in the MTF population. Similar rates of STI in the past 12 months were also seen in this study, although they did not assess herpes. A total of 6.3% had had rectal gonorrhea in the past 12 months and 4.9% had been diagnosed with *Chlamydia*. From other studies it is also clear that many transgender women are living with HIV and are unaware of their positive status (Schulden et al. 2008). Schulden et al. focussed on three cities in the United States and tested all participants for HIV; they found that 12% of the MTF people studied were HIV-positive and unaware, showing an increased need for more testing for this high-risk group to ensure treatment is being provided.

A project in Indonesia discovered high rates of HIV infection, at 31.6% in the transgender population (Guy et al. 2011). Compared to other high-risk groups, this was lower than for intravenous drug users (IVDUs), at 63.3%, but higher than the 7.7% and 9.3% rates seen in female sex workers and men who have sex with men (MSM) respectively. The data collected by Guy et al. focussed on centres in Jakarta and Bali and did not distinguish between MTF and female-to-male (FTM) individuals. Another study in Indonesia by Prabawanti et al. (2011), focussing on Java, found rates of HIV infection at 24.4% in MTF people. There were also high rates of other STIs: syphilis rates were 26.8% and rectal gonorrhea ± *Chlamydia* was 47%. Elsewhere in Asia, a 2011 study by Guadamuz et al.

(2011) from Thailand found HIV rates in the MTF population to be 13.5%, which, although still high, is much lower than rates seen elsewhere. This is also lower than the rates seen for MSM in Thailand, of 15.7%. Of participants, 68% had previously had an STI. When understanding HIV risks in Thailand it is important to be aware that the term "transgender" is a Western one, and in Thai culture men who express themselves as women are referred to as *kathoey*, a word with Khmer origins meaning "different kind of person" (Guadamuz et al. 2011). Its use in Thailand included homosexuality, where homosexuality was seen as a psychological mixing of the genders (Jackson 1998), but since the recent introduction of the Western term "gay," the use of *kathoey* has been used to denote what the Western world would understand as transgender (Barea 2012).

A 2012 study by Silva-Santisteban et al. in Lima, Peru, found a 30% prevalence of HIV in 450 transgender women. As seen in other studies, there were also high rates of coinfection with other STIs. Seventy-nine percent were found to have HSV-2, and 23% were also infected with syphilis. Notably, in this population 64% were involved in sex work as the main method of financial provision. Farias et al. (2011) in nearby Argentina looked at infection rates of HIV and other STIs in transgender women and also male sex workers (MSW). Rates of HIV were 34.1% in transgender sex workers compared to 11.4% in MSW. There were also high rates of hepatitis B virus infection in both the transgender sex workers and MSW populations, at 40.2% and 22.0% respectively. There was also a very high percentage of huma papillomavirus infection in transgender women, with 97.4% infected. These rates highlight a need for more provision and better access to public health care services for both of these population subgroups.

A systematic review by Baral et al. (2013) in Europe found similar rates for HIV in the MTF population, as seen elsewhere around the world. Results from three European countries—Italy, the Netherlands, and Spain—show rates of 24.5%, 18.8%, and 18.4% respectively (Baral et al. 2013). In all of these countries, male HIV infection makes up the majority of infections seen, ranging from 68.6% of the total proportion of HIV infections in Italy to 75.4% of the total proportion in Spain. Also, to compare the rates of infection seen within the transgender woman population, the overall HIV prevalence in these countries was found to be 0.49%, 0.28%, and 0.55% for Italy, the Netherlands, and Spain respectively, all significantly lower than the rates seen in transgender women (Baral et al. 2013).

Currently, data for the United Kingdom focus on the subgroups of male, female, MSM, IVDU, and maternal/blood infections and do not specify the rates of HIV infection in the MTF or FTM transgender population. Studies providing these data would be needed to ascertain whether HIV infection is a significant problem in this population, and whether rates in the United Kingdom are similar to elsewhere in the world.

HIV infection rates for FTM people were reported for the United States in a 2008 systematic review (Herbst et al. 2008). There were notably fewer studies into HIV infection in the FTM population compared to the MTF population.

Self-reported HIV infection rates ranged from 0 to 3%, and in one study that actively tested participants, rates were only 2%. This is considerably lower than rates reported in the MTF population. A more recent U.S. study recruited participants via the internet, aiming to reduce the geographic bias seen in other small U.S. studies that focussed on regional or urban centers (Feldman et al. 2014). A total of 60.42% of participants reported the results of HIV testing, with 2.2% reporting being HIV-positive. This study does not separate out the reported rates of infection between FTM and MTF, but the results are significantly lower than previous studies have reported, although similar to the rates reported for FTM people in the previous review. The low rates seen in this study are likely due to sampling from across the United States, and not just focussing on urban centers, as in the studies by Nemoto et al. (2004a) and Stephens et al. (2011).

As well as high rates of HIV infection in the MTF transgender population, there are very high mortality rates (Philip 2014). In an article in *The Times of India*, Philip (2014) noted that between 2009 and 2013 the mortality rate for HIV in the transgender population rose by 1,600%. Tamil Nadu is one of the four worst-affected states in the country and here there were only seven transgender deaths from HIV in 2009, rising to 113 in 2013 (Philip 2014). In this same period the mortality rates fell by 18.42% in the male and female populations. There is a clear discrepancy between the treatment of HIV in transgender and non-transgender individuals. While it is promising that infection rates for men and women, who make up the vast majority of cases, are falling, it is clear that the needs of the transgender community are not being addressed. This article does not distinguish between MTF and FTM but does show HIV to be a significant problem for these populations.

Risk Factors and HIV

A variety of risk factors and high-risk behaviors have been identified that increase the risk of acquiring HIV for MTF persons, such as transphobia, employment discrimination, financial situation, drug use, and relationship issues (Nemoto et al. 2004b). Nemoto et al. (2004b) used focus groups to highlight how MTF persons engage in casual sex with multiple partners to affirm their female gender identity, and how stress caused by factors such as sex work or depression can lead to substance misuse.

One of the risk factors for HIV infection is unprotected receptive anal intercourse (URAI). In a study undertaken in San Francisco by Nemoto et al. (2004a), 47% of those having receptive anal intercourse with a primary partner engaged in URAI. In all, 26% and 12% of those engaging in receptive anal intercourse had URAI with a casual partner and commercial partner respectively. A significant predictor of those engaging in URAI with a primary or casual partner was having sex under the influence of drugs. Focus groups also revealed that condom use in commercial sex work is affected by economic pressures, and the ability to earn more money for engaging in unsafe sex (Nemoto et al. 2004a).

Nuttbrock et al. (2009) reported that over half of MTFs have engaged in sexual encounters with commercial sex workers and many work as commercial sex workers themselves. Notably, MTF persons have a much higher lifetime number of non-commercial sex partners than others of the general population, and this increase in sexual activity with multiple partners puts them at increased risk of contracting HIV. Nuttbrock et al. (2009) also noted the androphilic (only attracted to men) subset of the MTF population may be at higher risk of acquiring HIV due to their increased sexual contact with MSM.

Melendez and Pinto (2007) interviewed MTF persons about their life and relationships and uncovered transgender women's own perspectives of gender roles and also the reasons for the high HIV infection rates. One respondent noted that due to "how hard the life is" ("the life" referring to life as a transgender woman), they just wanted "to be loved." After the abuse many of these people have been subjected to, when they find someone who may actually love them, they "risk a lot of things" in the hope of securing that love. Another participant noted that, while they may use condoms the first couple of times with a partner, if their partner wants to stop using one, "the woman side" wants to please and they acquiesce to these requests. This shows that the way they see themselves fulfilling their gender roles is essentially what is putting them at risk.

Another woman's perspective on her future risk of HIV infection stated that she "wouldn't be scared to get infected," as when she got older, and presumably less attractive to men, she wouldn't want to live a life alone, indicating that she seems to associate HIV infection with death (Melendez & Pinto 2007). It is interesting to note the impact that a desire to be loved and accepted as a transgender woman can affect the likelihood of these women acquiring HIV, as they will put their physical health and needs secondary to this requirement.

A 2007 study by Sausa et al. looked at transgendered women sex workers of color in San Francisco and the risks to this group. It is already established that there is heightened discrimination for each of these three groups individually. Their use of condoms when engaging in sex work depended on their financial situation. As noted previously, Sausa et al. found they were able to charge more for sex without a condom, and were also less likely to enforce condom use if they were in financial distress. Transgendered women of color were more likely to engage in high-risk behaviors such as drugs and sex work due to a lack of support and a sense of loneliness. They are also more likely to experience oppression and this "limited their employment opportunities," meaning sex work became a way to provide financial support.

Another factor that increases the risk of HIV infection for the MTF population is the lack of support they receive. Sevelius et al. (2011) found that, for those who are drug users, there are many negative experiences which deter them from seeking help. There are few programs that offer help appropriate to this population, with many shelters assigning beds based on birth gender. Within services transgender women may also suffer abuse from staff or other service users. Without appropriate services this population is left to continue with high-risk behaviors and is at subsequent increased risk of HIV infection.

Other risks found by Sevelius et al. (2011) that were associated with drug use or sex work include imprisonment, and there is an "overrepresentation of trans women in prison." In prison, cells are again assigned based on birth gender, leaving transgender women open to sexual assault, violence, and harassment, which increases their HIV risk. Sex work is a well-known risk factor for HIV infection, and for many transgender women is seen as a rite of passage, with rates of involvement reported as high as 80%. Those rejected by their families may find acceptance with other transwomen engaged in sex work, which can provide the sense of community and support required by the individual (Sausa et al. 2007). It may also provide gender identity acceptance through sexual encounters with clients, and money with which to pay for hormone therapy or surgery, to further aid gender confirmation.

The way in which MTF transgender individuals express their gender identity appears to be linked to their risk of HIV infection. According to Nuttbrock et al. (2009), those who chose to live in the male role were less likely to acquire HIV, whereas those who chose to dress in the female role, especially from an early age, were at greater risk of HIV or other STI. This increased risk is linked to those persons' involvement with the transgender community and greater "commitment to a transgender lifestyle." Nuttbrock et al. (2009) also noted that African-American MTFs' risk factors for HIV, namely commercial sex partners, androphilic sexual orientation, and expression of gender identity were all almost absent in the White American MTF population, suggesting an ethnic difference in HIV risk.

Drug use has been identified as another risk factor for HIV infection. In Los Angeles, Reback and Fletcher (2014) gathered participants from high-risk venues and the streets. They found 66.3% had injected illegal drugs or hormones at least once and there were also high rates of recent drug use, with 21.5% using methamphetamines. From analysis, results showed that injecting drugs/hormones and recent use of methamphetamines and/or crack cocaine increased the risk of having HIV-positive status. It is clear from this study and other research that safe and adequate provision of hormones to the transgender population may help reduce HIV prevalence, and prevent them from acquiring hormones illegally.

A study in Australia by Santos et al. (2014a) also looked at the use of alcohol and substances on the rates of HIV infection in transgender women. They found that 58% of the 314 respondents used alcohol and 43.3% used substances. They found those at greater risk of HIV infection reported weekly methamphetamine use, either during or before anal intercourse. Of the 314 studied, 20.1% used methamphetamines. This study shows methamphetamine use is associated with increased risk of acquiring HIV and, given the high rates of methamphetamine use in this population, there is a need for interventions aimed at reducing usage and preventing further HIV infections.

Syndemic Theory and HIV Infection in Relation to Sexual Health

Having looked at individual risk factors in isolation it is interesting to note the complex role of multiple risk factors, and how they may work together to increase an individual's risk. Studies have looked at what influences transwomen's HIV risk using the framework of syndemic theory (Brennan et al. 2012). The term "syndemic" is used to describe how a population's disease status is affected by a set of health problems that work together, in a context of physical and social conditions, to increase this. Brennan et al. (2012) looked into whether a range of factors—polysubstance use, partner violence, victimization related to trans identity, and low self-esteem—were syndemic with HIV infection and infection risk. Their results showed that HIV infection and sexual risk behaviors were significantly positively related to polysubstance use and intimate-partner violence. This suggests an additive effect of psychosocial factors on HIV infection.

Many factors highlighted by Brennan et al. (2012) are a part of, and directly impact on, an individual's sexual health (WHO 2006). It is important for clinicians to be aware of the additive effect of multiple psychosocial factors that compound a person's risk of HIV. It is also important to acknowledge that, in order to reduce the high rates of HIV seen in the trans population, then all aspects of an individual's sexual health need promoting.

HIV Treatment in Transgender People

In 2001 Clements-Nolle et al. reported that, of those found HIV-positive, only 50% were receiving medical care related to HIV. In this study only 65% of individuals knew they were infected, and of those unaware of their diagnosis, only 20% learned of this through the program and the other 15% never returned to collect their results. Only 58% of those who knew they were infected were receiving antiretroviral or prophylactic treatment for HIV. This indicates the increased need for testing of the MTF transgender population, and also the promotion of treatment. Most transgendered individuals' contact with health services was found to be for hormone treatment, so these services would be a good place to start for referral to HIV services.

Another study by Santos et al. (2014b) looked at treatment of HIV in transgender women in San Francisco. The study was conducted via respondent-driven sampling, with the aim of assessing participants' access to care and treatment, as well as their viral load. Of those diagnosed as HIV-positive, 77% had access to care within 3 months, but only 65% were actually on antiretroviral medication. In addition, only 44% were actually virologically suppressed. Housing instability was found to be a key link to poor treatment outcomes. With less than half of those infected virologically suppressed, there is a clear need for improved efforts in tackling HIV to prevent further forward transmission (Santos et al. 2014b).

In a recent study, 33.7% of participants reported having met a sexual partner over the internet, with no significant difference between transgender women and men (Benotsch et al. 2014). Among these individuals, transgender women reported significantly more lifetime internet sexual partners (median = 3) than transgender men (median = 1). Use of the internet to meet sexual partners was associated with lower self-esteem but not with depression, anxiety, somatic distress, or discrimination experiences. Although the internet is a common mode of meeting sexual partners among some transgender adults, it may also be a potential venue for prevention interventions targeting transgender individuals at particularly high risk for HIV acquisition.

HIV Reporting in the Trans Population

HIV reporting is important in determining the worldwide burden of the disease and those subgroups at greater risk of infection. Essentially HIV is a laboratory-based diagnosis, but the reporting of the disease and its burden relies on multiple factors, particularly when relating to subgroups. Such is the case in India, where "social stigma prevents the reporting of transgender deaths" (Philip 2014).

In 2012, as part of their national acquired immunodeficiency syndrome (AIDS) control program, the Indian government produced a technical report of HIV estimates. They used the tool Spectrum 4.53 Beta 19, which includes various models and packages, along with census data from 1981/1991/2001/2011 in order to improve the accuracy of HIV estimates. The population-specific estimates of subgroups were calculated using data from HIV Sentinel Surveillance data sites, for which there were only three for transgender people with none existing before 2005. MSM were found to be one of the top four at-risk groups, and transgender individuals were grouped into this category; however data were only available from 19 of the 34 states (Technical Report India 2012). This lack of appropriate surveillance and reporting of HIV in the transgender population highlights a need for improved services, in order to appropriately meet the needs of this group.

Historically India has shown notably more tolerance to transgender individuals, although this term is a modern one and a Western description (Ghosh 2015). One of the difficulties in comparing and evaluating attitudes to this population lies in individuals' and countries' differing interpretations of the term 'transgender'. Previously in India *hijra* was a term referring to transsexual people, transvestites, drag queens, and intersex people (Ghosh 2015). *Hijra* performances were once an important part of male childbirth and wedding ceremonies. There are many other descriptions of gender-fluid practices, key to many religious groups, such as the *rasiks* or *sakhis* of the Ramanandi monastic order of Hinduism, who "show effeminate behaviours" and also "wear female attire." However, when the country came under British rule, these practices were viewed as "failed masculinity," and laws were passed criminalizing "unnatural intercourse." The British also introduced the Criminal Tribes Act, which required registration and control of transgender communities, collectively referred to as "eunuchs." This marginalization penetrated into Indian society and continued after the end of British rule. It was only in 2015 that the Indian government recognized transgender people as a third sex (Ghosh 2015). Today in India transgender people still face difficulty with housing and employment due to the stigma attached, with many forced into sex work and subject to harassment, including from the police (Philip 2014).

Current attitudes towards the transgender population in the United Kingdom are improving, with a study in the North-East by Mitchell and Howarth (2009) showing that only 14% of people "felt negative towards trans people." Legislation is in place to protect transgender individuals and the Equality and Humans Rights Commission was set up with the aim of reducing discrimination. However, despite legislation these people still suffer discrimination at work and in school and are subject to hate crimes. Mitchell and Howarth (2009) found that 62% had been subjected to transphobic abuse, with 17% of this violent.

From looking at the changing attitudes of these two countries it is interesting to note that the once-accepting attitudes of traditional Indian society were radically changed by British rule, and now the United Kingdom is further ahead than when than when in the movement towards transgender acceptance (Ghosh 2015).

Overall attitudes are improving with regard to transgender people, mirroring the general move towards acceptance seen for other subpopulations such as lesbian, gay, and bisexual (Fisher 2013). Negative attitudes towards lesbian, gay, bisexual, and transgender people have become much less acceptable, so there has been a shift in the general subconscious views of society. However, this apparent increase in acceptance could be due simply to the "political correctness effect," and either way this is affected by a person's own interpretation of acceptance (Fisher 2013). Looking at how societal attitudes have changed towards homosexuality, particularly over the last 10–20 years, suggests transgender acceptance is a possibility. Although if this is achieved, will this help prevent the high rates of HIV infection in the MTF population? Perhaps one of the reasons for the lack of public understanding and acceptance of transgender individuals is the difficulty people have in accepting individuals who challenge the Western idea of gender as a binary concept (Toomey et al. 2013).

Practical Implications for the Clinician

From the literature it is evident that HIV rates are high in transwomen (De Santis 2009). This shows there is a need for targeted interventions for this population to address the increased infection rates. In 2009 the Pan American Health Organization (PAHO) created a document detailing appropriate methods of health promotion to MSM, and many of their suggestions are useful and can be applied to trans people (PAHO 2009). One particular focus was on outreach programs. The report stipulates that such programmes should be in settings appropriate and accessible for the population, in order to enable successful health promotion. This could help increase access to trans people who may feel current services are not appropriate for them or their needs.

Clinicians should be aware of the specific problems transwomen may face, such as problems with gender identity and expression. Individuals should educate themselves about these issues in order to provide an appropriate service. The focus should include improving an individual's self-esteem and help in achieving a positive identity, to help avoid the many psychosocial issues that increase the risk of HIV infection.

Research by Nemoto et al. (2004b) notes the complex and varied factors that increase an MTF person's risk of acquiring HIV. Key issues highlighted by Nemoto et al. (2004b) that increase a person's risk of HIV infection, such as drug use and mental health conditions, suggest that liaison with appropriate services may be of value in ensuring there is a cohesive approach to promoting sexual health, and that patients are not being missed. Also clinicians themselves should feel comfortable when advising and dealing with these problems.

In the United Kingdom most trans people come into contact with services via general practitioner referral to gender dysphoria clinics to be seen by gender consultants and specialists (Royal College of Psychiatrists 2013). Here, the assessment of individuals provides a good opportunity for clinicians to assess an individual's sexual health, take note of any high-risk behaviors such as ones noted previously in this chapter, and provide tailored sexual health information in addition to providing information on safe sex and testing services for individuals. However, it is important for all services to be aware of these high-risk behaviors and to consider any barriers there may be that would prevent transwomen from accessing the service and to look at ways of being more inclusive.

Conclusions

It is clear and well documented that the MTF transgender population has greater rates of HIV infection than other populations (Baral et al. 2013). From this research it is evident that gender identity and the way it is expressed are linked with this risk. Individuals' need to feel accepted in their gender identity often surpasses the value that they place on their own health (Melendez & Pinto 2007). MTF persons are also more likely to suffer discrimination in many aspects of life, leading to unemployment and other factors that increase their risk of HIV infection (Sausa et al. 2007; Sevelius et al. 2011). As such, it is important for clinicians to be aware of the many issues faced by the trans community, and how this is linked to their risk of HIV infection. Also, it is important to be aware that the promotion of their sexual health is very important and needs to be addressed from a holistic perspective. Finally, there are steps all clinicians can take to educate both themselves and their patients in order to provide an appropriate and inclusive service.

References

Baral, S. D. et al. (2013). Worldwide Burden of HIV in Transgender Women: A Systematic Review and Meta-analysis. *The Lancet Infectious Diseases.* 13(3): 214–222.

Barea, M. E. (2012). From the Iron to the Lady: The *Kathoey* Phenomenon in Thai Cinema. *Revista de letras y ficción audiovisual.* 2: 190–202. Available online: http://pendientedemigracion.ucm.es/info/sesionnonumerada/index.php/revista/article/viewFile/27/27 (accessed 16/9/15).

Benotsch, E. G., Zimmerman, R. S., Cathers, L., Heck, T., McNulty, S., Pierce, J., Perrin, P. B., & Snipes, D. J. (2014). Use of the internet to meet sexual partners, sexual risk behavior, and mental health in transgender adults. *Archives of Sexual Behavior.* DOI 10.1007/s10508-014-0432-x.

Brennan, J., Kuhns, L. M., Johnson, A. K., Belzer, M., Wilson, E. C., & Garofalo, R. (2012). Syndemic Theory and HIV-Related Risk Among Young Transgender Women: The Role of Multiple, Co-Occurring Health Problems and Social Marginalization. *American Journal of Public Health.* 102(9): 1751–1757.

Clements-Nolle, K., Marx, R., Guzman, R., & Katz, M. (2001). HIV Prevalence, Risk Behaviours, Health Care Use, and Mental Health Status of Transgender Persons: Implications for Public Health Interventions. *American Journal of Public Health. Lesbians, Gay, Bisexual and Transgender Health.* 91(6): 915–921.

De Santis, J. (2009). HIV Infection Risk Factors Among Male-to-Female Transgender Persons: A Review Of The Literature. *Journal of the Association of Nurses in AIDS Care.* 20(5): 362–372.

Farias, M. S. R., et al. (2011). HIV Prevalence, Substance Use, and Sexual Risk Behaviors Among Transgender Women Recruited Through Outreach. *International Journal of Infectious Disease.* 15(9): 635–640.

Feldman, J., Romine, R. S., & Bockting, W. O. (2014). HIV Risk Behaviours in the U.S. Transgender Population: Prevalence and Predictors in a Large Internet Sample. *Journal of Homosexuality.* 61(11): 1558–1588.

Fisher, M. (2013). A revealing map of the countries that are most and least tolerant of homosexuality. *The Washington Post.* Available online: http://www.washingtonpost.com/blogs/worldviews/wp/2013/06/05/a-revealing-map-of-the-countries-that-are-most-and-least-tolerant-of-homosexuality/ (accessed 26/1/15).

Ghosh, A. (2015). LGBTQ Activist Organisations as 'Respectably Queer' in India: Contesting a Western View. *Gender, Work and Organisation.* 22(1): 51–66.

Guadamuz, T. E., et al. (2011). HIV Prevalence, Risk Behaviour, Hormone Use and Surgical History among Transgender Persons in Thailand. *AIDS Behaviour.* 15(3): 650–658.

Guy, R., et al. (2011). Voluntary Counselling and Testing Sites as a Source of Sentinel Information on HIV Prevalence in a Concentrated Epidemic: A Pilot Project from Indonesia. *International Journal of STD and AIDS.* 22(9): 505–511.

Herbst, J. H., Jacobs, E. D., Finlayson, T. J., McKleroy, V. S., Neumann, M. S., & Crepaz, N. (2008). Estimating HIV Prevalence and Risk Behaviours of Transgender Persons in the United States: A Systematic Review. *AIDS & Behaviour.* 12(1): 1–17.

Jackson, P. A. (1998). Male Homosexuality and Transgenderism in the Thai Buddhist Tradition. In Leyland, W. (Ed.), *Queer Dharma: Voices of Gay Buddhists.* Available online:http://www.enabling.org/ia/vipassana/Archive/J/Jackson/homoBuddhaJackson.html (accessed 16/9/15).

Kozee, H. B., Tylka, T. L., & Bauerband, L. A. (2012). Measuring Transgender Individuals' Comfort With Gender Identity and Appearance: Development and Validation of the Transgender Congruence Scale. *Psychology of Women Quarterly.* 36(2): 179–196.

Melendez, R. M., & Pinto, R. (2007). "It's really a hard life": Love, Gender and HIV Risk among Male-to-Female Transgender Persons. *Culture, Health and Sexuality.* 9(3): 233–245.

Mitchell, M., & Howarth, C. (2009). Trans Research Review. *NatCen. Equality and Human Rights Commission Research Report* 27: 55.

Nemoto, T., Operario, D., Keatley, J., Han, L., & Soma, T. (2004a). HIV Risk Behaviours Among Male-To-Female Transgender Persons of Color in San Francisco. *American Journal of Public Health.* 94(7): 1193–1199.

Nemoto, T., Operario, D., Keatley, J., & Villegas, D. (2004b). Social Context of HIV Risk Behaviours Among Male-to-female Transgenders of Colour. *AIDS Care.*16(6): 724–735.

Nuttbrock, L., et al. (2009). Lifetime Risk Factors for HIV/Sexually Transmitted Infections Among Male-To-Female Transgender Persons. *Journal of Acquired Immunodeficiency Syndromes.* 52(3): 417–421.

PAHO. (2009). Blueprint for the Provision of Comprehensive Care to Gay Men and Other Men Who Have Sex with Men (MSM) in Latin American and the Caribbean. Available online: http://www.paho.org/hq/dmdocuments/2010/Blueprint%20 MSM%20Final%20ENGLISH.pdf (accessed 17/9/15).

Philip, C. M. (2014). Transgender HIV Deaths Rise Despite Drop in TN Fatalities. *The Times of India.* Available online: http://timesofindia.indiatimes.com/city/chennai/ Trangender-HIV-deaths-rise-despite-drop-in-TN-fatalities/articleshow/40312517. cms?intenttarget=no&utm_source=TOI_AShow_OBWidget&utm_medium=Int_ Ref&utm_campaign=TOI_AShow (accessed 26/9/14).

Prabawanti, C., et al. (2011). HIV, Sexually Transmitted Infections, and Sexual Risk Behaviour Among Transgenders in Indonesia. *AIDS and Behaviour.* 15(3): 663–673.

Reback, C. J., & Fletcher, J. B. (2014). HIV Prevalence, Substance Use, and Sexual Risk Behaviours Among Transgender Women Recruited Through Outreach. *AIDS and Behaviour.* 18(7): 1359–1367.

Royal College of Psychiatrists. (2013). Good practice guidelines for the assessment and treatment of adults with gender dysphoria. College report CR181. Available online: http://www.rcpsych.ac.uk/files/pdfversion/CR181.pdf (accessed 27/8/15).

Santos, G. M., et al. (2014a). Alcohol and Substance Use Among Transgender Women in San Francisco: Prevalence and Association With Human Immunodeficiency Virus Infection. *Drug and Alcohol Review.* 33(3): 287–292.

Santos, G. M., Wilson, E. C., Rapues, J., Macias, O., Packer, T., & Raymond, H. F. (2014b). HIV Treatment Cascade Among Transgender Women in a San Francisco Respondent Driven Sampling Study. *Sexually Transmitted Infections.* 90(5): 430–433.

Sausa, L. A., Keatley, J., & Operario, D. (2007). Perceived Risks and Benefits of Sex Work among Transgender Women of Color in San Francisco. *Archives of Sexual Behaviour.* 36(6): 768–777.

Schulden, J. D., et al. (2008). Rapid HIV Testing in Transgender Communities by Community-Based Organisations in Three Cities. *Public Health Reports.* 123(3): 101–114.

Sevelius, J. M., Keatley, J., & Gutierrez-Mock, L. (2011). HIV/AIDS Programming in the United States: Considerations Affecting Transgender Women and Girls. *Women's Health Issues.* 21(6):278–282.

Silva-Santisteban, A., et al. (2012). Understanding the HIV/AIDS Epidemic in Transgender Women of Lima, Peru: Results from a Sero-epidemiologic Study Using Respondent Driven Sampling. *AIDS and Behaviour.* 16(4): 872–881.

Stephens, S. C., Bernstein, K. T., & Philip, S. (2011). Male to Female and Female to Male Transgender Persons have Different Sexual Risk Behaviours Yet Similar Rates of STDs and HIV. *AIDS and Behaviour.* 15(3): 683–686.

Technical Report India, HIV Estimates. (2012). National AIDS Control Organization; Department of AIDS Control. Ministry of Health & Family Welfare, India. New Delhi – 110011 Available online: http://www.unaids.org/sites/default/files/en/media/unaids/contentassets/documents/data-and-analysis/tools/spectrum/India2012report.pdf (accessed 25/1/15).

Toomey, R. B., Ryan, C., Diaz, R. M., Card, N. A., & Russell, S. T. (2013). Gender-Nonconforming Lesbian, Gay, Bisexual, and Transgender Youth: School Victimization and Young Adult Psychosocial Adjustment. *Psychology of Sexual Orientation and Gender Diversity.* 1(1):71–80.

WHO. (2006). Defining Sexual Health. Report of a technical consultation on sexual health. Available online: http://www.who.int/reproductivehealth/publications/sexual_health/defining_sexual_health.pdf?ua=1 (accessed 27/8/15).

17 Reproduction and Fertility Issues for Transgender People

Petra De Sutter

Introduction

It is now well established that transsexualism and other forms of gender variance are not mental disorders, but conditions that need to be treated with state-of-the-art hormonal and surgical therapy to obtain reassignment to the desired gender (T'Sjoen et al. 2004; World Professional Association for Transgender Health 2011). Because of the effects of treatment on fertility, transition to the desired gender and reproduction appear to be mutually exclusive for transpeople. Therefore, loss of reproductive potential seems to be the "price to pay" for transition, at least if the reproductive organs are removed. In this chapter, we will only briefly touch upon possibilities for transpeople who retain their reproductive organs, and mainly focus on those who opt for full gender reassignment.

Although the reproductive needs and rights of transpeople were recognized 20 years ago (Lawrence et al. 1996), today, some medical experts—even those involved in the care of transpeople—are still critical when discussing possible procreation after gender reassignment. It was only in 2001 that the *Standards of Care* included a paragraph on the need to discuss reproductive issues with transpeople prior to the start of hormonal treatment (Meyer et al. 2001). At that time, the ethical debate as to whether transpeople should be helped with a desire for children in post-transition relationships was heavily discussed in the world of fertility specialists (Brothers & Ford 2000; Jones 2000). This debate dealt largely with donor inseminations in female partners of transmen. In essence, the question was whether transpeople can be "good" parents without negatively influencing the gender and/or sexual orientation of the child-to-be (Baetens et al. 2003; De Sutter 2003). The same discussion was held, many years before, regarding homosexual people (Hanscombe 1983). Just as it was offensive to homosexual people then, it may have been considered offensive to transpeople. The discussion was then broadened to address how to help fulfill the transperson's wish for children, rather than whether or not to help (De Sutter 2001). The overall well-being of transpeople after gender reassignment therapy has been well documented (Cohen-Kettenis & Gooren 1999), and many have ongoing relationships with children from their previous relationship or current partner. Although most scholars today believe this is not an issue any more (De Wert et al. 2014; Ross et al. 2014; T'Sjoen et al. 2013), we will discuss the ethical arguments before describing the medical possibilities and challenges.

Transpeople and Their Children

Before discussing the practical problems of fulfilling the wish for a child after transition, it may be worthwhile considering data from families of transpeople and children from a previous relationship. Not many studies have been performed, but from all available information, it seems that the transsexualism of one parent does not have any negative influence on the psychosexual or gender identity development of the children. The children may suffer from the separation or divorce issues occurring as a result of the gender problem of a parent, but this is not essentially different from the consequences of separation or divorce for other reasons (Green 1978, 1998; White & Ettner 2004, 2007).

Green reported on 34 children who remained in contact with their transsexual parents, and found no clinically significant cross-gender behavior. Although some children experienced teasing by peers, it was mild, transient, and resolved. All children had a reasonable understanding of the parent's gender variance and the treatment process. White and Ettner (2004) reviewed the experiences of therapists working with transpeople who had children, and found that younger children adapted better to the gender transition of a parent than older children, and children adapted better if the level of family conflict was low. In their 2007 study, White and Ettner interviewed 27 parents of 55 children and confirmed that children who were younger at the time of transition adapted better, and that parental conflicts which continued after the transition tended to reflect greater family conflict between parent and child.

In essence, these results are the same as those from earlier studies with children of lesbian couples (Brewaeys et al. 1997; Chan et al. 1998). In such children, psychosexual and gender identity development does not differ from that of other children. The only problems which sometimes occur are related to issues of non-acceptance of the parents' homosexuality and discrimination in the environment. Clearly, fighting societal bigotry and discrimination is the right approach, as opposed to refusing to give these couples their children.

For all these reasons, Green pleads against terminating contact between the transparent and his/her child(ren). Unfortunately, even today, courts all over the world are still not sufficiently aware of this. They continue to use transsexualism as sufficient cause to end contact between transpeople and their children. Often this is initiated by adversarial ex-partners, and is harmful to the children.

Ethical Arguments in Favor of Fertility Preservation

The Right to Reproduce

In today's reproductive medicine, it is accepted that every person has the right to reproduce (Chan & Ho, 2006; Robertson 1987; Schenker &

Eisenberg 1997). For the transman or transwoman, this does not seem obvious. Hormonal and/or surgical treatments render natural procreation biologically impossible. In daily infertility practice, however, there is another situation in which procreation is impossible by natural means: the lesbian couple. Reproduction within lesbian couples is now widely accepted, particularly among fertility specialists, and both simple donor inseminations and crossover in vitro fertilization (IVF) (one woman provides the oocytes which, after fertilization in vitro, are transferred to her partner) can help fulfill the wish for children. The argument that the transitioning transperson has deliberately chosen to abandon his or her reproductive potential is as specious as the argument that a woman becomes a lesbian by choice. If we accept that homosexuality is not a matter of choice, and lesbians may be helped with their wish for children, the same reasoning should apply to transsexual people (Murphy 2010, 2012).

However, even if homosexuality or gender variance were a matter of choice, this would not be sufficient ethical grounds to deny the possibility of reproduction to homosexual or gender-variant people. Indeed, even in more conventional situations, people have free choice to control their fertility, for instance, by means of sterilization procedures, and subsequent reversal surgery or assisted reproductive techniques in order to obtain a pregnancy.

The Legal Argument

In many countries, transsexualism is the only medical condition for which sterilization is a legal requirement before recognition of the new gender can be granted. This means that children born afterward cannot be legally claimed by the transperson. Although this requirement may have been inevitable in the past for technological reasons, preservation of reproductive material is currently feasible, and transpeople may now have genetic children after transition. The law must change to incorporate this fact.

Even if, at present, recognition of offspring in one's new gender legally may be impossible, this is not an ethical argument for withholding treatment. If a lesbian transwoman and her girlfriend require inseminations to create a child, one cannot seriously maintain that using donor sperm is preferable to the cryopreserved semen from the transwoman, even if she will not be able to claim legal parenthood.

Recently, several countries have started to remove from their legislation the requirement of sterilization in order to receive a legal gender recognition. In 2015 there were still 29 Council of Europe member states which require sterilization, while 18 have already changed their laws.

Transpeople and Fertility

The fact that many transgendered people, especially adolescents and young adults, are not preoccupied by their future opportunities for fertility is not an adequate argument for avoiding discussion of reproduction and possible gamete banking. Counseling young people on the issue of preserving sperm or ovarian tissue for possible later use is considered good clinical practice for cancer patients (Robertson 2005), but not (yet) for transgendered people. Like all young people, transitioning transpeople may not be thinking about their fertility, but when all gender issues have been successfully resolved, they may meet a partner with whom they will want to have children. Having their gametes preserved will greatly enhance the possibility of doing so. It is the responsibility of the psychiatrist and/or psychologist to discuss this issue before any treatment is started.

Transmission of the Transsexual Condition

Another ethical point of discussion often raised is the risk of transmission of the transsexual condition to the offspring. As far as we know, no solid scientific evidence concerning this issue is available. Since transsexualism, most probably, is multifactorial in origin (Wylie 2004), any such risk for the offspring will be minimal. If some transmittable genetic trait were identified in the future, it would still be the responsibility of transpersons themselves to determine whether they want children or not, just as in the case of other medical conditions or genetically transmittable diseases.

In conclusion, common ethical arguments used against reproductive options for gender-variant people are driven by societal fear of the transsexual phenomenon and by ignorance of the current technical possibilities available. Experience with lesbian couples shows that, when new techniques are available, new treatment options are sought and offered (Hodgen 1988). There is no legitimate reason why transsexual people should be refused these options.

Cryopreservation of Sperm for Transwomen

What follows is a brief discussion of the various theoretical options that are available. It is worthwhile mentioning that, although a majority of transsexual people will form heterosexual relationships after transition, many will not, illustrating the well-known fact that sexual orientation and gender identity are quite different entities (Leavitt & Berger 1990). Therefore, not all options are available for all transsexual people.

Feminizing hormonal therapy will induce hypospermatogenesis, and ultimately azoospermia, in transsexual women (Lubbert et al. 1992; Schulze 1988). The azoospermia will be irreversible after some time. Furthermore, gender reassignment surgery, with removal of the testes, obviously leads to irreversible sterility. The only option, therefore, is to perform sperm preservation by freezing a number of semen samples, preferably prior to starting hormonal therapy. These banked spermatozoa can then possibly be used later to inseminate a female partner if the quality is good, or else be used to perform IVF or intracytoplasmatic sperm injection (ICSI) (Figure 17.1). In theory, even a

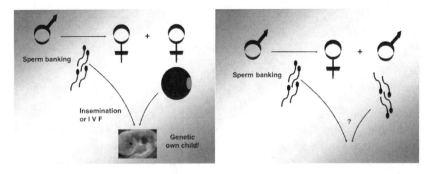

Figure 17.1 Reproductive options for a transwoman with a female partner (left) or with a male partner (right). IVF, in vitro fertilization.

testicular biopsy could be used, since very few sperm cells are needed to attain fertilization and pregnancy with the ICSI method. A recent study (Hamada et al. 2015) showed that the frozen semen of many transwomen is not of good quality, meaning that assisted reproduction will often be needed.

In the case of a future male partner, the situation is the same as with male couples today—there is little help available except when an oocyte donor and a surrogate mother are involved.

In 2003, we published a survey regarding the opinions of transwomen about sperm preservation (De Sutter et al. 2003). We received responses from 121 transwomen. The vast majority (77%) felt that the option of freezing sperm should be discussed and offered by the professionals treating them. A smaller majority (51%) would indeed have frozen their own sperm, or at least have seriously considered doing so, if the option had been presented. Most women who favored the idea of sperm freezing were under 40 years of age, and identified as lesbian or bisexual. A minority of respondents expressed concern about possible risks of genetically transmitting transsexualism to their children, or considered the whole idea of sperm freezing to be in conflict with their female core identity. Many transwomen expressed regret that they could not become pregnant and bear a child. From this study, it appears that younger transwomen who identify as lesbian or bisexual, and who would most benefit from having the sperm frozen, are willing to do so, if the possibility is offered.

Although sperm freezing has been an option for more than a decade in our clinic, only 15% of transwomen have chosen it (Wierckx et al. 2012a, b). Reasons for not freezing sperm in transwomen who identify as lesbians are financial and time constraints.

The possibility of transwomen becoming pregnant and delivering babies is still remote. Uterine transplantation has now been done successfully in a small series of women born without a uterus (Brännström et al. 2014; Johannesson et al. 2014; Tzakis 2015), but there are still many ethical and medical challenges to be overcome, such as the need for immunosuppressive therapy, the search for a suitable donor, medical risks, and financial issues. If uterus transplantation becomes a routine treatment for uterine infertility, there is no reason why transwomen should be excluded (Murphy 2015).

Donor Inseminations in Partners of Transmen

After transition, many transmen establish long-term relationships with female partners. Within these families, the wish for children may emerge. Although in the future there may be other options, currently, most of these couples will seeks donor sperm insemination. In theory, this approach does not in any way differ from the treatment of any other heterosexual couple with an untreatable male infertility problem. However, as earlier stated, there is some discussion in the literature regarding ethical issues (Baetens et al. 2003; De Sutter 2003). In our own department, we currently treat five to ten of these couples a year. In 2012, Wierckx et al. did a study on reproductive wishes in transmen. They questioned 50 transmen and found that 64% were currently involved in a relationship. Eleven participants (22.0%) reported having children; for eight, their female partner was inseminated with donor sperm, whereas three participants gave birth before hormonal therapy and surgery. More than half of the participants desired to have children (54%); 18 (37.5%) reported that they had considered freezing their germ cells, if this technique had been available previously. Participants without children at the time of investigation expressed this desire more often than participants with children. This study revealed that the majority of transmen desire to have children and the authors concluded that more attention should be paid to this topic during the diagnostic phase of transition and to the consequences for genetic parenthood after starting sex reassignment therapy.

Cryopreservation of Oocytes, Embryos, or Ovarian Tissue in Transmen

The situation for transmen is not quite the same as for transwomen. Masculinizing hormonal therapy will lead to a reversible amenorrhea, but ovarian follicles will remain in place. There is some discussion as to whether this leads to a condition physiologically similar to the polycystic ovarian (PCO) syndrome. At a minimum, the ovarian histology is very similar to that of women with the PCO syndrome (Grynberg et al. 2010; Pache et al. 1991; Spinder et al. 1989).

In cases where the uterus and ovaries remain in place, hormonal treatment can be stopped and fertility can be fully restored. Thomas Beattie (2008) and many others have shown that pregnancy and delivery are perfectly possible without any problem.

Of course, oophorectomy will provoke irreversible ovarian failure. To preserve procreational potential, three options are available: oocyte banking, embryo banking, and ovarian tissue banking. These are essentially the same

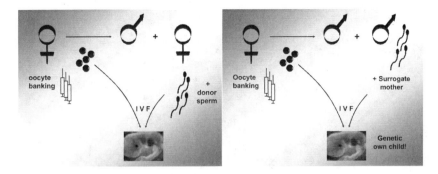

Figure 17.2 Reproductive options for a transman with a female partner (left) or with a male partner (right) after oocyte banking. IVF, in vitro fertilization.

options available for women undergoing chemotherapy or radiotherapy for malignant diseases (Seli & Tangir 2005).

Oocyte Banking

Oocyte banking (Figure 17.2) requires hormonal stimulation and oocyte retrieval (as for IVF), and subsequent freezing of the oocytes. Although oocyte freezing has been possible for a long time (Chen 1986), it has become a routine technique only since the last decade, because of better freezing methods (vitrification) (Porcu 2001). Oocyte freezing is now offered not only for medical reasons, but also for non-medical or so-called social reasons, so there is no reason why transmen could not have their oocytes frozen if they wished to (Harwood 2009). Since hormonal stimulation yields, on average, ten oocytes, more than one IVF cycle has to be performed in order to bank a sufficient number of oocytes. It remains to be seen how many transmen will choose to undergo this treatment in order to have their eggs banked. The IVF treatment obviously cannot take place while the patient is under androgen treatment (Wallace et al. 2014). Having oocytes banked would also require the later use of donor spermatozoa and a recipient uterus of a future female partner, or a surrogate mother, in the case of a male partner. The latter would allow the couple to have their own genetic child.

Embryo Banking

Embryo banking requires hormonal stimulation and oocyte retrieval (as for oocyte banking or IVF), as well as spermatozoa from a male partner (or donor) with subsequent freezing of the embryos (Figure 17.3). Embryo freezing is now a routine procedure in IVF and yields reasonably good results. Of course, it also would require a recipient uterus (female partner or surrogate mother). Again, to be efficient, this procedure should be repeated a few times, diminishing the

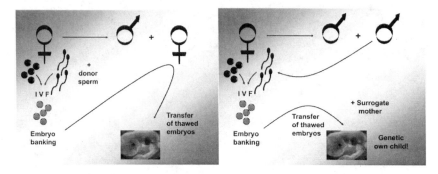

Figure 17.3 Reproductive options for a transman with a female partner (left) or with a male partner (right) after embryo banking. IVF, in vitro fertilization.

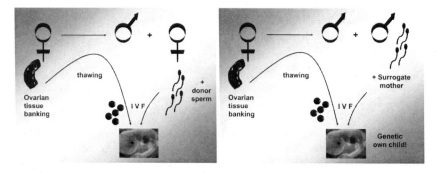

Figure 17.4 Reproductive options for a transman with a female partner (left) or with a male partner (right) after ovarian tissue banking. IVF, in vitro fertilization.

likelihood that many transmen would be willing to undergo such protracted treatment.

Ovarian Tissue Banking

Ovarian tissue banking (Figure 17.4) is being used by women who undergo chemotherapy or radiotherapy for a malignant disease. Ovarian tissue banking requires neither hormonal stimulation nor IVF, and is technically as easy as sperm freezing. Through means of a laparoscopy, ovarian tissue can be removed. The ovaries retain usable follicles even after hormonal therapy (Van den Broecke et al. 2001), which implies that removal of ovarian tissue can be performed at the time of oophorectomy. The PCO-like changes in the ovaries induced by androgen therapy apparently do not hinder subsequent successful follicle maturation and oocyte fertilizability.

Ovarian tissue banking would also require donor spermatozoa and a recipient uterus (a female partner, or a surrogate mother) in the case of a male

Table 17.1 Current options for fertility preservation in transwomen and transmen

	Future partner	
	Male	*Female*
Transwomen: sperm freezing	Oocyte donor and surrogate mother gestational carrier = genetic own child of transwoman or of partner	Insemination or IVF = genetic own child for both
Transmen: ovarian tissue banking	IVF with surrogate mother gestational carrier = genetic own child for both	IVF with donor sperm = genetic own child of transman
		Or
		Donor insemination of partner = genetic own child of partner

IVF, in vitro fertilization.

partner. The main problem of ovarian tissue banking, however, is not the freezing per se, but the question of what to do with the tissue after thawing. One has the option of grafting the ovarian tissue back into the patient (Donnez et al. 2004), but this is not an option for transsexual men. The only possibility would be the in vitro culture of the tissue fragments with follicular growth and oocyte maturation in vitro, but this has not led to pregnancies in humans yet.

So, although ovarian tissue banking seems to be the option of choice (Table 17.1), much research is needed to make this a viable possibility for transmen.

Future Possibilities

There may be other asexual ways of procreation awaiting discovery. The birth of Dolly, the cloned sheep, demonstrated that it is possible to obtain an individual, starting with an adult cell (Solter 1998). Although cloning may offer great potential to medicine in general and have many useful applications, reproductive cloning (reproducing a copy of a given individual) probably holds little interest and has been widely banned (Sandel 2005).

However, cloning and nuclear transfer technology may well offer other solutions to the problem at hand. In women who have no oocytes, and now need donor oocytes to reproduce, research is being conducted to produce artificial gametes by transfer of somatic cell nuclei into enucleated donor oocytes, inducing haploidization (halving the number of chromosomes), so that an artificial oocyte is created (Easley et al. 2014). This oocyte can then be fertilized in a normal way and yield a pregnancy. As an alternative for nuclear transfer, perhaps the induced pluripotent stem cell technology will also prove to be successful in yielding patient-specific gametes. Although functional artificial gametes have not yet been obtained in the human, they have been successfully produced in mice (Duggal et al. 2014). If this technology proves to be successful in humans as well, gamete preservation would no longer be necessary, as a simple skin biopsy would be sufficient to produce artificial gametes capable of reproduction with any partner. The ethical consequences of such a revolutionary technology are obvious (Palacios-González et al. 2014). Functional artificial gametes would allow homosexual procreation; however, with a male partner, the aid of a surrogate mother carrier will always be necessary.

In conclusion, this author acknowledges that, although these technological advances signal hope to many, the options are not universally available, and are often cost-prohibitive. Nevertheless, it behooves professionals who assist transitioning people to discuss the issues of fertility and reproduction. The heartfelt yearning to bear a child is seldom addressed in treatment, yet it is poignantly experienced.

References

Baetens, P., Camus, M., & Devroey, P. (2003). Should Requests for Donor Insemination on Social Grounds be Expanded to Transsexuals? *Reprod. Biomed. Online*, 6: 279–284.

Beattie, T. (2008). *Labor of Love: The Story of One Man's Extraordinary Pregnancy.* Berkeley, CA: Seal Press.

Brännström, M., Johannesson, L., Bokström, H., Kvarnström, N., Mölne, J., Dahm-Kähler, P., Enskog, A., Milenkovic, M., Ekberg, J., Diaz-Garcia, C., Gäbel, M., Hanafy, A., Hagberg, H., Olausson, M., & Nilsson, L. (2014). Livebirth after uterus transplantation. *Lancet*, S0140–6736(14)61728–61731.

Brewaeys, A., Ponjaert, I., Van Hall, E.V., et al. (1997). Donor Insemination: Child Development and Family Functioning in Lesbian Mother Families. *Hum. Reprod.*, 12: 1349–1359.

Brothers, D., & Ford, W.C. (2000). Gender Reassignment and Assisted Reproduction: An Ethical Analysis. *Hum. Reprod.*, 15: 737–738.

Chan, C.C., & Ho, P.C. (2006). Infertility, Assisted Reproduction and Rights. *Best Pract. Res. Clin. Obstet. Gynaecol.*, 20(3): 369–380.

Chan, R.W., Raboy, B., & Patterson, C.J. (1998). Psychosocial Adjustment among Children Conceived via Donor Insemination by Lesbian and Heterosexual Mothers. *Child Dev.*, 69: 443–457.

Chen, C. (1986). Pregnancy after Human Oocyte Cryopreservation. *Lancet*, i, 884–886.

Cohen-Kettenis, P.T., & Gooren, L.J. (1999). Transsexualism: A Review of Etiology, Diagnosis and Treatment. *J. Psychosom. Res.*, 46: 315–333.

De Sutter, P. (2001). Gender Reassignment and Assisted Reproduction: Present and Future Reproductive Options for Transsexual People. *Hum. Reprod.*, 16: 612–614.

De Sutter, P. (2003). Donor Inseminations in Partners of Female-to-Male Transsexuals: Should the Question be Asked? *Reprod. Biomed. Online*, 6: 382–383.

De Sutter, P., Kira, K., Verschoor, A., & Hotimsky, A. (2003). The Wish for Children and the Preservation of Fertility in Transsexual Women: A Survey. *Int. J. Transgenderism*, 6(3), http://www.europeants.org/profiles/kate_kira/ijtvo06no03_02.htm.

De Wert, G., Dondorp, W., Shenfield, F., Barri, P., Devroey, P., Diedrich, K., Tarlatzis, B., Provoost, V., & Pennings, G. (2014). ESHRE Task Force on Ethics and Law 23: Medically Assisted Reproduction in Singles, Lesbian and Gay Couples, and Transsexual People. *Hum. Reprod.*, 29(9): 1859–1865.

Donnez, J., Dolmans, M.M., Demylle, D., Jadoul, P., Pirard, C., Squifflet, J., Martinez-Madrid, B., & van Langendonckt, A. (2004). Livebirth after Orthotopic Transplantation of Cryopreserved Ovarian Tissue. *Lancet*, 364(9443): 1405–1410.

Duggal, G., Heindryckx, B., Deroo, T., & De Sutter, P. (2014). Use of Pluripotent Stem Cells for Reproductive Medicine: Are we There Yet? *Vet Q.* 34(1): 42–51.

Easley, C.A., Simerly, C.R., & Schatten, G. (2014). Gamete Derivation from Embryonic Stem Cells, Induced Pluripotent Stem Cells or Somatic Cell Nuclear Transfer-Derived Embryonic Stem Cells: State of the Art. *Reprod. Fertil. Dev.*, 27(1): 89–92.

Green, R. (1978). Sexual Identity of Thirty-seven Children Raised by Homosexual or Transsexual Parents. *Am. J. Psychiatry*, 135: 692–697.

Green, R. (1998). Transsexuals' Children. *Int. J. Transgenderism*, 2(4), http://www.glad. org/uploads/docs/publications/i._i_._Green_Transsexuals_Children_.pdf.

Grynberg, M., Fanchin, R., Dubost, G., Colau, J.C., Brémont-Weil, C., Frydman, R., & Ayoubi, J.M. (2010). Histology of Genital Tract and Breast Tissue after Long-term Testosterone Administration in a Female-to-male Transsexual Population. *Reprod. Biomed. Online*,20(4): 553–558.

Hamada, A., Kingsberg, S., Wierckx, K., T'Sjoen, G., De Sutter, P., Knudson, G., & Agarwal, A. (2015). Semen Characteristics of Transwomen Referred for Sperm Banking Before Sex Transition: A Case Series. *Andrologia*, 47(7): 832–838.

Hanscombe, G. (1983). The Right to Lesbian Parenthood. *J. Med. Ethics*, 9: 133–135.

Harwood, K. (2009). Egg Freezing: A Breakthrough for Reproductive Autonomy? *Bioethics*, 23(1): 39–46.

Hodgen, G.D. (1988). Perspectives in Human Reproduction. *Hum. Reprod.*, 3: 573–576.

Johannesson, L., Kvarnström, N., Mölne, J., Dahm-Kähler, P., Enskog, A., Diaz-Garcia, C., Olausson, M., & Brännström, M. (2014). The Uterus Transplantation Trial: 1-Year Outcome. *Fertil. Steril.*, S0015–0282(14)02201–8.

Jones, H.W. (2000). Gender Reassignment and Assisted Reproduction. Evaluation of Multiple Aspects. *Hum. Reprod.*, 15: 987.

Lawrence, A.A., Shaffer, J.D., Snow, W.R., et al. (1996). Health Care Needs of Transgendered Patients. *J. Am. Med. Assoc.*, 276: 874.

Leavitt, F., & Berger, J.C. (1990). Clinical Patterns among Male Transsexual Candidates with Erotic Interest in Males. *Arch. Sex. Behav.*, 19: 491–505.

Lubbert, H., Leo-Rossberg, I., & Hammerstein, J. (1992). Effects of Ethinyl Estradiol on Semen Quality and Various Hormonal Parameters in a Eugonadal Male. *Fertil. Steril.*, 58: 603–608.

Meyer, W., III, Bockting, W., Cohen-Kettenis, P., Coleman, E., Di Ceglie, D., Devor, H., Gooren, L., Hage, J., Kirk, S., Kuiper, B., Laub, D., Lawrence, A., Menard, Y., Patton, J., Schaefer, L., Webb, A., & Wheeler, C. (2001). The Standards of Care for Gender Identity Disorders – Sixth Version. *Int. J. Transgenderism*, 5(1): www.symposion.com/ijt/soc_2001/index.htm.

Murphy, T.F. (2010). The Ethics of Helping Transgender Men and Women have Children. *Perspect Biol Med.* 53(1): 46–60.

Murphy, T.F. (2012). The Ethics of Fertility Preservation in Transgender Body Modifications. *J. Bioeth. Inq.*, 9(3): 311–316.

Murphy, T.F. (2015). Assisted Gestation and Transgender Women. *Bioethics*, 29(6): 389–397.

Pache, T.D., Chadha, S., Gooren, L.J., et al. (1991). Ovarian Morphology in Long-Term Androgen-treated Female-to-Male Transsexuals. A Human Model for the Study of Polycystic Ovarian Syndrome? *Histopathology*, 19: 445–452.

Palacios-González, C., Harris, J., & Testa, G. (2014). Multiplex Parenting: IVG and the Generations to Come. *J. Med. Ethics*, 40(11): 752–758.

Porcu, E. (2001). Oocyte Freezing. *Semin. Reprod. Med.*, 19(3): 221–230.

Robertson, J.A. (1987). Procreative Liberty, Embryos, and Collaborative Reproduction: A Legal Perspective. *Women Hlth*, 13: 179–194.

Robertson, J.A. (2005). Cancer and Fertility: Ethical and Legal Challenges. *J. Natl Cancer Inst. Monogr.*, 34: 104–106.

Ross, L.E., Tarasoff, L.A., Anderson, S., Green, D., Epstein, R., Marvel, S., & Steele, L.S. (2014). Sexual and Gender Minority Peoples' Recommendations for Assisted Human Reproduction Services. *J. Obstet. Gynaecol. Can.*, 36(2): 146–153.

Sandel, M.J. (2005). The Ethical Implications of Human Cloning. *Perspect. Biol. Med.*, 48(2): 241–247.

Schenker, J.G., & Eisenberg, V.H. (1997). Ethical Issues Relating to Reproduction Control and Women's Health. *Int. J. Gynaecol. Obstet.*, 58: 167–176.

Schulze, C. (1988). Response of the Human Testes to Long-term Estrogen Treatment: Morphology of Sertoli Cells, Leydig Cells and Spermatogonial Stem Cells. *Cell, Tissue Res.*, 251: 31–43.

Seli, E., & Tangir, J. (2005). Fertility Preservation Options for Female Patients with Malignancies. *Curr. Opin. Obstet. Gynecol.*, 17(3): 299–308.

Solter, D. (1998). Dolly is a Clone – And No Longer Alone. *Nature*, 394: 315–316.

Spinder, T., Spijkstrat, J., van den Tweel, J., Burger, C., van Kessel, H., Hompes, P., & Gooren, L. (1989). The Effects of Long-Term Testosterone Administration on Pulsatile Luteinizing Hormone Secretion and on Ovarian Histology in Eugonadal Female-to-Male Transsexual Subjects. *J. Clin. Endocrinol. Metab.*, 69: 151–157.

T'Sjoen, G., Rubens, R., De Sutter, P., & Gooren, L. (2004). The Endocine Care of Transsexual People. *J. Clin. Endocrinol. Metab.*, 89: 1014–1015.

T'Sjoen, G., Van Caenegem, E., & Wierckx, K. (2013). Transgenderism and Reproduction. *Curr. Opin. Endocrinol. Diabetes Obes.*, 20(6): 575–579.

Tzakis, A.G. (2015). The First Live Birth Subsequent to Uterus Transplantation. *Transplantation*, 99(1): 8–9.

Van Den Broecke, R., Van Der Elst, J., Liu, J., Hovatta, O., & Dhont, M. (2001). The Female-to-Male Transsexual Patient: A Source of Human Ovarian Cortical Tissue for Experimental Use. *Hum. Reprod.*, 16(1): 145–147.

Wallace, S.A., Blough, K.L., Kondapalli, L.A. (2014). Fertility Preservation in the Transgender Patient: Expanding Oncofertility Care Beyond Cancer. *Gynecol. Endocrinol.*, 25: 1–4.

White, T., & Ettner, R. (2004). Disclosure, Risks and Protective Factors for Children Whose Parents are undergoing a Gender Transition. *J. Gay Lesbian Psychother.*, 8(1/2): 129–145.

White, T., & Ettner, R. (2007). Adaptation and Adjustment in Children of Transsexual Parents. *Eur. Child Adolesc. Psychiatry*, 16(4): 215–221.

Wierckx, K., Stuyver, I., Weyers, S., Hamada, A., Agarwal, A., De Sutter, P., & T'Sjoen, G. (2012a). Sperm Freezing in Transsexual Women. *Arch. Sex. Behav.*, 41(5): 1069–1071.

Wierckx, K., Van Caenegem, E., Pennings, G., Elaut, E., Dedecker, D., Van de Peer, F., Weyers, S., De Sutter, P., & T'Sjoen, G. (2012b). Reproductive Wish in Transsexual Men. *Hum. Reprod.*, 27(2): 483–487.

World Professional Association for Transgender Health. (2011). Standards of Care for the Health of Transsexual, Transgender, and Gender Nonconforming People. 7th Version. Retrieved from: http://www.wpath.org.

Wylie K. (2004). Gender Related Disorders. *BMJ*, 329(7466): 615–617.

18 Care of Aging Transgender and Gender Non-Conforming Patients

Tarynn M. Witten and A. Evan Eyler

Introduction

Gender non-conforming persons are now becoming visible in all age groups. This makes the question of how to manage the health care needs of this population a critical one, particularly with respect to the current and future generations of older adults. Many of today's older transgender persons transitioned gender at a young age, or in middle adulthood. Those who did not—perhaps due to adverse social circumstances, family needs, or the absence of necessary medical services—may still transition later in life. Future generations will likely have more opportunity to transition at earlier stages of their lives. Regardless of the timing of transition, there is no question that the population of transgender older adults is growing (Ippolito & Witten 2014; Witten 2003; Witten & Eyler 2012). As a result, the practices of many health care providers now include elderly patients who are also gender non-conforming or transgender-identified.

This chapter discusses the experiences of the current mid-life to older adult transgender-identified persons from a gerontologic and primary care medical perspective. In part, it relies on extrapolations made from the medical and social science literatures regarding non-transgender-identified elders and from general information regarding the human life-cycle experience. This remains necessary because aging, in general, and successful/positive aging in particular, although of increasingly greater research interest, remain minimally studied among gender non-conforming persons.

Successful Aging and its Predictors: The Concept of "Aging Well"

As a greater proportion of the world's population is reaching older ages, it has become important to consider the meaning of *aging well* or *aging successfully* (Rowe & Kahn 1997, 1998; von Faber et al. 2001). In recent years, words and phrases like *gero-transcendence* (Tornstam 1989, 2005; Wadensten & Carlsson 2003), *productive aging* (Biggs 2005; Butler 2002), *life satisfaction, robust aging* (Garfein & Herzog 1995; Menec 2003), and *creative aging* have become prominent in the gerontologic and geriatric literatures (Fisher & Specht 1999).

Additionally, terms such as *positive aging, healthy aging,* and *resiliency/robustness* have entered the discussion (von Faber et al. 2001) and are now beginning to appear in the transgender literature as well (Fabbre 2015; Fredricksen-Goldsen 2011; Fredricksen-Goldsen et al. 2015; McFadden et al. 2013; Stieglitz 2010; van Wagenen et al. 2013; Witten, 2013). Finally, Liang and Luo (2012) introduce the construct of harmonious aging.

According to the MacArthur Successful Aging Project (Rowe & Kahn 1997), three factors have a major influence on productive activity in older adults: health and functional capacity, social support networks, and personal characteristics. Although considerable cross-cultural variation exists, physical health, mental effectiveness, material security, social resources and relationships, and meaningful daily activity were seen as contributing to a "good old age" in most studied groups (Maylahn et al. 2005). Good physical health and functional status have been consistently associated with aging well (Fry et al. 1997; Tate et al. 2003; von Faber et al. 2001).

The research literature has demonstrated that a lifespan history of abuse, violence, or neglect leads to an increased risk of morbidity and mortality (Agahi et al. 2014; Felitti et al. 1998; Fors et al. 2009; Korten et al. 2014; Testa et al. 2012). This is significant when viewing the current generation of transgender-identified elders, as they have frequently experienced discrimination and abuse across the lifespan in multiple areas of including physical, mental and verbal abuse (Boza & Perry 2014; Redman 2011; Shipherd et al. 2011). Moreover, they have suffered at the hands of health care workers (Grant et al. 2011; Jauk 2013; Katari & Hasche 2015; Shires & Jaffee 2015). This history has profoundly affected the way in which members of the transgender-identified population, particularly the elders of the community, view and access all levels of health care, from one-on-one doctor visits to assisted living to nursing home use. A number of authors (Finkenauer et al. 2012; Jackson et al. 2008; Redman 2011; Witten 2014; Witten & Carpenter 2015) highlight a variety of challenges in this area. These range from simple care access to threats of suicide if the elder needs to enter an assisted-living or nursing home situation. All professional caring for members of the current elder cohort of trans-identified and gender non-conforming persons need this understanding as the background construct.

Transgender Aging and Psychological Health Care

Midlife aging challenges for trans-identified persons have been discussed in Witten (2004a, 2004b). Decisions made during midlife, such as going through gender harmonization while in a marital relationship, can have both immediate and long-term impact. Individuals can face divorce, loss of family relationships, loss of employment and income, and many other difficulties. The consequences of these challenges are likely to be carried on into later life and the end-of-life trajectory.

Geropsychology and Geriatric Psychiatry Challenges

The challenges in geropsychology and geriatric psychiatry revolve around the following major categories of medical and mental health care (Bush & Martin 2005):

1. the impact of neurocognitive and neurobehavioral changes arriving from cerebrovascular events;
2. assessment and treatment of Parkinson's disease, Lewy body dementia, and Alzheimer's disease;
3. traumatic brain injury due to falls or other impact events;
4. co-occurring psychiatric problems such as anxiety, depression;
5. pain and pain management;
6. substance abuse, including alcohol and other drugs.

While these problems may be a challenge to manage in those who do not identify as members of the transgender or gender non-conforming community, the gender non-conforming status of a trans-elder can readily increase their management difficulty. Practitioners should remain aware of the impact that gender non-conforming identities and the life histories may have in these areas.

Substance Abuse

Substance abuse in the elderly is a growing problem (Bogunovic 2012; Gum et al. 2009; SAMHSA/CSAT 2015; Steinhagen & Friedman 2008). Substance abuse among those 60 years and older (including misuse of prescription drugs) currently affects about 17% of this population. By 2020, the number of older adults with substance abuse problems is expected to double. Upwards of 15% of community-dwelling older adults have problems with alcohol and up to 20% of older adults misuse a combination of alcohol and medications (Hazelton Betty Ford Foundation 2015). It is believed that, as the baby boomer generation ages, there will be an increased use of marijuana that could lead to abuse as people age. While not focused specifically on transgender or on elders, Cochran and Cauce (2006) point out that, "openly LGBT [lesbian, gay, bisexual, or transgender] clients enter treatment with more severe substance abuse problems, greater psychopathology, and greater medical service utilization when compared with heterosexual clients" (p. 135). Reisner et al. (2015) and Richmond et al. (2012) both demonstrate results that suggest that, for transgender and gender-nonconforming individuals, suicidality, substance use, and tobacco use (Clark & Coughlin 2012) are further exacerbated. Many reasons are proposed for the elevated risks experienced by transgender-identified persons: social anxiety, ongoing stigma, loss of employment, homelessness, loss of social network. Nevertheless, the mistreatment of trans-identified persons can create challenges for these individuals even within addiction treatment settings, where social rejection, abuse, and stigma can induce premature exiting from the treatment program and further exacerbate a sense of isolation and conflict (Lyons et al. 2015). It is important to provide culturally competent substance abuse treatment (Nuttbrock 2012) by understanding the cultural context and history of today's members of the elder trans-community.

As people age, they experience pharmacodynamics changes (Shi & Klotz 2011): their bodies metabolize alcohol and other substances more slowly. Therefore, older adults have increased sensitivity to, and decreased tolerance for, alcohol. Older adults frequently use more prescribed medications and do not understand the potential interactions with alcohol and other substances, leading to serious medical and psychological problems. It is important for the health care worker to communicate the potential for interaction between medications and non-prescribed substances such as alcohol, marijuana, and other drugs.

Anxiety and Depression

Anxiety (Cassidy & Rector 2008; Wolitzky-Taylor et al. 2010) and depression (Carter 2011; Centers for Disease Control and Prevention 2015; Fiske et al. 2009) are common among the aging population. While there are few specific data regarding anxiety and depression prevalence in the elder transgender and gender non-conforming population, for the current elder cohort it is easy to make the hypothesis that the levels of anxiety and depression will be high given their overall history of stigma and abuse.

General studies of the trans-identified population show that levels of depression and anxiety exceed those in the non-trans/gender non-conforming population (Rotondi 2012). Budge et al. (2013a) found that the rates of depression symptoms (51.4% for transgender women and 48.3% for transgender men) and anxiety (40.4% for transgender women and 47.5% for transgender men) surpass the rates of those for the general population. Bockting et al. (2013) found a high prevalence of clinical depression (44.1% overall), anxiety (33.2% overall), and somatization challenges (27.5% overall). They found that peer support moderated the relationship between these disorders and the effects of minority stress. Other studies found similar results (Nuttbrock et al. 2014a, 2014b), though only Fredricksen-Goldsen et al. (2014) discussed the mental health status of transgender older adults and found significantly elevated levels of anxiety and depression with respect to the general population.

Overall, results from studies of transgender mental health show that practitioners should focus on interventions that reduce avoidant coping strategies, increase social support network connections and peer support systems, address body-centered issues, develop physical and mental activities, incorporate spirituality/religiosity where appropriate, and focus on person-centered care.

Cognitive Functioning

One of the central domains of positive aging is *cognitive functioning*. In particular, successful aging is related to the "ability to maintain the daily activities associated with overall health" (Hawkins 2005). Indicators of success in this area include self-esteem, perceived control, resilience, and mental well-being. Cognitive functioning can be impaired by dementing illnesses and mild cognitive impairment.

Mild cognitive impairment (MCI) is considered a transition state, along a continuum between normal cognitive aging and clinical dementia. Individuals identified with MCI have been shown to have an annual conversion rate to dementia of 12–15%, significantly higher than the population conversion rate of 1–2% (Petersen et al. 1999). Current estimates are that "1 in 3 seniors die with Alzheimer's or other dementia (Anderson 2013)." Witten (2015a, Table 1) suggests that, by the year 2030, based upon previous estimates of gender non-conforming population prevalence (Meier & Labuski 2013; Winter & Conway 2011; Witten 2003), there may be between 36,046 and 177,857 trans-identified individuals in the United States with some form of dementia. Moreover, by the year 2030, there may be between 21,268 and 152,127 trans-identified persons with the Alzheimer form of dementia. Among the transgender-identified population, later-life dementia is a significant worry (Witten 2014). In fact, Witten (2014, 2015b) points out that some of the survey respondents indicated that they had euthanasia plans in place should they need later-life care, whether it be in home or in a care facility.

> I am worried that I will development dementia and will not remember that I have transitioned. I am worried that I will not be able to support myself and that there will be no one to take care of me. I am already becoming so forgetful and unable to concentrate at 55yo that I worry I will not be able to hold or keep a job at some point within the next five years or longer. *I worry that I will not have the resolve to kill myself when I cannot support myself any longer* (Witten 2015a).

Given the already high estimates of suicide in the trans-community and the suicide rates of elder individuals in the general population (Clements-Nolle et al. 2006), these dementia-related facts must be given serious consideration.

As discussed in the following text, currently there is a significant lack of supportive care resources for transgender-identified persons. Therefore, loss of cognitive abilities may be particularly devastating to transgender older adults. Physicians and other clinicians should remain alert for signs of cognitive decline and emotional depression among their elderly transgender patients. Many older adults who experience the increased vulnerability of decreased cognitive functioning can continue to manage their lives with sufficient emotional and practical support. Early detection of cognitive decline can provide an opportunity for comprehensive assessment and planning for supportive services.

Another challenge to "aging well" for transgender elders is that they may be at higher risk for economic insecurity than their cisgender peers, due to midlife events such as loss of employment during gender transition, workplace discrimination, and the absence of legal protection against such transgressions (Agahi et al. 2014; Bradford et al. 2013; Fredricksen-Goldsen et al. 2014; Witten 2014).

Case History—James Retires from the Workforce and Becomes Susan

James was born in a Midwestern city. He was aware of his gender difference from an early age, but did not tell anyone. James attempted to maintain a masculine façade by pursuing traditionally masculine lifestyle choices. He worked as a skilled tradesman, got married, and sometimes engaged in heavy drinking.

When James was 57 years old, his wife died. At the age of 61, he decided to initiate an identity change. He began estrogen therapy, legally changed his name to Susan, and modified his legal documents accordingly. In addition to medical care for gender transition, she required treatment for hypertension and chronic lung disease.

Susan moved into a retirement community in a new city, easily making new female friends. She did not disclose her previous gender identity to anyone.

After living full-time as a woman for 2 years, Susan became interested in the possibility of having a sexual relationship as a female. At the age of 63, she underwent genital reconstruction surgery. Soon thereafter, Susan met an older bisexual woman at church with whom she had a sexual relationship.

Some time later, Susan moved to another community. She became active in religious service work, civic volunteer work, and teaching her hobbies. She has remained single and has many friends. None of them know about her gender transition. She had decided to avoid "coming out" following her move.

Susan is a vibrant, resilient individual. Her life course has been unusual, but she is aging successfully while making choices that are true to her heart.

Susan's journey demonstrates changes and concerns that sometimes accompany later-life transitions.

Transgender Aging and Medical Care

General Medical Care

The physical (morphological) realities of aging may facilitate social gender transition for many transgender older adults. For example, women and men share more physical similarities during the elder years than at any time since childhood. Loss of facial skin tone produces a softer appearance for many natal males; the natural diminishment of circulating estrogens, accompanied by a shift toward androgenization of the hair follicles, may facilitate the production of light new beard growth in natal females. In addition, the loss of muscle mass and increased body fat content, which is experienced by both male and female older adults, often results in phenotypic gender convergence of the body habitus (i.e., women and men appear more alike than before with regard to body fat distribution, girth, and posture). These physical changes can be accentuated by the use of hormonal medications, and used advantageously by older adults who transition gender.

Physical functioning, such as that required for the performance of the usual activities of daily living, is generally unaffected by gender transition, although androgen supplementation will result in increased muscle mass and, often, greater physical robustness.

In many ways, the health care experiences of women and men become more similar after the childbearing years. Emphasis is placed on preventive care, early detection of treatable illnesses, and maintenance of physical and mental functioning during the later years. Encouragement of physical activity and smoking cessation; normalization of blood pressure, serum glucose, and lipids; screening for non-genital cancers; and many other aspects of routine care are essentially the same for women and men, whether or not they have previously transitioned gender (U. S. Preventive Services Task Force 2014).

The routine medical care of transgender older adults does not differ from that of their non-transgender peers in most respects. The evidence-based recommendations of the U. S. Preventive Services Task Force, or similar guidelines, should be followed unless there are specific clinical reasons for doing otherwise. Recommendations and protocols for the primary care of transgender adults are available from a variety of sources (Center of Excellence for Transgender Health 2011; Feldman 2007, 2008; Feldman & Goldberg 2006; Gorton et al. 2005). The Center of Excellence for Transgender Health of the University of San Francisco document includes a section on aging, but due to the current limitations on transgender aging research, few specific recommendations are available (Center of Excellence for Transgender Health 2011).

Hormonal Treatment

Treatment with hormonal medications is a medically necessary treatment for many persons with gender dysphoria (Coleman et al. 2012). Although additional large sample research is needed, reasonable evidence-based guidelines for the use of hormonal medications by transgender adults are available to assist the practicing clinician in this area of practice (Coleman et al. 2012; Feldman & Safer 2009; Hembree et al. 2009). Specifics regarding the best clinical practices for use of estrogens and androgens by transgender older adults are substantially less clear. The use of hormonal preparations is affected by the aging process. While much is known about overall pharmacologic and hormonal changes of aging (Mangoni & Jackson 2004;

McLean & LeCouteur 2004; Roberts et al. 1996; Shi & Klotz 2011), research involving transgender older persons using supplemental hormones is much less robust, and prescribing practices often must be extrapolated from data regarding the non-transgender population.

Morbidity and Mortality

Despite the limitations, recent data regarding morbidity and mortality among transgender adults using estrogens or androgens are somewhat encouraging regarding long-term safety. In 1989, Asscheman et al. compared adverse events among 303 male-to-female and 122 female-to-male transgender adults to a similar reference group in the general Dutch population. Deaths among the transwomen were increased fivefold from expected levels, and non-lethal complications were also substantially increased, including thromboembolic events (45-fold), hyperprolactinemia (400-fold), and depressive symptoms (15-fold). There was no excess mortality among the transmen, but increases were observed in weight gain and elevation of transaminases. These findings were particularly concerning because the study population included relatively few older adults and persons who had used hormonal supplementation for long periods of time. The authors concluded, "Thus, the dilemma of prescribing cross gender hormones in view of the needs of these patients is not resolved."

In 2011, Asscheman et al. published a similar comparison, including data from a larger sample (966 male-to-female and 365 female-to-male trans-sexual persons) followed for a longer period of time (median 18.5 years, including 413 transwomen and 148 transmen who were followed for at least 20 years). Total mortality among the transwomen was increased 51% over the general population; though the authors concluded that use of ethinyl estradiol may increase the risk of death from cardiovascular causes, the excess mortality was "mainly due to non-hormone related causes (p. 635)," including suicide, HIV, substance abuse and "unknown cause," and was substantially lower than in the earlier study. Total mortality and cause-specific mortality were not increased among the transmen; the authors noted that "In the FTM transsexuals, use of testosterone in doses used for hypogonadal men seemed safe." Though data regarding the older adults in this sample were not reported specifically, the lengthy follow-up period is at least somewhat reassuring regarding safety of hormone use across the lifespan. Further research regarding specific risks and benefits of hormone use in older adulthood is currently needed.

Risks of Hormone Use

Until additional research on the care of transgender older adults is conducted, physicians and other health care providers must extrapolate from evidence-based recommendations regarding care of non-transgender geriatric patients. A general guideline is to consider both the usual effects of hormone supplementation for non-transgender patients and the medical characteristics of the individual transgender person.

For example, the risks of estrogen use among cisgender women increase with age, and it is very likely that transgender women are similarly affected. Therefore, initiating estrogen supplementation for an older transwoman patient with known coronary artery disease should be undertaken with extreme caution and careful monitoring. Similarly, androgen supplementation has been associated with a variety of risks in elderly natal males, and should be started cautiously when the patient has preexisting conditions, such as elevated serum hemoglobin or obstructive sleep apnea.

Counterbalancing the physiological risks of use of estrogens or androgens among older adults is the high level of psychological relief experienced by transgender persons who begin treatment with hormonal medications at any age. *Gender dysphoria*, "the distress that may accompany the incongruence between one's experienced or expressed gender and one's assigned gender" (American Psychiatric Association 2013, p. 451), can be a significant psychological burden across the lifespan. Many transgender older adults are willing to accept the risks that accompany treatment with estrogens or androgens in order to gain the psychological benefits that congruence between the psychological gender and the physical body can provide.

The risks of use of hormonal treatments by transgender adults have been extensively considered (Coleman et al. 2012; Eyler & Feldman 2008; Feldman 2007, 2008; Hembree et al. 2009), usually with acknowledgment that some risks rise with age. The World Professional Association for Transgender Health *Standards of Care* (version 7, Coleman et al. 2012) stratifies specific risks based on likelihood of increased risk and clinical significance.

Illnesses associated with a "likely increased risk" from feminizing hormones included: venous thromboembolic disease, gallstones, elevated liver enzymes, weight gain, hypertriglyceridemia—and cardiovascular disease if additional risk factors, including age, are present. A rating of "possible increased risk" was assigned to hypertension, hyperprolactinemia, or prolactinoma—and to type 2 diabetes with additional risk factors, including age. Illnesses associated with a "likely increased risk" from masculinizing hormones included polycythemia, weight gain, acne, male-pattern baldness, and sleep apnea. "Possible increased risk" with additional risk factors, again including age, was assigned to cardiovascular disease, hypertension, and type 2 diabetes. Specific aspects of transgender older adult hormonal care, with estrogens and androgens, are considered next (Coleman et al. 2012).

Estrogen Supplementation

Due to a current lack of data regarding the clinical experience of older transwomen, estrogen use in this population must be considered in light of information gained from the study of postmenopausal estrogen supplementation among (cisgender) women.

The use of supplemental estrogen by older non-transgender women remains somewhat controversial despite many years of research. For decades, it was believed that the longer average life expectancy enjoyed by women, relative to men, was in large part due to hormonal factors: higher levels of estrogen production, lower testosterone, or both. Therefore, it was argued, supplementing estrogen following the menopausal decline would continue this physiological advantage, reducing the risk of cardiovascular disease and prolonging life. In vitro evidence had demonstrated salutary effects of estrogen on physiological processes known to affect vascular functioning, such as the renin–angiotensin system, and nitrous oxide synthesis and secretion. Available clinical data, including the Nurses' Health Study (a prospective cohort study, including 70,533 nurses, 20-year observational data, Grodstein et al. 2001), supported this theory, at least in part.

Subsequent data from randomized controlled trials contradicted this viewpoint. The Heart and Estrogen/Progestin Replacement Study (HERS) trial failed to demonstrate any cardiovascular benefit—and found a probable increased risk—among women with preexisting coronary artery disease and taking estrogen and progestins postmenopausally (Grady et al. 2002; Roussouw et al. 2002). The Women's Health Initiative (WHI) trial studied the effects of hormone use among postmenopausal women without known cardiovascular disease. An increased risk of cardiac events was detected in the combined estrogen–progestin arm of the trial, while the estrogen-only arm found no increase in cardiac events, but an increase in cerebrovascular events (Curb et al. 2006; Cushman et al. 2004). (Some benefits of estrogen use were also detected, including reduced risk of osteoporosis.) Following publication of these results, estrogen supplementation was no longer recommended for either primary or secondary prevention of coronary artery disease among postmenopausal women, and women taking estrogen were encouraged to discontinue its use.

The HERS and the WHI conclusions were subsequently challenged on numerous methodological grounds (Speroff & Fritz 2005, pp. 689-777; Utian 2012). Concerns were raised regarding the heterogeneity of the HERS and WHI populations with regard to age of onset of supplemental hormone use, years elapsed since menopause, and concurrent risk factors for development of cardiovascular disease and other negative outcomes. Specific hormonal regimens, including use of estrogen with or without progesterone, estrogen dose, means of administration, and total duration of use, also became significant questions of interest. Reanalysis of the data from these studies and review of other relevant literature resulted in revised, more favorable, guidelines for use of estrogen in treatment of menopause by the International Menopause Society (jointly with the European Menopause and Andropause Society) (de Villiers et al. 2013; North American Menopause Society 2015), and other professional organizations. Though transgender women do not experience ovarian menopause as such, several aspects of this clinical evolution in the treatment of menopause are relevant to the care of older transwomen.

Age at Onset of Use

Although the average age of menopause in the United States is 51 years, the average age of enrollees in the WHI trial was 63.3 years. Twenty-five percent of the participants were 70–79 years old. Shortly after the publication of the HERS data, it was suggested (Phillips & Langer 2005; Speroff & Fritz 2005) that estrogen plays a beneficial role in preventing the formation of vascular plaque, but may have deleterious effects (e.g., increased likelihood of erosion and rupture) on existing plaque. Therefore, estrogen use begun at younger ages, such as at the time of menopause, when cardiovascular plaque would usually not yet be well established, would likely be safer, with regard to development of coronary artery disease, than estrogen begun later in life.

Analysis of the WHI data regarding women who began estrogen use at age 50–59 is consistent with that hypothesis (Hsia et al. 2006). Although the effects of estrogen on the cardiovascular system have not been well studied among transgender women, it is probable, or at least possible, that similar findings will emerge. Transwomen who begin hormonal transition after age 60 may have the same clinical experience as their cisgender peers who begin taking estrogen at older ages. Since natal males often develop coronary artery disease at earlier ages than natal females, it is possible that transgender women who begin estrogen use prior to age 50 will also experience an increased risk, though additional research will be needed to evaluate that question. In the meantime, transwomen who begin estrogen use in middle or older adulthood should be followed closely and offered comprehensive management of other risk factors for development of cardiovascular disease.

Type, Route, and Dosing of the Hormonal Preparation

Both the HERS and the WHI trials utilized conjugated equine estrogens (CEE), which were administered orally. It was subsequently suggested that transdermal administration may be associated with a lower thrombogenic risk (due to differences in hepatic metabolism), as might the use of other estrogen compounds, principally 17-beta-estradiol (E_2). Relatively small studies measuring physiologic endpoints have suggested an increased thrombotic risk among women taking oral CEE but not among those using transdermal E_2 (Girdler et al., 2004; Toorians et al. 2003; Vongpatanasin et al. 2003). Current research is attempting to determine whether differences between estrogen formulations and routes of administration are clinically significant.

The Kronos Early Estrogen Prevention Study is a randomized, placebo-controlled study designed to evaluate risks and benefits of estrogen early in the menopause years (middle adulthood). A total of 727 women, ages 42–58 (mean age 52), were randomized to receive estrogen replacement with either CEE 0.45 mg daily or 50 mcg transdermal estradiol, both with micronized progesterone 200 mg for 12 days each month, or placebo (Harman et al. 2005). Physiologic parameters were assessed, rather than actual events. Initial results suggest a mixture of benefits and drawbacks for both oral and transdermal estrogen (Manson

2013). Oral CEE was associated with favorable changes in lipid profile, with increased high-density lipoprotein and decreased low-density lipoprotein levels. Transdermal estrogen use did not result in any beneficial lipid effects, but was associated with a significant improvement in insulin resistance. Neither form of estrogen replacement increased blood pressure and both were associated with preservation of bone mineral density. Further follow-up is planned though questions remain regarding choice of estrogen preparation, changes in the estrogen program used may have contributed to the observed decline in thromboembolic events and all-cause mortality among transsexual women, over time, in the relatively large sample Dutch data (Asscheman et al, 1989; van Kesteren et al, 1997). Data regarding older transwomen followed over long periods of time are still fairly scant, but it is encouraging that observed mortality in the second study (van Kestenen et al, 1997) was not in excess of expected general Dutch population norms. Transwomen wanting to take estrogen in middle and older adulthood can be advised of the current state of available information, and programs of treatment adjusted as additional data become available.

Concurrent Health Risks

Cigarette smoking is the greatest modifiable risk factor for cardiovascular disease and thromboembolic events. Patients who use estrogens should not smoke. This is particularly important in the middle and older adult years, as the risk of these conditions rises with age. Other risk factors for estrogen-associated morbidity and mortality, particularly among the elderly, include uncontrolled hypertension, pathologic hypercoagulable states, any history of thromboembolic disease, uncontrolled diabetes mellitus, atypical migraine syndromes, obesity, and the use of unusually complicated pharmacologic regimens.

Clearly, additional clinical research regarding the use of estrogen by transwomen in older adulthood is needed. Current information suggests the following recommendations:

1. Use of estrogen can help to alleviate gender dysphoria at any age.
2. Though the available morbidity and mortality data are fairly encouraging, the risks and benefits of starting treatment with estrogen at older ages, and of taking estrogens for extended periods of time, have not been fully elucidated.
3. Treatment with estrogen during middle and older adulthood is associated with significant benefits and medical risks. Patients should be advised of the risks, benefits, and possible side effects of estrogen use, and assisted in making an informed decision about it.
4. Transgender women who begin hormonal treatment in midlife or at later ages should be evaluated for evidence of hypertension, cardiovascular or cerebrovascular disease, glucose intolerance, and other chronic conditions that may be worsened by the use of estrogen.
5. Estrogen preparations should be used with extreme caution, or not at all, by transgender older adults with uncontrolled concurrent health risks.

6. Minimal, clinically adequate estrogen doses should be used. There is no evidence to support the use of high doses of either estrogens or androgens for elderly persons.
7. Transwomen who use estrogen should not smoke. This is particularly important in older adulthood. Physicians and other clinicians should assist their older patients in smoking cessation.
8. Current data do not definitely support the use of one estrogen preparation or route of administration over another, including compounded "bio-identical" estrogen formulations.

Androgen Supplementation

Although morbidity and mortality data (Asscheman et al. 2011) suggest that use of testosterone therapy by transgender men is relatively safe, data regarding testosterone supplementation by older transmen, or over long periods of time (decades), are minimal. It is therefore necessary to extrapolate from the clinical experience of cisgender males taking androgens, despite the limitations of this approach.

Testosterone production in natal males declines slowly from midlife through old age, usually about 1–2% per year (Feldman et al. 2002; Harman et al. 2001), eventually by about 50%. Average serum testosterone levels among 30-year-old men are about 600 ng/dL, or 20.8 nmol/L; mean values for 80-year-old men are approximately 400 ng/dL, or 13.9 nmol/L. This "andropause" results in a decrease in muscle strength and mass, bone strength (although it is primarily the androgen-derived estrogen that maintains bone density), erythrocytosis, and subjective well-being. Frailty often increases over time.

Androgen replacement has been suggested as a means of maintaining vigor and robustness among elderly men. However, because of the associated risks, androgen supplementation is not recommended for routine use by most relevant professional bodies (e.g., U.S. Institute of Medicine, Endocrine Society, Endocrine Society of Australia). Supplemental testosterone is used primarily in deficiency states accompanied by clinical evidence of resultant problems (Conway et al. 2000), particularly if the morning serum testosterone level falls below 300 ng/dL (American Society of Andrology 2006). Some authors use 200 ng/dL as the value below which men should be considered hypogonadal, regardless of age and other factors (Wald et al. 2006). The Endocrine Society Clinical Practice Guideline on testosterone therapy in men with androgen deficiency syndrome recommends against screening for testosterone deficiency in the general population, and recommends treatment of androgen deficiency only when the serum testosterone levels are "unequivocally low" and the man is symptomatic (Bhasin et al. 2010).

Elderly transmen usually require ongoing testosterone supplementation, particularly if oophorectomy has been performed. At present, few data are available regarding optimal androgen dosing and monitoring in this population. Many clinicians recommend adjusting the testosterone dose to keep the serum level at the lower end of the normal male range, as would be the case for healthy older adult cisgendered males.

Informed consent for treatment with testosterone must include current information regarding potential benefits and risks. Potential benefits include relief of gender dysphoria, improved sense of well-being, increased muscle mass, and reduction in physical frailty.

Risks Associated with Supplemental Testosterone Use

Research among cisgender men using supplemental testosterone has identified the following side effects and health risks: acne and oily skin; breast enlargement and tenderness, especially early in treatment; fluid retention and peripheral edema; sleep apnea; the development of polycythemia; and possible negative effects on androgen-sensitive epilepsy and some migrainoid conditions (American Society of Andrology 2006; Conway et al. 2000; Wald et al. 2006). Testosterone use is also contraindicated in pregnancy and prostate disease, which is not among the concerns of transmen in older adulthood. Some transmen in middle and older adulthood report other symptoms that interfere with quality of life, including recurrent tendonitis, pelvic cramping that does not appear due to polycystic ovary syndrome, and uncomfortable increase in neck circumference, with or without development of obstructive sleep apnea (Ippolito & Sampson 2015). The Endocrine Society Guideline (Bhasin et al. 2010, p. 2545) recommends against use of testosterone in conditions in which "administration is associated with a high risk of adverse outcome," including breast cancer, polycythemia (hematocrit > 50%), uncontrolled or poorly controlled congestive heart failure. Some conditions, such as hypertension, type 2 diabetes, and cyclic or psychotic psychiatric disorders, may be increased in certain cases, such as when other risk factors are present (Coleman et al. 2012).

Although cardiac effects, in the absence of significant existing disease, have generally been neutral overall (Tan & Salazar 2004), the long-term impact of testosterone on cardiovascular disease remains unknown (Tenover 1999, reiterated in Wald et al. 2006) and may increase with age (Coleman et al. 2012). Supra-therapeutic androgen administration, which is sometimes used by male bodybuilders, is associated with cardiac disease and other serious complications, and is thoroughly contraindicated for both cisgender men and transmen.

Polycythemia

Testosterone supplementation results in increased erythrocyte production in both natal females and natal males. Although this may provide therapeutic benefit to elderly persons suffering from decreased erythropoiesis, occasionally hemoglobin and hematocrit elevate to pathologic levels, particularly if the serum testosterone is above the usual male range. Arterial and venous thromboembolic events may ensue, particularly if other cardiac risk factors (especially smoking) are present (Hachulla et al. 2000). Older adults are at higher risk due to the vascular changes that accompany the aging process. Wald et al. noted, "The main risk factor for polycythemia with testosterone administration appears to be age, "though risk is also increased with heavy smoking history, COPD, or obstructive sleep apnea" (Wald et al. 2006, p. 129).

Older transmen should be advised about the possible consequences of polycythemia, and should have hemoglobin and hematocrit monitored periodically. Annual evaluation may suffice when the testosterone dosage and hematocrit have stabilized over time; more frequent monitoring should be obtained earlier in the treatment process. The Endocrine Society Clinical Practice Guideline on the "endocrine treatment of transsexual persons" (Hembree et al. 2009) recommends obtaining a complete blood count and liver function tests every 3 months during the first year of testosterone treatment for transmen, then once or twice yearly. This is a slightly more frequent schedule than the recommendations of the same organization for hematocrit monitoring during androgen supplementation for cisgender men: 3–6 months after the start of treatment, then annually. This difference most likely represents the more robust nature of the data regarding cisgender men relative to transmen.

Reduction in testosterone dosage, or a moratorium on supplementation, is usually required when hemoglobin and hematocrit elevate to, or above, the upper limit of the normal male range (hematocrit 52% by American Society of Andrology (2006) guidelines, p. 133). Bhasin et al. (2010) recommend suspending testosterone use if the hematocrit exceeds 54%, evaluation for hypoxia and sleep apnea, then resumption of treatment with a lower testosterone dose. When hematocrit elevates above 54%, phlebotomy should be undertaken to reduce it below 45%, in order to prevent vascular occlusive complications (Pearson & Messinezy 2001). All of these recommendations were developed for the treatment of cisgender males. There is currently no evidence regarding whether this approach is appropriate for the treatment of older transmen. It may be prudent to reduce the testosterone dose, or temporarily stop administration, at a slightly lower hematocrit level in this population.

Choice of Testosterone Preparation

Testosterone can be administered by a variety of routes, including transdermally, intramuscularly, orally, and buccally. Hembree et al. (2009) recommend testosterone supplementation with parenteral testosterone enanthate, cypionate, or undecanoate; oral administration of testosterone undecanoate, or use of topical testosterone patches or gel. Bhasin et al. (2010) also recommend buccal administration and use of implantable pellets. Hepatic dysfunction and malignancies have previously been observed among men using oral testosterone preparations (Nieschalg & Behre 1998, in Wald et al. 2006) although a newer preparation of testosterone undecanoate dissolved in castor oil appears to be acceptably safe (Gooren & Bunck 2004) and is currently used in Canada and parts of Europe. Although intramuscular testosterone preparations have long been the mainstay of hormonal treatment for transmen, other routes of administration, particularly the transdermal patches and gels, offer some advantages in the treatment of older adults. Elderly persons generally have less muscle mass than young adults, and may experience more difficulties with injection pain and other problems. Transdermal administration also provides less variability in average testosterone levels than most injection programs. This offers the advantage of being able to more easily avoid supraphysiologic testosterone levels, that are most likely not appropriate for older adults, and of being able to obtain lab tests without the attention to timing that is needed with an injectable program.

Among natal males, transdermal patches, applied every night, produce a mean total testosterone profile that mimics the male circadian pattern (Mazer et al. 2005). Some patients cannot tolerate the dermal irritation that the patch can produce; this may be a greater problem among older patients because of age-associated dermal changes. Topical testosterone gel does not produce the circadian pattern associated with patch use (Mazer et al. 2005), but it is easy to use and is generally well accepted by transmen (Feldman 2005).

Buccal testosterone administration also appears to be safe and effective (Dobs et al. 2004), although its role in the treatment of older patients, who are more likely than younger individuals to experience problems maintaining oral health, remains to be determined.

It is clear that additional clinical research regarding use of hormonal treatments by transgender older men is needed. In the meantime, current information suggests the following recommendations:

1. Use of testosterone supplementation can help to alleviate gender dysphoria at any age.
2. Though the available morbidity and mortality data are fairly encouraging, the risks and benefits of starting treatment with testosterone at older ages, and of taking androgens for extended periods of time, have not been fully elucidated.
3. Treatment with androgens during middle and older adulthood is associated with significant benefits and medical risks. Patients should be advised of the risks, benefits, and possible side effects of testosterone use, and assisted in making an informed decision about it.
4. Transmen who begin hormonal treatment in middle or older adulthood should be screened for evidence of cardiovascular disease, obstructive sleep apnea, polycythemia, and other chronic conditions that may be worsened by the use of testosterone.
5. Testosterone preparations should be used with extreme caution, or not at all, by transgender older adults with uncontrolled concurrent health risks, or a history of breast cancer.
6. Older transmen wishing to begin treatment with testosterone should be advised that doses resulting in modest serum levels (i.e., generally not above the norms for natal males of similar age) should be used.
7. Hemoglobin and transaminase levels should be monitored periodically (at least annually when therapy is well established), and more often during initiation of treatment.
8. When possible, transdermal preparations (gel or patches) should be used.
9. Transmen who use androgens should not smoke. This is particularly important in the later years. Physicians and other clinicians should assist their older patients in smoking cessation.

Surgery

Research regarding the surgical experience of transgender older adults is scant. Many outcome studies have included small numbers of elderly participants, but none has specifically evaluated the experience of this population. Older age at the time of surgery has been associated with an increased likelihood of dissatisfaction or regret following male-to-female genital surgery in several studies (Eldh et al. 1997; Lindemalm et al. 1987; Rubin 1993), although not in others (Krege et al. 2001; Kuiper & Cohen-Kettenis 1988; Landen et al. 1998; Lawrence 2003). Overall, regrets have been uncommon.

Even the larger studies with "older" enrollees have included few participants over the age of 65 years. For example, in Lawrence's work (2003) involving 232 male-to-female transsexual adults, the mean age at the time of surgery was 44, with standard deviation of 9 years. Other recent studies (Asscheman et al. 2011; De Cuypere et al. 2005; Garaffa et al. 2010) have similarly included primarily persons who were in early or mid-adulthood at the time of surgery. Therefore, the current approach to sex reassignment surgery among elderly persons is based on extrapolation from the surgical experience of older adults undergoing other surgical procedures and from the emotional experience of younger adults.

Anecdotal information suggests that the results of genital surgery for older transgender patients are often not as good as those achieved by younger persons, due to the relative lack of tissue distensibility, the age-related genital shrinkage that may have occurred prior to initiation of hormonal supplementation, and the loss of tissue tone (W Kuzon and N Wilson personal communication). Nonetheless, older persons may experience the same emotional relief from gender dysphoria and sense of completion as would younger individuals. For many older persons, the joy of personal fulfillment is tempered by regret that the opportunity for gender transition, including gender confirmation surgery, did not arise until so late in the life course.

Decisions regarding candidacy for the surgical procedures associated with gender transition are made on the basis of the health status of the patient, rather than on the basis of chronological age, per se. Older adults who are in good health may be reasonable candidates for genital surgery, though a thorough preoperative evaluation should be performed. Medical and surgical history, current cardiovascular health status, and complexity of the planned procedure, including estimated anesthesia time, cardiovascular stress, and physiologic fluid shifting, should be weighed by the patient's personal physician and anesthesiologist (King 2000). Genital surgeries are usually scheduled far in advance of the surgery date, allowing ample opportunity for cardiopulmonary evaluation to be conducted on an outpatient basis during the months prior to the planned procedure.

Patients who are unable to undergo genital surgery due to lack of medical fitness may be appropriate candidates for less extensive procedures, such as breast augmentation mammoplasty and facial cosmetic surgery. For some transwomen, facial surgery may provide as much benefit with regard to social integration as genital surgery (Hage et al. 1997), although specific data regarding elderly persons are lacking in this regard. Facial rejuvenation surgeries, such as submental liposuction, are commonly performed in older adulthood (Pitanguy & Machado 2012) and may be chosen by older transwomen as part of the gender transition process.

For any surgical procedure, presurgical risk assessment should be performed according to evidence-based guidelines, with an emphasis on the balance between the anticipated cardiovascular demand of the procedure and the physiologic reserve of the patient.

Postsurgical recovery times generally lengthen with age. Older persons undergoing surgery usually need more in-home support during the weeks following surgery than would younger adults. Assessing the degree of family support and other available resources is a crucial aspect of the surgical planning process, particularly in the United States, where hospitalizations are often relatively brief, and much postsurgical recovery and care occur in the home setting. The recovery process may be further complicated if empathic, non-judgmental personal care assistants are not available during the postoperative period.

Osteoporosis

Osteoporosis is a medical condition that is of particular concern to transgender older adults, because of the crucial role of sex steroids in maintaining bone density. It is a common and painful condition. In the United States, 16% of women and 5% of men over the age of 50 will experience at least one vertebral fracture; 18% of women and 6% of men will experience at least one hip fracture. Fractures are less common among men because of the greater baseline adult bone mass and the slower decline in sex steroid production with aging. However, osteoporosis among men is increasing as they live to older ages and participate in lower levels of physical exercise early in life.

Osteoporosis has been reported among both transwomen and transmen, although there has, as yet, been little systematic study of this condition in the transgender population. Several small studies have indicated an increased risk of bone demineralization among both male-to-female patients who did not receive (or did not comply with) adequate estrogen replacement (Hierl et al. 1999; Ruetsche et al. 2005) and female-to-male patients following oophorectomy (van Kesteren et al. 1998a, 1998b). Other studies (Mueller et al. 2005; Reutrakul et al. 1998; Schlatterer et al. 1998; Sosa et al. 2003; Turner et al. 2004) have found mean bone densities at or above the usual range for age and natal sex, although these have utilized relatively short follow-up intervals and have included few elderly participants. One study with longer follow-up—mean 12.5 years for 24 male-to-female participants and 7.6 years for 15 female-to-male participants—found bone densities at or above expected norms, except for five cases of osteoporosis among male-to-female patients who did not comply with hormonal treatment (Ruetsche et al. 2005). More recently, Wierckx et al. (2012) evaluated 50 transmen and 50 transwomen who had used hormone treatments for an average of 10 years and who had had gender-confirming surgeries. None of the transmen showed evidence of osteoporosis, but one-quarter of the transwomen had osteoporosis of the lumbar spine and radius.

As is the case among all middle-aged and older adults, hormone deprivation appears to be a primary risk factor for the development of osteoporosis among both male-to-female and female-to-male transsexual patients. Van Caenegem et al. (2013) have also demonstrated lower bone mineral density in transwomen, prior to hormonal or surgical treatment, compared to matched cisgender male controls. Serum luteinizing hormone levels may provide the best predictor of adequacy of hormone replacement for osteoporosis prevention (Gooren et al. 2008; van Kesteren et al. 1998a, 1998b).

Osteoporosis prevention measures are discussed in several practice guidelines. Hembree et al. (2009) note that "fracture data in transsexual men and women are not available" but recommend measurement of bone mineral density "if risk factors for osteoporosis exist, specifically in those who stop hormone therapy after gonadectomy." The Center of Excellence for Transgender Health (2011) suggests consideration of bone density screening for transmen at age 50 or older if testosterone has been used for more than 5–10 years, and at age 60 or older if testosterone has been used for a shorter period of time. Both of these approaches reflect a degree of face validity and are evidence-based, though the evidence is not robust. Until more extensive evidence and therefore more specific guidelines for the prevention and treatment of osteoporosis among transgender persons become available, the following general recommendations can be offered:

1. Physicians and other clinicians should remain alert for the possibility of bone mineral loss among their transgender patients, particularly those with risk factors for the development of this condition (e.g., advanced age, smoking, treatment with anti-inflammatory steroid medications, gonadectomy with inconsistent hormone supplementation).

2. Transgender adults, particularly those who have received oophorectomy or orchiectomy, should be advised of the risk of subsequent bone demineralization, and advised to adhere to hormonal treatment over time. Many transgender middle-aged and older adults have not been informed of this possibility (Ippolito & Sampson 2015).

3. All patients should be advised to reduce their risk of osteoporosis development through lifestyle modification: smoking cessation, limited alcohol use, weight-bearing exercise (if able).

4. Calcium and vitamin D supplementation should be advised for persons in middle and older adulthood who are at risk for osteoporosis unless it is otherwise contraindicated (e.g., renal disease, recurrent nephrolithiasis).

5. If hormonal supplementation becomes contraindicated (e.g., for the older adult who develops a hormone-responsive malignancy), then bone mineral density should be monitored and alternate treatments (i.e., bisphosphonates, parathormone agonists) considered.

6. Serum luteinizing hormone (LH) levels may provide the best predictor of adequacy of hormone supplementation. Consideration should be given to checking luteinizing hormone levels at intervals. Densitometry should be

interpreted with natal sex norms, and followed over time when clinically indicated.

7. In older adulthood, use of the minimum adequate dose of estrogen or testosterone should be considered, as there is no evidence to support the use of high-dose hormonal supplementation among older adults of any gender.

8. Physicians and other clinicians should discuss bone mineral density evaluation with their patients who have taken hormonal medications for extended periods of time or who have had surgery with gonad removal.

9. Medical and nursing practices should update their osteoporosis screening and prevention protocols as additional evidence becomes available.

HIV in Later Life

The presence of human immunodeficiency virus (HIV)/acquired immuno-deficiency syndrome (AIDS) in the transgender population has been a matter of increasing concern (Hoffman 2015; Mizno et al. 2015; Nemoto et al. 2004, 2005; Pisani et al. 2004; Schwarz & Scheer 2004). However, while transgender and HIV/AIDS has been discussed in the literature for years (Bockting et al. 2005; Clements-Nolle et al. 2006; Pisani et al. 2004; Schwarz & Sheer 2004), little is known about HIV/AIDS among the current cohort of trans-elders (Witten 2004a). Regardless of the age of gender transition, beginning to socialize in the true psychological gender necessitates learning new "sexual negotiation skills," and new sexual relationships can provide an opportunity for exposure to HIV and other sexually transmissible infections. Older adults may be particularly vulnerable in this regard, due to having come of age in an era during which HIV infection was not yet a concern. Lack of familiarity with risk reduction techniques is also more common than among younger adults, who have often received this information in school or other group venues. Many transgender older persons report not having used any safer-sex techniques during first dating experiences in the new gender presentation.

Data comparing the risk of HIV infection for transgender and non-transgender-identified, single, older adults are currently lacking. However, the burden that infection places on transgender persons may be greater, due to the competing medical demands it creates. HIV infection in later life often leads to situations in which persons in middle and older adulthood are living with the burden of obtaining both antiretroviral chemotherapy and the medical treatments associated with other chronic conditions. The need to get (and, in some countries, finance) appropriate hormonal and surgical services for gender transition compounds this problem (Witten 2004b).

Physicians caring for transgender older adults should remain alert to the possibility of HIV risk and infection. Suggested interventions include:

1. Discussion of social and sexual behaviors prior to beginning gender transition and at intervals during this process;

2. HIV risk reduction education, tailored to the sexual practices and preferences of the individual;
3. referral to transgender community resources for additional support of healthy sexual behaviors, if this is indicated and resources are available.

Practical Concerns in Transgender Health Care

Privacy and Gender Identity Disclosure

Health care has both medical and social aspects. Obtaining health care and personal assistance services is more complex for persons who are transgender—and have not had genital reconstruction surgery—than for those who have had these procedures. Apparent mismatch between genital anatomy and gender of presentation can create difficulty in obtaining medical services (Bockting et al. 2004), practical nursing care, or even appropriate funeral arrangements (as in the case of Billy Tipton, whose female genitalia were "discovered" by the mortician and sensationalized in the American tabloid press).

Health Care and Financial Status in Old Age

Financial resources in later years usually depend on long-term economic status throughout much of adulthood (Choudhury & Leonescio 1997) and can be negatively affected if gender discrimination resulted in job loss. Such adverse events may impact the affordability of immediate and long-term health care, housing (Liebig 1996), and retirement (Vitt & Siegenthaler 1996). A comprehensive discussion of the midlife issues of aging among transgender persons may be found in Witten (2004b).

Transgender Aging and Social Adjustment

Gender transition at any age requires physical, legal, and social adaptation. Family relationships, community integration, and social support are important aspects of life for older adults, and are often significantly affected by the gender transition process.

Family relationships change with the older person's "coming out" regarding his or her gender identity. Fatherhood and motherhood, siblingships, grandparenthood, and other aspects of the family constellation may be reevaluated during the gender transition process. Children and young adults are usually, although not always, accepting of gender change (Ettner 1999). Therefore, concerns regarding the appropriateness of disclosing authentic gender to grandchildren and other young relatives are generally unwarranted; however, young children are also vulnerable to parental prejudice, and may react negatively if their parents reject the older person.

Gender transition within the context of a long-term marriage or partnership between elderly individuals remains relatively uncommon, but experience with middle-aged couples suggests several possible outcomes. Many middle-aged spouses or long-term partners will choose to maintain the relationship as their spouse or partner changes gender presentation, genital sex, or both; many others will not (Witten 2004b).

Couples who maintain a marriage or partnership may need to redefine their relationship. Persons who are more versatile can maintain a sexual relationship; other couples become "friends" or "sisters." In the former case, loss of the previous sexual orientation (usually as a heterosexual woman or lesbian; experience with male–transman couples is currently more limited) can be difficult for the non-transitioning partner. The wife or girlfriend may adjust by drawing a distinction between her relationship (which has changed) and her sexual orientation (which has not): "My husband is becoming a woman, but we're going to stay married."

Some older adults transition after loss of the primary relationship, as James did in the case study, above, although this requires reasonably good health and a high degree of self-efficacy, as many aspects of life are concurrently redefined.

Quality of life for older transgender persons can be related to previous social integration, as well as personal flexibility and available resilience for the development of new relationships. Social network support and community resources are important for the ongoing maintenance of well-being (Magai & McFadden 1996; Stallings et al. 1997; Turner 1996; Thompson 1996) and are slowly being researched in trans-identified populations (Budge et al. 2013b; Erosheva et al. 2016).

The patterns of participation in religious activities among transgender older adults are currently not well known. However, recent research indicates that many self-identify as belonging to a traditional religion or describe themselves as being highly spiritual (Kidd & Witten 2008; Porter et al. 2013).

Loss of a spouse, partner, or longstanding friendship group due to death; decreased ability to maintain a private residence; loss of the ability to drive; and moving from an independent residence to an assisted-living environment (and perhaps ultimately to dependent nursing care) all tend to erode personal control. These are significant problems in the lives of all persons who survive to become the "oldest old" (Witten 2010).

For transgender elders, the challenges described above are compounded by concerns relating to disclosure, privacy, isolation from transgender peers, specialized health care needs, and the potential for ostracism and negative judgment by health care professionals and caregivers (Finkenauer et al. 2012; Redman 2011; Witten & Kidd 2008). Those who previously obtained sex reassignment surgery (gender confirmation surgery) may avoid some of these difficulties, as they generally have a well-established gender presentation, and have shed most ties to pre-transition life with the passage of time. However, those who transition in later years must decide whether to share confidential—and potentially sensational or ostracizing—personal information with their caregivers.

Transgender older adults who have had genital, gender confirming surgeries must confide in their physicians and other health care professionals with regard to medical history, or risk inadvertent exposure. For example, a transwoman who medically and surgically transitioned gender in her youth still has a prostate. Ideally, she should receive her physical health care from a clinician who is familiar with her medical history. Otherwise, her prostate may be perceived as a "rectal mass" during physical examination.

Physicians can assist their transgender older adult patients by discussing the importance of routine health care, including preventive services; referring to colleagues who are empathic and supportive of transgender persons; and educating others involved in the patients' care about the realities of human gender diversity. This latter endeavor must include medical, nursing, and social work colleagues, as well as unskilled and semiskilled care assistants. In addition, facilitating the formation of a support group for transgender older adults (Slusher et al. 1996) may be of benefit. Finally, addressing family dynamics, and referring for family or individual counseling when difficulties are detected, can be crucial.

Graceful Exits: Living and Dying Well

Late-life and end-of-life support is important to older people. Increasing research evidence demonstrates that the incidence and prevalence of late-life medical problems are not different for transgender persons than for non-transgender persons. However, transgender identification can easily confound such problems if it sets up barriers to competent caregiving. Witten (2014, 2015a, 2015b) points out that these barriers, perceived and actual, are significant and induce a great deal of fear among elder respondents to her survey research. When this happens, it increases health care disparities for this group.

The following case study demonstrate such barriers:

> Vincent, a 71-year-old transman who had undergone chest reconstruction (but not genital) surgery 30 years ago, was experiencing early Alzheimer dementia. He was placed within a local-authority care home [a nursing home in the United Kingdom] where every other resident was female. Vincent had no visitors and no contact with any family. The staff stopped bringing him his mail, which included support group magazines, assuming he was not able to read or understand it.
>
> Vincent was extremely distressed with the incontinence pads used in his care. Vincent called them "sanitary towels" and regarded them as something for women (Witten & Whittle 2004).
>
> Janice is an 87-year-old transwoman who has been living in her true gender identity for over 15 years, but who never received genital surgery. She lost contact with her only son when she transitioned. She has no remaining friends or family. Janice suffers from incontinence and terminal cancer. When she was admitted to hospice care, Janice vigorously fought with the

staff over changing her underwear. The hospice nurses did not realize her reaction was due to the fact that, despite her female identity and life, Janice's genitalia were still male in appearance. She refuses a catheter and is wetting the bed, making caregiving difficult.

Physicians and other health care professionals can best serve their transgender older adult patients by understanding the need to retain psychological wholeness while preparing for death by having their true gender respected during medical examination and personal care.

Current research (Witten 2014, 2015b) has shown that a significant number of people within the trans-elder population are not well prepared for later-life challenges such as having legal and medical powers of attorney, legal wills, and other legal documentation. They should also be encouraged to obtain legal protection for their wishes regarding transfer of property and funeral arrangements. Spouses and significant others may be confronted with legal and insurance problems when carrying out the deceased person's last wishes (Witten 2010). Physicians should encourage their transgender patients to keep proof of their identity change, and identification-related documents, in a safe location.

Conclusion

As the population ages, physicians and other health care providers will need to be knowledgeable about the health care of gender non-conforming patients in general and elderly transgender-identified patients in particular. There will be obvious cohort differences as members of the younger cohorts will begin hormones earlier and therefore remain on them for longer periods of time (Levine et al. 2013). Research must be ongoing in order to understand the needs of these different generations. The military (Brown & McDuffie 2009) and the criminal justice systems also have aging trans-identified members. We know little about how trans-members of these populations experience the aging process, nor do we know what kinds of services they currently receive or will receive in the future. Much remains to be understood here.

Trans-identified individuals can maintain their dignity, autonomy, and positive social connections while seeking integration of the physical and psychological elements of their authentic selves. Health care professionals can assist in this actualizing process. Their alliances with transgender older adults can help them to age successfully and to live long, positive, and vital lives.

References

Agahi N, Shaw BA, Benjamin A, Fors A. (2014). Social and economic conditions in childhood and the progression of functional health problems from midlife into old age. *J. Epidemiol. Commun. Hlth*, 68(8): 734–740.

Ahern T, Wu FCW. (2015). New horizons in testosterone and the aging male. *Age Ageing*, 44(2): 188–195.

American Psychiatric Association. (2013). *Diagnostic and Statistical Manual of Mental Disorders, Fifth Edition: DSM-5.* Washington, DC: American Psychiatric Publishing.

American Society of Andrology. (2006). Testosterone replacement therapy for male aging: ASA position statement. *J. Androl.*, 27(2): 133–134.

Anderson P. (2013). 1 in 3 seniors dies with Alzheimer's or other dementia. *Medscape*, March 21, 2013. http://www.medscape.com/viewarticle/781180_print.

Asscheman H, Gooren LJG, Eklund PLE. (1989). Mortality and morbidity in transsexual patients with cross-gender hormone treatment. *Metabolism*, 38(9): 869–873.

Asscheman H, Giltay EJ, Megens JAJ, de Rond W, van Trotsenburg MAA, Gooren LJG. (2011). A long-term follow-up study of mortality in transsexuals receiving treatment with cross-sex hormones. *Eur. J. Endocrinol.*, 164(4): 635–642.

Bhasin S, Cunningham GR, Hayes FJ, Matusmoto AM. (2010). Testosterone therapy in men with androgen deficiency syndromes: An Endocrine Society Clinical Practice Guideline. *J. Clin. Endocrinol. Metab.*, 95(6): 2536–2559.

Biggs S. (2005). Beyond appearances: Perspectives on identity in late life and some implications for method. *J. Gerontol. Soc. Sci.*, 60B(3): S118–S128.

Bockting WO, Rosser S, Coleman E. (1999). Transgender HIV prevention: Community involvement and empowerment. *Int. J. Transgenderism*, 3(1+2): www.symposion.com/ijt/hiv_risk/bockting.htm.

Bockting WO, Robinson B, Benner A, Scheltema K. (2004). Patient satisfaction with transgender health services. *J. Sex. Marital Ther.*, 30(4): 277–294.

Bockting WO, Huang C-Y, Ding H, Robinson B, Rosser BR. (2005). Are transgender persons at higher risk for HIV than other sexual minorities? A comparison of HIV prevalence and risks. *Int. J. Transgenderism*, 8: 2–3, 123–131.

Bockting WO, Miner MH, Romine RES, Hamilton A, Coleman E. (2013). Stigma, mental health, and resilience in an online sample of the US transgender population. *Am. J. Publ. Hlth*, 103(5): 943–951.

Bogunovic O. (2012). Substance abuse in aging and elderly adults. *Psychiatr. Times*, http://www.psychiatrictimes.com/geriatric-psychiatry/substance-abuse-aging-and-elderly-adults (retrieved 28 June 2015).

Boza C, Perry KN. (2014). Gender-related victimization, perceived social support, and predictors of depression among transgender Australians. *Int. J. Transgenderism*, 15(1): 35–52.

Bradford J, Reisner SL, Honnold JA, Xavier J. (2013). Experiences of transgender-related discrimination and implications for health: Results from the Virginia transgender health initiative study. *Am. J. Publ. Hlth*, 103(10): 1820–1829.

Brown GR, McDuffie E. (2009). Health care policies addressing transgender inmates in prison systems in the United States. *J. Correctional Hlth Care*, 15(4): 280–291.

Budge SL, Adelson JL, Howard KA. (2013a). Anxiety and depression in transgender individuals: The roles of transition status, loss, social support and coping. *J. Consult. Clin. Psychol.*, 81(3): 545–557.

Budge SL, Katz-Wize S, Tebbe EN, Howard KAS, Schneider CL, Rodriguez A. (2013b). Transgender emotional and coping processes: Facilitative and avoidant coping throughout transitioning. *Counsel. Psychologist*, 41: 601–647.

Bush SS, Martin TA. (2005). *Geriatric Neuropsychology: Practice Essentials.* New York, NY: Taylor & Francis.

Butler RN. (2002). The study of productive aging. *J. Gerontol. Soc. Sci.*, 57B(6): S363.

Carter J. (2011). Depression in older adults. *Br. Med. J.*, 343 doi: http://dx.doi.org/10.1136/bmj.d5219.

Cassidy K-L, Rector NA. (2008). The silent geriatric giant: Anxiety disorders in late life. *Geriatr. Aging*, 11(3): 150–156.

Center of Excellence for Transgender Health. (2011). *Aging issues: special considerations.* http://transhealth.ucsf.edu/trans?page=protocol-aging.

Centers for Disease Control and Prevention. (2015). Depression is not a normal part of growing older. http://www.cdc.gov/aging/mentalhealth/depression.htm (retrieved 27 June 2015).

Choudhury S, Leonescio MV. (1997). Life-cycle aspects of poverty among older women. *Soc. Security Bull.*, 60(2): 17–36.

Clark MP, Coughlin JR. (2012). Prevalence of smoking among the lesbian, gay, bisexual, transsexual, transgender and queer (LGBTTQ) subpopulations in Toronto – the Toronto Rainbow Tobacco Survey (TRTS). *Can. J. Publ. Hlth*, 103(2): 132–136.

Clements-Nolle K, Marx R, Guzman R, Katz M. (2001). HIV prevalence, risk behaviors, healthcare use and mental health status of transgender persons: Implications for public health intervention. *Am. J. Publ. Hlth*, 91(6): 915–921.

Clements-Nolle K, Marx R, Katz M. (2006). Attempted suicide among transgender persons: The influence of gender-based discrimination and victimization. *J. Homosex.*, 51(3): 53–69.

Cochran BN, Cauce AM. (2006). Characteristics of lesbian, gay, bisexual and transgender individuals entering substance abuse treatment. *J. Substance Abuse Treat.*, 30: 135–146.

Coleman E, Bockting WO, Botzer M, Cohen-Kettenis P, et al. (2012). *Standards of Care for the Health of Transsexual, Transgender and Gender-Nonconforming People* [SOC v. 7]. World Professional Association for Transgender Health. Available at: http://admin.associationsonline.com/uploaded_files/140/files/Standards%20of%20Care,%20V7%20Full%20Book.pdf.

Conway AJ, Handelsman DJ, Lording D, et al. (2000). Use, misuse and abuse of androgens. The Endocrine Society of Australia consensus guidelines for androgen prescribing. *Med. J. Aust.*, 172(5): 220–224.

Curb JD, Prentice RL, Bray PF, Langer RD, Van Horn L, Barnabei VM, Bloch MJ, Cyr MG, Gass M, Lepine L, Rodabough RJ, Sidney S, Uwaifo GI, Rosendaal FR. (2006). Venous thrombosis and conjugated equine estrogen in women without a uterus. *Arch. Intern. Med.*, 166(7): 772.

Cushman M, Kuller LH, Prentice R, Rodabough RJ, Psaty BM, Stafford RS, Sidney S, Rosendaal FR. (2004). Women's Health Initiative Investigators. Estrogen plus progestin and risk of venous thrombosis. *JAMA*, 292(13): 1573.

Darby E, Anawalt BD. (2005). Male hypogonadism: an update on diagnosis and treatment. *Treat. Endocrinol.*, 4(5): 293–309.

de Cuypere G, T'Sjoen G, Beerten R, Selvaggi G, et al. (2005). Sexual and physical health after sex reassignment surgery. *Arch. Sex. Behav.*, 34(6): 679–690.

de Villiers TJ, Gass ML, Haines CJ, Hall JE, Lobo RA, Pierroz DD, Rees M. (2013). Global consensus statement on menopausal hormone therapy. *Maturitas*, 74(4): 391–392.

Dhejne C, Lichtenstein P, Boman M, Johansson ALV, Langstrom N, Landen M. (2011). Longterm follow-up of transsexual persons undergoing sex reassignment surgery: Cohort study in Sweden. *PloS ONE*, 6(2): 1–8.

DiPietro L. (2001). Physical activity in aging: Changes in patterns and their relationships to health and function. *J. Gerontol. Biol. Sci. Med. Sci.*, 56(2): 13–22.

Dobs AS, Matsumoto AM, Wang C, et al. (2004). Short-term pharmacokinetic comparison of a novel testosterone buccal system and a testosterone gel in testosterone deficient men. *Curr. Med. Res. Opin.*, 20(5): 729–738.

Eldh J, Berg A, Gustafsson LJG. (1997). Long-term follow-up after sex-reassignment surgery. *Scand. J. Plast. Reconstr. Hand Surg.*, 31: 39–45.

Endocrine Society of Australia. (2013). Position statement, use and misuse of androgens. http://www.endocrinesociety.org.au/position-statement-androgens.asp.

Erosheva EA, Kim H-J, Emlet C, Fredriksen-Goldsen KI. (2016). Social networks of lesbian, gay, bisexual and transgender older adults. *Res. Aging*, 38: 98–123. doi: 10.1177/0164027515581859.

Ettner R. (1999). *XVI International Meeting, Harry Benjamin International Gender Dysphoria Association*. London, U.K..

Ettner R, Wylie K. (2013). Psychological and social adjustment in older transsexual people. *Maturitas*, 74: 226–229.

Eyler AE, Feldman J. (2008). The transsexual male. In Heidelbaugh J.. (Ed.), *Clinical Men's Health; Evidence in Practice*. Philadelphia, PA: Elsevier, pp. 561–584.

Fabbre VD. (2015). Gender transitions in later life: A queer perspective on successful aging. *Gerontologist*, 55: 144–153.

Feldman J. (2005). Masculinizing hormone therapy with testosterone 1% topical gel (abstract). XIX Biennial Symposium of the Harry Benjamin International Gender Dysphoria Association, Bologna, Italy, April 8, 2005.

Feldman J. (2007). Preventive care of the transgendered patient: An evidence based approach. In Ettner R, Monstrey S, Eyler AE (Eds.), *Principles of Transgender Medicine and Surgery*. Binghamton, NY: The Haworth Press, pp. 33–72.

Feldman J. (2008). Medical and surgical management of the transgender patient: What the primary care clinician needs to know. In Makadon H, Mayer K, Potter J, Goldhammer H (Eds.), *Fenway Guide to Lesbian, Gay, Bisexual, and Transgender Health*. Philadelphia, PA: American College of Physicians, pp. 365–392.

Feldman J, Goldberg J. (2006). Transgender primary medical care. *Int. J. Transgenderism*, 9(3): 3–34.

Feldman J, Safer J. (2009). Hormone therapy in adults: Suggested revisions to the sixth version of the *Standards of Care*. *Int. J. Transgenderism*, 11(3): 146–182.

Feldman HA, Longcope C, Derby CA, Johannes CB, et al. (2002). Age trends in the level of serum testosterone and other hormones in middle-aged men: Longitudinal results from the Massachusetts Male Aging Study. *J. Clin. Endocrinol. Metab.*, 87: 589–598.

Felitti VJ, Anda RF, Nordenberg D, Williamson DF, Spitz AM, Edwards V, Koss MP, Marks JS. (1998). Relationship of childhood abuse and household dysfunction to many of the leading causes of death in adults: The Adverse Childhood Experiences (ACE) study. *Am. J. Prevent. Med.*, 14(4): 245–258.

Finkenauer S, Sherrat J, Marlow J, Brodey A. (2012). When injustice gets old: A systematic review of trans aging. *J. Gay Lesbian Soc. Serv.*, 24: 311–330.

Fisher BJ, Specht DK. (1999). Successful aging and creativity in later life. *J. Aging Stud.*, 13(4): 457–472.

Fiske A, Wetherell JL, Gatz M. (2009). Depression in older adults. *Annu. Rev. Clin. Pyschol.*, 5: 363–389.

Fors S, Lennartsson C, Lundberg O. (2009). Childhood living conditions, socioeconomic position in adulthood, and cognition in later life: Exploring the associations. *J. Gerontol. Soc. Sci.*, 64B(6): 750–757.

Fredricksen-Goldsen KI. (2011). Resilience and disparities among lesbian, gay, bisexual and transgender older adults. *Publ. Policy Aging Rep.*, 21: 3–7.

Fredricksen-Goldsen KI, Cook-Daniels L, Kim H-J, Erosheva EA, Emlet CA, Hoy-Ellis CP, Goldsen J, Muraco A. (2014). Physical and mental health of transgender older adults: An at-risk and underserved population. *Gerontologist*, 54: 488–500.

Fredricksen-Goldsen KI, Kim H-Y, Shiu C, Goldsen J, Emlet CA. (2015). Successful aging among LGBT older adults: Physical and mental health-related quality of life by age group. *Gerontologist*, 55: 154–168.

Fry CL, Dickerson-Putman J, Draper P, Ikels C, Keith J, Glascock AP, et al. (1997). Chapter 5 – Culture and the meaning of a good old age. In Sokolovsky J. (Ed.), *The Cultural Context of Aging – Worldwide Perspectives*. 2nd ed. Westport, CT: Bergin and Garvey.

Garaffa G, Christopher NA, Ralph DJ. (2010). Total phallic reconstruction in female-to-male transsexuals. *Eur. Urol.*, 57(4): 715–722.

Garfein AJ, Herzog AR. (1995). Robust aging among the young-old, old-old, and oldest-old. *J. Gerontol. B. Psychol. Sci. Soc. Sci.*, 50: S77–S87.

Girdler SS, Hinderliter AL, Wells EC, et al. (2004). Transdermal versus oral estrogen therapy in postmenopausal smokers: Hemodynamic and endothelial effects. *Obstet. Gynecol.*, 103(1): 169–180.

Gooren LJ, Bunck MC. (2004). Androgen replacement therapy: Present and future. *Drugs.* 64: 1861–1891.

Gooren LJ, Giltay EJ, Bunck MC. (2008). Long-term treatment of transsexuals with cross-sex hormones: Extensive personal experience. *J. Clin. Endocrinol. Metab.*, 93:19–25.

Gorton RN, Buth J, Spade D. (2005). *Medical Therapy and Health Maintenance for Transgender Men: A Guide for Health Care Providers*. San Francisco, CA: Lyon-Martin Women's Health Services.

Grady D, et al. (2002). Cardiovascular disease outcomes during 6.8 years of hormone therapy: Heart and Estrogen/progestin Replacement Study follow-up (HERS II). *JAMA*, 288(1): 49–57.

Grant J, Mottet M, Tanis J, Harrison J, Keisling H, Keisling M. (2011). *Injustice at Every Turn: A Report of the National Transgender Discrimination Survey*. Washington, DC: National Center for Transgender Equality and National Gay and Lesbian Task Force.

Grodstein F, Manson JE, Stampfer MJ. (2001). Postmenopausal hormone use and secondary prevention of coronary events in the Nurses' Health Study: A prospective, observational study. *Ann. Intern. Med.*, 135(1): 1–8.

Grodstein F, Manson JE, Stampfer MJ. (2006). Hormone therapy and coronary heart disease: The role of time since menopause and age at initiation *J. Women's Hlth*, 15(1): 35–44.

Gum AM, King-Kallimanis B, Kohn R. (2009). Prevalence of mood, anxiety and substance-abuse disorders for older Americans in the National Comorbidity Study – Replication. *Am. J. Geriatr. Psychiatry*, 17(9): 769–781.

Hachulla E, Rose C, Trillot N, et al. (2000). What vascular events suggest a myeloproliferative disorder? *J. Mal. Vasc.*, 25(5): 382–387.

Hage JJ, Vossen M, Becking AG. (1997). Rhinoplasty as part of gender-confirming surgery in male transsexuals: Basic considerations and clinical experience. *Ann. Plast. Surg.*, 39(3): 266–271.

Harman SM, Metter EJ, Tobin JD, Pearson J. (2001). Longitudinal effects of aging on serum total and free testosterone levels in healthy men. Baltimore Longitudinal Study of Aging. *J. Clin. Endocrinol. Metab.*, 86: 724–731.

Harman SM, Brinton EA, Cedars M, et al. (2005). KEEPS: The Kronos Early Estrogen Prevention study. *Climacteric*, 8(1): 3–12.

Hawkins BA. (2005). Aging well: Toward a way of life for all people. *Preventing Chronic Disease-Public Health Research. Practice and Policy*, 2(3): 1–3. Available at www.cdc. gov/issues/2005/jul/05_0018.htm.

Hazelton Betty Ford Foundation. (2015). https://www.hazelden.org/web/public/ ade60220.page.

Hembree WC, Cohen-Kettenis P, Delemarre-van de Waal HA, Gooren LJ, Meyer III WJ, et al. (2009). Endocrine treatment of transsexual persons: An Endocrine Society clinical practice guideline. *J. Clin. Endocrinol. Metab.*, 94(9): 3132–3154.

Hierl Th, Borcsok I, Ziegler R, et al. (1999). Osteoanabole Ostrogentherapie bei einem transsexuellen Mann. *Dtsch med. Wschr.*, 124: 519–527.

Hoffman B. (2014). An overview of depression among transgender women. *Depress. Res. Treat.*, 2014: 394283.

Hoffman BR. (2015). The interaction of drug use, sex work and HIV among transgender women. *Substance Use Misuse*, 49(8): 1049–1053.

Hsia J, Langer RD, Manson JE, et al. (2006). Conjugated equine estrogens and coronary heart disease: The Women's Health Initiative. *Arch. Intern. Med.*, 166(3): 357–365.

Ippolito J, Sampson J. (2015). *Baby Boomers and Gen-Xers: Exploring Aging Issues in Trans Male Communities.* 14th Philadelphia Trans-Health Conference, Philadelphia Convention Center, June 4, 2015.

Ippolito J, Witten TM. (2014). Aging. In Erickson-Schroth L. (Ed.), *Trans Bodies, Trans Selves.* New York, NY: Oxford University Press.

Jackson NC, Johnson MJ, Roberts R. (2008). The potential impact of discrimination fears of older gays, lesbians, bisexuals and transgender individuals living in small-to moderate-sized cities on long-term healthcare. *J. Homosex.*, 54(3): 325–339.

Jauk D. (2013). Gender violence revisited: Lessons from violent victimization of transgender identified individuals. *Sexualities*, 16(7): 807–825.

Katari SK, Hasche L. (2015). Differences across age groups in transgender and gender non-conforming people's experiences of health care discrimination, harassment, and victimization. *J. Aging Hlth*, Jun 16:089826431559028.

Kidd J, Witten TM. (2008). Assessing spirituality, religiosity and faith in the transgender community: A case study in violence and abuse – implications for the aging transgender community and for gerontological research. *J. Religious Gerontol.*, 20(1–2): 29–62.

Kimmel M. (2015). Theories of aging applied to LGBT older adults and their families. In Orel NA, Fruhauf CA. (Eds.), *The Lives of LGBT Older Adults: Understanding Challenges and Resilience.* Washington, DC: American Psychological Association Press.

King M. (2000). Preoperative evaluation. *Am. Fam. Phys.*, 62: 387–396.

King-Kallimanis B, Gum AM, Kohn R. (2009). Comorbidity of depressive and anxiety disorders for Americans in the national comorbidity survey – replication. *Am. J. Geriatr. Psychiatry*, 17(9): 782–792.

Kirmizioglu Y, Doqan O, Kuqu N, Akyüz G. (2009). Prevalence of anxiety disorders among elderly people. *Int. J. Geriatr. Psychiatry*, 24(9): 1026–1033.

Korten NCM, Mennix BWJH, Pot AM, Deeg DJH, Comijs HC. (2014). Adverse childhood and recent negative life events: Contrasting associations with cognitive decline in older persons. *J. Geriatr. Psychiatry Neurol.*, 27(2): 128–138.

Krege S, Bex A, Lummen G, et al. (2001). Male-to-female transsexualism: A technique, results, and long-term follow-up in 66 patients. *BJU Int.*, 88: 396–402.

Kuiper AJ, Cohen-Kettenis PT. (1998). Gender role reversal among postoperative transsexuals. *Int. J. Transgenderism*, 2(3). Revised Sept. 16, 2001 from Web publication www.symposion.com/ijt/ijtc0502.htm.

Landen M, Walinder J, Hambert G, et al. (1998). Factors predictive of regret in sex reassignment. *Acta Psychiatr. Scand.*, 97: 284–289.

Lawrence A. (2003). Factors associated with satisfaction or regret following male-to-female sex reassignment surgery. *Arch. Sex. Behav.*, 32(4): 299–315.

Levine DA and the Committee on Adolescence. (2013). Office-based care for lesbian, gay, bisexual, transgender and questioning youth. *Pediatrics*, 132: e297–e313.

Levitt HM, Ippolito MR. (2014). Being transgender: Navigating minority stressors and developing authentic self-presentation. *Psychol. Women Q.*, 38(1): 46–64.

Liang J, Luo B. (2012). Toward a discourse shift in social gerontology: From successful aging to harmonious aging. *J. Aging Studies*, 26: 327–334.

Liebig PS. (1996). Area agencies on aging and the National Affordable Housing Act: Opportunities and challenges. *J. Appl. Gerontol.*, 15(4): 486–500.

Lindemalm G, Korlin D, Uddenberg N. (1987). Prognostic factors vs. outcome in male-to-female transsexualism. *Acta Psychiatr. Scand.*, 75: 268–274.

Lyons T, Shannon K, Pierre L, Small W, Krusi A, Kerr T. (2015). A qualitative study of transgender individuals' experiences in residential addiction treatment settings: Stigma and inclusivity. *Substance Abuse Treat. Prevent. Policy*, 10: 17.

Magai C, McFadden SH. (1996). *Handbook of Emotion, Adult Development, and Aging*. San Diego, CA: Academic Press.

Mangoni AA, Jackson SHD. (2004). Age-related changes in pharmacokinetics and pharmacodynamics: Basic principles and practical applications. *Br. J. Clin. Pharmacol.*, 57(1): 6–14.

Manson JE. (2013). The Kronos Early Estrogen Prevention Study. *Women's Health*, 9(1): 9–11.

Manson JE, Hsia J, Johnson KC, et al. (2003). Women's Health Initiative Investigators, estrogen plus progestin and the risk of coronary heart disease. *N. Engl. J. Med.*, 349: 523–524.

Maslow K. (2013). Person-centered care for people with dementia: Opportunities and challenges. *Generations: J. Am. Soc. Aging*, 37(3): 8–15.

Maylahn C, Alongi S, Alongi J, Moore MJ, Anderson LA. (2005). Data needs and uses for older adult health surveillance: Perspectives from state agencies. *Prevent. Chronic Dis. – Publ. Hlth Res. Pract. Policy*, 2(3): 1–5.

Mazer N, Bell D, Wu J, et al. (2005). Comparison of the steady-state pharmacokinetics, metabolism, and variability of a transdermal testosterone patch versus a transdermal testosterone gel in hypogonadal men. *J. Sex. Med.*, 2(2): 213–226.

McAuley E, Blissmer B. (2000). Self-efficacy determinants and consequences of physical activity. *Exerc. Sport Sci. Rev.*, 28(2): 85–88.

McAuley E, Courneya KS, Rudolph DL, Lox CL. (1994). Enhancing exercise adherence in middle-aged males and females. *Prevent. Med.*, 23: 498–506.

McCann E. (2015). People who are transgender: Mental health concerns. *J. Psychiatr. Mental Hlth Nurs.*, 22(1):76–81.

McFadden SH, Frankowski S, Witten TM. (2013). Resilience and multiple stigmatized identities: Older transgender/intersex identified persons reflect on aging. In Sinnott J. (Ed.), *Positive Psychology and Aging*. New York, NY: Springer.

McLean AJ, Le Couteur DG. (2004). Aging biology and geriatric clinical pharmacology. *Pharmacol. Rev.*, 56: 163–184.

Meier SC, Labuski CM. (2013). The demographics of the transgender population. In Baumle AK (ed.), *International Handbooks on the Demography of Populations*, vol. 5. New York: Springer, pp. 289–327.

Menec VH. (2003). The relation between everyday activities and successful aging: A six-year longitudinal study. *J. Gerontol. Soc. Sci.*, 58B(2): S74–S82.

Mizno Y, Frazier EL, Huang P, Skarbinski J. (2015). Characteristics of transgender women living with HIV receiving medical care in the United States. *LGBT Health*, 2(20).

Mueller A, Dittrich R, Binder H. (2005). High dose estrogen treatment increases bone mineral density in male-to-female transsexuals receiving gonadotropin-releasing hormone agonist in the absence of testosterone. *Eur. J. Endocrinol.*, 153(1): 107–113.

Nemoto T, Operario D, Keatley J, Villegas D. (2004). Social context of HIV risk behaviours among male-to-female transgenders of colour. *AIDS Care*, 16(6): 724–735.

Nemoto T, Operario D, Keatley J, Nguyen H, Sugano E. (2005). Promoting health for transgender women: Transgender resources and neighborhood space (TRANS) program in San Francisco. *Am. J. Publ. Hlth*, 95: 382–384.

Nemoto T, Sausa LA, Operario D, Keatley J. (2006). Need for HIV/AIDS education and intervention for MTF transgenders. *J. Homosex.*, 51(1): 183–201.

Nieschalg E, Behre HM. (Eds.) (1998). *Testosterone: Action, Deficiency, Substitution* (2nd ed). New York: Springer.

North American Menopause Society. (2015). The North American Menopause statement on continued use of systemic hormone therapy after age 65. http://www.menopause.org/docs/default-source/2015/2015-nams-hormone-therapy-after-age-65.pdf.

Nuttbrock LA. (2012). Culturally competent substance abuse treatment with transgender persons. *J. Addict. Disord.*, 31(3): 236–241.

Nuttbrock L, Bockting WO, Rosenblum A, Hwahng S, Mason M, Macri M, Becker J. (2014a). Gender abuse and major depression among transgender women: A prospective study of vulnerability and resilience. *Am. J. Publ. Hlth*, 104(11): 2191–2198.

Nuttbrock L, Bockting WO, Rosenblum A, Hwahng S, Mason M, Macri M, Becker J. (2014b). Gender abuse, depressive symptoms and substance abuse among transgender women: a 3-year prospective study. *Am. J. Publ. Hlth*, 104(11): 2199–2206.

Pearson TC, Messinezy M. (2001). Idiopathic erythrocytosis, diagnosis, and clinical management. *Pathol. Biol. (Paris)*, 49(2): 170–177.

Persson DI. (2009). Unique challenges of transgender aging: Implications from the literature. *J. Gerontol. Soc. Work*, 52(6): 633–646.

Petersen PE, Yamamoto T. (2005). Improving the oral health of older people: The approach of the WHO global oral health programme. *Commun. Dentistry Oral Epidemiol.*, 33: 81–92.

Petersen RC, Smith BE, Waring SC. (1999). Mild cognitive impairment: Clinical characterization and outcome. *Arch. Neurol.*, 56: 303–308.

Phillips LS, Langer RD. (2005). Postmenopausal hormone therapy: Critical reappraisal and a unified hypothesis. *Fertil. Steril.*, 83(3): 558–566.

Pisani E, Girault P, Gultom M, Sukartini N, Kumalawati J, Jazan S, Donegan E. (2004). HIV, syphilis infection, and sexual practices among transgenders, male sex workers, and other men who have sex with men in Jakarta, Indonesia. *Sex. Transm. Infect.*, 80: 536–540.

Pitanguy I, Machado BH. (2012). Facial rejuvenation surgery: A retrospective study of 8788 cases. *Aesthet. Surg. J.*, 32(4): 393–412.

Porter KE, Oala CR, Witten TM. (2013). Transgender spirituality, religion and successful aging: Findings from the Trans MetLife survey. *J. Religion, Spirituality Aging*, 25(2): 112–138.

Redman D. (2011). Fear, discrimination and abuse: Transgender elders and the perils of long-term care. *Aging Today*, XXXII(2): 1–2.

Reisner S, Conron KJ, Scout Nfn, Baker K, Herman JL, Lombardi E, Graytak EA, Gill AM, Matthews AK. (2015). "Counting" transgender and gender-nonconforming adults in health research: Recommendations from the Gender Identity in US Surveillance Group. *Transgender Stud. Q.*, 2(1): 34–57.

Rejeski WJ, Mihalko SL. (2001). Physical activity and quality of life in older adults. *J. Gerontol.*, 56A(Suppl.2): 23–35.

Reutrakul S, Ongphiphadhanakul B, Piaseu S, et al. (1998). The effects of oestrogen exposure on bone mass in male to female transsexuals. *Clin. Endocrinol.*, 49: 811–814.

Richmond KA, Burns B, Carroll K. (2012). Lost in trans-lation: Interpreting systems of trauma for transgender clients. *Traumatology*, 18: 45–57.

Roberts J, Snyder DL, Friedman E. (1996). (Eds.), *Handbook of Pharmacology of Aging*, 2nd ed. Boca Raton, FL: CRC Press.

Rotondi NK. (2012). Depression in trans people: A review of the risk factors. *Int. J. Transgenderism*, 13(3): 104–116.

Roussouw JE, et al. (2002). Risks and benefits of estrogen plus progestin in healthy postmenopausal women: Principal results from the Women's Health Initiative randomized controlled trial. *JAMA*, 288(3): 321–333.

Rowe JR, Kahn RL. (1997). Successful aging. *Gerontologist*, 37(4): 433–440.

Rowe JR, Kahn RL. (1998). *Successful Aging*. New York: Pantheon Books.

Rubin SO. (1993). Sex reassignment surgery male-to-female. *Scand. J. Urol. Nephrol. Suppl.*, 154: 1–28.

Ruetsche AG, Kneubuehl R, Birkhaeuser MH. (2005). Cortical and trabecular bone mineral density in transsexuals after long-term cross-sex hormonal treatment: A cross-sectional study. *Osteoporosis Int.*, 16(7): 791–798.

SAMHSA/CSAT. (2015). Substance abuse among older adults: an invisible epidemic. In Substance Abuse Among Older Americans. http://www.ncbi.nlm.nih.gov/books/NBK64422/.

Satariano WA, McAuley E. (2003). Promoting physical activity among older adults: From ecology to individual. *Am. J. Prevent. Med.*, 25(Suppl. 2): 184–192.

Schechtman KB, Ory MG. (2001). The effects of exercise on the quality of life of frail older adults: A preplanned meta-analysis of the FICSIT trials. *Ann. Behav. Med.*, 23(3): 186–197.

Schlatterer K, Auer DP, Yassouridis K, et al. (1998). Transsexualism and osteoporosis. *Exp. Clin. Endocrinol. Diabetes*, 106: 365–368.

Schwarz S, Scheer S. (2004). HIV testing behaviors and knowledge of HIV reporting regulations among male-to-female transgenders. *J. Acquir. Immune Defic. Syndr.* 37(2): 1326–1327.

Shi S, Klotz U. (2011). Age-related changes in pharmacokinetics. *Curr. Drug Metab.*, 12(7): 1389–2002.

Shipherd JC, Maguen S, Skidmore WC, Abramovitz SM. (2011). Potentially traumatic events in a transgender sample: Frequency and associated symptoms. *Traumatology*, 17(2): 56–67.

Shires DA, Jaffee K. (2015). Factors associated with health care discrimination experiences among a national sample of female-to-male transgender individuals. *Health Soc. Work*, 40(2): 134–141.

Siu AL, for the U.S. Preventive Services Task Force. (2015). Behavioral and pharmacotherapy interventions for tobacco smoking cessation in adults, including pregnant women: U.S. Preventive Services Task Force Recommendation Statement. *Ann. Intern. Med.*, 163: 622–634.

Slusher MP, Mayer CJ, Dunkle RE. (1996). Gays and Lesbians Older and Wiser (GLOW): A support group for older gay people. *Gerontologist*, 36(1): 118–123.

Smith LC, Shin RQ, Officer LM. (2012). Moving counseling forward on LGB and transgender issues: Speaking queerly on discourses and microaggressions. *Counsel. Psychologist*, 40(3): 385–408.

Snyder PJ. (2004). Hypogonadism in elderly men: What to do until the evidence comes? *N. Engl. J. Med.*, 350(5): 440–443.

Sosa M, Jodar E, Arbelo E. (2003). Bone mass, bone turnover, vitamin D, and estrogen receptor gene polymorphisms in male-to-female transsexuals. *J. Clin. Densitometry*, 6(3): 297–304.

Speroff L, Fritz MA. (2005) *Clinical Gynecologic Endocrinology and Infertility*, 7th ed. Philadelphia, PA: Lippincott, Williams and Wilkins, pp. 689–777.

Stallings MC, Dunham CC, Gatz M, Baker LA, Bengston VL. (1997). Relationships among life events and psychological well-being: More evidence for a two-factor theory of well-being. *J. Appl. Gerontol.*, 16(1): 104–119.

Steinhagen K, Friedman MB. (2008). Substance abuse and misuse in older adults. *Aging Well*, 3: 250. http://www.todaysgeriatricmedicine.com/archive/071708p20.shtml.

Stieglitz KA. (2010). Development, risk and resilience of transgender youth. *J. Assoc. Nurses AIDS Care*, 21(3): 192–206.

Tager IB, Haight T, Sternfield B, Yu Z, van Der Laan M. (2004). Effects of physical activity and body composition on functional limitation in the elderly. *Epidemiology*, 15(4): 479–493.

Tan RS, Salazar JA. (2004). Risks of testosterone replacement therapy in ageing men. *Expert Opin. Drug Saf.*, 3(6): 599–606.

Tate RB, Lah L, Cuddy TE. (2003). Definition of successful aging in elderly Canadian males: The Manitoba follow-up study. *Gerontologist*, 43: 735–744.

Taylor HS, Manson JE. (2011). Update in hormone therapy use in menopause. *J. Clin. Endocrinol. Metab.*, 96(2): 255–64.

Tenover JL. (1999). Testosterone replacement therapy in older adult men. *Int. J. Androl.*, 22(5): 300–306.

Testa RJ, Sciacca LM, Wang F, Hendricks ML, Goldblum P, Bradford J, Bongar B. (2012). Effects of violence on transgender people. *Prof. Psychol. Res. Pract.*, 43(5): 452–459.

Thompson EH. (1996). *Men and Aging: A Selected, Annotated Bibliography*. Westport, CT: Greenwood Press.

Toorians AW, Thomassen MC, Zweegman S, et al. (2003). Venous thrombosis and changes of hemostatic variables during cross-sex hormone treatment in transsexual people. *J. Clin. Endocrinol. Metab.*, 88(12): 5723–5729.

Tornstam L. (1989). Gero-transcendence: A meta-theoretical reformulation of the disengagement theory. *Aging: Clin. Exp. Res.*, 1(1): 55–63.

Tornstam L. (2005). *Gerotranscendence: A Developmental Theory of Positive Aging.* New York: Springer.

Turner F. (1996). An interlocking perspective for treatment. In *Social Work Treatment: Interlocking Theoretical Approaches*, 4th ed. New York: The Free Press, pp. 699–706.

Turner A, Chen TC, Barber TW, et al. (2004). Testosterone increases bone mineral density in female-to-male transsexuals: A case series of fifteen subjects. *Clin. Endocrinol. (Oxf.)*, 61(5): 560–566.

U. S. Preventive Services Task Force and Agency for Healthcare Research and Quality. *The Guide to Clinical Preventive Services 2014.* Available at www.uspreventiveservicestaskforce.org.

Utian WH. (2012). A decade post-WHI, menopausal hormone therapy comes full circle – need for independent commission. *Climacteric*, 15(4): 320–325.

Van Caenegem E, Taes Y, Wierckx K, Vandewalle S, et al. (2013). Low bone mass is prevalent in male-to-female transsexual persons before the start of cross-sex hormonal therapy and gonadectomy. *Bone*, 54(1): 92–97.

van Kesteren PJ, Asscheman H, Megens JA, et al. (1998a). Mortality and morbidity in transsexual subjects treated with cross-sex hormones. *Clin. Endocrinol.*, 47(3): 337–342.

van Kesteren PJ, Lips P, Deville W, Popp-Snijders C, Asscheman H, Megens J, Gooren L. (1998b). The effect of one-year cross-sex hormonal treatment on bone metabolism and serum insulin-like growth factor-1 in transsexuals. *J. Clin. Endocrinol. Metab.*, 81: 2227–2232.

van Kesteren PJ, Lips P, Gooren LG, et al. (1998c). Long-term follow-up of bone mineral density and bone metabolism in transsexuals treated with cross-sex hormones. *Clin. Endocrinol.*, 48: 347–354.

van Wagenen A, Driskell J, Bradford J. (2013). "I'm still raring to go": Successful aging among lesbian, gay, bisexual and transgender older adults. *J. Aging Stud.*, 27: 1–14.

Vitt LA, Siegenthaler JK. (1996). (Eds.), *Encyclopedia of Financial Gerontology*. Westport, CT: Greenwood Press.

von Faber M, Bootsma van der Weil A, van Exel E, Gussekloo J, Lagaay AM, van Dongen Knook DL, van der Geest S, Westendorp RGJ. (2001). Successful aging in the oldest old. Who can be characterized as successfully aged? *Arch. Intern. Med.*, 161: 2695–2700.

Vongpatanasin W, Tuncel M, Wang Z, et al. (2003). Differential effects of oral versus transdermal estrogen replacement therapy on C-reactive protein in postmenopausal women. *J. Am. Coll. Cardiol.*, 41(8): 1358–1363.

Wadensten B, Carlsson M. (2003). Theory-driven guidelines for practical care of older people based on the theory of gerotranscendence. *J. Adv. Nurs.*, 41(5): 462–470.

Wald M, Meacham RB, Ross LS, et al. (2006). Testosterone replacement therapy for older men. *J. Androl.*, 27(2): 126–132.

Wierckx K, Muller S, Weyers S, et al. (2012). Long-term evaluation of cross-sex hormone treatment in transsexual persons. *J. Sex. Med.*, 9: 2641–2651.

Williams ME, Freeman PA. (2007). Transgender health. *J. Gay Lesbian Soc. Serv.*, 18(3–4): 93–108.

Winter S, Conway L. (2011). How many trans* people are there? A 2011 update incorporating new data. http://web.hku.hk/~sjwinter/TransgenderASIA/paper-how-many-trans-people-are-there.htm.

Witten TM. (2003). Transgender aging: An emerging population and an emerging need. *Rev. Sexol.*, XII(4): 15–20.

Witten TM. (2004a). *Lifecourse Issues in the Transgender and Intersex Populations.* Washington, DC: Gerontological Society of America Annual Meeting.

Witten TM. (2004b). Life course analysis: The courage to search for something more: Middle adulthood issues in the transgender and intersex community. *J. Hum. Behav. Soc. Environ.*, 8(3–4), 189–224.

Witten TM. (2010). Graceful exits: III. Intersections of aging, transgender identities and the family/community. In Fruhauf C A, Mahoney D. (Eds.), *Older GLBT Family and Community Life.* London: Routledge.

Witten TM. (2013). It's not all darkness: Resilience, robustness and successful aging in the trans-community. *LGBT Hlth*, 1(1): 24–33.

Witten TM. (2014). End of life, chronic illness and trans-identities. *J. Soc. Work End-of-Life Palliat. Care*, 10: 1–26.

Witten TM. (2015a). When my past returns: Loss of self and personhood – Dementia and the trans-person. In Westwood S, Price, E. (Eds.), *Lesbian, Gay, Bisexual and Trans (LGBT) Individuals with Dementia: Theoretical, Practical and Research Perspectives.* Routledge (in press).

Witten TM. (2015b). Elder transgender lesbians: Exploring the intersection of aging, lesbian sexual identity and transgender identity. *J. Lesbian Stud.*, 19: 1–17.

Witten TM, Carpenter B. (2015). Invisibility squared: The challenges of living as a transgender older adult. http://psychologybenefits.org/2015/03/09/invisibility-squared-the-challenges-of-living-as-a-transgender-older-adult/.

Witten TM, Eyler AE. (2012). *Lesbian, Gay, Bisexual, and Transgender Aging: Challenges in Research, Practice, and Policy.* Baltimore, MD: Johns Hopkins University Press.

Witten TM, Kidd J. (2008). Transgender and transsexual identities: The next strange fruit – Hate crimes, violence and genocide against trans-communities. *J. Hate Stud.*, 6(1): 31–63.

Witten TM, Whittle SP. (2004). TransPanthers: The graying of transgender and the law. *Deakin Law Rev.*, 9(2): 503–522.

Wolitzky-Taylor KB, Castriotta N, Lenze EJ, Stanley MA, Craske MG. (2010). Anxiety disorders in older adults: A comprehensive review. *Depress. Anxiety*, 27: 190–2010.

Wolf ECM, Dew MJ. (2012). Understanding risk factors contributing to substance abuse among MTF transgender persons. *J. LGBT Issues Counsel.*, 6(4): 237–256.

19 Transgender Health Care and Human Rights

Eszter Kismodi, Mauro Cabral, and Jack Byrne

Introduction

Transgender, gender-variant, and gender non-conforming people[1] may need a variety of health services during their lifetime. They may need to access transition-related health services, such as hormone therapy, hair removal, or a range of surgeries, including chest reconstruction or breast augmentation, and genital reconstruction surgeries, in order to express their gender identity. They may also require the same range of health services as other people, including primary care, gynecological, obstetric, urological, and HIV care, as well as mental health services, for example, to address the many consequences of stigma and discrimination. In addition to concerns about the availability, accessibility, or quality of health care, the health and wellbeing of transgender people depend on many other factors. These include whether there is a supportive interpersonal and family environment, and whether the social, cultural, and political climate provides and ensures social acceptance and respect, equality, and the full enjoyment of human rights without any form of discrimination or violence (UNDP 2013; WHO 2015a; WPATH 2012).

Addressing any of these factors requires an understanding of those experiences that are conceptualized as gender identity, gender expression, and bodily diversity and are fundamental to each person's dignity, self-determination, and full enjoyment of human rights. Furthermore, diversity in any of these areas reflects the breadth of human experience and is neither a disease nor a pathology (Council of Europe 2015; WHO 2015a; WPATH 2012). It requires detachment from a normative and pathologizing classification of gender identity and expression, and bodily diversity that neither recognizes the rich diversity of human beings nor the contingent hierarchies that organize, classify, and manage them. Instead, it requires understanding that "gender identity" refers to each person's deeply felt internal and individual experience of gender, including their personal sense of the body. This gender identity may or may not correspond with a person's sex classification assigned at birth. "Gender expression" refers to how a person expresses that gender identity externally, including through dress, speech, and mannerisms (OHCHR 2011; WHO 2015a; WPATH 2012; Yogyakarta Principles 2007).

The elaboration of health and related laws and policies; the establishment of health services; the development of standards of care and training for providers; as well as the provision of quality health services require understanding that identities, expressions, sexualities, and embodiments vary among and across cultures, regions, and societies. People may experience and express themselves in various ways, including those that contradict normative assumptions or expectations in their own culture, region, or society. There is a rich diversity of terms that people use to describe their gender identities, including transsexual, transgender, cross-dresser, genderqueer, third gender, no-gender or agender, gender non-conforming, gender-variant, and many culturally or linguistically specific terms (UNDP 2013; WHO 2015a; WPATH 2012).[2,3] Transgender people can have a range of different gender expressions, and different experiences of embodiment. None of these variations constitutes a health issue by definition; however, some transgender people may have specific health needs related to their transition. For some this involves bodily modifications through surgical procedures, hormonal treatments, prosthetic devices, while others may not wish to use medical intervention for expressing their gender identity.

The reality is, however, that many transgender people face challenges in having those needs met. There are still very few non-discriminatory, appropriate health services available and accessible to them. In those places where they are available, very few such services are non-pathologizing, supportive, and confidential, or prioritize an individual's informed decision making and self-determination over medical management (TGEU 2008; WHO 2015a). In many places in the world transgender people have to travel long distances—and even migrate to different countries—looking for clinics that may provide appropriate, comprehensive care. When they reach services, they are often rejected, mistreated, and discriminated against by health service providers (Castagnoli 2010; Eliason & Hughes 2004; Guevara 2009; Ojanen 2009; Sood 2009; Spanish Network 2010; WHO 2015a).

In those countries where health professionals are available, they often lack technical competence as very few countries have enabling laws, national health standards, medical curricula, and professional training that have incorporated a comprehensive approach to transgender health care (Bockting et al. 2005; Lombardi 2001; Lombardi & Van Servellen 2000; Sood 2009; WHO 2015a; WPATH 2012). Apart from the particular skills and experience needed for gender-affirming surgeries and other biotechnological procedures, few health professionals are knowledgeable about transgender health in general and are thus unable to provide sufficient information, let alone comprehensive, individualized, safe, and appropriate services (OSF 2013; UNDP 2013; Vancouver Coastal Health 2012; WHO 2015a; WPATH 2012).

As a result, transgender people worldwide experience substantial health disparities and barriers in accessing appropriate health care services. They often avoid seeking transgender health-related services, even if available, and miss out on essential health care, including emergency treatment for the consequences of violence or HIV-related care (Todahl et al. 2009; WHO 2015a). Disparities and barriers impact disproportionately on marginalized trans populations, including those who are poor, sex workers, trans migrants, trans people who are disabled, trans people who are intersex, trans people in prison, trans people who use drugs, trans people with HIV, and those who belong to racial and ethnic minorities (Baral et al. 2013; Health Policy Project 2015).

Respecting and protecting the human rights of transgender people require establishing trans-affirmative health services where people can receive various transgender health services and engage in an ongoing relationship with providers (if necessary and desired), to address the full spectrum of their health and wellbeing needs. Many of the barriers transgender people face are because of the stigma attached to experiences of gender identity, gender expression, sexuality, and bodily diversity that differ from normative, binary definitions. As later sections of this chapter describe, often this diversity itself is pathologized, either explicitly in classifications of disease or implicitly in judgments made by health providers. Both undermine transgender people's access to health services.

This chapter looks at laws, policies, health systems, standards of care, and providers' attitude in the context of human rights, all of which influence the provision of quality transgender health care. It explains the meaning and content of international, regional, and national health and human rights standards that are increasingly calling for the respect and protection of transgender people's human rights in relation to health care. Most pertinently for health professionals, it describes how these human rights standards have effectively been implemented and translated by ethical and professional organizations, professional bodies, and service delivery institutions.

The chapter acknowledges that the provision of services is highly dependent both on health providers' attitude in respecting and protecting transgender people's human rights and on the broader legal, policy, and health system environment that may enable or impair the provision of transgender health care. While health providers can inhibit the provision of rights-based services, they can be, and often are, pioneers in initiating and participating in the elaboration of rights-based laws, policies, standards of care, medical training, and curricula and provision of client-centered quality care itself.

Transgender Health Care and Human Rights

In order to meet the diverse health care needs of transgender people, enabling and rights-based health care-related laws, policies, and standards of care, training of health professionals and quality health services need to be in place. All these need to take into consideration the unique anatomic, social, or psychological situation of transgender individuals and be based on the respect and protection of their human rights, including in relation to non-discrimination, human dignity, self-determination, autonomy, privacy and confidentiality, and informed decision making (WPATH 2012).

In order to respect and protect human rights, health interventions (whether legal or health system or service-related) need to be based on the premise that gender identity, gender expression, and any transitional steps shall be solely determined by individuals themselves. Each person has the right to decide whether or not they seek transitional or other health services—including psychological, hormonal, or surgical interventions. This acknowledges that health interventions related to gender transition are desired for some, though not all, transgender people in order to experience, express, and embody their self-defined gender identity and expression. Other people make the transition socially through a change of name, dress, or other aspects of gender expression and bodily modifications without using any medical procedures (Health Policy Project 2015; OSF 2013; UNDP 2013; Vancouver Coastal Health 2012; WHO 2015a; WPATH 2012).

Non-Discrimination

Transgender and gender-variant people are often stigmatized and discriminated against because they are perceived to be defying socially accepted gender norms, because their gender identity or gender expression does not match their sex assigned at birth, or because their embodiment does not conform to expectations associated with that sex. Stigma and discrimination against transgender people are often aggravated by the fact that some forms of gender expression, such as cross-dressing, are criminalized in many countries. In the health sector, some of the discrimination against transgender women is linked to the perception that they are sex workers, drug users, or they are HIV-positive. All these dimensions of discrimination have an impact on transgender people's overall health and wellbeing (Health Policy Project 2015; Hill et al. 2007; UNDP 2013; United Nations 2011; WHO 2015a, 2015b). In addition, stigma, discrimination, marginalization, and violence related to gender identity and expression and bodily diversity are often exacerbated by other personal characteristics and factors, such as race, ethnicity, religion, socioeconomic status, being a migrant or residing in conflict settings, or being detained in incarceration facilities or mental health institutions (CEDAW 2010; CESCR 2009; OSF 2013; UNDP 2013; United Nations 2013).

   Provision of services, training, standards of care, and laws should aim at eliminating stereotypes and discriminatory attitudes that lead to the inaccessibility of respectful care for transgender people, and should guarantee non-discrimination on all grounds (WHO 2015a). International regional and national human rights standards increasingly recognize sex, gender identity, and gender expression among the prohibited grounds of discrimination. Human rights bodies have called on states to eliminate discrimination on these grounds in all aspects of life, including when accessing health care and social benefits (CEDAW 2010, 2015; CESCR 2009; CRC 2013). The Council of Europe, for example, has called on its member states to take appropriate legislative and other measures to ensure that the highest attainable standard of health can be effectively enjoyed without discrimination on grounds of gender identity. It has also urged them to take into account the specific needs of transgender people in the development of national health plans, including the integration of transgender health care into medical curricula, training courses, and when monitoring and evaluating the quality of health care services (Council of Europe 2011). In addition, a number of countries in all regions explicitly address discrimination on the basis of gender identity and expression in their legislation (Australian Government 2015; Council of Europe 2011; Fiji 2013; Serbia 2009; Thai National Legislative Assembly 2015; United Nations 2011).

De-Medicalization of Legal Gender Recognition

Legal gender recognition is key for people to live in accordance with their self-defined gender, in law and in fact, including being able to change their name and legal gender if they wish so. It encompasses both fundamental human rights and personal wellbeing issues.

Identification is required for most life activities, including accessing health services, social benefits, education, employment and housing, and traveling across borders. If the sex/gender indicated on a person's official identity card differs from that person's apparent gender, the person may be denied access to such services, or be treated in a discriminatory way that undermines that person's dignity (Council of Europe 2011; Köhler et al. 2013; TGEU 2008; UNDP 2013; United Nations 2011; WHO 2015a; WPATH 2015).[4] The immediate challenge is enabling people to amend official documents to reflect their self-defined identity. The broader concern is addressing discrimination against anyone who fails or refuses to conform to gender stereotypes, whether that is based on sex, gender identity, gender expression, or bodily diversity (Missé & Coll-Planas 2010).

Legal gender recognition is the formal recognition of an individual's personal decision about identity, under current and limited legal possibilities. Yet medical interventions, such as sterilization, surgery or hormonal treatment, mental health treatment, or diagnosis, are often required legally and administratively before a person's name or sex/gender can be changed on official documents. Such interventions may not be desired or needed by the individual, and are often financially or otherwise unavailable and inaccessible. They cannot be justified as a prerequisite for the legal recognition of gender identity (UNDP 2013; WHO 2015a). Some countries allow legal change of gender identity only if certain other requirements are also met, such as divorce or unmarried status (Council of Europe 2011; UNDP 2013; United Nations 2011; WPATH 2015). Administrative burdens and additional requirements, such as a period of "life experience" in the gender of choice, or an obligatory court hearing, make recognition procedures even more cumbersome (Missé & Coll-Planas 2010). Finally, a large number of countries have no provisions on gender recognition, making it impossible for transgender people to change the name and gender marker on personal identity documents and public registers (Council of Europe 2015).

Posing such arbitrary requirements are contradictory to human rights, including the rights to privacy, self-determination, personal development, and to physical and moral security and integrity (Austrian Administrative High Court 2009; Council of Europe 2011, 2015; ECtHR 1992, 2002; Federal Constitutional Court of Germany 2008, 2011; Italian Constitutional Court 1985; New Zealand Family Court 2008; United Nations 2011, 2013; WHO 2015a). It may also have a serious negative impact on transgender people's mental health by increasing levels of stress, anxiety, depression, and other forms of mental suffering (Hyde et al, 2014; WPATH 2015).

Human rights bodies increasingly urge states to enable legal gender recognition without such requirements and with a vision of respecting and protecting the rights of transgender people (Constitutional Court of Colombia 1993; HRC 2008a, 2008b). They have called for the elimination of any requirements for sterilization or any other compulsory medical treatment, including the need for a mental health diagnosis (Council of Europe 2015). Instead, human rights bodies have urged countries to develop quick, transparent, and accessible procedures, based on self-determination, for changing the name and registered sex of transgender people on birth certificates, identity cards, passports, educational certificates, and other similar documents. They have stressed the need to make these procedures available for all people who seek to use them, irrespective of age, medical status, financial situation, or police record (Council of Europe 2015).

Increasingly, countries are adopting laws that reflect such a human rights approach. Argentina was the first country, in May 2012, to pass a gender identity law that allows gender markers to be changed on birth certificates and all associated documents, through an administrative procedure, based solely on a person's request for such a change. Thus, there is no requirement for a medical diagnosis, surgery, and/or hormonal treatment (República Argentina 2012). Most recently Denmark, Ireland, and Malta have passed similar laws (Denmark 2014; Ireland 2015; Malta 2015).

In South Asia, a "third gender" has been legally recognized as a result of Supreme Court decisions in India, Nepal, and Pakistan (Supreme Court of India 2014; Supreme Court of Nepal 2007; Supreme Court of Pakistan 2011) and a Cabinet decision in Bangladesh. In addition, New Zealand and Australia have an optional third gender category on passports, and on birth certificates in one Australian territory (Health Policy Project 2015).

Informed Decision Making

The principle of autonomy, dignity, and the physical and mental integrity of a person expressed through free, full, and informed decision making is a central theme in medical ethics, and is embodied in human rights law. The respect of these principles requires that individuals have the opportunity to make autonomous choices about their own body, and are able to express their gender freely and without coercion of any kind. Accordingly, transgender people should be able to choose and to refuse any medical intervention conventionally associated with transitional health care, including sterilization and genital modifications. Respecting these principles requires that any counseling, advice, or information given by health care providers or other support staff or family members should be non-directive, enabling individuals to make decisions that are best for themselves, knowing the nature and content of all proposed medical interventions (WHO 2014).

Informed decision making that is based on autonomy and self-determination and the agency of the transgender individual to express gender identity and to choose transitional pathways excludes requirements that make one intervention conditional on the performance of another intervention that is medically not indicated. For example, the Argentinian law makes it clear that there should be no requirement for total or partial reassignment surgery in order to access comprehensive hormonal treatment (República Argentina 2012). Similarly, sterilization should not be required in order to access gender reassignment surgery or hormonal treatment (ECtHR 2015; WHO 2015a). In addition, imposing unjustified eligibility criteria for transgender health services, such as a mandatory 2-year waiting period, has been found medically unnecessary and undermines personal autonomy and informed decision making (ECtHR 2009).

Another frequently identified barrier for transgender people accessing trans-specific health care is the requirement of third-party consent or authorization from health care professionals, and/or from family members. Human rights bodies have frequently stated that requiring adults to obtain third-party consent or authorization in order to access health services, including from a spouse, medical practitioner, or public officer, is a violation of the right to privacy and self-determination (CEDAW 1994; CESCR 2000; WHO 2014). The specific consent requirements for children are addressed separately below.

In many countries mental health professionals are required to confirm that a transgender person has been diagnosed with "gender identity disorder" or "gender dysphoria" and lived according to the desired gender for a minimum number of years. In some countries, including China, additional requirements are needed before individuals are allowed to access gender-affirming surgeries. These include explicit consent of their family, a declaration that the person's sexual orientation after surgery will be heterosexual, and showing proof of no criminal record (China 2009; Health Policy Project 2015). This restriction excludes many transgender women, who have few employment options and are vulnerable to being arrested if they are doing sex work (UNDP 2013).

Such requirements for accessing transgender health services are often accompanied by over-medicalization of eligibility criteria assessments. For example, mental health assessment is often required before hormone therapy and surgery. This is a double standard when such requirements are not applied when cisgender people (those who are not transgender) access similar or identical medical interventions. Psycho-pathologization reinforces gender hierarchies and medical authority while undermining transgender people's self-determination. Human rights and professional health bodies have spoken out against mental health treatments that attempt to change a person's gender identity and against forced institutionalization of trans people, including as a prerequisite for legal gender recognition (Coleman et al. 2011; Health Policy Project 2015; Missé & Coll-Planas 2010; OSF 2014).

In addition, such assessments may be inaccessible to many transgender people, as the cost of consultations with mental health professionals very often exceeds the budget of the average trans person. Frequently these health services are unavailable or of insufficient quality, as very few psychiatrists and clinical psychologists specialize in gender-related mental health and transition issues. While the World Professional Association for Transgender Health *Standards of Care* recommend a mental health assessment before hormone therapy, it also notes that this can be done by an appropriately trained primary care or mental health provider (Health Policy Project 2015; Transvanilla 2014). In some countries, such as Argentina, such a mental health assessment is not required by law or policy (República Argentina 2012). This is also the practice in clinics that follow an informed-consent model of care (Callen-Lorde 2015; Radix 2014).

In order to make an informed decision about any medical intervention, comprehensive information, counseling, and support should be accessible for transgender people. However, many health providers have little information or are misinformed about transgender people's health needs, some actively discriminate against transgender people, and others are reluctant to prescribe hormones, sometimes fearing that doing so for trans people may be illegal. In this context, trans people look to each other to fill vital information gaps; many currently source most information from peers or online. Whereas peer support has been identified as an important enabling factor, such information may not always be accurate or sufficient to meet an individual's health needs. For example, advice about the type and amount of hormones received by trans peers can be inaccurate or outdated, leading to serious health hazards with long-lasting adverse effects. Administering hormones by unskilled people and/ or in unhygienic circumstances can lead to scarring and inflammation, and possibly the transmission of infectious diseases, including HIV. Hence, in many parts of the world, there is significant unmet need for information about safe hormone use, particularly in accessible formats, including in local languages (Health Policy Project 2015).

Individuals have the right to be fully informed by properly trained personnel, so they can make full and informed decisions, free from any form of coercion. Health care providers who are delivering the services have the responsibility to take into consideration each individual's health and social needs. They are required to convey accurate, clear information in a language and format that are readily understandable to the person concerned (Box 19.1). Censoring, withholding, or intentionally misrepresenting information about health services, including transgender health services, can put health and basic human rights of people in jeopardy (WHO 2014).

Box 19.1   Information required for making choices about transgender health care

Based on health and human right standards the information provided to transgender people so that they can make an informed choice about various procedures should emphasize the advantages and disadvantages, the health benefits, risks, and side effects of the particular intervention, enabling transgender people to compare various interventions. Counseling / the consultation should include the following points:

- the nature of the procedure, including benefits and consequences, and the permanent or temporary effects of the intervention;
- any necessary follow-up care;
- alternative options;
- risks, potential side effects, and follow-up care that may be required;
- the person's right to change his or her mind and withdraw consent at any time; and
- the voluntary nature of any intervention and that the decision to undergo any medical intervention is a decision to be made by the individual.

Information should be provided in a language and format, both spoken and written, that are understandable, accessible, and appropriate to the needs of the individual. Factors such as educational level, physical or intellectual impairments, and the age of the individual should be considered in the counseling / consultation. Alternative and augmentative formats—such as Braille, sign language, or simple communication—should be provided, as appropriate, to individual needs and preferences.

The right to effective access to information regarding one's health includes access to medical records. All people are entitled to know what information is being, or has been, collected about their own health. Lack of access to their medical records makes it hard for individuals to get information about their health status or receive a second opinion or follow-up care, and can block their access to justice, remedies, and redress when human rights violations occur (WHO 2014).

Availability, Accessibility, and Quality of Transition-Related Information and Health Services

According to recent studies, the overall lack of transition-related information and services in the public health system, with regard to both hormone treatment and gender-affirming surgeries, was seen as the greatest challenge to transgender people in achieving their highest attainable standard of health. The lack of coverage, absence of specialist expertise, few protocols for trans health care, and negative attitudes of many health care personnel drive trans people into the arms of unregulated and non-qualified health care providers (Health Policy Project 2015; WHO 2015a).

In some countries, such as Viet Nam, the first layer of barriers for accessing services lies in the law, that explicitly prohibits the provision of gender-affirming surgeries (Government of Viet Nam 2008). In either case, no counseling or support is available to transgender people who have to travel abroad for such interventions; those who find specialists or surgeons willing to perform operations do so at their own risk. In other instances, transgender surgery becomes forbidden because of religious reasons. For example, in Malaysia, gender-affirming surgeries were available at the University of Malaya Hospital between 1980 and 1982, and it was possible to change gender markers on identity cards. Subsequently, the National Fatwa Council issued a *fatwa* (a religious edict) against sex reassignment surgery, and the university closed its services to transgender people (Health Policy Project 2015).

One of the main barriers in accessing transgender health services, however, across the world is unaffordability and lack of reimbursement of transgender health services (Council of Europe 2011; ECtHR 2003; Health Policy Project 2015; TGEU 2008; United Nations 2011). Transition-related health care services do not always translate into funding for such care. Private and public insurers often do not offer, or may specifically exclude, coverage for medical procedures for gender transition; and there are substantial variations in which services are covered and what conditions are required (American Psychiatric Association 2012; Egale Canada 2004; Landén et al. 1998; WHO 2015a). Some state-based public health systems review requests for care on a case-by-case basis and they are often denied (Spade 2008).

As a result, trans people have to pay personally for the full cost of accessing health services, that often are available only in private hospitals or clinics and thus are prohibitively expensive for most trans people. Even for those who have private health insurance, it is very uncommon for these transitional health services to be reimbursed. Where health services are expensive and not subsidized, or are disrespectful of transgender and gender-variant people, transgender people often consider seeking cheaper and less clinically sound options, or delay or stop treatment (Health Policy Project 2015; WHO 2015a.) They may obtain hormones of dubious quality, outside the health system, over the counter, via the internet or illegally, without proper supervision of dosage or side effects (Cameron 2006; Clements Nolle et al. 2001; Grossman et al. 2006; McGowan 1999; Sanchez et al. 2009; Sood 2009; Teh 2001; Winter 2006; Xavier & Simmons 2000). The improper use of sex hormones may lead to serious health problems (Coleman et al. 2011; Hembree et al. 2009).

Lack of access to quality gender-affirming surgeries, because they are either not available or not affordable, can force transgender people to access unregulated or low-quality surgical procedures. For transgender women, this includes unregulated methods of castration by unqualified people, with serious risks such as urinary stricture, septic infection, and even death (Bockting et al. 2005; McGovern 1995; Sood 2009). Transgender women may choose to inject free-floating silicone, or other harmful substances such as cooking oil, as a faster and more accessible way to achieve the body they desire (Guevara 2009). These injected products may harden or migrate to other parts of the body, causing permanent disfigurement, serious pain, chronic infection, acute systemic inflammation, or death (Agrawal et al. 2013; Hariri et al. 2012; Visnyei et al. 2014).

The respect and protection of human rights call for the provision of accessible, affordable, and quality health information and services. Furthermore, all those seeking services should be treated with respect and dignity, free from discrimination and judgmental attitudes or the imposition of barriers in their access to care (CEDAW 2010; CESCR 2000, 2009; CRC 2013). Availability of quality transgender-specific health care requires the adoption of national standards of transgender health care that comprehensively reflect human rights. In turn there is a need for considerable long-term investment in capacity building, training, and sensitization, including the provision of regular rights-based pre- and in-service education opportunities to professionals from various disciplines (Council of Europe 2011; Health Policy Project 2015; WPATH 2012). Other requirements are necessary clinical and laboratory skills and infrastructure; and the reimbursement of related costs of care by national health and social security agencies (Health Policy Project 2015). When a specific health institution lacks trained professionals, it should provide information and referrals to trained providers, where available, and to offline and online peer support resources. Alternative technology, such as tele-medicine, may be a practical way to address gaps in access to appropriate transgender health care (WPATH 2012).

Affordability as a human rights matter has been addressed by various human rights bodies (Council of Europe 2011; ECtHR 2003; United Nations 2011). They have called on states to ensure that transgender health care is reimbursed by public health insurance schemes; and that any limitations on cost coverage must be lawful, objective, and proportionate (Council of Europe 2015). It is vital to take into consideration the complexity of funding mechanisms that hold power over individual care. Strategies for accessible and affordable transgender health care need to make clear allowances for each type of system, whether it is a private or public insurance scheme, publicly funded model, or mixture of each (TGEU 2008).

Recognizing the health benefits of such care, some professional associations have specifically called on public and private insurers to cover services that transgender people need (American Psychological Association 2008; WPATH 2008, 2015). An increasing number of countries have revised or are revising laws and regulations in relation to accessing transition-related services. In Argentina, for example, the 2012 Law includes provisions for coverage of all medical costs related to gender-affirming procedures and treatment for transgender people (República Argentina 2012).

Health Classifications, Transgender Health Care, and Human Rights

Health classification schemes have a great impact on the provision of health care, and the recognition of human rights. They can influence standards of care, utilization of services, provision of training, and reimbursement of services. Such classifications directly influence how people can access transition-related services, as well as other entitlements, including legal gender recognition (Drescher et al. 2012; WHO 2015a). Gender diversity is currently coded as mental health diagnoses in both the *International Classification of Disease* (ICD: WHO 2015b) and the *Diagnostic and Statistical Manual of Mental Disorders* (DSM) (American Psychological Association 2013). Until recently, both used the term "gender identity disorder."

In many countries, the existence of classification codes related to transgender health care enables people to access hormones, surgeries, and other gender-affirming medical interventions. Conversely, such codes contribute to negative perceptions of gender diversity by framing it as an illness. Specifically, mental health classifications may increase discrimination against transgender and gender-variant people, because of the unwarranted stigma attached to mental disorders, and because they undermine transgender people's autonomy. In addition, mental health diagnoses can pose unnecessary barriers such as requiring assessments by two or more psychiatrists over an extended period of time, or even psychiatric hospitalization (Bockting et al. 2005; Castagnoli 2010; Council of Europe 2011; Hill et al. 2007; WHO 2015a).

Authoritative international, regional, and national health and human rights bodies have critiqued the classification of gender diversity as a disease in international diagnosis manuals, noting that this is disrespectful of transgender people's human dignity and an additional obstacle to social inclusion (Council of Europe 2015; PAHO 2014). For example, the Council of Europe and the European Parliament called on member states to amend classifications of diseases used at national level and advocate the modification of international classifications, making sure that transgender people, including children, are not labeled as mentally disordered, while ensuring stigma-free access to necessary medical treatment (Council of Europe 2015; European Parliament 2015). In addition, transgender people, supported by many health professionals, are strongly advocating for transgender people's health needs to no longer be defined by a mental health diagnosis (GATE 2011, 2013; Health Policy Project 2015; Spanish Network 2010).

In 2013, the DSM reverted to an older term, "gender dysphoria," that appears in the fifth version of the U.S. *Diagnostic and Statistical Manual of Mental Disorders*, or DSM-5 (American Psychological Association 2013). It focuses more specifically on the distress some transgender people feel when their gender identity does not match their body. In some places the revised classification, "gender dysphoria," may offer a route to health care coverage without imposing a permanent label such as "gender identity disorder." However, it has been heavily criticized for, among other reasons, still heavily linking gender identity with a mental health condition (GATE 2011; Health Policy Project 2015).

While the DSM classification is strongly utilized in many places, most countries in the world follow the World Health Organization (WHO) classification system, and some use both (Drescher et al. 2012). Currently WHO is in the process of revising ICD-10, including the coding of "gender identity disorder" that is currently classified among "mental and behavioural disorders" (Drescher et al. 2012; WHO 1992). The new version, ICD-11, will ultimately be approved by the World Health Assembly. Proposed revisions include recommendations for deleting some subcategories (such as fetishistic transvestism) and creating a non-pathologizing code to be placed in a different chapter. Current proposals include that a "gender incongruence" code would be moved out of the ICD chapter on Mental and Behavioural Disorders and placed in a new chapter on Conditions Related to Sexual Health (Drescher et al. 2012; WHO 2015b). These recommended revisions aim to recognize gender identity and expression as a matter of self-determination, and transgender people's decision-making autonomy in regard to gender-affirming health care. They acknowledge the need for available, accessible, affordable, and quality transgender health services.

While the ICD-11 is awaiting approval by the World Health Assembly, some countries have already revised, or are in the process of revising, their national classification systems, to recognize transgender people's needs and human rights (Council of Europe 2011).

Recognizing Children's Rights in Relation to Transgender Health Care

When it comes to children, the past decades have brought a shift in addressing the needs, including health needs, and human rights of gender-variant and gender-diverse children. Clinicians, advocates, and policy makers have questioned the efficacy and ethics of conversion psychotherapies, designed to suppress gender non-conformity and enforce birth-assigned sex roles (Cohen-Kettenis et al. 2006; Delemarre-van de Waal & Cohen-Kettenis 2006; Hill et al. 2007, 2010; Olson et al. 2011; Riley et al. 2011; Speigel 2008; WHO 2015a; WPATH 2010, 2012). At the same time, current diagnostic labels of mental pathology face growing criticism regarding their validity and clinical utility and concerns about the harmful stigma they can elicit (Drescher et al. 2012; GATE 2013; WHO 2015a; Winters 2008; WPATH 2010).

Children and adolescents whose experience of gender does not correspond with their sex classification assigned at birth may experience rejection, harassment, and violence, particularly sexual violence. These each have a cumulatively negative effect on health (Cohen-Kettenis et al. 2006; Riley et al. 2011; WHO 2015a; WPATH 2010). The prerequisite for any action or intervention by health professionals and schools should be providing information for children, parents, and other caregivers that respects the human rights of children, is age-appropriate, and is based on respecting and understanding gender diversity and expression. Health care professionals can play an important supporting role in this regard (Health Policy Project 2015; WPATH 2012).

International, regional, and national standards call for the protection of children's rights, including their right to be free from discrimination, and to have the highest attainable standard of health, ensuring that their evolving capacity in decision making is recognized. National human rights bodies have increasingly applied these standards to protect the rights of gender-variant children and adolescents (CRC 2013). The Family Court of Australia, for example, stated that hormonal and surgical treatment and allowing change of name should be determined on a case-by-case basis, taking into account the child's rights to freedom of expression, non-discrimination, and privacy, in accordance with the child's best interest and evolving capacity (Family Court of Australia 2004, 2009, 2014).

Specific concern has been expressed about discrimination against transgender and gender-variant children in schools, and human rights bodies have called for the provision of effective protection against violence and discrimination based on gender identity in the educational system (CRC 2011; HRC 2010). National laws and programs have also recognized the need for public education about gender identity and expression, including in childhood and adolescence, in order to diminish and eliminate stigma and discrimination. For example, in the state of Tamil Nadu in India, the Health Department issued directives for a program of professional counseling and sensitization of teachers and families on transgender issues so that gender-variant children can enjoy better protection and care (Government of Tamil Nadu 2006). As another example, after passing the Gender Expression, Gender Identity and Sex Characteristics Act in 2015, Malta adopted a comprehensive education policy focusing specifically on trans, gender-variant, and intersex children. Among other things, the policy highlights the key issues to be addressed in order to make schools inclusive for trans, gender-variant, and intersex students (Malta 2015).

Privacy and Confidentiality

Individuals should not be subject to interference with their privacy and should enjoy protection of the law in this respect.[5] In the context of transgender health care, this right to privacy requires both non-interference with a person's decision making and expression of identity, and the availability of acceptable and respectful health services (Köhler et al. 2013; OSF 2014).

When the right to privacy is applied to gender recognition, it means that laws and practices should ensure that, once official documents have been amended, access to previous name and sex or gender details is limited strictly. Primarily, a transgender person should have power to authorize who can access this material, with provision for judicial authorization in limited, well-founded circumstances (República Argentina 2012).

The protection of an individual's privacy is critical when providing transgender health services. Transgender health care includes many sensitive issues that are not widely discussed in families or communities, and health care workers are often entrusted with such private information by their patients. Confidentiality implies a duty on providers to keep secret or private the medical information they receive from patients. Approaching a doctor, clinic, or hospital to ask for health support can be particularly difficult for many transgender people, as disclosing their gender identity can result in discrimination. When health providers use inappropriate names, titles, or pronouns it undermines a transgender person's dignity. Moreover, when that information is disclosed to others, without consent, it also breaches the right to privacy. This includes, for example, transgender people inappropriately being referred to as "it" in health care facilities, or transgender women being referred to as men, and transgender men being called women (Health Policy Project 2015; Transvanilla 2014). Health records often disclose a transgender person's sex assigned at birth and potentially expose that person to judgments or discrimination from other health providers. This includes being refused care or denied access to the appropriate sex-segregated hospital wards or clinics (Spade 2011; Suess 2014; UNDP 2013; WHO 2014).

If individuals feel that confidentiality and privacy are not guaranteed in the health care environment, trans people may avoid seeking care. This jeopardizes their own health and the exercise of their human rights, including their ability to make informed decisions about their gender identity and expression (Health Policy Project 2015; Transvanilla 2014).

Health care providers have a firm obligation to respect strictly the right to privacy and confidentiality, including with respect to counseling and other medical interventions related to providing transgender health care (CRC 2003). Health care providers have an obligation to keep medical information confidential, both written records and verbal communications. Confidential medical records may need to include personal information about a transgender person, including health-related information. However, all administrative details such as name, title, and gender identity should be based solely on a person's self-defined identity, whether or not that is legally recognized. Such information may only be disclosed with the consent of the patient/client. This may require training for health personnel about protecting privacy and confidentiality, and enacting laws or regulations setting out the right to confidential advice and treatment and avenues for addressing any privacy breach.

The 2012 Argentinean Gender Identity Law provides a good example of comprehensive privacy provisions that respect a person's self-defined gender identity. When individuals request to use a name different from the one recorded in their national identity documents, this must be respected in all administrative records and exchanges. The amendment of the recorded sex and the change in first name will never be published and access to the original birth certificate is legally restricted (República Argentina 2012).

Accountability, Participation, and Access to Remedies

Accountability is central to respecting and protecting human rights, ensuring that laws and standards of care are properly developed and that appropriate health services are provided.

Effective accountability processes include involving a wide range of stakeholders (including ministries of health, professional associations, service providers, and service users) in the development, implementation, and monitoring of laws, standards of care, and services. They require the participation of transgender people in all decision-making processes that affect their health, including law and policy making, setting of standards of care, or developing medical curricula.

Effective accountability also requires the availability of effective remedies and redress mechanisms. These can vary from country to country and may include access to national courts, effective operation of institutional patients' rights mechanisms, and ethics committees, national ombudsman institutions and other human right institutions and disciplinary bodies of professional associations. Effective remedies include the fair and effective investigations of human rights violations, ensuring they are not repeated, and compensation for victims (HRC 2004; WHO 2014, 2015a).

Conclusions

To have one's gender identity and expression recognized, without stigma, discrimination, exclusion, or violence, is important to any individual's health and wellbeing, and is too often denied to transgender people. Transgender people have the right to live in accordance with that self-defined gender identity, in law and in fact, and to access quality transgender health services based on informed decision making. Stigma, discrimination, and violence, inaccessibility of legal gender recognition, and the unavailability of transgender services based on self-determination and informed decision making can create life and health hazards for transgender people. This renders them vulnerable to economic, educational, and social exclusion. The development of rights-based laws, policies, and standards of care, availability and accessibly of quality transgender health services, and training of health care professionals are essential elements of rights-based transgender health services. Health services should be provided without stigma and discrimination, based on informed consent, and should be affordable. This requires that health care professionals are educated and trained about gender and bodily diversity and human rights, including the particular privacy and confidentiality concerns that transgender people may have. It also requires a focus on providing access to health services for transgender people without classifying gender diversity as a mental illness.

At the same time, human rights standards and an informed-consent approach to transgender health services require that transgender people are not coerced into having medical interventions against their will. The respect, protection, and fulfillment of human rights require that no one should be forced to undergo medical procedures, including gender-affirming surgeries, sterilization, or hormonal therapy. Human rights bodies and experts have identified and critiqued severely the coerced sterilization of transgender people, when legal gender recognition (and the protection it provides) is contingent on medical interventions that result in sterilization.

Arbitrary and medically unnecessary requirements for legal gender recognition jeopardize health and the enjoyment of human rights. These include non-medical requirements such as forced divorce, or excluding people based solely on their age, occupation, HIV status, or whether they have children.

In addition, transgender and gender-variant children need special protection. Their health and human rights should not be jeopardized by discrimination, violence, or stigma. They should be able to access health care services, on the basis of free informed consent, according to their best interest and evolving capacity. This includes recognizing the dangers of pathologizing gender diversity in childhood.

In order to respect, protect, and fulfill the human rights of transgender people in relation to health services, states need to set appropriate accountability mechanisms that will provide effective remedies and redress. This requires developing processes that enable effective participation of transgender people in the development of such accountability mechanisms.

Health care providers can be important actors in this regard, whether it comes to the reform of laws and policies, advocating for the development of rights-based standards of care, or training curricula. Most importantly, health care providers themselves are responsible for providing non-discriminatory, dignified health care services for transgender people that respect and protect each person's human dignity, privacy, self-determination, and autonomy.

Notes

1 Here and thereafter, the umbrella term "trans people" is used in this chapter, in the interests of consistency.
2 Various cultural and indigenous terms are also used to describe a wide and diverse range of gender identities, including *hijra* and *aravani* (India), *meti* (Nepal), *fa'afafine* (Samoa, America Samoa, Tokelau), *transpinay* and *transpinoy* (Philippines), *meme* (Namibia), *muxe* (Mexico), and *omeggid* (in Panama). Someone born male who identifies as female might use the term "male-to-female" (MTF), "transwoman," "transgender woman," "transfeminine," or simply "woman" to describe her gender identity. Someone born female who identifies as male might use the term "female-to-male" (FTM), "transman," "transgender man," "transmasculine," or simply "man" to describe his identity. There are also many transgender people whose gender identity fits outside the binary 'male' or 'female'. They may use terms such as non-binary, or gender non-conforming.
3 This chapter uses the term "transgender" as an umbrella term covering diverse gender identities.
4 Legal recognition of gender identity varies hugely across countries and is regulated through a range of civil administrative laws, including regulations controlling birth registries, state identity cards, passports, and other socially important identity documents. Often transgender people are able to change some documents but not others. This means an individual may have conflicting documents, reflecting different gender identities, causing major problems. Most countries recognize only "male" and "female" as constituting legal gender identity. However, legal recognition of a "third gender" has been implemented in a number of countries, as outlined later in this section.
5 *International Covenant on Civil and Political Rights*. New York, United Nations, 1966. Article 17.

References

Agrawal N, et al. (2013). Silicone-induced granuloma after injection for cosmetic purposes: A rare entity of calcitriol-mediated hypercalcemia. *Case Rep. Med.*, http://dx.doi.org/10.1155/2013/807292.

American Psychiatric Association. (2012). Position statement on access to care for transgender and gender variant individuals. Available at: www.psychiatry.org/File%20Library/Advocacy%20and%20Newsroom/Position%20Statements/ps2012_TransgenderCare.pdf.

American Psychological Association. (2008). Resolution on transgender and gender identity and gender expression non-discrimination. Available at: www.apa.org/about/policy/chapter-12b.aspx#transgender (accessed 3 May 2014).

American Psychological Association. (2013). *Diagnostic and Statistical Manual of Mental Disorders*, 5th ed., text revision. Washington, DC: American Psychiatric Association.

Australian Government. (2015). The Sex Discrimination Amendment (Sexual Orientation, Gender Identity and Intersex Status) Act 2013 (Cth). Australian Government 2015.

Austrian Administrative High Court. (2009). VwGH 27.02.2009, 2008/17/0054 (decided February 27th, 2009).

Baral SD, Poteat T, Stromdahl S, et al. (2013). Worldwide burden of HIV in transgender women: A systematic review and meta-analysis. *Lancet Infect. Dis.*, 13: 214–222.

Bockting WO, Robinson BE, Forberg J, et al. (2005). Evaluation of a sexual health approach to reducing HIV/STD risk in the transgender community. *AIDS Care*, 17(3): 289–303.

Cameron L. (2006). *Sexual Health and Rights. Sex Workers, Transgender People and Men who Have Sex with Men*. New York: Open Society Institute.

Callen-Lorde (2015). Transgender health services. Available at: http://callen-lorde.org/transhealth/.

Castagnoli C. (2010). Transgender persons' rights in the EU Member States. Brussels: Directorate General for Internal Policies, Citizens' Rights and Constitutional Affairs, Civil Liberties, Justice and Home Affairs, European Parliament.

CEDAW. (1994). *General Recommendation no. 21: Equality in Marriage and Family Relations*. New York: United Nations, Committee on the Elimination of Discrimination against Women. (Contained in UN Doc A/47/38.)

CEDAW. (2010). *General Recommendation 28: Core Obligations of States Parties under Article 2 of the Convention on the Elimination of All Forms of Discrimination Against Women*. New York: United Nations Committee on the Elimination of Discrimination against Women. (CEDAW/C/20107477GC.2.)

CEDAW. (2015). *General Recommendation 33: On Women's Access to Justice*. New York: United Nations Committee on the Elimination of Discrimination against Women. (CEDAW/C/GC/33.)

CESCR. (2000). *General Comment 14: The Right to the Highest Attainable Standard of Health (art. 12)*. Geneva: United Nations Committee on Economic, Social and Cultural Rights. (UN Doc E/C.12/2000/4.)

CESCR. (2009). *General Comment No. 20: Non-discrimination in Economic, Social and Cultural Rights (art. 2, para. 2, of the International Covenant on Economic, Social and Cultural Rights)*. Geneva: United Nations Committee on Economic, Social and Cultural Rights. (E/C.12/GC/20.)

China. (2009). Health Office of Medical Affairs No. 185. 2009. Sex Change Operations and Technology Management Standards. Available in Chinese at: http://baike.baidu.com/view/3140460.htm.

Clements-Nolle K, Marx R, Guzman R, Katz M. (2001). HIV prevalence, risk behaviors, health care use, and mental health status of transgender persons: Implications for public health intervention. *Am. J. Publ. Hlth*, 91(6): 915–921.

Cohen-Kettenis PT, Wallien M, Johnson LL, Owen-Anderson AFH, Bradley SJ, Zucker KJ. (2006). A parent-report gender identity questionnaire for children: A cross-national, cross-clinic comparative analysis. *Clin. Child Psychol. Psychiatry*, 11(3): 397–405.

Colema E, Bockting W, Botzer M, Cohen-Kettenis P, DeCuypere G, Feldman J, … Zucker K. (2011). Standards of care for the health of transsexual, transgender, and gender-nonconforming people, version 7. *Int. J. Transgenderism*, 13(4): 165–232.

Constitutional Court of Colombia. (1993). Decision T-594/93 (Dec. 15, 1993).

Council of Europe. (2011). *Discrimination on Grounds of Sexual Orientation and Gender Identity in Europe*, 2nd ed. Strasbourg: Council of Europe.

Council of Europe. (2015). Resolution 2048 (2015) Discrimination Against Transgender People in Europe. Strasbourg: Parliamentary Assembly of the Council of Europe. Resolution 2048.

CRC. (2011). *Concluding Observations: New Zealand*. Geneva: United Nations Committee on the Rights of the Child. (CRC/C/NZL/3–4.)

CRC. (2013). *General Comment No. 15: The Rights of the Child to the Highest Attainable Standard of Health*. Geneva: United Nations Committee on the Rights of the Child. (UN Doc CRC/C/GC/15.)

Delemarre-van de Waal HA, Cohen-Kettenis PT. (2006). Clinical management of gender identity disorder in adolescents: A protocol on psychological and paediatric endocrinology aspects. *Eur. J. Endocrinol.*, 155: S131–S137.

Denmark. (2014). Lov om ændring af lov om Det Centrale Personregister [Law on the amendment of the law on the central person registry]. Available at https://www.retsinformation.dk/forms/r0710.aspx?id=163824.

Drescher J., Cohen-Kettenis P, Winter S. (2012). Minding the body: Situating gender identity diagnoses in the ICD-11. *Int. Rev. Psychiatr.*, 24(6): 568–571.

ECtHR. (1992). *B v. France*. Application no. 13343/87, decided on 25 March 1992. Strasbourg: European Court of Human Rights.

ECtHR. (2002). *Goodwin v. United Kingdom*. Application no. 28957/95, decided on 11 July 2002. Strasbourg: European Court of Human Rights.

ECtHR. (2003). *Van Kück v. Germany*. Application no. 35968/97, decided on 12 June 2003. Strasbourg: European Court of Human Rights.

ECtHR. (2009). *Schlumpf v. Switzerland*. Application no. 29002/06, decided on 8 January 2009. Strasbourg: European Court of Human Rights.

ECtHR. (2015). *Y.Y v. Turkey. Schlumpf v. Switzerland*. Application no. 14793/08, decided on 10 March 2015. Strasbourg: European Court of Human Rights.

Egale Canada. (2004). Sex reassignment surgery (SRS). Backgrounder. October 2004. Available at: http://www.egale.ca/index.asp?lang=E&item=1086 (accessed January 17, 2012).

Eliason MJ, Hughes T. (2004). Treatment counselor's attitudes about lesbian, gay, and transgendered clients: Urban vs rural settings. *Substance Use Misuse*, 39 (4): 625–644.

European Parliament. (2015). A8-0230/2015 report on the situation of fundamental rights in the European Union (2013–2014) (2014/2254(INI)).

Family Court of Australia. (2004). Re Alex. FamCA 297. 2004.

Family Court of Australia. (2009). Re Alex. FamCA 1292. FamCA 1134. 2009.

Family Court of Australia. (2014). Re Isaac. FamCA 1134. 2014.

Federal Constitutional Court of Germany. (2008). 1 BvL 10/05 (27 May, 2008).

Federal Constitutional Court of Germany. (2011). 1 BvR 3295/07 (11 January 2011).

Fiji. (2013). Constitution of the Republic of Fiji. Available at: http://www.paclii.org/fj/Fiji-Constitution-English-2013.pdf.

GATE. (2011). *GATE, Global Action for Trans* Equality. It's Time for Reform. Trans* Health Issues in the International Classifications of Diseases. A Report on the GATE Experts Meeting.* The Hague, November 16–18, 2011. Available at: http://globaltransaction.files.wordpress.com/2012/05/its-time-for-reform.pdf.

GATE. (2013). Critique and Alternative Proposal to the "Gender Incongruence of Childhood" Category in ICD-11. GATE Civil Society Expert Working Group Buenos Aires, April 4–6, 2013. Available at: http://globaltransaction.files.wordpress.com/2012/03/critique-and-alternative-proposalto-the-_gender-incongruence-of-childhood_-category-in-icd-11.pdf (retrieved: August 17, 2014).

Government of Tamil Nadu. (2006). Social welfare – Rehabilitation of Aravani's (eunuchs): recommendation Sub-Committee – orders issued. G.O. (Ms) No.199; 21 December 2006. Available at: http://www.tn.gov.in/go_view/dept/30?page=4(accessed 4 May 2014).

Government of Viet Nam. (2008). Decree No. 88/2008/ND-CP of August 5, 2008, on Sex Reassignment, Article 1. Available at: http://kenfoxlaw.com/resources/legal-documents/governmental-decrees/2547-vbpl.html.

Grossman AH, D'Augelli AR, Salter NP. (2006). Male-to-female transgender youth: gender expression milestones, gender atypicality, victimization, and parents' responses. *J. GLBT Fam. Stud.,* 2(1): 71–92.

Guevara AL. (2009). *The Hidden HIV Epidemic: Transgender Women in Latin America and Asia. Compilation of Epidemiological Data.* Buenos Aires: International HIV/AIDS Alliance.

Hariri L P, et al. (2012). Progressive granulomatous pneumonitis in response to cosmetic subcutaneous silicone injections in a patient with HIV-1 infection: Case report and review of the literature. *Arch. Pathol. Lab. Med.,* 136(2): 204–207.

Health Policy Project. (2015). *Health Policy Project, Asia Pacific Transgender Network, United Nations Development Programme. Blueprint for the Provision of Comprehensive Care for Trans People and Trans Communities.* Washington, DC: Futures Group, Health Policy Project.

Hembree W, Cohen-Kettenis P, Delemarre-van de Waal HA, Gooren LJ, Meyer 3rd WJ, Spack NP, Tangpricha V, Montor VM. (2009). Endocrine treatment of transsexual persons: An Endocrine Society clinical practice guideline. *J. Clin. Endocrinol. Metab.,* 94(9): 3132–3154.

Hill DB, Rozanski C, Carfagnini J, Willoughby B. (2007). Gender identity disorders in childhood and adolescence: A critical inquiry. *Int. J. Sex. Hlth,* 19(1): 57–74.

Hill DB, Menvielle EJ, Sica KM, Johnson A. (2010). An affirmative intervention for families with gender variant children: Parental ratings of child mental health and gender. *J. Sex. Marital Ther.,* 36(1): 6–23.

HRC. (2004). *General Comment No. 31: The Nature of the General Legal Obligation Imposed on States Parties.* New York: United Nations Human Rights Committee (UN Doc CCPR/C/21/Rev.1/Add.13).

HRC. (2008a). *Concluding Observations: Ireland.* Geneva: United Nations Human Rights Committee. (UN Doc. CCPR/C/IRL/CO/3.)

HRC. (2008b). *Concluding Observations: United Kingdom of Great Britain and Northern Ireland*. Geneva: United Nations Human Rights Committee. (UN Doc. CCPR/C/GBR/6.)

HRC. (2010). *Concluding Observations: Mexico*. Geneva: United Nations Human Rights Committee. (UN Doc. CCPR/C/MEX/CO/5.)

Hyde Z, Doherty M, Tilley PJM, McCaul KA, Rooney R, Jancey J. (2014). *The First Australian National Trans Mental Health Study: Summary of Results*. Perth, Australia: School of Public Health, Curtin University.

Ireland. (2015). Number 25 of 2015 Gender Recognition Act 2015. Available at: http://www.oireachtas.ie/documents/bills28/acts/2015/a2515.pdf.

Italian Constitutional Court. (1985). Decision No. 161 of 1985.

Köhler R, Richer A, Ehrt J. (2013). Legal gender recognition in Europe. Toolkit. Transgender Europe, 2013. Available at: http://www.tgeu.org/sites/default/files/Toolkit_web.pdf (accessed 3 May 2014).

Landén M, Wålinder J, Hambert G, Lundström B. (1998). Factors predictive of regret in sex reassignment. *Acta Psychiatr. Scand.*, 97(4): 284–289.

Lombardi E. (2001). Enhancing transgender health care. *Am. J. Publ. Hlth*, 91: 869–872.

Lombardi EL, van Servellen G. (2000). Building culturally sensitive substance use prevention and treatment programs for transgendered populations. *J. Subst. Abuse Treat.*,19: 291–296.

Malta, (2015). *Trans, Gender Variant and Intersex Students in School Policy*. Malta: Ministry of Education and Employment.

McGovern S. (1995). Self castration in a transsexual. *J. Accid. Emerg. Med.*, 12: 57–58.

McGowan K. (1999). *Transgender Needs Assessment*. New York, NY: The HIV Prevention Planning Unit of the New York City Department of Health.

Missé M, Coll-Planas G. (Eds.) (2010). *El género Desordenado. Críticas en Torno a la Patologización de la Transexualidad*. Barcelona: Egales.

New Zealand Family Court. (2008). Michael v. Registrar-General of Births, Deaths and Marriages. New Zealand Family Court. 9 June 2008. FAM-2006-004-002325.

OHCHR. (2011). *Discriminatory Laws and Practices and Acts of Violence Against Individuals Based on their Sexual Orientation and Gender Identity. Report of the United Nations High Commissioner for Human Rights*. New York: United Nations. (UN Doc. A/HRC/19/41.)

Ojanen T T. (2009). Sexual/gender minorities in Thailand: Identities, challenges and voluntary-sector counselling. *Sex. Res. Soc. Policy*, 6(2): 4–34.

Olson J, Forbes C, Belzer M. (2011). Management of the transgender adolescent. *Arch. Pediatr. Adolesc. Med.*, 165(2): 171–176.

OSF. (2013). *Transforming Health. International Rights Based Advocacy for Trans Health*. New York: Open Society Foundations.

OSF. (2014). *J. Byrne. License to Be Yourself: Laws and Advocacy for Legal Gender Recognition of Trans People*. New York: Open Society Foundation.

PAHO. (2014). *Blueprint for the Provision of Comprehensive Care for Trans Persons and their Communities in the Caribbean and other Anglophone Countries*. Washington: Pan American Health Organization.

Radix A. (2014). Justus Eisfeld informierte Zustimmung in der Trans*-Gesundheitsversorgung. Erfahrungen eines US-amerikanischen. *Commun. Hlth Center. Z Sex-Forsch*, 27(1): 31–43.

República Argentina. (2012). Ley 26743: Derecho a la identidad de género. [Law No. 26743: Right to gender identity.]

Riley EA, Sitharthan G, Clemson L, Diamond M. (2011). The needs of gender-variant children and their parents: A parent survey. *Int. J. Sex. Hlth* 3: 181–195.

Sanchez NF, Sanchez JP, Danoff A. (2009). Health care utilization, barriers to care, and hormone usage among male-to-female transgender persons in New York City. *Am. J. Publ. Hlth* 99(4): 713–719.

Serbia. (2009). The Law on the Prohibition of Discrimination. (Unofficial translation by Labris Serbia.)

Sood N. (2009). *Transgender People's Access to Sexual Health and Rights: A Study of Law and Policy in 12 Asian Countries.* Kuala Lumpur: Asian-Pacific Resource and Research Centre for Women (ARROW).

Spade D. (2008). Documenting gender. *Hastings Law J.,* 59: 731–842.

Spade D. (2011). *Normal Life. Administrative Violence, Critical Trans Politics and the Limits of Law.* Brooklyn, NY: South End Press.

Spanish Network. (2010). *Best Practices Guide to Trans Health Care in the National Health System.* Spanish Network for Depathologization of Trans Identities.

Speigel A. (2008). Two families grapple with sons' gender preferences. National public radio: all things considered. Available at: www.npr.org/templates/story/story.php?storyId=90247842.

Suess A. (2014). Cuestionamiento de dinámicas de patologización y exclusion discursive desde perspectivas trans e intersex. *Rev. Estud. Soc.* 49: 128–143.

Supreme Court of India. (2014). *National Legal Services Authority* v. *Union of India & Ors.* [Writ Petition (Civil) No. 400 of 2012 ('NALSA').]

Supreme Court of Nepal. (2007). *Sunil Babu Pant and others* v *Government of Nepal and others.* Writ No. 917, 21 December 2007. English translation published in *NJA Law J.* 2008; 261–286.

Supreme Court of Pakistan. (2011). *Dr. Mohammad Aslam Khaki & Anr.* v. *Senior Superintendent of Police (Operation) Rawalpindi & Ors.* Constitution Petition No. 43 of 2009 decided on 22nd March, 2011.

Teh YK. (2001). Mak Nyahs (male transsexuals) in Malaysia: The influence of culture and religion on their identity. *Int. J. Transgenderism,* 5(3).

TGEU. (2008). *Transgender EuroStudy: Legal Survey and Focus on the Transgender Experience of Health Care.* Transgender Europe (TGEU) and The European Region of the International Lesbian and Gay Association (ILGA).

Thai National Legislative Assembly. (2015). Gender Equality Act B.E. 2558. Thailand: National Legislative Assembly.

Todahl JL, Linviole D, Bustin A, Wheeler J, Gau J. (2009). Sexual assault support services and community systems: Understanding critical issues and needs in the LGBTQ community. *J. Violence Against Women,* 15(8): 952–976.

Transvanilla. (2014). *TransCare – 'A transz* embereket egészségügyben érő diszkrimináció dokumentálása Magyarországon'* [Documentation of Discrmination Against Trans People in Hungarian Health Care]. Budapest: Transvanilla.

UNDP. (2013). *United Nations Development Programme. Discussion Paper: Transgender Health and Human Rights.* New York: UNDP.

United Nations. (2011). *United Nations High Commissioner for Human Rights. Discriminatory Laws and Practices and Acts of Violence Against Individuals Based on their Sexual Orientation and Gender Identity.* New York: United Nations General Assembly. (UN Doc A/HRC/19/41.)

United Nations. (2013). *Report of the Special Rapporteur on Torture and other Cruel, Inhuman or Degrading Treatment or Punishment*. New York: United Nations General Assembly. (UN Doc A/HRC/22/53.)

Vancouver Coastal Health. (2012). Transgender Health Program Guidelines for Transgender Care. Available at: http://transhealth.vch.ca/resources/careguidelines. html (accessed 17 January 2012).

Visnyei K, et al. (2014). Hypercalcemia in a male-to-female transgender patient after body contouring injections: A case report. *J. Med. Case Rep.*, 8(1): 71.

Winter S. (2006). Thai transgenders in focus: Demographics, transitions and identities. *Int. J. Transgenderism*, 9(1): 15–27.

Winters K. (2008). Gender madness in American psychiatry: essays from the struggle for dignity. Available at: www.gendermadness.com.

WHO. (1992). *International Classification of Diseases*, 10th ed. Geneva: World Health Organization.

WHO. (2014). *Interagency Statement on Forced or Coerced Sterilization*. Geneva: WHO.

WHO. (2015a). *Sexual Health, Human Rights and the Law*. Geneva: WHO.

WHO. (2015b). ICD-11 Beta Version. Available at: http://apps.who.int/classifications/ icd11/browse/l-m/en.

WPATH. (2008). *Clarification on Medical Necessity of Treatment, Sex Reassignment, and Insurance Coverage in the USA*. World Professional Association for Transgender Health.

WPATH. (2010). De-psychopatholisation statement. World Professional Association for Transgender Health. Available at: http://wpath.org/announcements_detail.cfm?pk_ announcement=1 (accessed 20 May 2013).

WPATH. (2012). Standards of care for the health of transsexual, transgender, and gender nonconforming people. 7th Version. Available at: http://www.wpa+th.org/ (accessed 10 January 2012).

WPATH. (2015). WPATH statement on legal recognition of gender identity. Available at: http://www.wpath.org/site_page.cfm?pk_association_webpage_menu=1351&pk_ association_webpage=3928.

Xavier JM, Simmons R. (2000). The Washington transgender needs assessment survey. Available at: http://www.glaa.org/archive/2000/tgneedsassessment1112.shtml (accessed 30 April 2012).

Yogyakarta Principles. (2007). Yogyakarta principles: The application of international human rights law in relation to sexual orientation and gender identity. Available at: http://www.yogyakartaprinciples.org/principles_en.htm.

Index